WESTERN POLITICAL THEORY:
The Modern Age

WESTERN POLITICAL THEORY:

The Modern Age

LEE CAMERON McDONALD

Pomona College

HARCOURT, BRACE & WORLD, INC.

New York · Burlingame

© 1962, BY HARCOURT, BRACE & WORLD, INC.

Library of Congress Catalog Card Number: 62-14227

PRINTED IN THE UNITED STATES OF AMERICA

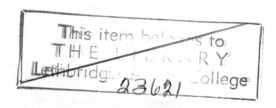

To My Parents

Preface

Western Political Theory: The Modern Age was not written to fill a long-felt need for a good book in political theory. There are many good books in political theory and, unlike books in astrophysics and backyard cookery, they age slowly. Nor, difficult as it is to believe, was it written to make money or to save the world.

The book was written mainly, I suppose, to fill a long-felt need in the author to write a book. The process of writing has been, by and large, a pleasure, and has provided me with some knowledge, occasional surges of creative euphoria, and a reliable excuse for not serving on committees. My needs being so well met, I therefore ask no more of the document. Should it, however, fill someone else's needs, I shall be most gratified. Should it, beyond this, make money and save the world, I shall be overjoyed.

The table of contents will reveal the distinctive—or perhaps I should say peculiar—form of organization: four chapters in the book are devoted to a survey of the political thought of a century, and each of these is followed by chapters dealing more intensively with the theories of the two to four men who have made, in my judgment, and in most people's judgment, the most original contributions to political theory in that century. The aim is to satisfy the sometimes divergent requirements for the understanding of political theory. For reasons given in the Introduction, the chapters on men are important chapters and, if I may say so, my favorites. But the chapters on centuries are probably necessary to convey something of the climate of opinion within which the men were working and to illustrate how patterns of thought widen and reverberate in the stream of history.

I do not claim "objectivity" for this book. Books on politics that place the goal of objectivity above all others fail to achieve that goal while succeeding in being dull. Politics is a matter of human conflict and cooperation, and thorough objectivity is a nonhuman attribute. The selection and treatment of every issue raised in these pages is affected by the predispositions, commitments and biases of the author. Since these will be far more evident to the intelligent reader than to the author himself, autobiography is unnecessary here.

If not pristinely objective, the book is, I hope, reasonably fair. Though not capable of standing in another man's shoes, we can give the other man a hearing and work at distinguishing between what he is saying and what we want him to say. Indeed, I was amazed at how conservative I felt in writing on Burke and how pragmatic I felt in writing on Dewey. If only some of this surprise at seeing as others saw is shared by the reader, I shall be content.

In the process of writing one comes to realize how thoroughly dependent he is on others for what he knows, however little the sum may be. My gratitude extends to many in the community of scholarship, among them: four dedicated teachers of political theory, the late Luther J. Lee, Jr., Thomas P. Jenkin, Carl J. Friedrich, and Louis Hartz; four stimulating Claremont colleagues devoted to political theory, Clifford Barrett, Martin Diamond, William T. Jones, and Herbert W. Schneider; a mentor, colleague, and friend whose helpfulness is beyond acknowledgment, John A. Vieg; one who carefully and critically read the entire manuscript, John P. Roche, and three who read parts, Paul Dale Bush, John A. Hutchison, and Maurice Shock; a host of conscientious typists, of whom Mrs. Zelda Leslie leads in conscientiousness; Gordon Ross for the index. Thanks are due the Haynes Foundation, the Ford Foundation, and the trustees of Pomona College for financial assistance during three summers. Finally, kudos to my patient wife, Claire, who gave birth twice while I was giving birth once, and to the youngest of my five children, who, at the age of four months, has agreed to accept full responsibility for all errors of fact or interpretation in the pages that follow.

L. C. M.

Claremont, California
January, 1962

Contents

.

WESTERN POLITICAL THEORY:
The Modern Age

CHAPTER 1

Introduction

IMITATING the practitioners of many human occupations, political theorists are not agreed among themselves what political theory is or what political theory should be. Some
men are inspired by the classical Greek example to attempt construction
of a model *polis*, an ideal state, a vision of rational perfection capable
of calling mankind forward into the good life. Others strive to generalize
about the governing of men with utter realism, to see into and through
all façades, all rationalizations, all ideologies. They would offer the world
a glimpse of politics as it really is, possibly with the hope that someone
else who knows the good life more intimately than they may use to
worthy ends the harsh truth they have revealed. Some think of political
theory as a branch of philosophy. Some say it is a field of political science.
"It is identical with the history of ideas," asserts Professor A. "Yes," says
Professor B, "but it should not be."

A survey of political theory deceives its readers if it ignores these
arguments. It is vain and pretentious if it tries to settle them. An author
is, of course, entitled to his opinion. No doubt his opinion will mark
every page of writing. But a descriptive book *on* political theory is not
primarily an exercise *in* political theory. This book will aim to point
the reader away from itself toward those most qualified in modern times
to be read as original political theorists. It will fail if it does not induce
movement in that direction. Neither the undergraduate nor any other
busy nonprofessional can read in depth more than one or two original
political theorists. This fact and this fact alone justifies the existence
of a history of political theory. Such a book, therefore, should try to

help the reader choose a theorist to be read in the original, and to expose a context of ideas and influences around that theorist which will help make the reading meaningful.

Without anticipating too much our conclusion in Chapter 20, it can be said that whatever else they have done, political theorists in the Western tradition have been conducting a dialogue with each other. The dialogue spans centuries and oceans and philosophies. The best way to grasp the nature of political theory is not to acquiesce in an abstract definition of its nature, but to participate in the dialogue that is the vehicle of its functioning; for, as we have suggested, the proper definition of political theory is itself one of the issues of political theory.

Premodernity

MOST of the durable issues of political theory have their origin and definition in premodern times. It would be fatuous to offer what pretended to be a complete summary of those issues here. It would be presumptuous to attempt even a sketchy review of the history of political theory in premodern times in the space of a few pages. That is a task for another book. Indeed, there are many "modern" movements and influences prior to the seventeenth century, which is the starting place for this volume. They, too, must be dealt with elsewhere. This volume breaks into the stream with Hobbes and the seventeenth century because here, in dramatic example, was the ripening of those forces we have come to call modern.

It might be useful, however, to state at the outset certain dominant assumptions and beliefs characteristic of premodern political theory, assumptions and beliefs that modern thought in part rejected and in part accepted, as is the way with movements of thought. Although the mere designation of these assumptions and beliefs by such labels probably means little, we may refer to three clusters of ideas as the transcendent community, natural law, and formalism.

TRANSCENDENT COMMUNITY

Although the early Greek *polis* (from which we derive the word "politics") may be translated "city-state," it meant to the Greek philosophers more than a collection of people in a given geographical area. It meant all the outward and inward expressions of civic virtue and civic taste: art, religion, drama, education. Whereas civic concerns in our day tend to be dominated by the economic aspect—tax rates, defense spending, highways, crop supports, welfare measures—at its best, the Greek *polis* relegated a good many of these mundane matters to household management (*oikonomia*, from which comes our "economy"), and in public discussion devoted more attention than we do to the qualitative aspects of the collective life. (We must remember, of course, that the citizenry was freed to participate in such elevated discussions in part because the social structure was built on a slave economy.) Patriotism to the Greeks was more than military heroism or ceremonial nostalgia. Ostracism was one of the worst punishments they knew, for an individual torn out of his community was assumed to be almost less than human.

The position of the individual vis-à-vis the community is nowhere better symbolized than in Plato's *Crito*, where Socrates, having been falsely condemned to death for corrupting the young of Athens, is given the chance to escape imprisonment and flee to Thessaly. Socrates declines, arguing that for him to disobey Athens now would be as impious as for a child to disobey his parents. It is, he feels, unjust to repay evil with evil; and to be such a subverter of the law that has prescribed his death would only confirm the false impression of subversion upon which the jury has acted. Beneath this action of sublime civic virtue lay Socrates' confident faith in the immortality of the soul: ultimately no evil could befall a good man. Socrates was hardly the typical Greek. But he stands for much that is important in the Greek influence on Western thought: the dignity and authority of law, the superiority of reason over passion, the importance of education in civic virtue. These were community ideals that were also individual ideals. In the end the value of the community was placed ahead of life itself.

Likewise, the philosopher in Plato's *Republic*, liberated by painful effort from the dark cave of ignorance where most of mankind lives, nevertheless is compelled by duty to leave the bright sunlight and go back into the forbidding cave to bring what light he can to his mocking fellows. In Aristotle's *Politics* perhaps the best-known statement is, "Man is by nature an animal intended to live in a polis." There are differences between Plato and Aristotle so basic that two separate traditions of thought can be traced from them. Plato aspired to discover a nonmaterial realm of ideal forms in which the perfect conceptions of man and *polis* are joined as harmonious parts of the transcendent idea of the good. The more empirically minded Aristotle saw the *telos*, or end, of both individual and community proceeding from the inherent nature, including material nature, of both. Form imposed itself on matter to help matter realize its potential. To Plato, form was the negation of matter. But for both Plato and Aristotle, the individual fulfills himself only as a part of a community whose purposes transcend his own egocentric purposes.

With the rise of Roman imperialism, the *polis* as a small, self-sufficient community was lost; but the *polis* ideal was not altogether alien to the Roman *imperium*. The Stoic philosophers extended brotherhood to all men through the bond of reason, an extension that makes the community of man a rather cool and impersonal entity. But still, the juridical status of equal citizenship under law supposedly bound men together in a political kinship that would forestall a wholly random and private individualism.

The most obvious example of the premodern transcendent community is the *corpus Christianum*, the Church viewed as the body of Christ on earth. The meaning of the concept sometimes seemed to imply a sharp opposition between this community and all secular communities, as in the case of St. Augustine's City of God and City of the Earth. Or at least it was made to imply a division of labor between two communities, as in the case of Pope Gelasius I's doctrine of the "two swords" of Church and state. Augustine's two cities were cities of love and self-love, respectively, and should not be identified directly with Church and state. But in any case, the secular and private realm could not be regarded as the source of moral value. Augustine accepted the classical assumption that the state, or perhaps better, society, is natural to man—at least to man in his fallen condition. But whereas the classical conception enabled the political community to fulfill the highest of man's needs, in Augustine and in Christian thought generally, the political community could at best do no more than maintain those conditions that would least interfere with man's fulfillment to higher purposes through the Church. Yet, however different Christian dogmatics may have been from classical philosophy, from the Greeks to the beginning of modern times— to Machiavelli, to be precise—politics was judged in a theoretical context of transcendent moral authority. The standard of the good life issued from what was thought higher and more divine than what today we would call subjective values.

NATURAL LAW

One form this transcendent norm took is natural law, an important concept for our study of modern political theory. That natural law is an expression of the transcendentalism discussed above will be clear enough. That transcendentalism in the broadest sense need not result in thinking in terms of natural law is evident if we recall any number of religionists who have emphasized the nonrational rather than the rational basis of religious insight. Defenders of natural law have traditionally identified reason as the element of objective orderliness in nature implied by the word "law." On these grounds, both Cicero and St. Thomas Aquinas qualify as outstanding spokesmen of natural-law thinking, whereas Augustine, who did not find reason to be the essential attribute of the human animal, does not. Plato's dialectical method of inquiry was not conducive to a legalistic construction of categories, and he is not often called a "natural lawyer." The varieties of natural law are many, however, and there are those who regard Plato as being very much in the natural-law tradition.

Cicero's definition of natural law is perhaps most frequently quoted today as the classical model:

There is in fact a true law—namely, right reason—which is in accordance with nature, applies to all men, and is unchangeable and eternal. By its commands this law summons men to the performance of their duties; by its prohibitions it restrains them from doing wrong. Its commands and prohibitions always influence good men, but are without effect on the bad. To invalidate this law by human legislation is never morally right, nor is it permissible ever to restrict its operation, and to annul it wholly is impossible.[1]

The essence of the natural-law position is that man is a rational animal and that by the proper use of his reason—"right reason"—universally true propositions for the direction of life may be discovered. The "self-evidence" of natural law is not evident to all men automatically, its defenders concede, but only after training and effort is bent in the proper direction. The question of whether man's "unassisted reason" is adequate to the discovery of natural law or whether some revelation is implied in every statement of it has become an issue both among exponents and between exponents and critics of natural law.[2]

Modern critics of natural law say that it involves a confusion between is and ought, for it is alleged to reveal not only the true but the good. They also contend that "nature" is applied to that which is actually unnatural, namely to rarefied moral insights that, measured by the historical record of conflict between natural-law interpreters, are actually

1 *De re publica*, Bk. III, sec. 22, trans. by George H. Sabine and Stanley B. Smith as *On the Commonwealth* (Columbus: Ohio State Univ. Press, 1929), pp. 215-16. Cicero is frequently treated as the epitome of the Stoic viewpoint. But Leo Strauss points out that for Cicero pure natural law and life in civil society were quite compatible and in this he follows Plato rather than the Stoics, who believed in natural law as a function of the contemplative life that could bear on civil society only in diluted form. *Natural Right and History* (Chicago: Univ. of Chicago Press, 1953), pp. 153-55.

2 See Felix Oppenheim, "The Natural Law Thesis: Affirmation or Denial?"; Harry Jaffa, "Comment on Oppenheim"; Oppenheim, "Non-Cognitivist Rebuttal," *Am. Pol. Sci. Rev.*, Vol. 51 (1957), pp. 41-66. Hans Kelsen, "The Natural Law Doctrine Before the Tribunal of Science," and Edgar Bodenheimer, "The Natural Law Doctrine . . . A Reply to Hans Kelsen," *Western Political Quarterly*, Vol. 2 (1949), pp. 481-513, Vol. 3 (1950), pp. 335-63. Alexander Passerin d'Entrèves, *Natural Law* (London: Hutchinson's Univ. Library, 1951).

non-self-evident. Defenders of natural law in its various forms would
uniformly disagree with present-day attempts to divide thought into
descriptive and normative aspects, or to divide statements into empirical
and valuational categories. They claim that the highest wisdom of which
natural law is an expression sees into the inextricable relationship between
is and ought, between the true and the good, between "being" and "essence." They say that the record of empirical description is but the beginning of truth, that truth is the substance of the reality that gives raw
data a human meaning.

As is frequently the case in disputes of this kind, the issue is not often
squarely joined. The "nature" of natural law is not the "nature" of nine-
teenth- and twentieth-century naturalism. Nature in the first instance
refers to essences, underlying principles, that which philosophy distills
out of the flux of history, whereby, for example, it is said that the nature
of a state is justice. In the second instance, nature is what may be observed
through sensory perception. It is physical process. That there is little
communication between holders of such radically different conceptions
of a basic term should not be surprising, but portentous confusion still
results.

Traditional exponents of natural law have rarely been as naïve about
the ease of its application to concrete situations as critics have suggested.
The urgencies of the human social conflict require a different kind of
judgment for the application of natural law than for the contemplative
discovery of it. Its defenders do, however, adhere to the belief that a
positive law that does not conform to natural law is not a true law.
In the words of St. Thomas Aquinas, ". . . every human law has just
so much of the nature of law as is derived from the law of nature. But
if in any point it deflects from the law of nature, it is no longer a law
but a perversion of law."[3] A variety of implications can be drawn
from this position, including the seldom drawn sanction for popular
revolt against law and the possibility of theocratic control of law. Although such issues are primarily identified with premodern thinkers,
they are not dead issues. Perhaps the most fundamental question in the
continuing debate over natural law is whether man's reason, even the
reason of an Aristotelian philosopher, can ever be as liberated from
passion as the discovery of natural law would seem to require.

FORMALISM
Belief in the validity of universal norms expressed in natural law
implies a formalism, a fixity of structures, categories, and explanations

3 *Summa theologica*, Part II, Ques. 95, Art. 2, trans. by English Dominican Fathers
(London: Oates & Washburn, 1927), Vol. VIII, p. 57.

that applies to premodern thought in many other ways. In looking at classical thought, for example, we find a delight in classification. Plato postulated three parts of the soul, the rational, the spirited, and the appetitive, which corresponded with three orders in society, the guardians, the warriors, the artisans. He classified states, in descending order from the ideal republic, as timocracy (rule of the warriors, or the spirited elements of society), plutocracy (rule of the rich), democracy (mob rule), and despotism. Aristotle followed suit, but stylized the arrangement somewhat more. For him there were good and bad forms, respectively, of the rule of one (monarchy, tyranny), the rule of some (aristocracy, oligarchy), and the rule of many (polity, democracy). Whereas monarchy was the best of the good and tyranny the worst of the bad, polity was the worst of the good and democracy the best of the bad. The Roman Polybius also prescribed a cyclical theory of government. These classical forms prevailed as standard categories for describing governments for almost two thousand years.

The concept of tyranny provides a study in formalism. Although throughout the medieval period reverence for authority was deep and often permeated with superstition, the unmitigated evil of one properly designated as a tyrant remained a categorical axiom. The concept did not seem to admit of degrees; one either was or was not a tyrant. As John of Salisbury wrote in *Policraticus* in the twelfth century, ". . . the prince is a kind of likeness of divinity; and the tyrant, on the contrary, a likeness of the boldness of the Adversary, even of the wickedness of Lucifer, imitating him that sought to build his throne to the north and make himself like unto the Most High. . . . The prince, as the likeness of the Deity, is to be loved, worshipped and cherished; the tyrant, the likeness of wickedness, is generally to be even killed."[4] The tendency to fashion political categories by analogy to theological categories was characteristic of the medieval period generally, and this tendency bred a certain static quality in political thought. Despite his creativity in synthesizing Aristotelianism with Christian faith, for example, Thomas in his defense of monarchy is as deductive and as analogical as John of Salisbury. In *De regno* Thomas argues for monarchy on the grounds that the world is one and the God who rules it is one and earthly rulers ought therefore to be one. Sometimes unfairly, but in general correctly, modern man has come to regard medieval patterns of thought as representative of a static and deductive approach to life.

4 *Policraticus*, trans. by John Dickinson as *The Statesman's Book* (New York: A. A. Knopf, 1927), pp. 335-36. John of Salisbury was not typical, it should be noted, in the casual manner in which he suggested tyrannicide.

Modernity

AGAINST this backdrop of transcendent communitarianism, natural law, and formalized thought stands the body of political thinking we call modern. What is the modern era? When did it begin and when will it be over—or is it already over? Etymologically the word "modern" refers to no special quality. It simply means "of the present." Like "mode," from which it comes, "modern" means the way things are done nowadays. Whether we are speaking of a brief now or an extended now is often a matter of taste. Future historians will probably not refer to our age as we do. The Renaissance was not known as such by those we now call Renaissance men. Perhaps the most recent three and one-half centuries that are the subject of this book will come to be called the age of science, or the nation-state period, or the Protestant era.

Yet the very fact that we can apply such labels to an era suggests that our more common designation, "the modern age," has some meaning and refers to a set of phenomena with some intrinsic unity. An urgent need is felt in many of the so-called underdeveloped nations today to "modernize," which indicates that the term "modern" refers to more than a block of time. And the fact that "to modernize" is almost a synonym for "to Westernize" suggests that the neglect of Eastern political thought in this volume is not wholly arbitrary. There is much to be learned from non-Western cultures, as Americans are only now becoming aware. But modernity is a product of Western culture and our task here is to seek understanding within the limits it imposes.

The start of the modern period in the West can be dated from some time between the birth of Charles V in 1500 and the Treaty of Westphalia in 1648. Where in that century and a half one could best locate the symbolic moment of birth is unimportant. One could perhaps choose 1517, with Martin Luther nailing his ninety-five theses to the door of the church in Wittenberg, or 1609, with Galileo setting up his telescope, or any of a half-dozen other dates. What is important is that there is such an entity as the modern age and that we are its children as inescapably as we are children of biological parents. Whether the fearful radioactive cloud that mushroomed over Hiroshima on August 6, 1945, marked the first date on a new, postmodern calendar, the reader is as qualified to judge as anyone else.

We have discussed three characteristics of premodern thought. What are the distinguishing marks of modern culture? Here again, three elements would appear most relevant to political thinking: experimental science, the nation-state, and individualism. They are not unrelated.

EXPERIMENTAL SCIENCE

In the post-World War II period we have become especially self-conscious about the philosophical origins and influences of scientific thought, and even the metaphysical presuppositions of science. Perhaps a certain disillusionment over the evil purposes for which science has been used, mixed with the quite opposite feeling of fascination with the prospects of space exploration, accounts for this self-consciousness. At any rate, one by-product is a fresh interest in the history of science. To look back on the birth of the modern scientific world view excites the imagination.

The birth pangs were not brief. Like those of the modern age itself, they continued for at least a century and a half, more or less the period between Nicolas Copernicus' *De revolutionibus orbium coelestium* in 1543 and Sir Isaac Newton's *Philosophiae naturalis principia mathematica* in 1687. The names that dot this stretch of time suggest the character and range of scientific revolution: Vesalius in anatomy, Mercator in geography, Galileo and Kepler in astronomy, Harvey in physiology, Boyle in chemistry, and, serving as a kind of "advertising philosopher" for the whole movement, Francis Bacon. Bacon's pen was devastating in its attack upon medieval scholastic science:

This kind of degenerate learning did chiefly reign among the schoolmen: who, having sharp and strong wits, and abundance of leisure, and small variety of reading, but their wits being shut up in the cells of a few authors (chiefly Aristotle their dictator) as their persons were shut up in the cells of monasteries and colleges, and knowing little history either of nature or time, did out of no great quantity of matter and infinite agitation of wit spin out unto us those laborious webs of learning which are extant in their books. . . . indeed cobwebs of learning, admirable for the fineness of thread and work, but of no substance or profit.[5]

The new method Bacon espoused was "to dwell among things" continually, for the "subtilty of nature" far exceeds that of cloistered logic. To know, one must "look into, and dissect the nature of this real world, must consult only things themselves."[6]

But we would miss a great deal if we thought this new method only a method. It represented a fundamental shift in intellectual orientation. That shift was not, as the casual observer of today is likely to imagine,

5 *The Advancement of Learning*, Bk. I, in James Spedding, R. L. Ellis, and Douglas Heath, eds., *The Works of Francis Bacon* (Cambridge, Mass.: Riverside Press, 1863), Vol. VI, p. 122.

6 *De augmentis*, Preface. Quoted in Basil Willey, *The Seventeenth Century Background* (New York: Doubleday [Anchor Books], n.d.), p. 33. Chapters 1 and 2 of Willey are especially relevant to the discussion above.

a change from an interest in piety to an interest in truth. Thomas was devoted to truth and John Locke was pious. The difference was one of conceptions of truth, or, one might better say, levels of truth. The School-men were more interested in the why than the how. "If the medieval mind wants to know the nature or the reason of a thing, it neither looks into it, to analyse its structure, nor behind it, to inquire into its origin, but looks up to heaven, where it shines as an idea. Whether the question involved is political, social or moral, the first step taken is to reduce it to its universal principle."7 Every problem, that is, tended to be viewed in the context of metaphysics. Take motion, for example. Following Aristotle, Thomas considered motion as a problem in actuality and po-tentiality: "the intention of everything that is in potentiality is to tend to actuality by way of movement."8 Every body, every thing, had its place in the divine order of creation, and the understanding of this divine order was all that was really important. Since sensory observation could in no case ultimately verify such order and purpose, such observa-tion tended to be unimportant.

When we compare the contingent and experimental character of mod-ern scientific postulates, the shift in conceptual orientation is evident. The new scientists of the sixteenth and seventeenth centuries did not so much refute the Scholastics as ignore them. They shared Bacon's fascination with *things*. In a sense they were describing rather than ex-plaining. The problem of motion, for them, did not have to be taken back to Aristotle's unmoved mover or any other first mover. Galileo claimed ignorance of the ultimate forces of the universe. He simply swung his pendulum, dropped his stones, and looked through his telescope. While, no doubt, fear, insecurity, and censoriousness largely impelled the now-ridiculed professor of Padua who refused to look through Galileo's telescope, we should not overlook the possibility that there may have been an element of genuine lack of interest as well. That we, who will look at, through, or into almost anything, find his attitude virtually in-comprehensible is but an indication of how much we belong to the scientific age.

These references to the birth of modern science have been made not merely to document the obvious fact that the scientific world view is characteristic of modernity, but also to suggest something of the per-vasiveness of this view. It is not coincidental that most of the political theorists who people this volume are concerned in some way with scientific methodology and the problems involved in the scientific study of political man.

7 Johann Huizinga, *The Waning of the Middle Ages* (New York: Doubleday [Anchor Books], 1954), p. 214.

8 *Summa contra gentiles*, Bk. III, Ch. 22, trans. by English Dominican Fathers (London: Oates & Washburn, 1928), Vol. III, p. 46.

THE NATION-STATE

Loyalty to the group of which one is a part is as typical a human trait as almost any we can think of. But the group that can claim the greatest devotion is different from one age to the next. The family is almost always the central group in one's ring of allegiances (even in our frantic, modern, urban society). But in some periods or places the city-state has been the dominant authority, in others, the Church, and in others, the gang. Our second mark of modernity is the dominant role of the large nation-state in men's hierarchy of allegiances. Not that all men, even in the twentieth century, live under their own politically organized nation-state; but those who do, accept it as natural and those who do not, fervently wish to. Hence, nationalism is one of the most potent forces to be considered if one is to understand modern politics. It affects the defensive feelings of former colonial powers. It enters into the aspirations of underdeveloped countries and thereby demonstrates how Western political ideas have spread along with Western industrial institutions. Nationalism is also related to totalitarianism, to the balance of power as a factor in international relations, and to centralizing trends in federal systems.

As a concept, "nation" derives much of its strength from its association with family groupings, despite the fact that from family to clan to tribe to nation are leaps of some distance. From primitive community to modern nation is an even greater leap. Linguistic unity and a traditional culture more than racial purity have been the marks of modern nationhood, and even these indices break down with newer "nations," such as Nigeria, which have a variety of religions, languages, and cultures. Nevertheless, every appeal to national patriotism is an appeal to an emotional counterpart of familial loyalty on a different plane.

The bulk of modern political theories, therefore, deals with nation-states and their problems. It is partly a reflection of our cultural bias that Mill probably seems more significant to us than Mazzini, or Voltaire than Vico; but another reason English and French theorists are given priority by American writers is that England and France became nation-states before Italy or Germany. Nevertheless, some of the most conspicuous theorists of national unity have been members of states not yet politically unified. One of the earliest and most important was the Florentine Niccolò Machiavelli who, because of his emphasis on power and his secular point of view, is often called the first modern political theorist. We shall not consider Machiavelli in detail here. But his relevance to nationalism is shown by the conspicuous departure from "scientific" detachment in the last chapter of his handbook for rulers, *The Prince* (1513). The chapter was aptly titled "Exhortation to Liberate Italy from the Barbarians." It was an appeal to Italian patriotism, an appeal to restore the glory that was ancient Rome and to unify Italy once again.⁹ Although Machiavelli was looking backward as well as forward, there is interest in noting that his departure from modern, scientific power analysis came in the name of modern nation-building. The fact that Italy, the early home of Renaissance science and national aspirations, was not finally unified until 1870 only adds a touch of irony. At any rate, the continuing relevance of Machiavelli's advice to problems of contemporary politics—even his argument for the superiority of conscripted citizen armies over mercenaries—is a testament both to his perception and to the national orientation of modern life.

The nation-state system was the successor to the feudal system. As any textbook of European history will reveal, feudalism was an intricate pattern of personal obligations (extending downward as well as upward) involving the division of European lands into fiefs, of which the more important were principalities, each with an army, law courts, and a treasury. Kings there were, but sometimes they were little more than figureheads. Toward the late Middle Ages monarchs began to assert their authority over the independent and often rebellious nobles. Sometimes using mercenary troops, the kings put an end to private warefare, sought to develop unified systems of law to replace the custom-dominated local courts, and imposed centralized tax-collecting authorities. Often the Church and townspeople were willing allies of the kings, finding in them a basis for counterattack against rapacious nobles. Eventually the strong monarchies not only crushed the nobles but reduced local town rights and the privileges of the clergy as well, relying in their place on a new personal allegiance from the mass of the citizens. Religious forces in the decline of feudalism and the rise of nationalism were, however, important.

The Reformation had much to do with [the new conception of monarchy]. The kings who denied Papal authority and confiscated Church lands added the powers of Pope to the powers of king and used both to stamp out feudalism. But the Papacy was so weakened by this defection that the Catholic kings gained an almost equal independence as a reward for their loyalty. Nationalism, in this religious aspect, was not a movement inspired by kings for their own benefit. It was a genuine movement among the people who willingly invested their national king with the powers of Emperor, Pope, Church, and Peerage. So far from being the unscrupulous and futile Prince of Machiavelli's imagining, the sixteenth century king became more than a

9 Leo Strauss argues that the last chapter of *The Prince* was a deliberate attempt to supply readers with a new secular religion of nationalism to replace the traditional values undermined in the earlier parts of the work. See his "Machiavelli's Intention: *The Prince*," *Am. Pol. Sci. Rev.*, Vol. 51 (1957), pp. 13-40; *Thoughts on Machiavelli* (Glencoe, Ill.: Free Press, 1959).

man. He was to embody in himself the whole territory he ruled, focussing its divergent provinces, centralizing its language and moulding its people into one. Shakespeare illustrates this process in *Henry V*, showing not merely the sixteenth century glory of kingship but the almost intolerable burden of responsibility which the king had now assumed.[10]

This new national allegiance, in one form or another, is the *sine qua non* of the modern nation-state. Its theoretical symbol is the concept of sovereignty, a symbol still powerful enough to agitate many people when the United Nations Security Council veto or the jurisdiction of the International Court of Justice is discussed. Not simply the nation-state, but the *sovereign* nation-state characterizes modernity.

The modern theory of sovereignty is usually associated with the six-teenth-century French lawyer Jean Bodin. Before Bodin's time sovereignty had been loosely used to refer to any authority that was the highest of its kind. In fifteenth- and sixteenth-century England a mere abbot had been called a sovereign. Sovereignty for Bodin was "the absolute and perpetual power . . . of commanding in the state."[11] It was that which distinguished a state from all other human associations; for all other human associations displayed power that was limited, restricted, hedged in by law. Bodin thought that universal acceptance of this supreme power, preferably ex-ercised through an absolute monarch, alone could prevent nations from being torn by bloody civil war. He had just seen such war in the bitter conflicts between Huguenots and French Catholics.

The ambiguities of Bodin's theory and the historical influences that help explain them we need not go into at this time. Suffice it to say that in both his political career and his writings, this peace-loving Catholic was a bridge between the theocratic, decentralized old and the secular, centralized new. While the moral weight of traditional natural law was always upon him, he met a practical problem of seemingly irre-solvable religious and political conflict with a theory of a new allegiance to a new kind of monarch, a theory more far-reaching than he realized. It remained for Hobbes, the first of the major theorists to be considered in this book, to produce a thoroughly secularized theory of sovereignty.

Theory usually follows rather than precedes the event. At least, avoid-ing complex methodological questions, we can say that it is easier to

10 C. Northcote Parkinson, *The Evolution of Political Thought* (Boston: Hough-ton Mifflin, 1958), p. 78.

11 *Les Six Livres de la République*, Bk. I, Ch. 8. Bodin wrote a Latin and a French version of his work, which differ in several important ways. They may be com-pared by reading excerpts from the Latin text of 1641 (originally 1586) in Francis Coker, *Readings in Political Philosophy* (New York: Macmillan, 1938), pp. 370-80; and excerpts from the French text of 1629 in W. T. Jones, *Masters of Political Thought* (Boston: Houghton Mifflin, 1949), Vol. II, pp. 55-84.

trace the influence of crucial events on theory than to trace the influence of theory on crucial events. The secular nation-state came into being not because of a theory but because the alternatives of national religious unity or interminable religious warfare became untenable as practical policies. The theory of sovereignty provided, as we shall see, a secular substitute for the unifying force of religious authority. The religious quality of this element in nation-state authority, a quality evoking a sense of majesty, awe, and destiny, did not, perhaps, become fully evident until the chiliastic nationalisms of the nineteenth and twentieth centuries appeared.

INDIVIDUALISM

The present American concern with "conformity," "other-directed-ness," and "togetherness" serves to remind us of what has been taken for granted during much of the modern period: the view that the human person ought to be independent, self-directing, autonomous, free—ought to be, that is, an individual, a unit distinguished from the social mass rather than submerged in it. This ideal—and it has been more ideal than reality—was encouraged by the two historical transformations we have already identified.

Although scientific research is almost always a collective enterprise, the scientific mentality tends to be an individualistic mentality. The experimentalist breaks the objects of observation into pieces for better viewing; and the social order, insofar as it, too, is an object of study, is likewise broken into pieces, which are usually the individual humans.[12] Moreover, what is now even more obvious, the technological revolution that ultimately followed in the train of the scientific revolution made mobility of population an economic necessity. A new mode of life was created that had to be justified by an economic theory of the "free" individual and the "free" market, the former so antithetical to the feudal system of status and the latter so antithetical to the mercantilist policy of governmental control of the economy. The individual worker was free to sell his labor where he could and the individual producer was free to sell his produce where he might. Individual greed, heretofore universally condemned, now became a universal necessity.

Such individualism was, of course, not always conducive to individuality. Karl Marx was neither the only nor the first, but simply the most

12 On the other hand, Western culture has perhaps always paid more attention to the gregarious attributes of man than has Eastern culture. See Betty Heimann, "Outsider in Society, a Study in the Social Psychology of Ancient India and the West," *Hibbert Journal*, Vol. 49 (1950), pp. 73-77; Norman D. Palmer, "Indian and Western Political Thought: Coalescence or Clash?" *Am. Pol. Sci. Rev.*, Vol. 49 (1955), pp. 747-61.

persuasive writer to point out that in the name of an individualistic ideology, workers were being uprooted from farms and cottage industries and placed in factory situations of oppressive discipline and social constraint. But this development could scarcely have been foreseen in clear outline by liberal political theorists of the seventeenth century. They may have voiced the political aspirations of the rising middle class, but it was not yet a class of industrial capitalists. In the seventeenth century the Bullionists, those who felt that national wealth in chunks of gold was the key to prosperity, still held sway. Even in England a factory system capable of absorbing the poor yeomen being pushed off the land by the enclosure movement did not yet exist. A self-conscious economics of the free market did not come until the late eighteenth century.

The second historical transformation, the overthrow of the pluralistic feudal order by the consolidation of power under national monarchs, also tended in the long run to liberate the individual. The nobility and the landed gentry were the mainstays of an intricate pattern of obligation that had put each person in his niche—his class, his town, his guild, his estate—and left him there for life. Legal rights inhered not in individuals but in families, towns, and pieces of land. As law courts were centralized, local custom lost its hold and the individual, already able to move about more freely, became the bearer of rights and obligations. It was James Harrington in his famous utopia, *Oceana* (1656), who noted that the Tudor monarchs, by ruining the feudal nobility and, to a degree, democratizing land ownership, had paved the way for monarchy's undoing at the hands of a bourgeois republic.

A third historical transformation, the Protestant Reformation, indirectly but nonetheless effectively contributed to the individualism of modernity. It did so through the channels of theology, political behavior, and economic behavior. Theologically, the Protestant Reformation gave the individual a new sense of independence by asserting on his behalf a claim to a direct, unmediated relationship with God. Martin Luther's concept of the "priesthood of all believers" opened the door to a society not dominated by ecclesiastical authority.[13] In today's sense, of course, Luther was neither "democratic" nor "individualistic." He did not trust Rome, or secular rulers, but least of all did he trust the mass of people to govern themselves. He agreed with St. Paul that "the powers that be are ordained of God" and argued that rebellion even against non-Christian tyrants was not to be condoned. One might take those measures

---

13 The nonindividualistic side of Luther's doctrine of the priesthood of all believers is often forgotten by today's Protestants. In addition to each man being his own priest, the doctrine holds that each man should be a priest to every other man. All laymen may minister and all ministers are laymen.

necessary to protect the proper worship of God from secular interference, but nothing more than this.

Nevertheless, the net effect of Luther's position was to encourage the individual's sense of autonomy, both religious and political. And the protection of worship from secular interference could be an invitation to rebellion. Both Luther's religious thought and his more or less incidental political thought were grounded on what Sheldon Wolin has aptly called a "simplistic imperative."[14] Each individual's relationship to God could be simple and direct, unmediated through a priestly hierarchy; and, in the same way, the individual's relationship to a secular ruler could be simple and direct, unmediated through a representative body. Luther's view of political representation was quite unrealistic for the years ahead and was not destined to prevail; but it also contained equalitarian implications, which were subsequently drawn from it.

By their political behavior in the sixteenth century, Reformation Protestants forever shattered the hope of a comfortable union of religious and secular authorities in Europe. In France, the Huguenots, relying on a skillful political organization as well as on religious zeal, fought their Catholic rulers. In Scotland, the Calvinists under the stern and intrepid John Knox resisted the pretensions of Mary Queen of Scots. Again we must remind ourselves that their behavior was not predicated on the "rights of individuals" in our present sense. Under Calvin, the Geneva theocracy (1541-64) was as bereft of individual liberties as one could imagine. A careless or playful oath could lead to the stocks or even banishment, and a bit of gay color in dress was strictly forbidden—not to mention that 150 heretics were burned to death in 60 years.

The Calvinists of this time did not sanction the general right of individuals to resist tyrants—even Catholic tyrants—but relied on an alleged right of special magistrates or "ephors" to resist for the community. In France, the author of the anonymous *Vindiciae contra tyrannos* (1579) and along the Dutch border, Johannes Althusius, relied on this and other semimedieval arguments. Quite apart from the kinds of arguments used, the mere fact of organized resistance to kings and Popes, and especially the denial of their religious authority, further cracked open the medieval edifice and nurtured a spirit of independence far beyond the imaginings of the original Reformers. In addition the new form of church organization that the Reformers brought had major political consequences. The Calvinist religious society (and, in Geneva, political

---

14 *Politics and Vision* (Boston: Little, Brown, 1960), Ch. 5. See also his "Politics and Religion: Luther's Simplistic Imperative," *Am. Pol. Sci. Rev.*, Vol. 50 (1956), pp. 24-42; and J. W. Allen, *A History of Political Thought in the Sixteenth Century* (London: Methuen, 1928), Part I, Ch. 2.

society) functioned effectively without a solitary head. Pastors, teachers, elders, and deacons were all ordained and in their different ways were equally responsible for church government. Oligarchy had replaced monarchy as the governing model. An active, participating laity was encouraged, however, and this encouragement was pregnant with equalizing and democratizing effects.[15]

The economic behavior of Reformed Christians promoted, or perhaps was a part of, modern individualism. In particular, the theology of Calvin seemed to dovetail with the economic aspirations of the rising middle class. (The Lutherans, more rural than urban, were economically much more conservative.) The doctrines of election and predestination gave Calvinists a "hunger for assurance" that drove them to diligent good works. Good works could not earn a man's election to sainthood; indeed no one in this life could be sure of election at all. But the capacity to do good works, as well as the blessings of material success, were taken as signs of God's favorable disposition toward the individual. The virtues of thrift, prudence, and industriousness, which Calvinism and Puritanism encouraged, corresponded nicely with managerial skills. As a pamphleteer of 1671 wrote, "There is a kind of natural unaptness in the Popish religion to business, whereas on the contrary among the Reformed, the greater their zeal, the greater their inclination to trade and industry, as holding idleness unlawful."[16]

The Calvinist belief in predestination, according to which the damned and the elect were foreordained by God to go their separate ways, has seemed to many an invitation to fatalism. But it would appear that the desire to be in step with the inevitable is a stronger goad than the challenges of utter freedom. We would do them an injustice, however, to assume that the Calvinists were opportunists using their doctrine as a cloak for self-interest. The religious zeal of the early Calvinists and their willingness to sacrifice were in many ways quite remarkable, as was their yoke of discipline in social matters. As R. H. Tawney points out, Calvin's doctrines could have resulted in a collectivist dictatorship as easily as in an intense individualism, but the subsequent political and economic environment, especially the minority position of the Calvinists, gave rise to the latter.

Despite—or perhaps because of—the indignities suffered by the individual in recent times, the "dignity of the individual" has remained a more concrete and less tarnished symbol even than "democracy," a term

15 See Wolin, *Politics and Vision*, Ch. 6; also his "Calvin and the Reformation: The Political Education of Protestantism," *Am. Pol. Sci. Rev.*, Vol. 51 (1957), pp. 428-53.

16 Quoted in R. H. Tawney, *Religion and the Rise of Capitalism* (New York: New American Library [Mentor Books], 1950), p. 172.

notable for its almost universal approbation in the twentieth century. We are now beginning, possibly, to leave an era in which individual autonomy is a cardinal value. Perhaps only with a measure of hindsight do we grasp the degree to which individualism has been a hallmark of modernity.

Character is a function of the authorities we serve, if "authority" is understood in its deeper psychological sense. Our character as children of the modern age has been determined in large part by the pervasive authority of three sets of values. We have named them experimental science, the nation-state, and individualism. These values are the modern in modern political theory.

Modern Political Theory

TO define the political is both easier and harder than to define the modern. It is easier in that the political can, if one so wishes, be defined in the abstract; it is unnecessary to sort out a plethora of historical details without which "modernity" would be an empty term. But it is harder if we try to see the political as a continuing aspect of human behavior, involved in all the ambiguities of human life itself. As we have said, political theorists disagree about the nature of political theory. How much more do they disagree about the nature of politics. Moreover, men of affairs who have nothing but scorn for what they call theory also participate in this disagreement. Theorists argue over whether law is part of politics or politics is part of law. Men of affairs argue over whether television should or should not be subject to political controls or whether a particular strike is or is not legal.

Let us designate the subject matter of politics as all that concerns the prescription of behavior for a public. If not immediately illuminating, this definition at least suggests some questions applicable to the political theories we shall study: How does a public know itself to be a public? Who prescribes its behavior (i.e., who is a ruler)? Who should prescribe its behavior? What happens when prescriptions are rejected and why are they rejected? But let us not polish and hone our own definition too much at this point. We shall do better to explore the explorers of definitions.

Definitions of theory are also troublesome. Theories are, let us say, general statements that attempt to explain or justify real or projected events and the relationships between them. But we have already seen in the case of natural law that whether explanation and justification can be separated is itself a matter of dispute. And the distance from the simple theories that merely try to state the general characteristics of two or three perceptions of concrete events (according to which "that is rain" is a perception and "rain is wet" is a theory) to theories about the nature of God and the cosmos is one that stretches the imagination of most men almost beyond their powers of intellectual control.

The bias in present-day political science seems to favor either descriptive theories, which make a statement of *what is*, or methodological theories, which prescribe *how* something is to be done. The bias throughout most of the history of political theory, Eastern and Western alike, has favored what we would today call normative theories, the construction of norms or goals or purposes (which may be more or less moralistic in the pejorative sense) for a society. In its pure form the latter type of theory is called utopian, from the Greek *ou topos*, no place. The purity of its detachment is typified by Plato's *Republic*. Plato, of course, wanted to be relevant and the fact that we still read him indicates that he was. But to the question of whether the ideal state visible to the mind's eye of the philosopher actually exists, Plato has Socrates answer, ". . . whether it exists anywhere or ever will exist is no matter; for this is the only commonwealth in whose politics he [the philosopher-king] can ever take part."[17]

If, by the conclusion of this volume, the reader has been helped to a slightly clearer conception of the nature of political theory, the author will be satisfied. Meanwhile, it might be useful to suggest what theory in general is not. First, theory is not practice. It may guide and criticize practice—indeed, it must guide and criticize practice if practice is not to be senseless improvisation. But there is many a slip 'twixt intention and deed, and many invisible links between a general proposition about men and a man acting.

Second, theory is not observation. The observer does not become a theorist until he ventures to say something about the *meaning* of the shapes and colors that fill his eye and the vowels and consonants that enter his ear. This may make unwitting theorists of us all; for meanings come out of memory and memory is not observed. However scrupulously we wish to describe only what we see, the general concepts inherent in our language force themselves upon us.

Finally, theory is not ideology. Or perhaps it is better to say that valid theory is not ideology. As a collection of generalized statements, ideology may be regarded as a form of theory. But the peculiar character of ideology, whether political or of some other variety, is that it is a weapon in a battle, a verbal club with which to nudge some and beat

17 *Republic*, Bk. IX, sec. 592, trans. by F. M. Cornford (New York: Oxford Univ. Press, 1945), p. 320.

others. As such, it is a form of action or practice. It lacks the disinterested quality of valid theory.[18] But, further, its interestedness is deceptive because it pretends to be disinterested. It masquerades as theory. It takes an idea and grafts on a "logic" to explain more than it is entitled to. The victim of an ideology that, for example, "explains" the universal superiority of the white race or the black race or the capitalist system or the socialist system thinks he has a hold on immutable truth, while the more sophisticated merely regard him as deceived.

It can be said with considerable plausibility, of course, that almost all expressions of sustained thought have a combative and deceptive role to play. It can be said by the cynic that our supposedly disinterested physical scientists are in reality always trying to prove someone else wrong and establish a claim for themselves when they propound a new scientific theory. Political theorists would be no less prone to such all too human vanity. But since this trait is only a manifestation of general human vanity, political theorists would likewise be no more afflicted as a class than anyone else. The special problem in political theory is not simply individual bias but group bias. Karl Mannheim has pointed us toward the view that social and political theories are indelibly stained by their combative origins:

Political discussion possesses a character fundamentally different from academic discussion. It seeks not only to be in the right but also to demolish the basis of its opponent's social and intellectual existence. . . . Political conflict, since it is from the very beginning a rationalized form of the struggle for social predominance, attacks the social status of the opponent, his public prestige, and his self-confidence. It is difficult to decide in this case whether the sublimation or substitution of discussion for the older weapons of conflict, the direct use of force and oppression, really constituted a fundamental improvement in human life.[19]

Continuing, Mannheim suggests that the spread of democratic practices in political discussion has served to reveal—by bringing out into the open heretofore unconscious group identifications—the extent to which all social and political thinking is conditioned by its group origins.

18 "Ideology" is a term widely used in present-day society but one that has been given almost as many stated or implied definitions as there are definers. Some stress the relationship of ideology to group goals, others the emotional content of the ideological statement, others the manner in which it is exploited by leadership. A useful definition is Gustave Bergmann's: ". . . a value judgment . . . in the disguise of a statement of fact." *The Metaphysics of Logical Positivism* (London: Longmans, Green, 1954), p. 310.

19 *Ideology and Utopia* (New York: Harcourt, Brace, 1949), pp. 34-35. Mannheim ultimately extends the point made here about social and political thinking to virtually all forms of thought.

Mannheim is highly persuasive; but to point to the political origins of political theory is not the same as saying that all political theory is mere ideology. A theorist worthy of the name is more than a mouthpiece for predetermined group interests, however much those group interests may consciously and unconsciously influence him. He is more than a public-relations man. Were this not true, the attention given to the thought of individual men in the chapters to follow would be unwarranted. Locke speaks to us as a Whig. But he also speaks to us as John Locke. Hume is a Tory Conservative. But he is also a philosopher for the ages.

It is a matter of degree, no doubt, but whereas the ideologue is trying to defeat an enemy, the theorist is trying to prove a point. Good theory aims at logical rigor, at clarity and precision, at explanation of the un-expected and uncomfortable fact, at fairness to alternative hypotheses, at a certain ingenuous heedlessness of consequences—all of which ideology is quick to sacrifice if its predetermined case is jeopardized. Ideology, if you will, is simply bad theory. This book is built on the assumption that there are good political theorists writing between the seventeenth and the twentieth centuries, theorists who are speaking *to* us and not merely *at* their contemporaries. If so, they are unusual men, and they deserve to be taken seriously.

2 | *The Seventeenth Century*

A MAGNIFICENT century, the seventeenth, and nowhere more magnificent than in England. In France
the monolithic rigidities of absolutism under Louis XIII and Louis XIV
seemed to freeze political speculation. England, by contrast, was going
through her great national travail: from Tudor absolutism, to Stuart
would-be absolutism, to revolution, the Commonwealth, the Restoration,
and finally, in the Glorious Revolution of 1688, the establishment of parliamentary supremacy on an enduring basis. Such contention seems to
force national self-examination and serious political thinking. America's
Revolution and Civil War were, in like fashion, her great periods of
political speculation. England was perhaps more fortunate than she knew
in having to work out her political adjustment to modernity earlier than
most nation-states, and fortunate, too, in that she was able to do so. England's island isolation, rather than some mystique of national character,
is perhaps most responsible for this happy state of affairs—although the
behavior of Englishmen, displayed in situations such as their lone stand
against the Nazis in 1940, will often inspire admiration for English national
character even in those who do not believe in the concept.

In political thought, the seventeenth century was indeed England's
century. Yet we must not let national political history crowd out theory.
The *theoretical* questions asked in the seventeenth century that are especially significant for us seem to be four in number, and these can usefully
serve as the framework of this chapter: (1) How can obedience to autocratic rulers be justified? (2) How can constitutional restraints on rulers
be justified? (3) How can a popular basis for political authority be

justified? (4) How do leaders respond to the need for reliable moral standards for political rule when religious standards are beginning to break down?

The Political Obligation of Subjects

THE first theoretical problem any political order must wrestle with, and quite possibly the last, is how to sustain a sense of political obligation on the part of the mass of citizens. We say "sustain" rather than "establish" because a sense of political obligation is of such a primal quality that social life can scarcely exist unless it is present. Dissolve the bonds of political obligation and one is close to dissolving the responsibility of one man to another, or vice versa. Social responsibility and political responsibility are intimately bound together, as any mayor, monarch, or prefect can testify. When both are gone, anarchy results; and in practice, anarchy has generally meant looting, pillage, rape, and casual murder. This "state of nature," the condition of man as he might be outside political society, was a concept that fascinated many seventeenth- and eighteenth-century thinkers. Such fascination was prerequisite to so-called social-contract theories. For, if the state of nature was a condition from which man needed to escape, what more logical way (to those living in a society where the commercial contract was becoming more and more important) than to enter a contractual relationship that established a joint partnership called government? Thomas Hobbes and John Locke are the most famous contractualists, and so important are they that we must devote separate chapters to them. (See Chapters 3 and 4.) Before the contractualists held sway, however, the conspicuous theorists were those who denied that man had been or could be free of his primeval obligation to rulers.

DIVINE RIGHT

There is irony, perhaps only the irony of all historical development, in the fact that while the divine ordination of monarchical rule was taken for granted for centuries, "divine right" as a well-articulated theory only became conspicious when monarchy itself was under attack. During that period, concern for the problem was intense. "From 1528, when Tyndale's book was issued, until the appearance of Hobbes' *De cive* in 1642, political thought exhausted itself almost wholly on *The Obedience of a Christian Man*."[1] As a basis for this political obligation of subjects the theory of

1 Charles H. McIlwain, ed., *The Political Works of James I* (Cambridge: Harvard Univ. Press, 1918), p. xx. See also J. N. Figgis, *The Theory of the Divine Right of Kings*, (2nd ed.; London: Cambridge Univ. Press, 1914).

divine right was most generously stated in seventeenth-century England by King James and by Sir Robert Filmer.

James I. "The wisest fool in Christendom," as James I (1566-1625) was known, came to the throne upon the death of Elizabeth in 1603. He was thirty-seven. Vain, slovenly, devout, widely learned, caustically humorous, shrewd, but erratic and explosive—these adjectives help to portray the man and, along with his unyielding view of monarchical supremacy, explain much of his trouble with Parliament. James had been born into an atmosphere of pervasive and often bloody intrigue. His father, Henry Stuart, earl of Darnley, was murdered in 1567, the year that the infant James became James VI, king of Scotland. It was one husband, several years, and several conspiracies later that his mother, Mary Queen of Scots, was executed at Fotheringhay. Although James' accession contravened the will of his great-uncle Henry VIII, he won out over his rivals, Lady Arabella Stuart and William Seymour, in part because of Elizabeth's wishes and in part because he was acceptable to all parties. Anglican churchmen knew he would support them ("No bishop, no King" was his oft-quoted maxim), Catholics expected at least toleration from the son of Mary Stuart, and Presbyterians took heart from the fact that he had been brought up in the tenets of the Scottish Kirk. All but the Anglican churchmen were destined to be disappointed.

The young king's tutor had been George Buchanan, "the Prince of Humanists," whose treatise *De jure regni apud Scotos* (1578) espoused the view, popular in Scotland, that a king's authority derived solely from the people. This view reflected the Huguenot influence in Scotland. But James, whose grandmother had been Mary of Guise, was more affected by another French influence on Scotland, that of the *Politiques*, a group of French Catholic promonarchists. James owed a debt of sorts to two early divine-right theorists, Scotsmen transplanted to France, William Barclay and Andrew Blackwood.[2] Barclay and Blackwood were Catholics, and *Politiques*, but other Catholics, especially the English Jesuits, were at this time developing antimonarchical doctrines that put them in an uncomfortable alliance with the Puritans, as the English Presbyterians, among others, were called. James would have no truck with either Catholics or Puritans, as such.

James' principal political works were written before he became king of England. They include *Basilicon Doron, or His Majesty's Instructions to His Dearest Son, Henry the Prince* (first published in 1599) and *The True Law of Free Monarchies* (1598). A "free" monarchy, for James, was one free of meddlesome parliamentarians. A number of his speeches to Parliament later follow the same theory. In the *Basilicon Doron* James

2 See J. W. Allen, *A History of Political Thought in the Sixteenth Century* (London: Methuen, 1928), Part 2, Ch. 10; Part 3, Ch. 7.

admonishes one who would be king to serve God and God alone and accepts the traditional distinction between the God-fearing king and the tyrant who feels no responsibility to God. The work reveals a rigorous conception of a king's duty to his people. But James also waxes indignant over those who dare challenge a king's sovereign authority: "I was oft-times calumniated in their popular sermons not for any evil or vice in me but because I was a king. . . . sometimes they would be informing the people that all kings and princes were naturally enemies to the liberty of the Church. . . . Take heed, therefore (my son), to such Puritans, very pests in the Church and Commonwealth. . . ." His son would do well to study history with care, but "not of such infamous invectives as Buchanan's or Knox's Chronicles. . . ."[3]

The True Law of Free Monarchies was a more systematic treatise. The core of the argument rested on no more than the analogy between a father's authority over his children and a king's authority over his people. Relying heavily on scriptural references to kingly power in ancient Israel, James finds a similar power implied by the coronation oath of Scotland, "as well as of every Christian Monarchy." "By the Law of Nature the King becomes a natural Father to all his Lieges at his Coronation: And as the Father of his family is duty bound to care for the nourishing, education, and virtuous government of his children, even so is the King bound to care for all his subjects."[4]

The dependence on analogy so important in divine-right theories meant, of course, that opponents could simply deny the validity of the analogy, which they did. Where James attempted more logical explications they generally failed. For example, when the law of nature was read into the law of primogeniture as a sign of God's preference for hereditary monarchy, one was faced with the practical problem of reconciling its operation in France, where female lines were excluded, with that in England, where women had their chance at the throne. As one writer has noted, this difference implied that God changed his mind about the law of nature whenever he crossed the Channel.

Logical arguments failing, James' tendency was to invoke an element of mystery in a somewhat arbitrary way and thunder at his opponents. Thus, in his famous speech in Star Chamber, 1616, James says, "It is atheism and blasphemie to dispute what God can do: good Christians content themselves with his will revealed in his word. So, it is presumption and high contempt in a subject, to dispute what a king can do, or say that a king cannot do this or that; but rest in that which is the King's revealed will in his law."[5]

3 *Political Works*, pp. 23-24, 40.
4 *Ibid.*, p. 55.
5 *Ibid.*, p. 333.

But James came a generation too late to act effectively on such sentiments. Neither common-law judges nor the Puritans in Parliament were
prepared to receive warmly his argument that God's law as interpreted
by the Church of England, ". . . most pure, . . . and . . . sureliest founded
upon the word of God, of any church in Christendom," stands above the
law of nature, which itself takes precedence over the common law and
statutory law. James agreed to maintain the common law, but "as to
maintain it, so to purge it. . . . For I will never trust any interpretation
that agreeth not with my common sense and reason, and true logic. . . .
As for the absolute prerogative of the Crown, that is no subject for the
tongue of a lawyer, nor is lawful to be disputed."[6]

The Puritans did not object to the theological flavor of James' statements. If anything, their arguments were more heavily theological than
his. Rather they objected to the finality with which he assumed power
for himself and the Church of England. The logical possibility that a
king's power might come from God indirectly *through* the people was
scarcely entertained by divine-right theorists of this time. Moreover, the
Lutheran doctrine forbidding resistance to tyrants was simply assumed
by them to be a part of the divine-right position, even though there
was no logically necessary connection between it and what James was
talking about. The divine-right theory was a popular theory rather than
a systematic theory with philosophic roots. We might properly call it
ideological in character.

Filmer.   The ideological use of divine-right theory is best illustrated
by noting the fate of *Patriarcha: A Defense of the Natural Power of
Kings against the Unnatural Liberty of the People,*[7] by Sir Robert Filmer
(c.1588-1653). Filmer, the eldest son of a family of eighteen children,
was educated at Trinity College, Cambridge, and received legal training
at Lincoln's Inn, but devoted most of his life to the duties of a country
gentleman at the family estate in Kent. These duties included service as a
county magistrate. His circle of friends embraced a rather distinguished
group of lawyers, clerics, historians, and businessmen, many of whom later
made their mark on the colony of Virginia. Members of this group often
wrote manuscript treatises on current intellectual questions for circulation
to one another and to their sons and cousins in London. Such was Filmer's discourse on usury of about 1630 and such was the *Patriarcha,*
written sometime between 1635 and 1642 to defend the royal prerogative.
Though not active in pursuing the Royalist cause during the Puritan
Revolution, Filmer was imprisoned from 1643 to 1645. It was only in his

---

6 *Ibid.,* pp. 331-33.

7 See Peter Laslett, ed., *The Patriarcha and Other Political Works* (Oxford:
Blackwell, 1949). This section rests heavily on Laslett's fine edition, which served
to resurrect Filmer from the oblivion into which Locke's attacks had cast him.

last years that any of Filmer's writings were published, and by his own request the *Patriarcha* was never published during his lifetime. It was resurrected in 1680 as an ideological weapon in a battle somewhat different from that for which it was written. Noting the judicious and critical wit displayed in some of Filmer's other writings, Laslett observes, "The worst of the injustices which have been done to him is that he should have been judged almost exclusively on *Patriarcha* alone."[8] Another, of course, is that most people have seen Filmer only through the scathing critique administered to him by Locke in *The First Treatise of Civil Government*.

What Filmer adds to the basic analogical argument of James I is an attempt at historical justification of divine right. His complete faith in the literal historical truth of the Bible is striking. In much the same way that the divinity of twentieth-century Japanese emperors has been traced back to the origins of man, Filmer traced the divine authority of European kings back to Adam. As the first man on earth, Adam was given authority by God over his wife, Eve, over his children, and over all the possessions of the earth. Adam, then, was the first king. "And indeed not only Adam, but the succeeding Patriarchs had, by right of Fatherhood, royal authority over their children. . . . I see not then how the children of Adam, or of any man else, can be free from subjection to their parents. And this subordination of children is the fountain of all regal authority, by the ordination of God himself."[9]

As do Biblical fundamentalists today, Filmer believed that all the races and kingdoms of man descended from the three sons of Noah, Shem, Ham, and Japheth, to whom the continents of earth were parceled out by their father, like field-work assignments, after the Flood. The Biblical command to political obedience was thus simple and clear: it was identical with the Fifth Commandment's enjoinder to parental obedience. Filmer, of course, could not actually trace genealogical lines back to Noah, and he had to admit the reality of various usurpations of kingly power and some disturbing breaks in hereditary lines. He came closest to granting the validity of election in stating that if the eldest male descendant of Adam could not be found in any given society, then the chief heads of families might establish the new royal house. But this provision was thought in no way to weaken the one true basis of governmental authority, namely paternalism.

On the negative side, Filmer's argument was directed against "The natural freedom of mankind, a new, plausible and dangerous opinion," and turned on the anarchic implications of any doctrine of individual consent. If consent were to be the moral basis of authority, it would be

8 *Ibid.,* p. 10 (Laslett's Introduction).
9 *Ibid.,* Bk. III, p. 57.

manifestly impossible to gather together all individuals to consult them or to achieve unanimity were they gathered. Even in the so-called mixed monarchy, fundamental disputes must be resolved by the will of one man, the sovereign monarch. The liberties of parliaments are "not from nature but from the grace of princes." In the assumption of the necessity of unitary sovereignty, Filmer was following Bodin quite closely. Moreover, secure in his own understanding of history, he could with some confidence deny the historicity of any genuine democratic society.

While the role of Adam and Noah in this argument no doubt strikes us as absurd (as it did Locke), we must not let incongruity lead us astray. The fact is that English society more nearly corresponded to the patriarchal image of Filmer than to the individualistic image of the liberals and radicals of that day:

It was simply not true that authority was being exercised by consent. How could it be pretended that the son consented to being commanded by the father? What conceivable sophistry could justify the obedience of the apprentice in going to church at his master's bidding, or the submission of the schoolboy to a beating, on the ground that they had given their assent? If authority could be exercised without consent, if in fact it was perpetually being so exercised, then there must be some other source of obligation. This other sort of obligation could only be by nature, not by choice, and observation showed that it was patriarchal.[10]

Today we think it strange that political power should be handed down from father to son, but not so with economic power: we still accept with equanimity the right of inheritance applied to property. Filmer took largely for granted the assumptions appropriate to his position as master of a huge household in East Sutton Park, Kent. Lesser patriarchs like Filmer were, of course, a minority of the population. "Nevertheless, in most of the places where the word 'people' is mentioned in the political writings of the time, even in such authors as Milton himself, it is possible to substitute the word 'patriarchs' or 'heads of households'."[11]

Filmer is a curious mixture of realism and unreality. There is a certain mystique that surrounds all political authority. It was Filmer's destiny to contribute to the mystique of monarchy and to capture the imagination of monarchical supporters through his use of the Genesis stories. We should not expect their acceptance to be tempered with critical reservations; many people in the seventeenth century still believed in the power of kings to heal scrofula by touching. Had Filmer been more critical, he would have been less effective. Nor was his argument held lightly by

10 *Ibid.*, p. 31 (Laslett's Introduction).
11 *Ibid.*, p. 25 (Laslett's Introduction).

supporters of the king. Just before his death on the scaffold in 1649, Lord Capel affirmed the core of Filmer's divine-right argument: "I die for keeping the Fifth Commandment, given by God himself and written with His own finger. It commands obedience to parents, and all divines, differ as they will on other points, agree in this, and acknowledge that it includes the magistrates."[12]

Bossuet. The seventeenth century was not a great period for political speculation in France. The atmosphere under the absolute rule of Louis XIII and Louis XIV could hardly have been less congenial for inquiries into the nature of the good state, and most literary efforts were confined to the writing of panegyrics on the regime. The best-known political writer of seventeenth-century France was Jacques Bossuet (1627-1704), bishop of Meaux and colorful funeral orator, who, as might be expected, furnished ideological fuel for the defense of absolute monarchy. Had he not been appointed tutor of the Dauphin in 1670, he might never have bothered with political studies; but with this responsibility he felt an obligation to train his charge in the political wisdom of the past. The Dauphin was an indifferent student; but the cause of refuting rebellious Protestant Monarchomachs was enough to keep Bossuet at his task, even in the face of such unpleasant diversions as mediating clashes between the Pope and Louis XIV.

Bossuet's principal political work was *La Politique tirée de l'Écriture Sainte*, published posthumously in 1709. He began with the same assumptions as had Filmer, the literal truth of the Bible, the patriarchal line from Adam to the present, and the rest. In his use of scriptural references to support detailed arrangements of the status quo, Bossuet outdid Filmer. Louis' lavish court, for example, was justified by reference to Solomon's extravagance: God, it seems, was using both courts to breed respect for monarchy. Bossuet made a problem for himself by arguing that one and only one ideal polity could be distilled from the Scriptures and that one was monarchy, yet maintaining the tradition (not accepted by the Jesuits) that resistance to any government was unjustified. This argument placed the believer living under a form other than monarchy in an ambiguous position. Filmer had rather naïvely assumed that monarchies had always existed and would always exist, with alternative forms being only transient, anarchic aberrations. Bossuet, writing at the end of the century, could not so confidently take for granted the historical normality of monarchy; but, in essence, like Filmer, he simply sidestepped the problem: "We have seen that, by order of the Divine Providence, the monarchical

12 Quoted by W. E. H. Lecky, *History of the Rise and Influence of the Spirit of Rationalism in Europe* (New York: Appleton, 1888), Vol. II, p. 181.

constitution was in its origin the most conformable to the will of God, as declared by the Scriptures. We have not overlooked therein the fact that other forms of government flourished in antiquity, of which God gave no special command to the human race, so that each people ought to accept as divinely ordained the form of government established in its country. . . ."[13]

Much influenced by the rationalist Hobbes' treatment of the horrors of the "State of Nature," Bossuet was able to adopt the description, but felt obliged to modify the explanation. It was the fall of man, the Augustinian concept of man's sin and corruption, rather than Hobbes' mechanistic psychology, that explained the need for an all-powerful sovereign ruler. "Far from the people being sovereign in this condition, as yet there is no such entity as a people. . . . There cannot be a people, since the existence of a people presupposes already some bond of unity, some settled behavior, and some established law; which things cannot exist until the multitude have begun to escape from this unhappy state of anarchy."[14]

While for Hobbes the authority of the sovereign was analogous to the central nervous system of the Leviathan, for Bossuet the analogy was the relationship of God to his whole creation.

If God withdrew His hand the universe would fall into annihilation. So if the authority of the King ceased in the Kingdom all things would fall into confusion. . . . Behold an entire nation united in the person of a single ruler; consider this sacred, paternal, and absolute authority; behold the hidden counsel which governs the entire body of the State, residing in one single head. Thus the image of God may be seen in Kings and the idea of their royal majesty.[15]

Bossuet composed a careful delineation of the differences between absolute monarchy, which he was defending, and arbitrary government, which he was not. But even as he wrote, the excesses of his own monarch dissolved the line in practice. Theories, even eloquent theories, that lose contact with the practice of men soon lose force and become anachronisms. Such was the fate of divine-right theories in the seventeenth century. But other theories dealing with the political obligation of subjects were destined to fare better. Of these, the theory of sovereignty lasted longest.

13 La Politique tirée de l'Écriture Sainte, Bk. II, Art. 2. Quoted in Norman Sykes, "Bossuet," Ch. 2 in F. J. C. Hearnshaw, ed., The Social and Political Ideas of Some Great French Thinkers of the Age of Reason (London: Harrap, 1930), p. 55.

14 Cinquième Avertissement, sec. 50. Quoted in Sykes, "Bossuet," p. 53.

15 La Politique, Bk. IV, Art. 4, Prop. 1. Quoted in Sykes, "Bossuet," p. 60.

SOVEREIGNTY

Should the general precede the particular or the particular precede the general? Strict logic might demand that we say nothing about such concepts as natural law, the social contract, the state of nature, and sovereignty until they can be spelled out in some detail. Such detail will appear in the subsequent chapters on Hobbes, the greatest political thinker of the seventeenth century, and Locke, the most influential. Yet perhaps we can avoid doing either Hobbes or ourselves an injustice if we first see him reflected, as it were, in the speculations of lesser men. In the seventeenth century, to set forth a theory of sovereignty was to explain, in more legalistic and less emotional terms than those of divine-right thinkers, why the citizen ought to accept the fact of a determinate center of governmental power in every society. (It is significant that while Locke's aversion to Hobbes led him to avoid the term "sovereignty," he could not avoid talking about "supreme power.") But the tremendous impact of Hobbes is recorded in the fact that, despite all differences of ability and nationality, pre-Hobbesian writers on sovereignty were more superficial on the topic than post-Hobbesian writers. In the former category are Bacon and Grotius, in the latter Spinoza and Pufendorf.

Bacon. An enthusiast and theoretician for the new world of science, Francis Bacon (1561-1626) was at the same time a practitioner and theoretician of an old world of politics. As Attorney General under James I he was thrust into the difficult position of defending the royal prerogative against the challenge of Chief Justice Coke. Bacon responded to the challenge with resourcefulness. While he did not sanction James' basic hostility to Parliament, it is probably correct to say that he was sincere in defending a strong royal prerogative. But his use of the concept of sovereignty was loose and unsystematic. When "there be other bands that tie faster than the band of sovereignty, kings begin to be put almost out of possession." Without much analysis, however, he takes for granted that there can be other such bands. "The wisest princes need not think it any diminution to their greatness . . . to rely upon counsel. . . . sovereignty is married to counsel." He seems to identify sovereignty with personal rulership in general rather than to see it as a concept of supreme power, which would make the problem of whether to accept counsel almost irrelevant. Yet in his warning to the common-law judges, Bacon placed sovereignty beyond the law: "Let judges also remember that Salomon's throne was supported by lions on both sides: let them be lions, but yet lions under the throne; being circumspect that they do not check or oppose any points of sovereignty."[16] But he did assume that,

16 The three quotations are from Bacon's *Essays or Counsels, Civil and Moral* (5th ed., 1625) (London: Dent, 1906), Nos. 15, 20, and 56, respectively.

somehow, sovereignty itself could be "checked." Submission to monarchy was as natural for Bacon as a child's submission to his parents, but he elaborated neither a sociological nor a legalistic theory of sovereignty. Brilliant man that he was, Bacon's political engagements, and even more his political frustrations, seemed to dry up the theoretical potential he possessed. As his contemporary Abraham Cowley wrote in a poem dedicated to Bacon, "For who on things remote can fix his sight/That's always in a Triumph, or a Fight."

Grotius. The Dutch jurist Hugo Grotius (1583-1645) was a far more systematic student of politics than Bacon, but his study of sovereignty was incidental to his basic purpose of formulating the law of nations.[17] His concern with sovereignty was mainly for the sake of determining which governments could rightly be parties to war, and he did not depart significantly from Bodin. The legalism of Grotius is well displayed in Chapter 14 of his great work *De jure belli et pacis*, entitled "Of the Promises, Contracts, and Oaths of Sovereigns," which concerns the lawful power kings have over their own actions, their subjects, and their successors. An ambivalence in Grotius between wanting to give the sovereign absolute power and wanting to impose moral obligations on him is reminiscent of Bodin; and the confusion of public authority with patrimonial power in land ownership is hardly modern. In modern usage, Grotius' sovereign is not really sovereign. True, a king is not bound by his own laws. No subject is legally wronged if the king revokes a law. And the king may bind his successors, but "this does not go to an infinite extent. For an infinite power of imposing such obligations is not necessary, in order rightly to exercise the government: as such power also is not necessary for a guardian or a Tutor; but only so much as the nature of the office requires."[18] Moreover, "if a free People had made any engagement, he who afterwards should receive the sovereignty in the fullest manner, would be bound by the engagement." Nor can sovereignty be received by usurpation. "Usurpers have no authority to bind the People" (or the "Legitimate Sovereign"). Private contracts of the sovereign do not have the standing of laws for all the people. The degree to which such contracts bind subjects is to be determined not by the consequences but by an inquiry (by whom?) into "the probable reason for doing the thing; if there be such a reason, the People itself will be bound."

These quotations are useful only because they convey the legalistic flavor of Grotius' concern with sovereignty and his disinclination to pursue the philosophic implications of the subject. Despite the distinction

17 See below, section on Pufendorf.

18 The quotations in this paragraph are from *De jure belli et pacis*, Bk. II, Ch. 14, sec. 12, trans. by William Whewell (Cambridge, Eng.: Cambridge Univ. Press, 1853) Vol. II, pp. 121-22.

made in the Prolegomena to *De jure* between sovereignty in the body politic as a whole and sovereignty in the government, for Grotius, the possibility of a systematic general theory of sovereignty was defeated by his concentration on a mass of details about the powers of specific governments.

After Hobbes no such evasive treatment of the problem of sovereignty was possible. And it *is* a problem. The problem, briefly stated, is this: if, as Bodin said, sovereignty is that which makes a state a state, and if sovereignty is that power to make and enforce law which is itself above law, then anything a sovereign chooses to do in the state is by definition lawful. Despite the obviousness of the conclusion, Hobbes was the first man to draw it and hold to it. Even today the stark conclusion is repugnant to many. The way the boldness and vigor of Hobbes' formulation affected later seventeenth-century writers on sovereignty is shown by the examples of Spinoza and Pufendorf.

Spinoza. The modest scholar Benedict Spinoza (1632-77) ranks as one of the major philosophers of modern times. A resident of Amsterdam, he was a descendant of persecution-driven Spanish Jews. But Spinoza bore a double burden: persecuted by Gentiles because he was a Jew, he was also excommunicated by Amsterdam Jewry because he was a nonconformist. His great work was produced during a rather short life, while working full time as a lens grinder, since scholarly occupations were closed to him. A highly systematic thinker, he poses something of a problem for one who would extract only the political elements of his system without distorting them in the process. A further problem is that we can easily exaggerate Spinoza's dependence on Hobbes simply because they share the same vocabulary. "As far as political theory is concerned, Spinoza is often described as a follower of Hobbes, and it is true that he borrowed many ideas and arguments from his great predecessor. But when he remarked that, unlike Hobbes, he kept natural right intact, he was not pointing to a minor deviation, but to a disagreement on fundamentals."[19] The point being made about natural right in the passage just quoted is that Spinoza goes one step further than Hobbes in maintaining a purely deterministic system. For Hobbes, man has a natural right to do all he can to preserve himself. This concept of natural right is far different from the definition that holds that man has a natural right to those things that are discovered by reason to be good by the standards of a universal moral order; but it still rules out a fairly wide range of behavior—aggression, assault, murder, etc.—that may not be justified by self-preservation. For Spinoza, man has a natural right to do

19 A. G. Wernham, in the Introduction to his translation of Spinoza's *Political Works* (Oxford: Clarendon Press, 1958), p. 35.

all that he can do—without qualification. Natural right is at last purged of any moral overtones and becomes simply a description of nature. It is a "given" of Spinoza's system that *every* human act is related to self-preservation. By this standard the Hobbesian qualification of natural right is irrelevant, if not inconsistent. Moreover, while Hobbes limits natural right to God, man, and beasts, Spinoza grants it to all of nature. In effect, then, for Spinoza the power of nature and the right of nature are identical.

Another way of putting this position is that Hobbes retains at least a slim distinction between what contemporary man would call natural behavioral laws and moral commands (what the theologian would call the existential and essential realms), both of which are willed by God. How much Hobbes personally believed in the latter is the subject of much argument, but the degree of his belief does not nullify the distinction. For Spinoza there is no such conflict. God wills what man does and what he ought to do simultaneously. It is impossible for Spinoza's man to break the law of nature.

This union of the natural and the moral in Spinoza bears directly on the questions of sovereignty and the social contract. For Hobbes, the presence of the sovereign is what gives a people unity. The duty of the subject to obey stems directly from his duty to preserve himself, a duty that can best be accomplished under conditions of peace. But having contracted to accept an all-powerful sovereign for this end, the subject has bound himself without reservation to obey the sovereign's commands —or rather with one reservation: he can resist a direct threat to his own life. And since "covenants without the sword are mere words," the sovereign can maintain the contract through continual force and threats of force. The contract has a prudential origin for Hobbes—it is established to save men from the anarchic state of nature—but it does not seem to have a prudential terminus. Once established it is fixed.

But Spinoza (who was more favorably disposed to republicanism than was Hobbes) does not give the same sanctity to contract that Hobbes does. The "duty" of the subject to obey the sovereign is purged of the last shred of moral obligation that remains in Hobbes. It is simply the inexorable workings of the laws of nature that if a sovereign misuses his power, his subjects will rebel and he will have destroyed himself. Since it is assumed that the people can in some fashion pick a new king, there must be a greater degree of unity in the absence of a sovereign than Hobbes would grant. For his own sake, then, Spinoza's sovereign takes on a greater burden of persuading his subjects that it is to their advantage to obey.

In the *Tractatus theologico politicus* (1670) Spinoza agrees with

Hobbes that all states had to begin with a contract, a contract that was a historical fact, a point in time. By the year of the *Tractatus politicus* (1677) he had modified his views to the extent of not even mentioning this contract. He sounds almost Aristotelian:

Since men, as I said, are led more by passion than by reason, their natural motive for uniting and being guided as if by one mind is not reason but some common passion; common hope, or common fear, or a common desire to avenge some common injury. . . . But since all men fear isolation, because no isolated individual has enough power to defend himself and procure the necessaries of life, they desire political society by nature, and can never dissolve it entirely.[20]

While the position of the sovereign in Hobbes' state would not be particularly enviable, even less so would be that of Spinoza's sovereign. In the face of the fact that (as for Hobbes) "men are by nature enemies," Spinoza's sovereign had the difficult task of bringing about in the state "a union or agreement of minds"—a task not altogether consistent, perhaps, with Spinoza's fervent advocacy of religious toleration.

It is not surprising that Spinoza, as the greatest of Hobbes' followers, was also the one who most modified and extended his thought. Given the naturalistic-deterministic orientation of Spinoza, sovereignty became more than merely a legal or moral concept. It became a principle of natural unity in the state itself, in whose service an individual monarch might be only an instrument.

Pufendorf. The German jurist Samuel Pufendorf (1632-94) was probably more famous than Spinoza during their parallel lifetimes, though certainly less notorious.[21] Since then, Spinoza's reputation has steadily grown and Pufendorf's has steadily receded. But this first professor of international law can serve as a further illustration of the impact of Hobbes on political thought. Pufendorf had opposed the German versions of Bossuet's divine-right ideas especially as expressed in the writings of Johann Horn. He also was assailed by Leibnitz for his attempt to separate natural law from theology. Pufendorf was noted for his rationalism both in content and style; that is, he avoided the citation of scriptural and classical authorities so characteristic of writing in his time. By his pedantic manner and continual qualification he managed to avoid offending anyone, but these qualities also vitiated much of his argument.

20 *Political Works*, p. 315.
21 An item in the New York *Times* of July 14, 1954, reported that the Jewish synagogue board of Amsterdam had refused to repeal the three-hundred-year-old order excommunicating Spinoza, as had been suggested by Prime Minister Ben-Gurion of Israel.

Pufendorf faced the task of attempting to reconcile the limited, moralistic sovereignty of Grotius with the absolutist sovereignty of Hobbes. Sovereignty was, for Pufendorf, the highest earthly power, but it was also to be limited by natural law and by custom. The unique element in his theory of sovereignty was his explicit distinction between absolute and restricted sovereignty. First distinguishing between authority over one's self and one's own things (which authority he called liberty) and authority over others and the things of others (which authority he called sovereignty), Pufendorf designated sovereignty as *absolute* "when its acts cannot be rendered void by any third person who is superior, nor be refused obedience on the part of those over whom sovereignty is exercised, upon the basis of some right which has been sought or retained by a pact entered into at the time when the sovereignty was established." Sovereignty was *restricted* "when one or the other, or both of those, can take place."[22] By contrast with Hobbes, Pufendorf argued that citizens, upon agreeing to place themselves under a sovereign, may at the moment of entering the contract make "the express reservation that they are unwilling to be bound by his orders in certain things. Such restriction is not at all repugnant to nature.[23] If it is the contract that makes a sovereign sovereign, and if the signatories have free will, it rests with them to determine the degree to which they will admit to control over them. Individuals, however, did not have rights that could stand in the way of a public sovereign acting for the general welfare. In this argument there is obviously a tinge of "consent of the governed," but stated in too abstract a form to have any practical effect.

Part of Pufendorf's popularity was based on the fact that his law of nature seemed full of pleasantly moral sanctions, yet not so many as to be an interference with strong government. The core of Pufendorf's system is a heavy weight of duty on sovereign and subject alike: "The general law of rulers is this: The welfare of the people is the supreme law. . . . They ought . . . to believe that nothing is to their private advantage, if it is not also to the advantage of the State." To this end, he must restrict his own "pleasures, delights and empty employments" and keep flatterers and triflers at a distance.[24] On the other hand, "To the rulers of the state a citizen owes respect, loyalty, and obedience. This implies that one acquiesce in the present regime, and have no thoughts of revolution. . . . A good citizen's duty towards the whole state is to

22 *Elementorum juris prudentiae universalis* (1660) trans. by William A. Oldfather, Carnegie Classics of International Law (New York: Oxford Univ. Press, 1931), p. 56.

23 *Ibid.*

24 *De officio hominis et civis* (1673) trans. by Frank Gardner Moore, Carnegie Classics in International Law (New York: Oxford Univ. Press, 1927), p. 121.

have nothing dearer than its welfare and safety, to offer his life, property, and fortunes freely for its preservation. . . ."[25]

Pufendorf's prescriptive-moralistic qualifications are enough to show that theorists of sovereignty are not necessarily absolutists; yet the fact remains that the most vigorous and systematic theorists of sovereignty—Hobbes and Spinoza—carried the concept in the direction of absolutism. The admonitions of a Pufendorf could in practice mean very little to a monarch unrestrained by any superior or even competing earthly power. Acutely aware of this weakness, other theorists were meanwhile working out theories that would not depend on the moral self-restraint of rulers but could justify institutional restraints on governing power. Such restraints are the essence of constitutionalism.

Restraints upon Rulers: Constitutionalism

COMMUNITY: ALTHUSIUS

A leading commentator on Johannes Althusius (1557-1638) has called him "the most profound political thinker between Bodin and Hobbes."[26] Althusius was, however, a much neglected thinker until the publication of Otto von Gierke's *Johannes Althusius und die Entwicklung der naturrechtlichen Staatstheorien* in 1880. The reason for this neglect appears to be that Althusius' theory of federalism had little application to France and England, where the reputations of political thinkers tended to be made and unmade for the next two centuries. Today we see his theory of federalism as highly relevant to modern political organization, and regard his definition of popular sovereignty—ultimate political authority residing inalienably in the whole people—as one of the earliest and clearest. That these two concepts should be related at all may seem remarkable. Even today (and all the more so in the seventeenth century) sovereignty signifies unity, while federalism signifies diversity. In the United States, where we have managed to live with and under a system of unity in diversity (*e pluribus unum*), we perhaps take too much for granted the kind of achievement our "dual sovereignty" represents. Only with a concept of sovereignty such as Althusius', divorced from any single ruler or government, can one visualize a federal allocation of powers that can maintain any higher degree of unity than that achieved by a mere alliance of separate, sovereign powers.

25 *Ibid.*, p. 144.
26 Carl J. Friedrich, in the Introduction to his edition of Althusius' *Politica methodice digesta* (3rd ed., 1614) (Cambridge: Harvard Univ. Press, 1932), p. xv.

Althusius' place in time and space can, of course, be given credit for part of his orientation. A devout Calvinist, he had visited Geneva and studied at Basel, where he received his doctorate in law in 1586. He shared the Calvinists' doctrine of resistance to tyrants through the use of the *ephors* or lesser magistrates[27] and shared, as well, the early Calvinists' strong sense of civic duty and community discipline. He left a professorship at Herborn in 1604 to become city attorney in Emden, East Friesland, in what is today northwest Germany. The nearness of the United Netherlands was significant, in practice because its troops protected Emden during the Thirty Years' War, and in theory because Althusius could observe and admire the federational elements in that body politic.

Althusius was a unique mixture of medieval and modern. The same comment is often made about Bodin and about the great English divine Richard Hooker. But the label, while no less applicable, has a somewhat different meaning for Althusius. Bodin was for repudiating the pluralism of the Middle Ages in favor of a sovereign monarchy, but he retained a medieval conception of abstract natural law. The result was an authoritarian yet individualistic society. Althusius retained or went back to the pluralism (Friedrich would say dualism) and corporateness of the Middle Ages, yet his theory was more naturalistic, in the modern scientific sense, than those of legalistic contemporaries such as Grotius, or especially Bodin. Like other Calvinists, Althusius identified natural law with the Decalogue, but this was the most superficially handled part of his thought. Like almost all except divine-right theorists in the seventeenth century, Althusius used the idea of a social contract, but in his hands it became less of a legal fiction and more of a description than in perhaps any other theorist of the time.

The key to Althusius' system was the conception of the basic social group; the *consociatio symbiotica*, a community living together by nature. The "sociological" orientation of Althusius is shown by his definition of politics: ". . . the science of those matters which pertain to the living together."[28] Man is a political *and* a social animal. In fact Althusius' *consociatio symbiotica* and Aristotle's *koinonia* would not be very far apart. According to Friedrich, Althusius is the first man to use the term *symbiotica* ("living together") with political connotations. This concept is at the heart of his contribution to the theory of contract, sovereignty, and federalism.

The *consociatio symbiotica* was not simply the political community. It was the generic form of a whole range of human associations. Thus marriage in later editions of the *Politica methodice* became *consociatio*

27 See above, p. 18.
28 Althusius, *Politica*, p. 15.

symbiotica conjugum. The *consociatio collegium* referred generally to the guilds, the *consociatio symbiotica universalis* or *civitas* or *respublica* referred to the state, and so forth. *Any* such community is marked by the operation of two kinds of law, one that establishes the pattern of relationships among members and the other that creates and limits the supreme authority in the group. The idea of a constitutional political order involves both these aspects of law, but modern constitutional theories are especially grounded in the latter.

The basic types of *consociatio* boiled down to five: the family, local voluntary corporations (*collegia*), the local political community, the province, and the State. At each level the members were related to one another by a contract—or rather contracts, for the formation of a community was clearly a two-stage matter. The first contract established the society itself (and the first kind of law); the second entrusted powers to specific leaders, or governments. In Locke we shall find the same division between the social contract proper and the governmental contract, but not stated so clearly. In addition to this network of contracts, there are also contracts relating each of the five levels to the next highest. Each community, therefore, bears rights and obligations vis-à-vis the others. The state itself results from the contracting not of individuals but of lesser communities. While comparable to the medieval network of feudal rights and obligations, and, of course, evolved from them, Althusius' scheme is also a somewhat rationalized structure suggestive of the modern "constitution-building" mentality.

If a sense of community is essential to the constitution-making process, so is a sense of law, which no one exemplified more dramatically than did Sir Edward Coke.

THE COMMON LAW: COKE

The common law is that body of judge-made law, supposedly common to all of England, that began to take shape during the thirteenth century with the rise of a legal profession, the development of systematic law teaching, and the secularization of the courts. Its primary characteristic is the rule of *stare decisis*, or the adherence to precedent in the decision of cases. It derives its authority not from the acts or decisions of one lawmaker or one judge but from the collective effect of a long line of judges and justices of the peace. It is accretive law. General rules are not formulated at one moment and codified, as under Roman-law systems, but rather are extracted from the pattern of precedents discoverable in a long series of concrete cases.[29] It may therefore seem anomalous to

29 Common-law systems, which prevail in most English-speaking countries, today use codes of law; but codified statutes are not the sole source of law, as they are

single out one man to illustrate the role of English common law in modern constitutionalism. Nevertheless, if any one man can be credited with preserving the integrity of the common law at a critical moment in history, that man would be Sir Edward Coke (pronounced "Cook," 1552-1634), "the oracle of the common law."

More than most men, Coke felt the weight of precedent on his shoulders. Perhaps this was indeed a prerequisite to his extensive contributions to the common law. The "law of the land" was available to him in the decisions of past courts, in Magna Carta of 1215, and in the writings of former judges: the twelfth century's Ranulf de Glanville, the great Justice Henry Bracton (whose thirteenth-century treatise *Of The Laws and Customs of England* was frequently quoted by lawyers), Chief Justice Sir John Fortescue (*De laudibus legum Angliae*, written in the late fifteenth century), and Judge Sir Thomas Littleton (*Treatise on Tenures*, on which Coke wrote a distinguished commentary). Despite these sources, Coke's *Institutes* (published in four parts between 1628 and 1644) and *Reports* (published in thirteen parts between 1600 and 1659) were the first systematic collation of English sources and precedents. The *Institutes* was the first work that could be used effectively as a textbook in teaching English law. During Coke's day, legal instruction in London's four Inns of Court was largely oral (Oxford and Cambridge taught no English law whatever and did not until Blackstone's first professorship in 1758). Coke's works were loaded with more medieval references than most people cared to handle, and it came to be tacitly agreed among English lawyers that one did not seek to go behind Coke's authorities. Thus Coke the writer became almost as binding as first-hand judicial precedent.

It would appear so far that Coke was primarily a scholar; but this designation would hardly fit his colorful career. Solicitor General, then Attorney General under Elizabeth, he was knighted by King James and elevated to the posts of Chief Justice of Common Pleas and Chief Justice of King's Bench, successively. For his stubborn resistance to James' attempts to extend the royal prerogative at the expense of the common law, Coke was removed from office in 1616. The specific issue was whether the king could command the common-law courts to desist from hearing a case. At the showdown his fellow judges gave ground, but Coke stood fast. "Tough old Coke," Carlyle called him, and the appellation fits. After various skirmishes and reconciliations, Coke got himself elected to

---

under Roman-law systems. In England, the common law drew precedents from historic charters, acts of Parliament, royal proclamations, and usages of the realm, as well as from court decisions. Roman law, the major alternative system, can be traced to the *Corpus juris civilis* of Emperor Justinian in the sixth century. Although there are today many overlappings, the responsibility of judges, prosecutors, and counsel are somewhat different in the two systems.

the Parliament of 1621. Although hardly friendly to the republican sentiments then growing in Parliament, Coke immediately became such a strong leader of the Parliamentary opposition to James that in December of that year he was arrested and put in the Tower of London, only to be released when Parliament was dissolved in January. A subsequent attempt by James to get Coke out of England by giving him an important post in Ireland failed when Coke refused to go. Upon ascending the throne in 1625, Charles I prevented Coke from being elected to Parliament by the neat trick of making him sheriff of Buckinghamshire. But by the 1628 Parliament Coke was able to get himself elected as knight of the shire for Bucks. In that year he drafted the Petition of Right, which Parliament forced Charles to sign. This, along with Magna Carta and later the Bill of Rights, became one of the great charters of England.

The two theories of greatest importance to which Coke contributed are, first, the general principle of the supremacy of the common law; and, second, the argument for "artificial reason" in the law, an argument that Coke used against James and against Francis Bacon. The general argument for the supremacy of common law was enshrined in Bonham's case (1610). The Royal College of Physicians had arrested Dr. Thomas Bonham for practicing medicine without a certificate. The court denied the right of the college to make the arrest on the grounds that it was acting as judge and party in the same case, a practice forbidden by the common law. Yet the authority of the College of Physicians existed by virtue of a parliamentary statute: ". . . it appears from our books," wrote Chief Justice Coke of the Court of Common Pleas, "that in many cases the common law will control acts of Parliament and sometimes adjudge them to be utterly void; For when an Act of Parliament is against common right and reason, or repugnant, or impossible to be performed, the common law will control it and adjudge such Act to be void."[30] There is some ambiguity in the statement because at this time an "Act of Parliament" could mean judicial decisions as well as statutory enactments. Moreover, the statement was attacked as an *obiter dictum.* But the intrinsic weight of the argument was far overshadowed by the historic uses to which it was put. John Adams, James Otis, and Patrick Henry were only three of the Americans who, almost two centuries later, found the Coke of Bonham's case a useful revolutionary ally. Actually, of course, Coke was anything but a revolutionary; the common law for him was a means of preserving the past. The monarchy may have been a barrier to change for Americans in 1776, but monarchical power seemed a threat of change to Coke in 1610.

30 Quoted in Catherine Drinker Bowen, *The Lion and the Throne* (Boston: Little, Brown, 1956), p. 315.

We do not grasp the essential contribution of Coke if we merely quote
Bonham's case. Even Bacon had said, "The common law is more worthy
than the statute law." The burning question of the day was the relation
of common law to the king's prerogative. The battle had begun when, as
Chief Justice of Common Pleas, Coke had issued writs of prohibition
against Archbishop Bancroft's Ecclesiastical Court of High Commission,
which James favored and which did not follow common-law procedures.

He was asked to discuss the matter with the clergy in the presence of King
James November 13, 1608, and he roundly asserted that he would not be able
to accept the Romanist interpretation of the clergy. James, taking exception
to this dogmatic view, declared that he was the supreme judge, and that
under him were all the courts. To this Coke replied: "The common law
protecteth the king." "That is a traitorous speech," King James shouted back
at him in great anger; "the king protecteth the law, not the law the king.
The king maketh judges and bishops." He then proceeded to denounce Coke so
vehemently, shaking his fists at him, that Coke "fell flat on all fower," before
the King and humbly begged his pardon.[31]

Coke was subsequently removed to the King's Bench, a lower-paying
job, but the conflict continued, now against Lord Chancellor Ellesmere's
Court of Chancery, which used Roman-law procedure, then against
Attorney General Bacon, who theorized about the Roman law of nature,
the "rule of right reason," as a part of the king's prerogative. To the claim
of James and Bacon that the "natural reason" of the king was sufficient
to establish law, Coke countered with a concept of "artificial reason,"
which he claimed could only be produced by the esoteric training of
the Inns of Court:

Reason is the life of the law, nay the common law itself is nothing else but
reason; which is to be understood as an artificial perfection of reason, gotten
by long study, observation and experience, and not as every man's natural
reason. . . . By the succession of ages [the law of England] has been fined
and refined by an infinite number of grave and learned men, and by long
experience grown to such a perfection, for the government of this realm,
as the old rule may be justly verified of it, that no man out of his private
reason ought to be wiser than the law, which is the perfection of reason.[32]

---

31 Carl J. Friedrich, *Constitutional Government and Democracy* (rev. ed.; Boston:
Ginn, 1950), p. 105. Compare the more extended description of this famous incident
in Bowen, *Lion and the Throne*, pp. 303-6, pieced together from a variety of
sources. Despite the necessity of humbling himself before James on this Sunday, on
the Monday morning following Coke issued another writ of prohibition against the
High Commission.
32 Quoted in Friedrich, *Constitutional Government*, p. 105.

The strength of the common law can be thought of as legal strength. But we would err if we concluded that legal checks in a formalistic sense guarantee what we have come to call constitutional government. There is a spirit in the stubborn resistance of Coke to James that could hardly be called legalistic. In was scarcely even judicious. (In his courtroom oratory against such victims as Essex and Raleigh, Coke was noted for surprise and caustic invective rather than calm, judicial demeanor.) This spirit, rather, involved an almost worshipful respect for tradition, a disposition that opposed yielding any one person too much power, and the courage to speak up when power became unduly personalized. We must admire this spirit even as we recognize that Coke's own conception of sovereign law was too divorced from political reality to operate as he hoped it would. Coke, making the law into a person, felt that real persons ought to keep their petty hands off it. "Magna Carta," he wrote in the *Institutes*, "is such a fellow that he will have no sovereign." But what this would mean in practice, as G. P. Gooch observes, is that not the rule of law, but the rule of lawyers would replace the rule of king and Parliament.[33]

PURITAN CONSTITUTIONALISM

Virtually any restraint upon a ruler, if we follow Friedrich, will be constitutional if it is public in character, effective, and regularized. The very idea of contract is such a restraint.

No single Puritan thinker can provoke us to as searching a reflection on the specific problem of contract as can Hobbes or Locke. The Puritan writers were not social contractualists as the term came to be used. Nevertheless, the Puritan movement as a whole (see pages 46ff.), a fascinating mixture of thought and action, conveys to us one unique dimension of contractualist thought. We might call it the covenant idea. We can recall from Althusius that the idea of contract does not necessarily presuppose individualism. We can infer from Hobbes ("covenants without swords are mere words") that the idea of contract does not necessarily presuppose consent. Moreover, Coke ought to be enough to remind us that not all legal, constitutional restraints on rulers presuppose contract. The common law, for Bracton as well as Coke, was above both king and people, not a contract between them. For Puritans, covenants were not simply contracts in the prudential, expedient, business usage, the final confirmation of a deal, a practical means of holding people to account, but rather the ordination of a *sacred* obligation shadowed over by the countenance of God himself.

The idea of a covenant is, of course, Hebraic in origin. God's covenant

33 *Political Thought in England from Bacon to Halifax* (London: Butterworth, 1914), pp. 64-65.

with Abraham and the children of Israel was the promise that gave meaning to the whole of Hebrew history, justifying the trials of the past and compelling Israel to look forward to an ultimate consummation in history. If the children of Israel are faithful to God (which they can never seem to be for any length of time), God will protect them. In any event, he will use them for his divine purposes. Puritans shared similar convictions. Moreover, they could and did draw from the early Calvinists a powerful sense of social concern, of hard discipline, of duty to the community. They made the religious sphere penetrate all things, even the activity of money-making. Their religious destiny might not be fulfilled on earth; but it had to be worked out on earth.

To this day there is something of the covenant flavor in our conception of a constitution. It is not, to American eyes, a mere contract, as Justice Marshall reminded us in the great case of *McCulloch v. Maryland* (1819). "We must never forget," he said, "it is a *constitution* we are expounding." A constitution implies solemnly held rights and duties, a sense of enduring fundamental law that casts a veil of sanctification over lesser, more expedient statute law. And in solemnity and sanctity the Puritans had no peers. The form was there even when the content was not. Note such magnificent names of the period of the Puritan Revolution as "The Solemn League and Covenant" between Parliament and Scotland (1643), and "The Solemn Engagement of the Army" (1647). No name was more symbolic than "Puritan" itself.

The term "Puritan" came from the Latin *puritas* and originally designated the rather diverse assortment of Englishmen who wished to "purify" the Church of England along Calvinist lines, to de-Romanize it further than had been done under Elizabeth. Worship in the Anglican Church was, in fact, not much different from what it had been before the break with Rome. The Puritans objected to the use of images and altars, the wearing of the surplice, the observance of saints' days, Archbishop Cranmer's *Book of Common Prayer*, and ceremonialism in general. The more unruly sometimes broke into Anglican services and forcibly ripped the surplices off the priests' backs.

Loosely speaking, "Puritan" was equated with "Nonconformist" and "Dissenter" and thus came to refer to anyone, English or American, who objected to the practices of the Church of England, not only to those who wished to purify the Church, but even to those who wished to leave it entirely.

A. S. P. Woodhouse classifies the Puritans of the period of the English Revolution into three groups:

(1) *The Presbyterians,* the only group to whom, strictly speaking, "Puritan" applied, wanted to organize the Church of England according

to Calvinist principles. They could be called the right wing of the Revolution. They stood for support of the "Solemn League and Covenant" negotiated with the Scots by Sir Henry Vane, Parliamentary representative, in 1643. By this agreement Scotland agreed to come to the aid of Parliament in the Revolution and, a bit reluctantly, Parliament pledged the "reformation of religion in the Kingdoms of England and Ireland, in doctrine, worship, discipline and government, according to the Word of God, and the example of the best reformed churches, and that popery and prelacy should be extirpated.[34] The Presbyterians tended to dominate Parliament, but the alliance of the Presbyterian faction with the Scots "was its potential military strength and its actual political weakness, for in moments when national feeling ran high its majority in Parliament became a minority."[35]

(2) *The Independents*, or Separatists, or Congregationalists, as they were later called (including the Plymouth Pilgrims), believed in leaving the control of church matters in the hands of local congregations. Distrustful of the Presbyterians' conception of an established church, they were nevertheless forced to cooperate with them to maintain a united front against the king. Despite their minority position in Parliament, the Independents, as the most consistent party of toleration, had considerable support among the general populace and especially in the city of London. The officer corps of the revolutionary army tended to be made up of Independents, and it was their scheme for settlement, called the "Heads of the Proposals," that was presented to King Charles by the Army in 1647. This proposal had some interesting features: the king was to surrender control of the militia for ten years, and a Council of State was to conduct foreign policy for seven years. Both the Episcopal (Anglican) and Presbyterian ecclesiastical systems were to be sanctioned and there was to be general religious toleration—except, of course, in the case of Catholics. Parliaments were to be biennial and were to be made more representative by reforms that would abolish the so-called rotten boroughs.

(3) Various *Left-wing sectarians and radicals* can be sharply divided into two categories: the somewhat secular radicals, interested in democratic reform—the Levellers, the Diggers, and so forth,[36] and the religious

---

34 Quoted in Godfrey Davies, *The Early Stuarts, 1603-1660* (Oxford: Clarendon Press, 1937), p. 134.

35 A. S. P. Woodhouse, in the Introduction to his edition of *Puritanism and Liberty, Being the Army Debates (1647-9) from the Clarke Manuscripts* (Chicago: Univ. of Chicago Press, 1951), p. 15. "But English Presbyterianism," Woodhouse continues, "is not to be confounded with Scottish. Few indeed wished to see the Scottish church duplicated in England."

36 See below, pp. 54, 59ff.

fanatics and doctrinaires, such as the Anabaptists and the Fifth Monarchy men. The more secular groups were especially representative of the rank and file of the Army.

Outside the Puritan category altogether were the Erastians, named or misnamed for Thomas Erastus, the sixteenth-century Swiss theologian who came to symbolize the position that the Church should be subordinate to state authority. Despite the fact that "Erastian" was something of an epithet, the Independents in Parliament often worked with the Erastians and were close to them.

Divided and quarreling as these groups were, they were nevertheless held together by a sense of divine mission and to a greater or lesser degree by—what is even more important to constitutionalism—a sense of history. "I cannot but see," said Army leader Oliver Cromwell, "but that we all speak to the same end, and the mistakes are only in the way. The end is to deliver this nation from oppression and slavery, to accomplish that work that God hath carried us on in, to establish our hopes of an end of justice and righteousness in it. We agree thus far. Further too: that we all apprehend danger from the person of the King and from the Lords. . . ."[37] This remark is taken from the so-called Putney debates, the rare and remarkable record of a revolutionary army debating its principles. Each regiment sent representatives or "agitators," to meet with the Army Council and express rank-and-file sentiment. Out of these debates (and an occasion for further debate) came *An Agreement of the People*, which we will look at more closely in a moment. It was a revolutionary document, drafted by the radical element in the Army known as the Levellers; but it was also a constitutional document, written with an eye toward the potential despotism of Parliament as well as the actual despotism of the king.

Cromwell and his son-in-law Ireton were moderates, at least within the group context of the Army itself, and did not at all like the business of extending the suffrage (Cromwell, like Pym and many other leaders of the Revolution, was, after all, a member of the landed-gentry class). The point at issue here, however, is neither Leveller hopes nor Cromwellian motives. The point is that the arguments that Cromwell and especially Ireton used against the *Agreement* were arguments of constitutional precedent. For example, to the question of giving the Commons extensive powers over the Lords, Ireton said, "I would fain know this: [since] that a Lord is subject to the common law, how can we take away that right of peers to be for the matter of fact [i. e., to decide] whether guilty or not guilty of the breach of such a law, when that it is a point of right for the Commons to be tried by *their* peers." Ireton

37 Woodhouse, *Puritanism and Liberty*, p. 104.

was an institutionalist, whereas the Levellers placed the subjective "inner light" of God's commands to them ahead of any institution.

With Colonel Rainborough, a Leveller, Ireton engaged in a spirited debate involving fine points of the status of monarchy before the Norman conquest, the position of the Commons under Edward I, and like topics.

RAINBOROUGH: [I think it well for us] to consider the equality and reasonableness of the thing, and not to stand upon [a] constitution which we have broken again and again. . . . besides the oath he [Ireton] found, [I would add] that one of the main articles against Richard the Second was that he did not concur with, and agree upon, those wholesome laws [that] were offered him by the Commons for the safety of the people. . . .

IRETON: You would have us lay aside arguments of constitution, and yet you have brought the strongest that may be. I have seen the Articles of Richard the Second, and it is strange that the Parliament should not insist upon that.

RAINBOROUGH: That is not the thing that I would consider of.

IRETON: I suppose no man will make a question that that may be justice and equity upon no constitution, which is not justice and equity upon a constitution. . . . I wish but this, that we may have a regard to safety—safety to our persons, safety to our estates, safety to our liberty. Let's have that as the law paramount, and then let us regard [the] positive constitution as far as it can stand with safety these. . . .

WILDMAN: I could wish that we should have recourse to principles and maxims of just government, [instead of arguments of safety] which are as loose as can be. [By these principles, government by King and Lords is seen to be unjust.]

IRETON: The government of Kings and Lords is as just as any in the world, is the justest government in the world. *Volenti non fit injuria.* Men cannot wrong themselves willingly and if they will agree to make a king and his heirs [their ruler], there's no injustice. . . . Any man that makes a bargain, and does find afterward 'tis for the worse, yet is bound to stand to it.[38]

It is surprising to find a conservative contractualist argument boldly stated in the midst of a revolutionary-army debate. The vigor of English constitutional tradition could hardly have a better testimonial. After Charles was beheaded in 1649, more and more people began to entertain the idea that perhaps a king was fairly useful, after all. Following the final defeat of the royalist forces in 1651, it became evident that the "rule of the saints" under a Council of State left something to be desired. *The Instrument of Government,* England's only operative or partly operative written constitution, was then (1654) set up, for all practical purposes creating a monarchy under a different name. Cromwell was

38 *Ibid.,* pp. 115, 120-22.

established as Lord Protector, to rule with a Council of State and a one-house Parliament. What has come to be a cardinal principle of sound constitution-making, the invulnerability of the basic law to easy legislative amendment, was well enough known to be attempted in the *Instrument* (as, in fact, had been planned in *The Agreement of the People*). Unfortunately, Parliament was unimpressed by this restraint and tried to amend the unamendable; this effort brought about its dissolution by Cromwell in 1655. The sole basis of right, Ireton had argued, was that "wee should keep covenant with one another." But how difficult to remain one big, happy family when the children are many, ambitious, and without a common enemy.

In the American colonies, where no revolutions were to be fought for a while, the impact of the covenant view on constitutional structure could be seen even more dramatically than in England. At the very beginning of the colonial experiment, in the Mayflower Compact of 1620, the tone was set: "We . . . having undertaken for the Glory of God, and Advancement of the Christian Faith, and The Honour of our King and Country, a voyage to plant the first colony in the northern part of Virginia; do by these Presents, solemnly and mutually in the Presence of God and one another, covenant and combine ourselves into a civil Body Politick, for our better Ordering and Preservation and furtherance of the Ends aforesaid. . . ." The Fundamental Orders of Connecticut, in 1639, strike a similar note.

The close-knit, congregational community paralleled to a considerable degree the town-government structure in New England, with the covenant relationship affecting both. While there was a theoretical, and to some degree a practical, separation of Church and state, secular authority was to take on the responsibility for punishing religious offenses, including idolatry, blasphemy, and heresy, and public taxes were to be used for church support. *The Platform of Church Discipline* adopted by the General Court of Massachusetts Bay in 1649 declared of church and civil government, "both stand together and flourish, the one being helpful unto the other, in their distinct and due administrations."

The constitutional element in the Massachusetts theocracy resided more in the selection of officials than in the subsequent control over them, although church officers "in case of manifest unworthiness and delinquency" might be removed by the membership. John Winthrop, governor of the Massachusetts Bay Colony until his death in 1649, once drew the analogy between the citizens' freedom to select civic officials and the freedom of a woman to select a husband. The initial freedom may have been genuine; but the relationship so chosen was more covenantal than contractual, for once the choice had been made, the wife was duty bound to obey the husband. Winthrop described the extant form of government as "mixed," neither tyranny nor "mere democracy"—"the meanest and worst of all forms of government."[39]

INDIVIDUAL LIBERTIES

The idea of individual liberties is perhaps implicit in every modern constitution that tries to restrict the powers of centralized authority. But every concrete claim for liberty (and every right is, in the last analysis, a claim) ultimately rests not upon the invocation of a constitutional rule but upon the appeal to moral principle. Apart from contractual arguments, apart from legal-traditional arguments, stand those arguments that attempt to speak for "the individual" and his right to freedom. Whenever an articulate spokesman is bold enough to make such claims, either on behalf of himself as a highly visible specimen, or on behalf of an abstract category "the individual," the powers that be feel the pressure of constraint from below. It is important to distinguish this kind of pressure from that operating only by virtue of the democratic or republican representational principle, which we will consider in a moment. Whatever the basis for the selection of the ruler, whatever the legal basis for his continuance in office, a cry for justice, an appeal to be let alone, an outburst in the name of freedom, can be regarded as a contributor to constitutional restraint, even though no claim for formal representation is made. It is hard to separate these appeals from democratic or republican representational arguments, for most often one author is voicing both. But there is a distinction. Put crudely, it is the distinction between libertarianism and equalitarianism. In the former the individual is seeking the freedom to be different from others; in the latter he is seeking to be treated the same as others.

Williams.   One of the outstanding seventeenth-century spokesmen of religious toleration and individual liberty was Roger Williams (1604-83). Always a religious seeker, he fought for the right of others to be the same. A protégé of Coke, he was an Anglican priest, but became a Puritan, later a Baptist, and still later a freethinker. He came to the Massachusetts Bay Colony in 1631, having known its leaders John Cotton and Thomas Hooker in England. But life was not tranquil in New England for one so courageous, obstreperous, and morally sensitive as Williams. He made an issue of the fact that for the sake of maintaining their charter from Charles I, the Massachusetts Puritans had never officially repudiated Anglicanism. He also had the audacity to stand up for the Indians, to point out that England really had no right to take their land

---

39 *A Modell of Christian Charity* (1630). Quoted in Alan P. Grimes, *American Political Thought* (New York: Holt, 1955), p. 29.

away from them. Over two hundred years later, liberty-minded Americans, not to mention heroes of the Wild West, were still callous to this kind of argument. And finally Williams insisted that a religious oath should not be imposed on anyone not voluntarily subscribing to the religious tenets implied by it. This was as clear a threat to the Puritan theocracy as his general advocacy of the separation of Church and state. Enough was enough, and Williams was banished in 1636.

Williams moved south and set up the Rhode Island colony, the Providence Plantations, remarkable both for its religious tolerance and its democratic constitutional structure. "Wee agree," stated the Plantation Agreement at Providence, August 27, 1640, "as formerly hath been the liberties of the town, so still, to hould forth liberty of Conscience." Williams returned to England to seek a royal charter, and in 1644, amid the strife of civil war, Williams and his friend John Milton each wrote tracts for the times in behalf of individual liberties, tracts that have endured beyond their times. Williams' great tract was *The Bloudy Tenent of Persecution for Cause of Conscience Discussed*; Milton's was the *Areopagitica*. Unlike Milton's work, Williams' was directed to the religious problem of the day, the toleration of religious deviation. Though perhaps less relevant to our own day, it was certainly more urgent for his own than Milton's plea for an unlicensed press. Williams' concern for conscience was not a product of religious indifference, but quite the reverse:

An enforced uniformity of religion throughout a nation or civil state, confounds the civil and religious, denies the principles of Christianity and civility, and that Jesus Christ is come in the flesh. . . . Whether thou standest charged with ten or but two talents, if thou huntest any for cause of conscience, how canst thou say thou followest the Lamb of God, who so abhorred that practice? . . . Without search and trial no man attains this faith and right persuasion. I Thes. v (21). . . . In vain have English Parliaments permitted English bibles in the poorest English houses, and the simplest man or woman to search the scriptures, if yet against their soul's persuasion from the scriptures, they should be forced, as if they lived in Spain or Rome itself without the sight of a bible, to believe as the church believes.[40]

Milton. The work of John Milton (1608-1674) on divorce had been published without conforming to the Law of 1643 requiring that all books be passed on by an official censor and registered with the Stationer's Company. The *Areopagitica* (from Areopagus, the law court of ancient Athens), is Milton's plea to Parliament to repeal the law.[41] In form, it

[40] Quoted in A. T. Mason, ed., *Free Government in the Making* (New York: Oxford Univ. Press, 1956), pp. 63-64.

[41] It failed to achieve its purpose but was so popular that the law ceased to be enforced.

is not so much a defense of the individual's rights as of the right of truth itself, or, to follow Milton's personification, *her*self: ". . . though all the winds of doctrine were let loose to play upon the earth, so Truth be in the field, we do injuriously, by licensing and prohibiting, to misdoubt her strength. Let her and falsehood grapple; who ever knew Truth put to the worse, in a free and open encounter?"[42] The strength of this faith in the power of truth to win, so characteristic of the liberal mentality in the past three centuries, has perhaps been shaken a bit in recent times, for we have seen what we take to be truth downed by a muscular false-hood even in "free and open encounter"; nevertheless, like the truth it refers to, this doctrine has a gratifying resiliency. Milton, however, like any first-rate pamphleteer, uses not only this but all available arguments. He is pragmatic in pointing out the intellectual accomplishments of free England by contrast with a policy that has "damped the glory of Italian wits." He invokes religious apprehension in saying ". . . as good almost kill a man as kill a good book. Who kills a man kills a reasonable creature, God's image; but he who destroys a good book, kills reason itself, kills the image of God, as it were in the eye." He is critical, in the highest sense, in showing the logical consequences of his adversaries' position: "I cannot praise a fugitive and cloistered virtue, unexercised and un-breathed, that never sallies out and sees her adversary, but slinks out of the race. . . . Assuredly we bring not innocence into the world, we bring impurity much rather; that which purifies us is trial, and trial is by what is contrary." He is also critical in the lesser sense of one who casts barbs at foolishness: "How many other things might be tolerated in peace, and left to conscience, had we but charity, and were it not the chief stronghold of our hypocrisy to be ever judging one another?"

From his literary fame John Milton might seem to belong in the com-pany of distinguished political theorists. But the regrettable fact is that apart from the *Areopagitica* he never produced a work of political theory of sufficient depth and consistency to grant him membership among the greats. His treatises against the bishops and his pleas for liberalized divorce had earned him a reputation for radicalism before he ever turned to strictly political subjects. Thus he was called a republican before his writings indicated as much. *The Tenure of Kings and Magistrates* (1649) was a bold defense of regicide and the right of revolution but contained nothing on republicanism. Power, he argued, belongs in the people; but this view entailed no concept of popular sovereignty and in fact was supported with little analysis of any kind. In his next political work, that same year, Milton turned against the people. *The Eikon Basilike* (King's

42 *Areopagitica*, Everyman Ed. (London: Dent, 1927). This and the immediately following quotations are from pp. 36, 25, 5, and 37, respectively. Like many other spokesmen for "toleration" in his day, Milton was unable to go so far as to favor freedom for Catholic or Unitarian views.

Book), a forgery by Gauden, was a eulogy to the recently executed Charles that captured the imagination of a wide host of readers. Milton, named by the Council of State to produce a reply, turned out *Eikonoklastes*, a bitter, inaccurate attack on Charles. In it the people were now seen as "an inconstant, irrational and hapless herd, begotten to servility." Nevertheless Milton became an avowed, if somewhat aristocratic, republican in the *Defensio populi anglicani* (1651), a reply to royalist Salmasius of Leyden. Of the two efforts, Hobbes commented, "They are very good Latin both, and hardly to be judged which is better; and both very ill reasoning, hardly to be judged which is worse." Though once praising Cromwell to the skies, Milton later was disturbed by his autocracy and in his most extreme of all polemical political writings, and his last, he lashed out at the evil of government by *any* one man. But his allegedly republican alternative to a lord protector or a restored monarch was a lifetime council of wise oligarchs![43]

The lesson we learn from Milton's example is that while Bacon may have been suffocated by too much practical political experience, Milton was rendered impotent by too little. A great poet, a master of the English language, a brilliant man, Milton was never at home with politics or in touch with common people. He possessed a burning passion for freedom and boldly identified himself with the great issues of his day in its service; but he had no understanding of the subtleties of power and of the compromises men must make to achieve a tolerable stability. Great political theory requires more than right ideals and a quantity of information. It requires a sense of politics.

The Levellers and the Independents (to be discussed shortly) are best examined in connection with equalitarianism. But it ought to be noted here that libertarianism as well as equalitarianism was flowing through the Army ranks, not as forcefully perhaps, and not without conflict, for libertarianism and equalitarianism are as often at odds as they are allies. *The Agreement of the People* opposed conscription as "against our freedom,"[44] and general immunity was asserted against being "questioned for anything said or done in reference to the late public differences, otherwise than in execution of the judgments of the present representatives, or House of Commons." A general principle of equality before the law —at least a negative freedom—was asserted: "That in all laws made, or to be made, every person may be bound alike, and that no tenure, estate, charter, degree, birth, or place, do confer any exemption from the ordinary course of legal proceedings, whereunto others are subjected." In the area of worship there is a slight ambivalence. While denying that

43 *The Readie and Easie Way to Establish a Free Commonwealth* (1660).
44 *The Agreement of the People*, in Woodhouse, *Puritanism and Liberty*. This and the immediately following quotations are from the Appendix, pp. 443-45.

the ways of God's worship are to be entrusted to any human power, "nevertheless the public way of instructing the nation (so it be not compulsive) is referred to their [Parliamentary representatives] discretion."

The anonymous Leveller tract *The Ancient Bounds* (1645) is more explicit than this:

I contend not for variety of opinions; I know there is but one truth. But this truth cannot be so easily brought forth without this liberty; and a general restraint, though intended but for errors, yet through the unskilfulness of men, may fall upon the truth. And better many errors of some kind suffered than one useful truth be obstructed or destroyed. . . . Moses permitted divorce to the Jews, notwithstanding the hardness of their hearts; so must this liberty be granted to men (within certain bounds) though it may be abused to wanton opinions more than were to be wished.[45]

But none, perhaps, could match Milton in forthrighteousness: "I have shown that the civil power neither hath right nor can do right by forcing religious things. I will now show the wrong it doth by violating the fundamental privilege of the Gospel, the new birthright of every true believer, Christian liberty. 2 Cor. 3. 17: *Where the spirit of the Lord is, there is liberty*."[46] That Milton was quite clearly twisting St. Paul's meaning of "liberty" in Second Corinthians, giving it a social rather than a psychological meaning, is beside the point. The point is that as a spokesman for the libertarians, Milton was obliged to fight first of all on the front against religious suppression. Later in the century, so also would Locke in his *Letters Concerning Toleration.*

Bayle. France does not have much to offer in the area of the theoretical defense of individual liberties in the seventeenth century. The best known defender of "toleration" was Pierre Bayle (1647-1706), who was anything but systematic. A French Calvinist who was converted into the Jesuit fold, only to relapse again, he was persecuted from right and left. After his banishment from France he settled in Rotterdam, and even in that tolerant spot, for his defense of atheists, he was hounded out of his professorship by a zealous Huguenot. His great work was the *Critical Dictionary* (1696-97). Skeptical, rambling, deliberately labyrinthine in order to fool the censors, betraying a fascination with the small fact, the work nevertheless communicated Bayle's critical curiosity. His penchant for examining all prejudices made him "the spiritual father of Voltaire." "Errors are none the better," said Bayle, "for being old."

45 *The Ancient Bounds*, in Woodhouse, *Puritanism and Liberty*, p. 247.
46 *Of Civil Power in Ecclesiastical Causes* (1659), in Woodhouse, *Puritanism and Liberty*, p. 226.

His defense of libertarian principles is best stated in the *Commentaire philosophique* (1681), directed against policies of forcible conversion, especially the "conversion by dragoon" of Louis XIV. Bayle was anything but irreligious, however. Though the term "Enlightenment," as the symbol of the eighteenth-century rationalist movement, came from Bayle, he was less secular in his interests than most of the eighteenth-century Enlightenment thinkers:

There is a vivid, natural light which enlightens all men from the first moment that they open the eyes of their minds and convinces them irresistibly of its truth. From this we must infer that it is God himself, the essential and substantial truth, who then gives us this direct enlightenment and causes us to contemplate in essence the ideas of the eternal truths. . . . God's will has given the soul an unfailing resource for discerning true and false; this resource is the natural light. . . .[47]

Although this could not be called a metaphysical basis for individual liberty—in its naturalism it is almost antimetaphysical—it is nevertheless a philosophical base. God does not ration his "natural light." Opinions ought to be free because they naturally gravitate toward truth. Milton personified truth fighting her own battles against falsehood and wanted to assure her a fair match. For Bayle, as De Jouvenel illustrates it, truth is more like a target at which all men are trying to aim. While no man may hit it, all men should be allowed to shoot, for the more shooting, the more the arrows will tend, by the operation of God's "natural light," to bunch around the bull's-eye.[48]

Williams, Milton, and Bayle spoke for the doubting individual and the subtlety of truth. They found doubt inescapable and useful, and rebelled against systems of orthodoxy that tried to forbid doubt. Their cry for justice was a cry to let "the individual" speak out. Parallel theories were devoted to letting "the people" have power.

The Ground of Political Authority: Populism

AMONG the many arguments for giving the ordinary man more power three would seem to be basic: (1) Healthy government requires a condition in which no one group has too much power. Unless ordinary people have a considerable degree of power, the few, the elite groups, have too much. Since power corrupts, it ought to be spread around as much as possible. (2) Since the ordinary man's fate is often decided by

47 Quoted in Bertrand de Jouvenel, *Sovereignty*, trans. by J. F. Huntington (Chicago: Univ. of Chicago Press, 1957), p. 282.
48 *Ibid.*

government, he has a moral right to be consulted, to affect by his consent or lack of it what government does. (3) The ordinary man is capable of a kind of wisdom that even the well-intentioned expert does not possess. Wise government therefore must be popular government. No flesh-and-blood theorists can be put in one or the other of such neatly divided categories without injustice. Nevertheless, James Harrington is close to the first position, the Levellers in general are close to the second, and one Leveller in particular, William Walwyn, is close to the third.[49]

HARRINGTON

Though he was a friend and counselor of Charles I, the historical studies and travels of James Harrington (1611-1677) had made him a confirmed republican. He had been especially impressed by the Venetian Republic. But he took no sides in the Puritan Revolution and had to use various wiles to prevent Cromwell from suppressing *Oceana*, despite the tributes the author paid him in the work. It was finally published in 1656. This utopia was a thinly disguised description of England, in which James I was Morpheus, Oliver Cromwell was Olphaus Megaletor, Hobbes was Leviathan, Westminster Hall was the Pantheon, and so on. Originally a monarchy, the country of Oceana had suffered a civil war because the constitution and the economic facts of life were out of adjustment. The commonwealth that replaced it was built upon a representative system of checks and counterchecks, what Harrington called "liberated" sovereignty.

What separated Harrington's theory from traditional "mixed-government" theories was the originality of his distinction between "external principles" of government derived from the economic position of the nation, and the "internal principles" derived from the nation's intellectual resources (we might speak of them as material and psychological causal factors). The former was the foundation of any political society, the latter was the superstructure; but not a superstructure in the Marxian, deterministic sense, for man retained considerable capacity to affect his environment. "The principles of government then are in the goods of the mind, or in the goods of fortune. To the goods of mind answers authority; to the goods of fortune, power or empire."[50] Harrington contrasts his distinction between authority and power with Hobbes' identi-

49 In France at this time there was virtually nothing that could be called populistic or democratic thought. Perhaps the closest approximation was the work of Claud Joly (1607-1700), an obscure opponent of Cardinal Mazarin. Bishop François Fénelon (1651-1715) is sometimes regarded as a liberal because he was a man of Christian charity and kindly tolerance, and because his *Télémaque* anticipated some of Rousseau's ideas on education. But Fénelon was certainly not a republican, let alone a democrat.

50 *Oceana*, in Henry Morley, ed., *Ideal Commonwealths* (London: Colonial Press, 1901), p. 185.

fication of them. Without quite disparaging power so conceived (for it is basic to his conception of economic influence), Harrington seemed to identify the neglect of true "authority" with monarchialism, Hobbism, and rule for lesser interests than the common good. Harrington's attachment to the classical republican ideal no doubt accounts for the moral quality he gave to authority. His chief distinction, however, is his persuasive argument for the proposition that political power follows economic power, an argument that combines the insights of Aristotle and Machiavelli. In illustration of this view, Harrington indicated that the ongoing shift in property ownership from the nobles to the people meant, inevitably, that the people would gain political power. What he did not see was that in the England of his own day the economic power of land was being replaced with the economic power of commerce.

The "internal principle," the intellectual resources of a people, was the clue to the freshness and vitality of any political system. The principle was applied, or perhaps enhanced, by rotation in office, one of Harrington's favorite reforms. Like the circulation of the blood, he felt, it was good for the system. Not that one man was as good as the next. Harrington was no democrat. He believed in a "natural aristocracy" of ability, and implicitly identified it with the gentlemen of the realm, excluding servants and wage-earners (but not yeomen) from citizenship. On the other hand, he did not impose restrictive property qualifications on political participation. The aristocratic element in his utopia would be represented in a senate, which would deliberate and propose policies. Its power would be balanced by an assembly of the people with power of veto. The magistracy, whose operation was outlined in overwhelming detail, would execute the laws. Harrington made no mention of a judiciary, but we have here, nevertheless, a system of separation of powers a hundred years before Montesquieu. All sorts of questions, including the choice of a poet laureate, were to be decided by popular vote. The people were to have the advantage of widespread public education. Liberty of conscience was guaranteed by the absence of all religious qualifications or penalities—except, as always, for Catholics, Jews, and "idolaters." The key to Harrington's balanced system was the prevention of an overconcentration of wealth. This end would be accomplished by the abolition of primogeniture and entail and the limitation of the value of land that any one man could own to that providing an annual income of £2,000.

Harrington's optimistic neglect of man's capacity to derail even so neatly balanced a system as this, can be, and was, subjected to much criticism; but the whole effort was nevertheless grounded in an impressive knowledge of historical examples. This concern for historical detail can be credited in part to Harrington's reading of Machiavelli, just as his interest in deterministic causality was stimulated by Hobbes— however much he criticized Hobbes.

Callously imprisoned after the Restoration, Harrington was driven insane and died in obscurity; but his work had a considerable effect on many subsequent thinkers, including the American Founding Fathers.

THE LEVELLERS

Although they were indefatigable tract writers, the Levellers were reformers first and theorists second. The moral urgency of their cause continually overshadowed their analytical tendencies. Yet the vitality, cogency, and prophetic relevance of their missives give them a special significance—perhaps, if we are honest, a sentimental significance. The term "Levellers," probably coined by Charles I or Cromwell, was an epithet intended to suggest that the purpose of the movement was to cut down every mark of status or privilege and level the nation to a flat and common uniformity. With justice, the Levellers insisted that this was not their aim; they had no designs at all on economic inequalities but were interested in equal political representation. Their appeals above human law to the natural law, which sanctioned every man's right to participate in government, and their assumption of natural equality in the ability of citizens, did, however, contain some of the anarchic implications attributed to them.

The rapid rise and fall of the Leveller movement suggests the pattern of almost all revolutions. At a certain point a wave of revolutionary feelings brings the radicals to the fore. The moderates are reluctantly induced to support the radicals by the increasing repressions of the now fearful government. Once the revolution occurs and the symbols of the past have been removed, however, the forms of the past creep back, and conservatism is once again in the saddle.

Lilburne. The most famous Leveller leader was John Lilburne (1614-57). A lieutenant colonel in Manchester's army, he became the civilian leader of the movement after the debate on *The Agreement of the People* in the Army councils had come to naught. The fluidity of his ideas is shown by the fact that when first arrested by the House of Lords, he asserted the sovereignty of the House of Commons. When later imprisoned by the House of Commons, he simply transferred sovereignty to the whole people. There, at least, it seemed to stay for Lilburne. For his attack on Cromwell and Ireton in 1649 he was tried and acquitted, after making a strong popular impression with his courageous speeches. He was banished in 1652, returned the next year only to be arrested again. His second trial generated intense public interest. Again he was acquitted and again banished. He returned in 1657 only to die, a leader without a movement, a few days before Cromwell himself.

The nature of Lilburne's appeals, the source of his support, is perhaps best indicated by his dramatic trials rather than by any of the many pamphlets he wrote. With great skill the amateur lawyer put the court on the defensive by challenges to its legality and won the crowd with references to the historic liberties of Englishmen, the laws of nature, and the laws of God. After his eloquent final plea to the jury at his first trial—"My honest jury and fellow citizens, who . . . by the law of England . . . having . . . alone the judicial power . . . you judges that sit there being no more . . . but ciphers to prounounce the sentence"—"the People with a lowd voyce, cried Amen, Amen," and more soldiers had to be rushed into the courtroom.[51] Here is the authentic voice of the demagogue.

In 1648 the various factions in the revolutionary army formed a tenuous alliance in resistance to Parliament. Involved were the "center party" of Independents under Ireton, the Fifth Monarchy men under Harrison (see below), and the Levellers of Lilburne and Richard Overton. Lilburne was made head of a committee to revise *The Agreement of the People* for presentation to Parliament. The new version proposed a Parliament of four hundred members, chosen by all men over twenty-one who were not servants, or recipients of relief. No member could sit for two successive Parliaments. Parliament was forbidden to legislate in the field of religion and could not grant monopolies or tax food. Prisoners were to be allowed counsel, tithes were to be abolished, and local congregations were to be free to make their own arrangements with ministers. These proposals were too radical for the Independent officers; they made further modifications before submitting the new version to Parliament, which was impressively unimpressed. Harrison was his usual millennial self and said, "God intends its failure." Lilburne was disgusted, and, as usual, appealed to the people, publishing the text of the original version of the *Agreement* in his *Foundations of Freedom* (1648).

Rainborough. Perhaps no utterance of the Levellers has been quoted more frequently than that of Colonel Thomas Rainborough (?-1648). In defending the first *Agreement of the People* in the Putney debates of 1647, he said, "For really I think that the poorest he that is in England hath a life to live, as the greatest he; and therefore truly, sir, I think it's clear, that every man that is to live under a government ought

51 Joseph Frank, *The Levellers, A History of the Writings of Three Seventeenth-Century Social Democrats—John Lilburne, Richard Overton, William Walwyn* (Cambridge: Harvard Univ. Press, 1955), p. 221.

first by his own consent to put himself under that government. . . ."[52]
Rainborough continues on to draw a revolutionary conclusion from
this premise, namely that citizens are not *presently* bound to the government unless they have given it their consent, a conclusion with immediate anarchic consequences. Behind both the premise and the conclusion
is an assumption about the natural reason of man that seems to anticipate
Locke. Replying to Ireton's rejoinder, Rainborough says.

I do hear nothing at all that can convince me, why any man that is born in
England ought not to have his voice in election of burgesses. It is said that
if a man have not a permanent interest, he can have no claim. . . . I do think
that the main cause why Almighty God gave men reason, it was that they
should make use of that reason. . . . And truly, I think that half a loaf is
better than none if a man be hungry: [this gift of reason without other
property may seem a small thing], yet I think there is nothing that God hath
given a man that any [one] else can take from him. . . . I do not find anything
in the Law of God that a lord shall choose twenty burgesses, and a gentleman
but two, or a poor man shall choose none; I find no such thing in the Law of
Nature, nor in the Law of Nations.[53]

If this natural law is above all constitutions, asks Ireton, rather sar-
castically, what is to keep you people from taking away all property?
To which Rainborough replies with some heat that God's law certainly
does not take away property. It assumes property, "else why [hath] God
made that law, Thou shalt not steal? . . . as for yourselves, I wish you
would not make the world believe that we are for anarchy." At this
point Cromwell himself, in characteristic role, leaps into the fray as a
soothing mediator, albeit a somewhat paternal one. He assures Rainborough and his Leveller friends that no one is calling them anarchists.
It is only that their argument "tends to anarchy, must end in anarchy. . . ."
But the important thing for the moment is that "we should not be so
hot one with another."[54]

Although they did not develop a formal contract theory, it is clear
from this and other passages in the Leveller literature—unusually spontaneous, grass-roots literature—that the idea of consent of the governed
was a basic Leveller tenet. Men had a moral right to choose their own
government. A second tenet was the essential equality of men "by nature."
Again, without constructing an extensive natural-law theory, they continually appealed to the natural equality of men, especially with reference to their reason. Despite the religious overtones of much of their

52 Woodhouse, *Puritanism and Liberty*, p. 53.
53 *Ibid.*, pp. 55-56.
54 *Ibid.*, pp. 58-59.

writing, compared to the millenarians and some of the Independents, the Levellers were almost rationalistic in their point of view, stressing what the eighteenth century would come to call self-evident truths. Finally, they clung firmly to the belief in liberty of conscience. In this they followed closely the argument of Roger Williams and often quoted him.

THE FIFTH MONARCHY

We have already made passing reference to the Fifth Monarchy men. A further note may be useful because the mere existence of this group illustrates the intricate intermixture, if not confusion, of religion and politics at this particular period. If a populistic or democratic theory is one that places ultimate authority in the people, then it is likely to be a secular theory, since for the man of religion ultimate authority must be placed in God. In this sense, then, the Fifth Monarchy men were more theistic than populistic. They regarded Christ alone as the source of ultimate authority; but unlike other Christians they expected him to assert this authority by setting up an earthly rule (the Fifth Monarchy) in a particular place, England, at a particular time, soon.

Their numbers included millenarian preachers John Canne and William Aspinwall, and Army leader Colonel Thomas Harrison. The ablest writer of the lot was John Rogers, whose best work was *Sagrir, or Doomesday Drawing Nigh* (1653). Laws are necessary, he argued, but they may be disobeyed when they do not conform to man's natural reason perfected by the light of God's word in the Scriptures. The principal purpose of law ought to be to restrain the lusts of the great and rich. This purpose, he said, had been perverted in England (and elsewhere) and explains why God, through the revolutionaries, was now striking down the great and rich of England.[55] The Fifth Monarchy men ardently supported Cromwell until he dissolved the Barebones Parliament, which contained many of their members, whereupon he was denounced as the Anti-Christ.

Two items suffice to convey the spirit and temper of this group. The year 1656 was anticipated with much eagerness by these men and was thought to be the year of the Second Coming, when England would be radically transformed and Christ would at last be set upon an earthly throne. The reason? The ages of the patriarchs in Genesis, if added up, come to 1,656 (although Rogers somehow calculated 1,666!). In 1661, after the Restoration, a group of Fifth Monarchy men, in one

55 For a good statement of Fifth Monarchy views, see Perez Zagorin, *A History of Political Thought in the English Revolution* (London: Routledge & Kegan Paul, 1954), Ch. 8.

of their last organized actions, broke into St. Paul's Cathedral and asked the first person they saw whom he was for. "For King Charles," he replied. "We are for King Jesus," they said, and shot the poor fellow dead.

THE DIGGERS: WINSTANLEY

In 1649 a strange little band went out from London to St. George's Hill, Surrey, to cultivate a patch of land in common and to share a communal existence. These were the so-called Diggers; their leader was Gerrard Winstanley (1609-1652). The experiment in communism was a dismal failure, if for no other reason than the hostility of nearby landlords and the action of troops who pulled down the two houses in which the group was living. But the ideas of Winstanley were precocious, whether or not influential.[56] Winstanley was a cloth merchant ruined by the depression of 1643 (ruined, he said, by the "cheating art of buying and selling") who moved through a tortuous religious odyssey. Beginning as a Baptist, he became an antinomian chiliast, then a somewhat mystical pantheist, and ended up as a Quaker. His philosophic communism, coinciding with his pantheism, bore seeds of the Enlightenment in its identification of God with nature and its stress on indwelling reason.

It was this that gave his radicalism its far-reaching implications. More than any man of his time he refused to admit the permanent and unalterable fact of a fallen world, and looked to the reintroduction of the pristine good. When this unyielding quest for an absolute justice was united to a philosophy whose ultimate bearings must . . . be regarded as naturalistic, we have a synthesis unlike anything in its day, a synthesis which essentially looks forward to the enlightenment and beyond.[57]

Winstanley's tract of 1649, *The True Levellers Standard Advanced*, challenged "the powers of England" and "the powers of the world" who by their actions denied that "the great creator Reason made the Earth a common treasury for beasts and man." Every landlord was a living violation of the commandment "Thou shalt not steal." "You Pharaohs, you have rich clothing and full bellies, you have your honours and your ease; but know the day of judgment is begun and that it will reach you ere long. The poor people you oppress shall be the saviours of the land."[58] Despite the fact that the small handful of men working

56 See Gerrard Winstanley, *Works*, George H. Sabine, ed. (Ithaca, N. Y.: Cornell Univ. Press, 1941).
57 Zagorin, *A History of Political Thought*, p. 47.
58 Quoted in Gooch, *Political Thought in England*, p. 126.

on St. George's Hill were peaceably occupying unused crown lands, it is not surprising that they were repudiated by one and all and their leaders arrested, fined, and forbidden to speak. Conservatives, not disposed to make fine distinctions among their enemies, regarded Winstanley as just another Leveller. And with some cause. " 'The poor shall inherit the earth.' I tell you," he wrote, "the scripture is to be really and materially fulfilled. You jeer at the name Leveller. I tell you Jesus Christ is the head Leveller."[59] But the Levellers themselves did not welcome his company, and in the second *Agreement of the People* any attempt to establish communism was made a penal offense.

Winstanley's major work was *The Law of Freedom* (1652), a utopia on a scale comparable to those of More, Campanella, and Harrington. Private property, wage labor, even money itself is abolished. Each worker has his quota to be produced for the common store. Education is universal. All offices are elective and of one year's duration. Everyone over twenty is eligible to vote; everyone over forty is eligible to be a candidate to Parliament. In place of the usual Christian worship, every Sunday shall see "gathered instruction" in moral precepts, laws of the society, and current affairs. One is reminded of Rousseau's "civil religion." At first Winstanley felt that repressive laws would be unnecessary once private property were abolished; but in the *Law of Freedom* he felt it necessary to provide a code of penalties, including the physical branding of anyone who was impious enough to declare that a piece of land was "owned" by someone.

Of Winstanley's later days little is known. His last work, *The Saints' Paradise* (1658), struck a more placid, quietistic tone that seems to confirm his supposed adoption of Quakerism.

For all the anachronisms in his thought and action, to Winstanley goes the prize as the most radical of the seventeenth-century radicals. For centuries private property had been regarded as the inevitable consequence of, and adjustment to, the fact of man's sinful nature. Winstanley turned the whole proposition upside down. Now it was the existence of private property that had made men sinful. Moreover, he pushed beyond the merely political reforms, which constituted the horizon of most reformers' vision, to fundamental economic relationships, and with simplicity and directness sought to put what he believed into practice, in itself a mark of uncommon radicalism.

WALWYN

One of the few reformers (he repudiated the label "Leveller") to carry his argument beyond the level of moral exhortation to somewhat systematic analysis was William Walwyn (1600-?). Early studies of

59 *Ibid.*, p. 129.

the revolutionary period scarcely mention him, but recent scholarship has done much to enhance his reputation. He was not the typical Leveller either in background or outlook. Grandson of a bishop, son of a country gentleman, himself a successful cloth merchant, he brought to the movement a breadth of view and an inquiring intelligence far surpassing those of the more famous Lilburne. Lacking Lilburne's or Richard Overton's directness and brashness in making mass appeals, Walwyn's greater consistency nevertheless made his a more fundamental radicalism. Against Lilburne's somewhat romantic rendering of English history and self-righteous identification with the principles of Magna Carta, we have Walwyn's sardonic view of Parliamentary history:

See how busie they have been about the regulating of petty inferior trades and exercises, about the ordering of hunting, who should keep Deere and who should not, who should weare cloth of such a price, who Velvet, Gold and Silver, what wages poore Labourers should have, and the like precious and rare business, being most of them put on purpose to divert them from the very thoughts of freedome suitable to the representative body of so great a people. And when by accident or intollerable oppression they were roused out of those waking dreams, then whats the greatest thing they ayme at? Hough wth [how with] one consent cry out for Magna Carta . . . calling that messe of pottage their birthright, the great inheritance of the people, the great Charter of England.[60]

Walwyn's pamphlet *The Power of Love* (1643) was a defense of liberty of conscience and the use of reason in examining all religious opinion. Now that the Bible was in English, he argued, every individual Englishman, whatever his capacity, had the means of religious enlightenment and ought to be allowed to employ it. History shows that the most learned men have been "the troublers of the world. . . . the poore and unlearned Fishermen and Tent-makers were made choyce of for Christ's Disciples and Apostles."[61] Walwyn was an antinomian, that is, one who believed that salvation depended on faith rather than on conformity to law, and held that to true faith the dogma of the churches was largely irrelevant. He also believed in universal redemption, that God's grace had been granted to all and not withheld for the elect few. Thus if God so bestowed his favor on all men, the state at the very least should grant due respect and the right of participation on all men regardless of station.

Despite his consistent religious orientation, on matters of political policy Walwyn tended to be pragmatic. Again his attitude on Magna Carta is indicative. If it does not provide protection for those rights

60 *Englands Lamentable Slaverie* (1645). Quoted in Frank, *The Levellers*, p. 65.
61 Quoted in Frank, *The Levellers*, p. 38.

deemed important in the present, then, said Walwyn, simply draft another charter. Perhaps one of his most pragmatic tenets, in the twentieth-century sense of that word, was the proposition that continual discussion is the basis of free government. Nothing "maintains love, unity and friendship in families: Societies, Citties, Countries, Authorities, Nations; so much as a condescension to the giving, and hearing, and debating of reason."[62]

Compared with their emphasis on the virtues and rights of the common man, constitutionalism was a marginal element in Leveller thought. But they were just Calvinists enough to question their own faith in the perfectibility of man and, in so doing, grant that a constitutional balance of power might be a necessary restraint on man's sin. Walwyn, at least, made the point:

> ... 'tis urged, That if we were in power we would bear ourselves as Tyranically as others have done: We confesse indeed that the experimentall defections of so many men as have succeeded in Authority, and the exceeding difference we have hitherto found in the same men in low and in an exalted condition, make us even mistrust our own hearts, and hardly beleeve our own Resolutions to the contrary. And therefore we have proposed such an Establishment, as supposing men to be too flexible and yielding to worldly Temptations, they should not yet have a means or opportunity either to injure particulars, or prejudice the Publick, without extreme hazard and apparent danger to themselves.[63]

Despite Walwyn's touch of realism, Don M. Wolfe is probably correct in summing up the Levellers as "last-ditch idealists, born centuries too soon, impatient, impulsive, unwilling or unable to gauge the barriers that barred the way to their utopian England."[64]

Natural Law, Reason of State, and Comparative Politics

THE bulk of this chapter has been concerned with prescriptive and ideological theory, for this was the character of most seventeenth-

---

62 *The Fountain of Slaunder Discovered* (1649). Quoted in Zagorin, *A History of Political Thought*, p. 29.

63 *A Manifestation* (1649). Quoted in Frank, *The Levellers*, p. 202. This tract was written by Walwyn in the Tower of London and signed by himself and three fellow prisoners, Lilburne, Overton, and Thomas Prince. The incarceration was distinguished by a protesting march of a crowd of Leveller women on the House of Commons, petition in hand, perhaps the first such participation of women in English politics.

64 Quoted in Frank, *The Levellers*, p. 203. See Wolfe's long Introduction to his edition of *Leveller Manifestoes* (New York: Nelson, 1944), pp. 1-108.

century theorizing. But what we might call descriptive and methodolog-ical theory was not wholly absent. The self-consciously "non-valuational" element in theory will become increasingly important as we move toward the "scientific" twentieth century. But we can briefly note at this point three seventeenth-century currents affecting descriptive theory: a new methodology applied to natural law, "reason of state," and comparative political studies.

GROTIUS AND NATURAL LAW

In our recent discussion of sovereignty (page 34) we saw that Grotius' concept of sovereignty was addressed to particulars rather than stated in the form of a general theory. It was at once both legalistic and moralistic. But Grotius made two other noteworthy contributions. First, he is the "father of international law." Though consciously following a long line of theologians and jurists—Victoria, Ayala, Suarez, Gentili, and others—who had contributed to the law of nations, the comprehen-sive and systematic character of his great work *De jure belli et pacis* won for international law general acceptance as a field. Second, and more central to our interests here, he introduced into the ancient natural-law tradition a new method that later did much to stimulate its secularization.

Grotius' break with the Scholastic tradition of natural law was not sharp. He was a dedicated Christian and took pains to avoid impiety. But his contemporaries and especially his follower Pufendorf saw what was new in Grotius. It was his rationalistic method. He sought to make law a science, modeled on mathematics, with clarity, self-evidence, and coherence the pervasive standards. His rationalism is most forcefully stated in his oft-quoted statement: "Natural Law is so immutable that it cannot be changed by God himself. For though the power of God be immense, there are some things to which it does not extend. . . . Thus God himself cannot make twice two not be four; and in like manner, he cannot make that which is intrinsically bad, not be bad."[65] This position was not meant to be irreligious. It can be compared to the traditional Christian view that the just is just not because God wills it but because God is just. But in the hands of Pufendorf and others this position becomes the vehicle of an extensive secularization characteristic of many modern natural-law theories. "What Grotius had put forth as a hypothesis has become a thesis. The self-evidence of natural law has made the existence of God perfectly superfluous.[66] Spinoza, as we have seen, identifies natural law with man's natural behavior. If not super-

65 *De jure belli et pacis*, Bk. I, Ch. 1, sec. 5, trans. by William Whewell (Cam-bridge, Eng.: Cambridge Univ. Press, 1853), Vol. I, p. 12.
66 Alexander Passerin d'Entrèves, *Natural Law* (London: Hutchinson's Univ. library, 1951), p. 53.

fluous, God for Spinoza has at least become synonymous with nature.

Thus the concept of natural law that entered the seventeenth century as a fairly uniform set of transcendental moral standards, the "right reason" of the Stoics and the Scholastics, had, by the end of the seventeenth century, taken off in a somewhat new direction. The old tradition was still in evidence, to be sure; but along with it was a new conception of an immanent (i.e., not transcendental), naturalistic standard. As we shall see, this new emphasis is a conspicuous part of the thought of both Hobbes and Locke.

REASON OF STATE

On a somewhat different level, a more practical level, the concept of "reason of state" also became an alternative to older conceptions of natural law. The doctrine of reason of state (or, as a result of its association with the *ancien régime, raison d'état*) postulates a rational standard for political action in the interests of a state, a standard supposedly recognizable by rulers and those who bear responsibility but not visible to others. The doctrine is not an offspring of the seventeenth century. The sixteenth century was its real parent. The term was first used in Italy in Guicciardini's *Dialogue Concerning the Government of Florence*, around 1521. By the second half of the sixteenth century it was a catchword. Giovanni Botero published his influential *Ragion di Stato* in Rome in 1589.[67] Later Don Quixote would be discussing *razon de estado* with his Spanish priest and barber. But considering the secularization and nationalization of politics that took place in the seventeenth century, if one cannot say that the doctrine was a child of the age it was at least a stepchild.

Carl Friedrich has pointed out with some insight how the concept of reason of state served as a tool for transferring religious allegiance from its traditional objects to a newly deified state. Understanding this ulterior function of the concept will help explain the loose way in which the concept was used in the sixteenth and seventeenth centuries. Reason of state ("principle" is perhaps a shade closer to *ragion* than "reason") was associated with any discussion of statecraft that followed non-ethical or Machiavellian lines. Botero was simply formulating principles of statecraft in the "mirror of princes" tradition. Later the doctrine came to be an alternative or perhaps foil to natural-law theories. Before Grotius lifted it into the realm of mathematics, the problem of natural law had

_____

67 See *The Reason of State*, trans. by P. J. and D. P. Whaley, (New York: Yale Univ. Press, 1956); Friedrich Meinecke, *Machiavellism, The Doctrine of Raison d'État and Its Place in History* (1924), trans. by Douglas Scott (London: Routledge & Kegan Paul, 1957); Carl J. Friedrich, *Constitutional Reason of State* (Providence: Brown Univ. Press, 1957).

always been the problem of how to explain a history in which wrong seems to triumph just as often as right. Theories that looked unblinkingly at the historical facts of political life and either explained or tried to justify political necessity or acts of expediency were called reason-of-state theories. They were at once both more empirical and less rational than natural-law theories.

In the hands of rulers, harried or unharried, the phrase became a useful piece of obfuscation implying "father knows best." In England, in Darnel's case (1627), Attorney General Heath was arguing for the Crown when he said that reason of state might justify the arrest and detention of men innocent of any breach of the law who nevertheless were dangerous to the state. That master of *raison d'état*, Louis XIV, wrote in his memoirs, "It is always worse for the public to control the government than to support even a bad government which is directed by Kings whom God alone can judge. . . . Those acts of Kings that are in seeming violation of the rights of their subjects are based upon reasons of state—the most fundamental of all motives, as everyone will admit, but one often misunderstood by those who do not rule."[68] Here, reason of state is not so much a theory of government as it is a privileged and probably impenetrable motive of rulers.

Reason of state has not been a characteristic feature of Anglo-American political thinking. During a House of Commons debate of 1621 one of the members protested James' use of the phrase and suggested petitioning the king to define what he meant by it. Doughty old Coke stood up and offered a definition of his own: "Reason of state is often a trick to put us out of the right way; for when a man can give no reason for a thing, then he flieth to a higher strain and saith it is a *reason of state*."[69] Yet even so perceptive and cautious a student of politics as George Savile, first marquis of Halifax, saw in the drive toward national self-preservation a fundamental principle of politics that has a kind of morality of its own, to which he applied the venerable phrase: ". . . there is a Natural Reason of State, an undefinable thing, grounded upon the Common Good of Mankind, which is immortal, and in all Changes and Revolutions, still preserveth its Original Right of saving a Nation when the Letter of the Law perhaps would destroy it; and by whatsoever means it moveth, carrieth a Power with it, that admitteth of no opposition, being supported by Nature."[70] Reason of state thus became in the seventeenth century a naturalistic law able to hold its own with the more ancient natural law.

68 Quoted in Parkinson, *Evolution of Political Thought*, p. 70.
69 Bowen, *Lion and the Throne*, p. 436.
70 *The Character of a Trimmer* (1684), in Walter Raleigh, ed., *The Complete Works of George Saville, First Marquess of Halifax* (Oxford: Clarendon Press, 1912), p. 60.

The Growth of Comparative Political Data

If reason of state implied a concern for the empirical realities of politics, even more was this concern implied by the striking growth of comparative political data in the seventeenth century. While not, strictly speaking, a part of political theory, the development is worth noting. In England Sir William Petty, who has been called the first man to apply statistics to public affairs, was specializing in population studies. Harrington, as we saw, relied heavily on historical data of a sociological type. In France, Pierre d'Avity in 1614 brought together and published a mass of political and anthropological data on the *"empires, royaumes, estats . . . et principautez du monde."* Dutch firms published some fifty treatises on the different states of the world, and in Germany one Werdenhagen mirrored the new interest in comparative politics with his *Introductio universalis in omnes respublicas* (1632).[71] Bacon's advice to "consult only things themselves" had penetrated even to the world of politics.

Conclusion

WHAT is important in the seventeenth century? England is important, for one thing. England was the dramatic center and remains the scholarly center of the seventeenth-century political transformations characteristic of the modern age. But issues, ideas, concepts—which of these are important? These seven are especially worth remembering:

(1) *Divine right*, because, unrealistic as most divine-right theories were, they assumed a reverential, majestic, "given" quality in political authority, a quality that often came closer to describing people's actual attitudes toward authority than the consent theories that replaced divine right.

(2) *Sovereignty*, because the major political theories for the next three hundred years would be inextricably bound up with the moral dilemmas it posed.

(3) *Constitutionalism*, because the ideas of common law, covenant, and contract served as restraints on rulers at a time when economic and nationalistic forces were encouraging a lack of restraint.

(4) *Religious toleration*, because the civil liberties we may today take for granted, especially freedom of expression, had to be fought for and established in a context of intense religious conflict and intolerance.

(5) *Populism*, because the "common man" as distinguished from a

71 See G. N. Clark, *The Seventeenth Century* (Oxford: Clarendon Press, 1929), pp. 213-14.

metaphorical "the people" came closer to the seat of power in the Puritan Revolution than ever before. He won no prizes, but the seeds of popular elections, universal suffrage, mass education, and perhaps even social security were planted there.

(6) *Natural Law,* because at this time natural law was rationalized and made deductive in a new way.

(7) *Reason of state,* because it reminds us that divine right can take many forms, even the form of supposedly hard-headed realism.

CHAPTER

3 | *Hobbes*

THE combination of an apparently hard-headed, power-centered conception of politics with an elaborately logical display of system-building accounts for the initial impact Thomas Hobbes still makes at first reading. The expedient as well as the moral difficulties surrounding present-day schemes of power politics account for the continuing relevance of Hobbes, a master political theorist by almost universal agreement.

Life[1]

MOST of what is known about the early life of Thomas Hobbes comes from his autobiography, composed in Latin couplets at the age of eighty-four, and from the *Brief Lives* of John Aubrey, who was least brief about his friend Hobbes. Neither source is infallible. Hobbes' mother

1 *A note on biography.* There are those who would say that biography is of little use in the study of political theory. Their position is that the validity of any particular theory cannot be confirmed by study of the life of the man who produced it, but only by study of the theory itself and the data it attempts to explain. If, on the other hand, one is attempting to understand how theories come to be produced, that is, to make a theory about theories, one would have to study systematically the biographies of a thousand or so theorists in order to say anything significant about the general relation of biography to the production of theory. Both of these points are well taken. Why, then, include biographical material on the thirteen men whose theories have been selected for special study in this book? The answer is twofold: (1) The undergraduate—and maybe the rest of us, too—can become more emotionally and therefore intellectually involved with a theory when he knows something about the man who produced it. The intellect is not so cold and detached that it

was supposedly fearful of the invasion of their town of Malmesbury by the threatening Spanish Armada and so gave birth to Thomas prematurely. He and terror were thus born twins, said Hobbes. His abiding passion for peace he attributes to his early timidity, which is somehow connected with his birth. His father, vicar of Charlton and Westport, was probably not so ignorant or unlearned as Aubrey said he was, but who would want to question the story of how the senior Hobbes once fell asleep in church after a Saturday night of cards and shouted out that clubs are trumps? There is no question that he did strike a man with his fists and had to flee Malmesbury because of it. He went somewhere "beyond London" and disappeared forever. Thomas and his older brother and sister were brought up by uncle Francis Hobbes, a glover.

SCHOLAR AND TUTOR

Thomas went to school at the Westport church and was an able student. Later, he had the good fortune to be taught at the school of Robert Latimer, a classicist and an unusually able teacher for the time and place. He worked Thomas long and hard, and in 1603, not quite fifteen years of age, Thomas set off for Magdalen Hall, Oxford. He was "tall, sallow, handsome, delicate . . . [with] hazel eyes that shone like 'a bright live-coal' " and such black hair that he had been nicknamed the crow. He did not like Oxford, according to his elderly reflections, because of the arid medieval curriculum; but possibly at the time it was the inept and somewhat degenerate tutors who more displeased him. "Athletic sports had not yet organized idleness," said Sir Leslie Stephen, "but Hobbes seems to have found sufficient excuses for not attending lectures." He much preferred, Aubrey notes, to visit bookshops and "lye gaping on mappes."

After Hobbes received his bachelor's degree in 1608, the principal of Magdalen, who must have known talent even when divorced from industry, recommended him as tutor for William Cavendish, later the second earl of Devonshire. Thus began an association of immense importance to Hobbes' future. He lived as a member of the family until

can do its work unstimulated by contact with personality. If so, teachers and colleges would be superfluous to education and isolated men would not go mad. Put crudely, an encounter with Hobbes the man may help us stay awake through soporific passages of his theory. (2) Of all theory political theory especially involves speculation about people, what they will do, and why. Even though a few bits of biography cannot provide a general theory about theories, we can, perhaps, understand better what Rousseau meant by "society" when we see what "society" did to him and for him. Whether or not Hobbes was a Christian may change our understanding of what he said about the church. We should not be scornful of fragmentary knowledge and ephemeral correlations. In many cases, this is all we can know.

the earl died in 1628. Devonshire House was more stimulating than a university. Nowhere, said Hobbes, was it easier "to study the liberal arts liberally." In 1610, Hobbes and his pupil and friend made the grand tour of Europe, where Hobbes learned French and Italian. Back home, he hunted, played the bass viol, and wrote a translation of Thucydides. Possibly he served as an occasional secretary to Francis Bacon.

With the death of the earl, Hobbes, now forty, somewhat reluctantly became traveling tutor to the son of Sir Gervase Clinton. It was during this time that Hobbes made his first acquaintance with geometry. Once, when in a gentleman's library, he noticed Euclid's *Elements*, opened to Proposition 47. Hobbes read the proposition and said, "By God, this is impossible." So he read the demonstration of it, which referred back to another proposition, which referred back to another, and so on, until he was convinced of its mathematical certainty. From that point on he was "in love with geometry." This love was to have a deep effect on his political theory. In 1631 he went back to Devonshire House, now as tutor to the third earl. Traveling with the earl in France, he became a good friend of Marin Mersenne, a Franciscan monk, who was close to Descartes and a leader in scientific circles. In 1634 or 1636 Hobbes met Galileo; but it is probably apocryphal that Galileo was the first to implant in his mind the idea that geometry might be applied to ethics.

Work and Politics

Back again in England, Hobbes developed an interest in politics. In the *Elements of Law*, which circulated in manuscript form in 1640, Hobbes wrote of the indissolubility of sovereignty in the king and made the first of his several cases for absolutism. The tract occasioned much talk and even resulted in threats on his life. " 'Tis time for me to shift myself," said Hobbes, and went back to France. There has been much discussion of whether this was an act of cowardice. It is probable that the intellectual congeniality of Mersenne and Paris was as much a factor in his move to France as was the hostility of London on the eve of revolution. Hobbes spent eleven years in France this time. He disputed with Descartes, wrote the *De cive* in 1642, and then wrote the *Leviathan*, which Michael Oakeshott has called "the greatest, perhaps the sole, masterpiece of political philosophy written in the English language." It is said that he carried an inkhorn in the head of his cane, and while on walks continually wrote in a notebook that had been subdivided into the sections of the proposed *Leviathan*.

Hobbes was about to run out of money when among the bedraggled royalist refugees flooding into Paris appeared the young Prince of Wales (who later became Charles II). Hobbes secured a position as his tutor in mathematics. Even this association alarmed some of the court who frowned at Hobbes' reputation as an atheist and skeptic. He was sternly advised to stick to mathematics and not to attempt any instruction in politics. However, the publication of the *Leviathan* in 1651 stirred up so much trouble that his situation at the exiled English court became impossible. On the one hand, the royalists said that the *Leviathan* was an endorsement of the Cromwellian status quo; some even claimed that it was but a deceitful expression of support for Cromwell, written so that Hobbes might go home in safety. On the other hand, supporters of the Commonwealth did not like his apparent irreligion and his association with monarchists. In any event, Hobbes did return to England the next year, to stay there for the rest of his life. That the *Leviathan* was not anti-Cromwellian seems suggested by the boast of Hobbes in 1656 that the work had "framed the minds of 1000 gentlemen to a conscientious obedience to the present government." As against this, however, he said it had been the distrustful French clergy rather than the exiled English court that had made him want to leave Paris. The evidence on Hobbes' underlying political loyalties justifies no more than a tentative conclusion. But it seems clear that he was more faithful to the practical implications of his theoretical tenets (namely, that *any* strong government was preferable to anarchy) than either royalist or Cromwellian could understand.

In 1655 Hobbes published his *De corpore*, an exposition of scientific materialism. Unfortunately he led himself up a blind alley by claiming to have squared the circle. This assumption provoked the long and bitter, if not insulting, controversy between Hobbes and John Wallis, the Oxford mathematician. Although never admitting his own errors, Hobbes was on the defensive in this fray. Perhaps hardest of all for him to accept was being outdone in mathematics by a mere minister. Other antagonists in the continuing forensic battles in which Hobbes was engaged were Seth Ward, professor of astronomy at Oxford, who, in his *Vindiciae academiarum* (1654), claimed that Hobbes had no understanding of what English universities were doing, and Bishop Bramhall, with whom Hobbes had been engaged in debate in Paris on the question of free will. The untimely release of some of Hobbes' statements rekindled this controversy in England during the fifties. Despite the support of Sir William Petty, who called him one of the great men of the age, Hobbes was never elected to the Royal Society, which was organized in 1662. The opposition of Wallis, Ward, Wren, and Robert Boyle was too much to overcome. Although Hobbes was not without distinguished friends —the poets Cowley and Davenant, the scientists Harvey and Sorbière, and the brilliant classicist John Selden—he had virtually no philosophical defenders and a host of critics. Some even said it was he who had brought down God's wrath in the London plague of 1665-66 and great fire of 1666. Nothing recedes like success.

REPUTATION

After the Restoration, Hobbes finally won the favor of his former pupil. Charles II liked Hobbes' repartee and likened him to a "Beare to be bayted." From Charles he received an annual pension of £100, which apparently was paid most of the time for the rest of his life. But the Church continued its rumblings against his "atheism." Samuel Pepys noted in his diary in 1668 that he had to pay twenty-four shillings for an eight-shilling copy of the *Leviathan* since the bishops had forbidden its reprinting. Charles himself forbade the publication of *Behemoth, or the Long Parliament,* as much to protect Hobbes as for any other reason. In 1675 Hobbes left London to retire to Chatsworth and Hardwick. There he died in 1679, at the age of ninety. According to Southwell, he died a "very good Christian." In any but a liturgical sense of "Christian," no one is qualified to make this kind of judgment about another person. All we can do is point to externals: Hobbes was overtly anticlerical and had a strong distaste for sermons. Yet he is known to have traveled a mile to take the Eucharist according to the Anglican rite. His cosmology and political theory stand on wholly secular assumptions. Yet he went to great lengths to find scriptural support and preserve the appearance of piety.

Throughout his long life Hobbes was noted for his sharp wit and genial sarcasm and for being, as he called himself, timorous. "There was not much poetry in him," as A. D. Lindsay has said.[2] Nor was he ever modest. "Natural philosophy is therefore but young," he wrote, "but civil philosophy yet much younger, as being no older (I say it provoked, and that my detractors may know how little they have wrought upon me) than my own book *De Cive.*"[3] In his old age he was said to be more "peevish," conceited, and disparaging of others than ever. But even his enemies admired his spirit. He was handicapped by palsied fingers, yet his nimble mind kept working. In his eighties he translated the *Illiad* and the *Odyssey,* not, he said, because his translation was better than previous ones, but because it would give his critics something to work on and divert them "from showing their folly on my more serious writings." At his death he left unfinished a critique of Coke aimed at showing him excessively worshipful of precedent.

2 In the Introduction to his edition of Thomas Hobbes, *Leviathan,* Everyman ed., (New York: Dutton, 1950), p. xiii.

3 *De corpore,* Epistle Dedicatory, in *The English Works of Thomas Hobbes,* Sir William Molesworth, ed. (London: Bohn, 1839-45), Vol. I, p. ix. Hereinafter cited as *Works.*

Hobbes was something of a health faddist, seeking to perspire as profusely as possible on the theory that "old men were drowned inwardly by their own moisture." To this end he played tennis until he was seventy-five and had rubdowns after his daily walk. He also felt that ventilation of the lungs was important and accomplished this by closing all the doors, getting into bed, and singing at the top of his voice.

For a man of his literary distinction, Hobbes died with a rather small library. A favorite theme of his was that most men read too much and cluttered up their minds. He early discovered, reports Bayle's *Dictionary*, that most books are simply quotations from other books and for this reason preferred the established classics.

Despite a life of probity, Hobbes' personal reputation suffered abuse. There was a time in England when all things evil were given the label "Hobbist." "A tract of 1686 describes the 'town-fop' as equipped with three or four wild companions, 'half a dozen bottles of Burgundy, and two leaves of *Leviathan.*' "4 It was not until the end of the century that Hobbes ceased to be the standard whipping boy for controversialists.

Motion and Matter, Geometry and Power

ONE of the first things to be said about the content of Hobbes' political theory is that, substantial as it is, it may be less important than the assumptions upon which it proceeded. Hobbes was probably the first modern political theorist to assert that "civil philosophy" and "natural philosophy" could not be treated in separate compartments but were indissolubly bound together. This is a contention honored in theory or in practice by most of the subjects of this book, but by almost none of Hobbes' contemporaries. Indeed, it was this position that made Hobbes so dangerous to orthodoxy. Francis Bacon was a great exponent of the new science, but of an inductive science. He was willing to let general principles take care of themselves while the great search for data went on. His name could be invoked by the pious scientists of the new Royal Society without fear of being branded heretics by religious or political authorities. But the science that Hobbes championed was deductive science. He cared very little for the gathering of empirical data, but wanted most of all to establish principles that should be right and logically consistent. He was passionately devoted to building a complete system, one that tied together physics, psychology, politics, and ethics. Any such devotion to logical completeness is a threat to orthodoxy; and Hobbes' unfortunate mixture of conceit and timidity compounded

4 Leslie Stephen, *Hobbes* (London: Macmillan, 1904), p. 68.

the threat. "Intellectual audacity combines awkwardly with personal timidity," Leslie Stephen rightly observed. Hobbes "shrank from no convictions to which his logic appeared to lead him; and he expounded them with a sublime self-confidence, tempered, indeed, by his decided unwillingness to become a martyr. Of course, like most men in whom the logical faculty is predominant he was splendidly one-sided."[5]

MOTION

The one universal phenomenon, the basic principle of all things for Hobbes, is motion. "Galileus in our time," he writes, ". . . was the first that opened to us the gate of natural philosophy universal, which is the knowledge and the nature of *motion*."[6] This statement means that the overriding task for scientists and philosophers (Hobbes would make little distinction between them) is to provide a mechanical explanation of the universe, including its political aspects. Audacious is the only word for it. But, more precisely still, what does Hobbes mean by calling motion ultimate? The world, for Hobbes, is reducible to particles—atoms—far beyond the threshold of human perception. These ultimate particles cannot be grasped or known; only the results of their interaction can be known. In themselves they have no properties, only motion: ". . . motion produces nothing but motion."[7] What we can know then, is how one state of motion passes into another, the laws of change. And for this knowledge, geometry is the only tool. "They that study natural philosophy," says Hobbes, "study in vain except they begin at geometry; and such writers and disputers thereof as are ignorant of geometry do but make their hearers and readers lose their time."[8] Thus the irreducibility of motion and faith in geometry are welded together.

Hobbes is not called a "motionalist," though he could be if there were such a word. He is called a materialist. What is the relation of motion as a fundamental principle and matter as a fundamental principle? Hobbes simply asserts with very little argument that the material world is the only world. Thought is a species of motion. Spirit is a species of motion. And only *things* can move: ". . . the whole mass of things that are is corporeal, that is to say, body; and has the dimension of magnitude, namely, length, breadth, and depth . . . and that which is not body is no part of the universe. . . ."[9] All of existence is simply matter in motion.

5 *Ibid.*, pp. 56, 71.
6 *De corpore*, in *Works*, Vol. I, p. viii.
7 *Leviathan*, Ch. 1. All quotations from the *Leviathan* in this chapter are taken from the Lindsay edition. Punctuation, spelling, and capitalization have been modernized. The results may be compared with Michael Oakeshott's edition (Oxford: Blackwell, 1946).
8 Quoted in Stephen, *Hobbes*, p. 81.
9 *Leviathan*, Ch. 46.

But of course it is not so simple. Descartes agreed with Hobbes on the fundamental character of geometrical laws of motion (though the two men were never eager to agree with each other); but he was no materialist. *Cogito ergo sum—Je pense, donc je suis*—"I think, therefore I am." Thought, for Descartes, was separable from, and prior to, the corporeal. He also denied Hobbes' contention that motion itself is the object of sense. We need not go into these arguments. The point is that motion and matter may be more separable than Hobbes imagined.

How does Hobbes explain thought, imagination, dreams, and spirit in bodily terms? The best way to answer this is to summarize the first few books of the *Leviathan*. The union of the physical and the political, the geometrical and the social, is seen at once in the first words of Hobbes' Introduction:

Nature (the art whereby God has made and governs the world) is by the art of man . . . imitated, that it can make an artificial animal. For seeing life is but a motion of limbs . . . why may we not say that all *automata* (engines that move themselves by springs and wheels as does a watch) have an artificial life? For what is the heart, but a spring; and the nerves, but so many strings; and the joints, but so many wheels giving motion to the whole body, such as was intended by the artificer? Art goes yet further, imitating that rational and most excellent work of nature, man. For by art is created that great Leviathan called a COMMON-WEALTH, or STATE (in latin CIVITAS) which is but an artificial man . . . in which the sovereignty is an artificial soul, as giving life and motion to the whole body. . . .[10]

Man is both the "matter" and the "artificer" of this artificial beast, the state. And he is very much the same in both capacities. For Hobbes, unlike almost all other political absolutists, assumes a natural equality of mankind. Although the objects of passions are diverse, the passions themselves are similar. By looking into ourselves we can see the passions of all other men. "He that is to govern a whole nation, must read in himself, not this or that particular man; but mankind." This is hard to do, "harder than to learn any language or science," but it must be done.

SENSE AND THOUGHT

Chapter 1 of the *Leviathan* begins with a discussion of sense. All thoughts, every mental conception, are but representations of sense impressions, singly or in train. "The cause of sense is the external body, or object, which presses the organ proper to each sense."[11] The qualities of sense—light, color, sound, odor, heat—are all forms of motion.

10 *Ibid.*, Introduction.
11 This and the immediately following quotations are from *Leviathan*, Chs. 1-8.

Though unrecognized by the Aristotelian universities, says Hobbes disparagingly, sight is caused by motion, not by something in the object itself. Imagination is "nothing but decaying sense" and is identical with memory, which can be simple or compounded, as when a man puts together the image of a horse with the image of a man to conceive a centaur. Much memory is called experience. The law of inertia forbids that motion itself decay, so Hobbes says that sense decays when one form of motion is overshadowed by another, a greater, closer, or more recent form, as when the sun's light blots out the stars' light without extinguishing it. Imagination during sleep is called dreaming. Hobbes' dream interpretations are not quite Freudian, but they are colorful. From the inability to distinguish between dreams and vision arose "the greatest part of the religion of the gentiles." Hobbes prudently exempts Christianity from this interpretation of religion, but does note the way "crafty ambitious persons abuse the simple people" with "this superstitious fear of spirits. . . ."

Hobbes belongs, partly at least, in the camp of English empiricists in that he denies the existence of any innate ideas in the mind apart from those ideas that derive from experience. "There is no other act of man's mind . . . naturally planted in him." Thus nothing beyond what is finite can be conceived, "therefore the name of God is used, not to make us conceive him; (for he is incomprehensible; and his greatness, and power are unconceivable;) but that we may honour him." If, however, we identify empiricism with experimental science, then Hobbes is not an empiricist. He was committed to deduction, or as he called it in *De corpore*, "the synthetical," rather than the inductive. But there is no doubt about his being a nominalist: "there being nothing in the world universal but names." Through the misuse of words and names, especially through metaphor, thinks Hobbes, men are apt to deceive themselves and others into believing that that which is fictional really exists. He anticipates twentieth-century semanticists in insisting "a man that seeks precise truth, had need to remember what every name he uses stands for . . . else he will find himself entangled in words, as a bird in limetwigs." Thus, settled definitions that can be used with geometrical precision are essential to truth. "For true and false are attributes of speech, not of things." The common-sense use of words is not often "excellently wise," but, then, neither is it "excellently foolish," as in the case of Schoolmen who value words "by the authority of an Aristotle, a Cicero, or a Thomas." Many statements based on false inference are called erroneous, says Hobbes, when they ought to be called absurdities, or senseless speech. In Chapter 5 of the *Leviathan* he gives some quite sophisticated examples of seven types of such absurdities.

WILL, FREE OR DETERMINED?

In animals, there are two kinds of motions, one called vital (pulse, breathing, nutrition, etc.), the other called voluntary (speech, motion of limbs, etc.). The "interior beginnings" of the latter are called the passions, or endeavor. Endeavor toward something is desire; endeavor "fromward" something is aversion. Desire and love are the same; and aversion and hate are the same. Contempt is the stationary middle, "an immobility, or contumacy of the heart." That which we desire is good. That to which we have an aversion is evil. In ethics, Hobbes is a complete subjectivist. The good is a product of motions having their center in the individual and is wholly relative to the individual. The words "good" and "evil" "are ever used with relation to the person that uses them: there being nothing simply and absolutely so; nor any common rule of good and evil to be taken from the nature of the objects themselves. . . ." Already we can begin to see the rationale for strong government. If there is no objective standard of good, men cannot be expected to cooperate in serving it, or get anywhere in trying to communicate what it is rationally. The only way men can adjust their differences is to balance their desires, or more accurately, to establish a tolerable harmony of behavior despite their subjective desires. This can only be done by an external unifying force, which, as we shall see, is for Hobbes the sovereign.

Hobbes rejects the Scholastic definition of will as "rational appetite." Will for him is simply the *last* desire or aversion pertaining to a given act. Will is therefore not free but determined. Moreover, "no discourse whatsoever, can end in absolute knowledge of fact, past or to come. For, as the knowledge of fact, it is originally sense; and ever after, memory. And for the knowledge of consequence, which I have said before is called science, it is not absolute, but conditional." We have, then, a picture of man moved by passions beyond his ultimate control, unable to achieve any fixed, absolute knowledge of anything because all of life is in flux. He is restless because happiness is never assured. Happiness resides in having (not in having had) a desired object. But "because the constitution of a man's body is in continual mutation, it is impossible that all the same things should always cause in him the same appetites and aversions: much less can all men consent in the desire of almost any one and the same object." Life is thus highly dynamic, uncertain, and naturally competitive.

A superficial reader may feel that Hobbes is inconsistent when later he talks of men *voluntarily* contracting with one another. How can a determined will act voluntarily? Hobbes effectively surmounts this difficulty by saying (in Chapter 21) that his conception of liberty or freedom is simply the absence of "external impediments to motion."

A free man is one "not hindered to do what he has a will to," whatever the source of that will. "When the words *free* and *liberty* are applied to anything but bodies, they are abused." Thus, "fear and liberty are consistent," as when a man pays a debt only for fear of landing in jail. He had liberty—i. e., physical liberty—to do otherwise. Thus, "liberty and necessity are consistent." In fact, "to him that could see the connection of . . . [all] causes, the necessity of all men's voluntary actions would appear manifest." Hobbes' determinism remains unshakable. If we were to say that men's thoughts are determined but that the movement of their bodies is free, we would not be far from Hobbes' meaning. This position does not actually reconcile liberty and necessity so much as it puts them in different compartments or at different levels of meaning. Liberty pertains to the superficially descriptive. Necessity pertains to underlying causes. Such a "consistency" does not give much cheer to defenders of free will.

Hobbes does not often provide what we would call experimental evidence on how men behave. He is, as we have stated before, not inducting but deducting. He is saying that *if* the nature of the universe is matter in motion, then men *must*, by and large, behave in a certain way. The "by and large" is important. We are familiar with theoretical models in contemporary physics and economics, but we are only beginning to use them in sociology and political science. Hobbes was constructing a theoretical model. That an individual acted altruistically here and there (as Hobbes himself did—he was notably generous to charitable causes) did not invalidate the system. Economists can assume that men will buy as cheap and sell as dear as they can, and build a fairly workable predictive model on the assumption, even though some men do not behave this way. Hobbes was doing much the same thing for the political order, and we are not being altogether fair if we dismiss him because our best friend has (apparently) unchanging, uncompetitive, altruistic values.

POWER AND POLITICS

In a few chapters of the *Leviathan* Hobbes has moved from the cosmological to the psychological and ethical. In Chapter 10 he enters upon the more strictly political with a discussion of power. "The power of a man (to take it universally) is his present means to obtain some future apparent good. . . . the nature of power is . . . like to fame, increasing as it proceeds; or like the motion of heavenly bodies, which the further they go make still the more haste."

"The greatest of human powers is that which is compounded of the powers of most men, united by consent in one person. . . . Therefore, to have servants is power; to have friends is power. . . ." But, above all, the sovereign of a commonwealth has power.

Hobbes does not miss the subtle psychological factors in power: "Reputation of power is power; because it draws with it the adherence of those that need protection. So is reputation of love of a man's country (called popularity) for the same reason. . . . Good success is power; because it makes reputation of wisdom. . . . Reputation of prudence is power. . . . Eloquence is power; because it is seeming prudence." No one who has watched the political hacks hustle away from a loser to cluster like bees around the winner can doubt Hobbes' realism at this point. But Hobbes tends to go further and make the esteem derived from political power the only esteem. "The value or worth of a man is, as of all other things, his price; that is to say, so much as would be given for the use of his power: and therefore is not absolute; but a thing dependent on the need and judgment of another." High and low honor therefore has meaning only "by comparison to the rate that each man sets on himself." That power is a fundamental concept for Hobbes may be indicated by one of the most famous statements in the *Leviathan:* "I put for a general inclination of all mankind a perpetual and restless desire of power after power that ceases only in death." This is not because man is incapable of being content with moderate power, "but because he cannot assure the power and means to live well which he has present, without the acquisition of more."[12] And so, the kings whose power is greatest are those who most seek additional power. The twentieth century can provide not a few confirmations of this tenet.

The State of Nature and Natural Law

THE subjective basis of the good and the dominance of the passions over the rational have denied to Hobbes' world the possibility of easy co-operation between men. But this does not make Hobbes an elitist, in the usual sense of the word. Hobbes is that rare creature, the equalitarian autocrat.

THE STATE OF NATURE
"Nature has made men so equal in the faculties of body and mind as that though there be found one man sometimes manifestly stronger in body, or of quicker mind than another; yet when all is reckoned together, the difference between man and man is not so considerable as that one man can thereupon claim to himself any benefit to which

12 *Ibid.,* Ch. 11.

another may not pretend as well as he."[13] And he thinks that by and large there is greater equality between men's mental faculties than there is in physical strength. We are not often aware of this because of "a vain conceit of one's own wisdom, which almost all men think they have in a greater degree than the vulgar, that is, than all men but themselves and a few others whom . . . they approve." Out of this equality of ability "arises equality of hope in the attaining of our ends"; but equality of hope means that when men desire the same ends, as they often do, they become natural enemies. They seek gain, or safety, or reputation, and this "is far enough to make them destroy each other." "Hereby it is manifest that during the time men live without a common power to keep them all in awe they are in a condition which is called war, and such a war is of every man against every man." This condition does not mean continual fighting but the continual threat of it, as foul weather may include the gloomy period between two showers of rain. If this is a startling thesis, Hobbes notes in one of his lapses into practical empiricism, let us look at our own experience. Do we not lock our doors at night, and even our chests? In so doing, does not a man "as much accuse mankind by his actions, as I do by my words?" Hobbes also pays brief, and quite erroneous, homage to the savage races of America, who are supposed to illustrate the historicity of the natural war of all against all, the "state of nature" in which the life of man is "solitary, poor, nasty, brutish, and short."

Where does justice lie in this kind of situation? Hobbes' answer is, Nowhere. "Where there is no common power, there is no law: where no law, no injustice." This point is of utmost significance. For centuries men had assumed that there was a level of justice behind or higher than men's daily practice of "justice" in punishing offenders. The Platonic form or ideal of justice might be greatly at variance with what the men of power were doing in the law courts; but the former stood as an immutable standard whereby the latter could be judged. The *jus naturale* of the Roman lawyers was thought to have a more immediate relevance to practice, in that the "right reason" of the judges could bring into operative law, especially the *jus gentium*, the tenets of the more exalted natural law. For St. Thomas Aquinas, positive law was not true law unless it conformed to natural (rational) or divine (scriptural) law. Different as they are, all of these positions assumed that there is a higher law, a higher justice, which either guides or condemns what rulers do. Hobbes wipes away this distinction. Without organized power in society, justice simply does not exist. It is the product of power and not the guide or judge of power. The concept of natural law remains

13 This and the immediately following quotations are from *Leviathan*, Ch. 13.

but it is transformed. It is not what men of right reason *ought* to do to live properly; it is what reason shows men of passion *must* do to stay alive. The difference can hardly be exaggerated.[14]

NATURAL LAW

We noted in the preceding chapter that Spinoza is even more thorough-going than Hobbes in pushing obligation out of natural law; for there is in Hobbes the injunction that a man is obliged to preserve his own skin and to permit others to do likewise. Not a very exalted moral obligation, most of us would say, but it is at least something. "The right of nature, which writers commonly call *jus naturale*, is the liberty each man has to use his own power, as he will himself, for the preservation of his own nature; that is to say, of his own life; and consequently of doing anything which in his own judgment and reasons he shall conceive to be the aptest means thereto."[15] From this one basic "right of nature" Hobbes derives a general "law of nature": "The right [*jus*] is the liberty to do or forbear; the law [*lex*] determines and binds." They are two sides of a coin. The law of nature forbids a man to do that which is destructive of his life. From this premise Hobbes logically derives some fourteen subsidiary laws of nature and hints at others.[16]

The first and most fundamental of these laws has two "branches," first, "to seek peace and follow it," and second, "by all means we can, to defend ourselves." In Hobbes' view, the two are simply positive and negative corollaries. The second law is to be content with as much liberty as one is willing to grant other men against oneself. This sounds like the golden rule, and indeed Hobbes cites the Scriptures on the point, later suggesting that if his deductions on natural law are too subtle, the golden rule is "one easy sum, intelligible even to the meanest capacity." But the chief burden of his argument at this point is to justify the basic concept of the covenant by which men give up control of all but one basic liberty to the government. This covenant is divested of all the religious overtones the term held for the Puritans. It is a purely secular arrangement. In fact, Hobbes specifically excludes covenants with God from his discourse: "To make covenant with God is impossible, but by mediation of such as God speaks to, either by revelation supernatural,

14 A traditional natural-law formulation will, as indicated above, stress "must" also, and minimize "ought"—or, rather, deny the distinction between them. There is an element of necessity in all natural-law thinking. But we might say it is long-run, even ultimate necessity that leaves man free to make a moral choice in day-to-day life. The necessity in Hobbes' natural law is immediate, practical, and, because he is a determinist, seems scarcely a matter of moral choice at all. How *much* morality resides in Hobbes' system we shall examine in a moment.

15 *Leviathan*, Ch. 14.

16 *De cive*, Chs. 2-3, lists twenty laws of nature.

or by his lieutenants that govern under him, and in his name. For otherwise we know not whether our covenants be accepted or not."[17] The supernatural and the natural were not to be dealt with in the same terms. This was one of the several bases of the charge of "atheism" cast at Hobbes. But atheism and amorality are not synonyms. Some of the other laws of nature derived from the basic tenet of self-protection have unmistakable moral overtones. They include the following pre-scriptions:[18]

(3) Men should perform covenants made.

(4) No man should show ingratitude for those gifts that are be-stowed upon him from another by "mere grace." Ingratitude "has the same relation to grace that injustice has to obligation by covenant."

(5) ". . . every man [should] strive to accommodate himself to the rest." This is the law of "compleasance."

(6) ". . . a man ought to pardon the offenses past of them that re-penting, desire it. For pardon is nothing but granting of peace" and aversion to peace is contrary to the law of nature.

(7) In taking revenge, returning evil for evil, men should look to the good that will follow the action rather than to the evil that is past. Revenge without respect to the profit to come is "vainglory, and con-trary to reason, and to hurt without reason tends to the introduction of war, which is against the law of nature. . . ."

(8) Because signs of contempt or hatred provoke fighting, no man "by deed, word, countenance, or gesture, [should] declare hatred or contempt of another." The breach of this precept is "contumely."

(9) Every man should acknowledge other men as his equal by nature. The breach of this precept is "pride."

(10) Upon entering into the condition of peace, no man should reserve to himself any right which he is not content "should be reserved to every one of the rest."

These precepts, it is clear, are "shoulds." They are not laws in the same sense as the law of gravity. There is genuine moral content in them. Yet they are but deductions from a precept that, given a non-theistic bias, has a kind of inexorability similar to that of the law of gravity; if a man does not preserve himself, he ceases to exist. The earth-bound, prudential, mechanistic ethics of Hobbes would seem to justify their designation as a-theistic, though not necessarily with all the diabolical connotations his seventeenth-century critics attached to the label "atheism."

17 *Leviathan*, Ch. 14.
18 All from *Leviathan*, Ch. 15.

Covenant, Commonwealth, and Sovereign

THE term "covenant" was a fairly technical one for Hobbes. In Chapter 14 he spells out the conditions of valid and invalid covenants. For example, covenants are invalid that are against the civil law, that require the parties to do the impossible, that take away from the individual the right to defend his own life when directly threatened, where the individual has already covenanted away the thing to be pledged by a previous valid covenant, and so forth. On the other hand, "Covenants entered into by fear, in the condition of mere nature, are obligatory."[19] There is a fine distinction between mere promises, words that do not bind, and covenants, which are more intractable. "The force of words being . . . too weak to hold men to the performance of their covenants, there are in man's nature but two imaginable helps to strengthen it, and those are either a fear of the consequences of breaking their word, or a glory or pride in appearing not to need to break it. This latter is a generosity too rarely found to be presumed on. . . ." Thus oaths are regarded by Hobbes as superfluous, adding nothing to the obligation incurred.

So central is the concept of covenant that justice itself rests upon it: ". . . the definition of injustice is no other than *the not performance of covenant*. And whatsoever is not unjust is *just*." The third of Hobbes' laws of nature, you recall, is that men should perform their covenants made. Men are therefore obligated to do that which they probably would not do in the absence of fear, and that is all they are required to do as far as society is concerned.[20] Hobbes' society (state and society are virtually synonymous for Hobbes) begins where fear begins and ends where fear ends. Society, it would seem, is perennially walking a tightrope of fear strung between the terror of a state of nature and a genuinely moral community.

Hobbes' concept of the valid covenant was a general concept applying to every aspect of life outside the state of nature. But by far the most crucial application of it was to the establishment of a commonwealth, for there could not be *any* valid covenants prior to that one. By the same token, social life could not last for long after a commonwealth expired. For "covenants without the sword are but words, and of no strength to secure a man at all. Therefore, notwithstanding the laws of nature . . .

19 This and the subsequent quotations are from *Leviathan*, Ch. 14.

20 In his argument against "breach of promise," however, Hobbes does seem to depart from his consistent egoism by calling the truly just man one who keeps his convenants without the need of fear. Hobbes would appear to be gratuitously praising a "higher" motive. But such a man is, in any case, so rare as not to upset the over-all mechanistic system. See below, pp. 89 ff.

if there be no power erected . . . every man will and may lawfully rely
on his own strength and art for caution against all other men."21

The only way to erect such a common power . . . is [for men] to confer
all their power and strength upon one man, or upon one assembly of men,
that may reduce all their wills, by plurality of voices, unto one will. . . . This
is more than consent or concord; it is a real unity of them all, in one and
the same person, made by covenant of every man with every man in such a
manner as if every man should say to every man, *I authorize and give up my
right of governing myself to this man, or to this assembly of men, on this
condition, that thou give up thy right to him, and authorize all his actions in
like manner.* This done the multitude so united in one person is called a
COMMON-WEALTH, in latin CIVITAS. This is the generation of that great LEVIA-
THAN, or rather (to speak more reverently) of that *mortal god,* to which
we owe under the immortal *God,* our peace and defence.

What is created by this act is an artificial person, who (or which) acts
in the name of every individual who is a party to the covenant; ". . . he
that carries this person is called SOVEREIGN, and said to have *sovereign
power;* and every one besides, his SUBJECT."

Let us examine some of the key phrases in this central declaration of
Hobbes and note some of the problems they raise. The covenant is more
than "consent or concord." The social contract is no romantic picture
of individuals agreeing in the sweet light of reason to follow a certain
course as long as it suits their fancy. It is no game. It is "a real unity," a
hard and inescapable unity in which diverse wills are ground into one by
the stark terror of diversity and the sheer power of the surrogate. Not
that Hobbes is able to make this transaction literal. There is still the "*as if*
every man should say to every man. . . ." It is a legal fiction of sorts but
still real, made real by the untenability of any alternative interpretation
of why men must and do accept government over them. "Generation,"
of course, refers to the process of begetting and not to the historical age.
The Leviathan has always gobbled up its subjects. But few before Hobbes
dared to call it a "mortal god" which, despite passing reference to the
immortal God, seems to be the overriding center of allegiance for mortal
man. The multitude is "united in one person." We may be confused by
the statement that this "person" can be an assembly of men. A person for
Hobbes is any entity "whose words or actions are considered as . . .
representing the words or actions of another man. . . . When they are
considered as his own then he is called a natural person. And when they
are considered as representing the words and actions of another, then he
is a feigned or artificial person."22 In the same way our corporations today
are persons in the law.

21 This and the immediately following quotations are from *Leviathan,* Ch. 17.
22 *Leviathan,* Ch. 16.

The sovereign created by this original covenant or contract is thus an "artificial person." He "personates"—not impersonates—every member of the commonwealth who formerly made up the headless multitude. It is important to note that as the creation *of* the contract he is not a party to it. The contract is between each and every subject. Therefore, there is no legal way by which the subjects can call the sovereign to account. His existence is the condition of their peace. Yet he speaks for them with a voice of his own; he is not a representative in the democratic sense of one who mirrors public opinion on all issues. Only by understanding this unique position of the sovereign can we make sense of Hobbes' controversial statement, "The law of nature and the civil law contain each other and are of equal extent."[23] He means that neither can become operative until the commonwealth comes into being. The sovereign is the sole source of civil law, yet because he personates all his subjects they are the authors of his every act, even the unwise ones, even the ones they disapprove of. This, as someone has said, seems a clear triumph of logic over common sense.

For all his skepticism, common sense does often seem to be crowded out of Hobbes' system. Yet we must always keep in mind that Hobbes is—or thinks he is—dealing with the *ultimate* basis of political obligation, which is fear. A man is *afraid* to disobey the sovereign for fear of the anarchy he might precipitate in a kind of chain reaction of disobedience. Remove the common tie of obedience to the sovereign and an explosion results. Since men's fearful nature and drive toward self-preservation are presumed to be basically the same from one man to the next, Hobbes' citizen can logically feel that if he does not obey, no one else will obey. In a sense, then, it is fair to say that this man has accepted and made his own the sovereign's command, even though it would not have been his command had he been sovereign. The questions this conclusion raises for us are not so farfetched. How much of our so-called morality does in fact rest on fear? Should we be thankful for any system that keeps our "natural" selves in check? Plato raised the same kind of question in the *Republic* with Glaucon's fable of the magic ring of Gyges, which made a man invisible at will and opened up all sorts of possibilities for unpunished mischief. Would we be our present decent selves if we could get away with anything?

Morality in the State of Nature

IN Hobbes' setting, this question becomes that of the existence of morality in the state of nature. There is no justice or injustice in his state of nature.

23 *Ibid.*, Ch. 26.

Is there no morality either? If none, if man is but an animal without a government over him, how can we expect him to live like a moral creature even with a government? Not surprisingly, these are the very issues that most divide contemporary Hobbes scholars. While we cannot do justice to the subtlety of their arguments here, the vitality of their disagreements helps to wash away any merely antiquarian attitude we might have toward Hobbes.

The arguments of these scholars fall basically into three categories. The first position is that there is little morality anywhere in Hobbes' system. Of the older commentators, Sir Leslie Stephen[24] seemed to hold the view that when Hobbes used the term "obligation" he used it in either a descriptive or, in some cases, a deceptive sense, rather than with truly moral connotations. George Sabine states that Hobbes "is saying merely that in order to cooperate men must do what they dislike to do, on pain of consequences which they dislike still more. In no other sense is there logically any obligation whatever in Hobbes' system."[25] The obligation here seems dependent *only* on the avoidance of punishment. Likewise, Bertrand de Jouvenel asserts that moral conduct for Hobbes rests solely "on the fear of repression—and on nothing else." He grants that Hobbes' sovereign will employ his wiles to keep this fear in the background of men's minds, but doubts that it thereby gains any moral stature: "It is by means of the desire to avoid the punishment that the will is made up against the prohibited act. This desire to avoid punishment forms by degrees good habits, with the result that the punishment becomes no longer present to the mind and the law comes to be obeyed from a respect now second nature. Let us note that this is to assimilate the training of citizens to the training of dogs."[26]

The second position is that man, for Hobbes, becomes moral only in the commonwealth, that morality is not natural but artificial, a product of social organization. Sterling Lamprecht, for example, finds that "Hobbes is insisting that any significant morality is social in character and presupposes the occurrence of regularized procedures. Morality is not significantly present when men are considered in their separateness as atomic individuals,"[27] even though there are "the beginnings of morality" in the state of nature. "Hobbes never maintained, as Hobbism attributed to him, that law creates moral distinctions by fiat." Michael Oakeshott is another

24 *Hobbes.*

25 *History of Political Theory* (New York: Holt, 1937), p. 469.

26 *Sovereignty*, trans. by J. F. Huntington (Chicago: Univ. of Chicago Press, 1957), p. 242.

27 This and the immediately following quotations are from the Introduction to his edition of Thomas Hobbes, *De cive* (New York: Appleton-Century-Crofts, 1949), pp. xxiii-iv. See also Lamprecht's "Hobbes and Hobbism," *Am. Pol. Sci. Rev.*, Vol. 34 (1940), pp. 31-53.

who argues that the concept of obligation in Hobbes is genuinely moral, but that it does not come into being until civil society is founded. By declining to label as moral an obligation stemming from rational self-interest alone, Oakeshott avoids making an easy but empty case. One

> . . . kind of obligation, which we will call *moral* obligation, is not the effect of superior power, or of the rational perception of the consequences of actions, but of Authority. . . . An Authority is a will that has been given a Right by a process called authorization. . . . the only sort of action to which the term moral obligation is applicable is obedience to the commands of an authority authorized by the voluntary act of him who is bound. The answer to the question, Why am I morally bound to obey the will of the Sovereign? is, Because I have authorized this Sovereign, 'avouched' his actions, and am 'bound by my own act.'[28]

As Oakeshott interprets Hobbes, physical, moral, and rational (self-interested) obligations are all necessary to preserve civil society. The mixture of the three Oakeshott calls *political* obligation.

The third position is that for Hobbes morality is an attribute of man in both the state of nature and the commonwealth, morality under the commonwealth being merely a new form of that which existed before. A. E. Taylor, for example, has argued that because Hobbes' laws of nature may be known by the use of reason they have the same kind of obligatory character as Kant's categorical imperatives.[29] In a tightly reasoned book Howard Warrender has examined with great care everything Hobbes has to say about obligation. He asserts, "A moral obligation . . . to obey the civil law cannot logically be extracted from a system in which man has *no* moral obligations before or apart from the institution of that law. Any view that assumes otherwise, contains a hiatus in the argument that cannot be surmounted, and if, in fact, this is Hobbes' position, he must be held to have failed in his main enterprise."[30] Warrender does not think Hobbes has failed. He finds that Hobbes relies upon two types of obligation, that which results from physical coercion and does not implicate the individual's will, and that which is voluntary and does implicate his will.

28 Michael Oakeshott, in the Introduction to his edition of *Leviathan*, pp. lix-lx.
29 "The Ethical Doctrine of Hobbes," *Philosophy*, Vol. 13 (1938), pp. 406-24. Kant's formulation is: "Act only on that maxim whereby thou canst at the same time will that it should become a universal law." One should bind oneself, in other words, to the same standard that one would impose on others. Compare Hobbes' second law of nature: "That a man . . . be contented with so much liberty against other men as he would allow other men against himself." (*Leviathan*, Ch. 14.) In both cases the rules are categorical in the sense of being offered as dictates of universal reason. In neither case are they categorical in the sense of being inescapable.
30 *The Political Philosophy of Hobbes; His Theory of Obligation* (Oxford: Clarendon Press, 1957), p. 6.

The former is physical and the latter is political or moral. The sovereign, the source of civil law, has, it turns out, relatively little physical power: ". . . the power of the sovereign is primarily the reluctance of his subjects to break natural law."[31] Their reluctance to break the natural law is never wholly divorced from fear of physical threats; but neither is it typically divorced from their own conception of duty. Says Hobbes in *Behemoth*: "For if men know not their duty, what is there that can force them to obey the laws? An army, you will say. But what shall force the army? Were not the trained bands an army? Were they not the janissaries, that not very long ago slew Osman in his own palace at Constantinople?"[32] The capacity and the willingness of men to do their duty is, then, a necessary, though not a sufficient, condition for the existence of society.

Leo Strauss is another who affirms the moral if not the moralistic characteristic of Hobbes' thought. In tracing its evolution he finds that the fear of death—to be distinguished from the fear of mere punishment— becomes for Hobbes the most significant of men's legitimate, moral motives and is set against pride and vanity. One obeys the law because the existence of law is the alternative to death.

Hobbes distinguishes no less precisely than other moralists between legality and morality. Not the legality of the action but the morality of the purpose, makes the just man. That man is just who fulfills the law because it is law and not for fear of punishment or for the sake of reputation. . . . In believing that the moral attitude, conscience, intention, is of more importance than the action, Hobbes is at one with Kant and the Christian tradition. He differs from this tradition at first sight only by his denial of the possibility that just and unjust action may be distinguished independently of human legislation.[33]

In the state of nature every action is permitted because every individual is his own judge; but even there not every *intention* is approved by Hobbes, only the intention of self-preservation.[34]

---

31 *Ibid.*, p. 317.

32 *Behemoth*, Frederick Tonnies, ed. (London: Simpkin, Marshall, 1889), p. 59.

33 *The Political Philosophy of Hobbes, Its Basis and Its Genesis*, trans. by Elsa Sinclair (Oxford: Clarendon Press, 1936), p. 23.

34 A fourth position might be that of John Laird, who cites quotations from Hobbes that would substantiate *both* positions two and three above and says, "I cannot see how these views can be reconciled." He further notes, "Very probably Hobbes would not have restricted his ethical theory to the problem of deliverance from civil tumult had the calamities of his own England weighed less heavily on his spirit." *Hobbes* (London: Oxford Univ. Press, 1934), pp. 184, 188.

Obligation in Hobbes Summarized

WHAT can we say in summarizing Hobbes' difficult theory of obligation? First of all, despite what many people casually say about him, Hobbes is not a might-makes-right man. Even in the state of nature, though external forces push us like animals, "pride, ingratitude, breach of contracts (or injury), inhumanity, contumely, will never be lawful, nor the contrary virtues to these ever unlawful, as we take them for dispositions of the mind, that is, as they are considered in the court of conscience, where only they oblige and are laws."[35] In the commonwealth, these good motives can be more safely externalized. It is the sovereign's specific moral obligation to provide for the safety of the people and to make good laws. "But what is a good law? By a good law, I mean not a just law; for no law can be unjust. . . . A good law is that which is *needful*, for the *good of the people*, and withal *perspicuous*."[36] True, no one but God can enforce this obligation on the sovereign, and remembering Hobbes' theology, this is not much of a restraint; but it is further evidence refuting the charge of amorality against Hobbes.

Second, the fear of death is not a despicable human motive for Hobbes, but rather a motive of some moral significance. A man can seek the preservation of life with some dignity and rationality—more dignity than when he merely seeks to avoid punishment and more rationality than when he seeks preferment for the sake of pride and vanity. We think of the fear of death as anxiety-ridden, irrational, egoistic. It is that, in part, no doubt. But Hobbes sometimes seems to make a much more positive affirmation out of this passion for safety. At one point in *De cive* he says, "By safety must be understood, not the sole preservation of life in what condition soever, but in order to its happiness. For to this end did men freely assemble themselves, and institute a government, that they might, as much as their human condition would afford, live delightfully."[37] This interpretation gives promise of an expanded and more positive hedonism than we usually associate with Hobbes. Of course, it may well be that any form of hedonism, if widely and rigorously followed in a society, would tear it apart, rather than hold it together as Hobbes expected. The contention here is not that Hobbes' morals are either adequate or realistic, only that they existed.

Third, Hobbes does have a theory of duty, closely identified with his natural-law principle of keeping covenants. Constraint is necessary to

35 *De cive*, Ch. 3, sec. 29, *Works*, Vol. II, p. 46.
36 *Leviathan*, Ch. 30. Italics in the original.
37 *De cive*, Ch. 13, sec. 4.

extract dutiful obedience from most men; but, as noted above, Hobbes does seem to concede moral superiority to the man who does his duty without constraint. To give his sense of duty Kantian overtones is, however, a bit strained. Hobbes' duty is not the universal ethical principle it is for Kant, either in scope of application to subject matter, or in its place in a hierarchy of values. Duty was a function of, and therefore subordinate to, the obligation to obey the sovereign.

Fourth, we cannot say that all morality was a product of society for Hobbes. Some of the evidence has been adduced above, and it seems ample, to indicate that goodness and rightness, and even conscience, have a place in the state of nature. In addition we would do well to recall that Hobbes is an individualist, a very thoroughgoing individualist for whom society is an artificial even if necessary creation. This position would seem to follow from his cosmology of atomic particles and his subjectivist epistemology. But more concretely we can see in his advice to the sovereign all sorts of individualistic assumptions. The wise sovereign would issue relatively few commands. Unnecessary laws do no good; they are but "traps for money." The purpose of the sovereign is "not to bind the people from all voluntary actions but to direct and keep them in such a motion as not to hurt themselves by their own impetuous desires. . . ."[38] Indeed, his major purpose seems to be to establish conditions for the safe pursuit of individual ends. He was close in many ways to the later laissez-faire school in matters of practical economics. All of this is enough to show that those who call Hobbes an early totalitarian do not know what they are talking about. The essence of totalitarianism is the absorption of the individual into the mass and the destruction of his privacy. Hobbes wanted to protect his privacy and was manifestly unmoved by high-flown collective ideals.

Revolution

WE must pass by many of the subjects Hobbes discusses in the *Leviathan*: the rights of the sovereign (Chapter 18); the nature of sovereignty under monarchy, democracy, and aristocracy (Chapter 19); the functions of public ministers (Chapter 23); the economy (Chapter 25); and others. The book qualifies as a major work on grounds of comprehensiveness as well as originality. But two problems, both related to sovereignty, are enough to command our attention for the rest of this chapter. The first is that of revolution.

If one contends that there is no moral obligation in Hobbes, then the difference between the state of nature and the commonwealth is simply

38 *Leviathan*, Ch. 30.

one of centralized force. This would seem to be an open invitation to continual rebellion and violence. We have rejected such a view of Hobbes, but problems remain. One problem is the general unsettlement produced by Hobbes' radical, atomic individualism. The core of Hobbes' critique of Coke[39] was directed against Coke's confidence in the wisdom embodied in the accidents of the historical past. Coke gave custom an authority superior to that of any living lawmaker. Such an exalted view of custom would inhibit the sovereign, and Hobbes had to reject it. To the sovereign Hobbes gave the power to eliminate undesirable customs at will. Thanks in part to the anthropologists, we now know more fully than Hobbes how absolutely inescapable is the authority of custom in any functioning society. To treat customs lightly or bend them to suit a sovereign's will is to invite rebellion. Hobbes the antirevolutionary is in this sense as revolutionary as anyone. Granted that Hobbes' advice to the sovereign is to rock the boat as little as possible, Hobbes could not guarantee that a sovereign would follow his advice.

A second weak spot stems from Hobbes' distinction between sovereignty by "institution" and sovereignty by "acquisition." In the former, men come together and by formal contract establish a sovereign; in the latter the sovereign simply takes over by conquest. The two differ "only in this, that men who choose their sovereign do it for fear of one another and not of him whom they institute: but in this case [acquisition] they subject themselves to him they are afraid of. In both cases they do it for fear."[40] Whatever the method of establishment, afterward the power and authority of the sovereign is identical. Yet it would seem from our earlier discussion of obligation that the requisite pattern of duties would be much more easily maintained by an instituted sovereign than by a conquering sovereign. Recall Hobbes' statement in *De cive* about safety meaning more than bare survival, but rather living "delightfully." This was the end for which men did "institute a government." This position certainly loses conviction if one says: living delightfully is the end for which men yield to a conqueror. Moreover, if elected sovereigns and bullying sovereigns have identical status, is this identity not an encouragement to the bully to foment rebellion wherever and whenever he can? You, too, can become a sovereign. Why delay? Though a moralist, Hobbes could not conceive of any moral grounds that could limit a sovereign's general grant of power, for such a conception would shatter the logic of his whole rationale for government. Thus, again, he seemed to invite the very revolution he hated.

Finally, a more practical problem: once a revolution has in fact started,

---

39 See *Dialogue Between a Philosopher and a Student of the Common Laws of England*, in *Works*, Vol. VI; and *Leviathan*, Ch. 26, secs. 6-7.
40 *Leviathan*, Ch. 20.

how does a subject know who is the sovereign? The problem was not altogether academic for Hobbes. He takes up the question at the very end of the *Leviathan*, in the appended "Review and Conclusion": ". . . the point of time, wherein a man becomes subject to a conqueror, is that point, wherein having liberty to submit to him, he consents, either by express words, or by other sufficient sign, to be his subject." Obligation to the former sovereign ends "when the means of his life is within the guards and garrisons of the enemy." A civilian can rightfully yield sooner than a soldier. As long as the old sovereign still has troops in the field, the soldier should be loyal to him. But even the soldier has no obligation beyond the point where the old sovereign can protect and nourish him. If a mess wagon blows up, this could presumably mean a change of sovereigns for a hungry foot soldier. If either soldier or civilian is thrown into jail by the conqueror, there is no obligation to the authority which does it. Every man, it seems, has a natural right to try to get out of jail. What constitutes the crucial difference between a predatory sovereign's protection when one is in jail and his protection when one is out of jail, Hobbes does not elucidate. Yet there are times, after all, when a man will be better fed in jail than out.

Lesser Corporations, Religion, and the "Kingdom of Darkness"

WE see what Leslie Stephen meant by talking about Hobbes' "splendid one-sidedness" when we look at his view of organizations that might stand between the individual and the sovereign. The idea of social stability being maintained by a balance of power between social organizations of less extent than the state was utterly alien to Hobbes' frame of mind: ". . . to leave to a [subordinate] body politic of subjects to have an absolute representative to all intents and purposes were to abandon the government . . . contrary to their peace and defence."[41] Hence his strong antipathy to factions: ". . . leagues of subjects . . . are, in a Commonwealth, . . . for the most part unnecessary and savour of unlawful design; and are for that cause unlawful, and go commonly by the name of factions, or conspiracies." Adopting an organic metaphor, Hobbes likened lawful corporations to muscles serving under the higher organs of the sovereign officials; but unlawful corporations were "wens, biles, and apostems."[42]

Hobbes was thoroughly consistent in disparaging institutional forms that jeopardized his conception of sovereignty. The traditional "mixed-

41 *Ibid.*, Ch. 22.
42 *Ibid.*

state" idea, for example, the balance of king, aristocracy, and people, Hobbes regarded as impossible: ". . . power is either without limit, or is again restrained by some other greater than itself; and so we shall at length arrive to a power which hath no other limit. . . . that same is called the supreme command."[43] Hobbes' hostility to Presbyterianism, best expressed in *Behemoth, or The Long Parliament* (1682, posthumous), is at least partly related to its mixed and therefore ambiguous form of ecclesiastical government, with neither the bishops of Anglicanism nor the congregational autonomy of the Independents.

Religion in general, however, is a subject of special concern for Hobbes. About one half of the *Leviathan* was devoted to scriptural exegesis and the subject of religion. Yet, paradoxically, the greater Hobbes' attention to religion, the more secular his thought became. Leo Strauss has traced this concern as it developed through the pages of the *Elements of Law* (1640), the *De cive* (1642), and the *Leviathan* (1651). The trend is consistently toward greater but more critical attention to the Scriptures, away from "natural theology" (i. e., the discovery of God's will through reason) toward revealed theology, and toward a more rigid political absolutism. The *Elements of Law* had three chapters on religion, the *De cive* had four, and the *Leviathan* seventeen. Yet while the *De cive* devoted two chapters to the scriptural proof of natural law, the *Leviathan* gave two paragraphs to the same subject. While in all three works Hobbes affirms that belief that Jesus is the Christ is all that is necessary for salvation,[44] the basis of religious authority shifts from the *Elements*, where it is the Church, to the *De cive*, where it is personal belief in Jesus, to the *Leviathan*, where it is the political sovereign who permits certain beliefs. After the *Elements*, says Strauss, "That scripture vouches for priestly rule is from now on not an argument for priestly rule, but an argument against scripture."[45]

Hobbes' aim, of course, is not to eliminate religious belief but to make it a tool of the state, this so-called Erastian position. To this end he discusses angels, miracles, the sacraments, redemption, the "office of our blessed saviour" and in the longest chapter of the book, Chapter 42,

---

43 *De cive*, Ch. 6, sec. 18, *Works*, Vol. II, p. 88.

44 Strauss, who is very sensitive to the pressures on writers in turbulent times to avoid extreme unorthodoxy if they are to live, regards this affirmation as merely conventional and in no way proof of Hobbes' Christianity or even his theism. See *Natural Right and History* (Chicago: Univ. of Chicago Press, 1953), p. 198*n*. Oakeshott, on the other hand, notes that Hobbes died "in mortal fear of hell-fire" and credits him with a more genuine concern with religion. To judge Hobbes personally an atheist seems quite unwarranted, even though the consequences of his writings would be no different were such a judgment warranted. Perhaps this is all that Strauss means.

45 *Political Philosophy of Hobbes*, p. 74.

"power ecclesiastical." His advice to those who wish to make religion rational has become classic: "For it is with the mysteries of our religion, as with wholesome pills for the sick, which swallowed whole have the virtue to cure; but chewed, are for the most part cast up again without effect."[46]

The long, involved, and heavily scriptural argument of Chapter 42 can be summarized quite briefly. "Preachers . . . have not magistral but ministerial power"; they are rightfully concerned only with faith, and "faith has no relation to or dependence upon compulsion." Compulsion is within the province of the sovereign, who, in the interests of peace, may find it necessary to exert compulsion that affects the externals of worship, and even teaching.

The last part of the *Leviathan*, the "Kingdom of Darkness" (Chapters 44-47), is a biting, savage indictment of the "confederacy of deceivers that, to obtain dominion over men in this present world, endeavor by dark and erroneous doctrines to extinguish in them the light both by nature and the gospel, and so to dis-prepare them for the Kingdom of God to come."[47] The Church of Rome took the brunt of this attack, but by no means all of it. These deceptive clergymen, the "children of darkness," were compared to the fairies who "inhabit darkness, solitudes and graves. . . . What kind of money is current in the kingdom of fairies is not recorded. . . . But the ecclesiastics in their receipts accept of the same money that we do."[48] It is only after Hobbes' Erastianism becomes overwhelming, toward the end of the *Leviathan*, that one is likely to go back to the beginning and note a short but incredibly audacious statement in his catalogue of passions. "Fear of power invisible, feigned by the mind, or imagined from tales publicly allowed, RELIGION; not allowed, SUPERSTITION."[49] This is surely the ultimate power of the sovereign, the power to define religion out of existence.

Conclusion: The Problem of Sovereignty

SHAKESPEARE would not be Shakespeare if he were not an Elizabethan. But neither would he be Shakespeare if he were *only* an Elizabethan. He is read both because he reflects his age and because he transcends his age. The same can be said for Hobbes. He, too, is a fascinating mixture of the old and the new, the parochial and the universal. We said in Chapter 1 that modernity was characterized by individualism, the nation-state, and the new science. Hobbes' thought can be hung on these three hooks with not much left over, and in each case the old is blended with the new.

46 *Leviathan*, Ch. 32.   47 *Ibid.*, Ch. 44.   48 *Ibid.*, Ch. 47.   49 *Ibid.*, Ch. 6.

Hobbes was an individualist in the extreme. As the atoms bounced back and forth within the individual, individuals were seen to carom off each other as each went his way in pursuit of individual ends. Despite his absolutism, Hobbes caught the spirit of laissez faire. The individual in his system was liberated from a wide variety of constraints. The natural law became a kind of background regulating principle comparable to what the economics of a subsequent century would call the invisible hand. There was very little by way of restrictive allegiances standing between allegiance to self and allegiance to the sovereign. The medieval *corpus mysticum* was thoroughly shattered. Yet Hobbes did not depart from the basic forms of medieval political speculations. He kept the concept of natural law and twisted it to his own ends. He did not repudiate the distinction between objective natural law and subjective natural right— he simply nullified it: the concept of sovereignty was preserved, but made precise and concrete; "the people" were still to be reckoned with, but as individuals, not as a community; the Scriptures were to be followed, but under new Erastian interpretations. He did not turn his back on earlier theorists. As Laird expresses it, "he beat them at their own game."

In his victory Hobbes erected a state that was absolute not merely in the sense of supreme social power but also in the sense of supreme religious authority. Obedience to God's laws "is the greatest worship of all," but the same natural reason that reveals these laws requires us to entrust their application to the sovereign. "It follows that those attributes which the sovereign ordains in the worship of God, for signs of honor, ought to be taken and used for such by private men in their public worship."[50] The political has superseded the religious. This is something new, at least in the postclassical period. Before Hobbes the state of nature was a theological term. Hobbes made it a political term, with civil society replacing the state of grace. Oakeshott says that he consciously or unconsciously went back to the Roman period in erecting a "civil theology."

Strauss points out with insight that despite his scientific interests, Hobbes' basic thesis grew out of a moralistic rather than a scientific tradition. He did not limit himself to the naturalistic observations characteristic of modern science, i. e., he did not merely describe what in his day was called natural appetite. Nor, on the other hand, did he adhere to traditional natural law, which sought to define an objective moral order. Hobbes was interested in natural right, a basis for subjective, juridical claims. His individualism and his political absolutism, thus, were not anomalous tenets, but at root were one. This philosophy is hedonism, for there is no good beyond the individuals' desires which can give a basis for community values. He does not stress wisdom, courage, or the "severe

50 *Ibid.,* Ch. 31.

virtues," but rather the "liberal virtues." "Just as Machiavelli reduced virtue to the political virtue of patriotism, Hobbes reduced virtue to the social virtue of peaceableness." The elimination of any standard but the subjective, meant, says Strauss, the elimination of God, in fact if not in name: ". . . political atheism and political hedonism belong together. They arose together in the same moment and in the same mind."[51] Michael Oakeshott gives a more positive construction to the virtue of peaceableness and denies that Hobbes is a hedonist. "Felicity" is the end of Hobbes' state, thinks Oakeshott. It seems rather arbitrary of Strauss to deny God access to the subjective; but whether a grubby sort of peace or a more elevated felicity is the highest of Hobbes' social goals, there is no doubt that neither of them transcends the secular. As author of a sovereign power and a social policy that owes nothing to the authority of transcendent values, Hobbes it a fit symbol for all that is secular in the modern state.

While undoubtedly a secular moralist, Hobbes was still very much involved with the new science. The extent of this involvement has been sketched above. The interweaving of practical politics, science, and morals in Hobbes' mind is succinctly registered in the beginning of De corpore: ". . . from the not knowing of civil duties, that is, from the want of moral science, proceed civil wars. . . ."[52] A good case can be made that Hobbes' interest in building an indestructible political science preceded his concern with validating absolute sovereignty as such. Strauss shows how Hobbes built his system by fusing parts of Platonic idealism with Epicurean hedonism. He retained Plato's concern for the political system, the ideal— or, ideational—polity; but he rejected Plato's transcendental perfectionism. He substituted for it the rather worldly Epicurean goal of the pleasant life, but rejected Epicurus' antipolitical bias. The combination is what has been referred to above as "political hedonism." It should not be understood as merely one more expression of what constitutes the good life. Hobbes thought he was constructing a scientific model of the political world as exact as any geometrical model. Given a cooperative sovereign (a flaw in the system, as we shall see), Hobbes could do what the Greeks had failed to do, produce a political science that works. A good many twentieth-century political scientists, especially in America, seem to be animated by very much the same kind of hope.

The mold into which all of these ingredients—individualism, absolutism, and scientism—were poured was sovereignty, the union of many into one, a center for earthly allegiance, the very foundation of law. The American economist and social theorist A. F. Bentley once said of sovereignty, ". . .

51 Natural Right and History, pp. 187, 169.
52 De corpore, Ch. 1, in Works, Vol. I, p. 10.

as soon as it gets out of the pages of a lawbook or the political pamphlet it is a piteous, threadbare joke." From Bentley's hard-headed, no-nonsense position it may well be a joke. But it is no joking matter to a diplomat in the United Nations who is invoking the concept in order to keep a UN inspection team out of his country, to a southern senator defending states' rights, or to anyone fighting to keep a state senatorial district from being abolished. "Sovereignty" has permeated our political vocabulary so deeply that we take "popular sovereignty" for granted. In this case, to say there is no sovereign, no single source of law, is akin to saying "the people" do not rule. We are accustomed to say that democracy is the only legitimate regime. By this we imply that legitimacy is not determined by the purposes to be served by the state but only by the locus of final social power—i.e., by the sovereign. Thus, if we deny the concept of sovereignty, we deny our only principle of political legitimacy; we are left adrift with no criteria of the good and the bad state. The theory of sovereignty bequeathed to us by Hobbes has, in our generation, made the legitimacy of majoritarian democracy dependent upon its form rather than its content. When majorities become inflamed or hysterical, we are uncomfortable with the theory. But we have not yet produced another theory powerful enough to displace it.

Apart from the overriding significance of the concept of sovereignty itself, what, for us, is true and false in Hobbes' system? Let us be more modest and ask, instead, where Hobbes fell down, and what may be salvaged for present use.

At least six failures may be noted:

(1) In trying to describe and prescribe at the same time Hobbes used the word "natural" to mean two different things, which he did not or could not distinguish. On the one hand, the natural was what reason would show to be necessary for our self-preservation; on the other hand, the natural was the consequences of our spontaneous passions. On the one hand it was what gave some men power over other men; on the other hand it was what prescribed the rights all men were to observe. In the early nineteenth century, Bentham and Austin were to propound a conception of sovereignty and law (the command of the sovereign) virtually identical with Hobbes' while deriding both natural-law conceptions and the social contract. By this time the rationalistic trappings had fallen off.

(2) Although revolution was forbidden by Hobbes' interpretation of natural right, by giving "sovereignty by institution" and "sovereignty by acquisition" equal standing, and by giving the subject no voice in the determination of lines of succession, Hobbes would seem to have made revolution virtually inevitable.

(3) As a thoroughgoing equalitarian, Hobbes endowed his sovereign

with no greater skill or wisdom than anyone else, yet he admits that to function the commonwealth needs "the help of a very able architect." When a state breaks up it is the fault of the sovereign, "the fault is not in men, as they are the *matter* but as they are the *makers*. . . ."[53] Hobbes is not reluctant to tell the sovereign what a difficult job he has—he must pick good counselors, be popular, reward and punish skillfully, avoid unnecessary laws, and much more. The mathematical probabilities that this almost accidentally selected sovereign will botch the job are overwhelming.

(4) Even putting the most elevated construction on Hobbes' conception of self-preservation, it is quite probable that a political system without sympathy, self-sacrifice, and compassion anywhere in it would fly apart like a smashed atom.

(5) By questioning the legitimacy and minimizing the importance of human associations intermediate between individual and sovereign, Hobbes was working with an image of society unlike that which has ever existed or probably ever will exist. Since the next two centuries made the same mistake, we should not be too harsh with him for this weakness.

(6) Finally, Hobbes did nothing to extend the logic of his analysis to the world scene. If avoidance of war is the dominant aim of life and an absolute sovereign is essential to this end, then a world sovereign would seem essential. Yet by giving each nation its own absolute sovereignty, Hobbes would (and history has) made world-wide conflict all the more likely. Yet, ironically, the natural law that has created this tense, warlike world is telling subjects everywhere to seek peace as hard as they can and as soon as possible.

The parts of Hobbes' system in no way add up in significance to the whole; but these insights do seem relevant to our situation:

(1) Moral obligation does require a degree of security. Without society, government, laws, and other restraints, men would probably be worse creatures than they are. International morality is as weak as it is in part because nations are their own masters and rarely have a common bond of security sufficient to risk trusting other nations. Though he made too much of the need for security and the fears that make men natural enemies, Hobbes is an invigorating antidote to some of the more romantic notions of brotherhood always with us.

(2) Those of us who lean toward equalitarianism like Hobbes' frank assertions about man's humanity and frailty, even, or especially, when it undermines his own theory of sovereign rule. This is a negative contribution to the so-called liberal tradition; but it is by no means the least desirable element.

(3) The implications of the theory of sovereignty are manifold, and,

53 *Leviathan*, Ch. 29.

from this writer's point of view, not all of them are good. The logic of
Hobbes, the constant pushing toward the extreme case, at least make
us aware of some of the implications of the theory of sovereignty which
later defenders have overlooked. For one thing, a consistent application
of it requires an Erastian view of Church-state relations. For another, it
would treat as a *non sequitur* the theory of "dual sovereignty," which
prevails in American constitutional law. Hobbes, as De Jouvenel has
pointed out,[54] is often more logical than his critics. If we are going to
play around with the theory of sovereignty, we would at least do well
to pay heed to its greatest exponent.

54 De Jouvenel observes that we often take our image of "economic man" from
Hobbes because it fits the economic model and simultaneously select a happier, more
rational "political man" to fit our democratic theories. We cannot have it both ways,
says De Jouvenel. If man is really as Hobbes described him, some form of absolutism
is inevitable. *Sovereignty*, pp. 239-41.

CHAPTER

4 | *Locke*

T HE portraits of John Locke display a man with a long face, a long, humped nose, a high, scholarly forehead, large, heavy-lidded eyes, and a large but well-contoured mouth. One receives an impression of reserve, a quiet, undefiant pride. Here is a man of moderation, of balanced judgment, suspicious of "enthusiasm" and complacency alike. Here is a man of caution and wit, whose influence insinuates rather than provokes, as did Hobbes'.

Life[1]

THERE are several parallels between the lives of Locke and Hobbes. Both were born in small towns in the southwest of England—Wrington in Somerset was Locke's birthplace. Both were Oxford undergraduates, disgruntled with the medieval curriculum, and both were lifelong bachelors. Some differences are conspicuous, too. Hobbes' relationship with his father was nonexistent; Locke's father was important to him in several ways. The elder Locke, a Puritan, was an attorney and clerk to Alexander Popham, the deputy lieutenant of Somerset County. Between 1634 and 1640 it was the senior Locke's unpleasant duty to collect King Charles' hated ship money; then came the Revolution and, outfitted as a captain, he followed Popham into battle in the Parliamentary cause—

---

1 The bulk of this biography has been drawn from Maurice Cranston, *John Locke; A Biography* (New York: Macmillan, 1957), a model of what historical biography should be.

with little success and less glory. The practical significance of his father's exploits for young John Locke was that, as a result of the Revolution, the Long Parliament took over the distinguished Westminster School in London, which event gave Mr. Popham, M.P. from Bath, the right to nominate candidates for enrollment. In 1647 he rewarded his friend and counselor, the elder John Locke, by naming his fifteen-year-old son to the school, thus launching a famous scholarly career.

THE YOUNG LOCKE

Despite the Puritan victory, Westminster School was decidedly royalist, due largely to its great headmaster, Richard Busby, called by Gladstone "the master of the public school system." The conflict between this new environment and his Puritan background was both disturbing and stimulating to Locke. In 1652, at the age of twenty—older than the typical undergraduate—Locke left London for Christ Church College, Oxford. He had won a scholarship, though at the bottom of a list of six winners. At Oxford he developed an interest in experimental science, not as a result of the curriculum, for it was still basically medieval (Aristotle and Galen were the principal authorities for the professors of medicine), but more in rebellion against it. Dissection, experimentation, and the teaching of new clinical techniques went on in the private homes of scientists, only some of whom were connected with the university. Locke was drawn into this remarkably distinguished group of men. He was not much of a practical experimenter himself, but he was fascinated by the principles upon which experiment proceeded. He was reacting against the excessive reliance on tradition that he associated with the royalists, as well as against the moral emotionalism—"enthusiasm," he called it—of the Puritans. By age twenty-four, the year he received his Bachelor of Arts degree, the empiricist in Locke was evident.

He was not yet, however, a liberal in politics. He felt, for example, that Catholics, Quakers, and various other dissenters were too dangerous to be tolerated. His grounds for this position were essentially practical: the fear of anarchy. In 1658, the year Cromwell died, Locke received his Master of Arts degree. The general uncertainty as to the future of the Commonwealth left their mark on young Locke. His letters reveal that he was gloomy about the future of England, despairing of mankind, and unsure what to do with his life. When the Restoration came, it was a cause for great rejoicing. Locke simultaneously welcomed the "happy return of his Majesty" and disparaged the "popular asserters of public liberty." The myth that Locke was at this stage of his life as much of a "liberal" as he was later rested for centuries on the mistaken attribution to him of an essay written in 1661 by a Walter Moyle. What Locke was writing in that year is more typically revealed by his reply to a pamphlet of Edward Bagshawe. Repudiating the latter's argument for religious toleration, Locke said that the magistrate "must necessarily have an absolute and arbitary power over all indifferent actions of his people."[2] In this and other writings Locke clearly borrowed heavily from the ideas of Hobbes, whose *Leviathan* Locke had read in his twenties. Yet he never acknowledged his debt to Hobbes; in fact he even denied it on at least one occasion, perhaps to avoid the distasteful label "Hobbist."[3]

Scientist and Diplomat

In 1661, shortly after his election to a lectureship in Greek at Christ Church, Locke was saddened by the death of his father.[4] The lawyer Locke left to his eldest son enough land around Pensford to provide him with a modest income for the rest of his life. But for all his gentleness, Locke tended to be an impatient and sharp-eyed landlord.

During his period as Oxford tutor, Locke became a close friend of Robert Boyle, "the father of chemistry," whose High Street home was the center for much scientific research. It is significant that Locke, like Boyle, brought no clearly formed metaphysical conceptions about nature to their experimental work. They were above all following Bacon's advice to examine *things*. It was only after this period that Locke read Descartes and began to speculate on the philosophy of inquiry.

With the encouragement of his friend John Strachey, Locke decided that travel was needed to round out his education. The diplomatic service was the tool to this end. In 1665 he left England to be secretary to the mission to Brandenburg, having learned shorthand to fit him better for the post. What soon impressed Locke in the town of Cleves was that Calvinist, Lutheran, and Roman Catholic religions were all tolerated. In a letter to Boyle he wrote, "They quietly permit one another to choose their way to heaven; and I cannot observe any quarrels or animosities amongst them on account of religion."[5] The practical possibility of a policy of toleration was beginning to change Locke's political orientation. But he had less admiration for the food, church singing, and merchandise of Cleves. The characteristic Lockean sense of humor crops out in a letter to Strachey, where he notes that he had spent three days finding a pair of gloves to buy and the next two days trying to put them on.

2 From the Locke manuscripts in the Bodleian Library, quoted in Cranston, p. 60.

3 A letter from John Aubrey to Locke in 1673 commending to him both the works and the person of Thomas Hobbes suggests the possibility that the two great philosophers met at least once. But Locke's reply to Aubrey is lost and the meeting is purely conjectural.

4 Locke's mother, of whom he spoke rarely but with affection, died when he was twenty-two. His younger brother, Thomas, died in 1663.

5 Cranston, p. 82.

Locke's success as a diplomat led to two subsequent offers of employment when he had returned to England in 1666, one with the ambassador to Spain, the other a like post in Sweden. After anxious ponderings, Locke refused both. He had decided to study medicine. Locke and a friend opened a small laboratory in Oxford and solicited funds from interested scientists to keep it going. The evidence indicates that Locke was primarily interested in applied medicine, in drugs and herbals. In 1667 he met and began to collaborate with Thomas Sydenham, the greatest English physician of his day and a pioneer of the clinical method. Locke had made an even more important friendship the year before, when Lord Ashley, later earl of Shaftesbury and Lord High Chancellor, met Locke on a trip to Oxford to drink mineral waters. Locke operated on Ashley for a cyst of the liver in 1668. Fortunately, the operation was a success, and Locke thereby won a lifelong patron. It was Shaftesbury's intervention with the king that gave Locke tenure at Christ Church without the necessity of taking holy orders, which Locke wished to avoid. He had earlier sought a Doctor of Medicine degree in order to teach there, but had been denied it by the suspicious medical faculty; they granted that he had done the requisite advanced work but noted sternly that he had no Bachelor of Medicine degree. Able to teach, but not to teach medicine, he had won a hollow victory.

About this time Locke began to read Descartes. He welcomed Descartes' advocacy of systematic doubt, but rejected his deductive, rationalistic reconstruction. He did not go as far as Hobbes and assert that matter or body is everything, but he did question whether more could be known of mind than of matter, as Descartes believed. In 1668, at the age of thirty-six, Locke was elected a fellow of the Royal Society. He had already moved to London to live in Lord Ashley's palatial establishment. That same year he became secretary to the Lords Proprietors of Carolina and later had a hand in drafting the *Fundamental Constitution* of that colony, a document carefully designed to avoid the dangers of "democracy." The colonists themselves had other ideas, and the constitution was never put into effect.

WHIG MAN OF AFFAIRS

As Shaftesbury moved higher and higher in the government, Locke moved with him. When Shaftesbury was made Lord Chancellor, Locke continued to serve him from the relatively obscure post of secretary of presentation, a position involving ecclesiastical relations. But after Shaftesbury found out about King Charles' secret pro-Catholic Treaty of Dover with France, he could scarcely conceal his disillusionment. In spite of his earlier policy of toleration, he became increasingly anti-Catholic.

His usefulness to Charles faded and he was dismissed. Locke, meanwhile, had prudently obtained a somewhat more secure job as secretary to the Council of Trade and Plantations; but a reorganization, ostensibly for economy, cut him out of this post in 1675. Displaying a breadth barely comprehensible to specialized, twentieth-century man, Locke had been all the while continuing his medical studies and in the same year received a Bachelor of Medicine degree from Oxford and a "faculty" to practice as a physician.

We shall later consider the tangle of Whig politics as a backdrop for the publication of the *Two Treatises of Government* in 1689. Suffice it to say at this point that Locke's financial journals reveal that he purchased a copy of Filmer's *Patriarcha* and *Inquest* for four shillings, sixpence on February 3, 1680. It is very probable that he began composing a reply shortly thereafter. There is no evidence that Locke wrote the treatises after the Glorious Revolution of 1688, as was believed for years. Shaftesbury, forced by his plottings of 1682 to flee England, went to Holland where he died of "gout of the stomach" in early 1683. After the Rye House Plot in June, 1683, several Whig writers were arrested, and Locke felt it expedient in the late summer to follow the example of his now-deceased patron and journey to Holland. Some said that among the papers he burned before leaving was a full-length biography of Shaftesbury.

The first lonely winter in Amsterdam (part of the time he felt it necessary to go under the assumed name "Dr. van der Linden"), Locke spent working on his *Essay Concerning Human Understanding*. He also wrote extensively to his English friends. His letters to Edward and Mary Clarke contained much advice on the raising of children, and some were published in 1693 as *Thoughts Concerning Education*. In November, 1684, by express order of the king, Locke's name was stricken from the rolls of Christ Church. Locke was in Utrecht in 1686, working on the fourth book of the *Essay Concerning Human Understanding*, when he took time out to write his influential *Letter on Toleration*, published in Latin in 1689. For two years, beginning in 1687, Locke was a paying guest in the Rotterdam home of Benjamin Furly, a famous, radical, and somewhat eccentric Quaker who undoubtedly nourished Locke's spirit of toleration.

In 1685 Charles II died suddenly and was succeeded by Catholic James II. Protestants were somewhat consoled by the fact that James had no heir and Protestant Mary of Orange was the heir presumptive to the throne. But in June, 1688, the birth of a son to the queen shattered these hopes. The English public was now receptive to a Lockean kind of political theory—that is, a theory of limited monarchy—as it had not been in 1683. Encouraged by the change in public temper, William of Orange set sail from Holland for England with four hundred ships under Admiral Herbert. On November 5, 1688, they landed at Brixham, and the insurgent forces moved toward London under Lord Mordaunt[6] with scarcely any opposition and much support. James subsequently fled to France.

WRITER OF PARTS

In February, 1689, Locke joined Lady Mordaunt and Princess Mary in the expedition taking them to England to their husbands, and, in Mary's case, to the throne. Locke went to live with a friend in London. He declined an appointment as English ambassador to the Elector of Brandenburg on grounds of health, noting, among other things, that he could not keep up with the "warm drinking" of the Germans, a diplomatic challenge that would be unavoidable. He declined other offers as well, and finally settled for the position of Commissioner of Appeals, a nondemanding post, if not quite a sinecure. Although he wanted back his place at Christ Church "as acknowledgment that he had been wronged," Locke withdrew the request when he learned it would mean displacing another, and concentrated on seeing his *Essay Concerning Human Understanding* through the printers. Meanwhile, he rejoiced over the Act of Toleration passed by Parliament. With his three most important books on press, 1689 was by any measure a big year for Locke.

To escape the debilitating London air, the asthmatic Locke in 1691 went to live at Oates, the country estate of his long-time friend and correspondent, Lady Masham, who was more than gracious in giving Locke the run of the place. The same year saw the publication of his book *Some Considerations of the Consequences of the Lowering of Interest, and Raising the Value of the Money*, which dealt with the highly pressing problems of interest rates, and the practice of "clipping" the edge off unmilled coins. Except for advocating a recoinage to cope with the latter problem, Locke favored minimal governmental interference with supply, demand, rates of interest, and the use-value of money. His economics as well as his politics were clearly Whiggish.

In 1692 Locke edited and in large part rewrote his late friend Robert Boyle's *History of the Air;* that year he also wrote his own *Third Letter for Toleration.* In 1695 the Act for the Regulation of Printing was repealed, in part because of the weight of Locke's arguments against it, fed through his friends on the House of Commons committee considering the matter. In Locke's memorandum the heaviest weight was given

6 Whose wife, in Holland, was at this time carrying on a genteel flirtation with Locke.

to the practical, even commercial, values of liberty of the press. "Unlike Milton, who called for liberty in the name of liberty, Locke was content to ask for liberty in the name of trade; and unlike Milton, he achieved his end."[7] This year also saw the anonymous publication of *The Reasonableness of Christianity*. Critics tried to prove that the author was a Socinian (in present day language, Unitarian) and that all Socinians were atheists. Although he did not remove the cloak of anonymity, Locke was provoked into a reply. He more effectively refuted the latter charge than the former.

LAST YEARS

Despite illness, in 1696 Locke surprisingly accepted appointment to a new Board of Trade, designed to deal with the threatening rise of Dutch trade, the disintegration of colonial administration, the problem of piracy, and other pressing matters. Locke moved back to London, and, though he was ailing and the duties were arduous, he clearly dominated the work of the board. During a convalescent absence at Oates, however, he wrote (though it was never completed) *The Conduct of the Understanding*. Despite its title, the book attacked a problem somewhat different from that of the *Essay*, namely, the nature of prejudice and its opposite, "clear thinking." In one passage he takes to task those who prefer to deal with only one sort of man and those who prefer books to any sort of man. The experience of practical politics, of coming to grips with a variety of strong viewpoints expressed by a variety of strong presonalities is, he felt, essential training for anyone who would seek truth. This passage helps to explain why Locke the truth-seeker would interrupt his scholarship to take on a heavy burden of public service. It also is a testament to the vitality of his questing spirit.

In 1697 Locke prepared a report for the Board of Trade on the problem of unemployment and pauperism. Although the report was not adopted, Locke's severe proposals for the treatment of beggars, including imprisonment and impressment into sea duty, suggest the limits of his "liberalism." Fortunately for the ailing bachelor, Locke had managed to draw full pay while spending a good part of his winters at Oates. In the spring of 1700, however, Lord Chancellor Somers, the man who had induced Locke to take the Board of Trade position, was removed from office by the exposure of Captain Kidd's Whig-approved piracy, and Locke felt it was expedient to resign.

He spent his last days at Oates, carrying on a wide correspondence, replying to critics, writing a commentary on the Epistles of St. Paul, and conversing with visitors who came, he gently complained, all too

7 Cranston, p. 387.

infrequently. John Locke, a great philosopher, died on October 28, 1704, at the age of seventy-two.

The Two Treatises: Political Philosophy or Tracts for the Times?

LOCKE'S *Second Treatise . . . of Civil Government*[8] is so famous that fame has become a barrier to its understanding. The phrases "life, liberty, and property," "consent of the governed," "the majority have a right to act and conclude the rest," have become commonplaces in the political vocabulary of the West, if not the world. If we were not aware of his originality, we would say the man was using clichés. Students of the American Constitution will find the phrase "life, liberty, and property" familiar because it refers to the rights singled out for protection against arbitrary federal action in the Fifth Amendment and against state action in the Fourteenth Amendment. In his natural-rights assumptions, his moderation, his reasonableness, Locke was an intellectual godparent of James Madison, "the Father of the Constitution." In 1783 Madison and two other congressmen compiled for their colleagues a list of books, which they titled "The American Statesman's Library." Locke's name was one of the most prominent on the list. (If today's congressmen have not read Locke, they have probably not read many of the other authors on the list either.) The polemical duties taken up by Madison and Locke were in many ways similar. Both were interested in making a case for the legitimacy of a government that either had been or would be born of rebellion. Even more obviously did this task fall to Thomas Jefferson in writing the Declaration of Independence. The weight of natural-rights terminology hung heavy on the Declaration, and the meaning of "life, liberty, and the pursuit of happiness" in the Declaration is not so different from Locke's "life, liberty, and property" as is often believed. Locke's defense of a sensible revolution, a reasonable revolution, was so congenial to the American situation and the American mentality that his ideas can be regarded as an important weapon in the defeat of his own countrymen four generations after he wrote.

Locke's skill as a polemicist may lead us to wonder if he was *only* a polemicist. Certainly the *Second Treatise* has none of the logical cohesion of the *Leviathan*. If it is only a tract for the times, perhaps we

8 The full title is: *Two Treatises of Government. In the Former the False Principles and Foundation of Sir Robert Filmer and His Followers are Detected and Overthrown. The Latter is an Essay Concerning the True Original, Extent, and End of Civil Government.*

should leave it to the historian of ideas and not bother to seek profound political theory in it. Actually, the *Second Treatise*, like many important works of political theory, can be dealt with on different levels, and the obvious meaning is not always the most important.

Let us first look at the *Second Treatise* as a tract for the times, as a weapon wielded in the Whig cause of Parliamentary supremacy. Will this point of view not explain Locke's reluctance to draw logical conclusions? Will this not make clear why a highly intelligent writer could tolerate inconsistencies? We have noted above that the *Two Treatises* were written in or about 1681, as a reply to Filmer's *Patriarcha*. The dispute that was the occasion of these writings was called the Exclusion Controversy. Locke's patron, Shaftesbury, was the leader of the Country Party, in general the ideological successors of the Roundheads of the Cromwellian period. Above all they feared a Catholic monarch and wished to remove the Catholic duke of York (the future James II) from the line of succession. A thoroughly unscrupulous and nefarious fellow named Titus Oates invented the elaborate Popish Plot, complete with falsified documents, claiming that the Jesuits were going to murder Charles and put James on the throne. Shaftesbury was willing to exploit the resulting furor in an attempt to remove James from the line of succession. An Exclusion Bill, as it was called, would have passed in 1679 had not Charles prorogued, then dissolved, Parliament. A second bill the next year was defeated only by action of the House of Lords. The conservatives, including most of the Anglican clergy, feared this assault on the king's prerogative. Desperate for ammunition, they resurrected Filmer's tract on monarchy and circulated it widely. The next year, 1681, Charles called Parliament to meet in Oxford in order to avoid Shaftesbury's "London mobs." But the London Whigs, as they came to be called,[9] simply moved into Oxford with ribbons on their hats. "No Popery. No Slavery," the ribbons said. Locke was there and described the tumultuous scene in a letter. Charles subsequently dissolved the Parliament. Four years of repressive monarchical autocracy followed until his death in 1685.

9 For a time the Shaftesbury men were called "Petitioners" because of the petitions to the king they drew up protesting the dissolution of Parliament; the royalists, the successors of the Cavaliers of the English Revolution, were called the "Abhorrers" because of their counter-petitions abhorring Shaftesbury's interference with the royal prerogative. It was during the Exclusion Bill debates that the terms "Whigs" and "Tories" came into use. Both were pejorative terms, as have been many party labels. Three theories have been suggested for the origins of the name "Whig": (1) that it was a derivative of "whey"—for the sour-milk faces of Scottish parliamentarians; (2) that it was derived from the slogan "We Hope In God"; (3) that it came from "Whiggem"— the call of Scots drivers to their horses. Any one is probably as reliable or as dubious as the others. The term "Tory" has a more certain origin. The outlaws who hid in the bogs of Ireland were called "tories."

Within a few months of the publication of Filmer, three of the ablest Whig minds were at work on a refutation, Locke's historian friend James Tyrell, Algernon Sidney, the dean of statesmen of the "old cause," and Locke himself. Charles' rage over Sidney's moderately republican *Discourses Concerning Government* led to Sidney's execution in December, 1683. Locke, who was by this time, as we have seen, in Holland, prudently held up publication of his own reply until 1689 and even then printed it anonymously.

With cutting polemical skill, Locke, in the *First Treatise*, dissected Filmer's claim that the authority of kings could be traced to the primeval authority of Adam and thence to God. Locke sneered at Filmer's "Description of his Fatherly Authority, as it lies scatter'd up and down in his Writings, which he supposes was first vested in *Adam*, and by Right belongs to all princes ever since. . . . If he has . . . any where in the whole Treatise, given any other Proofs of *Adam's Royal Authority* other than by often repeating it, which, among some Men, goes for Argument, I desire any body for him to shew me the Place and Page, that I may be convinced of my mistake. . . ."[10] The tone of the debater is unmistakable. The demolition was so complete that for centuries Filmer had the disadvantage of being known principally through Locke's critique of him. The historical argument was easy to discredit; but as Peter Laslett has pointed out,[11] Locke did not really come to grips with the fundamental problem posed by Filmer's writings: is not social authority, in the broadest sense, "natural," and is not political authority inevitably bound up with social authority?

Equality and the State of Nature

LOCKE begins the *Second Treatise* with a summary of his critique of Filmer, then explains that it is now his task to "find out another rise of government, another original of political power."[12] In a direct manner that would seem consistent with his stress on precise definition in the *Essay*, Locke defines political power: "Political power . . . I take to be a right of making laws with penalties of death and consequently all less penalties for the regulating and preserving of property, and of employing

10 *Two Treatises of Government*. I, Peter Laslett, ed. (London: Cambridge Univ. Press, 1960), pp. 165, 168. Italics in original.

11 In the Introduction to his edition of *The Patriarcha and Other Political Works* (Oxford: Blackwell, 1949).

12 *Two Treatises of Government*, II, Ch. 1, sec. 1. All quotations from the *Second Treatise* are taken from the Everyman edition, William S. Carpenter, ed. (London: Dent, 1924).

the force of the community . . . *and all this only for the public good.*"¹³
Note that Locke does not take what the twentieth-century political
scientist might call an empirical, nonvaluational approach to political
power. Presumably laws with penalty of death made and enforced without regard to the public good would not only be a bad exercise of power
but not power at all, a definition that seems to bring true power close
to justice. Locke's later discussion of the abuses of power, however,
ignores this definition. We could infer that he is merely planting a seed
in the reader's mind, a standard by which tyranny can later be recognized and judged. On the other hand, this troublesome sentence could
be but an unconscious mixing of the moral flavor of medieval Scholasticism
with the antiseptic definitionalism of modern science.

In Chapter 2, entitled "The State of Nature," Locke leans heavily
on Richard Hooker, the great English divine who wrote *The Laws of
Ecclesiastical Polity* in 1594. "The judicious Hooker," Locke called him,
and so has everyone else since. Hooker gives us, and Locke adopts, a kind
of legalized golden rule, which simultaneously invokes the concept of
nature and asserts a moral obligation concerning the equality of citizens.
"My desire . . . to be loved of my equals in nature as much as possible
may be, imposeth on me a natural duty of bearing to themward fully
the like affection; from which relation of equality between ourselves,
and them that are as ourselves, what several rules and canons natural
reason hath drawn for direction of life no man is ignorant."¹⁴ By
quoting Hooker, Locke gives his equalitarianism the sanctity of age and
revered authority and identifies it with a tradition of natural law which
goes back to the ancient Stoics. That Locke has the motives of a debater
rather than a scholar, however, would seem to be indicated by what he
omits from Hooker. Neither Hooker nor the preceding natural-law
tradition uses a concept of the "state of nature." In Hooker the "several
rules and canons [of] natural reason" operate on man seen as a naturally
social creature. But Locke uses Hooker to bolster his argument *for* the
state of nature.

The heart of any state-of-nature argument is that government is
"artificial" rather than natural, that government is a human contrivance, a
convention, and is not necessarily ordained of God (or a demiurge) by his
work of creation. It is not prior to the individual, either in the sense of
being a prerequisite to birth and life, or in the Aristotelian sense of
being essential to the individual's true fulfillment of himself. The device
could be used, as in Hobbes, to remove government from criticism by

13 *Second Treatise,* Ch. 1, sec. 3. Italics added.
14 *The Laws of Ecclesiastical Polity,* Bk. I. Quoted in Locke, *Second Treatise,*
Ch. 2, sec. 5.

theological standards, or, as in Locke, to justify criticism of arbitrary power by pragmatic standards. In one case it bolstered arbitrary government, in the other it undermined it. Hobbes and Locke could disagree as they did about government and the characteristics of the state of nature only because they agreed that there was a state of nature.

The question raised in our discussion of Hobbes about the moral obligations existing in the state of nature are answered early and specifically in Locke. "The state of nature has a law of nature to govern it, which obliges every one; and reason which is that law, teaches all mankind who will but consult it, that being all equal and independent, no one ought to harm another in his life, health, liberty, or possessions."[15] The range of protection of natural law is broadened beyond Hobbes' domain of self-preservation, and the possibility of natural cooperation is given greater weight. Self-preservation comes first, but man has at least the negative obligation not to "harm another in his life, health, liberty, or possessions." Life in the state of nature is not filled with the stark terror it was for Hobbes, only with "inconveniences" arising from the fact that every man has the right to judge and punish offenders, and "self-love" sometimes interferes with the perception of or obedience to natural law: ". . . yet it is certain that there is such a law, . . . as intelligible and plain to a rational creature and a studier of that law as the positive laws of commonwealths. . . ."[16]

Locke often finds it necessary to forget his ostensible target, the Kentish patriarch, for the sake of a dig at the Malmesbury sage—who is never named. For example, after granting that the creation of civil government is the "proper remedy" for the "inconveniences" of the state of nature, Locke admonishes those who are bothered by the thought of men being judges in their own cases "to remember that absolute monarchs are but men. . . . And if he that judges, judges amiss in his own or in any other case, he is answerable for it to the rest of mankind."[17] In such passages the common sense of Locke washes refreshingly over the forced logic of Hobbes.

Though Hobbes pays only indifferent attention to the problem of the historicity of the state of nature, Locke characteristically brings the question down to the everyday level. Since there is no common government over them, independent nations may be said to be in a state of nature with each other. Yet they do get along, somehow. "The promises and bargains for truck, etc., between two men in Soldania, in or between a Swiss and an Indian in the woods of America, are binding to them, though they are perfectly in a state of nature in reference to one another.

15 *Second Treatise*, Ch. 2, sec. 6.   16 *Ibid.*, sec. 12.   17 *Ibid.*, sec. 13.

For truth and keeping of faith belong to men as men and not as members of society."[18]

In Chapter 3 Locke takes an even more pointed thrust at Hobbes when he notes the confusion of some who have identified the state of nature with a state of war. One puts oneself in a state of war with another man, says Locke, only when one uses force and seeks absolute power over him. And all men do not seek such power at all times. At the expense, perhaps, of his theory of natural equality Locke observes that even in a state of war "when all cannot be preserved, the safety of the innocent is to be preferred."[19] The innocent are the most worthy. It is not surprising, then, that Locke the "liberal" Whig places on government a special moral obligation to protect the innocent. Not simply preservation of life is essential, as Hobbes seems to say, but preservation of a certain quality of life, which is related to the individual's right of self-determination. Hobbes had made the state of nature an inescapable category for political theorizing for the next century; but Locke was reluctant to accept Hobbes' dilemma: take the chaos of the state of nature or take absolute government, for there is no other choice. Both sides of this equation were too extreme for Locke. The state of nature is not hell and the power of government need not be absolute. The pressures to escape one's natural condition are not so terrible and the threat of dissolution of government is therefore not so terrible. Whether in a state of nature *or* under a government, felt Locke, "freedom from arbitrary power is so necessary to, and closely joined with, a man's preservation, that he cannot part with it but by what forfeits his preservation and life together."[20] Arbitrary power is clearly Locke's bête noire.

Thus a state of slavery is but a state of war between master and slave. And slavery is not natural either in the state of nature or under government. A man must consent to the power over him or it is arbitrary. If he is not in a position to give his consent, then by definition the power over him is illegitimate. Here is the crux of the distinction between Locke and Hobbes or even Filmer. For the latter two, the need for power or the fact of power was its justification; for Locke, the subject's consent was its justification.

Property

WE shall return in a moment to the problem of consent. At this point Locke's theory of property intrudes, for it is closely related to his ideas on the state of nature, arbitrary power, and the ends of government. In Chap-

18 *Ibid.*, sec. 14.   19 *Ibid.*, Ch. 3, sec. 16.   20 *Ibid.*, Ch. 4, sec. 22.

ter 5 of the *Second Treatise*, Locke analyzes what seems at first glance to be an extraneous subject in a work on government, the origins of property.

Locke is an early defender of the labor theory of value, a theory held by most of the classical economists, and by Karl Marx, but rejected by almost all contemporary economists. Stated simply, the theory holds that the value of a product is measured by the amount of labor invested in it. A ton of coal dug by five men in one hour is worth one half as much as a ton of copper dug by five men in two hours, or by ten men in one hour. Labor is also seen by Locke as the explanation of the origin of property itself. God gave the world to men in common; but whatever a man "removes out of the state that nature hath provided and left it in, he hath mixed his labour with, and joined to it something that is his own, and thereby makes it his property."[21] This argument does not mean, however, that a man should accumulate as much property as is physically possible in this way. God has given us goods to enjoy. "As much as any one can make use of to any advantage of life before it spoils, so much [a man] may by his labour fix a property in; whatever is beyond this, is more than his share, and belongs to others. Nothing was made by God for man to spoil or destroy."[22] Thus, even—or especially—in the state of nature, a man has no natural right to that which exceeds his own or his family's capacity to consume. The essentially agrarian basis of Locke's thinking is suggested by the fact that the same standard is applied to land ownership. A man has a natural right to as much land as he can personally cultivate for the sake of his own and his family's needs.

Certain highly imperishable commodities, however, are virtually exempt from the problem of waste. Things hard to come by like gold, silver, diamonds, "things that fancy or agreement have put value on more than real use," in time come to stand in the place of perishable produce. Plums that rot in a week are traded for nuts that last a year, which are traded for pieces of metal that last a lifetime. "And thus came in the use of money—some lasting thing that men might keep without spoiling, and that, *by mutual consent*, men would take in exchange for the truly useful but perishable supports of life."[23] Observe that the possession of money rests upon mutual consent and not on natural right. The natural rights of property relate to what is directly useful to the support of biological life. All possessions beyond this and all property in money rest on consent; that is, on social right and not on natural right. Those, therefore, who make speeches about the "natural rights of property" with reference to, say, corporate profits, are being, whether they know it or not, quite un-Lockean.

21 *Ibid.*, Ch. 5, sec. 27.   22 *Ibid.*, sec. 30.   23 *Ibid.*, sec. 47. Italics added.

Practical political applications can be read into Locke's chapter on property as easily as into other parts of the *Second Treatise*. On the one hand, men of property must know that "consent" not "nature" gives worth to their money. Economic position no more than political position is certified and fixed by divine sanction. On the other hand, since waste is the primary criterion by which violations of natural law are judged and since money can be stored up indefinitely without waste, men of great wealth need not fear that they are violating natural law simply because of their wealth. There is in this an ingenious mixture of equalitarianism and aristocracy. Here is an attack upon privilege that nevertheless, as far as economic classes are concerned, does not rock the boat. If we recall Locke's own rather penurious landlordism and the severity of his attitude toward paupers, we know that he was no economic do-gooder. Locke's theory of property, like his politics, was nicely suited to the Whig man of affairs.

Finally, however, we must recognize that beneath Locke's equivocal yet practical assertions lies an emphasis that is fundamental to an understanding of his political theory. Far from being marginal to politics, Locke's theory of property implies what man's chief aim in life is and should be, and therefore what standard should guide government. Property, which is something more than mere physical "estate," is at the heart of his conception of the good life and the good state, "the GREAT end of men's entering into society being the enjoyment of their properties in peace and safety. . . ."[24]

Consent

"CONSENT" is obviously an important concept for Locke. But what did he mean by "consent of the governed"? Even the most rabid of present-day majoritarians would not contend that each individual must have an opportunity to approve or disapprove every governmental act that might affect him. Among other things, it would be difficult to collect income taxes were this the practice. Here again we find that whatever else he was, Locke was not a doctrinaire. What Bertrand Russell said of his philosophy is applicable to his politics: "Locke aimed at credibility and achieved it at the expense of consistency. Most of the great philosophers have done the opposite."[25]

There are at least three vital qualifications that Locke imposed on his

24 *Ibid.*, Ch. 11, sec. 134.
25 *History of Western Philosophy* (New York: Simon and Schuster, 1945), p. 613.

theory of consent. The first is that the equality of subjects is not to be taken in a literal, mechanical sense:

Though I have said above (Chapter II) that all men are by nature equal, I cannot be supposed to understand all sorts of equality. Age or virtue may give men a just precedency. Excellency of parts and merit may place others above the common level. Birth may subject some, and alliance or benefits others, to pay an observance to those whom nature, gratitude, or other respects may have made it due. And yet all this consists with the equality which all men are in, in respect of jurisdiction or dominion, one over another; which was the equality I there spoke of as proper to the business in hand, being that equal right that every man hath to his natural freedom, without being subjected to the will or authority of any other man.[26]

Children, for example, "are not born *in* this full state of equality, though they are born *to* it,"[27] and are subjects of their father rather than the state until they come of age. Not *all* persons are equal and therefore not all persons are consent-givers.

The second is that the giving of consent is only relevant to a restricted function, "the business in hand," which is the *establishment* of the government itself. We might call this giving of consent the constituent authority residing in a people. Locke was no closer than Hobbes to saying that government should not make a man do what he might not want to do. Consent is not necessarily involved in the making of ordinary statutes and certainly not in their enforcement. The question Locke is raising and answering is: upon what fundamental base must the whole governmental structure rest if it is to be legitimate? Shall it be the mystique of divine right, the fear of death, or rational consent of naturally equal men? If we take Locke's question at face value and the three alternative answers available in his time, we shall no doubt be with Locke rather than with Filmer or Hobbes. Yet we must also recognize the circularity involved in the basic rationale for his answer: men are naturally equal, which is to say mainly in their constituent capacity. Why are they equal in their constituent capacity? Because they are naturally equal. It could be said that the empirical case goes to Filmer by default.

The third qualification is that, putting aside the difficulty of natural equality, how often does the average citizen have a chance to give or withhold his consent to the whole governmental structure? How do we know when people are consenting and when they are not? Since such clear-cut occasions arise rarely, Locke was forced to make a distinction between "express consent" and "tacit consent." The distinction, or at least Locke's

26 *Second Treatise*, Ch. 6, sec. 54.   27 *Ibid.*, sec. 55. Italics added.

application of it, was one of the more slippery elements in his theory. "I say that every man that hath any possession or enjoyment of any part of the dominions of any government doth thereby give his tacit consent and is as far forth obliged to obedience to the laws of that government as any one under it. . . ."[28] The possession may be as substantial as a large piece of land, or as transient as the right to travel freely on the highway. In either case, consent is assumed to have been given. This interpretation would seem to render the moral basis of the theory of consent rather empty, for who can exist in a country without some "possession" thus broadly conceived? The view also offers an ambiguous distinction between the kinds of duties falling upon those who give one or the other kind of consent. Since tacit consent rests upon some possession or other, if that possession is abandoned, says Locke, the obligation ends. The subject "is at liberty to go and incorporate himself into any other common-wealth. . . . Whereas he that has once by actual agreement and any express declaration given his consent to be of any commonwealth is perpetually and indispensably obliged to be and remain unalterably a subject to it. . . ."[29] This burden on, and discrimination against, the ex-press-consent people (e. g., those who take an oath in support of the government) seems oppressive. It also contradicts Locke's earlier statement that Filmer's idea of the natural, historical right of patrimony is discredited by the fact that many monarchies are scattered over the world and would not have existed "if men had not been at liberty to separate themselves from their families and their government, *be it what it will*, . . . and go and make distinct commonwealths and other governments as they saw fit."[30] At this point the freedom to pack up and leave is given the blessing of natural law. If the freedom issues from natural law, it is hard to see how the mere form in which consent is expressed can be allowed to nullify it. Moreover, when later discussing tyranny and the dissolution of government, Locke does not seem particularly concerned to deny those who have given their express consent[31] to the regime the right to rebel against it when it becomes tyrannical.

28 *Ibid.*, Ch. 8, sec. 119.   29 *Ibid.*, sec. 121.   30 *Ibid.*, sec. 115. Italics added.
31 If Locke was not perfectly clear as to the proper range of consent, how clear are we? Present-day pollsters can testify that the practical problem of measuring consent is by no means simple. Where is the line between consent and acquiescence? between acquiescence and complete indifference? There are moral questions that plague us as well. How important is the "intensity factor" in the worth of a citizen's choice? Assuming measurement were possible, should the involved voter's vote count more heavily than the apathetic voter's vote? These are questions our society has scarcely raised, let alone answered. Locke, at least, was aware of the apathy of most citizens. Indeed, he found it a useful contributor to political stability. See *Second Treatise*, Ch. 14, secs. 161 and 168. It is no doubt also fair to say that Locke was not really trying to look at the community as a sociological fact, but as a legal entity.

Part of the confusion is cleared up when we realize that rebellion against a ruler did not mean for Locke rebellion against the social order. There is the definite implication of *two* contracts, one between individuals as individuals, which establishes the social order, and another between individuals as members of a majority and a particular government. Thus those entering civil society by express consent may be indissolubly bound to that society and can never revert to the state of nature, although they *can* reject a particular ruler: ". . . the power that every individual gave the society when he entered into it can never revert to the individuals again as long as society lasts, but will always remain in the community, because without this there can be no community, no commonwealth."[32]

Locke certainly does not tax himself to make clear this distinction between the two contracts, however. In Chapter 8, where the key statement on contract appears, he first states that a man leaves the state of nature "by agreeing with other men to join and unite into a community." The "community" would seems to be more fundamental than a particular government. In the same paragraph, however, he continues, "When any number of men have so consented to make one community *or government*, they are thereby presently incorporated, and make one body politic, wherein the majority have a right to act and conclude the rest."[33] It would appear that the individual is the agency of choice in the first instance only. After that the majority alone possesses the right of rejecting an offending government: ". . . every man, by consenting with others to make one body politic under one government, puts himself under an obligation to every one of that society to submit to the determination of the majority, and to be concluded by it; or else this original compact . . . would signify nothing. . . ."[34]

The Majority

WHY does the majority rather than some other more select (or more extensive) group have such conclusive authority? Locke's answer is strictly utilitarian, even mechanistic: "For that which acts any community being only the consent of the individuals in it, and it being one body must move one way, it is necessary the body should move that way whither the greatest force carries it, which is the consent of the majority; or else it is impossible it should act or continue one body, one community."[35] If, on the one hand, we agree that one man with his vote is

---

32 *Ibid.*, Ch. 19, sec. 243.   33 *Ibid.*, Ch. 8, sec. 95. Italics added.
34 *Ibid.*, sec. 97.   35 *Ibid.*, sec. 96—"acts" is a verb.

roughly equal to another man with his vote, we are entitled to ask for more than a simple majority; but this demand is impractical, because if we wait for more than a simple majority to coalesce, we may wait too long. The community may move in no direction at all; it may simply stand still and be broken by the tide of events. On the other hand, if we settle for less than a simple majority, the few become unequal in power since they are pushing the many in a direction they do not want to go. If one asks, "But why precisely 50.01 per cent?" one can always answer, "Why not?" Do we really have any more exalted reason than this for advocating majority rule?

The term "majority rule," of course, raises the well-known dilemma concerning minority rights: if the majority rules, minority rights are not absolute. If minority rights are absolute, the majority does not really rule. Locke simply avoided raising the question in this form and, by and large, so has American society. If we listen to a speech by the President, watch a well-run Congressional committee hearing, or sit in a small-town planning commission, we discover that American political leaders tend to be impressed by both goals but unimpressed by the logical conflict between them. The illogic of Locke is possibly one clue to his continuing political relevance, and the illogic of our Anglo-American political system one clue to its continuing success.[36]

By citing his majoritarian passages, Wilmoore Kendall has been able to argue that Locke is at heart a collectivist rather than an individualist. Kendall also contends that Locke's treatment of the individual himself is nonindividualistic: Locke's individuals "always prove, upon examination, to be highly socialized individuals . . . and the rights he claims for them, even in the state of nature, are the rights which have their origins in social needs."[37] Kendall's study served to draw attention to a major defect of Locke's liberalism and perhaps all liberalism (a term, incidentally, that was not applied to politics until several generations after Locke), the too easy identification of individual interests with society's interest. The term "collectivism," however, is a twentieth-century concept with but a strained relationship to seventeenth-century problems. Locke and his Whig brethren were certainly against one kind of collectivism, namely, feudal corporativism. They wanted to "liberate" the individual from a

36 Whether cause or effect, the areas in which majority rights vis-à-vis minority or individual rights have been most precisely defined in American society have tended to be the areas most troublesome to us; e.g., racial segregation and free speech for radicals.

37 "John Locke and the Doctrine of Majority Rule," *University of Illinois Studies in the Social Sciences*, Vol. 26 (1940-42), p. 66.

rigidly hierarchical social order, hallowed by an official church and sanctified by mystery.[38]

Actually, the issue of individual versus majority was almost irrelevant
to the burning issue of the day, which was majority versus king, or, to
be more realistic, Parliament versus king. James II was very unpopular
and the anti-Jacobite Whigs had two thirds of the votes in the House of
Commons. Locke was giving the Whigs a political theory that was per-
suasively antimonarchical and pro-Parliament. The preferred position that
Parliamentary power had in Locke's theory is conspicuous. Parliament
alone would seem to be the vehicle of the majority. In a given government
"there can be but one supreme power, which is the legislative."[39] It must,
at least indirectly, control both the executive and the "federative" (that
which concerns "the power of war and peace, leagues and alliances").
There is a residual power in the people, the community, to save themselves from the possible wicked designs "even of their legislators," but
"this power of the people can never take place till the government be
dissolved."[40] The right of society or the community to break its bonds
with an unjust monarch is discussed at length. The possibility of the
legislative branch being tyrannical is barely mentioned. At the very end
of the *Second Treatise* Locke repeats for emphasis what he had stated
earlier: ". . . when the society hath placed the legislative in any assembly
of men to continue in them and their successors, with direction and
authority for providing such successors, the legislative can never revert
to the people whilst that government lasts. . . ."[41]

Thus the sovereignty—or, for Locke, "supreme power"[42]—of the people
never comes into play until all government is dissolved. This is the extreme case, what Locke calls "the appeal to heaven." Meanwhile, the
Parliament can be fairly well assumed to have the situation in control. In
any practical application the Parliament is "the people" in Locke's theory.
This was a theory of popular government, popular at least in the sense
that ultimately "the people shall be judge." It seems less popular when we
consider how thoroughly unrepresentative of the common man was the

38 Ironically, though he scorned medieval superstition and mystery, Locke was a
great lover of mystery, inventing a code for his diary, cutting the signatures off
letters he received, using various *noms de plume* in correspondence with friends—
especially women friends. Such eccentricities have not made easier the historian's
task.

39 *Second Treatise*, Ch. 8, sec. 149.

40 *Ibid.*

41 *Ibid.*, Ch. 19, sec. 243. Locke does, however, again mention the possibility of
forfeiture of legislative authority, in which case it "reverts to the society" and the
people "continue the legislative in themselves."

42 Probably because it was used by both Hobbes and Filmer, the term "sovereignty" was never mentioned in the *Second Treatise*. It was used in reference to
Filmer's theory in the *First Treatise*.

English Parliament of that time. In his incisive study of Locke's political theory, John Gough gives us an assessment that reflects a healthy sense of realism.

He appears to state his political theory in general philosophical terms, as if it were a purely logical deduction from general principles, but if we read between the lines we recognize the historic features of the English seventeenth-century constitution. . . . Locke's real starting point was not a mass of right-possessing individuals in a state of nature. . . . what he was really doing, under the guise of erecting a form of government on the basis of freely consenting individuals, was to describe the operation of the traditional English constitution in terms of the political philosophy current in his age.[43]

Conclusion: Politics and Philosophy

ONE can hardly blame a tract writer for couching his arguments in the most respectable philosophic trappings, even though they are only marginally relevant. Nor can we expect Locke to analyze at a sophisticated theoretical level the possible tyranny of legislatures when the king was the immediate enemy and the legislature was the ally in a good cause. But was Locke only a tract writer? If so, why is the *Second Treatise* invariably excerpted in anthologies of the political greats? Could it be that the *Second Treatise* has been carried along all these years by the reputation of its author as a philosopher and the popularity of his political ideas with succeeding generations? Alfred Cobban once described Locke as "the writer whose influence pervades the eighteenth century with an almost scriptural authority." Yet the *Second Treatise* contains a number of passages that can best be described as carelessly written, suggestive of a less than devoted preparation.[44] Many, in fact, would study Locke only as a "political prophet" (to use Parkinson's phrase), whose ideas reflected the seventeenth and influenced the eighteenth centuries. We can and have studied him in this way. But such study must inevitably have a slightly antiquarian flavor to a student of contemporary politics. How can Locke's politics clarify our own politics? This is the more urgent question.

Locke can help us understand the relationship between our own philosophical beliefs and our political beliefs. By themselves, Locke's political beliefs may appear to be historically limited, outdated. But his general philosophical position is more likely to be seen as relevant to the twentieth century. If the political corollaries of this philosophy can be recognized

43 *John Locke's Political Philosophy* (Oxford: Clarendon Press, 1950), pp. 70-71.
44 See, for example, secs. 3, 133, 150.

without their expression in seventeenth-century language, we may better see how close we are to Locke, after all. Although not universally recognized, there are, in fact, a number of parallels between Locke's epistemology and his politics.[45] Let us look first at his epistemology.

LOCKE'S EPISTEMOLOGY

A primary objective of Locke's *Essay Concerning Human Understanding* is to undercut the argument for "innate ideas," i. e., universal principles in the mind of man discoverable by a priori reasoning. If this seems an essentially negative task, Locke is characteristically modest about it: ". . . everyone must not hope to be a Boyle or a Sydenham; and in an age which produces such masters as the great Huygenius, and the incomparable Mr. Newton . . . it is ambition enough to be employed as an under-laborer in clearing the ground a little, and removing some of the rubbish that lies in the way to knowledge. . . ."[46] In the Introduction to the *Essay* he makes a lucid plea for us to be content with the limits of our knowledge, to employ our minds for those purposes which may be of most use to us, to avoid the futility of perplexing ourselves "out of an affectation of an universal knowledge." He insists we should not seek certainty "where probability only is to be had and which is sufficient to govern all our concernments."

Actually, of course, Locke does more than offer us reminders of our limitations. He offers us a new way of thinking. He lays the groundwork of British empiricism. And toward the end of the *Essay* he even forgets his disparagement of "enthusiasm" and the desire for universal maxims and rather ironically becomes most enthusiastic in stating the possibility of a universal mathematics of morals, setting forth a prospect of synthesis worthy of Hobbes:

They that are ignorant of algebra cannot imagine the wonders in this kind [sic] are to be done by it; and what farther improvements and helps, advantages to other parts of knowledge, the sagacious mind of man may yet find out, it is not easy to determine. . . . "where there is no property there is no injustice" is a proposition as certain as any demonstration in Euclid. . . . I can as certainly know this proposition to be true as that a triangle has three angles equal to two right ones.[47]

45 See Walter M. Simon, "John Locke: Philosophy and Political Theory," *Am. Pol. Sci. Rev.*, Vol. 45 (1951), pp. 386-99. Simon sets out to disprove George Sabine's contention that there is no clear connection between Locke's philosophy and his political thought. See the latter's *History of Political Theory* (New York: Holt, 1937), pp. 528-31.

46 *An Essay Concerning Human Understanding*, Epistle to the Reader, in *Works of John Locke*, J. A. St.-John, ed., (London: Bell, 1883), Vol. I, p. 121.

47 *Ibid.*, Bk. IV, Ch. 3, sec. 18, *Works*, Vol. II, pp. 154-55.

The basic contention of British empiricism in contained in Locke's famous assertion:

All ideas come from sensation or reflection—Let us then suppose the mind to be, as we say, white paper,[48] void of all characters, without any ideas; how comes it to be furnished? Whence comes it by that vast store which the busy and boundless fancy of man has painted on it with an almost endless variety? Whence has it all the materials of reason and knowledge? To this I answer, in one word, from experience.[49]

There are, in short, no innate ideas.

In their rejection of innate ideas both Locke and Hobbes might be called empiricists. In the customary sense of the term, however, Locke was empirical and Hobbes was not, in that Locke trusted to observation and experiment, what is generally called the inductive method, rather than the logically deduced, rationalistic system preferred by Hobbes. There were, however, even in Locke residues of Cartesian rationalism. The passage quoted above about the certainty of geometry and the principles of justice is one example. The quest for the "true idea," fixed and clear, is another. There is something of the rationalistic spirit in Locke's famous distinction between primary and secondary qualities. Primary qualities Locke regarded as those attributes of bodies wholly independent of our sensation: "solidity, extension, figure, motion or rest, and number." Secondary qualities were regarded as those arising in the perception of an object yet ultimately being merely reflections in the perceiver of primary qualities. The secondary qualities were thought to include bulk, texture, colors, sounds, tastes.[50]

The whole trend of Locke's thought, however, was away from abstract systematization and toward the particularization of ideas and words. Our ideas are produced in the reflection that follows perception. Complex ideas are but a compound of simple ideas. Very much as Robert Boyle put atoms together to make molecules and molecules together to make up more complex structures, Locke assembled the world of ideas: "Ideas of substances are nothing else but a collection of a certain number of simple ideas, considered as united in one thing."[51] Like Hobbes, Locke could be

48 Here and elsewhere Locke used the image of "white paper" as a symbol for the human mind at birth rather than the *tabula rasa*—blank slate—metaphor which is perennially attached to him. The latter term apparently became identified with Locke as a result of Leibnitz's constant use of it in criticizing him.

49 *Essay*, Bk. II, Ch. 1, sec. 2, *Works*, Vol. I, p. 205.

50 *Essay*, Bk. II, Ch. 8, secs. 9-10. Although Bishop Berkeley later pointed out that everything Locke said about secondary qualities could also be said about primary qualities and thereby demolished the distinction, practical physics followed Locke for generations.

51 *Ibid.*, Ch. 23, sec. 14, *Works*, Vol. I, p. 434.

called an atomist, although he avoids drawing the extreme case as Hobbes was prone to do, and he does not carry the whole of experience back to matter in motion. Also like Hobbes, Locke is a nominalist. "Words in the primary or immediate signification stand for nothing but the ideas in the mind of him that uses them," and at root their signification is arbitrary. One of the great sources of human error is that through force of habit men "often suppose their words to stand for the reality of things," especially when dealing with the general nature of phenomena, "this whole mystery of *genera* and *species* which make such a noise in the schools. . . ." Actually, "general and universal belong not to the real existence of things; but are the inventions and the creatures of the understanding, made by it for its own use, and concern only signs, whether words or ideas. . . . When therefore we quit particulars, the generals that rest are only creatures of our own making."[52]

EPISTEMOLOGY AND POLITICS

Locke's vivid analysis of the limits of abstract knowledge would seem to work against the success of any general theory applicable to a field as dynamic and complex as politics. Indeed, it is interesting that he chooses to call the loose words of ordinary conversation "civil words" as distinguished from more precise and exact terms, or "philosophical words."

The parallels that obtain between Locke's political thought and his philosophy are probably significant not so much for the direct causal relation one bears to the other—though this is not to deny that there is such a relationship—as for the suggestion they contain of a parallel between the prevailing *Weltanschauung* of the post-Lockean West and its political thought. Political thought is always a reflection of something more than simply the political. In this case a scientific world view is reflected in "liberal" politics. For example, the atomism of Locke's physics fits his view of the way complex ideas are compounded of simple ideas, which in turn corresponds to his picture of individuals coming together to form a state. Note also the mechanistic language in Locke's rationale for majority rule: a "body should move that way whither the greater force carries it." Again, his epistemological skepticism seems to be reflected in his nominalist view of the state. The good state for Locke is one that protects individual rights. But in the last analysis the rights are defined (by the legislature) subjectively rather than by reference to any objective standard of the good. To say this is to bring into question the whole concept of natural law as Locke uses it, and so we must do.

There is sometimes thought to be a contradiction between Locke's repudiation of innate ideas in the *Essay* and the stress on natural rights in

52 *Ibid.*, Bk. III, Ch. 2, secs. 2, 5; Ch. 3, secs. 9, 11, *Works*, Vol. II, pp. 5, 7, 13, 14.

the *Second Treatise*. The contention is that one cannot deny the force of a priori ideas in one place and affirm them in another; or again that men cannot have the same natural rights if they all have different experiences and all knowledge comes from experience. John Gough has effectively shown that such an argument misinterprets Locke's understanding of natural rights, the law of nature, and the relationship between them. A key phrase for understanding Locke at this point is the "light of nature," an expression we encountered in the thought of Pierre Bayle. The "light of nature" is, for Locke, a "combination of the interdependent faculties of sense perception and reason. . . . The law of nature is not innate; what is knowable by the light of nature is the kind of truth at which a man may arrive, by himself and without extraneous help, through the right use of the faculties with which he was endowed by nature."[53] There is little doubt that, by themselves, men can arrive at a kind of truth and can base legitimate claims—natural rights—upon it; but insofar as this represents the operation of a law of nature, such a law appears to be almost procedural in character, i. e., without a universal content that specifically commands certain acts. This position is a departure from traditional forms of natural law, which assume a universal, *objective*, moral order discoverable by the right use of reason.

If we recall the quotation from the *Essay* stating that "where there is no property there is no injustice" is as certain "as any demonstration in Euclid," we know that Locke hoped for a natural law as demonstrable as Euclid. But Locke could never elaborate natural law so conceived into a politically relevant code of particulars because he ran into the theological problem. Being a Christian, Locke felt that natural law came from God and must ultimately rest on otherworldly sanctions. But he could not honestly say that reason demonstrates the existence of the other world. Thus it was that in 1695 he published anonymously *The Reasonableness of Christianity*, which tried to show, not the reasonableness of belief in God or the other world, but the reasonableness of New Testament law. For this effort, as we saw, he was attacked, rightly, as being a Socinian, and, wrongly, as being an atheist. His argument for a distinction between "the law of works," which was "the law of nature, knowable by reason," and the "law of faith," which was belief in God and Jesus as the Christ, could not be validated by reason. In defending the reasonableness of the Scriptures he was led to repudiate the doctrine of original sin, the Athanasian Creed, and other Trinitarian expressions, and to try to rationalize the "simple teaching" of Jesus, "free from the corrupting and loosening glosses of the scribes and Pharisees."

53 Gough, *John Locke's Political Philosophy*, p. 14. It is probably safe to say that Jefferson's "inalienable" rights are not "innate" in the traditional sense, either.

But Locke is forced to grant that strict obedience to the "law of works" in the New Testament is not necessarily rewarded with political success. How many successful political—or other—leaders can consistently "turn the other cheek," "walk the second mile," "take no thought for their lives," "judge not," etc.? Really fundamental virtue, it seems, must rest on otherworldly sanctions; and the law of reason that has bearing on success and happiness in this world is therefore what Leo Strauss has called a "partial law of nature," closer to Hobbes' ideal of self-preservation than to the New Testament's command of self-sacrifice. Thus, in the last analysis, Locke's major political tenets—government by consent, majority rule, the rights of property, even the whole idea of the state of nature—are but dimly related to the law of nature Locke set out to establish. In the end he was left with fideism rather than the "reasonableness of Christianity." Is Locke's persistence in using natural-law terminology in his political theory therefore but a sign of his confusion and ineptness? If so, does he deserve to be placed among the great political theorists?

It is the conclusion of Strauss that the inconsistencies "are so obvious that they cannot have escaped the notice of a man of his rank and his sobriety."[54] Locke probably knew very well that he was deviating from traditional natural law toward a more utilitarian standard. Locke was a man of great prudence and caution who knew that revolutionary ideas cannot always be put forth in bold-faced terms. Recall that he held up publication of the *Two Treatises* until 1689 when the political revolution he defended would be acceptable to the victorious Whig revolutionaries, and even then he chose to remain anonymous. But the deeper intellectual-moral revolution, the shift from transcendent to utilitarian standards of political morality, might not be acceptable even to Whig revolutionaries, who would have liked to think that they were acting with God's blessing.

Thus, while there were major inconsistencies both within Locke's political thought and between his political thought and his philosophical writings, at the level of greatest significance there is a close correlation between the *Essay's* admonition to rest content within the modest limits of our knowledge, to let probability "govern all our concernments," to eschew universal knowledge and improve life within the frame of observation and experience, and the optimistic, common-sense, utilitarian conclusions to be drawn from the *Second Treatise*.

54 *Natural Right and History* (Chicago: Univ. of Chicago Press, 1953), p. 220. It is Professor Strauss' great contribution to our understanding of historical political theory to remind us of an author's need to conceal his true intent in much political writing of the past. Political theory is often more than meets the eye. Sometimes, however, as a result of making consistency an almost inevitable attribute of the theorist, Strauss is led to regard simple human mistakes as part of a grand esoteric design. But the application to Locke seems pertinent.

Those of us who live in modern, Western, "democratic" societies are indeed Lockeans, but not simply because we believe that man came out of a state of nature to form government by mutual consent or that natural law dictates what that government and its citizens should do. If we think about these things at all, it is probably with little conviction. We are Lockean because, however unsure we are about natural law, we feel God or nature or life has given us certain *rights*, and it was Locke even more decisively than Hobbes who transformed natural law into natural rights. He replaced faith in a universal, objective moral order with belief in the validity of subjective claims for earthly happiness. Locke's theory of property bears this out as much as any aspect of his thought. It is labor that produces the value of everything. In a sense, then, man can by labor create his own world; the role of government is simply to enable him to do so without necessarily involving him in the problem of defining the common moral ends of production.

We like Locke because he seems to be an individualist, but we are not sure individualism is relevant any more. We are beginning to have doubts about Locke's optimistic conclusions concerning a rights-oriented society. We are not quite Lockean any more, but we are not yet anything else. We still think of ourselves as citizens of a secularized, rights-claiming, theoretically individualized, economy-oriented world. This is Locke's world. But we are not sure that we can or should expect it to last much longer.

CHAPTER 5 | *The Eighteenth Century*

IN POLITICAL theory the eighteenth century belongs to France as surely as the seventeenth century belongs to England. Germany was beginning to be heard from, and a tiny group of American colonies produced some well-tailored constitutional speculations. But when we think of the eighteenth century we think of the Enlightenment, and when we think of the Enlightenment we think of France. As England's international and colonial power rose, the fertility of her political thought declined. In France, the reverse order obtained.

Political theory in the eighteenth century can be organized around five new developments that provide us with the structure of this chapter: (1) a new philosophical orientation called the Enlightenment, stressing faith in the unity of nature, human reason, and a secularized natural law; (2) the birth of laissez-faire economics; (3) a new emphasis on a progressive order of history; (4) a new concern with constitution-making; (5) a large block of data for speculation on the theory of revolution.

The Enlightenment

THE Enlightenment is the name we give to the philosophical movement that put its faith in reason by pitting reason against faith. Despite many antecedents in the seventeenth century, the movement is identified with the eighteenth century because that century produced a self-conscious rejection of religion as the guiding authority in art, morals, politics, and scholarship. A new spirit of critical inquiry, "reason," took religion's place. This movement had political causes as well as political effects. The eighteenth century was a period of intense struggle between dynastic sovereigns for control of colonies and heretofore semiautonomous provinces. By contrast with England, the Continental representative assemblies were the refuge of reaction, the seat of feudal privilege. In their struggle to gain ascendancy over them, such sovereigns as Frederick II (the Great) of Prussia, Joseph II of Austria, Catherine II (the Great) of Russia adopted the antifeudal ideology of the Enlightenment, thereby becoming "enlightened despots." They were much admired by French intellectuals.

The *philosophes*, or popular philosophers of France, applauded anyone, king or commoner, who attacked the old order. Their bitterness toward the Church was especially deep. Their success was phenomenal. "In the middle of the eighteenth century they constituted a literary clique in Paris, barely known outside of its walls; by 1789 it might be said that virtually the entire body of educated opinion was now on their side. A revolution in ideas had taken place. . . . In their war against the Old Regime the *philosophes* succeeded, in a remarkably short time, in completely discrediting its institutions and ideals. In religion they spread incredulity and indifference, even more than hostility."[1]

As the church bureaucracy lost power, the state bureaucracy gained it. A by-product of the monarchs' drive for control was the growth of centralized governmental administration, which fixed itself on the land with a permanence known only to bureaucracies. While designed primarily to prevent local magistrates from having their own way with loose interpretations of customary law, eventually the proliferations of bureaucratic rules came to operate as a check on the whims of the autocrat himself. By 1741 David Hume was able to observe, not with complete accuracy, "It may now be affirmed of civilized monarchies what was formerly said in praise of Republics alone, *that they are a government of laws not of men.*"[2] As economic prosperity came to commercial interests, they identified their own good fortune with governmental centralization and increased opportunity for individuals, and they identified both of these tendencies with the victory of "reason" over the shackles of the past. In England the Whig party represented a happy compromise of commercial interests with the country nobility. Their triumph in 1688 foreshadowed a relatively placid eighteenth-century domestic scene. But in France the antagonism between the commercial interests and the nobility grew and festered until it erupted in the French Revolution.

But along with the political tensions ran a sense of discovery and intel-

1 J. Salwyn Schapiro, *Condorcet and the Rise of Liberalism* (New York: Harcourt, Brace, 1934), p. 34.
2 "Of Civil Liberty," in C. W. Hendel, ed., *Political Essays* (New York: Liberal Arts Press, 1953), p. 106.

lectual excitement that was infectious. Let one of the *philosophes* describe it:

. . . the discovery and application of a new method of philosophizing, the kind of enthusiasm which accompanies discoveries, a certain exaltation of ideas which the spectacle of the universe produces in us—all these have brought about a lively fermentation of minds. Spreading through nature in all directions like a river which has burst its dams, this fermentation has swept with a sort of violence everything along with it which stood in its way. . . . from the principles of the secular sciences to the foundations of religious revelation, from metaphysics to matters of taste, from music to morals, from the scholastic disputes of theologians to matters of trade, from the laws of princes to those of peoples, from natural law to the arbitrary laws of nations . . . everything has been discussed and analyzed. . . .[3]

VOLTAIRE AND THE PHILOSOPHES

The central vision of the *philosophes* was the unity of nature under an overarching natural science. Denis Diderot, who with Jean d'Alembert edited the great French *Encyclopédie*, ranks with Bacon as a popular exponent of experimental method. Like Bacon, whom he helped restore to prominence, Diderot was uninterested in abstract mathematical systems but rather stressed the practical and technological side of science. The *Encyclopédie* was filled with drawings of industrial devices and gadgets. Voltaire played with science, collecting specimens of this and that to no particular end. Mixed with this practical, unspiritual bent, however, was an enthusiasm that took on an almost religious quality of its own. Diderot read Bayle and was stimulated by his faith in man's "inner light." Baron Paul Henri Dietrich d'Holbach, whose *System of Nature* was the most extreme and clear-cut statement of Enlightenment materialism and atheism, closes the work with a glowing devotional to nature, "the sovereign of all beings."[4]

All of these men followed Locke's sensationalist psychology and epistemology,[5] and none more enthusiastically than Voltaire (François Marie Arouet, 1694-1778). Voltaire spent the years between 1726 and 1729 in England and returned home an ardent disciple of Locke. Locke, he felt, had done for the human mind what Newton had done for nature, and Voltaire's mission in life became that of using his magnificent powers

3 Jean d'Alembert, *Elements de philosophie* (1759). Quoted in Ernst Cassirer, *The Philosophy of the Enlightenment*, trans. by F. C. A. Koelln and J. P. Pettegrove (Boston: Beacon Press, 1955), p. 4.

4 The passage may, however, have been written by Diderot.

5 Étienne Bonnot de Condillac tried to extend Locke's epistemology to more rigorous limits than Locke had done, and traced "reflection" back to language rather than simply a "power" produced by sensation. His psychology was both systematic and influential.

of ridicule to advance Lockean ideas. But Locke's politics tended to accompany his epistemology. It was ironic that while in England Locke's political theory was mainly a rationale for established interests, in France it became a radical attack on the status quo. Voltaire, who became famous as a radical reformer, never intended to be a political revolutionary. Like most *philosophes*, he considered enlightened despotism an acceptable (though not necessarily ideal) avenue of reform; and he was, for a while, a good friend of Frederick the Great. Moreover, most of the *philosophes* preferred talking to acting. While the political discussions in the Paris *salons* were scintillating, there was nevertheless an air of artificiality about them. No one was much moved to march out into the streets to organize the unsavory masses.

Voltaire, however, cannot be said to have been timid. His honest fear of the mob was mixed with his forthright hatred of oppressors. He served time in the Bastille, was chronically in exile for his attacks on revered authority, and saved a number of lives by virtue of his intervention on behalf of the unjustly condemned. That he was not a revolutionary cannot be blamed on either lack of courage or lack of intelligence. Voltaire had both. He simply could not sustain a really optimistic position. He hoped to make the world only a little better. "It is impossible in our melancholy world to prevent men living in society from being divided into two classes, one the rich who command, the other the poor who obey. . . . Equality, then, is at the same time the most natural and the most chimerical thing possible."[6] Candide's resigned, somewhat bitter advice at the end of Voltaire's novel may have been the author speaking: ". . . let us cultivate our garden."

How, then, did the *philosophes* come to be known as revolutionary figures? Part of the answer may come from their attitude toward religion. Voltaire's position could best be summed up by saying that the mass of men ought to believe in some religion so that they will behave themselves. Metaphysics, for most of the *philosophes*, was wholly subordinate to morals. But men cannot long believe in a God who is but a tool of expedience. The persistent efforts of the *philosophes* to lead men away from traditional faith, and their inability to replace it with something else, in time bred the passionate religion of the state that became the soul of the French Revolution. What began as indifference ended as hostility. "Nowhere except in France had irreligion become as yet an all-prevailing passion, fierce, intolerant, and predatory."[7]

6 "Equality" in *The Philosophical Dictionary*, in Lord Morley, ed., William F. Fleming, trans., *The Works of Voltaire* (New York: Dingwall-Rock, 1927), Vol. IV, part 2, pp. 262, 264.

7 Alexis de Tocqueville, *The Old Regime and the French Revolution* (1856), trans. by S. Gilbert (New York: Doubleday [Anchor Books], 1955), p. 149. De

Yet the Enlightenment supposedly was a period of great optimism. What of the religion of reason as a substitute for orthodox religion? For some men, such as Condorcet, the new faith could support continuing evangelism. Voltaire, however, was too much of a realist to be carried away by high hopes. His sense of new knowledge that could save the world was continually being mixed with disgust that the world was rejecting it. It was Carl Becker in his now-classic *Heavenly City of the Eighteenth-Century Philosophers* who, seeing the paradox of skepticism and faith, drew a parallel between the thirteenth and the eighteenth centuries. "There were, certainly, many differences between Voltaire and St. Thomas Aquinas, but the two men had much in common for all that. What they had in common was the profound conviction that their beliefs could be reasonably demonstrated. In a very real sense it may be said of the eighteenth century that it was an age of faith as well as of reason and of the thirteenth century that it was an age of reason as well as of faith."[8]

But the faith of Voltaire was scarcely untroubled. Touched by the suffering of men, he could be magnanimous. "What is toleration?" he wrote in the *Philosophical Dictionary*, "It is the appurtenance of humanity. We are all full of weakness and errors; let us mutually pardon each other our follies—it is the first law of nature."[9] More often he was incapable of pardoning others' folly. *Candide* was a classic of biting satire on the follies of extreme optimism. The parody of Leibnitz' philosophy that "all is the best possible" becomes a whip to lash the reader with a consciousness of man's persistent stupidity.

This disjuncture of hopes and reality helps to explain Voltaire's failure to produce a systematic political theory. It is too simple merely to attribute this failure to the "fatal flaw" of a mind "discursive and tangential

---

Tocqueville has also shown how the absolutism of the *ancien régime* made Frenchmen more and more like each other at the same time that citizens were erecting façades of separate interests to preserve their pride. Only by understanding this phenomenon, said de Tocqueville, can we understand "how it was that a successful revolution could tear down the whole social structure almost in the twinkling of an eye." *Ibid.,* p. 77.

8 Carl L. Becker, *The Heavenly City of the Eighteenth-Century Philosophers* (New Haven: Yale Univ. Press, 1932), p. 8. See also R. R. Palmer, "Thoughts on *The Heavenly City*," in R. O. Rockwood, ed., *Carl Becker's Heavenly City Revisited* (Ithaca: Cornell Univ. Press, 1958), pp. 123 ff. A criticism of Becker's emphasis on the rationalism of the Enlightenment is well made by Peter Gay in "The Enlightenment in the History of Political Theory," *Political Science Quarterly*, Vol. 69 (1954), pp. 374-89. See also Peter Gay, *Voltaire's Politics, the Poet as Realist* (Princeton: Princeton Univ. Press, 1959), especially the Prologue. The book has an admirable bibliography, pp. 355-95.

9 *Works*, Vol. VII, Part 2, p. 100.

rather than orderly and concentrated."[10] His hopes were at once too high and too low to produce a rounded political theory. The same kind of hopeless hopefulness, militant fatalism, passionate dispassion is evident in Diderot: "Self-interest has produced priests, priests have produced pre-judices, prejudices have produced wars, and wars will continue as long as there are prejudices, prejudices as long as there are priests, and priests as long as self-interest calls them into being."[11]

The closest thing to an orderly theoretical development in Voltaire comes in the *Essai sur les moeurs,* where he speaks of the two empires, the "Empire of Nature," which reveals itself in the unity of all mankind, and the "Empire of Custom," which accounts for the great diversity among groups, sects, and nations.[12] From a similar assumption of ultimate human uniformity Hume and Montesquieu are led to place great weight on the causal influence of institutions in creating diversity. Voltaire would seem to share this view, yet it is always the spirit rather than the form he stresses. He is only marginally interested in such things as the proper construction of constitutions. Abstract theories could never crowd out Voltaire's concern with questions of practical morals. Nevertheless, he thought it was the task of the philosopher to reconcile these two empires, to make custom conform to the more fundamental empire of nature. Thus, against legal codes he put natural law, against traditional Christianity he put natural religion, against the cramped privileges of the *ancien régime* he put natural rights.

He did pay enough attention to legal problems to deride the corpus of modern civil and criminal law. He compared it to the uneven, squalid, ramshackle growth of the large, unplanned cities. The law could be, he felt, as orderly and acceptable as the rules of chess if it were constructed rationally in the interests of the player-citizen. At that time it consisted of the irrational accretions of generations of special interest. In great im-patience he argued for wiping away *all* existing law, this baggage from the dead past. Give to contemporaries the task of formulating a simple, logical system of laws. Almost any group of reasonable men could do it. Coke would have shuddered. Yet not too many years later the Napoleonic Code came close to what Voltaire hoped for.

Voltaire's support of Locke and natural rights, however, did not make

---

10 J. B. Black, "Voltaire," in F. J. C. Hearnshaw, ed., *The Social and Political Ideas of Some Great French Thinkers of the Age of Reason* (London: Harrap, 1930), p. 136.

11 *La Promenade du sceptique* (1747), Discours Prélim., in *Oeuvres complètes* (Paris: Garnier, 1875), Vol. I, p. 183. There is more consistency to this pessimistic element in eighteenth-century French thought than is often recognized. See Henry Vyverberg, *Historical Pessimism in the French Enlightenment* (Cambridge: Harvard Univ. Press, 1958); and Peter Gay, *Voltaire's Politics.*

12 Ch. 197, *Oeuvres complètes* (Paris: Lefebvre, 1829), Vol. XX, pp. 307-25. See Black, "Voltaire."

him a believer in a state of nature. Man, he felt, was naturally gregarious, and, indeed, owed natural duties to the state.[13] Nor did inequality of possessions bother him. The *philosophes* were neither pie-in-the-sky optimists nor radical equalitarians. In the last analysis, however, we must mark these men down for optimists, and for liberals whose optimism marred their liberalism. They were great admirers of the English Constitution because it protected individual property rights. They were disturbed by autocracy in France because individuals suffered. Political problems that had dimensions other than the individual did not interest them. Even attacks on the Church were based primarily on the argument for individual freedom.[14] In one sense, there was no problem of society for these men, only problems of individuals. From them, in part, came the preoccupation of liberalism with the individual and the neglect of groups of which he must necessarily be a part. From them, in part, came liberalism's unbounded faith in education. Freedom is everything and knowledge is freedom. "In fact, what does it mean to be free? It means to know the rights of man, for to know them is to defend them."[15]

UTILITARIANISM: HELVETIUS

By utilitarianism we mean a general predisposition to judge social policies in terms of their "utility," or use-value, rather than by other presumably more metaphysical standards. We also mean, more specifically, a school of thought originating in England and France that accepted as a basic explanation of human behavior the desire to gain pleasure and avoid pain, and extended this principle into a general definition of the good: to maximize pleasure and minimize pain.

Despite his Lockean psychology, Voltaire remained largely the rationalistic moralist to the end. Diderot moved in the course of his life away from natural-law thinking toward utilitarian ethics. Claude Adrien Helvetius (1715-71), an important influence on Bentham, moved even further in this direction. Helvetius, a wealthy farmer-general whose *salon* was a frequent meeting place for the *philosophes,* is best remembered for the famous utilitarian standard "the greatest good for the greatest number," a standard that theoretically could be applied to ethical questions without reliance on natural law or natural rights. He also propounded what Elie Halévy has called "the principle of the artificial identification of interests."[16] That is, men can be assumed to act only in their

13 See Constance Rowe, *Voltaire and the State* (New York: Columbia Univ. Press, 1955).
14 See Diderot's *The Nun*, written in 1760, published in 1796.
15 Voltaire. Quoted in Cassirer, *Philosophy of the Enlightenment*, p. 251.
16 Elie Halévy, *The Growth of Philosophic Radicalism*, trans. by Mary Morris (Boston: Beacon Press, 1955), p. 19. This may be compared to Bernard de Mandeville (1670-1733) in *The Fable of the Bees*, who found in the world a natural identification of individual and public interests. If people were left alone, "private vices"

own self-interest, but a well-regulated system of punishments will enable the legislator to channel these interests toward the public good. Helvetius' aim was to "treat morals like any other science and to make an experimental morality like an experimental physics."[17]

The concept of "interest" was the key to this science, comparable to the laws of motion in the physical universe. The laws of interest were at one and the same time the key to how men behaved and how they ought to behave. Since the union of is and ought cannot be as simple as this concept would seem to assume, a distinction appeared in Helvetius between a misunderstod interest and a man's "true" interest, which it was the business of the legislator and the educator to point out to the individual. Here are the seeds, some of them, at any rate, of the welfare state. The importance of education and legislation in helping individuals achieve their own best interest is an important tenet in the liberal tradition. But so is the belief that, despite this helping hand, the individual's interests are still his own. And each man's (and woman's—Helvetius was a feminist) interest was worth about as much as any other man's. Even at this date the equalitarian drive inherent in utilitarian ethics was manifest. It was not the omnipotence of man, however, but the omnipotence of the environment that was ostensibly confirmed by Helvetius' theories. Man was a product of his environment—except that some men, the legislators, somehow transcended this limitation and were able to modify the environment. "Make good laws; they alone will naturally direct the people in the pursuit of the public advantage, by following the irresistible propensity they have to their private advantage. . . . It is of little consequence that men be vicious; it is enough that they be intelligent. . . . Laws do all. . . ."[18] In this way were the gates to limitless historical progress opened.

The shift from natural law to a simple pleasure-pain explanation of man appears to be fundamental, and, indeed, it is. But Helvetius was too much affected by the eighteenth-century environment to see this shift as we might. He shared with others the common faith in the unity of nature, the permanence of truth, and even the Cartesian ideal of a universal mathematics as the "alphabet of nature." In these ways he was closer to the natural-law tradition than most twentieth-century empiricists would be. He began not so much with the method of scientific inquiry as

---

would become "publick virtues." The connection between this view and the assumptions of the laissez-faire economics of Adam Smith is important. See below, p. 146.

17 *De l'Esprit*, Preface. Quoted in Halévy, p. 19. The similarity here to Hobbes is striking, a similarity Halévy overlooks.

18 *Treatise on Man*, II, 300-301. Quoted in Charles Frankel, *The Faith of Reason, The Idea of Progress in the French Enlightenment* (New York: King's Crown Press, 1948), p. 58.

with a metaphysical notion of "nature"—in whose name he attacked metaphysics. Moreover, Helvetius had no real psychology. His understanding of interests was largely external, and his tendency was to think in terms of manipulating individuals rather than understanding their inner motivations. He measured an individual's "enlightenment" more by action than by motive. In this way "freedom" itself became externalized. Yet the "free individual" is still important enough to Helvetius to make him spar with the problem: ". . . the freedom of man consists in the free exercise of his power; I say *his* power, because it would be ridiculous to regard as non-freedom our inability to pierce the clouds like an eagle, live under the water like a whale, or make ourselves kings. . . ."[19] This comes dangerously close to saying that man is free to do what he is free to do.

The certitude, simplicity, and mechanical qualities of Helvetius' utilitarianism fitted well into the *philosophes'* political program—or, rather, their political lack of a program—namely, enlightened despotism. For if the calculation of social goods is as scientific as Helvetius' utilitarianism would make it appear to be, then obviously lawmaking is a matter for expert determination rather than for bargaining and compromise. "Father knows best" has been the attitude of all autocracies. In recent times scientific authority—"the expert knows best"—has been added to the other sources of strength in the autocratic arsenal (sometimes with peril to the autocrat). In the history of ideas seen from a Western vantage point Helvetius' utilitarianism has often been put in the democratic ledger because of its influence on equalitarian thinkers. But its logic can just as easily lead in the opposite direction.

GODWIN

The principal English interpreter of the French Encyclopedists was William Godwin (1756-1836). Trained as a Calvinist clergyman, five years a pastor in a country parish, his faith was shaken by reading Holbach's *System of Nature*. He left his parish, no longer a Tory and no longer a Calvinist, but something of the Calvinist's stern moral discipline remained with him always.[20] Although he wrote novels, essays,

19 *De l'Esprit*, Disc. I, Ch. 4, in *Oeuvres complètes* (Paris: Garnery, 1793), Vol. I, pp. 298-99.

20 This Calvinist rectitude may appear to have deserted Godwin in his relationship with Mary Wollstonecraft, handsome and famous defender of the rights of women. She was thirty-seven, he was forty when they met. It was love at first sight, "the purest, most refined state of love," said Godwin. Whereupon they lived together without benefit of marriage until shortly before the birth of their only child. But this was a matter of moral principle, not immorality, for Godwin had already attacked the institution of marriage on moral grounds. The experience of marriage helped change his mind as to its value and, indeed, the short but blissful

histories, and other works in great profusion, Godwin's major work was *An Enquiry Concerning Political Justice*. Begun in 1791 and finished in 1793, it was a great statement of faith in the French Revolution—or at least the ideals of the French Revolution, for Godwin himself was opposed to revolutions.

Specifically, Godwin can be regarded as a disciple of Helvetius, sharing his view of the universe as a vast chain of cause and effect, a Newtonian mechanistic world, although Godwin could not go as far as Holbach and declare himself a materialist. The key argument, and, in fact, the core of his life's work, was on behalf of the perfectibility of the human species. Education can remake man. His character is not, as Montesquieu believed, formed by climate, nor, as Burke believed, cramped by dark, ineradicable passions. The vice in man results from error, which reason can correct.

Two quite different strains were at work in Godwin. On the one hand, he was a rationalist, declaring for a justice higher than any government and a reason higher than any positive law. Political institutions "to be good must have constant relation to the rules of immutable justice. . . . [which] uniform in their nature, are equally applicable to the whole human race."[21] Most laws should be abolished, for "Reason is a thousand times more explicit and intelligible than law; and when we are accustomed to consult her, the certainty of her decisions would be such, as men practiced in our present courts are totally unable to conceive."[22] On the other hand, Godwin adhered to a much more low-level, Helvetian pleasure-pain psychology. "The points in which human beings resemble are infinitely more considerable than those in which they differ. We [all] have the same senses. . . . Sensual pleasure on the one hand, or intellectual on the other is, absolutely speaking, the highest and most desirable."[23]

But of the two strains, the rationalist emphasis seems clearly to dominate. Take his discussion of forms of government, for example. The moralistic tone is overwhelming. Monarchy as a form of government is "essentially corrupt." It is "founded in imposture." Aristocracy, too, is "in direct opposition to all sound morality, and all generous independence of character." Both rest on deceitful assumptions of natural inequality. So-called mixed governments are likewise mere "imposture."[24] Only

relationship with Mary affected his whole philosophy, leading, he said, to a reexamination of the "empire of feeling." Mary died tragically a few days after childbirth. See C. Kegan Paul, *William Godwin* (London: H. S. King, 1876), Vol. I, p. 294.

21 *An Enquiry Concerning Political Justice*, 3rd ed., Bk. V, Ch. 1. F. E. L. Priestly, ed. (Toronto: Univ. of Toronto Press, 1946), Vol. II, p. 2.

22 *Ibid.*, Bk. VII, Ch. 9, Vol. II, p. 2.

23 *Ibid.*, Bk. III, Ch. 7, Vol. I, p. 240.

24 *Ibid.*, Bk. V, Chs. 6, 9.

democracy is in any way acceptable to Godwin and he is scarcely enthusiastic about that. Like Rousseau he felt that representative arrangements involved unwarranted abnegations of individual judgment; but
unlike Rousseau he worried over the protection of minorities (the argument had a close parallel to that of John Stuart Mill's "On Liberty"), and
he was not at all taken in by *vox populi:* ". . . the voice of the people is
not, as has sometimes been ridiculously asserted, 'the voice of truth and
God' . . . universal consent cannot convert wrong into right."[25]

Godwin was an extreme equalitarian who permitted property in his
system only that it might be given away. Yet he was not a communist,
for he did not like the thought of organized group cooperation either.
About all that is left is anarchism, so we call Godwin an anarchist. He
did believe in "anarchism" but not in "anarchy." The distinction is fundamental and may be Godwin's most striking contribution. "Anarchy" to
Godwin meant every man free to do as he liked, a condition he despised.
"Anarchism," by contrast, meant society functioning without a government. This Godwin dearly desired. But such a condition could not be
achieved as a result of every man going his own way; it required the
voluntary self-regulation of each individual for the public good. Here
Calvinist discipline and duty come again to the fore. Godwin's ringing
demand was for a spirit of "universal benevolence," attainable only by
education. It was the aspiration to this universal benevolence, each man
a brother to every other man, that led him for a time to advocate elimination of the family.

Godwin is fascinating because he marvelously combined the worst
and the best in Enlightenment faith. With a mechanical psychology that
trampled on moral subtleties, with a dogmatic conviction that science
would conquer evil as it conquered nature, he blended a simple faith
in man's capacity to reason, to improve himself, to feel the tides of "universal benevolence" out of which comes duty to the common good.
Though we cannot make Godwin into a great political theorist, he was a
good and courageous man whose aspirations reveal some of the positive
values that have given liberalism as a movement emotional force.

Economics and Politics

POLITICS and economics always go hand in hand. Tender souls repelled
by crass money matters sometimes hold this against politics, apparently
believing that if legislators talked more about the good life and less about

25 *Ibid.,* Bk. II, Ch. 5, Vol. I, p. 165. See David Fleisher, *William Godwin: A Study
in Liberalism* (London: Allen & Unwin, 1951).

the gross national income we would be better off. They may be right. The simple fact remains, however, that politics is particularly tied to common concerns—the things that bother most people—and staying alive and eating well has always bothered more people more insistently than knowing the truth or contemplating the beautiful. Even totalitarian dictators must see that people are fed and bridges are built before turning to the aesthetics and morals of the party line. Economics is fundamental.

But there was a time, in the feudal period, when economic relationships were welded to a status system that scarcely changed from one generation to the next. The ratio of births to deaths was stable. Geographic explorations were few. Economics was still basic but economic questions were fixed because, relatively speaking, the society was static. By the sixteenth and seventeenth centuries neither economics nor politics was static, and we can recall the theoretical interest in economics displayed by students of government, such as Harrington and Locke. But it was not until the eighteenth century that economic turmoil and the Enlightenment faith in science joined to produce a new "economic science." Whether the Physiocrats, or the Kameralists, or Adam Smith should receive the trophy as founder of modern economics is a moot point. All of them made their contribution.

THE PHYSIOCRATS

The founder of the school known as the Physiocrats was François Quesnay, a court physician to Louis XV who specialized in royal mistresses. Although he had written two articles for Diderot's *Encyclopédie* in the 1750's, it was late in that decade, when he was well into his sixties, before Quesnay published anything in economics. The birth of the Physiocratic school dates from an interview Quesnay had with Victor Riqueti, Marquis de Mirabeau, author of *Ami des hommes,* in July, 1757. The next year Quesnay published his *Tableau oeconomique,* an elaborate chart of the economy, modeled on the human circulatory system and not unlike some of the flow charts we see in introductory economics textbooks. The group, which originally was called simply *Les Économistes,* included, in addition to Quesnay and Mirabeau, Jean de Gournay, Mercier de la Rivière, Dupont de Nemours, and, though he disliked the label, Jacques Turgot. As Minister of Finance, Turgot in 1774 tried to put Physiocratic theories into practice, without much success.

The Physiocrats symbolize four phenomena: a reaction against the past, some economic axioms, a practical political program, and a set of philosophic assumptions. The reaction against the past was directed at feudal inefficiencies and mercantilist restrictions. Tolls, monopolies, privileged hunting—any of the feudal vestiges that were wasteful, choked off trade, or inhibited consumption were opposed. In France, mercantilism was most closely identified with the policies of Louis XIV's great finance minister Jean Colbert. It connoted strict state control of the economy, protective tariffs, centralized taxation, economic exploitation of colonies, and subordination of agriculture to commerce and manufacturing. Wealth, mercantilists felt, consisted in bullion, and nations could prosper only at each others' expense. It is not surprising that the Physiocrats opposed such policies. What followed these policies, and therefore seemed to be caused by them, was the economic malaise of France. Wars, fantastic monarchical extravagance, and the expulsion of Protestants had increased the debt and reduced the population. The French merchant marine had been ruined by the Seven Years' War. The population had declined by four million between 1660 and 1715. Two thirds of the tax revenues were being consumed by the cost of collection; agricultural production had fallen off precipitously.

The basic economic axiom that the Physiocrats hurled against mercantilism was the view that ultimately only agriculture can generate economic value. Though mistaken, their conclusion is understandable, not only on the basis of the economic facts just mentioned, but from the world scene as the French saw it. England, where there had been recent great strides in agriculture, was prosperous. Commercially oriented Holland was declining. Spain was declining, possibly because she had tried to develop her marine power at the expense of agriculture. Quesnay was aware that money was important to France, but its importance to him was mainly as a stimulus to agriculture. Agriculture is the "surest source of revenue" for the state, since only agriculture can produce a surplus profit for the owner. By contrast, trade and industry, operating on a narrower margin, were seen as sterile. In criticizing the shortcomings of Locke's labor theory of value, the Physiocrats went so far as to make human labor wholly subsidiary to land as the source of economic value.[26]

But if the land was to be productive, several requirements needed to be met: wastefulness and parasitical commercial elements had to be eliminated; large capital investments in land had to be encouraged (the larger the landowner, the greater the surplus profit); and a free market for goods had to be provided. Hence came a policy and with it a name graven deeply into the Western consciousness: *laissez faire, laissez passer.* The government was to keep its hands off trade.[27] The Physiocrats had no

26 See G. Wenlersse, "Physiocrats," in *Encyclopaedia of the Social Sciences* (New York: Macmillan, 1931), Vol. V, pp. 348-51; Henry Higgs, *The Physiocrats* (New York: Macmillan, 1897).

27 But their use of the term *laissez faire* did not mean the Physiocrats foreshadowed all that it came to mean. "Quesnay's *Maximes* were intended to provide [an omniscient] government with the viewpoints necessary to translate into practical

direct concern with such political questions as the right of suffrage or the proper construction of constitutions. Apart from questions of trade and colonialism they could not be said to be antigovernment. But their program had all sorts of political consequences. They defended various liberties regarded as corollaries of the right of private property: e.g., the right freely to sell one's services and the property in one's person, and the right to sell one's goods unchecked even by international conventions. This point of view assumes a legal equality of sorts, though it also takes for granted existing inequalities among participants in the economic process.

The philosophical underpinnings given these views probably came after the fact rather than before. These men were reacting more to conspicuous economic conditions than to subtle theories, which makes all the more impressive the degree to which they could bring the basic Enlightenment assumptions to bear on their policy. Employing the characteristic Enlightenment mode of geometric reasoning, they felt they had a hold on fixed a priori laws of nature concerning economic relations, laws that would stand forever. Government was not as irrelevant to the natural harmony of the universal order as it was to Adam Smith's concept of the "invisible hand" guiding market transactions, but there is no doubt that the Physiocrats believed in such an order.

Jacques Turgot was the most philosophically inclined Physiocrat. Possibly for that reason he was separated somewhat from the rest. He carried furthest the idea of inevitable progress. Indeed, his faith in the "ubiquity of reason" to use Charles Frankel's phrase, led him to the most un-*philosophe* extreme of lecturing in 1750 on the contribution Christianity had made to progress. "Turgot found continuity everywhere, and wherever he found continuity he inferred progress."[28] Thus every shred and tatter of history, however soiled, contributes something to the advance of mankind. Every "mutation" brings some advantage. Willy-nilly such reasoning brought Turgot to the dilemma of every monistic system. Either every act of history is directed, and we are but pawns, or no act of history is directed, and chance makes progress meaningless.

But men do not have to be good philosophers to make a contribution to political theory and the Physiocrats did make a contribution. They took Locke's individualism but rejected his labor theory of value. They

policy the principles of the *Tableau* on the basis of statistical data which he offered to have furnished periodically. The idea of a self-regulating system of markets had never as much as entered his mind." Karl Polanyi, *The Great Transformation* (Boston: Beacon Press, 1957), p. 135. The Physiocrats favored government protection of agriculture to such an extent that their position has been called an inverted, agrarian mercantilism.

28 Frankel, *The Faith of Reason*, p. 122.

took faith in a natural order from the *philosophes* and applied it to economics, where it has remained alive longer than in most other areas (examine, for example, the speeches of Herbert Hoover). By focusing on the concrete problems of France they helped push beyond the "Anglomania" of the *philosophes*. But, above all, their serious attempt at economic analysis gave birth to a science. Though more deductive than inductive, though mislabeled "moral and political science," their discipline was an important ancestor of nineteenth- and twentieth-century political economy. By no means the least of their descendants was Karl Marx, who, with different materials and different results, also built a theory on surplus value and sought to exorcise the parasites from the economic order.

THE KAMERALISTS

In the states of Austria and Germany during the mid-eighteenth century there arose a school of political economists who came to be known as the Kameralists (from *Kammer*, or chamber where the royal treasure was stored). The personalities of these men are, for most of us, hidden beneath a heavy veil of anonymity. Who has heard of Schröder, Hornick, Dithmar, Gasser, von Justi, Sonnenfels? They were mercantilists rather than free-traders and hence differed sharply from the Physiocrats. But whereas further west, mercantilism was focused especially on the need for colonial expansion, in Germany it was identified with the need for industrial and governmental centralization. The Kameralists were against freedom of trade on the grounds that population and food supply varied in direct relation to each other and that governmental stimulation was necessary to attract aliens, enlarge industry and agriculture, and achieve a balanced population.

The significant tendency for our purposes is the degree to which the Kameralists relied on the same philosophic tenets as the Physiocrats to achieve different ends. The Kameralists, too, invoked a doctrine of natural law, but following Pufendorf, used it to justify the extension of state power rather than individual rights. Along with this principle, and with some inconsistency, they postulated a kind of utilitarian general happiness of subjects toward which state action is directed. But most important, they tried to develop an administrative and economic science, making significant contributions to the use of statistics in public finance.

In Germany the Enlightenment had the advantage of somewhat more enlightened enlightened despots. By contrast with the conceited extravagance of the Louises or the dull stodginess of the Georges, governmental efficiency was sought after and rewarded. If efficiency is not necessarily enlightened, it is at least on the way to being "scientific." In Prussia, under

Frederick the Great, candidates for the civil service had to study Kameralism in the universities (Dithmar of Frankfurt was appointed to the first university chair of Kameralism by Frederick William I). Maria Theresa of Austria centralized tax-collecting and effectively reorganized the royal exchequer as a national treasury. The ends were already becoming out of date. But the means had the marks of the new.

ADAM SMITH

Even those who have never studied economics know the name of Adam Smith (1723-90). The name itself has a basic quality to it: what more primeval than Adam, or more common than Smith? Given the stimulus "Adam Smith," almost anyone can respond, "*Wealth of Nations,* 1776." Americans feel that their wealthy nation born in 1776 must have some connection with this work, even though Smith was a Scotsman. And rightly so: after 1776 "all of the Western World became the world of Adam Smith: his vision became the prescription for the spectacles of generations. . . . he gave the world the image of itself for which it had been searching."[29]

Adam Smith, a lecturer in moral philosophy at the University of Glasgow, was famous for his friendliness, his halting delivery, and his unbelievable absent-mindedness. He had already written *The Theory of Moral Sentiments* (1759) when he went to France as tutor to the duke of Buccleuch. There he met Voltaire, Turgot, and Quesnay. He was much impressed with Quesnay's *Tableau oeconomique,* even though he could not accept the Physiocrats' reduction of all productive value to land. Of the Physiocrats Smith once said, "[their] system with all its imperfections, is perhaps the nearest approximation to the truth that has yet been published on the subject of political economy."[30] While in France, Smith set to work on his *Wealth of Nations,* which, when published years later, would far overshadow the Physiocrats' efforts.

Smith's work was clearly an eighteenth-century creation, rambling, digressive, sweeping in subject matter and approach. It thoroughly incorporated the familiar Enlightenment belief in the natural order of history. Nor was its economic orientation new. The free-trade arguments of men as far back as Sir Dudley North in *Discourses on Trade* (1691) anticipated much of Smith's argument. But *The Wealth of Nations,* which was much more of a description than a proposal for reform, reflected, at one place and time, the realization of a completely new world of capitalistic eco-

29 Robert Heilbroner, *The Worldly Philosophers* (New York: Simon and Schuster, 1953), p. 32. Chapter 3 is a good summary of Smith's economics. See also Joseph Cropsey, *Polity and Economy: An Interpretation of the Principles of Adam Smith* (The Hague: Nijhoff, 1957).

30 Quoted in Henry Higgs, *The Physiocrats,* p. 2.

nomics and a new faith in the future of a system of competitive enterprise that was already here. The market-oriented society was a fact, and now it had a philosophic rationale.

The Wealth of Nations begins with a description of the principle of specialization of labor, the key to modern industrial society. One man working alone can make, perhaps, 20 pins a day. Ten men working together can make 48,000 pins a day. But this great leap in productivity requires a market capable of absorbing it. Smith sought for and found the laws of this market, the laws we have since labeled supply and demand. If the market is left free, the economic self-interest of thousands of isolated consumers and hundreds of isolated producers will unconsciously direct the system toward ends that are best for the economic welfare of the whole society. The driving force is called competition. To illustrate: if the price of commodity A becomes too high, two results automatically occur. Consumers begin buying other commodities, creating greater demand in those sectors, which will then require more labor, thereby absorbing some of the workers laid off or reduced in wages in industry A. Moreover, other producers rush in to take advantage of the consumer dissatisfaction with the present producers of commodity A, thus forcing the price down again. This process was a kind of balancing act, but it was seen as doing more than merely creating a static balance analogous to the national balance of trade the mercantilists sought. Smith put two dynamic factors into the system, which made progress a viable ideal. The system was continually expanding in such a way that the capitalist could accumulate surpluses, and these accumulations could and should be reinvested to tap an ever-expanding market. Smith opposed the use of accumulated capital for charitable purposes (which would only stimulate idleness), *or* for pretentious luxury for the capitalist. The great competitive machine would tolerate neither sloth nor ostentation.

The corollary of this law of accumulation was the law of population. The supply of laborers would, like the supply of goods, vary with the demand. As wages went up not merely would the number of workers for a particular industry go up, but the *total* number of workers would increase. And the converse if wages went down. "The liberal reward of labour, therefore, as it is the effect of increasing wealth, so it is the cause of increasing population. To complain of it, is to lament over the necessary effect and cause of the greatest public prosperity."[31] If this relation-

31 *The Wealth of Nations*, 6th ed., Bk. I, Ch. 8. Quotations from this work are taken from Bohn's Standard Library Ed. (London: George Bell, 1896). The Reverend Thomas Robert Malthus, in *An Essay on the Principle of Population As It Affects the Future Improvement of Society* (1798), took a less optimistic view of increasing population. Pointing out that while people multiply, the land does not, he concluded that the misery of bare subsistence would be the perennial lot of most of mankind.

ship between wages and the existence or nonexistence of human beings seems a bit strained, we must remember that,

In Smith's day infant mortality among the lower classes was shockingly high. . . . In many places in England, half the children died before they were four, and almost everywhere half the children only lived to the age of nine or ten. Malnutrition, evil living conditions, cold and disease took a horrendous toll among the poorer elements. Hence although higher wages may have affected the birth rate only slightly, it could be expected to have a considerable influence on the number of children who would grow to working age.[32]

The perfect competitiveness of the system, the inability of any one producer to affect prices or demand, the complete mobility of labor, the rationality of consumers—all of these assumptions upon which the system rested were not "facts" of Smith's day any more than they are "facts" of our own day. But though he may have exaggerated man's innate "propensity to barter, truck and exchange," and though he missed the vital role of credit, Smith's model nevertheless approached the reality of his day much more closely than it does the economic reality of our day. This was still a period of relatively small producers and of workers so close to starvation that they *had* to move if wages shifted. Certainly there is no greater mistake than to make Adam Smith a defender of giant corporate enterprise in the twentieth-century sense, a sense he could, after all, scarcely imagine. The "exclusive privileges of corporations, statutes of apprenticeship, and all those laws which restrain . . . the competition to a smaller number than might otherwise go into them . . . are a sort of enlarged monopolies [sic]," and, for Smith, monopolies are most unhealthy. "The price of monopoly is upon every occasion the highest which can be got. The natural price, or the price of free competition, on the contrary, the lowest which can be taken . . . for any considerable time together." The former is "the highest which can be squeezed out of the buyers. . . . Such enhancements of the market price may last as long as the regulations of police which give occasion to them."[33] We can see in this statement the basis of Smith's antipathy to government. It is the "police" whose power, alone among powers, can artificially prop up monopolies. This assumption, of course, is what makes Smith relevant to political studies.

We must, however, again remember that the "police" who upset the market price represented not the welfare state of the twentieth century, but the mercantilist state of the eighteenth. It is true that Smith had little use for "that insidious and crafty animal, vulgarly called a politician or

32 Heilbroner, *Worldly Philosophers*, p. 57.
33 *Wealth of Nations*, Bk. I, Ch. 7.

statesman,"[34] but neither was he opposed to every conceivable act of government, as Herbert Spencer very nearly was a few decades later. Smith granted, for example, the desirability of public education, admitted the possibility of some governmental action to cope with the more inhumane aspects of the factory system, and, indeed, charged government with the all-important responsibility of actively blocking threatening monopolies, collusions, and trade barriers. He supported government economic activity on behalf of defense or other requirements of national interest. On one occasion he urged that direct, government rule would be better for India than the exploitive rule of the private East India Company. There was, however, in the late eighteenth century, a general absence of economic legislation, the kinds of measures that make up the bulk of today's Parliamentary work, and Smith certainly did not favor a fundamental change in this respect.

In Adam Smith the acid of counting, calculating, clanking industrialism has gone a long way toward dissolving the feudal mystique of the community, the common bond of allegiance to the group, an influence that still held some sway in Locke's use of "the people." Locke's somewhat inconsistent identification of the individual's interest with society's interest has by this time become a consistent and conscious identification of particular, private interest and general, public interest. The individual "neither intends to promote the public interest, nor knows how much he is promoting it. . . . by directing . . . industry in such a manner as its produce may be of the greatest value, he intends only his own gain, and he is in this, as in many other cases, led by an invisible hand to promote an end which was no part of his intention."[35] The mystique of the feudal community has been ironically replaced by an even more esoteric power lurking behind the mechanical, impersonal economic system. The invisible hand—or at least its imaginary shadow—did, at least, buoy up the optimistic spirit of economists and businessmen during the rigors of industrial expansion, even though, being invisible, it afforded considerably less solace to tired and hungry laborers.

Although Smith himself was a good-hearted soul, with a genuine concern for public welfare, there were in his system the seeds of callousness, some of which came to fruition in Malthus and Ricardo. Neither he nor many of his successors were so addicted to material production that they hoped everyone would be prosperous; nor were they far enough away from Calvinism to regard happiness as a legitimate fruit of prosperity. On the one hand, the poor would benefit by the continuing up-

34 H. J. Laski, *Political Thought in England, Locke to Bentham* (London: Oxford Univ. Press, 1920), p. 194.
35 *Wealth of Nations*, Bk. IV, Ch. 2.

ward spiral of the productive system, yes; but there would always be the poor.[36] And since happiness is in large part an inner state of grace anyway, the poor are not necessarily less happy than the rich, and need not, certainly, be pitied as a class. On the other hand, while all men are basically equal, both by nature and even in the all-important ability to produce goods, the rich—at least the rich entrepreneurs—had become so by virtue of stout character, by will and fortitude, which had enabled them to use their more or less equal talents while others' talents lay idle through sloth. The result was an equalitarian system run by an elite.

The roots of industrial and colonial paternalism went deeper and deeper. The managerial class could go about its work without the ostentatious trappings of the nobility, yet with a sense of mission that had, and still has, a strong moral content. And by separating government from economics they could conceal even from themselves the degree to which they were running the government.[37] By leaning on necessity, they could beg the question of the good life. By sticking to business they could make business stick to everything.

ECONOMICS AND POLITICS IN THE EIGHTEENTH CENTURY: A SUMMARY
Three conclusions may be drawn from this section.

First, the eighteenth-century economists, even mercantilists like the Kameralists, were participants in the general fascination with the order of nature and with geometrical system. Economists have worked with abstract systems ever since. In order to make the system work, it appears as if Adam Smith abstracted the one motive of economic self-interest and made this the only motive of life. Actually, he did not. His central concern, at least in *The Wealth of Nations,* was with the way a system behaved, not the way individuals behaved. By assuming a sufficient degree of economic self-interest in the individual cogs to make the machine work, he had a theoretical system that, in fact, was not too far from reality. Although increasingly bothered by "nonclassical" and only partially calculable influences such as advertising, group cohesion values in labor unions, the pressure of public opinion, the desire to maintain good will on the part of big companies, government tax policies, and other imponderables, this is the system economists still believe in. They do not say that every man is driven to seek out the lowest price and the

36 The problem of poor relief was not great in 1776; but only a decade later it was acute. This helps explain some of Smith's optimism, which otherwise would be inexplicable.

37 Joseph Schumpeter has pointed out, however, the degree to which capitalists were dependent upon the "protecting strata" of the nobility in the advance of industrial society. For a richly insightful account of the social context of capitalist development, see his *Capitalism, Socialism, and Democracy* (3rd ed.; New York: Harper, 1950), Part II.

highest wage; but they assume most men do, make predictions accordingly, and are right often enough to continue to do so. What this assumption does to the mentality of the average citizen is more of a sociological and a political question than an economic one, and to this question we must return later.

It is sufficient at this point to note that for the last hundred years—from Auguste Comte to David Easton—some political theorists have felt that they were at the same point as the economists of the eighteenth century, that is, ready to offer the world a political system that could rationalize a complex set of factors and make possible predictions about future political behavior. This effort, too, will engage our subsequent attention.

Second, economic theorizing in the eighteenth century shared the vision of change, development, and progress manifest in political thought, narrowly conceived. The dynamic had won a clear-cut victory over the static. The open-endedness of the world ahead, both an effect and a cause of industrialization and individuation, came to be taken for granted. Quesnay's flow chart and Smith's law of accumulation testify to the hopeful, dynamic, expanding character of the era. Said Smith, with considerable accuracy and characteristic matter-of-factness, ". . . it is not the actual greatness of national wealth, but its continual increase, which occasions a rise in the wages of labour."[38]

Whatever the proper labels for the economic systems that are competing for dominance in the twentieth century—capitalism, communism, socialism, welfare economics—it is highly significant that they all share the progressive assumptions of eighteenth-century thought. A lag of a mere two centuries should not, by this time, surprise the student of political theory.

Third, the most cursory glance at the economic theorizing of the eighteenth century will confirm what we noted at the beginning of this section, that there is always a relationship between political and economic theory. But there is some irony in the fact that modern thinkers became least concerned about this relationship at that moment when they were most concerned to separate the two spheres of politics and economics. From ancient times men had assumed a close relationship between politics and economics but felt no need to develop a separate discipline of economics. Plato and Aristotle would no more have thought of omitting economic matters from their discussion of politics than they would have tried to discuss economics apart from politics. The *polis* embraced both—and more. But partly because men in the eighteenth century had a new vision of material progress and partly because they felt that to be

38 *Wealth of Nations*, Bk. I, Ch. 8.

scientific meant to compartmentalize, a political-economic theory came into being; and as a result, one set of phenomena was newly illuminated while another set was obscured. What was obscured was the degree to which the market economy was a political invention,[39] and the degree to which the commercial classes influenced governmental policy. The breakthrough of this separation was engineered by Marx, who turned more than Hegel upside down. In the early liberal creed, politics was not supposed to affect economics. In Marx, politics was nothing but a branch of economics. It is premature to expand on Marx here. The point is simple. To theorize means to theorize *about* something. There-fore, because politics and economics are never wholly separable, political theory and economic theory are never wholly separable. The laissez-faire theorists forgot this, and their forgetting helps us to remember.

History and Politics

FRANCE: CONDORCET
In a way that is not easy for the more disillusioned residents of the twentieth century to comprehend, the eighteenth-century *philosophes* were deeply aroused by the prospect of radical change in the course of history. A new way of thought was closing the door of the past and opening up a future of unlimited potentialities. It was more than simply a vision of a changed human environment—we, too, can construct our science-fiction cities of the future. It was, especially for the lesser *philosophes*, a vision of a wholly new, beatific quality of life.

In the list of *philosophe* historians, a list that would include Chastellux, Abbé Raynal, von Grimm, and many others, the best-developed yet typical philosophy of history belongs to Condorcet (Marie Jean de Caritat, Marquis de Cordorcet, 1743-94). The biography of Condorcet can tell us much of the political environment of the *philosophes*. He was the son of an impoverished army officer of noble birth and a mother of wealthy bourgeois background. The union, a conjunction of class decay and class ascendancy, was not atypical of eighteenth-century France. Condorcet was educated at a Jesuit college. "The man who was to become a skeptic in religion, a pacifist, and a democrat was brought up in the environment of priests, soldiers, and nobles."[40] Showing brilliance in mathematics and hating the profession of arms, Condorcet offended his father's family by chosing to live in Paris on a small allowance sent by

39 See Polanyi, *The Great Transformation*, especially Ch. 12.
40 Schapiro, *Condorcet and the Rise of Liberalism*, p. 67.

his widowed, overprotective mother. His mentor in mathematics was the great D'Alembert, and Condorcet was soon drawn into the intellectual life of the *salon*. Despite his timidity, the list of friends he made in this circle reads like an eighteenth-century *Who's Who*: Helvetius, Lafayette, La Rochefoucauld, Benjamin Franklin, Thomas Jefferson, Tom Paine, Diderot, Holbach, Quesnay, Adam Smith, and, above all, his "masters," Voltaire and Turgot, both of whom he honored with biographies. Condorcet scandalized this set by his prosaic puritanism: he fell in love, married happily, and never took a mistress. He wrote ably in mathematics, but turned to economics after Turgot appointed him inspector of the mint in 1774. When Necker and mercantilism returned to the saddle in 1776, Condorcet resigned. In politics he could be called a constitutional monarchist before the Revolution, a democrat after. With Lafayette, the younger Mirabeau, and others he helped organize and later became president of "The Friends of the Negroes," an antislavery society. He also worked diligently for woman suffrage.

Condorcet's role in the French Revolution was not decisive, but it was significant because he was the only *philosophe* to be an active participant —indeed, he was so active it cost him his life. A member of the National Convention, Condorcet was chairman of the committee to draw up a constitution in 1793. The document,[41] a product of years of reflection, meant as a model for all mankind, was coolly received by the Convention and was falsely labeled a Girondist scheme by the Jacobins. When Condorcet wrote a pamphlet attacking the hastily contrived Jacobin constitution, the Convention called for his arrest. For nine months he hid out, painfully but patiently writing his most famous work, *Outlines of an Historical View of the Progress of the Human Mind,* one of the most optimistic works ever written. When finally arrested, footsore and half-starved, he had only a copy of Horace in his pocket. He died his first night in prison, according to one report, from self-administered poison, according to another, from exposure. In either case, it was a sordid end for the last of the *philosophes.*

This last work gained some of its fame from the peculiar circumstances of its writing, almost as if readers were repaying the *philosophes,* intellectual godfathers of the Revolution, for the way the Revolution treated them. Its basic assumption was "that the perfectibility of man is absolutely infinite" and it set out to show that "the course of this progress

41 It proposed a unicameral legislature elected annually by direct manhood suffrage (women were sacrificed to expediency, presumably), with nominees to come from "primary assemblies" in each *département*. The *départements* were to nominate three times the number of candidates to be elected and a preferential ballot was to be used. Although this scheme does not reflect it, Condorcet had closely studied and much admired American state and Federal constitutions.

may doubtless be more or less rapid, but it can never be retrograde. . . .[42] Condorcet traced nine epochs in the history of mankind, beginning with men who lived in animal-like hordes, and continuing through the pastoral state, the era of first agriculture, the glory of Greece, and so on. Each age had to fight off and struggle through the "seductive influences" of prejudice. In the Middle Ages man was "plunged into darkness" by superstition, but apparently this plunge did not qualify as a retrograde movement, only a temporary delay in the upward spiral of history. The ninth epoch spanned the period from Descartes to the French Republic. The tenth stretched out into the limitless, bountiful future. Only in his own day, Condorcet felt, had man finally arrived at the knowledge of the true rights of man, deduced from a single principle: man "is a being endowed with sensation, capable of reasoning upon and understanding his interests, and of acquiring moral ideas."[43]

The naïveté of Condorcet strikes us as incredible. Without being aware that he was dealing in paradoxes as difficult as, and not dissimilar from, those of Christian theology, he described an omnipotent process of history that yet had given man consciousness of his freedom from historical limitations. He gave us a point in time, his own day, beyond which evil would be timelessly overcome. He gave us a new morality, which is man's understanding of his own interests.

Despite Condorcet's practical interest in constitutions, his theory of government seems almost wistfully divorced from practice. He cited Sidney, Locke, and Rousseau on the equality of all men, but waived away any contractual theory that would bind people to their government in perpetuity. No man can be bound except by himself; even acts of the majority can be validated only by the free acceptance of the individual, for the individual can never yield up his own reason to a majority if the result might be violation of individual rights. The practical result of this position would seem to be anarchy. But Condorcet preferred to think of it not as anarchy but rather as a universal reign of harmony and peace.

Condorcet has often been called the "perfect ideologue." He was the "man of principle," one who actually operated on certain social assumptions as if they were geometric axioms: the natural goodness of man, the evil effects of inherited institutions, the inevitability of progress. If the facts did not conform, so much the worse for the facts. For Condorcet, as for most of the *philosophes*, "the individual" was one of the most abstract of the abstractions. "History" was another. And because they were abstractions Condorcet could forget that individuals are *in* history as a fish

42 *Outlines of an Historical View of the Progress of the Human Mind* (Philadelphia: Carey, Rice, Orwood, Bache & Fellows, 1796), p. 11.
43 *Ibid.*, p. 185.

is in water, and they cannot, however exhilarating a new flash of self-consciousness may be, foresee the tides and currents of the far future.

And yet, reflecting on Condorcet's almost childlike trust in men and the devotion that led this shy, diffident man to enter the political fray for the sake of "the people," we cannot be too harsh with him for his naïveté. As with Godwin, it is not his logic but his impulsive departures from logic that lead us to admire this "theologian of political rationalism." It was at the expense of some of these impulses that Montesquieu was able to give us deeper insights into the nature of politics and history.

ENGLAND: BOLINGBROKE

In England in the eighteenth century, the greatest insights into history and politics, or, rather, to be more precise, into the political uses of history, are given to us by conservatives: Bolingbroke, Hume, and Burke. Hume and Burke are important enough to deserve separate treatment in Chapters 8 and 9, respectively. Bolingbroke is in no way a political theorist of the first rank, but the combination of his political writings and his political action can tell us something about the relationship of history to ideology.

Henry St. John, first viscount Bolingbroke (1678-1751) was "a man of headlong vehemence, a born partisan, whose gifts were all for fighting, and to whom it came naturally to seek reconciliation with an enemy by injuring a friend. . . ."[44] One of the organizers of the new Tory party, Bolingbroke was a political power while still young and spent most of his later years plotting to regain his earlier glory. A member of Robert Harley's two moderate Tory cabinets between 1704 and 1714, he overshadowed and outmaneuvered the older Harley. But in 1715, after the accession of George I, Harley and Bolingbroke were impeached by the new Whig majority in Parliament for their Jacobite sympathies. Bolingbroke fled to France. Pardoned in 1723, he returned to England but was kept from power by Robert Walpole, the new leader of the Whigs. Frustrated, Bolingbroke turned to writing. His three chief works are *A Dissertation on Parties* (1734), *The Study and Use of History* (1735), and *The Idea of a Patriot King* (1738).

We read Bolingbroke, if at all, less to discover great insights than to see what relationship his active life in politics bore to his writings. It is a case of the ancient problem of the man of thought versus the man of action. His felicitous style and his air of dispassion conceal what some of his letters reveal, the deep cynicism that lay behind much of what he did and wrote. We might suspect this cynicism upon considering the spectacle of Bolingbroke, a professed Deist, brilliantly arguing in the House of Lords

44 G. N. Clark, *The Later Stuarts, 1660-1714* (2nd ed.; Oxford: Clarendon Press, 1955), p. 235.

in 1714 for an act that forbade Dissenters to act as tutors or schoolmasters. It happened to be expedient for Tories to support this particular measure of the queen, and Bolingbroke was just the man to make the Established Church sound very good indeed—without, apparently, believing a word of what he was saying. In the *Dissertation on Parties* this most ardent of partisans argued against parties, at least against the only kind of parties that were known to history. Somewhat as in the case of the early Federalists in America, the *raison d'être* of Bolingbroke's faction was to get rid of factions. We still have, of course, pressure groups working to save us from pressure groups. Bolingbroke's early use of the concept of the separation of powers made this doctrine a conservative weapon against the centralization of ministerial power in Walpole's evolving cabinet system.[45]

The *Patriot King* was at once a plea for the dissolution of factions out of common loyalty to a monarch, and a statement of the ideal of a monarch fully loyal to the English Constitution—the rule of a man, yet the rule of law, the best of two worlds. Given such a man and such a system, "concord will appear, brooding peace and prosperity on the happy land; joy sitting in every face, content in every heart; a people unoppressed, undisturbed, unalarmed. . . ."[46] Bolingbroke once admitted that such a monarch would be "a sort of standing miracle," which led Harold Laski to observe that no other comment was needed. But it is of passing interest that while Bolingbroke's conception of monarchy would have earlier fitted nicely into the divine-right mold, by this time divine-right arguments had little ideological usefulness, and Bolingbroke was obliged to say, "A divine right to govern ill is an absurdity."[47]

Of greatest relevance to our present interest is Bolingbroke's *The Study and Use of History*. The book was a demonstration more than an explanation of how history may be used for political purposes. Notwithstanding some subtle insights, as, for example, in his treatment of self-love as a motive for the study of history, Bolingbroke's political generalizations, directed toward "a constant improvement in private and public virtue. . . . to make us better men and better citizens" are fairly vacuous and rest on random and arbitrary historical examples. Indeed, the examples are often clear, while the principles they are supposed to illustrate are not. But toward the end, recent history comes to the fore and Bolingbroke's partisan spirit shows its hand. The reader is swiftly carried from Olympian observations on universal history to complaints about local taxes.[48] Is this

45 See *A Dissertation on Parties* (10th ed.; London: T. Davies & T. Cadell, 1775).

46 *The Idea of a Patriot King* (new ed.; London: T. Davies, 1775), p. 217.

47 *Ibid.*, p. 79.

48 See *The Study and Use of History* (new ed., corrected; London: T. Cadell, 1770), pp. 381-82.

simply sophomoric sloppiness, in which case Bolingbroke is unworthy of our attention, or are these the wiles of a professional politician who knows how to use words in all sorts of contexts to further his ends? The latter would seem to be true (although, of course, we can never be completely sure of the degree of self-consciousness in Bolingbroke's deceptions). The use of words is a form of power; indeed, it is one of the chief forms of power for the politician. He, unlike the scholar, uses words, ideas, and principles as weapons of combat rather than as tools for the discovery of truth; and it is perhaps only the conceit of the scholar that believes the former requires less intelligence than the latter. That Bolingbroke had the power to sway is indicated not only by the response to his writings in his own day, but by the fact that George III, Chatham, and Disraeli were moved by them, especially by the image of the "patriot king."

The problem of the relationship between the man of action and the man of thought is as old as Plato and as young as the Atomic Energy Commission. The problem of the political use of history is as old as Thucydides and as young as *Pravda*. The problem is whether and to what extent truth and power can be joined together. It is more than the schism between "thinkers" and "doers." Condorcet was a politician, though a bad one, who sincerely thought he had historical truth by the tail. Hume, as we shall see, was an academic philosopher who wrote polemical history. Burke, and possibly Montesquieu, came closest to resolving the dilemma in one man. Whether they succeeded or not is one of the questions awaiting us in later chapters.

ITALY: VICO

Against the dominant progressive-optimistic-intellectualistic mood of the eighteenth century one man stands like a boulder in a stream. The disparity between his thought and the currents of his time—a measure, in one sense, of his genius—resulted in an almost total neglect in his lifetime. *Giambattista Vico* (1668-1744) was born in poverty and lived in obscurity. He took no part in public affairs. Tutoring and a modest income as professor of rhetoric at the University of Naples kept him alive. In 1725, after writing three major works in Latin, he significantly shifted to Italian for his greatest treatise, *Principles of a New Science Concerning the Natural Community of Nations.*[49]

The *New Science* is vast, complex, and often confusing. It moves in two apparently antithetical directions, creating a pervading tension. On the one hand, Vico is absorbed with infinite detail, the objective, concrete

49 *Principi di una scienza nuova intorno alla commune natura delle nazioni* (3rd ed., 1744), trans. by Thomas G. Bergin and Max H. Fisch as *The New Science of Giambattista Vico* (Ithaca: Cornell Univ. Press, 1948). All quotations are from this first and only English translation, hereinafter referred to as *The New Science*.

"reality" of history as conventionally understood. On the other hand, he is concerned with methodological principles, the theory of history, the subjective reality of history as it exists in the poetic memory of man. Against the cold, geometrical reason of the Enlightenment he puts an almost mystical reason working its way out of the long experience of the race: "Humanity's living consciousness of what it has done."[50] Against the optimistic hope for linear progress in history he puts a pessimistic theory of cyclical repetition in history. Against modern, scientific naturalism, which makes man a datum of nature, "Vico offers to modern man an alternative principle for the vindication of his own spirituality and subjectivity. That alternative is history."[51]

The "new science" was more of a new approach, a psychological approach, to history than it was a new method. It was grounded on the belief that "the true history of the human race is the history of its progressive mental states."[52] The scholar must penetrate these mental states by poetic-mystical participation; he must "enter into the imaginations of the first men who founded the gentile world."[53] There he finds man remaking the world in his own image: resinous trees weep, the wind whistles, fields are thirsty, the heavens smile. The "rational metaphysics" of most moderns does not take these transformations seriously, but Vico does. "Rational metaphysics" teaches that "man becomes all things by understanding them." But Vico's "imaginative metaphysics" teaches that "man becomes all things by *not* understanding them . . . he makes the things out of himself and becomes them by transforming himself into them." This negation of rational understanding must take place if the scholar is to know the past, and he must know the past to know the present. To do so is to "experience in his body a divine pleasure."

This participation in the past was more than a matter of capturing the mood of a given time. Vico actually tried to validate assertions about events and origins in this way. For example, after struggling to enter into the "primitive mind" of the Roman plebs, Vico concluded that it was impossible that they could have been governed by the laws of Solon. He thus denied the Greek origin of the Roman law of the Twelve Tables.

While basically a historian and historical methodologist, Vico qualifies as a political theorist on several grounds. One is his concern for law in its most exalted sense. The essence of humanity, he felt, was an indwelling

50 Benedetto Croce, "Vico," in *Encyclopaedia of the Social Sciences* (New York: Macmillan, 1935), Vol. XV, p. 249.

51 A. R. Caponigri, *Time and Idea, the Theory of History in Giambattista Vico* (Chicago: Regnery, 1953), p. 3.

52 H. P. Adams, *The Life and Writings of Giambattista Vico* (London: Allen & Unwin, 1935), p. 152.

53 The quotations in this paragraph are from *The New Science*, Bk. II, sec. 399; Bk. II, sec. 405; and Bk. I, sec. 345, respectively. Italics added.

desire for law ". . . man, fallen into despair of all the succors of nature, desires something superior to save him."[54] This was a rational desire, and the root of man's progress, but it was continually being transformed and cancelled out by the passions. Vico had a strong sense of the "fallen" nature of man, struggling half consciously toward the right and immortality. This aspiration for law is expressed in religion, customs, the whole "vulgar wisdom" (as contrasted with "the esoteric wisdom of the philosophers") of the race. In the course of this history-long quest, "Providence" has educated mankind. Part of this educative process involves the gradual realization in history of the meaning of justice, an eternal and universal idea that is in part embodied in, but also in part negated by, courts, judges, lawmakers, and every concrete political structure.

There is some difficulty here. In discussing justice, Vico suggests a uniformity of historical development which does not altogether coincide with his cyclical theory. He displays a Platonic concern with the ideal form of justice, a concern that is inconsistent with his criticism of Plato's "learned error," namely Plato's attribution of reality to products of speculation and his failure to see that ideas are products of history.[55]

Vico has some interesting things to say about the origins of states. Like Thomas Carlyle, he rejects the view that force accounts for the great movements of history, and he places heavy emphasis on the decisive role of great men. The state itself originates in the relationship between "giants" or "heroes" and their "clients," those who are protected or rescued by the hero. The hero may be cruel, his rages are often childish, but magnanimity is the trait that establishes his position. Not that Vico operates from the assumption of an idyllically innocent state of nature. The hero is feared, too, and fear plays its part in the growth of the state as it does in the growth of religion. But, says Vico, in the long run the stability of a political regime owes more to the ruler's contribution to progress than to his skill at repression.

Vico is not without ambiguities resulting from his inspired but lonely scholarship. He sometimes uses the word "Providence," for example, to mean the divine power of God shaping events. At other times Providence seems to be man's *belief* in this divine power. Men both are and are not in control of history. All in all, Vico with difficulty escapes the pitfalls of pantheism. But we can hardly underestimate his precociousness in relation to some key movements of thought in twentieth-century social science. Two centuries before Karl Mannheim and the "sociology of knowledge" he developed a theory about the way in which our location in the his-

---

54 *Ibid.*, Bk. I, sec. 339.

55 "The nature of things is nothing but their coming into being at certain times and in certain fashions." *Ibid.*, Bk. I, sec. 147.

torical stream conditions the very modes of our thought: ". . . we know only what we do . . . action and truth are mutually convertible."[56] In a day when the Enlightenment was pushing everything earlier than the eighteenth century into a box marked "superstitions of the past" and sealing it off, Vico was examining with great sensitivity the problems of language and myth in primitive culture as a clue to his own intellectual consciousness, an enterprise worthy of today's most sophisticated anthropologists and social psychologists.

Law and Constitutionalism

IF the eighteenth century was not a constitutional age, it was at least an age of constitutionalism. The faith in fundamental charters was a reflection of the faith in fundamental laws of nature, the "self-evident truths" of the American Declaration of Independence, and the "simple and incontestable principles" of the French Declaration of the Rights of Man and Citizen. Even in Germany, where the Prussian king was still consolidating his autocratic power over the *Landtage,* or representative assemblies, speculation on law was flourishing. Although the aim was not necessarily libertarian, the trend was at least toward systematization and a measure of equity.

GERMANY
Thomasius. Christian Thomasius (1655-1728) qualifies as a man of the Enlightenment for his religious toleration and his stout resistance to witch hunts and the use of torture in criminal procedings. He was also the first important professor to lecture in German (at Leipzig and Halle), an innovation that led to the appelation "the second Luther." Although he sought the same kind of systematization of law that Pufendorf had worked for, Thomasius made a much sharper distinction between law and morals. He elaborated on the law of nature, relating it more specifically to the common-sense element in reason than had many of his predecessors. But this law he regarded as a command of God, which teaches wisdom and is not connected in any direct way with positive law. The commands of governments embodied in statutory law are not necessarily related to these commands of God embodied in reason; and the systematization of positive law, desirable as this may be, does not necessarily establish the reign of natural law on earth.[57]
Wolff. A later professor at Halle, Christian Wolff (1679-1754), blurred the distinction Thomasius had so carefully made by developing a

56 Croce, "Vico."
57 See Carl J. Friedrich, *The Philosophy of Law in Historical Perspective* (Chicago: Univ. of Chicago Press, 1958), pp. 116-19.

theory of duty intended to synthesize Pufendorf, Thomasius, and Leibnitz.[58] Through this concept, Wolff sought to express a fundamental unity of law and nature. The result was equalitarian, in a way, but not at all democratic. He optimistically asserted that "inborn human duties" are the same for all men; consequently men are essentially equal and the state is obligated to treat them as such. A network of moral obligation binds together state, citizen, and law in a continuing quest for perfection. The substitution of a Stoic perfection for happiness as a goal of life fitted neatly with Wolff's predilection for benevolent despotism. Basically, Wolff was more interested in ethics than in jurisprudence; however, both his legal and his ethical writings were widely read and much admired. For a time his philosophy became almost authoritative for German scholars.

For our purposes the important influence of Thomasius and Wolff was on the codification and systematization of positive law. Combined with Frederick the Great's penchant for order and efficiency, this influence had a practical effect in the Germanic states, where codes were adopted in Bavaria in 1756, Prussia in 1794, and Austria in 1811. And though these codes had many feudal, corporative elements still clinging to them, separating them from the equalitarian, entrepreneur-oriented Code of Napoleon (1804), the latter was not wholly uninfluenced by German constitutionalism.[59]

Frederick the Great. Like Bolingbroke, Frederick II of Prussia (1712-86) is more important for what he did than for what he wrote. But it is impossible to ignore his writings: in addition to the political and military treatises there were histories, essays, poems, musical compositions, and sixty volumes of correspondence—and all of this on top of an exceedingly full life as military conqueror and conscientious autocrat. His precociousness is illustrated by his first political writing, produced at the age of nineteen in the prison where his father had thrown him for trying to flee the anti-intellectual environment of the court. In this *cahier* he not very modestly outlined his system for gaining political control of Europe. In 1740, the year he ascended the throne and marched into Silesia against Maria Theresa, he wrote *L'Antimachiavel*, a moralistic and not altogether fair critique of Machiavelli's *Prince*. This was followed by his two *Political Testaments*, the first in 1752 and the second in 1768. While, again,

---

58 Gottfried Leibnitz (1646-1716), a great metaphysician who also touched on the theory of law, had sharply criticized Pufendorf's attempt to secularize the law of nature. Leibnitz' view that the world is the best of all possible worlds (a much maligned view immortalized in *Candide* by Voltaire's viciously satirical characterization of Dr. Pangloss), his determinism, and his monism required the assumption of an underlying unity between positive law and the system of eternal ideas which he called the law of nature.

59 Friedrich, *Philosophy of Law*, p. 121. The Napoleonic Code, it should be noted, was not the first French code. The codes of 1667 and 1670, under Louis XIV, were significant predecessors.

the range of these works is impressive—touching on finances, the organization of the army, foreign policy, the training of princes, and so on—what
is significant is the degree to which Frederick, the absolute monarch, was
moved by considerations of natural law and "natural equity" to a clear
position of monarchical self-restraint. A king, he argued in the *First Political Testament*, should never interfere in a law case: ". . . in the tribunals
the law must speak and the sovereign be silent."[60] On the other hand, the
monarch must keep an eagle eye on the judges and be prepared to remove
them if they do not measure up.

Affecting and affected by the Kameralists' views of natural law and administrative science, especially those of von Justi, Frederick was willing
to put upon himself not only the burdens of absolute autocracy but the
burdens of legal restraint. *L'état c'est moi* was his slogan as much as it was
Louis XIV's, but to Frederick it was a weight of responsibility rather than
a badge of complacency. The extent of his detailed supervision of the
Prussian bureaucracy is astounding. His bureaucrats, selected by examination, well trained, and omnisciently watched, stand in marked contrast to
their class- and graft-ridden counterparts to the west. This contrast helps
explain German "autocratic" respect for bureaucracy and French "democratic" disrespect for bureaucracy, a difference that has carried down to
the twentieth century. The early reputation of Frederick was undoubtedly
excessively enhanced by the praise of his French admirers, especially
Voltaire and Diderot. Their praise, it should be recognized, was not entirely gratuitous; in fact, it can be compared to a well-paid public-relations job. But the fact that Frederick was shrewd enough to exploit a
newly self-conscious public opinion in this way is merely another evidence
of his imaginativeness.

The fatal flaw in Frederick's system of "everything for the people,
nothing by the people" was the problem of succession. The system could
work only so long as a man like Frederick was on the throne, and even
one such man in a century is rare. Frederick sensed this flaw—note his
lamentations over the weak nephew who would succeed him—but was
unable to draw the logical conclusion of a truly constitutional monarchy.
In the history of modern politics Frederick was a significant bridge between the autocratic and the modern constitutional state, but in the history of political theory he appears mainly as a fascinating anomaly. It was
not until after the French Revolution that the absolutism of Frederick was
seen as the fragile thing it really was. Only then, in the writings of Stein,
Hardenberg, and Humboldt, would German constitutionalism develop
deeper roots.

60 Quoted in G. P. Gooch's excellent study, *Frederick the Great* (New York:
Knopf, 1947), p. 293.

ENGLAND: BLACKSTONE

What William Blackstone (1723-80) illustrates is not a new set of ideas, or even a new depth in legal analysis, but the spread of a sense of law to the furthermost arteries of the English-speaking body politic. The influence of Blackstone's *Commentaries on the Laws of England* (which appeared in four volumes from 1765 to 1769) was phenomenal, and was as great in America as in England, where the roots of the common law already ran deep. The mental picture of ambitious young Abe Lincoln reading his Blackstone reminds us of countless other nineteenth-century lawyer-politicians developing or expressing a reverence for law by reading Blackstone.

If the *Commentaries* do not strike us as profound, we should remember that they were written for the layman as well as the law student, out of Blackstone's conviction that everyone ought to know some law. In many ways, this work can be called an introductory textbook. Blackstone's often-criticized inconsistencies stem in part from his strained attempt to be comprehensive and the fact that the textbookish definitions of Volume I are not always taken seriously in subsequent pages. Perhaps Blackstone's most serious running fault was that he repeatedly confused government and society. Partly because Blackstone was only trying to describe the law as it was, his former student Bentham, moved by a new conception of a science of law as it should be, attacked him with special virulence. Referring to the *Commentaries*, Bentham spoke of "the capital blemishes of that work, particularly this grand and fundamental one, the antipathy to reformation . . . [in addition to] the universal inaccuracy and confusion which seemed to my apprehension to pervade the whole."[61] Blackstone did indeed present certain structures of law as if they exhausted reality, while legal practice was in fact quite another thing.

He must have known that to talk of the independence of the branches of the legislature was simple nonsense at a time when king and peers competed for the control of elections in the House of Commons. . . . It was ridiculous to describe the Commons as representative of property so long as places like Manchester and Sheffield were virtually disfranchised. . . . What he did was to produce the defense of a nonexistent system which acted as a barrier to all legal, and much political progress in the next half-century.[62]

Nor can all the inconsistency be attributed to faulty definition. Within a few pages he seems to speak for both the supremacy of natural law and the absolute supremacy of the legislature. The purpose of society, says

61 Jeremy Bentham, *Fragment on Government*, Wilfred Harrison, ed., (Oxford: Blackwell, 1948) p. 4.
62 Laski, *Political Thought in England*, p. 120.

Blackstone, is to protect the "absolute rights" of individuals "vested in them by the immutable laws of nature."[63] If they are contrary to these laws of nature, "no human laws are of any validity." Elsewhere, however, Blackstone says that the legislature, "being in truth the sovereign power, is . . . always of absolute authority: it acknowledges no superior on earth." Blackstone meant by the "legislature" more than Parliament alone. He meant the whole law-making power, the "King in Parliament." But he certainly meant to defend the legislature so conceived from any superior power in "the people." He specifically criticized Locke's grant of authority to the people to remove an offending legislature. Two absolutes can hardly exist side by side; but Blackstone may not have been quite as inept as Bentham or Laski imply. John Gough suggests[64] that Blackstone is making a sharper distinction between law and morals than Bentham is capable of recognizing. If natural law is *morally* absolute, the legislature may still be *legally* absolute. Blackstone assumed that Parliament had an obligation under natural law, but he also blandly assumed that Parliament always had and always would fulfill that obligation. This complacency explains his tremendous appeal to visceral conservatives.

Complacent conservatism has always been an element of constitutionalism and is today. The law and order that stems from an unwillingness to rock the boat is at least a part of all law and order. Even in a century smitten with revolutionary ideals its influence was extensive. Today, in the more frantic twentieth century, the "new conservatives" or "radical conservatives," the zealous men who try to save us from ruin, make more noise but have less influence than the Blackstonian, let-us-count-our-blessings conservatives.

CONSTITUTIONALISM IN AMERICA

Strange, perhaps, that the young and revolutionary United States, whose example was an inspiration to the French Revolution, should turn out to be the standard-bearer to the world of sane and sensible constitutionalism. This is no place to expatiate once more on the miracle of the Founding Fathers or analyze the document they brought forth. But we can afford to observe, with many other writers, that they were great constitution-makers not merely because they were Americans, but because they were Americans steeped in the tradition of English law and Lockean liberalism. Although his own constitutional plan for America was not adopted, Alexander Hamilton was not greatly at odds with his brethren in declaring, "I

63 This quotation and the two immediately following are from the *Commentaries on the Laws of England*, 8th ed., William G. Hammond, ed. (San Francisco: Bancroft Whitney, 1890), Vol. I, pp. 290, 69, and 197, respectively.

64 *Fundamental Law in English Constitutional History* (Oxford: Clarendon Press, 1955), pp. 188-91.

believe the British government forms the best model the world has ever produced. . . . this government has for its object *public strength* and *individual security*.[65]

Even monarchially inclined Hamilton felt that a "mixed government," with power divided between the one, the few, and the many, did not depart too far from English practice. And even in the Revolutionary period the dominant American arguments were drawn from English legal precedents, which fact is support enough for the common judgment that the American Revolution was the most conservative revolution in history. James Otis of Massachusetts[66] was particularly eloquent in grafting the writings of Coke and Locke onto the English Constitution and from this base challenging the constitutionality of Parliament when it enacted such measures as the Sugar Act (1764) and the Stamp Act (1765). Since government rests on a contract drawn to ensure protection of life, liberty, and property, Otis argued, by taking property without granting representation to the property holder the English Parliament was violating the basic charter of government.

Ultimately, of course, it was up to the English king and Parliament to define the scope of the Constitution;[67] but be that as it may, the colonials did try very hard to keep their objections within a constitutional framework. They did not want a revolution; but if it had to come, they wanted to make it a revolution by due process of law. In mid-1774, when the more radical elements had infiltrated the Continental Congress, James Wilson of Pennsylvania[68] excoriated Parliament but still swore allegiance to the English king. He expounded what amounts to a theory of the British Commonwealth as it ultimately came to be. And even in 1776, when blood was being shed, the idea was still prevalent that America was merely asserting a legal claim against England.

Its reluctant revolutionaries illustrate the degree to which America identified with English traditionalism and the Blackstonian-conservative element in constitutionalism. But there were other constitutional influences at work. One was the typical eighteenth-century view of the universe and its natural laws, a mechanistic, optimistic view already aired a number

65 In the Constitutional Convention, June 18, 1787. Max Farrand, ed., *The Records of The Federal Convention of 1787* (New Haven: Yale Univ. Press, 1911), Vol. I, p. 299.

66 See his *Rights of the British Colonies Asserted and Proved* (1764) (London: J. Williams, 1766).

67 Which they did to the colonials' disadvantage. But by claiming that the Americans had "virtual representation" in Parliament even without having flesh-and-blood members sitting there, the British showed that they, too, wanted to be constitutional, if at all possible.

68 See his *Considerations on the Nature and Extent of the Legislative Authority of the British Parliament* (1774), in J. D. Andrews, ed., *The Works of James Wilson* (New York: Callaghan & Co., 1896), Vol. II, pp. 505-43.

of times in these pages. Its presence in the New World is nowhere better illustrated than in the justifiably famous *Federalist*, one of the few pieces of election propaganda to become a classic of political theory. "The science of politics," wrote Hamilton in *The Federalist*, ". . . like most other sciences, has received great improvement. The efficacy of various principles is now well understood, which were either not known at all, or imperfectly known to the ancients. The regular distribution of power into distinct departments; the introduction of legislative balance and checks. . . . These are wholly new discoveries, or have made their principal progress towards perfection in modern times."[69] The secret of the American Constitution's sure success, wrote James Madison, was in properly "combining the requisite stability and energy in government with the inviolable attention due to liberty and to the republican form."[70] The Constitution would work because it was designed to work, and it was designed according to natural principles of government discovered by rational men.[71]

The same spirit, as we have seen, animated the *philosophes* and sustained the hopes of the French revolutionaries. But there was an important difference between the French and American students of constitutionalism, a difference that gave the Americans an infinitely stronger constitutional tradition. The American leaders tended to be realists, while the French leaders tended to be visionaries. Despite the inherent optimism of their natural-law assumptions, Madison, Hamilton, and even Thomas Jefferson knew that "if men were angels no government would be necessary" and that men are not angels.[72] John Adams tended to focus his suspicions on the poor: "the idle, the vicious, the intemperate" who, without legal restraints, "would rush into the utmost extravagance of debauchery."[73] But he was hardly sentimental about the rich, either. For his part, Madison was able to look unblinkingly at the evils of "faction. . . . the most common and durable source of [which] has been the various and unequal distribution of property"[74] and, while giving up the hope of eliminating its cause, still work diligently and hopefully to control its effects.

69 Alexander Hamilton, John Jay, and James Madison, *The Federalist*, No. 9. (New York: Modern Library, 1937).

70 *Ibid.*, No. 37.

71 See Robert A. Dahl's imaginative critique of Madisonian theory in *A Preface to Democratic Theory* (Chicago: Univ. of Chicago Press, 1956), Ch. 1.

72 *The Federalist*, No. 51. Or again: "Why has government been instituted at all? Because the passions of men will not conform to the dictates of reason and justice, without restraint." *Ibid.*, No. 15.

73 *A Defense of the Constitutions of Government of the United States of America*, 1787. Quoted in Alan P. Grimes, *American Political Thought* (New York: Holt, 1955), p. 110. This work was a reply to Turgot's criticisms of the American state constitutions, especially their reliance upon separation of powers. Turgot regarded this principle as productive of inequality and division within the community.

74 *The Federalist*, No. 10.

The steady balance between the extremes of utopianism and despair has been the keynote of American political thinking from the beginning. It helps account for both the viability of our political institutions and the conventionality of our political theorizing.[75] Even in the colonial period our theorists tended to be men who had carried the burdens of governmental responsibility on their own shoulders. This practical experience of self-government had not been granted to the French revolutionaries, a deficiency that fostered their incipient utopianism and added to the consequent fragility of the French constitutional tradition.

The Theory of Revolution

WHILE the anatomy of revolution is strikingly constant, theories justifying revolution are highly volatile. From Aristotle to Crane Brinton[76] the standard pattern of revolutionary activity has been catalogued. An oppressive, inflexible ruling class is unable to recognize the demands a changing society makes upon it. Discontent produces more oppression which produces more discontent. Finally the vicious circle is broken by a *coup d'état*. The offending regime is expelled and the moderates attempt to take control. But the pent-up forces of revolt, suddenly released, surge beyond the control of the moderates, carrying them along on the tide for a while until the militarists or extremists replace them. Cromwell replaces Pym, Robespierre replaces Mirabeau, Lenin replaces Kerensky. Then, while idealistic programs and radical ideals are held aloft for public edification, consolidation through growing dictatorship takes place below. Finally, disillusionment sets in and the "Thermidorian Reaction"[77] takes place. Old forms creep back under new names. Charles II replaces Cromwell; Napoleon replaces Robespierre; Stalin replaces Lenin.

The particular doctrines that become the ideological weapons of a revolution cannot be classified in any such neat pattern. Revolutions are primarily waged against a great evil. They are negative efforts. And the positive ideas that become rallying cries are often taken up in catch-as-catch-can fashion. Therefore, while revolutionary eras seem to produce the greatest political theorizing, actual revolutions themselves rarely produce great ideas. They feed upon the ideas of the recent past.

75 See Louis Hartz, *The Liberal Tradition in America* (New York: Harcourt, Brace, 1955).

76 Aristotle, *Politics*, Bk. V; Crane Brinton, *The Anatomy of Revolution* (New York: Norton, 1938).

77 Thermidor was the "month of heat" on the new Revolutionary Calendar. It began July 19 on the Gregorian Calendar. With the execution of Robespierre on July 28, 1794, the Jacobian dictatorship and Reign of Terror ended.

The French Revolution is a prime example of these common patterns. With very little political experience (the Estates-General had not been called since 1614!), the Third Estate tried to drive a wedge between the monarchy and the nobility. When both collapsed, and the Third Estate was on its own, the ideas it turned to for guidance were naturally those of the *philosophes*. But for all the sparkling profusion of ideas associated with these men, not many were helpful to an ongoing parliamentary government. The *philosophes* had, at best, hoped for an enlightened despot like Frederick the Great, who could eliminate abuses of privilege, cut down inequalities of status, reform the law. But an enlightened despot was not a practical possibility in 1789, and the bland trust in the goodness of man characteristic of some *philosophes* like Condorcet was especially inappropriate to the passions of a revolution. For a time the great general Lafayette had hoped that the ideals of moderation, balance, and law developed by Montesquieu, and applied, he thought, in America, might find a reception in the form of a constitutional monarchy, with a responsible aristocracy serving as a mediator between monarch and Third Estate. But the collapse of monarchy made this view irrelevant. Thus, almost by default, Rousseau emerged as the philosopher of the Revolution, his poorly understood concept of the general will becoming a watchword.

Possibly the most revolutionary writer in France in the eighteenth century was Morelly. But the proposed communism of his *Code de la nature* (1755) was so radical and his critique of the whole structure of society was so fundamental that it had little effect on the exigencies of the French Revolution.[78]

One who shared many of Morelly's ideas but had a more direct effect on the Revolution was Gabriel de Mably (1709-85). Far more pessimistic than Morelly, Mably nevertheless felt that men had a natural, innate goodness, a harmonious bond with other men, which had been corrupted by the institutions of civilization, especially private property. To Mably equality was more important than liberty, a belief that he seemed to apply in his own life as he repeatedly refused posts, honors, and preferments and lived a frugal, constrained life rather than acknowledge the position of men he deemed unworthy or participate in the degrading system of rank and status. His *Rights and Duties of Citizens* (1758), one of fourteen major works, was not published until the eve of the Revolution. Some of the reforms he there proposes actually were attempted thirty years later: e. g., the calling of the Estates-General and the formation of executive

78 Morelly, whose first name no one seems to know, anticipates many of the ideas of Fourier. Both men are reviewed in Chapter 10, below. See Kingsley Martin, *The Rise of French Liberal Thought* (2nd ed; New York: New York Univ. Press, 1954), pp. 242-47; C. H. Driver, "Morelly and Mably," in Hearnshaw, *Great French Thinkers*, pp. 217-51.

committees. His advocacy of a mixed government, reflected in his phrase "republican-monarchy," found much support, and the phrase was widely quoted in the early days of the Revolution. He favored drastic cuts in state expenditures, a limitation on land holdings, and all sorts of sumptuary laws.

But more significant than the specifics of Mably's reforms, which provided fodder for the Revolution, was the underlying doctrine in both Morelly and Mably of man's natural goodness and of the evil character of certain institutions that were corrupting him. The idealistic phase of the Revolution was bursting with such sentiments, was full of a tingling spirit of newness. France, not only in the name of France but in the name of mankind, was sloughing off a decadent past and presenting a fresh face to the world. One cannot but note how in all innocence these men were offering categories in secular dress that were very close to traditional concepts of Christian theology: an original state of innocence, the Fall, and now, after despair (at least in Mably), a shattering regeneration and the emergence of a "new being." No wonder some Frenchmen acted as if the Revolution were Armageddon.

Sieyès. Among those who participated directly in the Revolution, only Condorcet had as much influence as Mably, and neither could touch the influence of Rousseau. But two other vigorous intellects stand out in the frenzied currents and countercurrents of the Revolution, Sieyès and Mirabeau. The Abbé Emmanuel Joseph Sieyès (1748-1836) is a phenomenon typical of Enlightenment France—the antireligious abbé. He is often passed by with a nod, although Lord Acton called him "the first political intellect of his age." His immediately popular yet unsuccessful attempt in *Qu'est-ce que le Tiers État?* to transform Rousseau's general will into majority rule, his odd mixture of passionate concern for the ideal state with short-run cynicism,[79] and his undistinguished writing, explain his lack of influence. But the combination of his moralistic zeal and realistic insight was, and is, unusual. "He understood politics as the science of the State as it ought to be, and he repudiated the product of history, which is things as they are. . . . [He] was essentially a revolutionist because he held that political oppression can never be right and that resistance to oppression can never be wrong."[80] On the other hand, he was not a rabid democrat. He favored indirect elections and a suffrage limited to taxpayers. Although a republican, he admitted that a properly checked monarchy could maintain individual liberties. He proposed one interesting constitutional

79 Asked what his greatest accomplishment was in the Revolution, Sieyès answered, "I survived." After his survival, he composed the Napoleonic Constitution of 1799, was made President of the Senate, and then passed into obscurity.

80 John E. E. D. Acton, *Lectures on the French Revolution* (London: Macmillan, 1910), p. 161.

check in the form of a supreme court composed, not of judges, whom he distrusted as reactionaries, but of veteran politicians. No contractualist, for him it was society and not "nature" that gave men their liberty. Yet Sieyès regarded his "society" as no more automatically wise than was the *philosophes*' "nature." The valid national will, he felt, did not spring full blown from the process of election, but arose from the give-and-take of sustained discussion. What a country thinks is less important than what it would think after enlightened men had debated the issues. In this view Sieyès is not so far from what some present-day critics have said about the public-opinion polls.

Mirabeau. An outstanding orator, Honoré Gabriel Victor Riqueti, Comte de Mirabeau (1749-1791), son of the Physiocrat, was perhaps as close to what some people call a statesman as any other figure of the Revolution.[81] He opposed Sieyès' republicanism and hoped to negotiate a new constitution with Louis XVI but failed. Knowing England well, Mirabeau also opposed followers of American precedent, such as Lafayette, who wanted a system of "checks and balances." Mirabeau wanted, rather, a parliamentary ministry that would bind together king and legislature. He was even attracted by Bolingbroke's idea of a patriot king under whom a national party might rally. But the chance for an English form of government was cut off by the Constituent Assembly vote of November 7, 1789, to exclude deputies from the ministry, a measure aimed directly at Mirabeau.

Despite the diversity of their positions, Condorcet, Lafayette, Sieyès, and Mirabeau all published their own model Declaration of Rights, and all had some influence on the Declaration of the Rights of Man and Citizen proclaimed by the Constituent Assembly on August 26, 1789. The Declaration[82] was quite similar in aim to the American Bill of Rights, though without the same practical bearing or legal effect. A wide variety of influences can easily be read into it. Rousseau's general will appears in Article VI; Blackstone's stress on innocence until proven guilty appears in Article IX; the Italian prison reformer Beccaria's hostility to *ex post facto* laws appears in Article VIII. Events of the times are also reflected. The storming of the Bastille in July can be read into Article VII, which prohibits arbitrary imprisonment. The attack on social distinctions in Article I mirrors the spirit of the day as well as recording Mably's basic theme. "The source of all sovereignty is essentially in the nation," in Article III, was a declaration of self-authorization by the National Assembly. But the under-

81 See J. P. Thompson, *The French Revolution* (New York: Oxford Univ. Press, 1945), pp. 208-16; Lord Acton, *Lectures*, Ch. 10.

82 The Declaration is reprinted in English in Lionel Laing, Manfred C. Vernon, and others, eds., *Source Book in European Governments* (New York: Sloane, 1950), pp. 79-81.

lying assumption of the whole document and, indeed, of an entire age, appears in the preamble: ". . . ignorance, forgetfulness or contempt of the rights of man are the sole causes of the public miseries and of the corruption of governments."

The American Revolution, as we have seen, was almost unique in its departure from the pattern of other revolutions. It was not a class revolution, a social revolution, or even an overturning of the men who had held governmental positions in the colonies. It had similarities to present-day nationalistic revolts but was without most of the equalitarian mass-democracy overtones of the colonial revolutions of the twentieth century.[83] Yet it may be significant that the two best-known "revolutionary theorists," in colonial America, Paine and Jefferson, were, in one way or another, associated with France.

Paine. Thomas Paine (1737-1809) was an Englishman who did not arrive in America until 1774. Although he eventually found himself in a French jail, his greatest popular adulation came when he visited France in the 1790's. Paine was more of a journalist than a theorist. He was an indefatigable pamphleteer and gadfly, with the simplistic bias essential to the true revolutionary. His pamphlet *Common Sense*, published in January, 1776, sold over 100,000 copies in a few months. An appeal more to emotion than to common sense, it did not hesitate to call for armed conflict with England and helped arouse the colonials to fighting temper. In it Paine pungently ridiculed monarchy, attacked the English Constitution, and criticized the separation of powers, the last two of which he, like a good many others at that time, tended to confuse. Monarchy and the separation of powers were, for Paine, mere encumbrances, since, "The more simple any thing is the less liable it is to be disordered." The simple life of Paine's state of nature was a glorious condition for its residents: "Some convenient tree will afford them a State House." But a series of at least superficially depressing moral failures leads to the present condition, wherein "Society . . . is a blessing, but Government, even in its best state, is but a necessary evil."[84] Later, when Paine tried to be more profound, he became less effective.

Jefferson. We can call Thomas Jefferson (1743-1826) a revolutionary theorist only because of circumstantial evidence. He wrote "A Summary

---

83 See Louis Hartz, "American Political Thought and the American Revolution," *Am. Pol. Sci. Rev.*, Vol. 46 (1952), pp. 321-42.

84 The quotations are from *Common Sense*, in *Political Works* (New York: Peter Eckler, 1892), pp. 3, 1. Paine's other major works are *The Rights of Man* (1791-92), a reply to Burke's *Reflections on the Revolution in France*; *The Age of Reason* (1794), a critique of Christianity; and *Agrarian Justice* (1797), a plea for welfare measures financed by a heavy tax on the inheritance of land. See M. D. Conway, ed., *The Writings of Thomas Paine*, (New York: Putnam, 1894-96); Cecilia Kenyon, "Where Paine Went Wrong," *Am. Pol. Sci. Rev.*, Vol. 45 (1951), pp. 1086-99.

View of the Rights of British America," a paper too revolutionary for the Virginia Convention to approve in 1774. In drafting the Declaration of Independence he substituted "the pursuit of happiness" for "property" in the Lockean phrase, "life, liberty, and property." He once wrote to Madison, "I hold it that a little rebellion, now and then, is a good thing."[85] Jefferson was a consorter with Parisian radicals while ambassador to France. But one who at the age of thirty-six is able to get himself elected governor of old Virginia is not likely to be regarded by his peers as a congenital insurrectionist. In his letter to Madison he was talking especially of "governments of force," or, with an unmistakable allusion to France, "a government of wolves over sheep." His advice to republican governors to keep their punishment of rebels "mild" was on the cautiously pragmatic ground that excessive repression is more dangerous than some "turbulence." "The pursuit of happiness" was not, as we have seen, at odds with Locke's conception of "property" and both phrases had appeared side by side in George Mason's Virginia Bill of Rights. As ambassador to France in the 1780's, Jefferson almost indiscreetly supported Lafayette's efforts to gain a compromise between absolute monarchy and a republic.

Jefferson was a respecter of law and order, a country gentleman, a patron of the arts and sciences, a believer in the natural rights of man, and a liberal. His sensitivity to humane values led him to resent the autocratic pretensions of New York City aristocrats, just as it led him to fear the outcroppings of urban, "artisan," leveling democracy. His view of revolution was essentially Lockean, which is merely to say that he believed that government should be the servant of the people, advancing the general interest while also protecting individual rights; when rulers forget this purpose and go astray, they may properly be regarded as tyrants, and men of good sense and sound judgment have every right—even a natural right —to throw the rascals out as adroitly as possible.[86]

85 From Paris, January 30, 1787. Quoted in Adrienne Koch and William Peden, eds., The Life and Selected Writings of Thomas Jefferson, (New York: Modern Library, 1944), p. 413.

86 The many other facets of Jefferson's thought must be left to other studies. The literature on Jefferson is voluminous (as is literature by Jefferson). See Julian P. Boyd, ed., The Papers of Thomas Jefferson (Princeton: Princeton Univ. Press, 1950–   ). Sixteen of a projected fifty volumes are presently available. See also Paul L. Ford, ed., The Works of Thomas Jefferson (New York: Putnam, 1904-05); Edward Dumbauld, ed., Political Writings (New York: Liberal Arts Press, 1955); Adrienne Koch, The Philosophy of Thomas Jefferson (New York: Columbia Univ. Press, 1943); Charles M. Wiltse, The Jeffersonian Tradition in American Democracy (Chapel Hill: Univ. of North Carolina Press, 1935; New York: Hill & Wang, 1960); Max Beloff, Thomas Jefferson and American Democracy (London: Hodder & Stoughton, 1949; Merrill D. Peterson, The Jefferson Image in the American Mind (New York: Oxford Univ. Press, 1960).

Conclusion

WE cannot understand twentieth-century politics without understanding eighteenth-century political theory for the following reasons:

(1) The urgent hope embedded in the secularized natural law of the Enlightenment, the hope that man can rationally know and rationally control his universe, is one important source of nineteenth-century utopianism and twentieth-century social science. The collapse of the hope has helped turn utopianism into totalitarianism and threatens to turn social science into social statistics.[87]

(2) The rise of the middle class, the triumph of the market economy, and the birth of economic science are aspects of a newly dynamic economy and herald a new kind of political interpenetration with the economy. Coeval with this development came a theoretical separation of politics and economics. The separation has produced problems not yet fully faced by the "capitalist West" and inadequately resolved by the "communist East."

(3) Western men for certain, all men perchance, are creatures of history. Darwin, Marx, and Freud; psychoanalysis, rockets to the moon, and presidential speeches, only make us more self-conscious creatures of history. We can wish-fulfill with history like Condorcet, or play politics with history like Bolingbroke, or think with history like Vico. We can and we do.

(4) The failure of men in the form of eighteenth-century enlightened despots transferred confidence to laws in the form of codes, bills of rights, and constitutions. But by the eighteenth century the medieval mystique that sanctified and dehumanized law was shattered by skepticism. The recurring controversies over the role of our own Supreme Court suggest that we have not yet found a simple answer to the question: If you cannot trust men, how can you trust the laws they make?

(5) We study revolutions because we cannot help it. We are drawn to revolutions as we are drawn to fights, wrecks, murders, violence of all kinds, because of something deep and dark within us. And so we learn about ourselves from studying revolutions. We learn that America is basically conservative and law-abiding—or at least law-respecting—because even her revolution was conservative and law-respecting. From studying the political *theories* of revolutionary periods we learn that ideologies come and ideologies go, but tyrants go on forever.

87 See Judith Shklar, *After Utopia; The Decline of Political Faith* (Princeton: Princeton Univ. Press, 1958); J. L. Talmon, *The Origins of Totalitarian Democracy* (New York: F. A. Praeger, 1960); Hannah Arendt, *The Origins of Totalitarianism* (New York: Harcourt, Brace, 1951).

6 | *Montesquieu*

CHARLES LOUIS DE SECONDAT, Baron de la Brède et de Montesquieu, is a somewhat enigmatic figure in the history of political theory. He was in but not of the Enlightenment, identified with but not attached to the *philosophes*, a mixer of ancient lore with modern sociology, an empirical but still unscientific historian. He poured years of work into *L'Esprit des lois*, "that apparently incoherent and alternately simplistic and obscure masterpiece of profound and benevolent guile."[1]

Life

THE life of Montesquieu is without the fascination of many eighteenth-century French lives and can be dealt with rather briefly. He was born in 1689 at La Brède, near Bordeaux, of a noble family. His mother died when he was seven, and at eleven he was sent to a school near Paris for a classical education. Perhaps because of his limited home life, he was shy and somewhat aloof even as an adult. But he was always a good student, with a strong attraction to languages and the classics. His admiration for the Stoic philosophers is explicit in an essay written when he was twenty-two, in which he argued that the Church was wrong in its position that the Stoics could not know salvation. He also displayed an early interest in natural science, studying and writing on botany, anatomy, physics, and related subjects.

1 David Lowenthal, "Book I of Montesquieu's *The Spirit of the Laws*," *Am. Pol. Sci. Rev.*, Vol. 53 (1959), p. 487.

In 1716 the uncle of M. de la Brède, as Montesquieu was then named, died and bequeathed to him the presidency of the *parlement* of Bordeaux. We would describe the post today as the chief justiceship of a local court. The *parlements*, of which the one at Bordeaux was the most venerated of all those outside Paris, had at one time been the agencies by which the centralized monarchy gained ascendancy over the feudal nobility and the clergy. Later, because seats were gained by hereditary right, they were able to become more independent of the king. Some of this independence rubbed off on Montesquieu and he was to become, in his way, a champion of the provincial *parlements* in their essentially conservative resistance to the monarchy. He kept this post for ten years, but sold it and moved to Paris after the literary fame brought about by the publication of the *Persian Letters* in 1721.

The *Persian Letters* were published anonymously in Cologne and purported to be the account of two Persian travelers visiting France. The format was devious enough to permit Montesquieu to get away with some sharp criticisms of French government and Parisian society, and his inclusion of both French and allegedly Persian erotica was then, as it would be now, conducive to sales. The book was a literary sensation; and when the author was identified, Montesquieu was famous. That the court was displeased with the *Persian Letters* may be inferred from the objection raised to the initial proposal of Montesquieu's name for membership in the French Academy. (In 1728 he was finally elected to this select circle of literary men.)

In 1729 Montesquieu departed for a lengthy trip through Europe, terminating in England, where he stayed for two years. There he studied English government with diligence and restrained admiration (though he ignored social problems), was a favorite at the court of Queen Caroline, and was elected to the Royal Society. Upon his return to France he spent more time at the family estate at La Brède; in 1734 he produced *Considerations on the Greatness and Decline of Rome*.

After a lifetime of study, in 1748 Montesquieu published his great book, *The Spirit of the Laws*. A work of apparently formless design, it exerted a profound influence on historical method and the study of the sociological basis of forms of government. The Jesuits attacked its apparent determinism. The *philosophes* welcomed much of the book but were unhappy with its conservative implications.[2] Voltaire was provoked to list, in his *Sur l'Esprit des lois*, all of Montesquieu's historical inaccuracies—or at least all those Voltaire knew about.

2 For the influence of Montesquieu on the *philosophes*, see Kingsley Martin, *The Rise of French Liberal Thought* (2nd ed.; New York: New York Univ. Press, 1954), pp. 137-62; and Joseph Dedieu, *Montesquieu; L'Homme et l'oeuvre* (Paris: Boivin, 1943), Ch. 11.

In 1755, only a few years after the publication of *The Spirit of the Laws*, Montesquieu, his sight failing, died in Paris.

The Spirit of the Laws: Organization and Aim

ORGANIZATION

Scholars are still not agreed on the organizational logic of *The Spirit of the Laws*, nor on the relationship of the organization to the work's underlying purpose, nor, indeed, on what this underlying purpose may be. George Sabine professes to find very little by way of an orderly pattern in *The Spirit of the Laws*. "There is not in truth much concatenation of subject matter and the amount of irrelevance is extraordinary." David Lowenthal, on the other hand, finds a rigorous design deliberately hidden from the "vulgar reader" (to use D'Alembert's phrase in dealing with the same problem). C. E. Vaughn sees in the opening chapter of *The Spirit of the Laws* a forthright declaration of "the vital principle which gives unity to the necessarily scattered details, the torch, in the light of which every detail is seen to take its place as part of an ordered and intelligible whole." David Cabeen finds the disorder, or better, the irregularity of Montesquieu's writing an inevitable result of the elusive concept of *esprit*, which it was his aim to communicate.[3]

Part of the problem of the organization of *The Spirit of the Laws*, therefore, is whether it needs to be taken as a problem. A quick outline of the work is enough to indicate that as written it is not what one would call conventionally systematic. Montesquieu begins with a short book (the *livres* are generally of chapter length), "Of Laws in General," and is soon immersed in more or less practical considerations pertaining to three basic forms of government—monarchy, republic, despotism—including the relation of each of the three forms to "sumptuary laws, luxury, and the condition of women." (Bks. II-VIII). There follow two books on defense and the laws of war (IX, X), and three on the subject of liberty (XI, XII, XIII). Perhaps the most famous part of the whole work is Book XI, in which the principle of separation of powers is developed, related to the subject of liberty, and illustrated in large part by reference to the English Constitution.

3 The above quotations are from Sabine, *History of Political Theory* (New York: Holt, 1937), p. 556; Lowenthal, "Book I," p. 486; Vaughn, *Studies in the History of Political Philosophy* (Manchester: Manchester Univ. Press, 1925), Vol. I, p. 257; Cabeen, "The *Esprit* of the *Esprit des Lois*," *Publications of the Modern Language Association*, Vol. 54 (1939), pp. 439-53. See also Gustave Lanson, *Montesquieu* (Paris: Felix Alcan, 1932), pp. 5-7; and Franz Neumann's Introduction to his edition of *The Spirit of the Laws* (New York: Hafner, 1949), pp. xxix-xxxv.

Books XIV to XXV, which have been shuffled around in a variety of ways by different students of Montesquieu, all relate in one way or another to the influence of environmental factors, especially geography and climate, on forms of government, social and economic forces, morals and manners, and religion. The last books, XXVI to XXXI, have been called the work of the pure historian, or fragmentary contributions to the history of law, or the incidental residue of Montesquieu's legal interests. He discussed the Roman law of succession, the origins of feudal law in France, and, in a rather technical treatment, "Of the Manner of Composing Laws" (XXIX).

C. E. Vaughn feels that the first eight books are of secondary importance but that Montesquieu put them first because they dealt with some of the more practical aspects of statesmanship and were therefore more likely to be read. The heart of *The Spirit of the Laws*, in Vaughn's view, is Books XIV to XXV (despite the greater fame of XI to XIII), in which the influence of geographic environment on cultural life is developed. The final books, in this analysis, are intended to make up for the neglect of historical continuity in the earlier books, which tended (though much less than did the writings of the *philosophes*) to stress cultural unity from a nonlinear point of view. Others feel that the concept of liberty and its relation to forms of government is, as its position would indicate, the central concern of the work. But to decide what is most important we must, temporarily at least, forget about organization and first take seriously the title of this strange work *The Spirit of the Laws*.

OF LAWS

Montesquieu begins Book I, "Of Laws in General" (*Des lois*) as follows:

Laws, in their most general signification, are the necessary relations arising from the nature of things. In this sense all beings have their laws: The Deity His Laws, the material world its laws, the beasts their laws, man his laws.

They who assert that a blind fatality produced the various effects we behold in this world talk very absurdly; for can any thing be more unreasonable than to pretend that a blind fatality could be productive of intelligent beings?

There is, then, a prime reason; and laws are the relations subsisting between it and different beings, and the relations of these to one another.[4]

God's creation and preservation of the universe, Montesquieu explains, presupposes invariable laws. Among "particular intelligent beings" the term describing their proper relations is "justice."

4 *The Spirit of the Laws*, Bk. I, Ch. 1. All quotations are from the translation by Thomas Nugent, ed. by Franz Neumann (New York: Hafner, 1949).

To say that there is nothing just or unjust but what is commanded or forbidden by positive laws, is the same as saying that before the describing of a circle all the radii were not equal.

We must therefore acknowledge relations of justice antecedent to the positive law by which they are established. . . .[5]

The intelligent world is not so well governed as the physical, since particular intelligent beings are finite and liable to error. Beasts are governed by natural laws (here Montesquieu is using the term "natural law[s]" in the nontraditional sense of descriptive behavioral laws) but not positive laws since beasts do not have knowledge as humans do:

Man, as a physical being, is like other bodies governed by invariable laws. As an intelligent being, he incessantly transgresses the laws established by God, and changes those of his own instituting. He is left to his private direction, though a limited being, and subject, like all finite intelligences, to ignorance and error: even his imperfect knowledge he loses; and as a sensible creature, he is hurried away by a thousand impetuous passions. Such a being might every instant forget his Creator; God has therefore reminded him of his duty by the laws of religion. Such a being is liable every moment to forget himself; philosophy has provided against this by the laws of morality. Formed to live in society, he might forget his fellow creatures; legislators have, therefore, by political and civil laws, confined him to his duty.[6]

First of all we must note that while Montesquieu is speaking "Of Laws in General" he is not speaking of law in the abstract. Every reference to law in this chapter is plural. Montesquieu is developing a theme rather than proving a proposition. In his reference to justice he is clearly conscious of the natural-law tradition behind the term, and in the analogy of the circle and its radii he seems to adopt a Grotius-like, rationalistic, deistic view of natural law. But it is also clear from the last paragraph quoted above that he does not share the traditional optimistic view of man as a rational being. Although possessed of intelligence, man forgets God in using his intelligence; he forgets his own knowledge when hurried by a thousand passions; and he forgets his fellows. Law is used in three senses in this paragraph. There are physical laws, which cannot be violated. There are religious laws of God (who here seems rather isolated from physical laws) and moral laws of philosophers, which can be and are violated. Finally there are "political and civil laws" of the legislator, which can confine men to their duty.

Antecedent to these three types of laws, continues Montesquieu in

5 *Ibid.*   6. *Ibid.*

Chapter 2, "are those of nature, so called," derived entirely "from our frame and existence." In this chapter Montesquieu looks at natural man and finds him to be one who thinks first of self-preservation, as Hobbes contended, but weak and without the strong power impulse that Hobbes found. Indeed, war, said Montesquieu, was not possible until *after* man entered society, since before society was formed each man would be isolated and "would fancy himself inferior." The natural laws Montesquieu talks about at this point are simply nonmoral drives, such as sex and gregariousness. Montesquieu's view of man, David Lowenthal concludes from this chapter, lies somewhere between Hobbes' egoism and the traditional natural-law view.

In Chapter 3, "Of Positive Laws," Montesquieu explains the distinction between political and civil laws referred to at the end of Chapter 1. Here, for the first time, *droits* replaces *lois* (although not in the chapter title). Political laws (rights) deal with the constitutional structure, the relations of the governors to the governed, the union of strengths, forces, and powers. Civil laws (rights) stem from the conjunction of individual wills. Montesquieu is obscure at this point, but the civil would seem to be an ideological substructure or prerequisite to the political. Though both are aspects of the same society, each type of law is a product of a different kind of state, the "political state," or constitutional body politic, on the one hand, and the "civil state"—perhaps we could say consensual state— on the other. A third type of law is the law (right) of nations whose principle is to do as much good in peace and as little harm in war as is possible "without prejudicing . . . real interests." By this law, nations are united in their relations to each other, even though there is between them no common state.

Given the specialized and esoteric character of these conceptions, it is all the more surprising to find that Montesquieu concludes the chapter and the book by stating:

Law in general is human reason, inasmuch as it governs all the inhabitants of the earth: the political and civil laws of each nation ought to be only the particular cases in which human reason is applied.

They should be adapted in such a manner to the people for whom they are framed that it should be a great chance if those of one nation suit another.

They should be in relation to the nature and principle of each government: whether they form it, as may be said of politic laws; or whether they support it, as in the case of civil institutions.

They should be in relation to the climate of each country, to the quality of its soil, to its situation and extent, to the principal occupation of the natives. . . . in all of which different lights they ought to be considered.

This is what I have undertaken to perform in the following work. These relations I shall examine, since all these together constitute what I call the Spirit of the Laws.

I have not separated the political from the civil institutions, as I do not pretend to treat of laws, but of their spirit; and as this spirit consists in the various relations which the laws may bear to different objects, it is not so much my business to follow the natural order of laws as that of these relations and objects.[7]

This passage shows Montesquieu's almost paradoxical combination of universalism and relativism. It also shows that he is neither unaware of what he is about nor careless of the reader's expectations. If the reader is subsequently bothered by Montesquieu's purpose, it may be the result of a misunderstanding of *esprit*.

L'Esprit

Given the subject of the spirit of the laws, (or, as Mme. de Deffand revised it, "Of the spirit in the laws"), Montesquieu was bound to follow the elliptical, uneven, ambiguous approach that marks his writings. *L'Esprit* cannot be pursued directly. Montesquieu himself said, "When one runs after spirit, one catches foolishness [la sottise]."[8] Cabeen has listed the stylistic techniques Montesquieu necessarily employs in trying to communicate *esprit*: "irony (rarely), sarcasm, affected naïveté, *pointes* (sometimes with a trace of *préciosité*), an occasional paradox, metaphor, or gasconnade, with some humor of understatement or dryness."[9] Montesquieu operates from the assumption that he can omit nonessentials for the reader who is also seeking *l'esprit* rather than the mere forms of knowledge. Only such a reader can, in any case, grasp what the writer is after. "My business is not to make people read, but to make them think."[10] This helps explain the many abrupt starts and stops in *The Spirit of the Laws*. Cabeen feels that Montesquieu was often led to restrain his natural brilliance deliberately in order to win the wide readership he knew the book deserved, and thus to impart its liberalizing effect both to those who did and to those who did not also truly seek *l'esprit*.

But still we are not completely sure what *esprit* means. It must be a word able to signal the paradoxes that delighted or perhaps only fascinated Montesquieu. In the rules of the physical universe, he says, "each diversity is uniformity, each change is constancy."[11] Everything seems to act in relation to everything else, in physical and nonphysical

7 *Ibid.*, Ch. 3.

8 *Pensées et fragments inédite*, quoted in Cabeen, "The *Esprit* of the *Esprit des Lois*," p. 440.

9 *Ibid.*, pp. 447-48.

10 *The Spirit of the Laws*, Bk. XI, Ch. 20.

11 *Ibid.*, Bk. I, Ch. 1.

worlds; yet somehow Montesquieu hoped to find an element of constancy in this fluid network of relationships. The word *esprit* has many English translations: "wit," "mind," "intellect," "character," "spirit," even "bodily fluids" (compare *âme*, "soul" or "mind"). But its protean character should not be allowed to obscure its systematic possibilities. "Something like intelligence or reason is only one level within 'esprit.' Temperament or disposition typify another and more physical level, and animal spirits another and even more evidently physical level. . . . There is reason to believe that the psychology and physiology of man, set within a wider natural philosophy, supply a continuing framework to Montesquieu's analysis. And to indicate these various ingredients of his concern, the word 'esprit' was admirably chosen."[12]

A search for *the* definitive objective of *The Spirit of the Laws* runs the risk of what Montesquieu warned against, chasing *l'esprit* only to catch *la sottise*. But if his opening declaration of purpose is to have any meaning at all, the assumption of underlying unity of purpose must be granted. The scope of this purpose is, in any case, more definable than its substance, ranging through the relations of climate to political structure and of political structure to "liberty." As students of politics, we have been given ample material.

Climate and Causation

Cold air constringes the extremities of the external fibres of the body; this increases their elasticity, and favors the return of the blood from the extreme parts to the heart. It contracts those very fibres; consequently it increases also their force. On the contrary, warm air relaxes and lengthens the extremes of the fibres; of course it diminishes their force and elasticity. People are, therefore, more vigorous in cold climates. . . .[13]

People are, in Montesquieu's view, many other things in cold climates: they are more courageous, industrious, liberty-minded, and capable of bearing pain, but also more likely to commit suicide. They are less erotic, romantic, indolent, and other-worldly than their southern brethren. In northern climates one needs a certain amount of strong liquor "without which the blood would congeal." In the south, where "the aqueous part of the blood loses itself greatly by perspiration," the Moslem law properly forbids wine.

Some of Montesquieu's observations about climate and soil are now

12 Lowenthal, "Book I," p. 498.
13 *The Spirit of the Laws*, Bk. XIV, Ch. 2.

obviously incorrect; but others are still illuminating: The greater relative equality of women in Europe results from monogamy. Monogamy results from climate. In warmer climates, girls mature more rapidly and are suitable for marriage at an earlier age, which makes them grow old and wrinkled faster, which leads to the practice of adding a new wife every so often.[14] The great plains of Asia make for despotic rule; but the natural subdivisions created by rivers and mountains in Europe encourages less centralized authority.[15] ". . . Monarchy is more frequently found in fruitful countries, and a republican government in those which are not so."[16] "The inhabitants of islands have a higher relish for liberty than those of the continent."[17] A trading and navigating people require a much more extensive code of laws than agrarian peoples.[18] The advent of a money economy increases the kinds and degrees of injustice.[19] The Moslem religion is conducive to despotism, the Catholic to monarchy, the Protestant to republicanism.

Climate is made to explain almost everything in Montesquieu: morals, economics, religion, forms of government. Much of this strikes us as a bit silly. But we are never quite sure how much of it Montesquieu himself takes seriously. And, on the other hand, at the level of every general causal explanation in history, climate is certainly no less absurd than any of the other single-factor explanations of historical process that men have advanced. Montesquieu at least warns his readers "to notice that there is a vast difference between saying that a certain quality, modification of the mind, or virtue, is not the spring by which government is actuated, and affirming that it is not to be found in that government. Were I to say such a wheel or such a pinion is not the spring which sets the watch going, can you infer thence that it is not to be found in the watch?"[20] Montesquieu was sensible enough to see that the factors of climate and soil were more determining in the earlier stages of civilization than in the later stages. If climate is implausible as an over-all explanatory cause, in time the economic influences that are now weighed so heavily in the causal scales may seem equally implausible.

Montesquieu drew from his observations the logical conclusion that the institutions of a particular nation are not easily changed. Indeed, he could scarcely have drawn any other. Not only was he skeptical about change, but pessimistic as well. A strong strain of pessimism runs through the *Persian Letters*. Progress is seen as ambiguous. "Of what advantage has the invention of the mariner's compass been to us, and the discovery

14 *Ibid.*, Bk. XVI, Ch. 2.   15 *Ibid.*, Bk. XVII, Ch. 6.   16 *Ibid.*, Bk. XVIII, Ch. 1.
17 *Ibid.*, Ch. 5.   18 *Ibid.*, Ch. 8.   19 *Ibid.*, Ch. 16.
20 *Ibid.*, Author's Explanatory Notes, No. 2.

of so many nations who have given us more diseases than wealth?"[21]
The best councils of France did not last long and neither did the good
they accomplished[22] Every man ought to have a right to commit
suicide;[23] in fact, "men should be bewailed at their birth and not at their
death."[24] Statesmen, it would appear from both *The Spirit of the Laws*
and from *Considerations on the Causes of the Greatness and Decline of
Rome*, have a limited capacity to control history. Time moved too rapidly
for Roman emperors. Rome grew too fast for effective management, and
crumbled. Unforseen reactions and counterreactions thwart the shrewdest
calculations, as when Henry VIII broke from Rome and hoped thereby
to strengthen the monarchy, only to help create a Protestant force that
eventually weakened the monarchy.

Yet Montesquieu was not a blind fatalist. As man increased his control of nature the possibility of more libertarian political forms was
enhanced. Political change could not be abrupt; but it was not impossible:
". . . when a prince would make great alterations in his kingdom, he
should reform by law what is established by law, and change by custom
what is settled by custom; for it is very bad policy to change by law what
ought to be changed by custom."[25] In a famous illustration Montesquieu
noted the futility of Peter the Great's law ordering the Muscovites'
beards to be cut off. Laws apply to the actions of subjects (here Montesquieu means positive laws). Manners and customs apply to the actions
of men as men rather than as subjects. Manners relate to interior conduct
and custom to exterior conduct. The wise legislator, says Montesquieu,
is aware of these distinctions.[26] It is clear that positive laws are but a
junior part of the family of laws whose *esprit* Montesquieu is exploring;
but it is also true that positive laws have a constructive, possibly even
a progressive, role to play in the life of man.

Relativism and Justice

THAT what works in one society will not necessarily work in another
is a judgment of common sense that few men would now question. If
this is all that is meant by the relativism of Montesquieu, it does not
amount to much. What is today called ethical relativism implies that
no truly independent judgment of moral worth can be made in comparing
different societies or cultures. Every moral judgment grows out of, is

---

21 *Persian Letters*, No. 106. Quotations are from John Davidson, trans., *Persian
and Chinese Letters*, (New York: Walter Dunne, 1907).
22 *Ibid.*, No. 138. 23 *Ibid.*, No. 76. 24 *Ibid.*, No. 40.
25 *The Spirit of the Laws*, Bk. XIX, Ch. 14. 26 *Ibid.*, Ch. 16.

relative to, is valid for, a particular culture only. Is Montesquieu a relativist in this sense?

Montesquieu sought to isolate the nature and the principle of different types of governments and evaluate them largely in their own terms. "Nature" and "principle" in his context are not the same.

There is this difference between the nature and principle of government, that the former is that by which it is constituted, the latter that by which it is made to act. One is its particular structure, and the other the human passions which set it in motion.

Now, laws ought not less to relate to the principle than to the nature of each government.[27]

The three basic types of government are republican, monarchical, and despotic. Their "nature" is that in the first, the whole people or a part have supreme power (a republic may be a democracy or an aristocracy depending upon the size of the ruling group); in the second, one person rules by fixed laws; and in the third, a single person rules by caprice. (Book II) The "principles" these forms require are, for the republic, virtue; for monarchy, honor; and for despotism, fear. Education (IV) and legislation (V) must be calculated to support and advance the relevant principle of government if it is to survive. If the principle becomes corrupted, the best laws can do little to preserve the system (VIII).

By comparison with his contemporaries Montesquieu symbolizes a remarkable detachment in trying to understand and not simply pass judgment on diverse institutions. If Ernst Cassirer is correct, Montesquieu was the first in history to grasp the concept of "ideal-types" as used in the twentieth century by Max Weber and others, that is, abstracted but nonutopian, historical-sociological models[28]

Nevertheless, despite his sensitive awareness of diversity, in at least three respects Montesquieu would seem to depart from any kind of strict ethical relativism. In the first place there are scattered in profusion throughout *The Spirit of the Laws* what we would call personal value-judgments, statements whose factual content is low and whose emotional content is fairly high: a despot "is naturally lazy, voluptuous, and ig-

27 *Ibid.*, Bk. III, Ch. 1.
28 Ernst Cassirer, *The Philosophy of the Enlightenment*, trans. by Fritz C. A. Koelln and James P. Pettegrove (Boston: Beacon Press, 1955), p. 210. While representing a brilliant insight into the spirit of types, Montesquieu's accomplishment, says Cassirer, is essentially static. Principles of functions as distinct from forms elude him.

norant";²⁹ despotism "glories in the contempt of life";³⁰ it has produced "horrid cruelties."³¹ The people in a democracy are "always either too remiss or too violent."³² The establishment of unlimited power is one remedy to prevent the dissolution of an empire, "but how dreadful the remedy."³³ A full listing of such statements would be endless, and perhaps without very great significance in any case. Montesquieu was, like almost every eighteenth-century writer, something of a moralist, influenced by the belletristic tradition of such writers as Montaigne. Stylistic intrusions of moral judgments, as well as his failure to be wholly detached, are not necessarily a failure of his fundamental orientation.

In the second place, Montesquieu was unable to be wholly detached from the gross evils and extravagances of the French monarchy under Louis XIV and Louis XV. Lightly concealed beneath the analytic surface of *The Spirit of the Laws* lie a series of barbs aimed directly at that target. Repeatedly Montesquieu assures his readers that to designate honor as the principle of monarchy is not to suggest that virtue is absent therefrom. His assurances are not altogether convincing; or perhaps it is better said that they convince us only that Montesquieu was anxious about the reactions of certain monarchists. Certainly most of Book VIII, Chapter 6, "Of the Corruption of the Principle of Monarchy," can be regarded as an elliptical attack on the Louises. China is the ostensible source of the illustrative material, but when Montesquieu says that monarchy "is destroyed when the prince, directing everything entirely to himself, calls to the state his capital, the capital to his court, and the court to his own person" it is not hard to imagine whom he is talking about. The privileges of provincial cities are regarded tenderly, and effeminacy in the ancient Lydian court is criticized pointedly and unhistorically.³⁴

Scholars have challenged the accuracy of much of Montesquieu's historical evidence. To prove by historical example that the institution of the grand vizier is the "fundamental law" of despotism³⁵ is an effort that suggests either that Montesquieu was not the best of historians or that he had objectives other than merely writing history as it "really was." Both suggestions are undoubtedly correct, and, indeed, the latter partly explains the former. That Montesquieu was less than accurate on many historical points reflects in part, of course, the limitations of the sources available to him and especially the dubious character of many Asian chronicles. But it was more the character of his interest than a

---

29 *The Spirit of the Laws*, Bk. II, Ch. 2.
30 *Ibid.*, Bk. III, Ch. 8.   31 *Ibid.*, Ch. 9.   32 *Ibid.*, Bk. II, Ch. 2.
33 *Ibid.*, Bk. VIII, Ch. 17.   34 *Ibid.*, Bk. X, Ch. 12.   35 *Ibid.*, Bk. II, Ch. 5.

defect in his talent that affected his historiography. His long excursion into the Salic law of France demonstrates his prowess as a historian. If the grand vizier became a slightly exaggerated target, it makes sense to believe that Richelieu and not a hoard of Moslem functionaries was being delicately deflated. As in most other political writers, there is in Montesquieu a quantity of polemics mixed with the history and social theory.

The third departure from ethical relativism is the most significant. It lies in Montesquieu's acknowledgment of a standard of justice that transcends the differences of place and time, being based on the "relations of justice anterior to the positive law by which they are established."[36] It is his feeling about this standard that permits and encourages his personal judgments against despotism in general and the French monarchy in particular. Montesquieu's condemnation of dehumanizing practices is evident throughout the *Persian Letters*. In Book XV of *The Spirit of the Laws* his mock defense of slavery is one of the most biting satires one could imagine; and in Book XXV his attack on religious persecutions is equally devastating. Montesquieu is incapable of saying: to each culture its own. Yet he still recognizes the irremediable fact of moral diversity. What we have, then, is a tension between an eternal standard of justice and the passionate creature man, who in practice seems continually to ignore it. One of the *Persian Letters* is most graphic on the contrast:

Justice is a true relation existing between things, a relation which is always the same, whoever contemplates it, whether it be God or an angel, or, lastly, man himself.

It is true that men do not always perceive these relations: often indeed, when they do perceive them, they turn aside from them, their own interest being always that which they perceive most clearly. Justice cries aloud; but her voice is hardly heard in the tumult of the passions.[37]

There would seem to be in Montesquieu a fundamental distinction parallel to that drawn in Book I between the political state and the civil state. At one level there are various political rights *(droits)* peculiar to given bodies politic, rights that from historical necesssity must be accepted as natural reflections of national differences.[38] At this level, and it is a fairly inclusive one, Montesquieu's advice seems to coincide with that of a gentleman he quotes: "leave us as we are . . . and nature will repair whatever is amiss."[39]

36 *Ibid.*, Bk. I, Ch. 1.
37 *Persian Letters*, No. 84.
38 *The Spirit of the Laws*, Bk. XIX, Chs. 5-6.
39 *Ibid.*, Ch. 6.

Yet there linger over or behind or in all bodies politic more fundamental human rights, especially rights of freedom of movement and individual expression and personal justice derived from the "relations of justice antecedent to . . . positive law." Such rights cannot be neatly codified nor easily isolated from standards of personal morality, yet it is clear that for Montesquieu they have a universal and not merely national sanction. These, too, are touched by necessity; indeed, they would seem to be necessary in a more profound sense than merely historical-political rights: "If I know of a thing useful for my nation which, however, would be ruinous to another, I would not propose it to my Prince, because I am a man before being a Frenchman, or, better, because I am a man by necessity and a Frenchman only by accident."[40]

On the record, we cannot call Montesquieu a moral relativist.

The Separation of Powers and Liberty

IN dozens of books and hundreds of lectures and thousands of examination papers the name Montesquieu means one thing—separation of powers. Folklore has it that we Americans owe the separation of powers to Montesquieu via Madison and the Founding Fathers, and Montesquieu owes it to a misunderstanding of the English Constitution. A man's reputation tends to be made by his followers and we cannot deny that Montesquieu's significance for us necessarily reflects the importance we attach to the principle of the separation of powers. Let us give the subject its due, but let us also avoid exaggeration if possible.

With the taste for cultural variety that has become his trademark, Montesquieu begins Book XI of the *Spirit of the Laws* by noting the tremendously wide range of conceptions of liberty. (Once again he "makes hay with a beard" by noting the fact that for the Russians under Peter the Great the greatest liberty was the privilege of wearing a long beard.) But liberty, even in a democracy, does not consist of doing anything one pleases to do. "We must have continually present to our minds the difference between independence and liberty. Liberty is the right of doing whatever the laws permit, and if a citizen could do what they forbid he would no longer be possessed of liberty, because all his fellow citizens would have the same power."[41]

Montesquieu specifically dismisses "philosophical" conceptions of liberty from his concern. He is here interested in the well-ordered society,

40 *Cahiers* (1716-55), quoted by Franz Neumann, ed., *op. cit.*, Introduction, p. xv.
41 *The Spirit of the Laws*, Bk. XI, Ch. 3.

not the deep places of the individual psyche. Moreover, as Neumann observes, he is without a counterpart to Rousseau's general will, or any other concept that might justify the subordination of individual interests to general law without the abandonment of liberty as a goal. Unlike his conception of justice, Montesquieu's conception of liberty is basically negative. If we remember his general attitude toward toleration, it is clear that he really wants to authorize not only those acts that the laws permit, but all acts that the laws do not forbid. This is close to the traditional liberal view of liberty, quite consonant with Locke, for example.

In particular, Montesquieu found in the principle of separation of powers a guarantee of the kind of restraint on government that, given the right setting, could assure liberty, that is, a condition in which the laws were appropriate to a well-ordered society and also permitted a considerable degree of individual and group independence.

Although all seem to seek self-preservation, different governments have many different ends: war, commerce, tranquillity, princely pleasure, and the like. But one eighteenth-century nation has as its end political liberty, thinks Montesquieu, and that nation is England. Chapter 6 of Book XI is entitled "Of the Constitution of England" and begins: "In every government there are three sorts of powers: the legislative; the executive in respect to things dependent on the law of nations; and the executive in regard to matters that depend on civil law." This terminology at first glance seems to correspond to Locke's separation of powers into legislative, executive, and "federative" in Chapter 12 of the *Second Treatise of Civil Government*. But Montesquieu, it soon appears, combines Locke's executive and federative into one, and calls the executive in regard to matters that depend on the civil law the "judiciary."

The heart of Montesquieu's theme was that where these three functions were combined in the same person or body of magistrates there would be the end of liberty. Not only did he point to the dangers of allowing one agency to be prosecutor and judge, but he also argued for the safety of having popular feeling represented in one house of a legislature and "persons distinguished by their birth, riches, or honors" represented in another. They would have "a right to check the licentiousness of the people, as the people have a right to oppose any encroachment of theirs."[42] Plausible arguments are offered for frequent but not continuous meetings of parliaments, and for entrusting the power of summoning and proroguing to someone outside the legislative body. The American Founding Fathers were influenced by Montesquieu's arguments for both separation of powers and bicameralism, though, of course, the parallelism between Lords and Commons and Senate and House was not exact.

42 *Ibid.*, Ch. 6.

What Montesquieu was describing was not the English government as it actually operated but the English government as it might operate. He was fully aware of the distinction. His *Notes on England* show that he was familiar with the realities of English politics, including the use of bribes and influence in high places. He had heard the famous Dunkirk debate in the House of Commons, during which Bolingbroke and Walpole argued the theory of the separation of powers. If he attached great weight to this theory, which came to earth more concretely in America than ever it did in England, it is partly because the system of centralized cabinet government that we have come to know in modern Britain was, at the time of Montesquieu's visit, in barely nascent form. It is also because he avowedly cared more about the theory than the practice: "It is not my business to examine whether the English actually enjoy this liberty or not. Sufficient it is for my purpose to observe that it is established by their laws; and I inquire no further."[43]

Actually, much more space is devoted to the principle of the separation of powers in the early Roman government than to England. But with that, Montesquieu stops. "I should be glad to inquire into the distribution of the three powers in all the moderate governments we are acquainted with, in order to calculate the degree of liberty which each may enjoy. But we must not always exhaust a subject, so as to leave no work at all for the reader."[44] The work given to the reader was the contemplation of an ideal-type construction of a system of liberty built on the separation of powers. Though rooted in historical contingency, it had no exact counterpart in England, or anywhere else. Certainly it could not serve as a blueprint for the reform of political societies wholly unlike England. But it did provide a standard of orderly and liberal government by which different existing governments could be compared—a measuring stick, so to speak. Montesquieu could hardly have been unaware of the likelihood that such comparison would be disadvantageous to the French monarchy.

Conclusion

IT is the fate of men of genius who do not fit into conventional categories to be neglected until such time as new categories emerge. Perhaps this has been the fate of Montesquieu. As Vaughn has observed, he was neither in the camp of the *philosophes* with their emphasis on abstract rights and their antihistorical bias, nor was he at one with the mechanical "expediency" of the utilitarians. Like later conservatives (and Montes-

43 *Ibid.*, Bk. XI, Ch. 6.   44 *Ibid.*, Ch. 20.

quieu's influence on Burke and De Maistre was profound), he saw the individual not as an atomistic entity but as a member of an ineluctable community. The variety of communities fascinated Montesquieu. The concept of immutable, inalienable, and universal rights to be hurled against these communities was not compatible with his mentality. Moreover, as an aristocrat, he defended the privileged position of aristocratic classes, where he did not take it for granted.

Yet justice and liberty meant a great deal to him, and he had a sensitivity for organic growth toward or away from such ideals, ideals that had a kind of universality similar to, yet distinct from, traditional natural-law principles. As we have seen, he was not an ethical relativist and was even capable of rousing moral denunciation. If such moralistic exercises seem inconsistent with the image of Montesquieu as an inductive scientist describing the diversities of cultures with an air of utter detachment, it is well to note that this was not necessarily the image Montesquieu had of himself. He knew, on the one hand, that admidst the vast sea of uncertain and often unreliable historical data he could not conform to the rigorous canons of Baconian induction. On the other hand, he was interested in much more than mere description and correlation. The spirit of those necessary relations that he called laws was much too elusive for a two-dimensional exposition. "I have laid down the first principles," he says in the Preface to *The Spirit of the Laws*, "and have found that the particular cases follow naturally from them. . . ." This is not induction. Montesquieu was subtly interweaving the general with the particular and offering a complex series of judgments about the "necessary relations" of many things. Vaughn quaintly but perhaps accurately calls this process divination. This accounts for the difficulty of summarizing Montesquieu and the difficulty of appreciating him in capsule form.[45] Montesquieu requires an inquisitive, thorough, and leisurely reading.

Such a reading can almost be viewed as an end in itself. The political thought it reveals is not by itself compelling in the way that Hobbes' political system is compelling. But there emerges from the pages the voice of a wise and witty man who saw, as did almost none of his contemporaries save Vico, the degree to which we are prisoners of our historic situation. Despite this perception, which at times bred a deep pessimism, he was able to communicate with genuine moral conviction a sense of justice and a sense of liberty. Politically they could be expressed

45 See A.-J. Grant "Montesquieu," in F. J. C. Hearnshaw, ed., *The Social and Political Ideas of Some Great French Thinkers in the Age of Reason* (London: Harrap, 1930), pp. 114-35. This article is an example of the distortion and even caricaturization which can result from overcondensed summaries of too many points. By such means Grant is able to say that in Montesquieu "the English constitution is traced to the London fogs"! (p. 119.)

only in different institutional forms in different places and times, but in *esprit* they could unite the parts into a whole. By looking intently and separately at Frenchmen, Englishmen, Indians, and Chinese, Montesquieu was finally able to see them all as men.

CHAPTER

7 | *Rousseau*

JEAN-JACQUES ROUSSEAU is an endlessly fascinating character. Few respect him as a man. Some do not respect him as a thinker. But almost everyone seems impelled to pay attention to him. The man is better known and discredits the thinker. But the thinker breaks through again and again and redeems the man. Rousseau's life and writings both are and are not at odds. The life seems amoral, the writings seem moralistic; yet the erratic character of his life seems also to have a parallel in the apparently inconsistent development of his thought. Rousseau recognized this self-contradiction as well as any of his critics and, as usual, bared it to the world in the strikingly titled *Rousseau juge de Jean-Jacques*.

What did he really believe? Did he believe that society is the enemy or the savior of man, that objective law kills the spirit or liberates it, that virtue or happiness is the supreme good? Is there consistency in either his life or his thought? Many commentators on Rousseau—John Morley, Émile Faguet, Irving Babbitt, to name three—have found him in confusion and have left him there, a colorful and influential, but second-rate, figure in the history of ideas. Other scholars—Gustave Lanson, E. H. Wright, Albert Schinz, Ernst Cassirer, Alfred Cobban—have found an underlying unity and profundity to Rousseau's thought.[1] But our first

1 C. E. Vaughn found unity in the movement from one extreme to the other, from Rousseau's individualism to his final collectivism. For a cogent discussion of these and other Rousseau interpreters, see Peter Gay's Introduction to his translation of Ernst Cassirer, *The Question of Jean-Jacques Rousseau* (New York: Columbia Univ. Press, 1954), pp. 3-30. For works by the above-named men, see the bibliography.

problem in dealing with Rousseau is to do justice to the relationship between his life and writings without getting wholly carried away by morbid fascination with his life.

Life

EARLY LIFE

Rousseau was born in Geneva, the center of Calvinism, in 1712. His mother died at his birth. His father was a watchmaker, who preferred to be a dancing master when he could get away with it in that austere environment, and was apparently a man of flabby character. Among other things, he kept young Jean-Jacques up till all hours of the night reading adult romances to him. A good time was had by all, but "I soon acquired by this dangerous practice," wrote Rousseau,

not only an extreme facility in reading and comprehending, but, for my age, a too intimate acquaintance with the passions. An infinity of sensations were familiar to me; without possessing any precise idea of the objects to which they related—I had conceived nothing—I had felt everything. The impact of this confused succession of emotions did not retard the future efforts of my reason, but through them I was given some extravagant, romantic notions of human life of which experience and reflection have never been able to cure me.[2]

When Jean-Jacques was ten, his father, who after a brawl felt it necessary to flee Geneva, abandoned him. Jean-Jacques drifted from job to job, learning how to lie and steal with considerable proficiency. When he was sixteen he found himself locked out of the city of Geneva one night, so he left for France. His natural charm and wit found him many friends, especially women friends, but his capacity to attract was matched only by his capacity to infuriate, and most of his friendships broke up after bitter quarrels.

Rousseau's greatest benefactress was Mme de Warens, his beloved "Mamma," who time after time took him back into her country estate at Chambéry. At Mme de Warens' establishment Rousseau took advantage of the opportunity to absorb the book learning that was essential to his later literary conquests. For a time he was one of two paramours living amicably in the household, but Rousseau could not accept as blandly another, later one of his mistress' lovers and thus departed for Paris in 1742.

In Paris Rousseau was, for a time, a different person. In the big city

2 *Confessions*, Bk. I, Louis Martin-Chauffier, ed. (Paris: Gallimard, 1951), p. 8.

he was aware of the time of day. He was orderly and dutiful and unchildlike. But though he had secured letters of introductions to various *salons*, he was only tolerated and never fully accepted into the tight circle of conventional society. He wrote an opera and invented a system of musical notation that was politely rejected by the French Academy. Finally in 1743, to get rid of him, someone secured for him a job at the French Embassy in Venice. Rousseau did his routine chores with considerable diligence but soon quarreled with his employer, the wanton ambassador, and with magnificent disdain walked out of the embassy, never to return. He stayed in Venice awhile to taunt the ambassador with his presence, and to taste, with mixed feelings, a bit of Venice's vaunted vice.

Returning to Paris, where he alienated more people by expounding the superiority of Italian to French music, he formed a liaison with an ignorant housemaid named Thérèse Levasseur. Devoted to each other in their fashion, they lived as common-law man and wife from that time on. Rousseau actually worked to support both her and her innumerable voracious relatives. But also during this time, in his most universally condemned action, he turned all five of his newborn infants over to a foundling home, despite the tears of their mother. With a slight trace of remorse, he explains in the *Confessions* that they probably had a better life being reared by the state and even cited the authority of Plato's *Republic* for this policy. Yet, even though in debt, this warm-hearted irresponsible, who was prone to gush tears at the drop of an eyelid, sent money to the now-improverished Mme de Warens. To make a living he copied music (mostly wrong, says Hearnshaw) and wrote some hasty articles on music for Diderot's *Encyclopédie*.

A Crucial Essay

In 1749 the Academy of Dijon sponsored an essay contest on the subject "Has the Progress of the Sciences and the Arts Contributed to Corrupt or Purify Morals?" With the perversity of his genius, Rousseau took an antiprogressive stance and won the prize. (Diderot later claimed that he had suggested this approach to Rousseau, but Diderot was angry when he claimed it, and was given to lying.) This was perhaps the decisive point in Rousseau's life. "In a moment," he said, "I saw a new world and became a new man." Rousseau's defense of the simple life, of the natural innocence and goodness of man corrupted by civilization, struck the artificial, effete Paris society with tremendous force. Now that he had rejected society, society at last sought him out. He was lionized, fêted, and bothered by the curious. But seeking vengeance, he churlishly abused them. Once again heedless of time and regularity, he sold his watch. Deliberately dressing sloppily, he gave up his favorite linen shirts—with the help of Thérèse's brother, who stole them. His opera *Le Devin du village* was now produced. The king attended the opening and asked to see the composer; but Rousseau did not bother to drop around.

In 1754 came the so-called *Second Discourse*, "On the Origin of Inequality," also written for a Dijon Academy contest. It did not win the prize, but it became even more famous than its predecessor; and justly so, for there Rousseau revealed his basic principles, so he said, "with the greatest boldness." In 1755 he wrote the "Discourse on Political Economy" for the *Encyclopédie*, which, in its original form, anticipated much of the *Social Contract*. In 1756 he left Paris for a cottage in the country, "The Hermitage," prepared for him by Mme d'Épinay, a long-time admirer. For a while his existence was quite idyllic and his humor good, except for the insidious depredations and backbiting of his mother-in-law—or mother-out-of-law.

DISPUTES AND DERANGEMENTS

With the terrible Lisbon earthquake of 1755 came shocked debates over the role of Providence in this disaster. This was the occasion of Rousseau's first dispute with Voltaire and a revelation of his concern with the problem of theodicy. He penned his *Lettre sur la Providence* to uphold an optimistic view of a beneficent divinity against Voltaire's forthright pessimism. About this time, during his morning stroll in the woods, the time usually devoted to writing, Rousseau began to experience amatory daydreams and delusions. Some of these emerged on paper in the novel *Julie, ou la Nouvelle Héloïse*. Also at this time came Rousseau's last grand passion, an affair with the sister-in-law of his hostess, which led to not a few quarrels and misunderstandings between Mme d'Épinay and her "dear bear." When Diderot kept badgering him to return to Paris, Rousseau's emotional distress turned to paranoia. Had he lived in the twentieth century, much of Rousseau's later life would no doubt have been spent in a mental hospital. What this would have done to his literary output no one knows. In any event, Rousseau was not the first nor the last madman whose utterances have made more sense than those of normal people.

In 1758 Mme d'Épinay happily got rid of Rousseau, and Rousseau happily got rid of Mme Levasseur. He left The Hermitage for (as always) a borrowed cottage at Mont-Louis and packed the old lady off to Paris. Soon thereafter Rousseau found himself in a spirited exchange of letters with D'Alembert over the wisdom of establishing a theater in Geneva. Rousseau's opposition, on the grounds that the arts in general

contaminated morality, placed him in company with the most conservative religious groups. This alliance, in turn, led to further and more
intemperate exchanges between Voltaire and Rousseau. Those who explain Rousseau as a lifelong seeker after status can no doubt see in this
episode an attempt to identify himself with the hidebound town of his
youth, a town that had rejected him.

   La Nouvelle Héloïse was published in 1760 and was an immediate
success. It gave jaded Parisians what they had long been wanting, a good
cry. Riding the crest of popularity, Rousseau in 1762 published his two
best-known works, *The Social Contract* (which had originally been intended as part of a greater but now abandoned work, *Institutions
politiques*) and *Émile*. *Émile*, the story of an orphan correctly tutored by
Rousseau himself, expounded a theory of child-centered, naturalistic
education, in which rationalistic, second-hand, or mere "verbal" knowledge would be deliberately kept at bay so that through a constant intercourse with "nature" the child could learn by himself and for himself.
"Society" was still a culprit for Rousseau. The unorthodox opinions, especially about religion, that *Émile* contained led the Parliament of Paris
to order it burned and its author arrested. Rousseau had to flee to Mont-
Louis, leaving Thérèse behind. He went first to Berne, but was driven
out. He then went to Neuchâtel, where, thanks to the tolerance of Frederick the Great, whom Rousseau had earlier criticized, he was able to stay
three years; Thérèse joined him here.

Last Days

This period saw little literary work. The *Constitution for Corsica* was
one of the few substantial enterprises. Rousseau did write a vigorous reply
to Beaumont, archbishop of Paris, who had denounced *Émile*, and was
drawn into the colorful dispute between factions in Geneva over
whether the ban there on Rousseau's person and books should be lifted.
The center of violent controversy, denied the sacraments by the Reformed Church (whose services he regularly attended), Rousseau finally
had to leave Neuchâtel. He lived happily for a while on an island in
Lake Bienne until he was driven on again, this time into Germany. Finally,
he accepted David Hume's invitation to visit England in 1766. Inevitably
the two men quarreled as Rousseau's paranoia grew more and more out
of control, and Hume unwisely chose to make public his defense against
Rousseau's charge of a conspiracy to humiliate him. Rousseau left England
the next year, and until 1770 lived here and there about Europe. In 1768,
to impress the bored, alcoholic, and now neglectful Thérèse, he married
her—at least he recited a ceremony in the presence of two witnesses.
Thérèse, however, was not impressed.

In 1770 he returned to Paris, where he was given to understand that if he did not make a nuisance of himself he would not be bothered by the authorities. He gave up the quaint Armenian dress he had adopted and settled down to his old vocation of copying music at ten sous a page. As many expected, however, he was unable not to make a nuisance of himself. Partly for self-vindication he began giving readings from his *Confessions* to private groups (one lasted seventeen hours) until Mme d'Épinay, in self-defense, had the police put a stop to it. He composed *Rousseau juge de Jean-Jacques*, in which the signs of persecutory paranoia are unmistakable. Yet the work also was a penetrating self-analysis with passages of some philosophic significance.[3] He then wrote the *Dialogues*, the *Rêveries d'un promeneur solitaire*, and the *Considérations sur le gouvernement de Pologne*, a sober, workmanlike job. For eight years he remained in Paris; but ill and tormented, he finally took to the country again, living at Ermonville, ten miles from Paris, in a little cottage lent to him by the Marquis de Girardin. In May, 1778, his old enemy Voltaire died, and Rousseau felt that somehow his existence was tied up with Voltaire's. "He is dead, and I shall soon follow," he wrote. Scarcely two months later, on July 2, he did. Thérèse, stupid and coarse to the end, lived on until 1801.

Conflicting Evaluations

It is easy, too easy, to make fun of this sad life, and, worse, to explain too much of Rousseau's writings in terms of it. F. J. C. Hearnshaw, for example, divides Rousseau's life into five periods: "the undisciplined boy," "the super-tramp," "the would-be man of the world," "the inspired maniac," and "the hunted fugitive." "So intimately," writes Hearnshaw, "were Rousseau's writings associated with his life that it is impossible to comprehend them without a detailed knowledge of his curious and re-markable career."[4] In the view of Hearnshaw and others, Rousseau's glorification of the simple presocial state of nature was but the outward manifestation of Rousseau's inner rejection of a society that had rejected him. The contradiction between the individualism of the *First* and *Second Discourses* and the collectivism of the *Third Discourse* ("On Political Economy"), and the latter parts of *The Social Contract*, as well as many other contradictions, are found to be reflections of his erratic personality. "He was an unsystematic thinker, untrained in formal logic. He was an

3 To foil his delusory "enemies" Rousseau planned to leave the manuscript on the altar in Notre Dame Cathedral, but when he found a gate locked against him he knew that even God was on their side.

4 F. J. C. Hearnshaw, "Rousseau," in F. J. C. Hearnshaw, ed., *The Social and Political Ideas of Some Great French Thinkers of the Age of Reason* (London: Harrap, 1930), p. 172.

omniverous reader with undeveloped powers of assimilation. He was an emotional enthusiast who spoke without due reflection. He was an irresponsible writer with a fatal gift for epigram."[5] There is some truth to this, of course; but the "fatal gift for epigram" may also have been fatal to many of Rousseau's critics. Peter Gay writes, ". . . it was Rousseau's eloquence rather than his extravagance that created difficulties for the commentators. Rousseau was, unhappily, the coiner of happy phrases. Read in context, they were usually elucidated by the argument in which they were embedded. Taken out of context, their rhetorical power obscured the fact that they were only elliptical pronouncements. Used as slogans, they twisted or destroyed his meaning."[6] Gay believes that Rousseau was neither confused nor inconsistent in the essentials of his thought, but, like another inspired madman, Nietzsche, *invited* misunderstanding. Given such a challenge, can we do less than seek for consistency—and understanding?

Nature and Society

FROM the time of his prize-winning essay, Rousseau is absorbed by the conflict between something called "nature" and something called "society." Compared to the *philosophes'* easy assumptions about natural law and their often shallow individualism, Rousseau's position was highly original. It was also boldly stated. "I shall be at no pains to please either intellectuals or men of the world," he wrote in the *First Discourse.*[7] (However, he flattered the Academy of Dijon to an extent the twentieth century would call inordinate.)

"Nature" for Rousseau did not refer to man as he is so much as to man as he might have been: ". . . nature makes man happy and good, but . . . society causes him to be depraved and miserable," he wrote in *Rousseau juge de Jean-Jacques.*[8] The famous openings of his most famous works strike the same note. Book I of *Émile:* "Everything is good as it comes out of the hands of the Author of things, everything degenerates in the hands of man."[9] Book I of *The Social Contract:* "Man is

5 *Ibid.,* p. 186.
6 In the Introduction to his translation of Cassirer, *The Question of Jean-Jacques Rousseau,* p. 13.
7 All references to the three *Discourses* ("On the Arts and Sciences," "On the Origin of Inequality," and "On Political Economy" respectively) are taken from G. D. H. Cole, trans., *The Social Contract and Discourses,* Everyman Ed. (London: Dent, 1913).
8 *Oeuvres complètes de J.-J. Rousseau,* (Paris: Hachette, 1909), Vol. IX, p. 287. There is a certain parallel between Rousseau's nature-society distinction and Aristotle's *physis-nomos* distinction.
9 *Ibid.,* Vol. II, p. 3.

born free but yet we see him everywhere in chains."[10] Note well that Rousseau does not promise to remove these chains. "Those who believe themselves the masters of others cease not to be even greater slaves than the people they govern. How this happens I am ignorant; but if I am asked what renders it justifiable [*légitime*], I believe it may be in my power to resolve the question." Society has forged the chains that are the condition of our lost innocence and in so doing has helped destroy something precious; but at least in *The Social Contract* and *Émile*, Rousseau is mainly trying to teach us how to live in our state of lost innocence, for, once lost, innocence can never be recaptured.

Nor was there a period in his life, as some have thought, when Rousseau took seriously a literal back-to-nature movement, his Armenian dress notwithstanding. The *First Discourse* does deal with a state of nature, but it is not simply a foolish idealization of the happy savage. If Rousseau does idealize the ancient primitives in passing, he also parades before us some historical facts about the depravities of advanced civilizations. If he twists Socrates' praise of ignorance slightly, he also uses him well against civilized vanities. The significance of Rousseau's assertion that "the arts and sciences owe their birth to our vices"[10a]—astronomy to superstition, geometry to avarice, moral philosophy to human pride, and so on,—is a contention the significance of which many learned men never grasp. He overdoes, to be sure, the decline of military courage and fortitude and the pernicious character of most philosophizing; yet, if he does not quite prove his case that good morals are injured by the arts and sciences, he does (and his slightly ironic, biting tone helps) make the reader reflect seriously on the proposition that the moral quality of man's life is very little improved by the advances of "society," that is, by scientific information, elegant architecture, or personal luxury.

The very proposition flew in the face of the prevailing optimism of the eighteenth century and also the material hopes that underlay it, hopes that Rousseau was not above ridiculing: "The politicians of the ancient world were always talking of morals and virtue; ours speak of nothing but commerce and money. . . . According to them, a man is worth no more to the State than the amount he consumes; and thus a Sybarite would be worth at least thirty Lacedaemonians."[10b]

Those who chide Rousseau for the idyllic raptures of his state of nature overlook the hypothetical-imaginative character of almost all of Rousseau's writings save his model constitutions. In the *Second Discourse* he suggests most clearly of all what he is doing, trying to look not at men

10 All quotations from *The Social Contract* are from an eighteenth-century translation rev. and ed. by Charles Frankel (New York: Hafner, 1947).
10a "Arts and Sciences," p. 130.
10b *Ibid.*, p. 132.

but at man in order to arrive at a standard of his true nature that can be set against almost all forms of contemporary knowledge. In the first two *Discourses* Rousseau is more radical than any naïve state-of-nature literalist. His call for a return to nature is a call to purge ourselves of moral dependence upon social convention and to consult only the uncorrupted conscience hidden in our innermost being. This is an "impossible possibility" comparable only to the Christian understanding of redemption. Even theoretical statements on natural right and natural law, Rousseau points out in the *Second Discourse*, are developed with the language and the conceptions that are products of society's artifice. Most natural-law theories, therefore, are really artificial rather than natural.

The state of affairs Rousseau wishes to look at "perhaps never did exist, and probably never will exist."[11] His is a hypothetical history of government. "Let us begin," he says, "by laying facts aside, as they do not affect the question. The investigations we may enter into in treating this subject must not be considered as historical truths, but only as mere conditional and hypothetical reasonings, rather calculated to explain the nature of things than to ascertain their actual origin. . . ."[11a] In one sense the bulk of Rousseau's literary effort is a gigantic "as if."

This distinction between historical truth and nature is fundamental to Rousseau, and little sense can be made of him until this distinction is understood. He considers what man ought to be as much a part of his nature as what man does. To this extent Rousseau parallels most natural-law thinkers. But for several reasons Rousseau does not fit into the category of natural-law thinker. He does not agree with the classical natural-law view that was without the state-of-nature concept and held that man is naturally a social animal. Man for Rousseau is naturally independent of society. This does not mean that man can be studied empirically outside of society. Indeed, Rousseau says the reverse: "It is necessary to study society through men and men through society: those who would wish to treat separately politics and morals will never understand a thing about either."[12] Rousseau accepts the fact of society—far more, indeed, than did the *philosophes*—but wishes to set the individual off from it, to give the individual a vision of radical independence which can preserve him from submersion in society. The state of nature was a literary device used toward this end.

On the other hand, Rousseau does not conform to either the secular or religious forms of modern natural law. Rejecting a theological base for law, his intuitionist naturalism is at odds with what we have come

11 "Origin of Inequality," p. 155.
11a *Ibid.*, p. 161.
12 *Émile*, Bk. IV, *Oeuvres complètes*, Vol. II, p. 206.

to call the Thomistic view. And he does not regard the pursuit of happiness and its derivatives as a natural right in the fashion of Locke or
Paine. On this point Rousseau sided with the classicists, for he was more
concerned with goodness and virtue than with happiness, or even the
prudential security of Hobbes. But basically, he does not agree with either
classical or modern schools of natural law because he rejects reason as
nature's ultimate standard for moral guidance.[13]

Feeling, Conscience, and Reason

REASON is artificial in the sense that it is a part of man's advanced cultural heritage. Conscience, or compassion, reveals the essence or nature
of man. "I think I can perceive in [the human soul] two principles prior
to reason, one of them deeply interesting us in our own welfare and
preservation, and the other exciting a natural repugnance as seeing any
other sensible being, and particularly any of our own species, suffer pain
or death." From these, "all the rules of natural right appear to me to be
derived—rules which our reason is *afterwards* obliged to establish on
other foundations." It follows that "if I am bound to do no injury to
my fellow creatures, this is less because they are rational than because
they are sentient beings [*un être sensible*]. . . ."[14]

Likewise in the first part of the *First Discourse* Rousseau is ostensibly
describing the state of nature, but the form scarcely conceals his intent
of demonstrating the priority of the passions to reflective thought without
reference to time or place. Physical prowess is, but intellectual discrimination is not, required of the natural man. While the proliferation of
speech and its application to general ideas require intellect—indeed general ideas are impossible without speech—the origin of speech is probably
the work of children trying to communicate with their mothers rather
than the deliberate act of learned men. So much that we know depends
upon society and the arts that very little can be assumed about the natural state—not even Hobbes' assumption about egotistical warring. But
the essence of what does apear is the "force of natural compassion." "It
is . . . certain that compassion is a natural feeling which, by moderating
the violence of love of self in each individual, contributes to the preserva-

13 Yet even on this conclusion there is no consensus on Rousseau. Robert
Derathé has traced traditional natural-law influences on Rousseau and concludes
that he is really a rationalist, although one who is unusually sensitive to the limits
of reason. See his *Le Rationalism de J.-J. Rousseau* (Paris: Presses Universitaires de
France, 1948).

14 *Second Discourse*, Preface. Italics added. French interpolations in all quotations
are from *Oeuvres complètes*.

tion of the whole species." This natural compassion is utterly divorced from thought: ". . . a state of reflection is a state contrary to nature . . . a thinking man is a depraved animal [*l'homme qui médite est un animal déprave*]."[15] This statement is frequently castigated, and perhaps justly so, as an example of Rousseau's tendency to hyperbole. But the phrase cannot be dismissed as mere exaggeration. Rousseau was fully aware of the audacity of his position at the very start of his literary career: "Will we dare take the side of instinct against reason? That is precisely what I ask."[16] And at the very end of his life he could write to Mirabeau the elder: ". . . I am perfectly sure that my heart loves only that which is good. All the evil I ever did in my life was the result of reflection; and the little good I have been able to do was the result of impulse."[17]

Rousseau has, of course, been most severely attacked at this very point. In making feeling, sentiment, or emotion, rather than reason, the test of the good, he is said to have thrown away all hope for a well-ordered society with dutiful, self-restrained citizens. His emotional subjectivism leads to anarchy, it is claimed, which in turn leads to the kind of oppressive external restraints suggested by Rousseau himself in the *Social Contract*.

This, indeed, is a fundamental issue in Rousseau. The character of these restraints we will examine in a moment. But first, what does Rousseau really mean to do in putting impulse, instinct, and sentiment ahead of reason? What are the obligations between men arising from the fact that they are naturally sentient beings rather than rational beings? Two things must be said:

(1) To make reason subsidiary is not to eliminate reason. Were we to change Rousseau's famous statement to "a man who *only* thinks is a depraved animal" it would make more sense and would not be at odds with his general argument. Rousseau does not belittle every act of reason, nor disregard the need for laws to restrain men's unruly emotions: ". . . the more violent the passions are, the more are laws necessary to keep them under restraint."[18] This is not the "deliberately courted giddiness" that Babbitt accuses Rousseau of elevating into a principle. Whatever his ambiguities, Rousseau's guide to the good life was not a function of adrenal secretions.

(2) "Sentiment" had a double meaning in Rousseau. On the one hand

15 *Ibid.*, Part 1.
16 "Dernière Résponse à A. M. Bordes" [in defense of the *First Discourse*]. *Oeuvres complètes*, Vol. I, pp. 62-63.
17 Letter of March 25, 1767. In Theophile Dufour, ed., *Correspondance générale de J.-J. Rousseau* (Paris: Colin, 1934), Vol. XVII, pp. 2-3. Quoted in Cassirer, *The Problem of Jean-Jacques Rousseau*, p. 127.
18 "Origin of Inequality," p. 186.

it meant mere feeling, a psychological affect stemming from memory or sensory stimuli (*sens*). On the other hand it meant a spontaneous impulse or action of the soul with genuine ethical content and with overtones almost of divinity. This impulse was part of natural man but not simply physical man: ". . . my will is independent of my senses," Rousseau wrote in the controversial "Profession de foi du Vicaire Savoyard" in Book IV of *Émile*. In what could only be a deliberate metaphorical transplanting of the organ of thought, the Savoyard vicar revealed what "I think in the simplicity of my heart," and asked his auditor to do likewise. "It is said that conscience is the product of prejudice; however, I know by my experience that it insists on following the order of nature against the laws of men."[19] Although it is not that of logic or calculation, there is a kind of rationality, or at least a self-evidence, in this "order of nature." And it is directly related to man's destiny in society; for it would appear that the innocent savage in the state of nature scarcely has need of such insights. His passions, Rousseau holds in the *Second Discourse*, are *less* violent than those of modern man, especially as related to sexual conquests, because they are more simply animalistic and prosaic. The more imaginative and "moral" and less simply physical aspects of love are the marks of man in society. But the impetuosity of modern lovers is a source both of greater delight than the savage knows and of more violent trouble.

Ernst Cassirer, Platonizing Rousseau somewhat, makes this distinction between simple animal feeling and natural moral sentiment fundamental to the understanding of Rousseau:

Beside the self-evidence of feeling, then, there stands the self-evidence of ethical insight; but the two do not have the same origin. For one is a passive, the other an active power of the soul. In the case of self-evidence of feeling, our faculty of devotion is at work; it alone can unlock nature to us, and it allows us to blot out our own existence, so that we may live solely in and with nature. In the case of self-evidence of ethical insight, we are concerned with elevating and intensifying this existence of ours; for thus only may we survey the task of man in its true magnitude. This task remains insoluble for the individual as such; it can be accomplished only within the community and by means of its powers.[20]

The two elements may be seen concretely in, first, the image of Jean-Jacques on his solitary morning walks, losing himself in the sound of singing birds. Here self-love (*amour de soi*) is an innocent and natural instinct for self-preservation. And, secondly, it may be seen in the image

19 *Oeuvres complètes*, Vol. II, pp. 236-37.
20 *The Question of Jean-Jacques Rousseau*, p. 108.

of Rousseau in the afternoon taking pen in hand to wage regretfully
necessary battles for equity and justice, battles in which "society" compli-
cates everything unmercifully, self-love is corrupted into selfish love
(amour-propre), and pride and vanity are at stake. Here the "order of
nature" is infinitely harder to follow, but no less authoritative.

As Rousseau is pulled reluctantly but inexorably from morning to afternoon, so mankind is driven or led to its present state. There is both irony
and a double paradox in this development: ". . . human perfectibility, the
social virtues, and the other faculties which natural man potentially possessed," he writes in the Second Discourse, were only developed by "the
different accidents which may have improved the human understanding
while depraving the species and made man wicked while making him
sociable."[21] There is a paradox in man's becoming simultaneously wicked
and sociable, and there is a paradox in his being "perfected" in this way
by historical "accidents." Man's capacity to perfect himself is shown by
that which fortuitously happens to him to make him less perfect! What
are we to make of this?

Obviously we can say that Rousseau is confused or we can say that
he has struck deep into the paradox of life: the better we are the worse
we are; we make ourselves yet we are made; we are individuals only
in a group; society and the individual are simultaneously guilty of evil.
The Christian relates this same complex of ideas to the doctrine of original
sin, but Rousseau was too much a child of the Enlightenment, albeit a
precocious and spoiled child, to use this terminology. Rousseau sought a
way out of this, man's condition, not through divine grace but through
education and political reorganization. The tangible goal was the achievement of a special kind of freedom for man.

Freedom

NATURAL man is perfectible precisely because he is in a state of innocence, without pride; but being innocent, he is also without freedom. In
being perfected, man loses his innocence and becomes infected with
artificiality. He now has the capacity to become free, but is nevertheless
a slave to his own spurious appetites and those of his fellows. His condition, we have seen, is both better and worse than that of natural man;
but in any event there is no turning back. What one must strive for is
freedom (liberté), which Rousseau many times defines as freedom "to
obey a law which we prescribe for ourselves."[22]

This conception of freedom is subjectivistic, for it points back into the

21 "Origin of Inequality," p. 190.
22 Social Contract, Bk. I, Ch. 8.

individual. But, as we have seen, the law man prescribes for himself as a sentient being is not the product of mere emotional whim. Rousseau was not an Epicurean. His quest for freedom did not lead to pleasure; nor, in one sense, did it lead to "goodness," which he tended to associate with the state of innocence; but rather to virtue in the classical sense of *virtus*, manly strength, excellence, and self-control. This goal was made necessary by society, but was also in part made possible by society. Rousseau's frequent praise of ancient Sparta was not accidental. Nor could Kant have been as impressed as he was by Rousseau had his freedom meant only lack of restraint: "Rousseau's ethics is not an ethics of feeling, but the most categorical form of a pure ethics of obligation [*Gesetzes-Ethik*] that was established before Kant."[23]

It was the nineteenth-century romantic literary movement, the *Sturm und Drang*, that later perverted Rousseau's writings into a symbol of irrationalism and irresponsible individualism. That freedom is not a synonym for license for Rousseau is made clear in the dedicatory section of the *Second Discourse:* "I should have wished to live and die free, that is, so far subject to the laws that neither I nor anybody else should be able to cast off their honorable yoke. . . . no one within the State should be able to say he was above the law." Nor was Rousseau, that great revolutionary influence, one who encouraged revolutions: "Peoples once accustomed to masters are not in a condition to do without them. If they attempt to shake off the yoke they still more estrange themselves from freedom, as, by mistaking for it an unbridled license to which it is diametrically opposed, they nearly always manage, by their revolutions, to hand themselves over to seducers, who only make their chains heavier than before."[24]

Many critics of Rousseau have ignored all this qualification of freedom, and by mixing the right proportions of his life with his teachings have managed to come to a conclusion the exact opposite of the foregoing. Irving Babbitt said that Rousseau's "general readiness to subordinate his ethical self to his sensibility is indubitable."[25] And W. H. Hudson wrote, ". . . he talked unceasingly of freedom; but freedom for him meant not that true liberty which is to be achieved only through cheerful obedience to the eternal laws of life, but simply absence of obligation and responsibility. He had no will-power and no moral fibre."[26]

23 Cassirer, *The Question of Jean-Jacques Rousseau*, p. 96. See also Immanuel Kant's "Idea for a Universal History" (1784), in Carl J. Friedrich, ed., *The Philosophy of Kant* (New York: Modern Library, 1949), p. 126.
24 "Origin of Inequality," Dedicatory section, p. 145.
25 *Rousseau and Romanticism* (1919) (New York: Noonday Press [Meridian Books], 1955), p. 130.
26 William Henry Hudson, *Rousseau and Naturalism in Life and Thought* (Edinburgh: T. & T. Clark, 1903), p. 111.

Rousseau's ethical position was, to be sure, relativistic. He appealed to no fixed metaphysical standard; but this lack of absolutes merely strengthened the logic of his call for community, rather than the logic of anarchy. For without a metaphysical base from which to challenge the norms of a given society, Rousseau's individual found his salvation in community or nowhere.[27] The individual alone can never be emancipated from his slavery. All of us in a given society are free or we are all slaves. Politics for Rousseau was thus central to the very existence of the individual, central in a way minimal-government liberals were never quite able to understand.

Sovereignty and the General Will

STANDING alone, *The Social Contract*, Rousseau's most famous political work, is something of a puzzle. In the context of his problem of freedom, however, it can be understood as an unsuccessful yet inspired attempt to make man free while in society, that is, to make legitimate his chains. Seen in this light, the alleged contradiction between the "individualist" first part and the "collectivist" second part dissolves, or at least resolves into an understandable tension.

Rousseau is concerned with what is right in society. "I shall endeavor to unite what right [*droit*] permits with what interest prescribes," a hopeless task, no doubt, but well worth the effort. He first establishes that society, while basic, is nevertheless artificial: ". . . the social order is a sacred right which serves as a basis for all other [rights]. Yet this right comes not from nature; it is therefore founded on conventions. The question is, what those conventions are."[28] Immediately we see that the convention known as the social contract does not serve the same purpose at all that it did for Hobbes, Locke, or Paine, i. e., to preserve natural rights. For Rousseau, all rights are born out of the social order. And we already know that man has no real choice of whether or not to be brought out of the state of nature. The accidents of history drag him out. *The Social Contract* is not, therefore, an aptly titled work.

NATURAL SOCIETY

Since civil society is not natural, the family is the only natural society. But even families are natural only so long as the children need the father's protection. If they manage to hang together after that time, they become

27 Of course it is just as plausible to say that his avoidance of metaphysics was a deliberate result of his faith in community as to say that the absence of a metaphysical base left him with no alternative but faith in community.

28 *Social Contract*, Bk. I, Introduction and Ch. 1.

for Rousseau conventional. Although in the *Second Discourse* he had opposed the paternalism of Filmer and Bossuet, Rousseau was not opposed
to the family as an institution; but perhaps on the basis of personal experience, he could not regard it as the kind of purely ethical community
he was seeking. Thus, if Rousseau's concept of nature was deeper than
Locke's, it was narrower than Aristotle's. When Aristotle spoke of natural slaves, for example, he mistook, said Rousseau, the effect for the
cause. That society can give a man a slavish mentality is no proof that
it was natural and proper that it should have done so. Grotius opposes
slavery, but on equally specious grounds. Grotius seeks to establish
rights by appeal to fact, says Rousseau, not entirely accurately. Rousseau,
ever the moralist, does not appeal to "facts." He wants to establish what
is right, it would seem, not simply what is existent. His critique of the
position of might makes right is classic in its simplicity, a model for all
who follow: "Force is a physical power; I do not see what morality
can result from its effects. . . . If it is necessary to obey by force, there
can be no occasion to obey from duty. . . . If in saying, 'Let us obey the
powerful,' they mean to say 'Let us yield to force,' the precept is good,
but it is superfluous, for it never is or can be violated."[29] Nor can a man
voluntarily give up his liberty, says Rousseau in a direct rebuttal to
Hobbes, for liberty is of the essence of the "quality of man" and to give
up liberty is to give up being a man.

CONTRACT AND SOVEREIGN

In Chapters, 6, 7, and 8 of Book I Rousseau takes up the social contract,
the establishment of the sovereign, and the civil state. The contract
amounts to an "act of association" that "produces a moral and collective
body" and involves "the total alienation of each associate, and all his
rights, to the whole community." What is formed by this association is a
"public person," which took formerly the name of 'city'[30] and now takes
that of 'republic' or 'body politic.' It is called by its members 'State' when
it is passive, 'Sovereign' when in activity. . . ." Rousseau's political community is really a modern version of the ancient Greek *politeia*, or
"soul of the *polis*." In describing it, he is clearly reacting against the
excessive individualism and atomism of the English contractualists. For
the latter, the body politic was an artificial, constitutional structure; for
Rousseau, it is a natural, moral association.

The sovereign created by this association is not the determinate figure
it was for Hobbes but is rather the whole body of citizens. The concept

29 *Ibid.*, Ch. 3.
30 Houses do not make a city, houses make a town. *Citizens* make a city; but
few French authors seem to realize this, says Rousseau in a stern footnote.

gives rise to the same questions of the moral basis for obedience by subjects and command by sovereigns that we discussed in connection with Hobbes, but in addition Rousseau's "popular sovereignty" raises the special problem of protecting individuals from themselves. Each individual "contracting, as it were, with himself, is engaged under a double character," as a member of the state acted upon and the sovereign acting. The sovereign cannot be bound by law since it is the source of law. There is no cause for alarm here, Rousseau assures us somewhat too hastily, because "the Sovereign, being formed only of the individuals who compose it, neither has, nor can have, any interest contrary to theirs. . . . The Sovereign, by its nature, is always everything it ought to be."[30a]

FORCED TO BE FREE

It is difficult to accept the notion that the individuals who compose the sovereign are always everything they ought to be. Rousseau thinks they are, however, when in their sovereign capacity, for then they are guided by the general will and then only are they true citizens. The general will (*volonté général*) is the perfect expression of common interest. Each individual partakes of it, but each individual also has a private will (*volonté particulière*), which is the expression of noncommon, particular, selfish, and hence potentially dangerous interests, which if given sway could "cause the ruin of the body politic . . . therefore, to prevent the social compact from becoming an empty formula . . . whoever refuses to obey the general will shall be compelled to it by the whole body: this in fact only forces him to be free. . . . This alone renders all civil engagements justifiable, and without it they would be absurd, tyrannical, and subject to the most enormous abuses."[30b] This is the most significant of the several contradictions with which Rousseau has been charged. Force can have no moral effect, but man can be forced to be free. To prevent tyranny, individuals may have to be tyrannized. Though possibly mistaken, Rousseau was not venally deceptive and we have no grounds for questioning the genuineness of his objective of a free individual in a free society. We must give him the chance to follow through.

By entering the social contract the individual gives up his "natural liberty," the "unlimited right to all which tempts him," but he exchanges it for "civil liberty, which is limited by the general will. . . . In addition we might add to the other acquisitions of the civil state that of moral liberty, which alone renders a man master of himself; for it is *slavery* to be under the impulse of appetite, and *freedom* to obey a law which we prescribe for ourselves. But I have already said too much on

30a *The Social Contract*, Bk. I, Ch. 7.
30b *Ibid.*

this head, and the philosophical sense of the word 'liberty' is not at present my subject."[31]

Rousseau has taken us into some murky waters but deliberately avoids the "philosophical" discussion that seems necessary if we are to follow through. Actually, the problem is not so much how force, which is unfree, can free a man. We know, do we not, how students can be forced to read books by the threat of an examination and by this process learn to read books of their own volition? It is a simple case of immoral but necessary means being used toward a moral end. The problem is much more the practical one of deciding whether the process of forcing to be free is the action of one group, the sovereign citizens, on another group, the nonsovereign, nonfree, noncitizens; or the action of one part of the individual's psyche, that motivated by the general will, acting upon another part, that motivated by the particular will. Rousseau also leaves somewhat obscure whether or not this process is an ideal not yet attained, or is an ongoing function existing in some sense in actual bodies politic. In one of his most controversial statements Rousseau says that "the general will is always right and tends always to the public advantage." Does he mean that the general will is a standard of rightness by which to judge the imperfections of present policies? Or does he think the general will is actually embodied in some present policies? Does he think there is a mysterious force (it cannot be a rational idea, for *volonté* and *raison* can scarcely be made synonyms) actually at work in society leading all of us to do what is right?

Rousseau apparently meant all of these things (and more, for the "Legislator" is yet to be heard from). He characteristically wanted to have his cake and eat it too. In the fashion of a romantic who distrusts abstract formulas, he wanted to go to the heart of reality, to deal with the concrete actualities of life. At the same time he was driven by a vision of the good society and the good individual in that society that had a counterpart nowhere on earth.[32] He invented a new term, the "general will," and perhaps without quite knowing what he was doing, he used it in two different ways. Who or what is forcing us to be free makes a great deal of difference. If it is our better selves winning a battle over our worse selves, that is one thing. If it is a mob, or a man with shiny buttons and a rubber truncheon, that is quite another thing. It is in many ways unfortunate that the power of Hobbesian logic pressed Rousseau into a mold not best adapted to his argument.

31 *Social Contract*, Bk. I, Ch. 8.
32 However: "There is still in Europe one country capable of receiving legislation: it is the island of Corsica. . . . I have a presentiment that this little island will some day astonish Europe." *Ibid.*, Bk. II, Ch. 10. One is reminded of Plato's temporal hopes for Syracuse.

THE GENERAL WILL ILLUSTRATED

There are many helpful illustrations of the general will conceived as our better self: our general will tells us that we ought to get up at seven A.M.; our particular will leads us to turn off the alarm and roll over. Our general will tells us that we need a strong army; our particular will wants to keep us out of the draft. The drunkard's general will tells him that he should have stopped drinking several hours ago, his particular will gives him one more for the road. If the police throw him in jail, he is really throwing himself in jail. And he is free because his restraint is self-imposed. He really wants to do right and in his heart of hearts knows better. That is why, when sober, he accepted the law against public drunkenness and chose to remain a member of the community that adopted this law. So far so good. But we are talking about this or that individual. When we bring the sovereign into the picture, when we try to institutionalize the operation of the general will and make it produce binding rules for all men, then confusion returns. It has been said that the sovereign is like the quarterback on a football team. When he calls the signals, every team member carries out the play to the best of his ability, even though other players might have called different signals. They know and accept the fact that the whole team has to follow signals or be ruined and someone has to call them. Thus every signal represents the operation of the general will for that miniature society.

The trouble is, of course, that the political society of, say, France is not a football team with its single, simple objective and face-to-face relationships. And the sovereign is not a quarterback but "a collective being" that cannot be represented except by itself: "the power may be transmitted but not the will." Rousseau was firm in denying the possibility of delegating sovereignty. If a people give themselves a representative, they are no longer free, for their laws are no longer self-prescribed. The "city" is destroyed. It is interesting to note that Rousseau identifies representation with the "absurd and iniquitous" feudal system, and is led back to the classical ideal of a state small enough for all citizens to participate. In such a state, public affairs more and more replace merely private affairs "in the minds of the citizens."[33] Sovereignty is hence "inalienable." It is also "indivisible." "For the will is general or it is not; it is

---

[33] *Social Contract*, Bk. III, Ch. 15. That thought, morality, and excellence were above all aspects of the public as opposed to the private realm in the classical world, by contrast with the reverse in modern times, is a point made with much force by Hannah Arendt in *The Human Condition* (Chicago: Univ. of Chicago Press, 1958), Ch. 2. She attaches the greatest significance to Rousseau as the theorist of the intimate who, for the sake of protecting the intimate, resurrected a classical ideal of politics to be used against the "leveling demands of the social." After Rousseau came the rise of the novel, "the only entirely social art form," and a "decline of all the more public arts, especially architecture."

either the will of the whole body of people, or only of a part." Law and the general will must be absolutely general, and many things that have been regarded as acts of sovereignty are not so. They are not acts of law but particular applications of law. Declaring war is one example.[34]

It would seem, then, that the sovereign is the body of people as a whole *when* they agree on a general policy for the common good, which may be called law. In this sense, ". . . the voice of the people is in fact the voice of God."[35] But when it comes to the practical determination of this will, Rousseau runs into trouble. In an important footnote he says, for example, "To make the will general it is not always necessary that it should be unanimous, but it is indispensably necessary that every vote be counted: any formal exclusion destroys generality."[36] Again, after saying that the general will is always right, he says "but it does not follow that the deliberations of the people have always the same rectitude. Our will always seeks our own good, but we do not always perceive what it is. The people are never corrupted, but they are often deceived, and only then do they seem to will what is bad."[37] He then distinguishes between the general will and the will of all, which is the "sum of private wills."

Thus the general will not only does not have have to be discovered through unanimity, it is not assured even through unanimity: ". . . the generality of the will depends less on the number of voters than on the common interest which unites them.[38] It must be general in its object as well as its essence." Every vote must be counted, but in the last analysis the votes do not tell us anything. Rousseau is reluctant to transform mere quantity into quality, yet he does not give us any test beyond generality by which to recognize the general will when we see it. It cannot be represented, yet its power may be delegated.[38a] No wonder that both the ideal of popular sovereignty and the ideal of totalitarian uniformity have been found in the concept of the general will; and no wonder that hard-headed analysts have for generations been suspicious of its vagaries.

34 *Social Contract*, Bk. II, Ch. 2.
35 "Political Economy," p. 238.
36 *Social Contract*, Bk. II, Ch. 2.
37 *Ibid.*, Ch. 3.   38 *Ibid.*, Ch. 4.
38a Kant overcame most of these difficulties by simply lifting the general will unequivocally into the normative realm and declaring that only that which is always right can be the general will. Given a social order symbolized by a wholly normative general will and given the existence of a government somewhat at odds with this symbol because it must, as a practical matter, be involved with representation, we can see in this situation what Frederick Watkins has seen, a counterpart of medieval dualism. See his *Political Tradition of the West* (Cambridge: Harvard Univ. Press, 1948), pp. 104-05. Chapter 4, on the general will, is excellent.

Voting, Unanimity, and General Will

Rousseau himself seems to backtrack in Book IV of *The Social Contract* when he discusses the suffrage: ". . . the general will is found by counting the votes. When, therefore, the motion which I oppose carries, it only proves to me that I was mistaken, and that what I believed to be the general will was not so." If a reconciliation of this statement with earlier ones is in any way possible, it is by looking carefully at the context of the second statement. In the first place, Rousseau is trying, almost against his nature, to appeal to his reader at a practical level. It is also clear that, although the distinction is not mentioned here, Rousseau is still very conscious of the substantive difference between the general will and the will of all, a difference that belies their surface similarity. He cites elections in the Roman Republic, where from fear or flattery the people abandon deliberation. On such occasions their votes, while unanimous, are not true votes at all but become mere acclamations. The general will is not found by such a vote. Careful precautions must be taken to prevent such invalid demonstrations, precautions "which must vary as the general will is more or less easy to ascertain."[39] The larger the groups and the more factions there are the harder it is to ascertain the general will. And again the generality of the object of the general will must be recalled. "When the people of Athens, for example, nominated or cashiered their chiefs, decreed honors to one, imposed punishments on another . . . the people, properly speaking, had then no longer a general will; they acted no longer as Sovereign but as magistrate."[40]

Yet there is only one law that requires unanimous consent, and that is the social contract. He who opposes the social contract is simply a foreigner, a noncitizen. Thereafter, as in Locke, residence constitutes consent (note, however, that the dissidents are never referred to as being put back into a state of nature; society will exist regardless). In other votes a majority is necessary to bind the voter. Rousseau is not blind to the problem this requirement raises in light of the priority he attaches to his particular conception of freedom in society. He poses the question himself: "How are the opposers free when they are in submission to laws to which they have never consented?"

I answer that the question is not fairly stated. The citizen consents to all the laws, to those which are passed in spite of his opposition, and even to those which sentence him to punishment if he violates any one of them. The constant will of all the members of the State is the general will; it is by that they are citizens and free. When any law is proposed in the assembly of the people, the question is not precisely to inquire whether they approve the proposition

<hr/>

39 *Social Contract*, Bk. IV, Ch. 2.   40 *Ibid.*, Bk. II, Ch. 4.

or reject it, but if it is conformable or not to the general will, which is their will.[41]

Even if the theory is unambiguous, the practice most certainly is not. The general will seems clearly relevant only to acceptance of the idea of law itself, yet Rousseau speaks as if many propositions could be passed in conformity to it. But at this level the voter's will is somehow made separable from his preference for or against any concrete proposal, and a practical test whether a vote is cast in the true spirit of the general will or as an unreflective piece of selfishness is never offered. Rousseau does offer two practical rules of thumb: the more serious and important the deliberations are, the closer the number of votes should approach unanimity; and the greater the necessity for swift action, the smaller may be the majority. Any skillful politician would be delighted to use these as loopholes by which to jam or railroad suggested legislation.

The Legislator and Civil Religion

EARLY in *The Social Contract* Rousseau urged the necessity of avoiding factions or "partial societies" in order that "every citizen should speak his opinion entirely from himself."[42] But apparently many citizens or potential citizens are incapable of grasping and expressing the general will that is within them. The problem of counting votes, thus, is not the only practical problem connected with the general will.

Men can be made moral and free by obedience to the general will but not until they have seen it—or felt it. All men are equal as citizens but not until the city has been achieved. This achievement does not fall willy-nilly on the people, but upon one among them who is superior, the legislator. He it is who must protect the people from "the seducing voice of private wills." The challenge to the legislator, therefore, is no small one:

Those who dare to undertake the institution of a people must feel themselves capable, as it were, of changing human nature, of transforming each individual, who by himself is a perfect and solitary whole, into a part of a much greater whole, from which he in some measure receives his being and his life. . . . of substituting a moral and partial existence instead of the physical and independent existence which we have all received from nature.

The legislator is a man of "superior intelligence, acquainted with all the passions of men but liable to none of them . . . whose happiness was

41 *Ibid.*, Bk. IV, Ch. 2.   42 *Ibid.*, Bk. I, Ch. 3.

independent of ours, but who still condescended to make us the object of his care. . . ."[43] The image is strikingly similar to that of Plato's philosopher-king, and it is significant that with the exception of Calvin, all Rousseau's examples of great lawmakers are taken from antiquity. When we understand the magnitude of Rousseau's problem and the daring of his solution we are not surprised by his statement that "legislation is at the highest point of perfection which human talents can attain."[44]

Nevertheless, unlike Plato's philosopher-king, this genius among men must only propose laws and not directly command men, or else "private aims" might "defile the sanctity of his work." He is not the sovereign, for his proposed laws in each case must be submitted to the free vote of the people so that each citizen has the opportunity to be free by imposing his own restraints. No dictator here, apparently.

But such wise men who try to address themselves to the vulgar in their own language instead of the language of the vulgar "cannot possibly make themselves understood." And not being understood, they will be rejected. "It is not enough to say to the citizens, *be good;* they must be taught to be so; and even example, which is in this respect the first lesson, is not the sole means to be employed; patriotism is the most efficacious. . . ."[45] And the most efficacious form of patriotism is "civil religion." The legislators' wisdom must be clothed in the authority of divine sanction. They must "attribute to the gods what has proceeded from their own wisdom."

Whatever its potentialities, Rousseau's "civil religion" was conceived not as a device to enslave people but to free them. It was the necessary tool of communication by which the legislature could channel popular feeling toward the general will and away from particular wills. It is also a reflection of Rousseau's classicism, a harking back to the period when "each State, having its peculiar cult as well as its own form of government, did not distinguish its gods from its laws."[46] In that time men did not fight for their gods, since each nation had its own gods, which were not assumed to watch over other nations or require the conversion of foreigners. Men fought wars for themselves. Israel was a limited exception; but Christianity, of course, was the great exception, bringing with it "a perpetual conflict for jurisdiction which has made any system of good polity impossible in Christian states."[47] Rousseau praises the intention of Hobbes' clear-cut Erastian solution to this problem, but almost wistfully observes that the interest of the priesthood

43 This and the preceding quotation are from *ibid.*, Bk. II, Ch. 7.
44 *Ibid.*
45 "Political Economy," p. 246.
46 *Social Contract*, Bk. IV, Ch. 8.   47 *Ibid.*

would in fact defeat it. Rousseau sets apart from the religion of the priest the "simple religion of the Gospel, the true theism" which is the "religion of man" as distinguished from the "religion of the citizen." The former should be no bother at all to the latter and, presumably, vice versa. The religion of the priest is a dangerous confusion of the two. Rousseau makes out a plausible case that a society of dedicated Christians with their eyes focused only on the other world would fly to pieces, indeed would probably be impossible.

What remains for Rousseau is,

a purely civil profession of faith, the articles of which it is the business of the Sovereign [Legislator? Magistrate?] to arrange, not precisely as dogmas of religion, but as sentiments of sociability, without which it is impossible to be either a good citizen or a faithful subject. The Sovereign has no power by which it can oblige men to believe them, but it can banish from the State whoever does not believe them, not as an impious person, but as an unsociable one. . . . But if any one, after he has publicly subscribed to these dogmas, shall conduct himself as if he did not believe them, he is to be punished by death. He has committed the greatest of all crimes: he has lied in the face of the law.[48]

The civil religion was not conceived as pre-empting the rights of all religions: ". . . all religions that tolerate others ought to be tolerated, so long as their dogmas discover nothing contradictory to the duties of a citizen." This tolerance, Rousseau made perfectly clear, did not apply to the Roman Church, which, he said, holds that there is no salvation outside its confines.

It is not hard to imagine how an elite group can control a populace by manipulating the symbols of an ingenious ideology. It has been done before and it will be done again. But even the most vigorous of Rousseau's defenders are hard put to explain, let alone justify, how the sovereign, i. e., all the citizens motivated by a general will, can put over an *ersatz* religion on all the people and punish by death the somewhat subjective crime of lying about one's beliefs, without surrendering entirely the condition of every citizen speaking his opinion "entirely from himself."

There is no reason to question Rousseau's goal at this point. He thought that civil religion was a necessary mythological mechanism for deceiving the unfree into freedom; but the relationship created suggests that of oppressor-oppressee much more than teacher-pupil. Belief would not be induced so much as the outward appearance of belief would be compelled. Thus, in a work that skillfully defends the thesis that Rousseau is a liberal, John W. Chapman nevertheless grants that "the

48 *Ibid.*

purpose of the civil religion may be to preserve man's political freedom, but it is a means which destroys his moral freedom and dignity. This is surely sufficient to make it totalitarian."[49]

Conclusion

ALL things begin in mystique and end in politics, said Péguy. Rousseau had good reason to believe this. Preoccupied with the torments of his own soul, he could nevertheless say toward the end of the *Confessions,* "Everything is related to politics." His drive to make life whole, to reconcile the warring demands of individuality and sociability, was overwhelming. The goodness, not to say the holiness, of unity was his underlying theme, and this led him inevitably to attempt political-historical solutions.

The "solution" of the general will was not enough to bridge all disunities and answer all questions. Many lines of Rousseau's thought were truncated and incomplete. For one thing, there was the problem of his relativism, which can be illustrated at both ends of the political scale. Each human group, Rousseau recognized in the *Discourse on Political Economy,* has its own general will; but this general will, judged by the interests of a higher community, becomes a particular will. Thus factions were a great social evil for Rousseau because they threatened unity. But the unity of the general will itself is destroyed if general wills in one context become particular wills in another. Do big general wills from little general wills grow, or don't they?

The city-state, or, at the most, national, limits of Rousseau's political community seemed to preclude any general will for the world. Is the problem of law, then, irrelevant to the world as a whole? Must war be the normal method for determining international policy? Rousseau had no answer. He seemed less cramped by temporal limits, however, than he did by spatial limits. His thought leaped about history more easily than it leaped about the eighteenth-century world. In shielding Émile from the influence of his own society, for example, Rousseau may merely have been preparing him for life in a future and greater society.

Another problem is the subjectivism of Rousseau's religious, metaphysical, and epistemological views—insofar as he had any. Every man, in a sense, stands alone. Although he can find freedom only in a com-

---

49 *Rousseau—Totalitarian or Liberal* (New York: Columbia Univ. Press, 1956), p. 86. Chapman argues that despite Rousseau's divergence from the early so-called classical liberalism, his theory of the general will is "remarkably similar to the modern liberal doctrine of the deliberative state." *Ibid.,* p. 92.

munity, the more free he is the more alone he is: he must vote for himself, speak for himself, think for himself, believe for himself. The virtuous man, like the natural man, listens to his own heart and that is enough. Man is made free in this way, as he is for the twentieth-century existentialist; but is such freedom conducive to the particular kind of social unity Rousseau wanted?

A third problem is presented by a strongly stated but weakly reinforced goal of equality. As freedom was Rousseau's great positive goal, inequality was his great negative evil. As with the early liberals, however, equality and inequality were treated as political concepts having little to do with economics. Although he denounced the rich for their political machinations, Rosseau was plainly uninterested in the inequalities of property *per se*, or even in the plight of the poor. But can an economically divided community be a politically united community?

These and many other questions Rousseau leaves unanswered. Nevertheless, his enduring greatness derives from his having raised the right questions, not from his having answered them. His vision of a long-outdated and even irrelevant *polis* was so graphic, his attempt to erect a community that could absorb the individual while still freeing him was so poignant, that his influence is still felt.

The French Revolution, only half understanding Rousseau, clumsily tried to make the new society and the new man he called for. Romantic poets and novelists tried to ascertain the quality of the "real man" and lay his inner self before the public, in part because Rousseau had done so. Criminologists and educators began to consider the power and guilt of society in producing individual behavior, kindergartens were started, and child-centered education eventually developed, in part because Rousseau had raised some questions. At second or third or twentieth hand, perhaps, dictators adapted Rousseau's "civil religion" to their own use. And democrats were given a concept of law and a standard of popular participation in politics that still have much to commend them. For we still worry—or perhaps we have only begun to worry—about passive conformism, political apathy, and a weak sense of community as problems for the "highly civilized" democratic nations.

CHAPTER

8 | *Hume*

DAVID HUME'S cool skepticism appears to be equally characteristic of his philosophy and his life. To the age of rationalist enthusiasm he was a brake. But to the subsequent age of empiricist enthusiasm he was a stimulus. Always he seemed to fit into a position of dual influence: a liberal who was conservative, a secularist who accepted religion, a man of the Enlightenment with doubts about the source of light.

Life

THIRST FOR FAME

Hume was born in Edinburgh, Scotland, on April 26, 1711, the son of Joseph Hume (or, as it was then spelled, Home), offspring of a long and distinguished Scottish line, which the son mentions with pride in his briefest of brief autobiographies.[1] His genius, his love of learning, and his "thirst for literary fame" (which, he tells us, was his life's "ruling passion") appeared early in life. Yet Hume was a long time in finding himself. The schools of Scotland did not challenge him; the profession of the law, which his family sought for him, did not excite him, though his skill at handling legal phraseology was unquestionable. For a brief time he tried employment as a clerk to a trader in Bristol, with little satisfaction.

---

1 *My Own Life*, reprinted as Appendix A to Ernest Campbell Mossner, *The Life of David Hume* (Austin: Univ. of Texas Press, 1954). The discussion above is indebted to this distinguished recent work.

Overcoming a great melancholy and an attack of scurvy, he finally left England for France, where, following a plan of "very rigid frugality," he stayed for three years and wrote his greatest work, the *Treatise of Human Nature*. This young man who was so slow to find himself had written one of the world's masterpieces of philosophy by the age of twenty-five. Book I, "Of the Understanding," and Book II, "Of the Passions," were published in January, 1739; Book III, "On Morals," the next year. "Never literary attempt was more unfortunate than my *Treatise of Human Nature*. It fell *deadborn from the press. . . .*" Hume exaggerated. By those who read it, the work was well received; but its author had hoped for a best-seller.

Later, Hume condensed and rewrote Book I of the *Treatise* as the *Essay Concerning Human Understanding*. The book was more readable but less substantial, and it is one of the sad facts of Hume's life that his concern for popular literary fame seemed to lead him away from the continuing extension, testing, and development of the ideas in the *Treatise*, a task of which he was fully capable. Fame was, at least in part, the spur that induced Hume to spend his later years on political and historical subjects at the expense of deeper philosophical penetration. Political theory has been blessed in this way, and perhaps we should ask no more than one masterpiece from any man. But neither can we deny the fact of unfulfilled promise.

Back in Edinburgh, Hume published anonymously *Essays Moral and Political* (in two volumes, 1741 and 1742). Of the twenty-seven essays in that collection, some of the lighter, Addison-like efforts were purged by the author in the long series of later editions. Of the rest, the political essays—"Of the First Principles of Government," "That Politics May Be Reduced to a Science," "Of the Parties of Great Britain," and so on— were more popular than the philosophic ones. Hume has been accused of deleting indiscreetly democratic passages from his essays as they moved through subsequent editions. Although, through cutting and re-editing, he moved continually in the direction of greater political caution, it is fair to say that he did not seriously alter any expressions of his basic convictions.

TRAVELS AND FURTHER PUBLICATIONS

In 1746 Hume joined General St. Clair in his ill-fated expedition to Canada, serving him as secretary and later as judge advocate. When St. Clair went to the court of Turin, Hume went along with him as aide-de-camp, "so that the philosopher was obliged to encase his more than portly, and by no means elegant, figure in a military uniform."[2] The

2 Thomas Huxley, *Hume* (London: Macmillan, 1881), p. 28.

Enquiry Concerning Human Understanding (first titled *Philosophical Essays*) was published in 1748, while Hume was away from England. Between 1749 and 1751, Hume was back at the family home in Ninewells, in Berwickshire along the Tweed River valley, writing the *Dialogues of Natural Religion, Enquiry Concerning the Principles of Morals,* and the *Political Discourses.* The last-named, published in 1752, contained twelve essays, seven of which dealt with economics from a free-market perspective, reflecting and affecting Hume's friendship with the young Adam Smith.

In that same year Hume was elected librarian of the Edinburgh Faculty of Advocates, despite the charges of irreligion made against him, charges that had kept him from an Edinburgh University post years before. The new post was negligible except that it gave him access to a large library, which he used to good advantage in writing the *History of England,* published in volume after volume between 1754 and 1762. During this period he also wrote the *Natural History of Religion,* published in 1757.

In 1763 Hume went to France as secretary to Lord Hertford, the new ambassador. The bland countenance of *"le gros David, le bon David"* was the delight of Parisian society, for whom any visiting philosopher was a good show. His acquaintance there with Rousseau led to Rousseau's nightmarish trip to England, referred to in Chapter 7, and his introduction to the Comtesse de Boufflers led to a delicate but hopeless love affair. Moving up the administrative ladder, Hume became Under-Secretary of State in London for two years, beginning in 1767. By contrast with our twentieth-century image of the harried bureaucrat, Hume's life in this post was quiet and leisurely, and he casually mixed wide reading and personal correspondence with affairs of state.

He returned to Edinburgh in 1769, more or less to retire; he built his own house there the next year in order to live the comfortable and somewhat complacent life of a bachelor, whose hobby, incidentally, was cooking. In correspondence he fulminated against the English and radicals like Wilkes,[3] and worked over another edition of the *History* to "soften or expunge [he said] many villainous seditious Whig strokes which had crept into it." There he died, on August 25, 1776, of an intestinal disorder, after writing his will and the memorable five-page autobiography, *My Own Life.*

Skepticism, Empiricism, and Causation

HUME was a skeptic, which meant that he asked doubting questions about everything imaginable. But he was also part of a philosophic tradi-

3 See below, Chapter 9.

tion. The critics of rationalism and its religious offshoot, deism, included some of the most distinguished men of Hume's century: the earl of Shaftesbury, Bishop Berkeley, and the professor of moral philosophy at the University of Glasgow, Francis Hutcheson, prominent member of the "moral sense" school. Hume was respectful of this tradition, but his originality would not be contained by it. Back to Locke, Newton, Hobbes, Descartes, Bayle, Bacon, Cicero, and Seneca he went in his readings; and from the richness of his knowledge came a dedication to detached analysis that pruned away the theological speculations that marked Berkeley's and Hutcheson's attack on rationalism. Hume sent Hutcheson the manuscript of Book III of the *Treatise*. The older man commented that it "wants a certain warmth in the Cause of Virtue," to which Hume replied, ". . . I am perswaded [sic], that a Metaphysician may be very helpful to a moralist; tho' I cannot easily conceive these two Characters united in the same work. Any warm Sentiment of Morals, I am afraid, wou'd have the air of Declamation amidst abstract reasonings, & wou'd be esteemed contrary to good Taste."[4] Cool and cautious—that was Hume.

The caution that restrained his own passion enabled him to see and accept more readily the passions of others. "Reason is, and ought only to be, the slave of the passions," he wrote in the *Treatise of Human Nature*.[5] Despite his differences from the "moral sense" school, he agreed with them that a priori reason is not the source of morality and also that man is a naturally sympathetic creature and not one of Hobbes' warring beasts. On the other hand, by his close attention to Berkeley's argument for God, Hume was able to carry nontheological empiricism to a point of independence scarcely yet exceeded. By disproving the reality of the external world apart from our own perceptions, Berkeley had found God to be the inescapable ordering principle. Granting the irreducibility of our disconnected perceptions, Hume went further to ask the question: Is not the idea of God, like the idea of Matter, necessary to hold our perceptions together only so long as we assume the necessity of a continual operation of cause and effect in the world? Can we get along without assuming that everything is caused? Hume thought that we could.

The sweeping character of this assertion can hardly be exaggerated. All conclusions based on causal inference—obviously an overwhelming number of conclusions—become uncertain. Hume himself spoke of this proposition as a "revolution in philosophy." Ironically, Hume's doubts about causal inference, which would seem to imply abandoning the quest for universal knowledge and living from experiment to experiment, were

4 Mossner, *Hume*, p. 134.
5 *Treatise of Human Nature*, Bk. II, Part 3, sec. 3, L. A. Selby-Bigge, ed. (Oxford: Clarendon Press, 1896).

developed in the *Treatise of Human Nature* as part of a more or less traditional attempt to systematize all human knowledge. Moreover, in some ways, even his radical empiricism leaned heavily on the past. Hume's distinction between "impressions" (we might say "feelings") and "ideas" was largely a reaffirmation of Locke's empiricism and therefore retained the tincture of rationalist faith lurking in Locke's "true ideas."

Hume's unique contribution rested on another distinction, one that is crucial for all of modern logical empiricism: that between "demonstrable" and "moral" (we might say "experiential") knowledge. The former deals with the logical relations of ideas and is governed by rules of mathematics. The latter deals with matters of fact. In this realm there are no absolutely necessary propositions. Logically there is no logic of facts, and anything is possible. This, says Hume, is the realm of experience. In experience we *assume* a future conformable to the past. From causes that appear similar, we have come to expect similar effects. But our causal inferences cannot be proven by logical demonstration nor even validated by intuition. They are based, says Hume, on custom or habit.

However unprovable they may be, we nevertheless lean on causal inferences to survive. We piece together and make sense of our perceptions by noting their resemblance, their contiguity in space and time, and their constant conjunction. The operation of these three principles appears to Hume to be an invariable tendency of the human mind, a tendency that makes possible a belief in the external world and in true causation (i. e., a *necessary* connection between events). But it is habitual belief and natural impulse, not necessity, that permit us to act on these causal assumptions, just as it is individual preference and not necessity that designates our values. Each human being constructs his own world.

Hume was not fully content with his system of "moderate skepticism," especially in coping with the problem of the self and self-consciousness; and he was reluctant to draw radical conclusions from it. As he demonstrated in the *Dialogues Concerning Natural Religion*, his disinclination to be dogmatic led him to grant the tenability of common beliefs about religion.

The Critique of the Contractualists

SUCH skepticism not only tended to eliminate the easy faith in natural law characteristic of many Enlightenment writers, but also seemed to eliminate the historical optimism that was a part of that faith. This Hume accomplished without an appeal to a supernatural mystique, simply by using the tools of critical analysis so favored by the Enlightenment.

"Hume was something more than the Enlightenment incarnate, for his significance is that he turned against the Enlightenment its own weapons. And herein lies his importance as a conservative thinker."[6] He was a conservative without sentimental emotion. He was a utilitarian without grand schemes of reform. Using a variation of the associationist psychology adopted by Locke and later by the English utilitarians, he came to more realistic conclusions than either concerning the possibility of rational self-interest operating toward social harmony.

What strikes upon [men] with a strong and lively idea commonly prevails above what lies in a more obscure light . . . as everything that is contiguous to us, either in space or time, strikes upon us with such an idea . . . and commonly operates with more force than any object that lies in a more distant and obscure light. . . .

   This is the reason why men so often act in contradiction to their known interest; and in particular why they prefer any trivial advantage, that is present, to the maintenance of order in society, which so much depends on the observance of justice. The consequences of every breach of equity seem to lie very remote, and are not able to counterbalance any immediate advantage that may be reaped from it. They are, however, never the less real for being remote; and as all men are, in some degree, subject to the same weakness, it necessarily happens that the violations of equity must become very frequent in society, dangerous and uncertain.[7]

If men's interests cannot be assumed to be clearly perceptible to them, if natural sympathy rather than rational calculation draws men together, it follows that the contractualist view of society is defectively simple. Hume addresses himself to the subject in the essays "Of the Origin of Government" and "Of the Origin of Contract."[8] "Man, born in a family, is compelled to maintain society from necessity, from natural inclination, and from habit," thus Hume begins the first-named essay. All men are conscious of the need to maintain peace and order and of the contribution of justice to this end, he goes on. Yet because of "the frailty or perverseness of our nature" men do not follow the paths of justice unerringly. Sometimes a man's interest is promoted by fraud or rapine, but more often, as the foregoing quotation from the *Treatise* argued, present transient interests overshadow greater and more important ones. "This

   6 Sheldon Wolin, "Hume and Conservatism," *Am. Pol. Sci. Rev.*, Vol. 48 (1954), p. 1001.
   7 *Treatise*, Bk. III, Part 2, sec. 7.
   8 Charles W. Hendel, ed., *David Hume's Political Essays* (New York: Liberal Arts Press, 1953), pp. 39-61. All quotations from the *Essays* in the remainder of this chapter are taken from this book, which is reprinted from the last edition in Hume's lifetime (1777) of *Essays Moral and Political*. See also *Treatise*, Bk. III, Part 2, secs. 7-8.

weakness is incurable in human nature." As an agency to induce habits of obedience in support of justice, "government commences . . . casually and . . . imperfectly." And though strong and superior leaders may develop habits of good order, "in all governments there is a perpetual intestine struggle, open or secret, between Authority and Liberty, and neither of them can ever absolutely prevail in the contest." While liberty may be in one sense the principle of perfection in a civil society (Hume was not much bothered to distinguish between state and society), "still authority must be acknowledged essential to its very existence." Consequently, those governments commonly called "free"—the quotation marks are Hume's—are those that have managed to divide power and can keep the monarch in check without overturning him.

In "Of the Original Contract" he more systematically examines first the divine-right theorists, then the contractualists. With surprising sympathy and patience he neatly demolishes the theory of divine right. All men are under God and no "peculiar sacredness" can be discovered in the persons of kings. Again, seeking agreement rather than exploiting disagreement with the position he examines, Hume grants that in a sense there must have been a kind of consent exercised for primitives to have banded together for protection; however, "no compact or agreement, it is evident, was expressly formed for general submission, an idea far beyond the comprehension of savages." And the idea of rational consent to government in the contemporary world is even more hypothetical. In a sly dig at Locke, Hume refers to "philosophers who have embraced a party—if that be not a contradiction in terms." If these men would "look abroad in the world" they would find, whether in Persia or China, France or Spain, Holland or England, that political connections are "independent of our consent." "Obedience or subjection becomes so familiar that most men never make any inquiry about its origin or cause, more than about the principle of gravity. . . ." Moreover, "were you to preach, in most parts of the world, that political connections are founded altogether on voluntary consent or a mutual promise, the magistrate would soon imprison you as seditious. . . ." The simple and incontestable fact is that almost every present and past government has been "founded originally either on usurpation or conquest or both, without any pretence as a fair consent or voluntary subjection of the people."

Hume points out that the much-fêted Revolution of 1688 was really less of a revolution than a change in the succession and involved no contractual arrangement with the people. The bulk of ten million people acquiesced, to be sure, but did they have any choice in the matter? Hume thinks not, and his examination of governments of the past leads him to conclude that they were not much different in this respect. "My intention here is not to exclude the consent of the people from being one just foundation of government. . . . I only contend that it has very seldom had place in any degree, and never almost in its full extent and that, therefore, some other foundation of government must also be admitted."

Locke, of course, had said that acquiescence could be regarded as consent since a man was free to depart and live under another government. Again, Hume the realist speaks: "Can we seriously say that a poor peasant or artisan has a free choice to leave his country when he knows no foreign language or manners and lives from day to day by the small wages he acquires?"

Hume is concerned with reality but also with what is justifiable. And so, in a quite Burkean paragraph, he shows how a constant stress on individual consent would rip open the social fabric and lead to violence. The process of history cannot be stopped dead in its tracks to take a vote: ". . . as human society is in perpetual flux, one man every hour going out of the world, another coming into it, it is necessary in order to preserve stability in government that the new brood should conform themselves to the established constitution. . . ." Hume is careful not to base his conception of civic duty on a monistic conception of moral duties. He contrasts natural moral impulses—love of children, gratitude to benefactors, pity of the unfortunate, etc.—with moral duties arising only out of a sense of obligation—the keeping of promises, respect for others' property, and so on. Civil authorities are needed precisely because the latter actions, while moral, do not arise spontaneously; a bit of prodding is sometimes necessary. The authorities cannot rely on our promise to obey, given in some hypothetical contract, because we can and often do fall short of our promises. They need power as well as a promise. On the question "But to whom is allegiance due . . . who is our lawful sovereign?" Hume hedges a bit. He retreats into historical examples of usurpation, conquest, and succession, and concludes that in sovereignty, as in property, possession seems to be nine points of the law—which does not tell us whether it should be. Such a conclusion appears to be more statically conservative than Hume elsewhere appears. But the gist of his argument is not affected by this evasion. It can be summed up by his answer to the question of why government must be obeyed, "I readily answer, 'Because society could not otherwise subsist.' "

Politics as a Science

THE skepticism that shattered the bland Lockean assumptions about the origins of government might easily be thought to have dissolved as well the Lockean hope for a science of morals and, by implication, a science of politics. But in this respect, Hume seems more a child of the Enlightenment than its critic. He addresses himself to this question in the essay "That Politics May Be Reduced to a Science."

The title may be deceptive unless we note carefully what Hume means by "science." Hume's conception of a science of politics is not in accord with that of some of our more mathematically inclined contemporaries. Sophisticated algebraic formulas for handling questionnaire responses and voting statistics were not yet relevant. Basically, he was trying to prove, like Aristotle, that forms of government have certain predictable influences on the course of political development, influences that, if not absolutely causative, may be more determinative than the personalities of specific leaders. Nevertheless, the image of mathematical certainty does creep into his usage: "So great is the force of laws and of particular forms of government, and so little dependence have they on the humors and tempers of men, that consequences almost as general and certain may sometimes be deduced from them as any which the mathematical sciences afford us."

Note the prudent qualifications: "*almost* as general and certain may *sometimes* be deduced. . . ." The empirical evidence to support such generalizations about politics was to be drawn from the common materials of history. For example, Hume shows how, as was true in the Roman Republic before the Caesars, a democratic form that vests power in a collective rather than in a representative body leads with almost complete certainty to tumult, licentiousness, and anarchy. The methodology of this science of politics is the methodology of history, with the canons of sound evidence being very close to common sense. From the experience of England and Ireland he generalizes that "free governments" are likely to be the most oppressive to their provinces. "And this observation may, I believe, be *fixed* as a maxim of the kind we are here speaking of."

For all his caution, Hume was hoping for a kind of fixity that contemporary social scientists would be unlikely to expect. Moreover, he was seeking a science of morals antithetical to the value-free methodology of the contemporary social scientist and seemingly antithetical to his own epistemology, with its sharp distinction between matters of fact and matters of value. At least at a low level, an understanding of the good as well as the real was to be accomplished by Hume's method: "It may, therefore, be pronounced as a universal axiom in politics *that a hereditary prince, a nobility without vassals, and a people voting by their representatives form the best monarchy, aristocracy, and democracy.*" He cites an observation of Machiavelli concerning Alexander the Great as "one of those eternal political truths which no time nor accidents can vary."

This concern for the good and the wise and the eternal in political relationships is in keeping with a distinguished tradition of political speculation as well as with some of the special assumptions of the Enlightenment. But it does not always seem in keeping with Hume's analysis of causation earlier discussed. Is it a lapse of judgment, or methodological schizophrenia, that permits him to say in the essay "That Politics May Be Reduced to a Science": "Effects will always correspond to causes, and wise regulations in any commonwealth are the most valuable legacy that can be left to future ages"?

We would do well, on the one hand, to remember that in the eighteenth century "science" was still roughly a synonym for "philosophy" and philosophy was the term attached to the love of wisdom, not merely the pursuit of empirical truth. Science had not yet become essentially experimental, nor philosophy largely analytical. Hume could scarcely draw all the skeptical implications out of his epistemology that later students did. On the other hand, there is unquestionably a gap between his epistemology and his social theorizing. To say in one place that causality is an inference not amenable to rational proof, and in another place that a science of politics can prove that nonrepresentative democracy is a cause of anarchy does seem rather contradictory. Technically, Hume has no right to talk about historical causes in the way that he does. But he never questioned the inevitability of causal inference nor the fact that there were more and less reliable causal inferences. He simply denied their rational certitude.

His antirationalism does not, of course, make Hume "value-free." His attack on partisan zeal as a source of social instability becomes almost partisan in its zeal. And, ironically, it was probably this conception of the danger of faction that, sanctified as a conclusion of "science," most influenced James Madison's famous position on factions in the *Federalist* and afterward.[9] But if we rule Hume and other members out of the fraternity of social scientists on the grounds of partisanship, there would be few left.

Lest we oversimplify the contrast between Hume's political science and his epistemology, three things ought to be said. First, his philosophical works, especially Book III of the *Treatise* and parts of the *Essay Concerning Human Understanding*, are not devoid of the considerations raised in the essay on politics as a science. In the *Essay Concerning Human Under-*

9 See Douglass Adair, "'That Politics May Be Reduced to a Science': David Hume, James Madison, and the Tenth *Federalist*," *Huntington Library Quarterly*, Vol. 20 (1957), pp. 343-60. Adair effectively shows how Madison and his colleagues in the Convention were, in the eighteenth-century sense of the term, "making a genuinely 'scientific' attempt to discover the 'constant and universal principles' of any republican government in regard to liberty, justice, and stability."

standing[10] he asks, "How could *politics* be a science, if laws and forms of government had not a uniform influence upon society?" And he argues that the chief use of history "is only to discover the constant and universal principles of human nature, by showing men in all varieties of circumstances and situations, and furnishing us with materials from which we may form our observations and become acquainted with the regular springs of human action and behavior." There is a basic unity to all of Hume's work.

Second, like Locke, Hume displayed a practical bent, a bias toward action which led him into the world of affairs and kept the man of thought at least familiar with the man of action. This propensity tended to restrain any tendency toward a wholly radical and irresponsible subjectivism. Or perhaps a better way to put it would be to say that Hume was skeptical enough to be skeptical even of skepticism itself. In the final pages of the *Essay Concerning Human Understanding* he criticizes what he calls Pyrrhonism or excessive skepticism. And it is interesting to note that what overcomes Pyrrhonism is "action," "employment," and "the occupations of common life." Hume was neither a visionary nor an intellectual escapist. "Be a philosopher," he wrote, "but amidst all your philosophizing, be still a man."[11]

Third, having noted Hume's consistency and down-to-earthness, we are obliged also to recognize that both fail when Hume discusses natural law and his idea of a perfect commonwealth.[12] For one thing, reason, which has been eliminated as a source of morality and subordinated to passion, creeps back in disguise. "Calm" passions, which permit farsighted judgments, are recognized as superior to "violent" passions, which do not. This distinction reinforces Hume's conservatism, for he finds that men of education and property tend to be the most calm. And it is a requirement of Hume's political science that such calm judgments are necessary for the perception of "general and Universal rules." Moreover, while Hume's epistemology undermines natural law, it does not do so with finality. Rules of natural law, says Hume, are "invented" by man to cope with what may, without such rules, be natural and unrestrained appetites. Although for Hume they seem to have prudential rather than metaphysical sanction, he appears to believe in their necessity as strongly as any natural-law thinker. Yet their scope is narrowly conservative, in that they are confined exclusively to the domain of property rights. The "three fundamental laws of nature" are those "*of the stability of possession, of its transference by consent,* and *of the performance of promises.* It is on the strict ob-

10 Sec. 8, Part 1.
11 *Essay Concerning Human Understanding,* Sec. 1.
12 *Treatise,* Bk. II, Part 2, secs. 1-6; "Idea of a Perfect Commonwealth," in *Political Essays.*

servance of those three laws that the peace and security of human society entirely depend. . . . Society is absolutely necessary for the well-being of men; and these are as necessary to the support of society."[13]

The Balance of Power

THE political theorist is sometimes accused of spending all his time talking about what can and cannot be done, while the political scientist is, figuratively at least, out in the world doing it. By this test, Hume should be more acceptable as a colleague of political scientists than most of the men discussed in these pages. That Hume had an insight into the realities of politics transcending most of the legalistic and prescriptive theories of his day may be illustrated by looking at his discussions of the balance of power and the system of influence in English politics.

The term "balance of power," which today is usually applied to the relations between nations, was applied by Hume in the same way in his essay "Of the Balance of Power" (1752). In the essay he was able to point to the necessity of balancing nation against nation in the ancient world as a "desirable check" against top-heavy concentrations of power, and also to see England's military policy as an attempt to contain the assertive power of Austria and France. But he was detached enough to observe that England tends to err on the side of excess rather than prudence once a war has begun.

The balancing, moderating tendency that Hume both described and praised was found to operate not only in the realm of international relations, but also in domestic politics and the economy. Hume, the friend of Adam Smith, shared some of Smith's optimism about the balancing process that was supposed to take place automatically in a free market unhampered by mercantilist restrictions. But he also saw, as few of the early economic liberals did, the fact of and the necessity for a reciprocal relationship between public state power and private economic power: "As the ambition of the sovereign must entrench on the luxury of individuals, so the luxury of individuals must diminish the force and check the ambition of

13 *Treatise*, Bk. II, Part 2, sec. 6. Frederick Watkins observes that this is by no means an outmoded point of view. "Under the influence of scientific empiricism liberal theorists have been prone to adopt a position of mildly conservative utilitarianism. Rejecting *a priori* standards of political morality, they have tried to defend the institutions and practices of constitutional government as empirically superior manifestations of historical evolution. An aristocratic and conservative bias quite similar to that of Hume has normally been characteristic of the Western liberal attitude toward the traditions and aspirations of the non-Western majority of mankind." Frederick Watkins, ed., *Hume: Theory of Politics* (Austin: Univ. of Texas Press, 1953), p. xxv.

the sovereign."[14] His defense of equal opportunity in acquisition of property and the enjoyment of the fruits of one's labor was not based upon abstract rights of the individual, but upon the contention that "a too great disproportion among the citizens weakens any state."

The results, if not the rationale, behind Hume's preference for balance and moderation often place him close to the liberal tradition. It is the praiseworthy attribute of "civilized monarchies" as of republics that *"they are a government of laws, not of men."*[15] The liberty of the press is to be stoutly defended, not because it is a right, but because it is an advantage. Liberty of the press and mixed government mutually support each other. The spirit of the people must frequently be roused in order to curb the ambition of the court; ". . . the liberty of the press is so [thoroughly] essential to the support of our mixed government, this sufficiently decides the . . . question: *Whether this liberty be advantageous or prejudicial*, there being nothing of greater importance than the preservation of the ancient government, especially if it be a free one." The common sense of Hume's approach is conspicuous. "A man reads a book or pamphlet alone and coolly. . . . The liberty of the press . . . however abused, can scarce ever excite popular tumults or rebellion. . . . the *people* are no such dangerous monsters as they have been represented, . . . it is in every respect better to guide them like rational creatures than to lead or drive them like brute beasts."[16]

Though Hume was calm about the threat of a wholly popular government, he did conceive of it as a threat if unchecked by another power. Popular government would see the tyranny of faction subdivided into new factions. But, on the other hand, absolute monarchy would be a less spectacular but equally certain cause of death to the English Constitution, a "true Euthanasia" he called it. ". . . we have also reason to be more jealous of popular government because that danger is more terrible. This may teach us a lesson of moderation in all our political controversies."[17] Hume's opposition to parties, therefore, was not based on their challenge to monarchical power, which he regarded as healthy, but on their tendency to be immoderate.

Power and the System of Influence

SINCE, in terms of numbers, force is always on the side of the governed rather than the governors, the ultimate power and authority of govern-

14 "Of Commerce" (1752).
15 "Of Civil Liberty."
16 "Of the Liberty of the Press."
17 "Whether the British Government Inclines More to Absolute Monarchy or to a Republic."

ments, says Hume, always rests on opinion. In "Of the First Principles of Government" Hume finds this base of opinion to be composed of three aspects, opinion of "public interest," opinion of the "right to power," and opinion of the "right to property." He shows, with perhaps somewhat more realism than Machiavelli, the limits of fear as an instrument of governance, but he also deals with the limits of affection. More significant than either, thinks Hume, is the individual's capacity to invest the acts of governments with his own self-interest.

The remarkable perceptiveness of Hume the political analyst is nowhere better shown than in his explanation and defense of the system of influence in the English government. Like Madison, Hume accepted factions or parties as necessary evils that ought to be tolerated because to eliminate them would be a remedy worse than the disease. What could be hoped for was to keep them in check. Most dangerous were parties or factions of principle, for they tended to crystallize opinion around inflexible positions and to generate the intractable "enthusiasm" that Hume saw as the bane of orderly political life. In "Of the Parties of Great Britain" he found the Whigs and Tories to be far more agreed on fundamental assumptions than was commonly thought. The ambiguity of principle, the tendency to follow men rather than ideas, the pressures toward moderation, Hume approved of. "The Tories, as men, were enemies to oppression; and also, as Englishmen, they were enemies to arbitrary power. Their zeal for liberty was perhaps less fervent than that of their antagonists, but was sufficient to make them forget all their general principles when they saw themselves openly threatened with subversion of the ancient government."[18]

As Sheldon Wolin has pointed out,[19] admirers of the "balanced" English Constitution, such as Blackstone and Burke, failed to see as Hume did the degree to which the system of influence—patronage, bribes, ties of family, contracts, and so on—was an integral part of the balancing process between king and Commons. It was partly because this network of influence was hidden from view and involved with deeply habitual behavior that Hume could say, "To tamper . . . or try experiments merely upon the credit of supposed argument and philosophy can never be the part of the wise magistrate, who will bear a reverence to what carries the marks of age; and though he may attempt some improvements for the public good, yet will he adjust his innovations as much as possible to the ancient fabric and preserve entire the ancient pillars and supports of the constitution."[20]

18 In *Political Essays.* See also "Of Parties in General," reprinted in Watkins, *Hume: Theory of Politics,* pp. 168–76.
19 In "Hume and Conservatism."
20 "Idea of a Perfect Commonwealth."

The History of England and the Uses of History

AT about the age of thirty-five, Hume shifted from philosophy to history as his primary preoccupation. Even before, however, he had been more concerned than were most thinkers identified with the Enlightenment with the methodology of history.[21] As against some who would use his own skepticism to discredit historical studies altogether, Hume was able to vindicate historical knowledge by showing it to be a system of reasonable beliefs based on testimony. If such knowledge did not have absolute certitude, neither, in Hume's view, had any other kind of knowledge.

But when it came to *writing* history, Hume's accomplishments are more equivocal. In the first place, he was rather careless about sources, especially in dealing with the period before the Tudor monarchs. Sharing to some degree the antireligious and antihistorical bias of the Enlightenment, he was not really interested in historical epochs prior to his own. Hume's somewhat parochial history certainly did not always square with the tone of detachment he urged in many of his other writings: ". . . there is no subject in which we must proceed with more caution than in tracing the history of the arts and sciences, lest we assign causes which never existed and reduce what is merely contingent to stable and universal principles."[22]

Hume's reputation as a historian is blemished by the belief that he was mainly a Tory partisan. Such a judgment is derived not so much from the work itself as from the reaction to the work in some Whig quarters and Hume's exaggerated and somewhat bitter statement in his autobiography that after the "senseless clamour" of the Whigs over his book, alterations in future editions were "made all of them invariably to the Tory side." Hume's volume on the Stuarts had been greeted by the more rabid Whigs with charges of being Jacobite. But Horace Walpole himself wrote that the book, though "certainly with faults, I cannot help liking much. It is called Jacobite, but in my opinion it is only not *George-abite*." And Hume's publisher had early been impressed that "it is neither whig nor tory but truely imparshal." This was Hume's feeling also: "I have the impudence to pretend that I am of no party and have no bias. . . . With regard to politics . . . I think I am very moderate. My views of *things* are more conformable to Whig principles, my representations of *persons* to Tory prejudices."[23]

21 See *Treatise*, Bk. I, Part 3, secs. 4, 13.

22 "Of the Rise and Progress of the Arts and Sciences."

23 Quotations are from Mossner, *Hume*, pp. 614, 310, 303, and 311, respectively. See E. C. Mossner, "Was Hume a Tory Historian? Facts and Reconsiderations," *Journal of the History of Ideas*, Vol. 2 (1941), pp. 225-36.

Hume also produced reactions from some of the clergy, who charged him with irreligion. But the *History* much more than the *Treatise* was written with income in mind and Hume was not ashamed to admit that he wrote with an awareness of his audience: "A few Christians (and but few) think I speak like a Libertine in religion; be assured I am tolerably reserved on this head. . . . I composed it *ad populum* as well as *ad clerum*, and thought that scepticism was not in its place in a historical production."[24] In a later edition Hume actually removed two passages that had offended the clergy.

By our standards the *History* is neither dispassionate nor a testament to original research. But although it is a work based largely on the synthesis of others' research, and was loaded with what we would call value-judgments, it is by no means a mere partisan tract. The work has great literary merit, and this distinction overshadows its shortcomings as a history. In addition to the technical defects of Hume's history, however, there is a deeper difficulty, as R. G. Collingwood has pointed out. There was in the Enlightenment quest for a science of an unvarying human nature a remnant of what Collingwood calls classical "substantialism," that is, the view that only that which is unchanging is knowable. Because the essence of history is change, substantialism is antithetical to any view that takes the problem of history seriously. "Hume substituted for the idea of spiritual substance the idea of constant tendencies to associate ideas in particular ways, and these laws of association were just as uniform and unchanging as any substance."[25] Hume could not simultaneously think historically and in terms of constants of human nature, and in the balance his treatment of history suffered.

Nevertheless, we must grant, on the one hand, that Hume was more sophisticated about the historical process than most of the conservatives *or* Enlightenment progressives of his day. Blackstone found in the mere longevity of institutions a sign of their naturalness and rationality. The rationality of habitual institutions was not so clear to Hume. On the other hand, the progressives assumed that a science of politics applied to the world would automatically lead to reform. Hume made no such assumption and did not pretend to possess the key to the good life on earth. If his historical skepticism was not pure, neither was it naïve.

24 Mossner, *Hume*, p. 305.
25 *The Idea of History* (Oxford: Clarendon Press, 1946), p. 83. What to us are historically conditioned traits of Western man, to Hume were trans-historical constants of human nature.

Conclusion

IN the eighteenth-century sense of "moral," Hume's political writings were moral through and through. The whole thrust of his social thought was to find a basis for distinguishing between justified and unjustified institutions. From his empirical and experimental premise Hume sought to extract reliable principles from both the psychological and the social worlds. From the former came his "natural principles" of human nature expounded in the *Treatise*. On the basis of these plus further observations of whole societies came his "artificial principles" of society sketched in the *Political Essays*. Like the later utilitarians, Hume believed that the natural obligation in social relationships was the obligation of interest. But he also believed that this interest was a function of passions less mechanical and more elusive than, say, Bentham would admit. He further assumed that individual interests and social interests are ultimately (though he would not have liked this word) capable of harmonious adjustment. Hume found no evidential basis for believing in a natural disharmony of individual and society. But his subjectivism was such that he saw more clearly than Bentham the scope of individual differences in values; and he could explain a great many social disharmonies by noting the dominance of immediate interest over the possibly greater but more distant interest in the affairs of men.

Using the general criterion of utility, Hume concluded that social stability must be the cardinal goal of policy. Such stability was not, for him, accidental, nor the result of the simple operation of natural principles of human nature, nor the result of superimposed rules. It was rather the result of a system of "conventions," which were the product of both human understanding and natural human affections.[26] In this view he anticipates much of Burke's reverence for the human community. Hume is in the unique position of influencing Bentham's radicalism and Burke's conservatism by virtue of categories that transcend them both. Rousseau's paradoxical blend of radicalism and conservatism may also owe something to Hume. By divorcing the demands of community from a rational sanction, Hume left the way open for his contemporary Rousseau to introduce a nonrational "civil religion" as the ideological basis of a romanticized community.

Hume's methodological skepticism, meanwhile, turns out not to be so skeptical after all. He was cautious about grand schemes and fixed models; he had little faith in radical transformations based on rational plans. The passionate character of men's interests was most real to him. These qualities

26 See W. Gordon Ross, *Human Nature and Utility in Hume's Social Philosophy* (Garden City: published by the author, 1942), pp. 98ff.

made him a conservative with a probing concern for the consequences of each new social step and a deep affection for social stability. But, despite this outlook, he was an optimistic conservative, a man with limited hopes, perhaps, but virtually no sense of despair. After the French Revolution, this relaxed brand of conservatism would no longer suit the times, and urgent metaphysical varieties would take its place.

CHAPTER

9 | *Burke*

I<small>N</small> E<small>DMUND</small> B<small>URKE</small> we have the theorist as statesman, or, to be more precise, the statesman as theorist.
We also have a man who has become a symbol of conservatism. Put the
two together and we have the myth that the man of affairs, the responsible
man, the man in constant daily touch with political reality, tends to be
conservative. The myth is not necessarily false; but it *is* a myth, a proposition more easily believed than proved. Thus arises the problem of the
relationship of political thought to political action, a problem that makes
the biography of Burke especially relevant.

Life

EDUCATION AND EARLY WORKS
Burke was born in Dublin, Ireland, January 12, 1729, one of several offspring of an irritable Church of Ireland (Anglican) attorney and a gentle
Catholic housewife. The mother was a remote descendant of Edmund
Spenser, whence came our subject's name. In delicate health, Edmund
spent periods of physical quiet studying history and dreaming dreams of
the past, a romantic fascination that affected his whole life. From his
mother he learned to tolerate Catholics, from his Quaker schoolmaster at
Ballitore School, Dublin, he learned to tolerate Quakers, and from the
many French Huguenot boys enrolled there he learned to tolerate Calvinists. But he was always a strong Church of England man and never
comfortable in the presence of the irreligious.

In 1744 Burke entered Trinity College, Dublin University, at that time a better school than either Oxford or Cambridge. He went through a series of infatuations and disillusionments with mathematics, metaphysics, history, and poetry, of which only the last two left a positive mark. Metaphysics became Burke's chief whipping boy, a "Serbonian bog" he called it. While an undergraduate, he wrote a play, and in 1748, the year of his Bachelor of Arts, he produced pamphlets attacking mercantilism and examining Bolingbroke's *Idea of a Patriot King*. He also wrote but did not publish a treatise on aesthetics, *The Sublime and the Beautiful*, and edited thirteen issues of a periodical called (ironically enough, considering his subsequent reputation) the *Reformer*. The journal paid special attention to economics and the drama. Altogether not a bad start for a boy of nineteen.

In 1750 Burke entered the Inn of the Middle Temple in London to study law, but spent as much or more time studying literature. By 1755, fearing that he had become a wastrel, his disgusted father cut off his allowance. Burke never was admitted to the bar. But fame and his own income began with the publication of his *Vindication of Natural Society* in 1756. History, he maintained, is a history of wars. Wars are mainly the result of the subversion of "natural society" by atheists, divines, and politicians. In a natural society, labor produces the ownership of goods. In an artificial or "political" society, those who labor the most tend to have the least— witness, said Burke, the terrible conditions of the miners in northern England (when, in 1765, a mellower and more "political" Burke was running for Parliament, he felt it necessary to issue a preface to the new edition of *The Vindication of Natural Society* assuring readers that the design of the work was "entirely ironical").

The success of the *Vindication* led Burke to publish in the same year *The Sublime and the Beautiful*. But suddenly his health broke. Fortunately, he found in Bath a skilled (though Presbyterian) doctor with a gentle, charming daughter. The doctor cured him, the daughter married him, and Burke managed to get his father-in-law to pay some of his mounting bills. In the same year he published *An Abridgement of English History*, which, by contrast with most of the histories of the Enlightenment period, did not disparage the past.

From 1758 to 1791 Burke was the unacknowledged editor of the *Annual Register*, a journal devoted to the review of major events in history, politics, and literature.[1] Journalists were looked down upon in the eighteenth century, and Burke's self-chosen anonymity left a cloud of ob-

[1] The *Register* had limited space for reviews, but Burke's careful choice of books for review brought to the reader's attention almost all those contemporary works that time has vindicated as great, works by such men as Rousseau, Hume, Sterne, Samuel Johnson, and Adam Smith. See Robert H. Murray, *Edmund Burke, A Biography* (New York: Oxford Univ. Press, 1931), pp. 83ff. This biographical section draws heavily on Murray's book.

scurity over much of this journal's authorship.[2] But it can be said that the tone of the publication was consistently moderate and dispassionate. Here is evidence that the man of thought and the man of action can to some degree exist in the same person at different times. For whatever else Burke's oratory and political tract-writing were, they could not be called dispassionate. The mixture of moderate reason and immoderate passion is perhaps a large part of Burke's fascination.

INTRODUCTION TO POLITICS

In 1759 Burke was introduced to William Gerald "Single Speech" Hamilton.[3] This was his first contact with statesmanship. He became Hamilton's secretary, and when Hamilton went to Ireland in 1761 as chief secretary of the Lord Lieutenant, Burke went with him. Fascinated by politics, Burke soon faced a dilemma: whether to become an Irish politician, in which case his Catholic sympathies would be an asset, or to strive for greater rewards by going back to England to become an English politician, in which case his Catholic sympathies would be a liability. He chose the latter. While his choice gave England one of its greatest parliamentarians, it also imposed tragic elements on Burke's life.

Burke was not one to shun an unpopular cause. During his Irish stay he wrote his *Tracts on the Popery Laws*,[4] which attacked the terribly oppressive—even if largely unenforced—laws against Catholics in Ireland. Schools, professions, and politics were closed to Catholics by these laws. Special taxes lay against them. The Mass was forbidden. Attempts to gain conversions were considered high treason. The nearest Protestant relative could claim an inheritance ahead of a Catholic heir. Burke's consistent position against such measures was later to encourage political reprisals against him.

In 1763 Burke went back to London with Hamilton and joined a notable fellowship called simply The Literary Club, founded by the painter Sir Joshua Reynolds. Meeting once a week for supper at the Turk's Head in Soho, the society debated issues of the day, enabling Burke to sharpen his wit and try out his flow of bad puns on such friends and fellow raconteurs as Samuel Johnson and Oliver Goldsmith. (Later the group came to include such distinguished men as Boswell, Gibbon, Adam Smith, Fox,

2 See Thomas W. Copeland, *Edmund Burke, Six Essays* (London: Jonathan Cape, 1950), Chs. 3-4.

3 Hamilton, who subsequently held many administrative posts, attracted Prime Minister Walpole's attention with his maiden speech in the House of Commons, November 13, 1755. According to legend, he never again spoke in the House. The legend is false.

4 In *The Writings and Speeches of Edmund Burke* (Boston: Little, Brown, 1901), Vol. VI, pp. 301-60. Hereinafter referred to as *Works*.

Windham, Sheridan, and David Garrick, the actor.) At this time, after some unpleasant disagreements, Burke broke with Hamilton. He was poor again, despite which he, and even more his brother Dick and cousin Will Burke, ran up great debts and generously befriended all sorts of acquaintances.[5]

In 1765 a new career began for Burke. He became private secretary of Lord Rockingham, leader of the Whigs, and entered Parliament. Burke could not have chosen a more critical time. William Pitt the Elder, under whose aggressive leadership Britain had defeated the French in the Seven Years' War, had been abruptly dismissed by George III in 1761, almost two years before the Treaty of Paris had ended the war. No one got along very well with the king, that man of "unforgiving piety," as Junius called him, that "conscientious bull in a china shop."[6] Seven ministries came and went in less than ten years: those of Pitt, Bute, Grenville, Rockingham, Grafton (twice), and North. It was during Rockingham's ill-starred government that Burke became his secretary and also became a member of the House of Commons from Wendover in Buckinghamshire, a pocket borough of Lord Verney that Cousin Will had helped Burke line up.

ORATOR FOR THE UNDERDOG

The Rockingham government is remembered for repealing the Stamp Act, which had so infuriated the Americans when first passed, and for "an almost suicidal incorruptibility"[7] in an age of awesome corruption. Among the first speeches Burke made in the House were those for repeal of the Stamp Act. The speeches, said Dr. Johnson, were so impressive they "filled the town with wonder."[8] Until 1794, for virtually the rest of his life, Burke was, as every writer seems to term it, "mentor, guide, and philosopher" of the Whig Party, or at least that faction of it originally led by Rockingham. Yet for all his fame and prestige, Burke was more often on the losing than the winning side and never became a minister.

Burke's first major political publication was *Thoughts on the Cause of*

5 Burke assisted for years one Joseph Emin, an Armenian refugee he happened to encounter in St. James Park. Copeland has documented how much of the scathing personal criticism Burke received during his life was due to the reputation of his relatives, especially Dick and Will, who were virtually part of the family. "The Burkes" as a whole were commonly regarded as erratic, irresponsible, sly, and quite charming. *Edmund Burke, Six Essays*, pp. 36-58.

6 Richard Pares, *King George III and the Politicians* (Oxford: Clarendon Press, 1953), p. 67. The anonymous *Letters of Junius* (1769-72) attacked George III and defended John Wilkes.

7 Quoted in Ross J. S. Hoffman and Paul Levack, eds., *Burke's Politics, Selected Writings and Speeches of Edmund Burke on Reform, Revolution, and War* (New York: Knopf, 1949), p. 3. This excellent collection is a good introduction to Burke.

8 *Ibid.*, p. 4.

the Present Discontents (1770). King George, no longer worried about a Jacobite restoration, was actively seeking to build up the Tories in hopes of making them a personal court party. The beleaguered Whigs were split into factions. The *Present Discontents* was an eloquent critique of the ideas used by the court cabal to advance their cause. The separation of the court from "the sentiments and opinions of the people," argued Burke, and the system of corruption and favoritism that had grown up around the cabal, was threatening the Constitution itself. The traditional balance of the English Constitution required Parliamentary men of independent judgment, working together in political parties, responsible to the people, though not necessarily subservient to them. George's efforts to dominate Parliament were largely frustrated by his own bungling. "Yet," says Harold Laski, "in the long run, the real weapon which defeated George was the ideas of Edmund Burke, for he gave to political conflict its real place in philosophy."[9]

In 1771 Burke became the English agent for the colony of New York.[10] This position furthered his identification with the American colonists, in whose interests some of his greatest speeches were made. The Irish also benefited from Burke's sometimes outraged solicitude for their rights, although the cause of Ireland was the source of major political headaches for Burke. In 1774 Burke became Member of Parliament for the industrial city of Bristol in western England. In that year Lord Verney, a bit short of cash, had put up for sale his four Parliamentary seats, and Burke, one of the incumbents, was unfortunately too poor to buy his own. He was therefore much pleased to be asked to run in a genuine election in Bristol. The city fathers liked his views on trade with America, and he was elected. But Burke's principled independence was too much for them, especially as regards Ireland. Not only Bristol's anti-Catholicism, but its ardent support of trade restrictions on Ireland harmed Burke. For he went on pressing for relief of Catholic disabilities and, loyal to the economic views of his friend Adam Smith, opposed restrictions on Irish commerce. When the Savile Act for the relief of Catholics was passed in 1778, the so-called Gordon riots broke out in London. Over three hundred people were killed and at one point Parliament was invaded. Burke was one of the major objects of hostility. By the time of the election of 1780 Burke knew it was hopeless to stand for re-election from Bristol. He abandoned the seat and picked up one in Malton, Yorkshire, a family borough of Lord Rockingham. Thus ended Burke's direct encounter with grass-roots democracy.

9 H. J. Laski, *Political Thought in England, Locke to Bentham* (New York: Oxford Univ. Press, 1920), p. 146.
10 See Ross J. S. Hoffman, *Edmund Burke, New York Agent* (Philadelphia: American Philosophical Society, 1956).

India and France were two other stimuli to Burkean thought and action. Many Englishmen were disturbed by the plunder of India and the mismanagement in the East India Company, though their concern was sometimes as much fiscal as humanitarian. Burke, concerned as always with the dignity of the British heritage, also spoke of Indian rights. One of his rare references to the "natural rights of mankind" came during the debate on Fox's East India Bill of 1783. Not that Burke was free of partisan influences. He had opposed Lord North's India reform bill in 1773 on the grounds that it would violate the East India Company's charter rights and create a source of government patronage. When the Whigs later came to power under Charles James Fox and attempted a similar reform, the same arguments could be and were used against Fox and Burke. But part of the forensic ammunition in the debate was a Parliamentary committee report drafted by Burke that bluntly revealed the injustices heaped on Indian natives and the collusion of East India Company officials with native princes. It was Burke who, from 1788 to 1794, pushed through the impeachment of Warren Hastings, governor general of Bengal, on grounds of extortion, brutality, and other crimes. Hastings was in the end acquitted, but the trial was nevertheless a landmark in the reform of the British Empire.

Closing Years

The work for which Burke is most widely known is *Reflections on the Revolution in France* (1790), a book that might best be described as a protracted explosion. Important as it is in the history of ideas, perhaps too much of Burke's popular reputation depends upon this one tract. At any rate, it made him many friends and many enemies and touched off one of the most vigorous running debates in modern times. Burke was shocked in 1791 when his friend, Whig leader Charles James Fox, praised the new French constitution as "the most stupendous and glorious edifice of liberty. . . ." The resultant conflict between the two men led to an open break that never healed. The Whigs voted to follow Fox rather than Burke, and he was, in effect, read out of the party he had served for almost thirty years. In this context he wrote *An Appeal from the New to the Old Whigs* (1791), the classic statement of Burke's "idea of a people" and defense of "natural aristocracy."

The year 1794 appeared to be a sad, depressing end of the road for Burke. His beloved son died on the eve of a promising career. Hastings was acquitted. Old and weary, repudiated by his party, Burke retired from political life. But until his death in 1797 he continued to write, with no reduction of his literary powers. His last work was *Letters on a Regicide Peace* (1796), which developed his conception of the whole of Europe as a Christian commonwealth threatened by the rise of Jacobinism. *A Letter to a Noble Lord* (1796) has been called his valedictory. It was a reply to the duke of Bedford's petty attack on the pension Burke received upon retirement. Burke was masterfully satirical and ironic, joining the issue with vigor, yet without loss of humor or perspective. He demonstrated what his friends knew by experience, that strong-willed and testy as he was, he was incapable of being petty. They knew that he was a great man as well as a great politician. To the very end, the man of thought and the man of action remained united.

"Burke's magnificent speeches," wrote Sir Leslie Stephen, "stand absolutely alone in the language. They are, literally speaking, the only English speeches which may still be read with profit when the hearer and the speaker have long been turned to dust."[11] Burke's dazzling command of the English language and his principled avoidance of systematization create a strong temptation to deal with his political theory by simply stringing together a long series of pungent epigrams. Though contrary to his own belief, it has been necessary for the sake of exposition to impose an external, somewhat abstract structure on the Burkean materials discussed in the pages that follow. But the reader will forgive frequent and lengthy quotations within that structure. The temptation to quote at length Burke's flowing prose is irresistible. Of this, Burke would no doubt approve. For him, the mode of action was always as important as the end of action, and flowing prose was his primary mode of action.

Nonconservative Elements in Burke

EDMUND BURKE is almost universally regarded as the archetypal conservative.[12] In the vernacular of our day, "conservative" is regarded as the opposite of "liberal." A conservative supposedly opposes and a liberal supposedly favors innovation (even though a self-designated conservative may argue for a wholly new tax structure and a self-designated liberal may labor to conserve civil liberties). The confusion presently surrounding these terms suggests that their use as antitheses may be unwarranted. If so, to call Burke antiliberal, hence conservative, may be too simple.

Liberalism—if we may digress a moment—more clearly than conservatism refers to a particular movement of thought occurring within a given historical period. Although the name was not used until the early nineteenth century,[13] scholars now apply it to the general body of Western

11 *English Thought in the Eighteenth Century* (2nd ed.; London: Smith, Elder, 1881), Vol. II, p. 219.

12 See below, footnote 26.

13 By the *Liberales*, a Spanish party. See J. Salwyn Schapiro, ed., *Liberalism: Its Meaning and History* (Princeton: Van Nostrand, 1958), p. 9; Guido de Ruggiero,

European thought deriving from the attempt to justify the "liberation" of the individual from the confinements of feudal status and privilege. Three characteristics of liberal thought are basic: (1) Private interest (or conscience) is given priority over public (governmental) authority. That is, individualism replaces communitarianism.[14] (2) Scientific judgments are given priority over religious insight. Liberalism has almost always been sympathetic to scientific inquiry, and even when not antireligious, has been anticlerical. (3) The economy is given priority over the polity. The liberal movement is identified with the middle classes of industrial civilizations for whom the maximization of economic productivity takes precedence over noneconomic public goods. By these three tests, Burke is clearly nonliberal.

In one of its aspects, conservatism is not so much a definable body of social thought as it is a temperamental predisposition in favor of caution. We speak of conservative tastes in music and architecture but we do not speak similarly of liberal tastes. There will be conservatives even in societies where the term "liberalism" has no meaning. In its more clearly political connotations, conservatism suggests a reverence for tradition, but often the plurality of traditions appealed to generates confusion and even a lack of caution. Burke, for all his reverence for tradition, could be incautious. In his attitude toward religion, class, and community, Burke was no liberal. But in his defense of the free-market economy, the rights of free speech, and justice for underprivileged colonies, he shared some of the policies born of liberal assumptions. Though not a liberal, he could sometimes be a nonconservative reformer.[15]

A Free Parliament: George iii and the Wilkes Case

It was Burke's great virtue to deal with general moral principles without ever losing touch with the situation at hand. Or perhaps it is better to say that he dealt with a prodigious quantity of practical political issues without

---

The History of European Liberalism, trans. by R. G. Collingwood (New York: Oxford Univ. Press, 1927; Boston: Beacon Press, 1959); Harold J. Laski, *The Rise of European Liberalism* (London: Allen & Unwin, 1936); John H. Hallowell, *The Decline of Liberalism as an Ideology* (Berkeley: Univ. of California Press, 1943); Louis Hartz, *The Liberal Tradition in America* (New York: Harcourt, Brace, 1955).

14 One student of liberalism has argued that faith in the "autonomy of human reason" is the key to liberal individualism. John H. Hallowell, *Main Currents in Modern Political Thought* (New York: Holt, 1950), Ch. 4. Sheldon Wolin argues convincingly, on the other hand, that faith in mechanism rather than faith in reason characterizes the liberal tradition. *Politics and Vision* (Boston: Little, Brown, 1960) Ch. 9.

15 Arnold A. Rogow argues convincingly that Burke has little in common with the American conservatives who invoke his name most fervently, those who define the right "by what economic man does to achieve success." "Edmund Burke and the American Liberal Tradition," *Antioch Review,* Vol. 17 (1957), pp. 255-65.

losing sight of their moral dimensions. In every dispute, save one, said Stephen, Burke had "taken the generous side." The exception Stephen grants was the dispute over the French Revolution, to which ought to be added the proposed reform of the rotten boroughs. In the Wilkes case he was on a generous and courageous side, but also, this time, the popular, underdog side. John Wilkes was expelled from the House of Commons in 1764 for libeling the king and was prejudicially convicted at King's Bench for publishing an allegedly obscene poem. He first fled to France, but returned, served his sentence, and was elected to Parliament from Middlesex in 1768. But Parliament, cowed by the king, refused to seat him. Three more times he went back to his constituency and was re-elected, and three more times Parliament refused to seat him. His plight became a *cause célèbre* and Burke took his stand with Wilkes.[16] With qualifications, Burke at the same time took his stand with the people:

I am not one of those who think that the people are never in the wrong. They have been so, frequently and outrageously, both in other countries and in this. But I do say that in all disputes between them and their rulers the presumption is at least upon a par in favor of the people. . . . the people have no interest in disorder. When they do wrong, it is their error and not their crime. But with the governing part of the state, it is far otherwise.

Is this conservatism or liberalism? Maybe it is only a debater's point. Maybe it is only good sense. But in the context of the times it did not please the powers that be, and the powers that be were crudely suppressing an individual politician and his individual supporters. The persecution of Wilkes, Burke observes, nay, demonstrates, was but a pretense to achieve the "separation of the representatives from their constituents. . . . a precedent . . . tending to show *that the favor of the people was not so sure a road as the favor of the court even to popular honors and popular trusts.* . . ." Such a precedent would be disastrous for good government. "The power of the people, within the laws, must show itself sufficient to protect every representative in the animated performance of his duty, or that duty cannot be performed." The court party, to be sure, says that this power to disqualify is in good hands and will not be abused. "Until I find something in this argument differing from that on which every mode of despotism has been defended, I shall not be inclined to pay it any great compliment. The people are satisfied to trust themselves with the exercise of their own privileges. . . ."[17]

16 See *Speech on Wilkes* in *Works*, Vol. VII, pp. 61-67; *Thoughts on the Cause of the Present Discontents* (1770), in *ibid.*, Vol. I, pp. 435-537.

17 The quotations are from *Present Discontents*, pp. 440-41, 496-97, 503, and 506, respectively. Italics in the original. At times Burke's words could be used to make him

The argument is characteristic of Burke's method of operation, which is the same in his writings as in his speeches. As his friend Goldsmith said, he winds into his subject like a serpent. The values to which he appeals are implicit rather than explicit. In many men this approach would be a sign of superficiality or confusion, but in Burke it was a way of life. The appeal to reason is not dogmatic, axiomatic, or geometrical. The good sense of what he says insinuates itself in a series of pithy, medium-level generalizations until the hearer finds himself lured into thinking the speaker is expressing sentiments with which he, the hearer, has agreed all along. This particular skill with words is the trait of the good politician. The good politician does not bludgeon his hearers with logic. Cold logic pitted against warm emotion wins only perfunctory assent and loses votes. Nor does he put them to sleep with a catalogue of dusty bits of data. He charms them. He woos them.

Yet even subtle, insinuating logic does not produce the values Burke ultimately appeals to. These are either shared or not shared. They cannot be demonstrated. These values—that the blatant persecution of Wilkes is wrong, that a constituency's right to pick its own representative should not be trampled on—are "givens," are products of the historical community in which both Burke and his hearers reside. This pointed view raises the fundamental problem of the political community as a source of values, a problem to be examined later in this chapter.

The Responsibility of Authority: America and India

If solicitude for the rights of constituencies and the integrity of Parliament in their struggle against external control reflects a nonconservative side of Burke, so does the corollary of these rights—the *duty* of Parliament to grant the same kind of integrity to other governing bodies that it would wish for itself. Those in authority do not have to keep everyone happy. Burke would grant them no authority to do wrong in order to be popular. But political wisdom, Burke's everlasting goal, does not sanction paternalistic interference with orderly governments run by grown men. To claim a right is also to claim a responsibility, but if the responsibility is accepted, it ought to be respected by others.

As usual, the principle is not stated by Burke in the abstract but emerges from the discussion of tangible disputes, such as those concerning America and India. Burke's first major utterance on the American colonies

---

out a revolutionary: ". . . a decent attention to public interest in representatives [may require] *the interposition of the body of the people itself*. [The remedy is] most unpleasant. But if it be a legal remedy, it is intended on some occasion to be used; to be used then only when it is evident that nothing else can hold the constitution to its true principles." (p. 521.) Or again, in defense of party government: ". . . he that supports every administration subverts all government." (p. 523.)

occurs in the long pamphlet, *Observations on a Late Publication Intitled "The Present State of the Nation."* Written in early 1769, it was a reply to Lord Grenville's attack on the Rockingham Whigs in the preceding year. The pamphlet was not his best, but it reveals his warm, almost elegiac, feeling for the worth of the American colonies in the course of contending what a mistake the Stamp Act and the Townshend Acts were. It is important to note that the affection for America was not an affection for all mankind. Burke was parochial enough and patriotic enough to be moved by the fact that Americans were not just anybody: ". . . the people who are to be the subjects of these restraints are descendants of Englishmen, and of a high and free spirit. To hold over them a government made up of nothing but restraints and penalties, and taxes in the granting of which they have no share, will neither be wise nor long practicable. . . . The British colonist must see something which will distinguish him from the colonists of other nations."[18] There is dignity without crass sentimentality in this statement; and if there is also a tincture of British chauvinism, we can at least remember that most of Burke's colleagues had greater difficulty identifying with white-skinned, English-speaking colonials three thousand miles away, not to mention dark-skinned Eastern natives six thousand miles away in India.

On April 19, 1774, Burke offered the House his *Speech on American Taxation*. In it he stressed the critical function in political relations of confidence—what today we would call rapport, a quality that the *philosophes*, with their concern for the geometrically precise statement of equity, tended to overlook. "The spirit of practicability, of moderation and mutual convenience will never call in geometrical exactness as the arbiter of an amicable settlement. Consult and follow your experience."[19] Burke's experience revealed to him that the Americans could not be browbeaten into subservience. If told "that sovereignty and their freedom cannot be reconciled, which will they take? They will cast your sovereignty in your face. Nobody will be argued into slavery."[20]

On March 22, 1775, Burke gave one of his greatest speeches, the *Speech on Conciliation with the Colonies*. Its pervasive flavor is the delicate combination of passionate involvement and detached observation that we associate with Burke's kind of political responsibility and that, in fact,

18 *Observations on a Late Publication Intitled "The Present State of the Nation,"* in *Works*, Vol. I, pp. 395-96.

19 *Speech on American Taxation*, in *Works*, Vol. II, p. 71. To the objection that Parliament should worry about the solution of the problem and not its origin, Burke posed a sarcastic restatement, "We are to consult our invention and reject our experience." He refused to be drawn into categorical definitions of rights and their limits. "I do not enter into these metaphysical distinctions; I hate the very sound of them."

20 *Ibid.*, p. 73.

is the necessary art of political leadership. It is remarkable to find an analysis of the American situation, made in the heat of debate, that after two hundred years is still a sound and perceptive exposition. Burke outlines six major causes for America's "fierce spirit of liberty." If the accent falls somewhat more heavily on the moral than ours would, Burke does not therefore neglect hard economic realities. But it is the keen sensitivity to the moral interdependence of nations that strikes us: ". . . in order to prove that the Americans have no right to their liberties, we are every day endeavoring to subvert the maxims which preserve the whole spirit of our own. To prove that the Americans ought not to be free we are obliged to depreciate the value of freedom itself. . . ."[21] At the same time, Burke cautioned against attempting to weaken the Southern states by declaring the slaves to be free, as some had suggested. No friend of slavery, Burke could nevertheless make highly practical arguments for the inexpedience of such a dictate from London. As to criminal charges against the Americans, "I do not know the method of drawing up an indictment against a whole people."[22]

After eliminating all other alternatives, Burke concludes that the only solution is "to admit the people of our colonies into an interest in the constitution."[23] Had Burke's advice been followed, the United States might today be a Dominion of the Commonwealth. By "an interest in the constitution," however, Burke did not mean perfect equality with England. Though he raises questions about the concept of "virtual representation," in the end he sanctions it, being unable seriously to propose Parliamentary representation for America. The heart of his six resolutions was that the taxation of America should be by grant of colonial assemblies and not by "imposition."[24]

India was, as we have seen, a somewhat different case, the honor of English officials being as much at issue as the rights of distant subjects. Yet, though Burke's references to India were often in terms of interest rather than some other standard, it was interest in its most refined and inclusive sense, a conception that called for men of circumscribed mind to stretch their imaginations. "The scene of the Indian abuse is distant, indeed; but we must not infer that the value of our interest in it is decreased in proportion as it recedes from our view. In our politics, as in

21 *Speech on Conciliation with the Colonies,* in *Works,* Vol. II, p. 130. The implied prophecy was fulfilled when, after the Revolution began, England suspended habeas corpus for the colonies. Burke attacked this action in his *Letter to the Sheriffs of Bristol,* April 3, 1777. *Works,* Vol. II, pp. 187-245.
22 *Speech on Conciliation,* in *Works,* Vol. II, p. 136.
23 *Ibid.,* p. 141.
24 On this question see also *Observations on a Late Publication,* in *Works,* Vol. I, pp. 271-432, esp. pp. 370-76.

our common conduct, we shall be worse than infants if we do not put our sense under the tuition of our judgment, and effectively cure ourselves of that optical illusion which makes a brier at our nose of greater magnitude than an oak at five hundred yards distance."[25]

Parliament was made to remember and Warren Hastings was not allowed to forget the "scene of the Indian abuse." Through them the whole nation was reminded that authority and power are not synonyms. Burke's intense personal hatred of all forms of cruelty had nothing to do with partisan politics, but the consequences he drew in political action were not unlike those drawn by many who later called themselves liberals.

Burke as a Conservative

IF Burke's concern for the national interest was more compatible with a sensitivity to individual rights than some have imagined, other facets of his thought seem to fit appropriately under the conservative label. Three seem central, Burke's conceptions of (1) the limits of abstract reason, (2) representation, (3) the nature of social freedom.[26]

25 *Speech on the Nabob of Arcot's Debts*, in *Works*, Vol. III, p. 15. To get around the rule against accepting gifts from native princes, East India Company men often loaned money to them at fantastic rates of interest, sometimes without any initial cash transfer whatsoever. Such graft was involved in the case Burke was discussing: ". . . the Nabob of Arcot and his creditors are not adversaries but collusive parties, . . . the whole transaction is under a false color and false names." *Ibid.*, p. 28.

26 Russell Kirk lists six attributes of the "conservative mind," drawn largely from Burke, whom he regards as a kind of godfather of modern conservatism: (1) the belief that divine intent rules; (2) affection for the mystery of tradition; (3) the belief that civilization requires orders and classes; (4) the belief that property and freedom are inseparable; (5) faith in prescription as a check on man's will; and (6) the view that change and reform are not identical. *The Conservative Mind from Burke to Santayana* (Chicago: Regnery, 1953), Ch. 1. This is a useful check-list, although (1) is not confined to conservatives, and (6) is a rather empty truism. Burke, incidentally, made a special contribution only to (5).

Clinton Rossiter, who is less precise but also less dogmatic than Kirk, does not offer a conclusive definition of the conservative, but sketches different types of conservative minds: temperamental, possessive, practical, and philosophical. The last type is the "highest kind," and, is found in "the genuine conservative," one who with "some degree of disinterestedness" can "justify the established order and guard it against careless tinkering and determined reform" by reference to intellectual principles which he has "found . . . good" after "hard thinking." By this standard, it might be noted, a Soviet Communist could qualify as a "genuine conservative." *"Conservatism in America"* (New York: Knopf, 1955), p. 9. Burke, for Rossiter as for Kirk, is "the father of all Conservatives" (p. 22).

Peter Viereck speaks of a continuum from "authoritarianism" running through "conservatism" to "liberalism." Burke is placed on the borderline between the latter two. Those in the middle ground, says Viereck, tend to stress experience

THE LIMITS OF ABSTRACT REASON

There are points of contact between almost all schools of thought. Though he would have been alarmed by the tinkering propensity of the contemporary pragmatist, Burke would share with him a distrust of metaphysical speculation and abstract reason.[27] As Godwin or Condorcet was the man of principle, Burke was the man of experience. Principled men are not blind to experience; experienced men cannot ignore every principle. But there is a difference.

Burke's final thoughts on the dangers of metaphysical abstractions in politics were violently pulled out of him by the events of the French Revolution. Not that he had concealed them before this time. In one of his earliest speeches, the Commination Service speech, he referred disparagingly to "refining speculatists," "political aeronauts," "smugglers of adulterated metaphysics," and "metaphysical knights of the sorrowful countenance."[28] In his *Letter to the Sheriffs of Bristol* (1777) he observed that the propensity of a people to resort to theories is "one sure symptom of an ill-conducted state." "Civil freedom, Gentlemen, is not, as many have endeavored to persuade you, a thing that lies hid in the depth of abstruse science. It is a blessing and a benefit, not an abstract speculation."[29] "Abstract liberty," he said in his *Speech on Conciliation with the Colonies*, "like other mere abstractions, is not to be found. Liberty inheres in some sensible object."[30]

The continuity of Burke's opposition to abstract principles is clear. Yet this antimetaphysical position did not, in his earlier days, automatically parallel a hostile attitude toward a possible French revolution, as it later bolstered opposition to the actual French Revolution in 1789. In *Observations on a Late Publication* (1769) he had referred to "injudicious" and "oppressive" taxation in France. In the *Annual Register* for 1770, Burke wrote sympathetically of the forces struggling against the oppressive French monarchy. Of the latter, he wrote, "How long this destructive power may continue to desolate the country, or whether, as has frequently been the case, it may at length fall by its own enormous weight

---

against apriorism, the organic against the atomistic, liberty against equality, and aristocracy against plutocracy or democracy. *Conservatism from John Adams to Churchill,* Anvil Series (Princeton: Van Nostrand, 1956), Preface and Chs. 1-2.

27 Charles Parkin, in *The Moral Basis of Burke's Political Thought* (London: Cambridge Univ. Press, 1956), however, subtly infers the existence of an abstract design in Burke's writings almost tantamount to natural law.

28 Quoted in John MacCunn, *The Political Philosophy of Burke* (New York: Longmans, Green, 1913), p. 1.

29 *Letter to the Sheriffs of Bristol,* in *Works,* Vol. II, pp. 230, 229.

30 *Speech on Conciliation,* in *ibid.,* p. 120.

must be left to time to disclose."[31] Finally, once when discussing the American Revolution he noted that "revolts of a whole people. . . . are always provoked."[32]

These sentiments would seem to lead in a direction other than his thoroughgoing condemnation of the Revolution in the *Reflections*. Indeed, it required for Burke an uncharacteristic narrowness of view to blame the Revolution solely on a conspiracy of men, particularly one that included such moderates as Mirabeau and Lafayette. Burke was usually especially keen on the deep historic roots of any emerging conflict. Was it a sign of age, or the frustrations of repeated Parliamentary defeats, that led Burke to vitriolic denunciation: "Is it because liberty in the abstract may be classed among the blessings of mankind that I am to felicitate a mad-man who has escaped from the protecting restraint and wholesome darkness of his cell, on his restoration to the enjoyment of light and liberty?"[33]

Burke's first task in the *Reflections* was to show, as against the Reverend Dr. Richard Price and other English admirers of the Revolution, that the Glorious Revolution of 1688, which had given the Whigs their charter, had little in common with the French Revolution. James II was "a bad king with a good title" who, confronted with a true charge of papist subversion, chose to abdicate at an auspicious moment. "No experience has taught us that in any other course or method than that of an *hereditary crown* our liberties can be regularly perpetuated and preserved sacred as our *hereditary right*. An irregular, convulsive movement may be necessary to throw off an irregular, convulsive disease. But the course of succession is the healthy habit of the British Constitution." If the French admirers in England can restrain themselves, said Burke, law and order is secure in England. France, meanwhile, has burst asunder. The new principle of absolute equality, which made France "let loose the reins of regal authority" has "doubled the licence of a ferocious dissoluteness in manners, and of an insolent irreligion in opinions and practices. . . ." Authority has been placed in the hands of men "not taught habitually to respect themselves" and so now "intoxicated with their unprepared greatness. . . . a handful of country clowns, who have seats in [the] assembly, some of whom are said not to be able to read and write . . . and by not a greater number of traders who . . . had never known anything beyond their counting-house." The National Assembly is a body "with every possible power and no possible external control

---

31 *Annual Register*, 1770, p. 53. Quoted in Alfred Cobban, *Edmund Burke and the Revolt Against the Eighteenth Century* (New York: Macmillan, 1929), p. 120.
32 Cobban, *Edmund Burke*, p. 120.
33 *Reflections on the French Revolution*, in *Works*, Vol. III, p. 241.

. . . a body without fundamental laws, without established maxims, without respected rules of proceeding. . . ." And due to the manner of election, "If possible, the next Assembly must be worse than the present."[34] Of the men in the *Tiers État* some had rank and talent, "but of any practical experience in the state, not one man was to be found. *The best were only men of theory.*" The army, a result of "mixing mutinous soldiers with seditious citizens," has gone to pot. The officers are only able "to manage their troops by electioneering arts. They must bear themselves as candidates, not as commanders."[35]

The mistreatment of Marie Antoinette touches off Burke's most agonized lament:

. . . little did I dream that I should have lived to see such disaster fallen upon her in a nation of gallant men, in a nation of men of honor, and of cavaliers. . . . But the age of chivalry is gone. That of sophisters, economists, and calculators has succeeded; and the glory of Europe is extinguished forever. . . . The unbought grace of life, the cheap defense of nations, the nurse of manly sentiment and heroic enterprise, is gone! It is gone, that sensibility of principle, that chastity of honor, which felt a stain like a wound, which inspired courage whilst it mitigated ferocity, which ennobled whatever it touched, and under which vice itself lost half its evil, by losing all its grossness.[36]

But how can one whose very philosophy is to operate from the facts ignore the facts of monarchical oppression and a successful revolution? In distinguishing France in 1789 from England in 1688, why does he ignore England in 1641? Is not what Burke laments in France the loss of principle, the destruction of standards? How can the loss of principle be blamed on the love of principles? Is Burke's rage so apoplectic that he does not know or care that he is contradicting himself right and left?

There is in this situation a triple irony. The first is that, despite his continuing criticism of reliance on abstractions and principles, Burke's peculiar genius as a political thinker was to take concrete, mundane political events and appraise them in the light of general principle. "A mere politician he could not be. When he encountered a political problem it was not in him to deal with it in ordinary fashion. . . . No politician, either in ancient or in modern times, has had so irrepressible a faculty of lifting even the passing incidents of the political hour into the region of

---

34 *Ibid.*, pp. 261, 263, 280, 287, 288, and 495, respectively. Italics in original.
35 *Ibid.*, pp. 284 and 522, respectively. Italics added.
36 *Ibid.*, pp. 331-32. Thomas Paine, commenting on this passage in his *Rights of Man*, said of Burke, "He pities the plumage but forgets the dying bird." In *Political Works* (New York: Eckler, 1892), Part 2, p. 25.

great ideas."[37] Even where the futility of mere theory was his theme, he could not but place his confidence in theories, and uphold right principles: "The pretended rights of these [French] theorists are all extremes; and in proportion as they are metaphysically true, they are morally and politically false. The rights of men are in a sort of *middle*, incapable of definition, but not impossible to be discerned."[38] Politics, Burke said elsewhere, is not so much concerned with the true and the false as with the good and the evil. But this does not mean reason has no place in politics. Quite the contrary. He tells his French friend Dupont in 1789, "The moment *will* is set above reason and justice, in any community, a great question may arise in sober minds in what part or portion of the community that dangerous dominion of will may be the least mischievously placed."[39] This question was at the heart of his dispute with Rousseau. We know that Burke is, despite himself, a theorist. But he is not even a thoroughly antitheoretical theorist. For an antitheoretical theorist could never put those abstractions "reason and justice" ahead of "will."

The second irony is that this advocate of caution, deliberation, and concrete facts was, in his attacks on the French Revolution, highly incautious in his assertions and without reliable information to support his "facts." Yet his prophecies, constructed from confused bits of data in 1790, in the long run proved right. From a mixture of intuition and analysis he sensed that France was headed for ever more serious trouble that would lead eventually to armed conflict with England. It is dubious logic to say, as Alfred Cobban does, that the success of Burke's prediction "is a vindication of the virtue of just theory."[40] Cobban does, however, call our attention to what is often overlooked, that Burke's concern was not only domestic but was directed as well at the international consequences of the Revolution and the possibility of just such an expansively nationalistic force as Napoleon's troops turned out to be. The concern was more implicit than explicit, but it was there. Burke quotes the French Secretary of State for War to the effect that the domestic disorders are not the greatest evil. "*The nature of things requires* that an army should never act but as *an instrument*. The moment that, erecting itself into a deliberative body, it shall act according to its own resolutions, *the government, be it what it may, will immediately degenerate into a military democracy*." Burke comments, "It is not necessary to add much to this finished picture."[41] Burke might have been just as vigorous had the internal factors been discussed in isolation, but his half-concealed perception of their relation to external

37 MacCunn, *Political Philosophy of Burke*, p. 3.
38 *Reflections*, p. 313.
39 Hoffman and Levack, *Burke's Politics*, p. 279.
40 Cobban, *Edmund Burke*, p. 123.
41 *Reflections*, p. 514. Italics in original.

factors is what gives his work a special kind of historical significance. Indeed, in the view of Cobban, this significance is what makes the *Reflections* "the greatest and most influential political pamphlet ever written."[42]

In this significance is our third irony. Against the new nationalism of Frenchmen Burke was appealing to a not quite so new nationalism of Englishmen. Because aristocratic leaders in England, William Pitt and others, could not see the potential threat in France that Burke saw, he spoke in the *Reflections* over the heads of the aristocrats and directly to the English public—on behalf of an aristocratic cause. Without implying a blatant, manipulative intent on his part, it may be suggested that Burke's emotion and not his reason was what weighed most heavily with his readers. He employed terms of abstract reason—"justice," "equity," "rights" —to disparage reliance on abstract reason. Many theorists have done the same. But Burke used the terms in a particularly forceful and emotional way. Just as Burke always insisted, the how is as important as the what. The act, not the word, validates the principle of the limits of abstract reason in political affairs. Perhaps Burke's greatest contribution, then, was not in exalting the concrete over the abstract in politics, but in showing in the concrete how false is the dichotomy between abstract reason and concrete emotion.

REPRESENTATION AND THE PEOPLE

Just after they had elected him to Parliament, on November 3, 1774, Burke faced his new constituents at Bristol and told them that as their representative he would do his own thinking:

Certainly, Gentlemen, it ought to be the happiness and glory of a representative to live in the strictest union, the closest correspondence, and the most unreserved communication with his constituents. Their wishes ought to have great weight with him; their opinions high respect; their business unremitted attention. It is his duty to sacrifice his repose, his pleasure, his satisfactions, to theirs—and above all, ever, and in all cases, to prefer their interests to his own.

But his unbiased opinion, his mature judgment, his enlightened conscience, he ought not to sacrifice to you, to any man, or to any set of men living. These he does not derive from your pleasure—no, nor from the law and the constitution. They are a trust from Providence, for the abuse of which he is deeply answerable. Your representative owes you, not his industry only, but his judgment; and he betrays, instead of serving you, if he sacrifices it to your opinion.

42 Cobban, *Edmund Burke*, p. 129. As Cobban notes, however, along with his prescience, Burke conspicuously fails to see that though France might be less of a state after the Revolution, it might also be more of a nation. Given his nationalistic and generally peaceful premises, Burke could not otherwise have called for the invasion of France.

. . . Parliament is not a *congress* of ambassadors from different and hostile interests . . . but Parliament is a *deliberative* assembly of *one* nation, with *one* interest, that of the whole. You choose a member, indeed; but when you have chosen him he is not a member of Bristol, but he is a member of *Parliament*. If the local constituent should have an interest or should form a hasty opinion evidently opposite to the real good of the rest of the community, the member for that place ought to be as far as any other from any endeavor to give it effect. . . . Your faithful friend, your devoted servant, I shall be to the end of my life: a flatterer you do not wish for. . . .[43]

Here is a man of independent judgment, the kind of man we say we want for our congressman, and the kind of man we consistently vote against, especially if he is bold enough to speak as Burke spoke. Burke could get away with this kind of talk partly because it was the eighteenth century and partly because he was Burke, but even he did not get away with it for long in Bristol, as we saw. What Burke was speaking against was the practice of constituencies instructing their M.P.'s how to vote on specific measures. After the Wilkes agitation in Middlesex, a number of the more radically democratic constituencies had begun to do this. Bristol was such a constituency and Burke was not pleased by the fact. He clearly felt himself above the kind of errand-running that democratic constituencies require their representative to do (representatives of pocket boroughs had a different kind of errand-running). It is, at any rate, a tribute to the man's influence that the practice of instructed M.P.'s almost died out. And even though a flatterer is what most constituencies *do* wish for, especially in less "deferential" nations than England (to use Walter Bagehot's phrase), the idea that members of a legislative body must have more freedom to deliberate than ambassador-delegates to an international conclave is fairly well fixed in the Western democracies.

Yet, as Carl Friedrich has pointed out, the deliberative and the representative functions of legislative bodies are never easily compatible, since the former reflects the reason of the expert and the latter the will of the masses. The problem of democratic leadership remains one of the thorniest of all contemporary political problems. How can a man lead the public and still follow it? Burke leaned on the side of strong leadership and was, at least verbally, a bit too hopeful that the national interest existed as a clearly visible guide that could triumph over the legislator's self-interest as well as over local interest. His plea for deliberation overlooked the value in the tension between aristocratic deliberation and democratic representation.

On these aristocratic grounds Burke opposed a bill for triennial elections

[43] *Speech to the Electorate at Bristol*, in *Works*, Vol. II, pp. 95-97. Italics in original.

in 1780, believing that too many elections were a disturbance to orderly government. In 1782 he opposed Pitt's plan to eliminate rotten boroughs. The argument for "virtual representation" on which this opposition rests is the one argument among all aristocratic arguments that many of us find most difficult to accept today. The theory was that the areas without men in Parliament could count on the faithful service of others in Parliament just as much as their voting brethren who had "actual representation." The theory smacks of rationalizing paternalism and that is what it was. Burke nevertheless claimed advantages for the system: "It corrects the irregularities in the literal representation, when the swifting currents of human affairs . . . carry it obliquely from its first line of direction. The people may err in their choice, but common interest and common sentiment are rarely mistaken."[44] The argument no doubt benefits if seen as an admonition to the M.P. to take seriously his responsibilities even for those who cannot vote for him. As a message to the unrepresented that they are really better represented than those who elect their men, the argument does not make much sense.

That the idea of virtual representation had some limits in Burke's mind is evident not only by his speeches on America, but by his position on Ireland, where he included disfranchisement in his catalogue of protest. English laws, he said, had divided Ireland "into two distinct bodies, without common interest, sympathy or connexion. One of these bodies was to possess *all* the franchises, *all* the property, *all* the education: the other was to be composed of drawers of water and cutters of turf for them. . . . If you treat men as robbers, why, robbers sooner or later they will become."[45] And if you treat men as incapable of significant electoral choice?

Burke was not an aristocrat by default. Indeed at the heart of his politics was the belief that a natural aristocracy was essential to keep society running. But it was a *natural* aristocracy he favored, not a propped-up, artificial aristocracy of unchecked and irresponsible privilege. He was honest enough to see that rulers as well as the ruled have passions requiring external checks. In *An Appeal from the New to the Old Whigs*, Burke's attack on arbitrary power and "the vulgar of every description" was not limited to the rampant majority but to their power-thirsty servants, willing victims of the fact that "the democratic commonwealth is the foodful nurse of ambition." The rule of a "true, natural aristocracy" on the other hand, requires men who have not only had good breeding and the leisure to read, who are habituated to command and possessed of the virtues of "diligence, order, constancy, and regularity," vital as these are; but also men who are "habituated to the censorial inspection of the public eye;

44 *Letter to S. H. Langrishe*, quoted in Murray, *Edmund Burke*, p. 110.
45 *Ibid.*

[who] look early to public opinion; [and] stand upon such elevated ground as to be enabled to take a large view of the wide-spread and infinitely diversified combinations of men and affairs in a large society. . . ."[46]

Burke's conception of representation, or rather, his conception of the priority of deliberation over representation, rested on an aristocratic premise not only overly idealistic for its own day but largely irrelevant to our own nonaristocratic age. Yet, despite this premise, Burke somehow has the capacity to evoke in us an image of aristocracy at its best, an image which may never be irrelevant.

The Nature of Social Freedom

Burke seems to stand most sharply at odds with the whole liberal tradition in his conception of the individual's proper relationship to the social fabric. The liberal tradition was and is concerned to liberate the individual from the chains of social restraint, to make him a "free man." Burke did not believe that the "autonomous individual" of the liberals could or should exist. All men are and inevitably will be bound by an elaborate network of social obligations not wholly of their own choosing. To seek to escape these obligations is, to put it bluntly, immoral. Not only should we accept them, we should accept them reverently. Man "should approach to the faults of the state as to the wounds of a father, with pious awe and trembling solicitude."[47] Society is a contract, but not in the mechanical sense of the Lockeans. "It is," wrote Burke in his most famous statement,

a partnership in all science; a partnership in all art, a partnership in every virtue, and in all perfection. As the ends of such a partnership cannot be obtained in many generations, it becomes a partnership not only between those who are living, but between those who are living, those who are dead, and those who are to be born. Each contract of each particular state is but a clause in the great primeval contract of eternal society. . . . a necessity that is not chosen, but chooses, a necessity paramount to deliberation. . . .[48]

The basic theme of the *Reflections* is that an individualist revolt against society is impossible and that the attempt can only lead to the crippled half-society of the mob. Against liberal clichés about liberty, Burke hurled brilliant metaphors: the commonwealth crumbling "into the dust and powder of individuality," or men severed from prior generations becoming "little better than the flies of a summer."[49] In the *Appeal* he spoke of "a people" breaking up into "a number of vague, loose individuals, and nothing more." As against grand words about mankind in general, Burke

---

46 *An Appeal from the New to the Old Whigs*, in *Works*, Vol. IV, pp. 164, 175.
47 *Reflections*, p. 358.   48 *Ibid.*, pp. 359-60.   49 *Ibid.*, pp. 358, 357.

spoke warmly of the necessity of loving "the little platoon" each of us belongs to. Clearly belongingness was essential to Burke. He saw man as a group being and a familial being and regarded speculation about him in a condition of isolation as unrealistic and dangerous.

Yet we should err to conclude from this that Burke was an organicist who gave society a life of its own. "The idea of a people is the idea of a corporation. It is wholly artificial, and made, like all other legal fictions, by common agreement."[50] Nor could he be regarded as scornful of the dignity of the individual. He lamented what the French Revolution had done to humanity, compassion, and "tenderness to individuals." His anguish over oppression anywhere and his personal life confirm the genuineness of this solicitude. Nevertheless, by focusing on the necessary restraints society imposes on the individual, Burke allied himself with those who had and would submerge the individual completely in an organismic conception of society. His frequent failure to distinguish between state and society furthered this alliance.

He also edged toward the Germanic Reaction in sometimes stressing freedom as an inner quality. "Men of intemperate minds cannot be free. Their passions forge their fetters."[51] The idea was in no sense novel; but it was a new emphasis for Whigs who, like the *philosophes*, generally meant to refer to prisons, civil liberties, and the like when they spoke of "freedom." Burke, in his attack on the supposed libertarian excesses of Rousseau and the Revolution, put discipline ahead of absence of restraint. He was not in the least interested in developing a new, esoteric philosophy of internalized freedom, as Hegel was. He was simply impressed with how tenuous and valuable a creation society is. Prudence was his watchword: ". . . to make a government requires no great prudence. Settle the seat of power; teach obedience: and the work is done. To give freedom is still more easy. It is not necessary to guide; it only requires to let go the rein. But to form a *free government*; that is, to temper together these opposite elements of liberty and restraint in one consistent work, requires much thought, deep reflection, a sagacious, powerful, and combining mind."[52]

Surprising, perhaps, that Burke should place as much faith as he did in party government to achieve this delicate end. If the philosopher discerns the ends of government, said Burke, the politician, who is the "philosopher in action," discovers the means to the end. And to reach that end, he must associate with others, even, Burke might have said, at the expense of his own individuality. Admitting the narrow bigotries that sometimes beset party factions, Burke's case for participation in political associations is

---

50 *Appeal*, p. 169. The preceding quotation was from p. 170.
51 *Letter to a Member of the National Assembly*, in *Works*, Vol. IV, p. 52.
52 *Reflections*, pp. 559-60.

still relevant and is couched in infinitely better prose than most "good citizenship" tracts of our day.

> When bad men combine, the good must associate else they will fall, one by one, an unpitied sacrifice in a contemptible struggle. . . . it is not enough that [a man] never did an evil act, but always voted according to his conscience. . . . duty demands and requires that what is right should not only be made known, but made prevalent; that what is evil should not only be detected but defeated. . . . For my part, I find it impossible to conceive that anyone believes in his own politics or thinks them to be of any weight, who refuses to adopt the means of having them reduced into practice.[53]

Burke's famous definition of party—"a body of men united for promoting by their joint endeavors the national interest upon some principle in which they are all agreed"[54]—is often held to be hopelessly idealistic. Read in the context of the *Present Discontents* it appears much less so. Politicians, it is true, talk more of principle and less of interest than the facts would warrant; but nonpoliticians often see more of interest and less of principle than the facts would warrant. Our inability to grant that men with sharply different principles from ours sincerely believe them, helps to obscure the role that ideological principles play in the party politics of even "nonideological" political systems, such as that of the United States. Burke is not so naïve but that he can note with a touch of skepticism the degree to which men confuse the desire for power with their own consciences. The well-run party is a counteractive to such confusions. That Burke suffered from his own party is insufficient reason to say that his own faith in party government was misplaced. It is this faith in "free parties" as a bulwark of "free government" that keeps Burke from complete identification with the group of thinkers known as the Reaction (Hegel, De Maistre, De Bonald, Adam Müller, Friedrich Schlegel and so on). The Reactionaries who followed Hegel (even more than Hegel himself), allowed the concept of internalized freedom to become a cloak for despotism as Burke could never have done.

Conclusion: Prescription and Rights

WHAT Burke the conservative wishes to conserve is the historic community, the partnership in all science, art, and virtue, the necessity that is not chosen, but chooses. The name that Burke gives to this necessity is "prescription." Prescription means that the past legitimizes what it produces, that a moral presumption rests in favor of "any settled scheme of government against any untried project," that "the individual is foolish

---

53 *Present Discontents*, p. 526.   54 *Ibid.*, p. 530.

. . . but the species is wise." The contemplation of prescription produces two problems whose consideration can serve to close our examination of Burke: What does prescription do to individual rights? What ground of value does prescription offer?

PRESCRIPTION AND RIGHTS

Thomas Paine wrote *The Rights of Man* in 1791 as a reply to Burke's *Reflections*. With disarming directness, Paine grants the power of Burke's prescription but rejects its authority. "Paine's doctrine may be given in two words. Kings, like priests, are cheats and impostors."[55] Their power and that of aristocracies rest on superstition and should be swept away. Paine accused Burke of making dead men more important than live ones, of advocating rulers accountable to nobody because they ruled by prescription, and of treating the mass of men as contemptible fools. Paine's constructive theory of natural rights did little to advance earlier conceptions, but his searing criticism of Burke sometimes came close to home.

Burke often spoke of rights. He spoke of "natural rights," "sacred rights," "*real* rights," "the great rule of equality grounded upon our common nature," "the fundamental rule" of all civil society that "no man should be a judge in his own cause," and so forth. The many references display very little consistency, which, no doubt, is itself consistent with Burke's most pervasive view of rights, that "their abstract perfection is their practical defect." As abstractions he was against them and as legal practices he very nearly took them for granted. The important thing for Burke was a clear perception of the national interest derived from the collective experience of the whole society. We should not waste time arguing over the precise boundary of the right to make people miserable, he said in the *Speech on Conciliation with the Colonies*, but explore our interest in making people happy.

John Locke took the rights in the English Constitution and by justifying them in natural-rights terminology made them central to his thought. Edmund Burke took the English Constitution and justified it by prescription, which made the Constitution central and the rights it contained peripheral to his thought.

Thus in answer to the question of what prescription does to individual rights, we can say that in theory it demolishes them and in practice it leaves them untouched—*if* the constitution history has prescribed happens to be the English Constitution.

PRESCRIPTION AND THE GROUND OF VALUE

But what if the constitution is not the English Constitution? Or what if the English Constitution prescribes that all Whig babies be executed at

55 Stephen, *English Thought in The Eighteenth Century*, Vol. II, p. 262.

birth? that M.P.'s shall own no property? that only Jacobins may ascend the British throne? On what grounds could Burke challenge such a constitution if, hypothetically speaking, it were a genuine product of history? Burke would decline to answer on the grounds that since they are always here before us, we cannot speak hypothetically about constitutions, even though metaphysicians may try.

In defense of his various policies Burke appealed at different times to "moral law," to "experience," to "the national interest," to "Providence," to "utility," to "prudence." In all these cases what he was really appealing to was what we all know down deep to be right because we are, after all, Englishmen. In the case of Irishmen, Americans, Indians, and Frenchmen, they were judged *as if* they were Englishmen (which, if we may judge Burke *as if* he were an American, was not in the least uncharitable of him). Burke did not see his own ground of value—though he no doubt felt it—because he was too antiphilosophical to articulate the extreme historical relativism he was continually forced to act on in good faith and in blind faith. As men of action, we are not much different.

But as a man of thought, Burke was needlessly cramped. This inarticulate and (to the twentieth-century scholar) unsophisticated relativism, more than any policy he did or did not support, or any argument he did or did not use, is what makes Burke a conservative. And it is this same relativism that dooms any attempt to make a philosophy out of the various ideological excrescences of conservatism. Though the conservative is often deeply troubled by the spectacle of diversity, diversity is exactly what this type of relativism produces. For if the established order is taken as the ultimate measure of political wisdom, there is no basis of choice among established orders.

CHAPTER

10 | *The Nineteenth Century*

A CENTURY can be a mental image as well as a span of years. If we wish to be metaphorical, we can think of the nineteenth century as the parent of the twentieth century; and the fact that, each in our own way, we *are* the twentieth century makes the nineteenth century the parent of our own most cherished ideologies. Seen in this way, the nineteenth century begins not in 1801, but in 1789, with the French Revolution, or possibly in 1815, with the Congress of Vienna. From our viewpoint, which may still be too close for good focus, the essence of nineteenth-century thought would seem to center around process, growth, and evolution. The eighteenth century was also progressive, but in what now seems an abstract and mechanical way. (The eighteenth century is our grandparent, respected, but distant and outmoded.) Men were concerned in the eighteenth century with choosing the most rational method by which to order society and the world. In the nineteenth century society and the world seemed to be charging blindly forward by natural impulse, and scholars were bent on finding the key to growth. The geometrical mode of thinking had been replaced by the biological.

A sense of hard but rewarding destiny flavors the work of Hegel, who discovered process as a philosophical concern. Growth as a nonrational, subconscious pattern was part of Darwin's biological thinking and ultimately of Freud's psychological thinking. The simple atomistic individualism of early liberal thought was done for. In relation to this new emphasis Bentham must be regarded as basically an eighteenth-century figure, neat and tidy and rather static. But his vigorous influence on nineteenth-century English politics warrants that he be given a separate chapter (Chapter 11) as a nineteenth-century figure. Hegel (Chapter 12) is without question a nineteenth-century thinker, as are his inverted disciple, Marx (Chapter 13), and most members of the socialist movement. In the name of the individual, Nietzsche (Chapter 14) revolted against everything the nineteenth century stood for, and in so doing delighted paradox-lovers by affirming a good part of what the nineteenth century stood for.

Of these four men, more later. First we must sketch a backdrop for their solos, a crude backdrop, no doubt, with some oversimplified issues and a few one-dimensional bit-players; but what more can be done for a century so ripe with contention and so alive with change?

Thanks in part to Hegel, with the nineteenth century we enter the age of ideology, the age of "isms," so in what more appropriate way can we organize this chapter than around the symbols "liberalism," "conservatism," and "socialism," serving as background and foreground to Bentham, Hegel, and Marx, respectively?

Liberalism

ONE has only to recall the distance we have traversed from Locke to Harrington to Montesquieu to Godwin to be struck by how complicated liberalism as a movement was. Its central tenet was, apparently, that the free individual, the liberated individual, is the proper goal of social policy. "Free" had meaning not in some obscure metaphysical sense but rather in the more practical sense of being unbound by traditional hierarchical authority. Individuals were empowered to seek private ends which, it was more or less assumed, were at least somewhat inhibited by a rational propensity toward decent behavior in man as man. Optimism was a recurring ingredient in liberalism. Yet, except for a few figures like Condorcet and Godwin, almost everywhere it was a qualified optimism. The legislature in Locke and the legislator in Bentham were not without quite restrictive responsibilities.

ENGLISH UTILITARIANISM

The mechanical practicalism implicit in the English empiricist tradition came to full flower in the utilitarianism of Jeremy Bentham (1748-1832) and his immediate followers. Without trespassing on Chapter 11, it can be said at this point that the essence of Bentham's system was his "felicific calculus," whereby the legislator could calculate the worth of any legislative proposal by examining the more or less quantifiable pleasures and pains of the mass of the citizens, each citizen counting for one and no more than one. Bentham's basic assumptions were: (1) through the index of pleasure and pain, is and ought can be united (what is most pleasurable to man is what is best for him); (2) social reform, "improvement," is necessary to maximize pleasure and can only be achieved by the elimination of "fictions," superstition, and mystique (typified, for example, by natural law) and the rationalization of laws, penal systems, and social programs; (3) the only legitimate end of government is "the greatest good of the greatest number."

James Mill. Although the influence was reciprocal, Bentham inspired no man more fully than he did James Mill (1773-1836). This stern Scots journalist, the archetype of the ex-Calvinist, carried the utilitarian gospel to the world and with the aid of skillful agitators like Francis Place helped create a climate favorable to the English Reform Bill of 1832. After Mill wrote *The History of India* in 1817, which lifted him out of poverty, he was able to turn to more fundamental issues, namely, the principles of associationist psychology expounded in his *Analysis of the Phenomena of the Human Mind* (1829). Valiantly as he tried, it can hardly be said that he succeeded in bridging the gap between the realm of simple sensations of pleasure and pain and the world of ideas. Nevertheless, he provided a base of sorts for utilitarian ethics and politics. This base Bentham himself hardly needed, but he did need Mill to change him from an aristocratic to a democratic reformer.

James Mill's political thought is most clearly revealed in the article on *Government* that he wrote for the *Encyclopaedia Britannica* in 1820. More explicitly than in Bentham's writings, this article reveals the middle-class bias of utilitarianism. Government exists to protect and extend individual interests—i.e., pleasures—the foremost of which is the enjoyment of property. Distrusting Montesquieu's system of checks and balances to keep rulers on the straight and narrow, Mill places his faith in a system of perfect representation. The suffrage must be universal, but the flavor of legislation would come from one class:

There can be no doubt that the middle rank, which gives to science, to art, and to legislation itself, their most distinguished ornaments, the chief source of all that has exalted and refined human nature, is that portion of the community of which, if the basis of Representation were ever so far extended, the opinion would ultimately decide. Of the people beneath them a vast majority would be sure to be guided by their advice and example.[1]

Mill's approach was deductive, which no doubt made it possible for him to plump for a radically equalitarian politics without seeing the

[1] *Government*, in E. A. Burtt, ed., *The English Philosophers from Bacon to Mill* (New York: Modern Library, 1939), p. 888.

possible implications of this for his equally deductive bourgeois economic theories. On the other hand, there was at the time not much more evidence supporting Mill's opponents, men like Macaulay, who argued that the extension of the suffrage would inevitably lead to the destruction of property rights.

John Stuart Mill. James Mill's son, John Stuart Mill (1806-73), possessed a far more subtle mind than his father. Despite, or possibly because of, the "forced draft" education imposed by his father, a ruthlessly rigorous regime which denied him every pleasure of childhood, John Stuart saw progressively more clearly the weaknesses of utilitarianism as a doctrine. But his liberation from his father came too late to permit his natural genius to break through into the new philosophy of which he was capable. Having organized a "Utilitarian Society" at age sixteen, he called himself a utilitarian to the end.

Young Mill's strengths and weaknesses are well illustrated in his famous *On Liberty* (1859). In this essay he defended freedom of thought, action, and association with rhetoric so felicitous that readers are still moved by it today. "If all mankind minus one were of one opinion, and only one person were of the contrary opinion, mankind would be no more justified in silencing that one person than he, if he had the power, would be justified in silencing mankind."[2] Any suppression of speech implies the infallibility of the suppressor, a futile possibility, as Mill showed with ample historical evidence; it overlooks the needed truth that is buried in every erroneous statement; and it denies to individuals the opportunity to test truth by the challenge of error, a challenge without which oncetruthful propositions dry up and become "dead dogma, not a living truth."

Despite its eloquent libertarian appeal, *On Liberty* is marked by the uncertainties of Mill's position. Still an equalitarian, he was nevertheless bothered by the psychological "tyranny of the majority" (a term borrowed from De Tocqueville), which can fetter the development of unique individuals. His criterion of good social policy was still determined by the essentially negative utilitarian proposition that ". . . the sole end for which mankind are warranted, individually or collectively, in interfering with the liberty of action of any of their number, is self protection. . . . the only purpose for which power can be rightfully exercised over any member of a civilized community against his will is to prevent harm to others."[3] Yet throughout he revealed an implicit faith in a positive concept of evolving truth against which good and bad social policy is presumably

2 *On Liberty*, in *Utilitarianism, Liberty, and Representative Government*, Everyman Ed. (New York: Dutton, 1951), p. 104.

3 *Ibid.*, pp. 95-96. Note the exemption of those not in "civilized communities," in which category Mill explicitly placed children and members of "barbarian nations."

measured. (Since Mill had read Hegel—with, as he said, "a kind of sickening feeling"—it is possible that his concept of truth born of clashing opposites was influenced by Hegel.)

He was still tied to the utilitarian standard of pleasure and pain, but spoke now of "utility in the largest sense, grounded on the permanent interests of a man as a progressive being."[4] This interpretation took all the precision out of the old standard. In fact, there was not much left of Bentham's simple, almost physiological, units of pleasure and pain when Mill said, in *Utilitarianism*, "It is better to be a human being dissatisfied than a pig satisfied; better to be Socrates dissatisfied than a fool satisfied."[5]

Mill's outstanding economics textbook, *The Principles of Political Economy* (1848) dominated its field for half a century, but became less laissez-faire in orientation with each of many succeeding editions until Mill was finally admitting, as against the old "iron law of wages" theory, that trade unions could raise real wages. Like his father, John Stuart was interested in schemes of representation, and in *Representative Government* (1861) he put upon the Hare system of proportional representation an impossibly heavy burden of reform, hoping not only that it could give minority parties a voice in government but that it could thereby stimulate rationality and individuality in the body politic—even though, ironically, Mill did not trust individuals with a secret ballot. He did trust women, however, as "superior in moral goodness" (especially Mrs. Taylor, who became his wife after a twenty-year courtship), and Mill worked hard for woman suffrage, both during his four years in Parliament and by writing *The Subjection of Women* (1869).

Mill's greatest intellectual effort was probably the *System of Logic* (1843), noted especially for its four methods of experimental inquiry. The last section, "On the Logic of the Moral Sciences" is of special interest to us here. It deals with a subject that still fascinates us today—the methodology of the social sciences. Much influenced by the sociology of Auguste Comte,[6] Mill considered and rejected as inappropriate to social studies the loose empiricism of the "chemical or experimental" method and the unreal generalizing of the "geometrical or abstract" method, for which he singled out Bentham himself as an example. The special sociological method he suggested was the "physical or concrete deductive" method, by which general propositions common to "large classes of observed facts" were to be obtained. The complexity of social data

4 *Ibid.*, p. 97.
5 *Utilitarianism*, in *Utilitarianism, Liberty, and Representative Government*, p. 12.
6 See below, p. 282. Mill, in his own *Auguste Comte and Positivism* (3rd ed.; London: Turner, 1882), calls Comte as great as Descartes or Leibnitz, although he criticized some of his canons of proof, and was also, of course, highly critical of Comte's repressive social views.

required, felt Mill, use of both direct and "inverse" deductive operations. Sometimes generalizations could be deduced by reasoning and then confirmed by observation. Sometimes one must begin with conclusions obtained "provisionally from specific experience" and afterward connected "with the principles of human nature by *a priori* reasonings."[7] The latter technique was particularly appropriate to historical data.

The "principles of human nature" referred to above were in essence the "laws of mind" that Mill assumed were largely demonstrated by associationist psychology. He hoped to bridge the gap between this psychology and large-scale sociological generalizations with a new science of character formation called "ethology," which would study the causes and effects of successive "states of mind" in their sociological context. By thinking of character as the effect of habitual will he evaded the old pleasure-pain axis. Recognizing that such a science could not be as exact as physics, he nevertheless hoped it might be as exact as meteorology.

Mill's hopes were, of course, unfulfilled, and his methodology would not be of much practical use today. The important point, however, is that in the *Logic* "science" conceived on a close analogy to physical science was being applied to man in his social setting in a new and more rigorous way, yet without the disregard for historical insights characteristic of earlier utilitarianism.

Mill was very much a "man in the middle," placed in a state of tension by virtue of the sympathetic insights of his quick and open mind which could see the worth in competing trends: democracy versus aristocracy; laissez faire versus welfare state; the autonomous individual versus the value of social cohesion; a nonmoral social science (called, ironically, "moral science") versus humane reformism. As L. T. Hobhouse wrote, ". . . in his single person he spans the interval between the old and the new liberalism."[8]

Austin. Another utilitarian with a quite different kind of influence was John Austin (1790-1859). London neighbor of Bentham and James Mill, Austin was appointed by their intervention to the chair of jurisprudence at the new University College, London. Though he failed as a lecturer, he succeeded in founding a new school of legal theory. Mainly through *The Province of Jurisprudence Determined* (1832) and to some extent *Lectures on Jurisprudence* (1863) he became the spokesman of "analytical jurisprudence." He was fearful of universal suffrage and more conservative than Bentham. But he must be discussed under the general heading of liberalism because his strong utilitarian beliefs, which com-

---

7 *System of Logics*, Bk. VI, Ch. 9, sec. 1 (8th ed.; London: Longmans, Green, 1925), p. 585.
8 *Liberalism* (New York: Holt, 1911), p. 107.

plemented if they did not determine his theory of law, were directed at the same traditionalist targets battered by Bentham: natural law, social myths, nonrational legal custom, and metaphysics generally. He believed that the good of society was merely the aggregate of individual interests. He believed in education, free trade, limited government, and Locke's empiricism. He disparaged attempts to erect a good of the whole which would transcend all private values.[9]

Austin's jurisprudential mission owed much to Hobbes' theory of sovereignty, and was dedicated to clearness, precision, and concreteness. He concerned himself with "positive" law in the full sense of the word —the exposition of law as it is, not confused with considerations of what it ought to be. "The science of jurisprudence . . . is concerned with positive laws, or with laws strictly so called, as considered without regard to their goodness or badness."[10] Law is, very simply, the command of the sovereign. And who is the sovereign? ". . . if a determinate human superior, not in a habit of obedience to a like superior, receive habitual obedience from the bulk of a given society, that determinate superior is sovereign in that society." And what of ancient law? ". . . (borrowing the language of Hobbes) 'the legislator is he, not by whose authority the law was first made, but by whose authority it continues to be a law.' "[11]

Austin added fuel to the reformist fires of Bentham's legal criticisms by his claim that law properly conceived must be clear, determinate, positive; but the very strength of his logic restricted his theoretical impact. To overcome loose social fictions, legal obscurantism, and the dead hand of the past, he sought to erect a hard logical structure, eschewing moralism, delineating law as only a means to an end, while holding in abeyance consideration of the ends of society. He, like Hobbes, clearly distinguished between the legal and the moral.[12] To this extent his efforts were toward a wholly formalistic theory of law, i.e., a *science* of law.

But he also wanted a science of *law* and not mere power, a theory of authority and not mere force. He was unwilling to make sovereign anyone who could grab power momentarily. To make this clear he was forced to enter the empirical realm through his definition of sovereignty. The sovereign is one who receives "*habitual* obedience from the *bulk*

9 Utilitarians did not believe, he said, that "the lover should kiss his mistress with an eye to the common weal." For the dry Austin, an unexpected burst of humor. Quoted in John Bowle, *Politics and Opinion in the Nineteenth Century* (New York: Oxford Univ. Press, 1954), p. 73.

10 *Lectures on Jurisprudence*, Lec. 5, in W. Jethro Brown, ed., *The Austinian Theory of Law* (London: J. Murray, 1906), p. 35.

11 *Ibid.*, Lec. 6, pp. 97, 96.

12 For the implications of this distinction see the exchange between Huntington Cairns and Stuart M. Brown, Jr., in Carl J. Friedrich, ed., *Community* (New York: Liberal Arts Press, 1959), Chs. 2-3.

of a given society." Once the habits of the masses are involved we are faced with an empirical sociological determination of no mean proportions. Bentham preferred to talk about the pleasure-pain calculations of individuals and legislator rather than the habits of large masses. This definition would have made it much easier to build a logical system, although the resulting system would have been further removed than Austin's from social reality.

English utilitarianism, though subject to many mutations, was still doing at the end of the nineteenth century what it was doing at the beginning: trying to reform fellow Englishmen by telling them to be logical, a difficult if not impossible task in any age and place, but a liberalizing task notwithstanding.

CONTINENTAL LIBERALISM

We frequently read that liberalism in England was concrete, grounded in tangible electoral, parliamentary, and judicial practices, whereas French liberalism was abstract, inflated by revolutionary rhetoric never brought to earth. But the Charter of the Bourbon restoration in 1814 moved sharply away from revolutionary ideology, and instead of expounding the Rights of Man it itemized a few rights of Frenchmen. High property qualifications prevented it from being a democratic instrument so far as representation was concerned, but it did grant religious liberty, freedom of speech, equality before the law, and, above all, the inviolability of property—for although it was granted by Louis XVIII, this was a bourgeois charter. The old aristocracy had been decimated by the French Revolution. Its spokesmen were, as we shall see, the very reactionary writers such as De Maistre and De Bonald, who were more officeholders than landowners. The bourgeoisie, by contrast, were strong, having won over the peasant proprietors, but their economic wealth came from commerce and finance rather than manufacturing. Hence the clash, as someone has noted, was between aristocrats without land and capitalists without factories, and the pressing task of liberal theory was to mediate between the two.

Royer-Collard. Among those who tried to mediate were the badly named Doctrinaires, so few in number that "they could all find room on a sofa," but with considerable influence. Their leader was Pierre Paul Royer-Collard (1763-1845),[13] the philosopher of the Charter; another prominent member was the historian François Guizot (1787-1874), who

13 Royer-Collard's political thought is almost wholly contained in his speeches, many of which are collected in A. G. P. Brugière de Barante, *Vie politique de M. Royer-Collard* (Paris: Didier, 1861), 2 vols. The best exposition of his thought in English is Harold J. Laski, *Authority in the Modern State* (New Haven: Yale Univ. Press, 1919), Ch. 4.

ultimately became Premier. To the left of these two was the novelist Benjamin Constant (1767-1830), organizer of the Liberal Party in 1817. Unlike the moderate Doctrinaires, he regarded the Charter as but a stepping stone to something better and often attacked the men who supported it.

Despite a tentative move toward practicalism, we find in Royer-Collard's theory of sovereignty a recurrence of the visionary faith in words which has so plagued France. Royer-Collard tried to elaborate a conception of sovereignty that, because it was divorced from individual interests, could not be attached to any concrete political institutions. Yet, haunted by the memory of the Terror, he also insisted on the safeguards of a system of separation of powers. He distinguished between two types of interest in society: liberty, especially of speech, press, and judicial process, which he associated with the popular (actually, the bourgeois) Chamber of Deputies; and stability, which was maintained by the power of the elite group of Peers.

Royer-Collard saw more clearly than most liberals that government must necessarily reflect the social structure around it, and this was his major theoretical strength. Yet at the same time he tended to exaggerate the causal force of written constitutions, making almost a fetish of the Charter. Moreover, if government must accurately reflect the realities of society, it seems a bit disproportionate to give monarchy and the nobility roughly two thirds of the political power, as his system did. The bourgeoisie were possibly short-changed, but even more so were the masses, whom he regarded as both politically inexperienced and corruptible. His hope that a deep affection for the constitution would rise up out of the masses was therefore quite unrealistic. Later in life, Royer-Collard's idea of sovereignty in reason began to take on a more explicitly middle-class coloration. Invoking Aristotle's idea of reason as a mean, he made the median position of the middle class in society an argument for the rationality of its having a disproportionate share of power.[14]

Constant. Benjamin Constant was as antidemocratic as Royer-Collard or Guizot, but the tool he used as a check on popular sovereignty was an eighteenth-century conception of natural rights which the historicism of the Doctrinaires had destroyed. In this sense, Constant was a throwback to an earlier period. But in another sense, he was ahead of the Doctrinaires. In his use of the word "sovereignty" he brought the term back to earth from the abstract "sovereignty in reason" as used by Royer-Collard:

14 Guizot, a more prolific political writer and also more the expedient politician, was close to Royer-Collard in most respects. He also stressed the value of middle-class moderation as against the dangerous "power of the word Democracy." A touch of cynicism is apparent in such phrases as: "All are in turn democrats as against those above them, aristocrats as against those below." *Democracy in France,* trans. anon. (New York: Appleton, 1849), pp. 11, 25.

. . . one must not build upon an abstract idea in the illusion that it can increase the sum of individual liberty. . . . there is a part of human life which necessarily remains individual and independent, and has the right to stand outside all social control. Where the independent life of the individual begins, the jurisdiction of the sovereign ends. Rousseau failed to see this elementary truth. . . .[15]

Constant also saw more clearly than most of his contemporaries the importance of a party system as a prerequisite for effective cabinet government (an insight which De Ruggiero interestingly attributes to Constant's Protestant background) and possessed in general a realistic grasp of the subtleties involved in making a parliamentary machine run. Equipped with this realism, he could see the futility of the recurring quest for a new *polis*. In the most famous of his essays, "Ancient and Modern Liberty," he contrasts the Greek *polis*, which has the power to control everything but is in turn controlled by the freemen who participate in it, with the modern state, in which, because of its size and complexity, this kind of participation is impossible. In such a society, liberty has meaning only in the negative sense of freedom *from* state interference. This was Constant's answer to Rousseau and, as well, an assertion of middle-class independence.

De Tocqueville. It is a mark of the difference between the two countries that one of the best known of the French liberals of this period, Alexis de Tocqueville (1805-1859), is called a conservative by citizens of the America he studied so engagingly in *Democracy in America* (1835). That a "conservative liberal" is not really a contradiction in terms need not invalidate the contrast between a France uncertain of its future and the lively frontier equalitarianism that so impressed De Tocqueville in the United States. The great virtue of De Tocqueville as a thinker is that, though an aristocrat, he could appraise the virtues and faults of democracy with cool detachment. Without rebelling against his class, he could, unlike the other French liberals, rise above class feeling. He traveled in America and wrote about it with one eye on France, which helps to explain the almost deductive quality of his comments. The theme of *Democracy in America*, insinuating itself between pungent comments on associations, religion, lawyers, and popular manners, is that equality is dangerous but may nevertheless be a price worth paying for liberty. The danger is tyranny, the new and subtle tyranny of the majority: ". . . the majority possesses a power which is physical and moral at the same time; it acts upon the will as well as upon the

15 *Cours de politique constitutionelle* (1839), p. 64. Quoted in Guido de Ruggiero, *History of European Liberalism*, trans. by R. G. Collingwood (Boston: Beacon Press, 1959), p. 161.

actions of men, and it represses not only all content, but all controversy."[16]

But De Tocqueville also recognized that the centralizing tendencies of modern industry and the machine mentality arising from the division of labor, rather than merely pernicious doctrines, were causal roots of what he thought was a growing equalitarian conformity. Moreover, he was open-minded enough to see, in the words of one of his chapter titles, the "causes which mitigate the tyranny of the majority in the United States." In the restless, competitive, fluid side of American life he found an alternative to the compartmentalization of French society, the "great number of watertight compartments, small, self-contained units, each of which watched vigilantly over its own interests and took no part in the life of the community at large."[17] This tendency of French life was what had enabled the Revolution to be so swift and sweeping, yet even when De Tocqueville wrote it had not been eliminated, nor, indeed, has it been wholly eliminated even today. His hopes for keeping equality libertarian were no doubt based too heavily on a parallel hope that political equality need not necessarily lead to social equality; but whatever the basis of his hopes and fears, De Tocqueville had a more clear-eyed perception of the irreversibility of the revolutionary forces than any of the reactionaries or most of the liberals of his day. He "dispelled a nightmare by showing that the democratic idea, far from being a revolutionary aberration, stood upon the highway of French history."[18] Had middle-class theorists been as flexible as De Tocqueville and held less tightly to their class positions, possibly the middle class itself would have been better able to surmount the jab from the Right in the Revolution of 1830 and the jolt from the Left in the Revolution of 1848. Even though they saw the relationship of social structure to politics more clearly than did the English utilitarians, historically speaking, the French liberals could never lead the nineteenth-century parade.

Von Gneist. If the French liberals were not conspicuous successes, how much less so were the German liberals. Liberalism in Germany reflected the divided nation and the antiquated feudal system within which the theorists wrote. The typical liberal concern for rights took on a legal, if not a legalistic, bent. But in trying to make individual rights into an objective reality immune from practical politics, the theorists succeeded mainly in making them abstract. Rudolph von Gneist (1816-1895), leader of mid-century German liberals, aimed in his theory of

16 *Democracy in America*, Ch. 14, trans. by Henry Reeve, Oxford World's Classics (New York: Oxford Univ. Press, 1946), p. 192.
17 *The Old Regime and the French Revolution* (1856), trans. by Stuart Gilbert (New York: Doubleday [Anchor Books], 1955), p. 77.
18 De Ruggiero, *European Liberalism*, p. 191.

Der Rechtstaat to define a sphere of popular freedom in such a way that it would not weaken the force of unified monarchical authority, and he thought he found an answer in administration. The result was a highly circumscribed bureaucratic liberalism.[19]

Von Treitschke. A more fundamental attack on the problem was to follow the lead of Hegel and redefine the concept of freedom. Heinrich von Treitschke (1834-1896) in *Freedom* (1861), a reply to Mill's *On Liberty*, offered the classic exposition of the German alternative to English liberalism. He supported freedom, but of a somewhat different brand from Mill's. "Whoever sees the state as only a means for the ends of the citizens must logically demand . . . freedom from the state not freedom in the state."[20] Only the latter would suit Treitschke. By English standards this was half-hearted liberalism at best. In their preoccupation with law many German scholars in the latter half of the nineteenth century (typified by C. F. von Gerber, Paul Laband, and Georg Jellinek) showed a similar fascination with an abstract "will of the state"; only now as "analytical jurisprudence" it was a will divorced from moral values as well as from the power of a flesh-and-blood monarch. Suspended in this no-man's-land between power and morality, legality itself became a kind of self-justifying and dangerously elusive entity, either powerless morality or amoral power, depending on factors the scholars did not care to discuss. At least the analytic-positivist jurisprudence of Austin gave the sovereign human form and deferred to a realm of social morality beyond the law, which might hold him accountable. Theories tend, however, to become more abstract as the possibility of free choice between the practical political alternatives associated with those theories declines. In this respect Germany was an ideal locale for abstract theory.

Mazzini. In Italy, too, the divided character of the once-proud nation affected the political theory of liberalism, and the lack of a strong middle class made republicanism futile. Ths situation spawned the sometimes pathetic, always romantic idealism of that diverse group of nationalist agitators called the *risorgiomento* ("resurrection"). The best-known member was Joseph Mazzini (1805-1872), whose cosmopolitanism came from the fact that he was forced to spend most of his life outside the country he was trying to save. Somewhat in the fashion of Rousseau, Mazzini was impressed by a natural goodness in man which drives him toward cooperation and community, an inclination to be at one with

19 See *Vier Abhandlungen über das constitutionelle prinzip*, (1864), discussed in Leonard Krieger, *The German Idea of Freedom* (Boston: Beacon Press, 1957), pp. 356ff.
20 Quoted in Krieger, p. 367.

something greater than the self. Mazzini's brand of liberalism was several steps removed from atomistic individualism. His major book was not on the Rights of Man, but on the *Duties of Man* (1840-43). The message was liberal to the extent that Mazzini insisted on a criterion of meaningful duty as being self-imposed duty, which in turn required a democratic environment.

There is much of Rousseau in this doctrine, but Mazzini's great contribution is that he applied his criterion of self-imposed duty not only to the state but to all associations, and he welcomed a plurality of associations within the state as Rousseau had not. At least on the theoretical level, Mazzini was therefore much more than a mere nationalist. But the possibilities of this theory of free associations were unfortunately unrealized. A neo-Hegelian nationalism hung over Mazzini's attempt to make the state a very special association, the one that was common to all men, while at the same time he somewhat fuzzily tried to set apart from both state and lesser associations an inviolable realm of individual freedom.

SOCIAL DARWINISM

"Social Darwinism" is a handy label for a school of antipolitical theorists who flourished spectacularly in the second half of the nineteenth century. By means of rather clumsy analogies they were able to seize upon Charles Darwin's theories of biological evolution, and, stressing terms like "natural selection" and "survival of the fittest," to transfer this authority to the much older theory of laissez faire. Their theory was liberal in that it would free the individual from governmental restraints, but perhaps not so liberal in respect to the socio-economic restraints from which it did not free the individual.

Spencer. As Karl Polanyi labored to demonstrate,[21] the free-market doctrines of the economic liberals were implemented only by carefully organized planning, as nonspontaneous as any planning; but they nevertheless insisted that the free market was in some sense prior to government, "natural," and that governmental economic policy could do little more than get in the way. "The policy of *laissez faire* as applied to the workers was a policy of negation, derived from a philosophy of complacency compounded with antipathy to the unsuccessful. It received its harshest justification at the hands of the last of the bourgeois liberals, Herbert Spencer."[22] The harshness of Herbert Spencer (1820-1903) was, however, coated with a generous layer of historicist optimism:

21 *The Great Transformation* (Boston: Beacon Press, 1957).
22 J. Salwyn Schapiro, *Liberalism and the Challenge of Fascism* (New York: McGraw-Hill, 1949), p. 105.

Pervading all nature we may see at work a stern discipline which is a little cruel that it may be very kind. That state of universal warfare maintained throughout the lower creation, to the great perplexity of many worthy people, is at bottom the most merciful provision which the circumstances admit of. . . . By the aid of . . . purifying process, as well as by the fighting so universal in the pairing season, all vitiation of the race through the multiplication of its inferior samples is prevented, and the maintenance of a constitution completely adapted to surrounding conditions, and therefore most productive of happiness is assured.[23]

Spencer at least had the virtue of greater consistency than most liberals. He could and did point with some alarm to state interventions his lax liberal brethren had let slip by: enforced vaccination, rural drainage, coal-mine safety regulations, laws preventing the exploitation of boy chimney sweeps, and many other horrendous measures. There were, of course, some exceptions to Spencer's proscription on state meddling. He approved laws restraining the blowing of locomotive whistles (Spencer suffered from insomnia) and the making of boned corsets for women (they deformed the female figure).

All this makes it appear that Spencer approved of no coercion whatsoever; but he was, of course, not this hopeless. As Sheldon Wolin has suggested,[24] the liberals were forced to face the reality of society; but by making it a separable, natural backdrop to an evil government, they were better able to condemn the latter while ignoring the former. Hence, "freedom" meant freedom from government, not escape from all coercion. Man "must have a master; but the master may be Nature or may be a fellow man. When he is under the impersonal coercion of Nature, we say that he is free; and when he is under the personal coercion of some one above him, we call him . . . a slave, a serf, or a vassal."[25] It is curious, but in passages like this we find it possible to put this extreme opponent of state power and enemy of metaphysics alongside the most idealistic, antiliberal German statist: in one case the individual is free (and helpless) before Nature, in the other, before the state.

The naturalism expressed in this passage was by no means casual.[26] The

23 Herbert Spencer, *Social Statics* (abridged and rev. ed.; New York: Appleton, 1892), pp. 149-50. This book was originally published in 1851, eight years before Charles Darwin's *The Origin of the Species*. It was Spencer, not Darwin, who coined the phrase, "survival of the fittest." Social Darwinists *used* Darwin, but their ideas were not generated by him.

24 *Politics and Vision* (Boston: Little, Brown, 1960), Ch. 9.

25 Spencer, *Essays, Scientific, Political, and Speculative* (New York: Appleton, 1896), Vol. III, p. 450.

26 The chapter titles of *Man Versus the State* (Caldwell, Idaho: Caxton Printers, 1954) suggest the content: "The New Toryism," "The Sins of Legislators," "Over-Legislation," and so on. The London unemployed Spencer explains very simply: "They are simply the good-for-nothings, who in one way or another live on the good-for-something . . ." (p. 23).

revival of Spencer by today's right-wing publicists has only added to the obscurity into which his nonpolitical writings have fallen, but he thought of himself as a synthesizer of all human thought. His scheme for the *Synthetic Philosophy* was, in conception, as ambitious as Comte's. As part of the plan he wrote *First Principles* (1862), *Principles of Biology* (1864-67), *Principles of Psychology* (1872), *Principles of Sociology* (1876), and *Principles of Ethics* (1896). In ethics Spencer belonged to the utilitarians, sharing their faith in an ultimate happiness divorced from transcendental values, and sharing their inability to see society as an organic whole. But now a theory of historical evolution was grafted on and loosely drawn scientific laws were invoked in behalf of political conclusions. For example, the Lamarckian theory of the inheritance of acquired characteristics was used to explain why the better society of the future would be populated with the competitive English types whom Spencer so admired (a non-Darwinian theory, incidentally).

Thanks in a small measure to Comte, from whom he continually tried to distinguish himself, Spencer moved steadily from a social biology toward a social physics; but it remained a pseudo-science of society nevertheless. "The fundamental confusion which he never surmounts is due to the fact that *a priori* conceptions of individual rights with which he starts do not and cannot accord with the organic and evolutionary conception of the State which he attains through the use of natural science. . . . Spencer's logic is really bare and mechanical. It is a matter of constant antitheses which are too clear-cut to correspond to life."[27] By this means Spencer could with the utmost certainty announce that society was evolving beyond war and that war would soon disappear from the earth.

Evolution was indeed Spencer's God. But "His God has betrayed him. We have evolved beyond Spencer."[28]

Sumner. Spencer's American disciple William Graham Sumner (1840-1910) was both less pretentious and more realistic than his English counterpart. Without attempting a *Synthetic Philosophy*, he focused an unsentimental eye on what he took to be the fine fruits of unregulated struggle. Yet no more than in Spencer could his lucid, commonsensical prose conceal the confused philosophy of history that lurked behind every premise. The struggle that was so natural and so productive referred in the end not to military, moral, or power struggles at large but to a very special kind of economic struggle that required "liberty under law" to insure "peace for the laborer and security for the capitalist."

27 Ernest Barker, *Political Thought in England, 1848 to 1914* (2nd ed., rev.; London: Oxford Univ. Press, 1947), p. 71.
28 Crane Brinton, *English Political Thought in the Nineteenth Century* (Cambridge: Harvard Univ. Press, 1949), p. 227.

The cooperative emotions required to build that kind of liberty under law were left unexplored, because the results of such inquiry would have contradicted the basic Social Darwinist dogma that "Competition . . . is a law of nature. Nature is entirely neutral; she submits to him who most energetically and resolutely assails her. She grants her rewards to the fittest. . . ."[29] Another, deeper, contradiction is embedded in this passage. Nature is entirely neutral. Yet "she" (neutral, though not, please note, a neuter) seems invariably to abandon her neutrality when it comes to handing out prizes. For the "fittest" (a term with unmistakable moral connotations in both Spencer and Sumner) always win.

Social Darwinism is important because so many people have believed in it, both before and after it was given that label. From Lord Brougham to Andrew Carnegie to Senator Barry Goldwater, economically successful men have copied or created similar theories to justify their success. The whole nineteenth century, a century of industrial upsurge and progressive cosmology, was a stimulus to such theories. The apex was certainly the Victorian era, toward the caricature of which we all look at times with nostalgia; for there life was real, the struggle was heroic— but the good always won.

Conservatism

TO conserve something is easier than to liberate something, so the term "conservatism" is not one which imposes rigorous definitional limits. Under its broad canopy we may and will group such diverse figures as the reactionary-technocratic-positivistic Comte, the half-liberal Green, the romantic elitist Carlyle. If anything holds them together it is the assertion of social tradition as a value superior to privately determined individual rights (and even to this statement must no doubt be added, to fit Carlyle's case: "by ordinary individuals"). At bottom, a social good prior to and greater than individual goods was what liberals could not assert. Though in many ways flourishing in the nineteenth century, the liberals had a more difficult time ignoring the factor of social tradition and the organic wholeness of political orders after the disruption of the French Revolution than they had had before. By the same token, conservatism as a whole in the ninetenth century was deeply marked by memories of

29 "The Challenge of Facts," in A. G. Keller and M. R. Davie, eds., *The Essays of William Graham Sumner* (New Haven: Yale Univ. Press, 1934), Vol. II, p. 95. Sumner, it should be pointed out, was no apologist for American "robber barons." He opposed the protective tariff and the Spanish-American War even at the risk of losing his Yale professorship.

the Revolution. The early and most intense reactors turned their reaction into a name for the group to which they belonged.

THE REACTION

Edmund Burke was the best-known exponent of these anti-revolutionary feelings; but his own temperament, as we have seen, and the stable constitutional pattern of his nation, restrained him from the extremism that characterized France then as it does today. The explosive mixture of Revolutionary equalitarianism, Bourbon absolutism, and Napoleonic militarism created a poor climate for the constitutional moderates of France. Although they, too, lived with the memory of Revolutionary excesses, a man like De Maistre seems better to fit the dark mood of the times.

De Maistre. A nobleman and civic official who was Sardinian ambassador to Russia from 1803 to 1815, Joseph de Maistre (1776-1847), was a fanatic absolutist and ecclesiast. He did not simply disapprove of unorthodoxy and democracy. He loathed, despised, and raged against them. He dismissed the argument for popular suffrage by noting that children and lunatics may be represented in court by persons they have not chosen, and since the people are "a perpetual child, a perpetual lunatic," why not let another speak for them?[30] To give power to the people, De Maistre felt, was to unmuzzle a tiger. Absolutism was essential for the simple reason that society would fall apart without it.

Perhaps the greatest significance of De Maistre is his role as a negative critic of liberalism and some of its easy claims, especially in its quest for a secular freedom. His criticism, however, at best tended to be extreme. Locke, Voltaire, and Rousseau alike were ridiculed for envisioning a mythical state where there are so many "wills loose in the world" that anarchy followed by slavery is inevitable. The idea of the social contract is a foolish abstraction. Popular sovereignty is an altogether empty concept which merely bemuses the liberals. The rash of legislation with which revolutionaries always indulge themselves can only weaken the body politic, for authority is best accepted *in toto* and not chopped up into nothing by an attempt to put everything into legal terminology.

De Maistre's negative attack did nevertheless stem from a rich theological base. Like St. Augustine, he felt that government was made necessary by original sin. The most that one can do with sinful, emotional, unreasoning, prejudiced man is to pound him over the head with the correct prejudices until he behaves himself sufficiently to maintain social

30 *Considérations sur la France* (1796), Ch. 4. Quoted in Roger Soltau, *French Political Thought in the Nineteenth Century* (New Haven: Yale Univ. Press, 1931), p. 21.

order—until, in effect, he does the right thing for the wrong reason. This is why the Roman Church is the model for all government. Man must be ruled by mystery, and the supreme authority of the Pope is the highest mystery. "*Infallibility* in the spiritual order and *sovereignty* in the temporal order are perfectly synonymous words."[31] But mystery alone is not enough. Another essential cement of the social fabric is the restraint of terror produced by the *bourreau*, the executioner, whose mission is painted in ghastly hues in the dialogues *Soirées de St. Petersburg* (1822), all the more ghastly because of the proper pride De Maistre gives the executioner after he has expertly and professionally tortured a hapless soul.[32]

Such bizarre strains aside, De Maistre is probably most original in relating his ideas on authority to the process of language formation. Somewhat in the manner of Vico,[33] he regarded the creation of language as a mysterious, mythical process which is destroyed as soon as it becomes self-conscious. Like primitive religion—indeed, like all religion—language is simply *there*, its origins shrouded in mystery, yet inseparable from even the most rational activity of the human mind. The absolute identity of thought and language, in which De Maistre believed, imprisons man in the culture that produces language without possibility of escape, for moral conscience itself is subsequent to language. Perhaps, then, De Maistre was being consistent and not merely chauvinistic in finding a cause for unity in the spread of French as the international language.[34]

De Maistre, finally, treated the problem of war with poetic, sardonic, morbid insight. He saw war as a universal expression of blood lust, collective guilt, and ritual sacrifice peculiar to the human animal. His discussion of sacrifice is ingenious. An essential part of society's need to live, he felt, was the process—called "reversibility of merits"—whereby the innocent are made to atone for the sins of the guilty (De Maistre is not clear on the matter of where Louis XVI stood in this exchange!)[35]

De Maistre made the dark side of the human psyche the characteristic side, and the necessity of its control by mysterious and unquestioned political authority became for him virtually self-evident. Twentieth-century conservatives have surpassed De Maistre in logic, but none has surpassed him in the power of expression, and for a defender of mystery the power of expression becomes in a practical way all-important. A less, or possibly more, charitable way of assessing this talent was Lamartine's comment on

31 *Du Pape*, Ch. 1, sec. 1. (Paris: Garnier, n.d.), p. 21.
32 *Soirées de St. Petersburg*, Disc. 1 (Lyon: E. Vitte, 1924), Vol. I, pp. 31ff.
33 See Elio Gianturco, *Joseph De Maistre and Giambattista Vico* (Washington, D.C.: privately published, 1937). This book includes an excellent bibliography on De Maistre.
34 See the discussion of language in Gianturco, Ch. 4.
35 *Soirées*, Disc. 9, Vol. II, pp. 120ff.

De Maistre that the man was superior to the writer and the writer was superior to the thinker.[36]

De Bonald. De Maistre's contemporary Louis de Bonald (1753-1840)[37] likewise saw religion as the only firm basis for social organization and shared De Maistre's nostalgia for the feudal past. Bonald was fascinated by triads and molded his whole thought to fit a triangular pattern. The basic triad was cause, means, effect. The cause of society was God, its means absolute sovereignty, and its effect man himself, who was, needless to say, utterly a social creature. Society itself, thus, was the ultimate authority, because man was made by and for society, or by and for God, which amounted to very much the same thing. Analogous triads existed for religion: God, priests, believers; for politics: king, nobility, people; and for the family: father, mother, children.

De Bonald indulged in a more elaborate empirical study than De Maistre to prove that man is shaped by society, but he did not have De Maistre's sense of historical development and was not much concerned to explain how it is that men rebel *against* the society that controls them, though he granted that this, like rebellion against God, was part of man's grim fate. Speaking of the French Revolution he said, ". . . a people who, in their desire for written laws, have lost their customs, impose on themselves the hard necessity of writing everything, even their customs."[38] De Bonald took Rousseau's general will, and, by denying that all individuals harbored it, turned it into a rationale for simple monarchy. But at least he took pains to distinguish between absolute power, which he defended, and arbitrary power, which he did not.

In general, De Bonald's more static position enabled him to cling to the present with a tenacity even greater than De Maistre's, and the authority of language as the symbol of man's inability to remake his society was even more important to him. Yet in a curious lapse he attacked the contractualists at one point by postulating the inevitable development of a future society somewhat comparable to the old governmentless state of nature that was the heart of his enemies' doctrine.

Fichte. Germany, still essentially an agrarian nation at the beginning of the century and politically but a collection of feudal principalities, had early begun to develop a self-conscious national philosophy with strong romantic elements. Romanticism in Germany had a profound influence on conservative thought at this time, as did French romanticism later in the century. Johann Gottfried von Herder, the eighteenth-century "champion

36 Cited by Jules d'Ottange, Preface to *Du Pape*, p. 5.
37 Exiled during the Revolution, De Bonald was minister of instruction in 1808, a deputy in 1815, a peer in 1823. He refused to take the oath of allegiance to Louis Philippe. His chief works were *De la législation primitive* (1802) and *Recherches philosophiques sur les premiers objets des connaissances morales* (1818).
38 *Législation primitive* (Paris: A. Le Cere, 1857), title page.

of intuition against analysis, of faith against the intellect, of history against science,"[39] was the movement's mentor, and the scientific rationalism of the *Aufklärung* was its target. Its leaders opposed the search for universal laws and gloried in subjective relativism. Herder had been largely apolitical, but fear of the anarchy that, the romantics felt, accompanied the analytic thought of the Enlightenment (the French Revolution was, of course, the great example) led them to stress a religion and a community safe from analysis. The stress on subjective individuality on the one hand and the sanctity of the community on the other suggests an inner tension in romanticism which is not illusory. The romantics did in fact tend to exempt only the man of genius from the heavy hand of duty.

The poet Johann Friedrich von Schiller (1759-1805), who gave Hegel his beginning tenet—"*Die Weltgeschichte ist das Weltgericht*" ("World history is world justice")—and the reformer Wilhelm von Humboldt (1767-1835) were more individualistic than the romantics and favored less state interference. But they too criticized reason as the key to enlightenment. The unsavory features of later German nationalism are often traced back to Johann Gottlieb Fichte (1762-1814), first rector of the University of Berlin. Fichte began his career as a rationalist and never abandoned rationalist categories (his self-designation as the inheritor of Kant's mantle led to a repudiation by Kant himself), but he became increasingly divorced from this tradition in fact and is generally considered in the camp of German romantics. In practical politics he moved from Jacobinism to conservative nationalism.

Fichte incorporated some liberal symbols, such as contract and freedom of thought, in his political theory, but his devotion to communal unity seemed to contradict their typical meaning. He rejected separation of powers on the grounds that the state's will must be single and free of the taint of private interests. The three ascending stages of civil contract, as Fichte saw it, were property, which was self-oriented; protection, which involved mutual security; and association, in which all men agree to a rule of law made and administered by a single fixed will to which they all subordinate themselves. The subordination was to be more than merely external; it also included a subjective feeling of trust. The state thus created was endowed with a mystical quality. It was, as he said, "not merely a *compositum* but a *totum*. In the organic body every part continuously preserves the whole and by preserving it the part itself is preserved; the citizen's relation to the state is precisely the same."[40]

39 H. S. Reiss, in the Introduction to his edition of *The Political Thought of the German Romantics, 1793-1815* (Oxford: Blackwell, 1955), p. 2.

40 *Grundlage der Naturrechts* (1797), in Reiss, pp. 44-73. The passage quoted occurs on p. 73. See the editor's commentary in the Introduction, pp. 11-22.

In *The Closed Commercial State* (1800)[41] Fichte describes his ideal of a state fully self-supporting and economically independent. The entire economy is controlled by the state, all individuals are assigned their work, a rigid hierarchy of classes is established, foreign trade is abolished, and war is sanctioned if necessary to establish "natural" frontiers. The only right available to the citizen is the right of emigration. Perhaps the most famous work of Fichte is *Addresses to the German Nation* (1808), made up of inflamed appeals to German nationalism. Obviously stirred by Napoleon's defeat of Prussia, Fichte points to the need to bring together the high culture of German life with the power which can make it effective in the world. This great mission requires economic self-sufficiency, proper pride in nationhood, and the devotion and sacrifices of individuals to the state.[42]

Georg W. F. Hegel (1770-1831) followed Fichte at the University of Berlin and shared many of his nationalistic sentiments and to some extent his mode of exposition. Hegel can be called part of the Reaction, but he fits into no categories neatly because as a man of genius he transcended the old to invent new categories. For that reason he deserves a chapter to himself (Chapter 12). What Hegel gave to the nineteenth century was a sense of the dynamic movement of history. What the Reaction as a whole gave to the nineteenth century was a conception of man as a dependent, nonself-directing member of a predetermined social group. The conception would be ignored or rejected by the liberals, but would return again in different form with the socialists.

POSITIVISM

Positivism, as Charles Frankel points out,[43] is a double-barrelled word. It suggests first of all a matter-of-fact orientation—concern for what is rather than what ought to be, distrust of metaphysics, support for science. In this sense, it is not so much conservative as scientifically neutral on those questions on which conservative and radical emotions are spent.

The term is also identified with certain specific attempts to systematize social knowledge by the use of methodologies akin to those of the natural sciences, the most famous if not the first of which is the "Positive Philosophy" of August Comte. John Stuart Mill, as we have seen, made an exploratory effort in the same direction in his *System of Logic*. He was an economic liberal and a political reformer. Herbert Spencer likewise contributed to what he called positive philosophy. He was an economic liberal and a political conservative. The disparity in the social views of these three

41 *Der Geschlossene Handelstadt*, in Reiss, pp. 86-102.
42 See the Thirteenth Address, in Reiss, pp. 102-118.
43 Charles Frankel, "Positivism," in Virgilius Ferm, ed., *A History of Philosophical Systems* (New York: Philosophical Library, 1950).

men is enough to suggest that positivism itself does not necessarily fit under the general heading of "conservatism." But whether or not he was conservative, positivist Comte was indubitably antiliberal. He was directly influenced by De Maistre (as well as by utopian socialism). We shall discuss Comte under the heading of conservatism, therefore, because he fits this category not well but better than any other.

Comte. A one-time secretary to the utopian socialist Claude Henri de Saint-Simon, Auguste Comte (1798-1857) was a troubled and impoverished tutor of mathematics. He published a six-volume *Cours de philosophie positive* from 1830 to 1842 and a four-volume *Système de politique positive* from 1851 to 1854.[44] Both works were marked by an unbelievable intellectual arrogance. Comte refused to read any of his contemporaries' writings because he knew, a priori, they were unworthy of him. Though not a qualified scientist he undertook in the *Cours de philosophie* to cover the frontiers of knowledge in all the natural sciences. His arrogance was not, however, a substitute for work. He worked and wrote with a fearful zeal, and made life even harder for himself by arbitrary self-imposed rules, such as writing seven chapters of seven sections of seven sentences with no repetition of words in consecutive sentences—all this to improve, he said, his style. Thus he did not exempt even himself from what Mill called his "frenzy for regulation."

For all its massive bulk, the Comtean system can be summarized rather briefly. History, he said, falls into three distinct stages, the theological, the metaphysical, and the positive. The first stage, progressing from primitive polytheism to monotheism, lasted until the end of the Middle Ages. As man shed the superstition of supernatural religion he began to put his faith in impersonal gods, in metaphysical abstractions such as "nature" or "natural rights" and in fictions such as "social contract" or "sovereignty of the people." The eighteenth century was the apex of the metaphysical stage, a necessary step in the progressive unfolding of history, but still laden with errors. By the nineteenth century the positive stage was ready to be born, and Comte generously offered himself as midwife. It may be an index of Comte's egocentricity that two of the three stages of human history were telescoped into the last two of twenty or thirty centuries.

The positive stage is the stage of science. Theology and metaphysics are now set aside in order to look at the positive facts of society, the world as it is. Using the understanding that is gained from this look, mankind, through the agency of certain men, will be able logically to induce "invariable laws of phenomena" which may then be manipulated in order to

44 See Comte, *A General View of Positivism*, trans. by J. H. Bridges (Stanford, Cal.: Academic Reprints, n.d.). This represents the first volume of the 1848 edition of the *Système*, which has been widely reprinted.

establish a reign of perfect harmony on earth. The basic tool for this reconstruction of society was of course science, but all sciences, it seems, are not equal (nor are all men, as it turned out). Comte arranged the sciences in a hierarchical order from the simplest and most basic, mathematics, at the bottom, to the most complex at the top. Here was the queen of them all, "sociology" (Comte invented the term after "social physics" proved inadequate), perched atop the pyramid, giving imperious orders. There can be no doubt that Comte earned his title, "the father of sociology."

The technocracy Comte describes in his *Système de politique positive* as appropriate to the positivistic age is a magic mixture of De Maistre's reactionary theocracy and Saint-Simon's or Fourier's gadget-filled socialist utopia. The temptation to make fun of it is almost irresistible. A committee of three bankers will handle industry, commerce, and agriculture, respectively. In the elaborately constructed thirteen-month Positivist Calendar there will be special days for honoring "the higher dignity of the banking element." There will also be a "Festival of the Proletarian" at which great inventors will be fêted. Education of the young until age fourteen will be entirely in the hands of women, whom Comte regarded as superior to men in morality and "social feeling." A rigorous educational regime will be imposed on everyone until age twenty-one. An "Occidental Committee" is charged with the responsibility of spreading the Positivistic gospel slowly but surely around the world. In what Comte thought a perfectly reasonable scheme of representation, the committee will be made up of eight Frenchmen, seven Englishmen, six Germans, five Italians, and four Spaniards. The committee meetings will always be in Paris. Outside, the green Positivist flag will fly, with "Order and Progress" on one (the "male") side, and "Live for Others" on the other (the "female") side. This flag must be distinguished from that used for religious services, which is adorned with the image of a woman thirty years old, holding her son in her arms.

Having taken the old religion away from positivistic man, Comte felt obliged to give him a new religion, "Catholicism without Christianity," as it is frequently called. The "Religion of Humanity" had hymns, meditations on great men, a trained positivist priesthood, and even a trinity: the Great Being (humanity), the Grand Fetich (earth), and the Grand Medium (space). "Love . . . is our principle; Order our basis, and Progress our end."[45]

The details of Comte's political-social-religious dream world could be spelled out interminably. But rather than look at details we must look at what is important in his over-all effort to reorganize society. Part of what

45 *General View*, p. 355.

is important in Comte is, of course, simply the typical nineteenth-century traits that he, like many others, represented: hopefulness and confidence in the progressive character of historical evolution; fascination with industry and technology and the possibilities of extensive social regulation; faith in science. But the most important part of Comte is what he did not share with many, a recognition of the problem of separating "heart and intellect," and of the role society plays in such a separation. The theological stage of history had failed because it was unintelligent. The metaphysical stage of history had failed because it was only intelligent: it had failed to produce a social system that did justice to the affective side of man and his need for the warmth of belonging. In a graphic metaphor, Comte said that, as in the old fable a man died when he saw his own ghost, each age passed away when it saw the ghost of itself in the succeeding age.[46] The failure of the French Revolution to provide orderly emotional substance behind the individualistic abstractions it espoused led directly, Comte felt, to the anarchic denouement of that particular drama, a drama very much on Comte's mind. The elaborate artificiality of Comte's Religion of Humanity is apt to lead us away from the fact that his insights into the social necessity of some kind of religion were often penetrating. As Comte put it, "the principal religious difficulty is to secure that the external shall regulate the internal without affecting its spontaneity," a problem of special difficulty when "the intelligence is in insurrection against the heart."[47] But eventually, positivist science gives back, as Caird puts it, what it has seemed to take away, namely a basis for religious belief. John Stuart Mill approved of the taking away, but was dismayed by what was put back. "Others may laugh, but we could rather weep at this melancholy decadence of a great intellect."[48] Mill was not complaining merely of the quaint excesses of the Religion of Humanity, but of the presumptuous way Comte was trying to make over man: "Like the extreme Calvinists, he requires that all believers shall be saints, and damns them (after his own fashion) if they are not."[49]

In his peculiar way, despite his frightening solutions, Comte had an insight into the deficiencies of his own society: the abstract, impersonal, mechanical quality of life in the new industrial age; the loss of traditional faith, which called for some kind of substitute; and the exaggeration of economic values at the expense of the affective.

46 Quoted in Edward Caird, *The Social Philosophy and Religion of Comte* (New York: Macmillan, 1885), p. 18. This is a first-rate sympathetic interpretation of Comte from Caird's neo-Hegelian point of view.

47 *Ibid.*, p. 27.

48 Mill, *Auguste Comte and Positivism*, p. 199.

49 *Ibid.*, p. 145.

IDEALISM

The term "idealist" has two quite distinct meanings. In its popular sense it refers to anyone who is altruistic, who thinks well of his fellow man, who is hopeful and charged with good will. In the technical philosophical sense it refers to one who believes that ideas and the ideational, rather than matter, spirit, or something else, are the substance of ultimate reality. Although these generalizations should not be taken too seriously, it may be said that the popular idealist tends to be nonconservative as a matter of temperament, simply because he is willing to venture forth to make improvements in an imperfect world and, possibly, to let others have free rein in their attempts at improvement. On the other hand, insofar as his views affect politics at all, the philosophical idealist tends to be conservative to the extent that he regards the realm of ultimate truth in ideas as accessible only to the few rather than to the many. Most philosophical idealists seem to find themselves in this position. Plato, paradoxically, was conservative to the point of being utopian. Kant, with his individualism, did, it is true, bring a new liberal spirit into idealism. But Hegel, though his "spirit" absorbed "idea," and his conservatism was of a uniquely dynamic variety, must be counted both an idealist and a conservative.

Green. The so-called Oxford Idealists, neo-Hegelians all, displayed the incipient tendencies toward conservatism that one might expect. But practical English individualism kept creeping in, sometimes in disguise, to divert and even thwart authoritarian conclusions. Thomas Hill Green (1836-1882), the dominant figure in the group,[50] was the most liberal; or, one might better say, he rejected the old liberalism in such a way as to help create a new liberalism. Green was an idealist in both of the preceding senses, and as a hard-working elected member of the Oxford City Council and School Board, a temperance leader, and a philosophy professor, he knew political thought and action from many angles.

Liberty was, in a way, Green's fundamental concern; but not liberty in the old liberal sense of absence of restraint, or negative liberty. His concept of liberty or freedom is positive, not freedom *from*, but freedom *for*, and it is part of a long tradition:

. . . freedom is in some sense the goal of moral endeavor; . . . there is some will in a man with which many or most of his voluntary actions do not accord, a higher self that is not satisfied by the objects which yet he deliberately pursues. Some such notion is common to those different theories about freedom

50 Others were F. H. Bradley, Bernard Bosanquet, D. G. Ritchie, and Edward Caird. Their influence continued into the twentieth century through such figures as A. D. Lindsay, the Master of Balliol College. See Lindsay, *The Modern Democratic State* (New York: Oxford Univ. Press, 1947).

which in the rough we have ascribed severally to the Stoics, St. Paul, Kant, and Hegel. . . . So far as the proposition means anything it would seem to represent Kant's notion . . . of there being two wills or selves in a man, the "pure" will or ego and the "empirical" will or ego, the pure will being independent of a man's actual desires and directed to the fullfillment of a universal law of which it is itself the giver. . . .[51]

The problem in Green and the Oxford Idealists stems not so much from this Kantian view of selfhood, but from the attempt to identify this "higher self" with the purposes of the state. The state is at one point called a "society of societies" but it is not the simple existential phenomenon the utilitarians took it to be. "It is a mistake to think of the State as an aggregation of individuals under a sovereign. . . ."[52] It is a moral entity, somehow identical with the "true selves" of all. It "secures and extends the exercise of powers which men, influenced in dealing with each other by an idea of common good, had recognized in each other as being capable of direction to that common good. . . . It is not a state unless it does so."[53] As against the legalistic utilitarians, Green goes to great lengths to illustrate the degree to which we all depend upon some conception of the common good to maintain social life itself. His existential and experiential evidence on behalf of this contention was perhaps Green's strongest feature.

One of the latter-day members of the movement said of the Oxford group: "[They] went for their philosophical inspiration to some very undemocratic sources, to Plato and to Hegel, as well as to Kant and the seventeenth century Puritans; but their purpose in so doing was to carry out better and more thoroughly what the Utilitarians had begun."[54] Such a statement tends to minimize the sharp differences which in fact separated the idealists from the utilitarians. For one thing, Green was not much interested in the mechanics of democracy, systems of representation and the like. The Lectures on Political Obligation were addressed to questions that were more ethical than legal or political, in the narrow sense of those words. His thought was democratic only in the sense that its premise was also a democratic premise, namely (in the words of one of Green's chapter titles) "Will, not force, is the basis of the state."[55] While most utilitarians regarded rights as the expression of individual self-interest, Green saw rights as but one aspect of the necessity for all moral acts to be directed toward a common good. Rights, thus, inhere in individuals only insofar

51 Lectures on the Principles of Political Obligation, sec. 19. (London: Longmans, Green, 1941), pp. 18-19.

52 Ibid., sec. 134, p. 139.   53 Ibid., sec. 132, p. 138.

54 A. D. Lindsay, in the Introduction to Green, Lectures on Political Obligation, p. ix.

55 Lectures on Political Obligation, p. 121. See the discussion in Barker, Political Thought in England, pp. 30f.

as those individuals are members of a society which recognizes such rights. Society (or, rather, the state) is the determiner of the good, instead of the individual, as was the case in both contractualist and utilitarian thought.

Green is not, however, it must be hastily added, as authoritarian as this might make it appear. ". . . if we regard the state as the sustainer and harmonizer of social relations it would follow that the individual can have no right against the state; that its law must be to him of absolute authority. But in fact as actual states at best fulfill but partially their ideal function, we cannot apply this rule to practice." There follows what is, perhaps necessarily, a somewhat cloudy discussion of when the individual can resist the dictates of his state, from which Green concludes that the individual has no rights against the state "founded on any right to do as he likes. Whatever counter-rights he has must be founded on a relation to the social well-being, and that a relation of which his fellow citizens are aware. He must be able to point to some public interest, *generally recognized as such*, which is involved in the exercise of the power claimed by him as a right; . . ."[56] Although Green read and admired John Stuart Mill, there is a world of difference between Green's reliance upon what is generally accepted and Mill's one man who is justified in standing alone against the whole world.

The problem of rights takes us to the central problem in Green, one we have already hinted at—the problem of the relationship between state and society, or, what is almost the same thing, between the state as power and the state as moral consensus. On the one hand, Green speaks in this fashion: "To ask why I am to submit to the power of the state, is to ask why I am to allow my life to be regulated by that complex of institutions without which I literally should not have a life to call my own. . . ."[57] The state here appears to be the natural force of the social whole from which we can never escape and to which we owe everything. Government is but a minor part of this complex. On the other hand, the state also seems to be a specific institution, a part and not the whole. It is the "sustainer and harmonizer of social relations," a function which "actual states at best fulfill but partially."[58] In this context the state is finite and partial. It is creature not creator. It is not the source of moral standards, but is to be judged by moral standards arising elsewhere, from society at large, or, perhaps, from T. H. Green at large: ". . . the state, or the sovereign as a characteristic institution of the state, does not create rights, but gives fuller reality to rights already existing. It secures and extends the exercise of powers, which men, influenced in dealing with each other by an idea

56 *Lectures on Political Obligation*, secs. 143-44, pp. 148-49. Italics added.
57 *Ibid.*, sec. 114, p. 122.   58 *Ibid.*, sec. 143, p. 148.

of common good, had recognized in each other as being capable of direction to that common good. . . . It is not a state unless it does so."[59]

Contemplating this confusion between state and society, Leonard Hobhouse, who regarded himself as a spokesman for post-utilitarian liberalism, said, "it is only misleading to identify the entire [social] fabric with a state organization which is only one of its necessary components. . . . By playing between these two meanings, we get the worst of both worlds."[60] Hobhouse found many other inconsistencies: for example, in one place Green regards rights as "made by recognition"; in another place, rights "remain rights though any particular state or all states refuse to recognize them." But Hobhouse did more than merely point out discrepancies. He launched a devastating attack on the fundamental tenets of the whole school, namely, that true individual freedom lies in conformity with our "real will'; that our "real will" is identical with the "general will"; that the "general will" is embodied in the state. All of this, finds Hobhouse, rests upon metaphor rather than evidence, sentiment rather than logic.

Hobhouse, we must confess, seems to win his argument; but on pragmatic grounds he was opening the door to more state regulation than the older liberals would have liked, and, on nonpragmatic grounds, the net effect of Green's doctrines was precisely the same. Though his specific economic ideas are strictly middle-class, Green sees the function of the state as a moral one: to improve the character of its individual members. In the simplest terms it can be said that he helped to justify the positive state by metaphysical arguments, while men like John Stuart Mill and Hobhouse were accepting the positive state without abandoning as decisively the tenets of early liberalism. It should not be surprising that as it was refined and extended, political idealism moved in both conservative and liberal directions; conservative in men like Bosanquet in England and, to the far right, Giovanni Gentile in Italy; liberal in men like Benedetto Croce in Italy, Ernest Barker in England, or William E. Hocking in the United States.

Political idealism corrected the error of those liberals who failed to take the independent moral worth of society seriously and made the individual unrealistically autonomous. In so doing, idealism, like virtually all movements of thought, overcorrected and made possible authoritarian extension.[61] But no system is perfect, and despite his inconsistencies, we

59 *Ibid.*, sec. 133, p. 138.
60 Leonard T. Hobhouse, *The Metaphysical Theory of the State: A Criticism* (London: Allen & Unwin, 1918), p. 82. Hobhouse at this point is actually attacking Bernard Bosanquet, but the point is valid against Green as well.
61 Perhaps Green's clearest and most conspicuous departure from Hegel's conservatism was his erection of universal brotherhood as a political goal and his vigorous attacks on war as a solution to international tensions.

can hardly help but be grateful for the good will that animated everything Green wrote.

ELITISM

If idealism is only tenuously related to conservatism, how much more so is elitism, by which we mean any view that assigns the capacity to govern to a specially selected group or type of individual. If we wish to play with labels we could call Burke a conservative, half-liberal elitist, Comte a reactionary-radical elitist, and Marx a radical-socialist elitist. Perhaps the purest kind of elitism is that which looks longingly to "great men," almost irrespective of ideology. Nietzsche, as we shall see in Chapter 14, is a writer in this category.

Carlyle. Another such writer is Thomas Carlyle (1795-1881), and we shall pay him brief attention here. He cannot be called typical of nine-teenth-century elitists, since the genre is without common markings, but he could probably only have happened in the nineteenth century. Carlyle had no system. System is probably impossible for one who believes that history is nothing but the biography of great men. A simple conception of history, you say, and it is: ". . . no time need have gone to ruin, could it have found a man great enough, a man wise and good enough."[62] But, though simple, not without mystery. "History is the essence of innumer-able Biographies. But if one Biography, nay, our own Biography, study and recapitulate it as we may, remains in so many points unintelligible to us, how much more must these million, the very facts of which, to say nothing of the purport of them, we know not, and cannot know!"[63] In the dazzling stylistic pyrotechnics of Carlyle's essays one finds doubt and faith, compassion and cruelty. He is wholly subjective and egocentric, a former Calvinist infected by German romanticism, building little coffer-dams against the democratic tides.

Carlyle detested the industrial revolution and what it did to men:

I will venture to believe that in no time, since the beginnings of Society, was the lot of these same dumb millions of toilers so entirely unbearable as it is even in the days now passing over us. It is not to die, or even to die of hunger, that makes a man wretched; many men have died; all men must die, —the last exit of us all is in a Fire-Chariot of Pain. But it is to live miserable we know not why; to work sore and yet gain nothing; to be heart-worn, weary, yet isolated, unrelated, girt-in with a cold universal Laissez-faire; it is to die slowly all our life long, imprisoned in a deaf, dead, Infinite Injustice,

62 *Heroes, Hero-Worship, and the Heroic in History* (1841), Lec. 1 (New York: A. L. Burt, n.d.), p. 15.
63 *On History* (1830), in *Critical and Miscellaneous Essays* (new ed.; New York: Appleton, 1871), p. 220.

as in the accursed iron belly of a Phalaris' Bull! This is and remains forever intolerable to all men whom God has made. Do we wonder at French Revolutions, Chartisms, Revolts of Three Days?[64]

Yet Carlyle had no reforms in mind to correct the evils of industrialism other than paternal reliance on great men, in this case the "Captains of Industry," who, "if Industry is ever to be led, are virtually Captains of the World! If there be no nobleness in them, there will never be an Aristocracy more."[65] By the same token, utilitarian slogans about liberty were nothing as against the need for men who could keep the ignorant masses from destroying themselves. "You do not allow a palpable madman to leap over precipices; you violate his liberty, you that are wise. . . . Every stupid, every cowardly and foolish man is but a less palpable madman: his true liberty were that a wiser man, any and every wiser man, could, by brass collars, or in whatever milder or sharper way, lay hold of him when he was going wrong, and order and compel him to go a little righter."[66] Democracy is only an option when men despair of finding heroes who can lead them. That the casting of a vote in a polling booth constitutes a significant act of self-leadership is a nonsensical and superstitious fiction of "our National Palaver." That all men are in some sense equal is nothing less than ridiculous.

As he grew older Carlyle seemed less and less charitable toward the working man; but at all periods he seemed to think that the need to worship great men was psychologically necessary as well as socially useful. ". . . if worship even of a star had some meaning in it, how much more might that of a hero! Worship of a hero is transcendent admiration of a great man. I say great men are still admirable; I say there is, at bottom, nothing else admirable."[67] Little wonder that, given Carlyle's latent Calvinism, the duty of obedience to superiors becomes a prime virtue and the style of leadership of the hero over the masses becomes comparable to that of a drill sergeant handling raw recruits. Fluctuating between humanitarian concern for the victim of laissez faire and castigation of their idleness, between praise of great men and blame of the mere "talkers" in Parliament, Carlyle offered few solutions to "the condition of England." To call him a feudal socialist is misleading. But the term is, perhaps, appropriate to his admirer, Ruskin.

Ruskin. John Ruskin (1819-1900) was not a socialist in our meaning of the term. The label "feudal socialism"[68] is a testament to the power of

64 *Past and Present* (1843), Bk. III, Ch. 13, in *Works* (London: Chapman & Hall, n.d.), Vol. X, pp. 210-11.
65 *Ibid.*, Bk. IV, Ch. 4, p. 271.   66 *Ibid.*, Bk. III, Ch. 13, p. 212.
67 *Heroes, Hero-Worship, and the Heroic in History*, p. 13.
68 Also applied to William Morris (1834-1896), the eccentric poet, Oxonian, and furniture manufacturer who helped organize the Socialist League in 1884. Like

the socialist symbol in the late nineteenth century, and also to the power of the individualistic assumptions against which socialism fought. Any alternative to the competitive-individualistic society that produced and was produced by the machine tended to be shunted into the socialist camp, since there the anti-individualists seemed to have their headquarters. Ruskin, artist, art critic, Oxford professor, and supporter of a fantastic variety of good causes, has been a much neglected figure in the history of political thought. His call for the reorganization of a decadent society in the interests of creating the necessary preconditions for great art has a disorderly pungency about it that is still compelling. The materialism, the blindness to economic misery, the cheap standards he saw everywhere around him evoked a passionate appeal for a cooperative rather than a competitive society, one which sanctified honest craftsmanship rather than tawdry success.

Ruskin criticized classical economics for its disregard of man's "social affections," for treating him like a "covetous machine." To stimulate a sense of craftsmanship in all men he would pay good and bad workmen identical wages, on the analogy of physicians' uniform fees, so that the motives for doing better work would be intrinsic to the job and not tainted by mercenary feelings. And he would establish government workshops and factories which would turn out model creations of every necessity and art at model prices. This would hold aloft a standard of excellence for private enterprise and enable every man to know the experience of buying "bread that was bread, ale that was ale, and work that was work."[69]

Ruskin scarcely considered the bureaucratic implications of his proposals, although a deep-seated paternalism rode along with these sometimes progressive, sometimes regressive notions. He blamed the system for unemployment, but he blamed the unemployed even more. He would have had the government give work to the unemployed but withhold wages until the worker "has come to a sounder mind respecting the laws of unemployment."[70] Like Plato he made rulership a restricted profession and equated democracy with anarchy. A brilliant but erratic man, almost the equal of Carlyle in literary powers, Ruskin (with the help of William Morris) inspired the subsequent Guild Socialist movement. In his desire to make every man an artist he would have treated men as children; yet his vision of a society dominated at every level by a soothing blend of cooperative affection and pure artistic value is as much an indictment of

---

Ruskin, he was dedicated to the elimination of the "eyeless vulgarity" of Victorian culture, but, as revealed in his fictional utopia, *News From Nowhere* (1890), he was more willing to entertain thoughts of revolution.

69 *Unto This Last* (1860), in *The Seven Lamps of Architecture, Sesame and Lilies, Unto This Last* (Boston: Estes, n.d.), p. 144.

70 *Ibid.*, p. 145.

the twentieth-century machine age as it was of the society of its own day.

Racism. The elitism of certain nineteenth-century racists is different in kind from that which we have been discussing. Its significance is more historical than intrinsic. Today we look at these writings to find the roots of Nazi and Fascist race theories. But we can also regard them as one manifestation of the concern for biology as a key to history peculiar to the Darwinian age. Their content is less rewarding.

The two best-known racists of the later nineteenth century were Count Arthur Joseph de Gobineau (1816-1882), a Frenchman claiming German blood, and Houston Stewart Chamberlain (1855-1926), an Englishman claiming German blood.[71] De Gobineau resurrected and polished up the label "Aryan" to designate those people he thought biologically superior, the Persians in Asia and the Teutons in Europe. Europeans in general (except for the "somewhat inferior" Jews) were superior to the Chinese, and the Chinese were superior to the Negroes. De Gobineau's training in poetry led him to the "scientific" conclusion that the process of polluting Aryan blood with that of inferior races had better stop or we would all be in trouble. Chamberlain likewise thought that the Teutons were responsible for everything good in philosophy, politics, economics, science, culture, and lager beer. The most Teutonic people of all, the Germans, were, it follows, a "master race," a concept defended by reference to the indisputable fact that there are many, many different breeds of dogs, and some can bark louder than others.

Socialism

LIBERALISM established the authority of the individual, against which the conservatives reasserted the authority of the community. Socialism in the nineteenth century was groping toward the establishment of the authority of the class. But this culmination in the work of Marx was preceded by a wide variety of non-Marxian socialisms. Perhaps the best known are the works of the utopian socialists, of whom we may look briefly at three, Saint-Simon, Owen, and Fourier.

71 See De Gobineau, *Essai sur l'inégalité des races humaines* (1853-55), trans. by A. Collins as *The Inequality of Human Races* (London: William Heinemann, 1915); Chamberlain, *Die Grundlagen des neunzehnten Jahrhunderts* (2nd ed., 1900), trans. by J. Lees as *The Foundations of the Nineteenth Century* (London: J. Lane Co., 1912). An important disciple of De Gobineau in France was Hippolyte Taine (1828-1893), who attacked the "metaphysical concepts" of general will, social contract, and consent of the governed, stressed in the manner of Hegel and Treitschke the naturalness of conflict and the "positive fact of force," and sought a return to the "organic rules of society," namely: (1) rule by aristocracy, (2) regionalism combined with naturalism, (3) heightened race consciousness. See also the American, Madison Grant, *The Passing of the Great Race* (New York: Scribner, 1916).

Utopian Socialism

Every age seems to produce its utopias. From Plato to More to Orwell men have been fascinated by tales of what might be but is not. A utopia (literally, "no place") may be optimistic or pessimistic. Today's utopias, called "science fiction," run toward the pessimistic. In the nineteenth century they were generously optimistic.

Saint-Simon. The colorful character of Count Claude Henri de Rouvroy de Saint-Simon (1760-1825) has perhaps spread an undeserved veneer of glamor over all subsequent utopians. Defiant, egoistical, and impulsive, he dashed off to fight—and fight well—in the American Revolution, and afterwards headed for Mexico to try to persuade the viceroy to build something like the Panama Canal. Back in France he renounced his title, supported the Revolution, but nevertheless wound up in jail. There came his great vision. Charlemagne appeared to him in a dream and commissioned him to become a great philosopher. He spent the rest of his life and his fortune trying—unsuccessfully. In poverty, he attempted suicide in 1823, but the shot was not fatal and he lingered on for two more years.

Saint-Simon left behind a mountain of writings demonstrating that the workers (*les industriels*) produced the most of what was valuable but received the least by way of reward. He proposed that the whole society be organized as a factory with each man rewarded solely on the basis of his work. The politics of this transformation Saint-Simon left wholly unexplored; and though he left behind a dedicated band of disciples, they were not much help on the point.

Owen. Of considerably greater influence were Robert Owen (1771-1858) and Charles Fourier (1772-1837). Owen's is the story of a successful businessman who became a radical reformer. Rising from a draper's apprenticeship to become a prosperous Manchester cotton manufacturer, he decided to attempt an experiment when he took over what was supposed to be a model factory at New Lanark, Scotland. This factory had been blessed with schools for children, which they attended *after* their eleven-and-a-half-hour working day (in twelve years only fourteen children had died from overwork). The town saw large families crowded into one room, garbage piling up in the streets, pubs galore, and every Saturday night a wild, despairing debauch. Owen cleaned up the place. He introduced sanitation, nursery schools, and good cheap whisky combined with fines for drunkenness. By the time he came to America to set up his New Harmony, Indiana, experiment he was so famous he was asked to address Congress. The Indiana experiment, incidentally, cursed with a democratic constitution, gave Owen all kinds of trouble. But with or without trouble, Owen became a symbol of encouragement to popular education, workers' cooperatives, and labor unions.

Philosophically, Owen began as a Benthamite, but one major deviation put him on a distant shore: he rejected self-interest as the basis of happiness. Furthermore, man is, he felt, a product of his environment, and society can therefore transform self-interest into altruism. ". . . there is no fixed standard, in any part of the world, of a good or a bad man; both terms have ever been the creation of the prejudices and imaginations of the human mind, according to the education it has received. . . . Men are made to be what they are, by their organization, and the external circumstances which act upon and influence it. None are or can be bad by nature; their education is always the business or work of society and not of the individual."[72] Owen does recognize inherited, "constitutional" factors, but he does not seriously examine the interaction between inheritance and environment, nor does he wrestle with the philosophic problem of how a completely determined man can transform the environment which makes him what he is. He simply *assumes* that the essential nature of man is altruistic, using rather conventional English notions of altruism.

If one were to eliminate, therefore, such encumbrances as property, family, and orthodox religion, the spontaneous urge for human solidarity would burst forth:

The individuality of man, unavoidable by his nature, which is, now, through ignorance, a cause of so much disunion of the human race, will become the cause of the more intimate union, and of the increase of pleasure and enjoyment. Contrasts of feelings and opinions which have been, hitherto, causes of anger, hatred and repulsion, will become sources of attraction, as being the most easy and direct mode to acquire an extended knowledge of our nature and of the laws which govern it.[73]

The shallowness of Owen's thinking is apparent. Good and bad are wholly relative and dependent upon peculiarities of environment. Change certain nineteenth-century environmental conventions and the true laws of man's good nature will be revealed. The two propositions can hardly be made compatible.

Owen's deepest faith was in industrial efficiency, and his great antagonist was the "pandemonium" of a society constructed around and hence perpetuating egocentric economics. As long as society was based on such economic assumptions, all the "political devices" attained by the liberals—equal representation, extensions of the suffrage, and so forth—were worthless. Almost by default, therefore, Owen reduced political problems to unimportance and was blind to the totalitarian possibilities of his ideal society. Without such "political devices" for self-protection the individual was wholly absorbed in the social unit. Owen's ideal society was held together by a rigid class structure based wholly on age. He loved children—they were so malleable. Children were the trainees. The middle-aged did the work, the old governed, and the oldest handled foreign affairs (his ideal-sized unit was, of course, the town, not the nation).

What about conflict within the community? There would not be any, since altruists do not have conflicts. Government would be, therefore, merely the administration of things rather than the rule of men (in anticipation of the Marxist utopia). The general will would reign supreme. But even Rousseau had wrestled with the problem of controlling the particular will. Owen simply ignored such problems. He could not imagine the possibility of an individual wanting to leave an Owenite association.

Owen was a practical as well as a theoretical failure. The working class had already found cause for some hope in political participation, in achieving the liberal reforms which Owen scorned. Actually he had a distaste for hard political conflict. A genteel and benevolent paternalist, he thought he could persuade wealthy men to see the light and that would be enough. He had a falling out with one of his lieutenants in 1834 when he accused the man of stirring up class hatred in articles calling for a general strike. Owen approved of the general strike but somewhat inconsistently thought agitation for it should be carried on in a spirit of complete magnanimity, "merely by an overwhelming moral influence, which influence individuals and nations will speedily perceive the uselessness and folly of attempting to resist."[74] Workers were not interested, however, in harmony for its own sake. They hated the bosses and wanted to get out of them what they could. Hence, ironically, Karl Marx was to call Owen a "class collaborator."

Fourier. Charles Fourier was a slightly insane traveling salesman who, with amazing perseverence and enthusiasm, wrote mounds of repetitious prose in hotel rooms all over Europe. On the surface, he seems to be the opposite of Owen. Owen was a radical environmentalist; Fourier was a radical nonenvironmentalist. Human nature was not malleable; it was fixed, static; human passions have been the same in all periods of history. This would seem to provide a solid base for conservatism. But Fourier argued that these fixed passions are good as well as fixed and that existing social organization has frustrated and perverted them. Hence, by changing the social organization, man's natural goodness would be liberated. In practical results, then, Fourier is very close to Owen. One changes man, the other liberates the real man.

Like Bentham, Fourier had a mania for classification and worked out a catalogue of the twelve basic human passions. He, like Owen, attacked the competitive chaos of the new capitalistic society, but he admired

74 Quoted in G. D. H. Cole, *Robert Owen* (London: Benn, 1925), p. 216.

its efficiency and productivity. Like the French reactionaries, he stressed the value of solidarity within small communities, to which he gave the name phalanxes *(phalanstères)*. His descriptions of life in the phalanxes were incredibly detailed (we shall charitably omit his similarly detailed descriptions of life on other planets), with heavy emphasis on the centralized kitchen which turned out the fabulous meals that Fourier, a bachelor, probably never enjoyed in reality. Given free play, the twelve passions of man (the five senses, the four "group passions" of friendship, love, family feeling, and ambition; and the three "distributive passions" for planning, change, and unity) will automatically combine into the one supreme passion of love for others. When people come together in phalanxes of from four hundred to two thousand, share a great central building, and work at the tasks they most enjoy (mainly agricultural), everyone is happy. Even the dirty work of garbage collection and slaughtering gets done voluntarily because, as we all know, this is what children most love to do.

Reflecting the capitalist mentality Fourier thought he was expunging, the economics of the phalanx is that of a joint stock company. All invest in the enterprise and the profits are split five twelfths to labor, four twelfths to capital, and three twelfths to talent. The government was more democratic than in Owen's associations, since officers were elected, but with everyone so full of joy, little government was needed. Movement between phalanxes was possible without hindrance, as was movement between jobs within phalanxes. If Owen erred on the side of too little movement, surely Fourier erred on the side of too much movement. Harmony would become anarchy.

Yet despite what seems extreme impracticality Fourierism was tried in France and worked with some success,[75] and some forty Fourierist phalanxes were established in the United States. The most famous was Brook Farm in Massachusetts (the subject of Hawthorne's novel *The Blithedale Romance*), which had been established earlier by George Ripley, but was converted to the Fourier gospel through the efforts of Albert Brisbane in 1844. The New England transcendentalists—Emerson, Thoreau, Alcott, Hawthorne—looked on approvingly. All the Owenite and Fourierist experiments failed eventually, but the spirit of new life in America was an encouraging atmosphere for such ventures and it was great fun while it lasted.[76]

75 See industrialist Jean Godin's description of his "familistère" in *Social Solutions*, trans. by Marie Howland (New York: Lovell, 1886).

76 Not that Fourierism was the last display of sentimental utopianism in America. Edward Bellamy's charming utopian romance *Looking Backward* (1887) touched off a wave of "Nationalist Clubs" in the late eighties and nineties devoted to Bellamy's technocratic anticapitalist principles.

ANARCHISM

Proud'hon. Pierre-Joseph Proud'hon (1809-1865) is hard to classify, but he was probably the first man to call himself an "anarchist" (i.e., one opposed to all organized government), so we shall accept the designation.[77] An impoverished printer's compositor who read everything he set and seemed to forget none of it, he criticized Owen and Fourier for inadvertently substituting a new despotism for an old. He drove sharply to the root of their defect, their assumption of inherent human goodness. Somewhat in the terms of traditional religion (though he was strongly anticlerical), Proud'hon saw man, rather, as characterized by an inner struggle between good and evil, and responsible for his own condition as much as conditions are responsible for him. Man's passions are not all evil, but they need to be contained.

It follows that real advance is always spiritual advance. On these grounds Proud'hon attacked the materialist emphasis of *both* capitalism and socialism, being one of the few political theorists in the nineteenth century who did. His first well-known book was *What Is Property?* (*Qu'est-ce que la Propriété?* 1840). The answer to the question made him notorious: "Property is theft." Property is "the mother of tyranny," the "negation of equality." Not property but labor is the basis of production and under capitalism labor is denied its rightful reward. He was proud of his answer and proud of his notoriety, but it made him appear more radical than he actually was. He did, it is true, reject the whole political and religious structure of his day as a tool of economic interests, and in this came very close to Marx. And he had the radical's disdain for "solutions." "I build no system. I ask an end to privilege, the abolition of slavery, equality of rights, and the reign of law. Justice, nothing else; that is the alpha and omega of my argument: to others I leave the business of governing the world."[78] Yet like Saint-Simon and Comte he hoped for a science of politics, and he was fascinated by the possibility of Lockean contract applied at the nongovernmental level. In order to diminish the power of the central government, he wanted to see a network of contracts between producers for specific purposes, creating "a world of spontaneous self-governing producers."

The aim of Proud'hon's scheme was also radical in its simplicity. He sought the promotion of human dignity conceived in the light of his own stolid peasant virtues, his somewhat puritanical humanism. Though more pessimistic than Owen and Fourier, he felt that by exercising his own personal responsibility man could conceivably reorganize society.

77 The classification of Proud'hon continues to be a problem. J. Salwyn Schapiro regards him as a "herald of fascism." *Liberalism and the Challenge of Fascism*, Ch. 14.
78 *What Is Property?* trans. by Benjamin R. Tucker (New York: Humboldt, 1876), p. 14.

He called himself a theorist of poverty, a defender of the poorer classes. What is generally regarded as his major work was *The Philosophy of Poverty* (1846),[79] which led to Marx's brilliant refutation, *The Poverty of Philosophy*. Marx called Proud'hon "utopian" because he did not recognize the necessity for a large-scale, class-based revolution, the same criticism Marx made of Owen and Fourier. But Proud'hon called Owen and Fourier utopian on quite different grounds, namely, their acceptance of the idea of ultimate harmony, a coming age when moral struggle would cease. On these grounds, as we shall see, Marx, too, is utopian. Alone among the four, Proud'hon does not share the progressive eschatology characteristic of the nineteenth century.

Bakunin and Kropotkin. More consistently anarchistic were two exiles from the Russian nobility, Michael Bakunin (1814-1876) and Prince Peter Kropotkin (1842-1921). Bakunin exercised greater influence by his activity in organizing and guiding revolutionary secret societies throughout Europe than he did by his disorderly writings,[80] though he felt that he had established the scientific validity of his theories. Private property, religion, and all political authority, he felt, were institutions appropriate for the containment of passions and fears in man's lower stages of development; but evolution had now brought man to a new stage in which coercion could be replaced by enlightened persuasion once the demoralizing hold of the entrenched power-wielders was broken. Kropotkin traced historically the cooperative as distinguished from the competitive traits of men and concluded that mutual aid rather than conflict explains the survival of human groups. The law of the state was made necessary only after society was divided into hostile classes by pernicious economic doctrines. Like Ruskin, Fourier, and various other nineteenth-century thinkers, he envisioned a future society of free association, where men would work for the joy of creativity and share the fruits of their labor in the spirit of brotherhood. The hopeful background provided by such ideas as these is not, as we shall see, irrelevant to the supposedly more hard-headed Marxist socialism.

THE VARIETIES OF SOCIALISM

The nineteenth century was the gestation period for a new approach to political and economic organization, called "socialism," a name that first appeared in an Owenite magazine. The mosaic of its many youthful

---

79 *Système des contradictions économiques ou la philosophie de la misère*. Perhaps Proud'hon's best work was *De la justice* (1861), in four volumes.

80 The Russian nationalist Theodore Herzen relates how Bakunin and Proud'hon fell to arguing about Hegel one night and in the best bohemian tradition continued arguing until the next morning, neither man changing his physical or intellectual position.

varieties is a colorful sight, one that we can scarcely begin to reproduce here. The seemingly unrelenting march of industrialism across Europe brought forth in its wake reactionary feudal socialists like Ruskin and Morris, slightly mad blueprinters of the future like Fourier, and unclassifiable geniuses like Proud'hon. The list of utopian fiction the age produced is quite remarkable: Étienne Cabet's *Voyage to Icaria* (1839), Lord Lytton's *The Coming Race* (1870), W. H. Mallock's *The New Republic* (1877), Edward Bellamy's *Looking Backward* (1887), Theodor Hertzka's *Freeland* (1890), William Morris' *News from Nowhere* (1890), Eugene Richter's *Pictures of the Socialistic Future* (1893).

Socialist organizations were being founded, merged, dissolved, and founded again in bewildering profusion. From the Chartist uprising in 1848, England's milder version of the revolutions occuring all over Europe that year, until sometime in 1854 a group of dedicated "Christian Socialists" met in London for weekly Bible reading and discussion of social problems. Their leader was the distinguished theologian F. D. Maurice, and a member was Charles Kingsley, the cleric and novelist, whose novels of social protest, *Alton Locke* (1850) and *Yeast* (1851) were widely read. Before the abortive Chartist march of workers on Parliament, April 10, 1848, Kingsley and John Ludlow, a Fourierist, had stayed up all night writing placards calling for justice. The group sponsored a Workingmen's College in London, which Maurice headed until 1872.

In 1879 the American Henry George published *Progress and Poverty*, a discerning attack upon the wage-fund theory of economics in particular and landlordism in general. His less discerning solution of the single tax on land nevertheless evoked tremendous response at home and abroad, and Henry George Schools of Social Science were founded that still survive in the 1960's. George made five trips to England, impressing such men as George Bernard Shaw, William Morris, and the Marxist Henry Hyndman. In Germany Ferdinand Lassalle and August Bebel, in France Fernand Pelloutier, in England the Fabian Society[81] in their quite different ways labored for the triumph of the working class. Trade unionism, syndicalism, anarchism, Fabianism, guild socialism, Marxian socialism, and other isms more numerous than we care to remember bear witness to a new society struggling both to understand and to correct itself.

81 Founded by George Bernard Shaw, Sidney and Beatrice Webb, and Graham Wallas, and later joined by H. G. Wells, Ramsay MacDonald, Keir Hardie, and G. D. H. Cole. The faith of Fabianism was a faith in facts: rigorous factual analysis of specific social conditions "without fear or favor" would open the way to reform. The faith prompted some brilliant essays. See George Bernard Shaw, *Essays in Fabian Socialism* (Edinburgh: R. and R. Clark, 1932); *Fabian Tracts*, Nos. 1-181 (London: The Fabian Society, 1884-1916); *Fabian Essays* (London: The Fabian Society, 1931).

Ideas need organizations to make them socially effective, although the best ideas are not always, of course, matched with the best organizations. The political strength of socialism, especially Marxian socialism, was certainly increased by its connection with workers' organizations that in greater or lesser degree reflected the new society born of industrialism. Yet, paradoxically, it was the old liberal ideas of individual freedom that sparked the socialist protest and gave it much of its moral content at the very time it was speaking for a class to which old-fashioned liberal individualism was becoming irrelevant.

A tremendous change, from the heyday of the small private entrepreneur struggling to be free of feudal restrictions, to the day of the mass, class-based party stuggling against the large capitalists, had occurred in one century. The sweep of this change can be seen by comparing the work of Bentham with the work of Marx, both of whose writings we shall soon examine.

Bentham

To MAKE Jeremy Bentham a nineteenth-century great rather than an eighteenth-century near-great takes a bit of justifying. His utilitarian descendant John Stuart Mill, who was indubitably a nineteenth-century figure and had as well a richer, more sensitive intellect, might better seem to deserve this chapter. But Bentham can be regarded as great not for what he was but for what he did. An eighteenth-century *philosophe* in mentality, he was a necessary bridge between that frame of mind and nineteenth-century democratic reforms. He speaks with an eighteenth-century distaste for medieval superstition and could scarcely have understood the warm reverence for a sense of community that animated the feudal socialists of later nineteenth-century England. Yet he also represented a practical, calculating, counting kind of logic that was both typically English and typically middle class. The political fruit of this logic was the extension of the suffrage—one man, one vote—symbolized by the Reform Bill of 1832, which was being born as Bentham died. Jeremy Bentham was an eighteenth-century man, yes; but by being democratized, he carried the whole liberal tradition with him into the more democratic nineteenth century.

Life

JEREMY BENTHAM, the eldest son of a modestly successful London attorney, was a remarkably precocious child, writing Latin at five and reading Voltaire at six. The small, weak, and excessively sensitive boy had a miserable time when he was sent to the Westminster School in 1755 and was not much happier when at the age of twelve he entered Queen's College, Oxford. He early wrote, it is said, more easily in French than in English, which may have some significance in explaining his attraction to the French utilitarians.

After his B.A. in 1763 he began to study law at Lincoln's Inn, mainly to please his father. He also returned to Oxford to hear Blackstone's popular lectures on the British Constitution, and noted that they were full of fallacies and illogical doctrines. This iconoclastic reaction became a public indictment with the publication of Bentham's *Fragment on Government* in 1776. Bentham went to the bar as a "bear to the stake" and to the despair of his father his career as a barrister was brief and utterly unsuccessful.

In retreat from the world of affairs, Bentham turned with relief and joy to speculation and reform. But for some time it was only a speculative kind of reform. Bentham preferred to inform the powers that be, rather than to challenge them directly. Although critical of the self-evidence of natural-law propositions, Bentham took for granted another kind of self-evidence, inasmuch as he fully expected that those in power, having been shown the correctness of a course of action, would naturally follow it. Bentham's reading during these years, the early seventies, indicates the tradition of which he was a part: Locke, Montesquieu, the Italian Beccaria's work on prison reform, Helvetius' *De l'esprit*, Hume's *Treatise of Human Nature*, and Daines Barrington's *Observations on the Statutes* (1766), which helped focus Bentham's attention on the specifics of legal reform. If one can grant the distinction, Bentham was first and foremost a legal reformer rather than a political reformer, although political reform eventually came to hold his attention. His study convinced him that English law was irrational, cruel, cluttered, and burdened with historical irrelevancies from which only lawyers benefited. English law was "a mere jungle of unintelligible distinctions, contradictions, and cumbrous methods through which no man could find his way without the guidance of the initiated, and in which a long purse and unscrupulous trickery gave the advantage over the poor to the rich and to the knave over the honest man."[1]

From all of this emerged Bentham's "fundamental axiom," the keystone of his whole outlook, "the greatest happiness of the greatest number . . . is the measure of right and wrong."[2] The phrase itself Bentham attributes to Beccaria, although it actually originated with Francis Hutcheson.

[1] Leslie Stephen, *The English Utilitarians* (London: Duckworth, 1900), Vol. I, p. 278.
[2] Preface to *Fragment*, in John Bowring, ed., *Works* (Edinburgh: William Tait, 1838-42), Vol. I, p. 227. All quotations from Bentham in this chapter are taken from this edition, hereinafter referred to as *Works*.

The conception is not, at any rate, novel. What Bentham did with it is what counts.

The *Fragment*, published anonymously, did not stay anonymous, and it brought Bentham a modicum of fame, enough at least for him to make the acquaintance of the sometime premier Lord Shelburne, which led in turn to contacts with other important people, including one who came to be a chief interpreter and disciple, the Swiss Étienne Dumont.

In 1787 Bentham's *Defense of Usury* was published. The book was an application of Adam Smith's economic principles in a way Smith himself had not condoned; but Bentham respectfully appends a letter to Smith at the end of the book. Two years later came Bentham's greatest work, *An Introduction to the Principles of Morals and Legislation*, which was originally to be but the first part of a massive system. The inability to finish schemes once begun was a special Bentham trait. He was continually being aroused by new ideas that led him away from old projects. The result of this penchant was that most of his writings had to be assembled for publication by his disciples if they were to be assembled at all. Fortunately, Bentham had a flair for attracting disciples.

If Bentham was a philosophic reformer rather than either a philosopher or a politician, he was also a powerful critic. His incisive criticisms of everything from Pitt's Poor Law Bill to French colonialism were acute and disinterested, and often effective. But his fascination with an immense variety of inventions and schemes of reform was largely divorced from considerations of political strategy. Bentham was incapable of being a true party man. Metropolitan police reform, a new type of interest-bearing note, a "frigidarium" for preserving foods, and, above all, his model prison, the "Panopticon," consumed his attention. The Panopticon, which supposedly required the most in the way of prisoner industry and the least in the way of supervisory time, drained from Bentham much money and energy before the final frustration of having it rejected by the government.

In 1802 Dumont published *Traités de legislation de M. Jeremie Bentham*, a collection of translated and original French pieces that, thanks to Dumont's editing, gave a more straightforward picture of Bentham's thought than the master himself could have put together.

Some time before 1809 (according to Bentham himself) and after the failure of the Panopticon, Bentham awoke to the fact that mere assertion of the best course did not lead governors to adopt it. At this point he began to move in the direction of equalitarian democracy. It was James Mill (who had met Bentham in 1808) who really converted Bentham to political radicalism. Moreover, as Elie Halévy put it, Bentham gave Mill a doctrine and Mill gave Bentham a school. Francis Place, the tailor turned practical politician, also helped turn utilitarianism into a popular political movement. With Bentham's funds the group began in 1824 to publish an organ, the *Westminster Review*, edited by John Bowring, which turned out to be a first step toward the Reform Bill of 1832. The year before, young John Stuart Mill had organized a group devoted to discussing morals and politics and called it the Utilitarian Society.

Bentham's work with codes of law was remarkable for its extent. For ten years he worked on his *Rationale of Evidence*. James Mill published part of it as *An Introductory View of the Rationale of Evidence* in 1812 and John Stuart Mill edited a five-volume version in 1827. The *Constitutional Code* came in 1830, two years before his death. The *Plan of Parliamentary Reform* had appeared in 1818. This work drew the attention of scholars and officials in Spain, Portugal, Tripoli, and Greece, as well as such diverse figures as John Quincy Adams, then the American ambassador in Britain, Aaron Burr, who was cooking up nefarious schemes for Mexico, and Simon Bolivar. In 1811 Bentham wrote to President James Madison proposing a "Pannomion" or code of laws for the United States.[3]

In *The Book of Fallacies* (1824) he ridiculed all sorts of old and irrational customs and those who were "alive to possible imaginable evils, dead to actual ones, eagle-eyed to future contingent evils, blind and insensible to all existing ones."[4]

To the end, as Leslie Stephen points out, Bentham remained something of a child. Untouched by tragedy or profound love, he was aloof from the realities of practical politics or bitter struggles of any kind. He was an amiable and crotchety bachelor who lived simply, loved gardening and cats and mice (a juxtaposition that, as Stephen put it, "suggests problems as to the greatest happiness of the greatest number"), followed a rigid daily work and walk schedule, and had no use at all for poetry. Yet his amazing intellectual vigor compensated for his shallowness and preserved an example, in Stephen's words, "of the power which belongs to the man of one idea."[5]

The Critique of Blackstone

THE first and possibly the most fundamental task that Bentham performed was the negative one of undercutting the easy assumptions of conservative

3 Bentham delighted in making up new names: the frigidarium, the Panopticon, a "Chrestomathic school." To him we owe such terms as "codify," "international," "maximize," "minimize."

4 *The Book of Fallacies*, in *Works*, Vol. II, p. 410.

5 Stephen, *The English Utilitarians*, Vol. I, pp. 231, 234.

brands of eighteenth-century natural law. This he did most effectively in *A Fragment on Government*. The audacity of Bentham's attack on Blackstone, it must be confessed, accounts for no small part of the *Fragment's* appeal, even today. Bentham cites on the title page a statement from Montesquieu's *The Spirit of the Laws* to the effect that nothing retards the progress of knowledge as much as a bad work by a celebrated author, because, once having been instructed by it, one must then begin to undeceive oneself. With the greatest energy and enthusiasm Bentham chose to undeceive the reader about the great Blackstone. Fortunately, Bentham in 1776 was not yet afflicted by the prolix style that marred his later work.

But as the preface shows, this is not simply a work of negative criticism. For Bentham is sharing from the outset his great discovery for the reformation of the moral world and the challenge of applying this discovery: "with so little method and precision have the consequences of this fundamental axiom, *It is the greatest happiness of the greatest number that is the measure of right and wrong*, been as yet developed."[6] On this premise, with but a modest show of reluctance, Bentham is brought to point out "some of what appeared to me the capital blemishes of that work [Blackstone's *Commentaries*], particularly this grand and fundamental one, the antipathy to reformation; or rather, indeed, of laying open and exposing the universal inaccuracy and confusion which seemed to my apprehension to pervade the whole."[7] But, of course, it is not merely Blackstone that Bentham is after but what Blackstone represents, the English law in all its constraining, stagnating mumbo-jumbo; for example, "*Equity*, that capricious and incomprehensible mistress of our fortunes, whose features neither our Author, nor perhaps anyone is well able to delineate."[8] And the "tyranny of judge-made law" which was about as bad in Bentham's eyes as the tyranny of "priest-made religion."[9]

Bentham frankly aspires to be a "censor" rather than an "expositor;" that is, to be a teacher of the art and science of legislation rather than one who merely explains what is. Beccaria he finds the "father of censorial jurisprudence." Montesquieu he admires as author of a work "of a mixed kind." But before Montesquieu "all was unmixed barbarism."[10] Bentham's objection to Blackstone includes the charge that he is a censor in disguise. He pretends merely to explain the law as it is, but actually goes out of his way to justify it.

Two major prongs of Bentham's attack are against contract theory

6 *Fragment*, in *Works*, Vol. I, p. 227. Italics in original.
7 *Ibid.*   8 *Ibid.*, p. 228.
9 *Codification Present*, in *Works*, Vol. V, p. 92.
10 *Fragment*, p. 231 *n*.

and the separation of powers. He was boring from within the liberal tradition, so to speak, and in the name of common sense knocking the props from under what other liberals had thought the natural products of reason. With telling accuracy Bentham points out how Blackstone in one place uses "society" as a synonym for "government" and in another makes it compatible with the state of nature. In one place it is an original contract in society that produces the state. In another place there seems to be no such thing as an original contract.

Bentham wishes to replace contractual assumptions with utilitarian principles. Promises of past subjects to past kings, and vice versa, or even contemporary agreements between kings and subjects, provide in themselves no adequate criteria of good government. Only utility can do that, the utility "which alone depends not upon any higher reason, but which is itself the sole and all-sufficient reason for every point of practice whatsoever."[11] In simplest form, Bentham's argument aimed to show that the original contract, however conceived, must have rested on utility, and if so, there were no logical grounds by which utility in the present could be superseded by an out-of-date contract.

In addition to directing assaults upon Blackstone's naïve contractualism, Bentham waged war against his simple faith in England's "mixed constitution" and the classical conception of government that it implied. The classical typologies were primarily useful to Blackstone, said Bentham, so that "he may save himself the expense of thinking."[12] This typology, you may recall, consisted of: government of one, monarchy, whose cardinal virtue was power; government of the few, aristocracy, whose virtue was wisdom; and government of the many, democracy, whose virture was goodness. Each had its corrupt forms: tyranny, oligarchy, "and then," notes Bentham, "a sort of government fit to break one's teeth, called an *Ochlocracy*."[13] Blackstone thought the magic of the English Constitution was that it combined the best of each form in its mixed system. Bentham noted that this was shown solely by demonstration, not by empirical evidence, and that the same logical argument could be used to prove that England combined the worst of the three corrupt forms. Along the way Bentham showed how empty of content was the idea of supposedly classical democracy, the government of "all over all," since anything short of this impossible and anarchic extension would by definition be aristocracy or oligarchy.

Bentham's examination of Blackstone's classical conception of democracy suggests two things. First, Bentham was bent on rejecting all theories that were defended mainly on grounds of traditional sanctity. At least he wished to subject all such time-honored views to the corro-

11 *Ibid.*, p. 272.   12 *Ibid.*, p. 275.   13 Ibid., p. 276.

sive test of utility. Second, he was not yet a democrat. The dissection of the classical conception of democracy implied no substitution of a modern conception. Bentham's picture of pure democracy comes close to that of Tom Paine, whose *Common Sense* was inflaming the American revolutionaries in the same year of 1776. But Bentham was showing the concept to be irrelevant, while Paine was showing it to be the ideal for a good society. Conservatives like Blackstone and Burke, on the other hand, were identifying government and society. Bentham was thus neither a conservative nor a revolutionary democrat.[14] The utilitarians and the Tories were together in rejecting the Whig contract theory. This union of utilitarianism and conservatism was, as we have seen, uniquely personified in Hume. Hume had made Blackstone more defensive, and had made Bentham's work that much easier. Bentham had the honesty to acknowledge Hume's contribution, and even more generously to grant that contract theory may not always have been bad. "With respect to this, and other fictions, there was once a time, perhaps, when they had their use. . . . But the season of *Fiction* is now over. . . ."[15]

Bentham was not much more respectful to other forms of natural-law reasoning. Certain practices men universally acceded to, which, because they were so widely accepted, had no need of proof. "In theory they were assumed for axioms: and in practice they were observed as rules. If, on any occasion, it was thought proper to make a show of proving them, it was rather for form's sake than for anything else. . . . On such an occasion the commonplace retinue of phrases was at hand; *Justice, Right Reason* required it, the *Law of Nature* commanded it, and so forth; all which are but so many ways of intimating that a man is firmly persuaded of the truth of this or that moral proposition, though he either thinks he *need not*, or finds he *can't*, tell *why*."[16]

People wish to be governed by the principle of utility, that is, by the standard of their own happiness, but simply do not yet understand that this is so. Their faith in obedience to the king results from his governing in their interests, and not vice versa. Bentham punctures the theory of general obedience by showing that it is impossible to rule out altogether the extraordinary situation when obedience to the letter of the law is disastrous, by which means he brings the reader back again and again to the consideration of utility. Promises, in short, are not and should not be self-enforcing. They are kept for a reason. Subjects should obey kings only "so long as the probable mischiefs of obedience are less than the probable mischiefs of resistance" and the

14 See Elie Halévy, *The Growth of Philosophic Radicalism*, trans. by Mary Morris (Boston: Beacon Press, 1955), pp. 129-30.

15 *Fragment*, p. 269.   16 *Ibid.* Italics in original.

duty to obey is synonymous with the interest in obeying.[17] There are overtones of contemporary pragmatism in Bentham's attempt to reduce disputes over the legitimacy of legislation to questions of "conjecture concerning so many future contingent matters of fact," in which evidence —almost by itself—seems to play the deciding role. "Men, let them but once clearly understand one another, will not be long ere they agree."[18]

Bentham's touching faith in the social harmony that springs from a common understanding of future consequences has radical implications; but at this stage Bentham cannot be said to have given defenders of rebellion even a foothold from which to transform utility into practical political radicalism. By what sign shall it be known that the mischiefs of rebellion are less than the mischiefs of submission? In general, "it is impossible to find an answer." A particular person must count on "his own internal persuasion of a balance of *utility* on the side of resistance." But without a common sign of such a point, the supreme governor's field of authority "must unavoidably, I think, *unless where limited by express convention*, be allowed to be *indefinite*."[19] The supremacy of the existing English constitution seems to have crept back into Bentham's theory under a different but no less intractable rule than that of natural law. Moreover, although Bentham expressly denies that he intends to stifle reform, his sematic realism plays into the hands of governors. The word "duty," for example, "if applied to persons spoken of as supreme governors, is evidently applied to them in a sense which is figurative and improper. . . ."[20]

In the *Fragment* Bentham had not yet formulated an ideal theory of government; indeed, he was hardly interested in forms of government. Like Hume, from whom he had gained so much, he felt that the quality of the laws meant much more than their source, and, in hard reality, the habit of obedience may mean more than any logic. The invitation to rebellion that Paine's conception of natural rights gave to the Americans had no place in Bentham's conception of utility at this time. Hence he supported the king against John Wilkes and opposed the American rebels. Later, making friends with the Whigs (the Crown had declined to pay Bentham a sum he claimed), he seemed to deviate from his earlier position to the extent of praising the separation of powers in the English Constitution (*On the Influence of Time and Place in Matters of Legislation and Indirect Legislation*, 1782). Still later, he returned to

17 *Ibid.*, p. 270. In the original, the phrase is italicized. "Mischiefs" is one of the vital, but undefined, terms in Bentham's lexicon.
18 *Ibid.*, Vol. IV, p. 228.   19 *Ibid.*, p. 216. Italics in original.
20 *Ibid.*, p. 236.

a more rigorous, if somewhat different, line, and attempted to have these passages suppressed.

Utility and Legislation

THE *Fragment* was a masterful critique. *An Introduction to the Principles of Morals and Legislation* (1789) was instead a constructive effort, less successful but more important than the *Fragment*. The nature of Bentham's interest is shown by the fact that *Morals and Legislation* was meant to be merely the preliminary statement of principles upon which was to be built a penal code. His temperament is shown in his failure to complete the project. Here Bentham attempted to spell out the principles of utilitarianism (the word is actually James Mill's). The opening words of the work are so succinct, they reveal so forcefully Bentham's strengths and biases, that they are worth quoting at some length:

Nature has placed mankind under the governance of two sovereign masters, *pain* and *pleasure*. It is for them alone to point out what we ought to do, as well as to determine what we shall do. On the one hand the standard of right and wrong, on the other the chain of causes and effects, are fastened to their throne. They govern us in all we do, in all we say, in all we think: every effort we can make to throw off our subjection, will serve but to demonstrate and confirm it. In words a man may pretend to abjure their empire: but in reality he will remain subject to it all the while. The *principle of utility* recognizes this subjection and assumes it for the foundation of that system the object of which is to rear the fabric of felicity by the hands of reason and of law. Systems which attempt to question it, deal in sounds instead of sense, in caprice instead of reason, in darkness instead of light.

Then, impatiently, as if ashamed of grace in style, "But enough of metaphor and declamation: it is not by such means that moral science is to be improved."[21]

The first thing that strikes us about this opening is the bold way in which Bentham admits to an attempt to unite the is with the ought. Granted his premises, a factual judgment and a value judgment are identical. Pleasure and pain determine not only how we live but how we ought to live. If they are also "sovereign masters" it would seem to follow that man is incapable of doing other than he does, and a fatalistic pantheism would appear the only logical conclusion. But being roundly irritated by theological questions Bentham was incapable of seeing these

21 *An Introduction to the Principles of Morals and Legislation,* in *Works,* Vol. I, p. 1.

implications, and preferred instead to do battle with the "caprices" of those who disagreed with him. For despite the alleged sovereignty of pleasure and pain, the "fabric of felicity" is for some reason not yet generally understood. The "felicific calculus" theme must be erected to the position of a standard tool for the determination of public policy. This, in turn, implies the "addibility of happiness" as a practical operation. In 1822 Bentham added a footnote to the above reference to the principle of utility and noted that the greatest-happiness or greatest-felicity principle is an acceptable if not preferable substitute for the original term. For "the word *utility* does not so clearly point to the ideas of *pleasure* and *pain* as the words *happiness* and *felicity* do."[22]

What this means is that every action, whether private or governmental, should be judged by the degree to which it augments or diminishes the happiness of the parties in question. Benefit, advantage, pleasure, good, or happiness are all regarded as synonyms, as are, on the opposite side of the scale, "mischief, pain, evil, or unhappiness." These terms must have reference to individuals, for apart from such concretions they have no meaning. "The community is a fictitious body. . . . The interest of the community then is—what? The sum of the interest of the several members who compose it."[23]

Bentham is the pure nominalist. Words have no intrinsic meaning, and do not refer to any universal entities. Their meaning is wholly from usage, and, in a sense, arbitrary.[24] The central concept of interest, upon which almost everything else hangs, is deliberately left undefined. ". . . not having any superior *genus*, [it] cannot in the ordinary way be defined." Other value words, as we might call them, have meaning only within the system of utility. When related to it "the words *ought*, and *right* and *wrong*, and others of that stamp, have a meaning: when otherwise, they have none."[25] But Bentham is at least honest enough and perceptive enough to grant that the structure is assumed rather than validated: "Is it susceptible of any direct proof? It should seem not; for that which is used to prove everything else, cannot itself be proved: a chain of proofs must have their commencement somewhere."[26]

With considerable cleverness, Bentham shows how arguments supposedly opposed to the principle of utility are actually drawn from that very principle, as he conceives it. Asceticism, for example, a supposed

22 *Ibid.*   23 *Ibid.*, p. 2.

24 Bentham thought "happiness" was such a good word on which to base an ethical system because it was so unequivocal. On one occasion, noting that the authors of *The Federalist* had tried to make justice the end of government, he argued that justice was always a matter of dispute whereas "what happiness is every man knows." *Constitutional Code*, in *Works*, Vol. IX, p. 123.

25 *Morals and Legislation*, p. 2.   26 *Ibid.*

alternative to utility, merely tries to demonstrate that a good many pleasures are purchased at too high a cost in pain to be worth fooling with. Then, using a technique probably borrowed from Hume, Bentham challenges his reader: If there is any principle superior to utility by which to judge what a man should pursue, show us what it may be!

After this somewhat satirical review of "principles adverse to that of utility" Bentham leads us into the marvels of the felicific calculus. His taxonomic gyrations leave us breathless. For example, there are, Bentham tells us, fourteen simple pleasures: sense, wealth, skill, amity, good name, power, piety, benevolence, malevolence, memory, imagination, expectation, association, and relief. There are as well twelve simple pains: privation, sense, awkwardness, enmity, ill name, piety, benevolence, malevolence, memory, imagination, expectation and association. Each of these is subdivided into its components. Sense, for example, is broken down into taste, intoxication, smell, touch, ear, eye, sex, health, novelty, privation includes desire, disappointment, regret, and so forth. Each simple pleasure or pain can be mixed with another to comprise a complex pleasure or pain. The simple forms are supposedly irreducible. They are also supposedly equal. In an oft-quoted tribute to this equality, Bentham somewhere says that "pushpin is the same as poetry if it gives the same pleasure." To help in the comparison, the weighing, measuring, drawing and quartering of all these lumps of pleasure and pain, Bentham gives us seven criteria: intensity, duration, certainty or uncertainty, propinquity or remoteness, fecundity (i.e., the tendency to repeat), and "purity" (i.e., the chance of not being followed by opposite reactions). The seventh is trans-personal, "extent" (i.e., the number of persons affected). Armed with these categories, one can judge the worth of all things.[27]

Much fun can be made of all this, and has been. Bentham asked for ridicule by calling himself "the Newton of the Moral World." But let us see if we cannot make a case in his behalf. As psychology, Bentham's "addibility of happiness" is absurd. To make mechanical the subtlest and most subjective of feelings is pathetic. But the system did force Bentham to assume the equality of each individual with every other individual in the sense of the equal worth of his interest. Despite the memory of Hobbes, this kind of thoroughgoing equalitarianism stood in sharp contrast to the assumptions of the age, indeed perhaps any age.

27 See Bentham's modest *Table of the Springs of Action Shewing the Several Species of Pleasures and Pains of which Man's Nature is Susceptible together with the Several Species of Interests, Desires & Motives Respectively Corresponding to Them and the Several Sets of Appellatives, Neutral, Eulogistic, and Dyseopistic by which each species of Motive is wont to be Designated* (1815). The full title is even longer—by eighty-five words! See *Works*, Vol. I, pp. 195-218.

Moreover, once this assumption is granted, it is not so far-fetched to talk of at least a crude equation of pleasures and pains distributed among members of a given society. It is at least possible to ask whether the amount of pleasure from security distributed to a large number of people, brought about by the execution of a poor sheep-stealer, is equal to the amount of pain inflicted upon him and his family. It can be asked whether the pleasures of a millionaire landlord are intense enough to balance the pain of several hundred agricultural laborers kept in abject poverty. Perhaps these were questions that needed to be asked.

By his crude equalizing of all pleasures Bentham sought to avoid the problem of values and the question of whether some values are not more fundamental than others, but in any concrete application of the system, it is not surprising that Bentham's solid middle-class virtues crept into positions of priority. Benevolence turned out to be an uncommonly important pleasure. Property was a remarkably useful interest. Moreover, Bentham was no utopian. Contrary to what some writers have said of him, his object was not to eliminate all pain. In *Traités de legislation* he recognized that some pleasures must be bought with pain. "We are searching only for the possible," he wrote.[28]

The calculus, though hopeless as psychology, was not hopelessly unsuited for the task for which it was designed—legislation. The aim of Bentham was always the rationalization (in the non-Freudian sense) of the process of lawmaking. If a lawmaker attempts, as lawmakers must, to weigh the pain of a slight increase in taxes inflicted on a large number of people against the pleasures of a new public-housing project benefiting relatively few, he is at least analogically going through Bentham's felicific calculus. How many people will be affected? How much do these people desire this project? By what amount will their average income be reduced? What percentage of the population is unemployed? These are not mathematical questions, but they are quantitative, and they illustrate the kind of question the legislator must ask in his effort to get at something more solid than mere whim. Bentham could be called a rationalizer of the welfare state long before the welfare state came into existence.

Although a listing of pleasures and pains such as Bentham's would logically involve an examination of the motives of each individual, in practice the list was nearly always used to assess the *general* felicific

28 Sheldon Wolin has tried to correct the view that liberal theory was infected throughout with utopian optimism: ". . . the liberal's desperate insistence on the privacy of the pleasure-principle as the dominant motivation was meant to compensate for the real source of his worries: the predominance of pain in the world." *Politics and Vision* (Boston: Little, Brown, 1960), p. 326. Bentham, he argues, was closer to this position than he was to Condorcet or Godwin.

consequences of given social actions. Hence we have a bad psychology in the service of a not-so-bad social policy: examine in as much detail as possible the effect of proposed policies and justify them always in terms of these effects rather than by a priori, abstract principles. Surely here is a forerunner of contemporary pragmatism. If the assumption that understanding by itself produces agreement was no more valid for Bentham than for Dewey, this is not to deny the value of first looking unblinkingly at the consequences of a proposed action before seeking agreement.

Ethical Difficulties

TO SAY that Bentham provided a stimulus for legislative action based upon a rational calculation of general numerical happiness is not to say that he provided a philosophically tight rationale for such calculation. Despite his elaborate *Table of the Springs of Action* he never overcame the gap between an understanding of motives and the evaluation of consequences, a pitfall for most systems of social ethics. If one grants, as Bentham did, that the same motive could be bad or good depending upon the consequences of the action it induced, then it would seem incumbent upon the legislator to ignore motives altogether and evaluate only the consequences of actions. But in *Morals and Legislation* Bentham notes that the legislator in measuring the "mischievousness" of acts must distinguish between "primary" and "secondary" effects. Loss of useful goods is a primary effect of robbery. But a secondary effect is the suggestion of the possibility of robbery to others, which has a weakening influence on the "tutelary motive" of respect for property. At this point one's judgment on consequences gets mixed up with the change in motives that constitutes the consequence. This is why the administration of justice can never be wholly mechanical. The dilemma is not at all novel. But Bentham did not see that it was a dilemma.

He blithely felt that he could capture goodness in a code. His whole system of ethics was, like most of what he did, wrapped up in his passion for codifying. In *Chrestomathia* (1817) he applied what he called the "dichotomous" or "bifurcate" or "bipartition" method in which, as if he were classifying crustaceans, he would divide ethical actions into two mutually exclusive but exhaustive classes, then subdivide each of these, and so forth. He granted that it might take centuries to compile in this way a perfectly adequate and accurate catalogue of the ethical life, but he believed that it would come. No wonder that he considered metaphysics to be but a minor branch of logic.

Hence a major failure of Bentham was that he confused what was essentially a legal doctrine with a system of private ethics. This confusion, in turn, was possible only because Bentham could rather simple-mindedly and single-mindedly assume that a single motive could be separated out from the welter of human drives and inclinations and attached to a single action. He did not deny, of course, that a bundle of intentions could create a predisposition to act that might never be realized in action; but an understanding of such potential action was only background data for the legislator. Neither law nor morals really came into play until there was action.

Now private ethics has happiness for its end: and legislation can have no other. Private ethics concerns every member; that is, the happiness and the actions of every member of any community that can be proposed: and legislation can concern no more. Thus far, then, private ethics and the art of legislation go hand in hand. The end they have, or ought to have, in view, is of the same nature. The persons whose happiness they ought to have in view, as also the persons whose conduct they ought to be occupied in directing, are precisely the same. The very acts they ought to be conversant about, are even in a *great measure* the same.[29]

What, if anything, is the difference between ethics and law? There is no case, Bentham continues, in which the individual should not seek his own happiness "and that of his fellow creatures." But there are some cases in which the legislator ought not ("in a direct manner at least") to interfere. These are the cases discussed in an earlier chapter, in which such interference would be "groundless . . . inefficacious . . . unprofitable . . . needless." They include cases when punishment is badly timed; when infants are involved; when evil acts of minor consequence are incoveniently mingled with good acts of major consequence; when the simplest possible punishment would exceed the magnitude of the offense; when, as in the case of fornication, the possibility of future detection is too slight for present punishment to have much effect; when, as in the case of offenses such as rudeness, any punishment is likely to involve the innocent "in the fate designed only for the guilty"; and so forth.

What all this adds up to, then, is that the division between private morality and public law is created only in that realm of behavior that the legislator finds it inconvenient to bother with. In this conclusion there is a kind of Hobbesian deference to omnipotent legislative authority, but without the limitation of a contractual myth.

Are there any limitations upon this central figure of the legislator in Bentham? The answer of course is yes. Three seem especially worth notice. First, despite the unrealism of many aspects of the felicific calculus,

29 *Morals and Legislation*, p. 144.

there is nevertheless in Bentham a certain earthy realism that, at least in a true Benthamite legislator, would keep him from running wild. The sensibly noted inconveniences mentioned above are an example. The best touches of reality often appear in Bentham's footnotes, although even here mechanical quantification will time and again make Bentham appear a bit silly. At one point, he says that a man should not receive the same punishment for giving another man ten blows as for giving him five blows, since he then has the pleasure of giving the second five blows "for nothing." Making the punishment fit the crime is, not illogically, a fetish with Bentham.[30] But the reverse of this precept is that punishment must never be more than what is absolutely necessary to bring behavior into conformity with the desired social behavior.[31] There is not a trace of vindictiveness in Bentham's system. Neither is there much compassion. But there is enough humanity to impose some self-denying qualities upon the legislator. He is to concern himself not with intimate, private matters in which each man must be assumed to know what best conduces to his own happiness, but rather confine himself to "those broad lines of conduct in which all persons, or very large and permanent descriptions of persons, may be in a way to engage. . . ." Even here his "interference" can and should be open to dispute. "At any rate he must never expect to produce a perfect compliance by the mere force of the sanction of which he is himself the author. All he can hope to do is to increase the efficacy of private ethics, by giving strength and direction to the influence of the moral sanction."[32] Bentham is quite aware, as we would expect, that a man often knows too little of what would conduce to his own happiness (i.e., produce the good); "but is it so certain that the legislator must know more?" At this point Bentham reminds any would-be legislator to remember the story of the oculist and the sot. The former, while himself drinking, prescribes that the latter give up drink if he is to save his eyes. When reminded of the discrepancy in his own behavior, the oculist replies, " 'That's very true, my friend . . . but you are to know I love my bottle better than my eyes' "[33] If Bentham has a defective sense of moral community, at least he has some respect for the sanctity of moral choice in the individual. This respect may not square with his psychology, but we like him the better for it.

30 Bentham was not unaware of possible reactions to this mechanization: ". . . my fear is, that in the ensuing model, I may be thought to have carried my endeavors at proportionality too far. Hitherto scarcely any attention has been paid to it. Montesquieu seems to have been almost the first who has had the least idea of any such thing. In such a matter, therefore, excess seemed more eligible than defect. The difficulty is to invent: that done, if anything seems superfluous, it is easy to retrench." *Morals and Legislation*, p. 90.
31 *Ibid.*, p. 88.   32 *Ibid.*, p. 146.   33 *Ibid.*

Second, like all his fellow liberals, Bentham did not conceive of a government capable of regulating an entire economic system. Since Bentham did not believe in natural rights, he could not erect natural rights of property as a barrier against governmental action. But he did not need to. The happiness of men was so obviously advanced by leaving them free to borrow, spend, save, invest, and scramble for wages, that socialism and utilitarianism could scarcely be spoken of in the same breath. In his *Defense of Usury* (1787) Bentham adopts almost completely the fundamental economic ideas of Adam Smith. What Halévy calls "the principle of the natural identity of interests," the view, that is to say, that there is an "invisible hand" which sums up individual egoisms into a social harmony, was as compatible with Bentham's economics as with Smith's. Given this assumption, the government's function in the economic sphere was simply that of enabling men to know their own self-interest better. Hence Bentham spoke of the government publishing new processes and lists of prices, giving prizes for new technological discoveries, protecting inventors through patents, and so forth. Beyond this, the government had no special competence and was too solitary and cumbersome to itself invest capital in industrial enterprises.

On the question of usury, Bentham went even beyond Smith, who felt that usury laws were permissible so long as they did not impinge upon the going market rate of interest. Bentham once wrote "You know, it is an odd maxim of mine, that interest, as love and religion, and so many other pretty things, should be free.[34] While the language had made "usurer" an ugly word, in fact, argued Bentham, the usurer makes an important contribution to the progress of the economic system and is envied mainly because he has sacrificed in order to save as others have not. The exemption of usury from Bentham's long list of crimes may be taken as symbolic of the distinction Bentham made ironclad: the juridical function of the state was exalted almost in proportion as its economic function was minimized. It seems inconsistent to give the legislator a crucial role in consciously educating the individual through penal laws to a consciousness of his own (and therefore society's) true interest, while at the same time the legislator is denied such a role with reference to the individual's economic interest. Here the identity of individual with social interests was presumed to take place spontaneously. It seems inconsistent and it is inconsistent, and the failure to assimilate economic activity into its view of politics can only be regarded as a major failure of liberal thought. Yet it is too simple to chalk up this lapse to Bentham's unrealism and let it go at that. Or perhaps we could say that though Bentham is unrealistic, he is not utopian. He carries over into

34 Quoted in Halévy, *Growth of Philosophic Radicalism*, p. 110.

the political sphere the idea of an economy of scarcity—a scarcity of pleasures. The failure of the individual to buy future pleasures with present pain is automatically punished by the economic system. In the more vaguely defined political system a legislator is needed to provide the punishment.

Third, the legislator is not unchecked in Bentham's system, at least not in his later system, because there are elections to contend with. With his penchant for elaborate terminology, Bentham could not simply call this the principle of elections. He had to call it the principle of the "universal dislocability of officials." Even earlier he had revealed himself as a somewhat uncertain and qualified democrat. At the time of the French Revolution he had written *An Essay on Political Tactics*, a handbook of essentially English parliamentary procedure intended for the guidance of the new Estates-General. And later in the same year he had written for the French a code of judicial procedure that featured a qualified system of elected ("amovable") judges. One of the interesting qualifications was the principle of "patriotic auction" in which the candidates are invited before the election to offer to pay a sum of money to the state, a sum determined by their own estimate of how much this will impress the voters. This is supposed to assure disinterested judges; but it also weighs the scales on behalf of the rich. Yet, in this code Bentham notes, "I have not that horror of the people. I do not see in them the savage monster which their detractors dream of. . . . When the Athenians were cruel and unjust, were the Dionysuses and Artaxerxeses less so?"[35] If Bentham never had a thoroughgoing faith in the wisdom of the common man, at least he also had a healthy distrust of uncommon men who held power.

Conclusion

BENTHAM is still important because utilitarianism is still important. As philosophy and psychology its force has dissipated; however, as a practical criterion for legislation in democratic countries the maximization of pleasure and minimization of pain for the greatest number of people is demonstrably alive. Much of the argument for such welfare measures as social security, farm parity payments, the minimum wage, and so forth is couched in latter-day utilitarian terminology. And even college students have been known to declare with reverent voices their faith in the principle of the greatest happiness for the greatest number.

In adapting Bentham's eighteenth-century mechanisms to the nineteenth

35 *An Essay on Political Tactics*, in *Works*, Vol. IV, pp. 262-63.

century's belief in process, John Stuart Mill, it is true, succeeded mainly in vitiating utilitarian's emotional appeal. Unable to live with Bentham's oversimplifications, Mill was forced to make what were, in effect, qualitative distinctions between short-run and long-run utility. The pleasure of poetry was placed on a different plane from the pleasure of pushpin. Too sensitive to be mechanical about majority rule, Mill worried about the "tyranny of the majority" and its psychological effect on the free expression of critical ideas.

But even in Mill the utilitarian distrust of metaphysical abstraction and respect for the concrete fact remains, as does the willingness to use law for educational and reformist purposes. And, finally, the autonomous individual, the man able to decide and act on the basis of his own calculation of self-interest, is still there. The last-named is the most troublesome. For despite Bentham's praise of security when threatened by equality,[36] and despite Mill's eventual appreciation of the role of groups in political society, utilitarianism has tended to beg one basic question: can every individual be permitted to seek his own happiness, and that alone, without utterly destroying the social fabric? Perhaps alone among utilitarians David Hume did not beg this question, but the vigor of Bentham is nowhere better shown than in the way he eclipsed Hume in conventional histories of the movement. Although Bentham made an ambiguous distinction between self-regarding and nonself-regarding motives, both of which were part of self-interest rightly understood, this was no way out of the conflict we see between individual welfare and the social good. Bentham simply assumed that in the long run the pursuit of self-interest clarified by a legislator would coincide with the greatest happiness of the greatest number, and so, in essence, did Mill.

Perhaps the problem of individual and society is irresolvable in philosophic terms; but we would like our political philosophers to agonize over the problem as Rousseau did. That Bentham did not feel it was necessary is a clue to his early influence and also to his eventual fall from grace.

36 Bentham, we often forget, was never a thoroughgoing equalitarian, least of all in property matters. The legislator should seek to maintain the existing distribution of property lest the security of all be attacked. "When security and equality are in opposition there should be no hesitation: equality should give way. . . . The establishment of equality is a chimera: the only thing which can be done is to diminish inequality." *Principles of the Civil Code*, Ch. 11, in *Works*, Vol. II, p. 311.

12 | *Hegel*

W HAT shall we do with Hegel? He is too systematic to summarize; too cumbersome to quote; and too influential to ignore. Most chapters and many books which presume to simplify Hegel for the casual reader are doomed to failure. So be it. Let us bravely dare to fail together, for without knowing something about Hegel one can scarcely understand how fully he has penetrated into contemporary thinking about politics, economics, and history, and how much the mood of present-day nationalism owes to his categories.

Life

GEORG WILHELM FRIEDRICH HEGEL was born in Stuttgart in 1770, the son of a fiscal official for the Kingdom of Württemberg. He attended grammar school at Stuttgart, where his record was adequate but not distinguished, and in 1788 entered the University of Tübingen as a theological student, receiving a Doctor of Philosophy degree in 1790 and a certificate in theology in 1793. Along with his fellow students Holderlin, the poet, and F. W. J. Schelling, the philosopher, he tended to neglect the prescribed theological studies in favor of reading the classics. Hence he was early knowledgeable in Platonic metaphysics and attracted to the *polis* as a model of the ethical community. It was the disunity of the German peoples, the particularity of existing political institutions, that made the Greek ideal so attractive to Hegel and his contemporaries. Yet Hegel was determined to correct the failure of the Greeks to make freedom the

central attribute of man as man. This same disunity had for Hegel, therefore, religious dimensions as well. Though disillusioned by formalistic,
ecclesiastical religion, Hegel was concerned even at this time about the
divisive political effects of secularism and, at the personal level, bothered
by its egocentric influences.

After leaving Tübingen, Hegel went as a private tutor first to Berne
and then to Frankfurt, but when in 1799 his father died and left him a
small inheritance, he set himself up in Jena and plunged into the intellectual life of the university in hopes of qualifying for a university position.
In 1801 he was licensed as a *privatdozent* and began lecturing on logic
and metaphysics. Finally in 1805 he won the professorship he had long
sought. Scarcely had his professorial career begun, however, when the
armies of Napoleon invaded the area and the great general himself rode
through the streets of Jena. "The Soul of the World" commented Hegel
on Napoleon, after seeing him. It is doubtful that Hegel so admired
Napoleon that his philosophy was touched by that man's affection for
power, as some have suggested. The groundwork of the philosophical
system was already laid, and Hegel soon changed his mind about Napoleon.
Perhaps more significant was Hegel's respect for Machiavelli, a theorist
who understood the nature of power and the role of great men in the
integration of peoples. It is certain, however, that the French Revolution
had a profound effect on Hegel as on most of his German contemporaries.
The Revolution constituted an intellectual and ideological challenge
to the hierarchical organization of German social life. It symbolized the
possibility of reorganizing society on a rational basis, of liberating the
individual from the last remnants of feudal authority and establishing
his autonomy. However critical he was of the Terror, Hegel felt deeply
the need for coming to grips with the French claims of having rationalized society. He did so while affected by German romantic intuitionism,
converting both rationalism and intuitionism into a magisterial vision of
the world. The multiplicity of interpretations of the Hegelian system
is an index of its scope and complexity. Hegel has been called everything
from inspiring to dangerous. Schopenhauer repeatedly called him a
charlatan. Yet his significance is indisputable and his influence far-reaching,
and nowhere more so than in political theory. Every major political
thinker discussed in the remainder of this book will show the mark
of Hegel's conception of history and the political order.

In 1807 came Hegel's first major work, *The Phenomenology of Spirit*,[1]

1 John Baillie's noted translation of *Phaenomenologie des Geistes* is entitled *Phenomenology of Mind* (2nd ed.; New York: Macmillan, 1931), but "spirit" is often considered a more appropriate translation of *Geist*. Hegel had published two works prior
to this time, *The Constitution of Germany* (1802), and *The History of Philosophy*
(1805).

an analysis of the consciousness of the self in which "spirit" is seen as the essence of man and history. Close on the heels of this academic success Hegel was forced to take a job as editor of a newspaper due to the disruption of Jena by the Napoleonic wars. From 1808 to 1816 he was headmaster of a *gymnasium* in Nuremberg. While there he married the charming and well-educated Marie von Tucker, twenty-two years his junior. Always a "good family man" (he was addicted only to snuff), his affection for wife and children perhaps gave him a keener appreciation of the organic elements in society than that held by the long line of British bachelors we have been studying.

In 1816 Hegel published the last volume of his greatest work, *The Science of Logic*, which contained the systematic working out of the dialectic. The success of *The Science of Logic* was so great that Hegel was immediately offered professorships from Erlangen, Berlin, and Heidelberg. He accepted the Heidelberg position, but remained there only until 1818, when the death of Fichte left a vacant chair at Berlin which Hegel gladly filled. In 1821 he published *The Philosophy of Right*. By this time he was a prominent and noted man. More and more conservative as he aged, he was in high favor with the Prussian government, and was decorated by the King of Prussia in the year of his death. Made rector of the university in 1830, he died in November, 1831, after a one-day's illness of cholera.

Published posthumously were *The Philosophy of History*, a series of lectures delivered between 1822 and 1831; *Lectures on the Philosophy of Religion;* and *Lectures on Aesthetics*, first delivered in 1818. Though he was worshiped by many as a scholar and teacher, Hegel's lectures were apparently delivered in a weak-voiced, painful manner with a broad Swabian accent. Nor was he particularly admired as a person. He was, it is said, "a hard dry man"; but even so, the greatest philosopher of his century.

The Dialectic

IT IS impossible to review secondary materials on Hegel without being struck by the diversity of "key concepts" that are offered as aids to understanding the system. Reality, spirit, and dialectics, says one. Hegel's six attitudes of consciousness toward reality (simple consciousness, self-consciousness, reason, spirit, religion, and absolute knowledge), says another. Thesis, antithesis, synthesis (terms Hegel did not actually use), says still another. Freedom, mind, subject, and notion, says a fourth. It is a tribute to the richness (some would say the ambiguity) of the system that so many thoughtful men could accentuate such different aspects of it. Actually, everything in the Hegelian system is related to everything else, and if one is concerned with the over-all cohesiveness of the whole he can break into the chain at many different places. But all commentators would agree that Hegel's great methodological contribution is the new logic of the dialectic. It will be helpful if we go back to the problem Hegel was trying to solve. From the first it was a problem with both political and metaphysical dimensions.

A philosopher usually begins by correcting someone else. In the case of Hegel it was primarily the Greeks and Kant. The pursuit of the "empty" abstractions Hegel associated with the idealism of Plato and Kant was, he felt, as ultimately disillusioning as the drive of private egoism. He much admired Kant's ethical philosophy, but was determined to transcend its hypothetical character. Dissatisfied with the static logic of mathematics and the geometrical philosophizing of Descartes and Spinoza, he was determined to invent a logic that could capture the ebb and flow of life itself. The result was the Hegelian dialectic.

The dialectic of the Platonic dialogues was simply a method of discourse whereby truth was approached through questions and answers and the repeated examination of the diametrical opposites of any given statement. It was a winnowing-out process directed toward the single center of the Idea of the Good, from which all other categories were a deduction. In the even more rigorous logic of "abstract universals" by which Aristotle attempted to classify all things into genus and species, it was necessary to assume absolute dichotomies. A and not-A were necessarily in a fixed position of complete opposition. Kant felt that he had reduced the problem of human knowledge to more manageable proportions by working out the twelve irreducible epistemological categories through which all is known.

Hegel's logic of "concrete universals," however, denied the monistic center of Plato's Good, denied the principle of contradiction in Aristotle's logic, denied that Kant's epistemological categories were fixed in number. He made the seemingly impossible contention that all categories of thought could be deduced from any one category, and that anything that is could be an example of any category. "Hegel found that a concept may contain its own opposite hidden away within itself, and that this opposite may be extricated or deduced from it and made to do the work of the differentia, thus converting genus into species."[2] Traditional logic, Hegel granted, was suitable for analysis, the breaking up of wholes. This produces "understanding" (*Verstand*), a valuable but limited form of knowledge. The higher logic of the identity of opposites was required for

2 W. T. Stace, *The Philosophy of Hegel* (New York: Macmillan, 1924), p. 90.

synthesis, the restoration of wholeness. This logic produces "reason" (*Vernunft*). "Understanding meets every question with an inflexible 'either . . . or'. . . . A thing either is, or is not. Reason breaks up this hard and fast schematism of the understanding, sees that A and not-A are identical in their very difference, that the truth does not lie, as understanding supposes, either wholly in A, or wholly in not-A, but rather in the synthesis of the two."[3]

Hence the form of human knowledge is triadic. A concept (called by some the "thesis") contains and gives birth to its opposite ("antithesis"), both of which are known by analysis and both of which are overcome, absorbed, and transformed by "reason" in the stage of "synthesis." But not only did Hegel claim this triad to be the form of human knowledge, he claimed it to be the form of the world itself, that which knowledge knows. From the beginning, epistemology and the philosophy of history are one for Hegel, and are made one by a more fundamental ontology.

Like all ontologists, Hegel began with the concept of Being, that which is, that without which nothing can be. His dialectical interpretation of Being served as a model for the dialectical interpretation of all categories. At the lowest level, Being, mere "isness" purged of all specific determinations, is so minimal that it "passes over" into Nothing. If one can say of an object only that it is, one is saying nothing about it. Being passing into Nothing is "decease," and Nothing passing into Being is "origination." Taken together the two terms describe Becoming. The synthesis of Becoming absorbs and transcends but does not annul Being and Nothing.

On the basis of this elemental triad Hegel attempted the magnificently ambitious task of embracing all the forms of knowledge known to man, a vast and complicated network of triadic processes each flowing into the others. The simplest description is found in Part I of Hegel's *Encyclopedia of Philosophic Sciences* (1817), often referred to as the "Smaller Logic." The most extensive treatment is in *The Science of Logic* (1812-16). But subsequent works such as *The Philosophy of Right* (1821), concerned with political and historical subjects, built upon the system in such a way that later commentators were able to outline in tabular form the interrelationships of all the various parts of the Hegelian system. Some idea of these interrelationships may be obtained from the quite incomplete diagram on pages 324-25.[4]

In trying to make sense of the foregoing table, it is important to

3 *Ibid.*, p. 101.
4 Adapted from G. R. G. Mure, *A Study of Hegel's Logic* (Oxford: Clarendon Press, 1950), p. 370. See also the table of *Encyclopedia* categories in Stace, *The Philosophy of Hegel*, p. 526; and the table in W. H. Johnston and L. G. Struthers, eds. and trans., *The Science of Logic* (London: Allen & Unwin, 1929), Vol. I, p. 24.

The Hegelian System

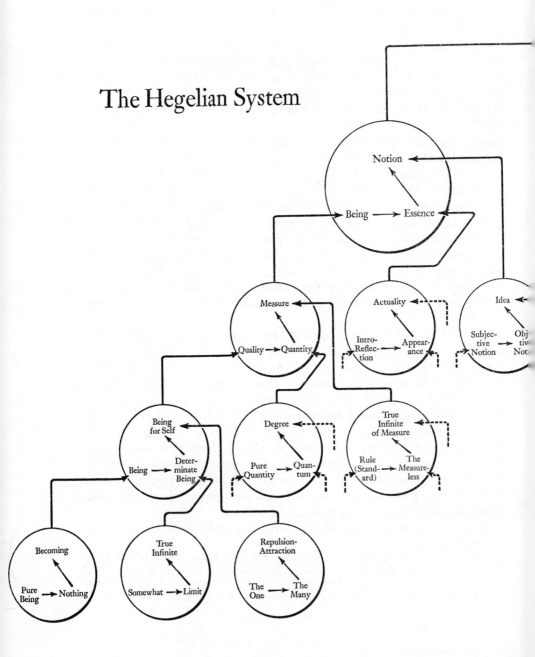

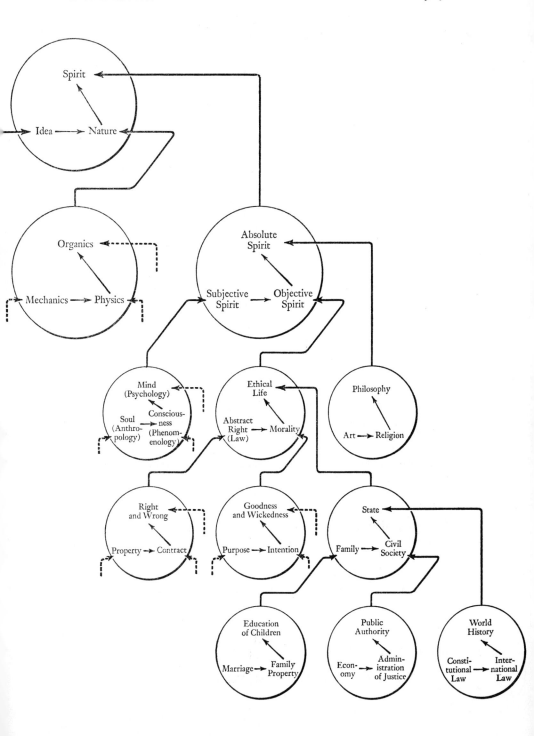

understand that these triads are not simply a set of building blocks. Each triad represents a process wherein the synthesis absorbs and completes the two prior terms, following which the *entire* triad is absorbed into the next higher process. Moreover, every term of every triad is itself the culmination of lower processes, so that in a sense, it serves a dual function. It is simultaneously part of two networks. Finally, it must be noted that in what is probably the basic chain, that from Being-Nothing-Becoming to Being-Essence-Notion, the term Being appears at three different levels. The reader of Hegel is forced to remember (in such ways Hegel some-times seems to be deliberately obscurantist) that these are three different terms—even though each is partly the same as the others!

Let us return to the basic dialectic of the logic and try once again to clarify its essentials. It is, first of all, not traditional logic at all. It is a new mode of thought, adapted to and reflecting the continual movement of the world. It is neither a series of set, mathematical relationships, nor a manner of a priori deductive reasonings. Hegel firmly believed that it was descriptive of the way thought must apprehend the real world. In this sense there is in the dialectic something of the intuitive quality lauded by the German romantics. The history of human thought, Hegel be-lieved, was in fact a manifestation of the dialectic, with the power of negation asserting itself again and again to contradict what its authors regarded as settled systems of thought and by that "contradiction" lifting them to higher and higher levels:

. . . there are no traces in [traditional] Logic of the new spirit which has arisen both in Learning and in Life. It is, however (let us say it once for all), quite vain to try to retain the forms of an earlier stage of development when the inner structure of spirit has become transformed; these earlier forms are like withered leaves which are pushed off by the new buds already being generated at the roots.[5]

Being, at its first beginning, at the bottom of the far-left triad in the foregoing diagram, is most barren and least determinate, and therefore, as we have seen, passes over into Nothing; both then move on into Be-coming. The whole triad then moves on, or rather is transformed into the thesis of a new dialectical triad, the first term of which is also called Being. At the lowest level Being is most immediate, that is, it most stands by itself and does not mediate between itself and other categories. Actu-ally, Hegel is interested in showing this mediacy at all levels, but it varies in degree. Without trying to explain the subsequent triads of Being–Deter-minate Being–Being for Self, and Quality-Quantity-Measure (political

5 *Science of Logic*, Preface to 1st ed., Vol. I, p. 35.

theory must leave *something* for the philosophers), we can look at the key arch in the edifice of the *Logic*, the triad of Being-Essence-Notion (some would translate *Begriff* as "Conception" rather than "Notion"). At this level, Being, which includes all its subcategories, becomes the symbol for immediacy (despite the fact that Hegel has been attempting to show that the immediacy of all the subcategories was in part illusory, since they did not in fact stand apart, but flowed into each other). Essence is the factor of mediation. And Notion is the unity of immediacy and mediation which swallows them both by virtue of the conception of self-mediation.

Absolute Idea, the unity of subjectivity and objectivity, is alone fully self-mediate. It transcends the whole logic and is the first term of the most exalted triad all, Idea-Nature-Spirit. The dialectic of course operates in the world of nature and spirit as well as idea. It is in the realm of spirit, which is "thought in the full sense, knowing itself not merely as thought, but as thought-of-object," that we come at last to political thought.

Criticism of Hegel's logic is frequent. A succinct example:

Hegel assumed that because thought is dynamic, logic also must be dynamic. It is as if we were to suppose that because (in Locke's phrase) we have difficulty in adjusting a "standing measure" to a "growing bulk" a running measure would do better. . . . The trouble is that Hegel tried to do two things in a single operation. On the one hand, he wanted to give a systematic and logically structured account of the basic categories or concepts by means of which we understand our world. On the other hand, he wanted to describe the self-transcending character of meaning. Each of these was an entirely proper undertaking, but put together as Hegel put them together they resulted in confusion. First, he attributed self-transcendence to the various categories of logic; then he turned around and attributed logical formality to the process of self-transcendence and expansion of meaning.[6]

This confusion is shown in the imprecise way Hegel used logical terms like "contradiction," "negate," and the like—at least imprecise according to the standards of the old logic, and, unless one is a Hegelian to begin with, this is the only standard by which his logic can be judged.

The Dialectic in History

OLD-FASHIONED logical imprecision, however, little inhibited one who claimed as validation the whole historical process. Not that Hegel played

6 W. T. Jones, *A History of Western Philosophy* (New York: Harcourt, Brace, 1952), p. 879.

the role of prophet. Although there is a sense in which it was necessary for him to assume that he and he alone had the secret of the universe by the tail, he nevertheless disavowed claims to any special insight into the future or into what the world "ought to be." In a famous passage in the Preface to *The Philosophy of Right*, Hegel says:

One word more about giving instructions as to what the world ought to be. Philosophy in any case always comes on the scene too late to give it. As the thought of the world, it appears only when actuality is already there cut and dried after its process of formation has been completed. The teaching of the concept, which is also history's inescapable lesson, is that it is only when actuality is mature that the ideal first appears over against the real and that the ideal apprehends this same real world in its substance and builds it up for itself into the shape of an intellectual realm. When philosophy paints its grey in grey it cannot be rejuvenated but only understood. The owl of Minerva spreads its wings only with the falling of the dusk.[7]

If, as Hegel believed, "abstract" metaphysics is empty, if historical knowledge is all the knowledge we can command, it follows that we can only know what history gives us. The future is a blank wall because it has not yet become history. In this respect, as Carl Friedrich points out, Hegel's philosophy of history was far more profound than the "bald generalities" of Spengler and Toynbee.[8] If "reason" is a name for all in history that overcomes negativity and recreates the substance of life,[9] then it is not so puzzling to read in the same *Philosophy of Right* what has puzzled so many: "What is rational is actual and what is actual is rational."[10] By "actual" (or, as *wirklich* is sometimes translated, "real") Hegel is not referring to mere existence, but to the synthesis of existence and essence. For example, if we say that President Harding was not a real statesman, we do not mean that he had no existence. We mean that he fulfilled the external appearance but not the essence of statesmanship.
    The Philosophy of Right, therefore,

7 *The Philosophy of Right*, trans. by T. M. Knox (London: Oxford Univ. Press, 1942), pp. 12-13.
    8 Carl J. Friedrich, in the Introduction to his edition of *The Philosophy of Hegel* (New York: Modern Library, 1953), p. iii.
    9 The sovereignty of reason amounts to an article of faith for Hegel, and he so recognized it: "I have proclaimed at the outset that reason rules the world and I have stated this as our presupposition and faith." *The Philosophy of History*, Introduction in Friedrich, ed. and trans., *The Philosophy of Hegel*, p. 16. The Sibree translation has "hypothesis and belief" for "presupposition and faith." *The Philosophy of History*, trans. by J. Sibree (London: George Bell, 1905), p. 26. We would do well to remember that Hegel's *Philosophy of History*, like Aristotle's *Politics*, was prepared from notes.
    10 *Philosophy of Right*, Preface.

containing as it does the science of the state, is to be nothing other than the endeavor to apprehend and portray the state as something rational. As a work of philosophy it must be poles apart from any attempt to construct a state as it ought to be. . . . To comprehend what is, this is the task of philosophy, because what is, is reason. Whatever happens, every individual is a child of his time; so philosophy, too, is its own time apprehended in thoughts. It is just as absurd to fancy that a philosophy can transcend its contemporary world as it is to fancy that an individual can overleap his own age, jump over Rhodes.[11]

If we take seriously these declarations, it may serve to mitigate two insistent and related criticisms of Hegel's political philosophy; first, that he seemed to stop the dialectic with the ascendancy of the German nations in his own time (much as Marx would stop the dialectic with the triumph of the proletariat); second, that because he could envision no higher form of political life than the sovereign nation-state, he glorified the wars which result from conflict between sovereign nation-states.[12]

It is quite true, as we shall see, that Hegel regarded the Germanic nations as the high point of a long cultural development. But a high point is not necessarily a terminus. This writer finds nothing in Hegel to indicate that he stops the dialectic with the Prussia of 1820. But more to the point, if Hegel is correct in believing that no philosophy can "transcend its contemporary world" perhaps the glories of German culture were all that he could know fully enough to praise. It is no doubt ironic that Hegel sought to explain more with his temporally restricted conception of philosophy than did half a dozen run-of-the-mill philosophers without such a limitation. Historical relativism ought to induce humility; but perhaps this is asking too much of one who virtually invented historical relativism.

As for war, there was certainly a romantic strain in Hegel's treatment of it. It is by war that "the ethical health of peoples is preserved," as

11 *Ibid.*

12 Some examples: (1) "Hegel seemed to think that the Prussian state of his professional maturity was the end of the process, the perfect synthesis." Crane Brinton, *The Shaping of the Modern Mind*, (New York: New American Library [Mentor Books], 1953), p. 158. (2) ". . . at this point an importation from the actual put an end to logic. Hegel simply took over, and arbitrarily idealized, the political organization with which his private sympathies lay. He thought well of the Prussia of 1820; therefore, it must be the terminus of the forward-moving logic. . . ." W. T. Jones, *A History of Western Philosophy*, p. 885. (3) Hegel "seems to think everything important takes the form of war. . . . his admiration of the nation state is carried so far as to become inconsistent with his general preference of wholes to parts." Bertrand Russell, *A History of Western Philosophy* (New York: Simon & Schuster, 1945), p. 739. (4) "History completes itself in the Prussia of his day." Morris Cohen, "Hegel," in *Encyclopaedia of the Social Sciences* (New York: Macmillan, 1932), Vol. VII, p. 313.

the wind preserves the sea from foulness.[13] The sacrifice of oneself to the higher purposes of the state is a "universal duty."[14] But if we remember that Hegel's avowed purpose was not to change the world but to understand it, we recognize that he was trying to *justify* war rather than to *glorify* it. Indeed, in contemplating the violence and passions of historical conflict, in "looking upon history as this butchery," Hegel noted that "we can end up by feeling sorry for this vainglory."[15] War is just *there*, in the world as a fact of life. If national unity is regarded as a good, and if war generates national unity (as it certainly does) then war has within it elements of good. It must also be noted that Hegel's view of war is nothing like twentieth-century conceptions of total war. He invokes "the proviso of the *jus gentium* that the possibility of peace be retained (and so, for example, that envoys be respected), and, in general, that war be not waged against domestic institutions, against the peace of family and private life, or against persons in their private capacity."[16] To be "rational" war must be within the framework of law.

It is not inconsistent with the dialectic to see wholes and the conflict of parts simultaneously. On the contrary, this is the essence of the dialectic. And that Hegel, speaking out of history and for history, could not see as did Kant the possibility of a world state, does not by itself invalidate the dialectic, or even make it irrelevant to such a possibility. All of which makes Bertrand Russell's statement that Hegel's doctrine of the state "if accepted, justifies every internal tyranny and every external aggression that can possibly be imagined"[17] rather absurd.

Hegel began by taking seriously the Christian problem of theodicy, i.e., how a good God can permit evil in the world, and sought to find the good that came out of evil rather than to deny the reality of evil. He also took the Incarnation seriously and accepted what it implied about the meaningfulness of history. Hegel's view of history is consequently Christian at least with respect to the conclusion that the ultimate good in history is not always coincident with the pleasure of individuals: "The History of the World is not the theater of happiness. Periods of happiness are blank pages in it, for they are periods of harmony—periods when the antithesis is in abeyance."[18]

It is manifestly unfair to make Hegel a totalitarian in the twentieth-century sense. In his constitutional writings Hegel favored trial by jury, local self-government, at least partial freedom of the press, and

13 *Philosophy of Right*, sec. 324.   14 *Ibid.*, sec. 325.
15 *Philosophy of History*, Introduction, Friedrich trans., p. 14. Compare Sibree trans., p. 22.
16 *Philosophy of Right*, sec. 338.   17 *History of Western Philosophy*, p. 742.
18 *Philosophy of History*, Sibree trans., p. 28.

other conditions identified with liberal constitutionalism. Unlike reactionaries of the stamp of De Maistre, he favored separation of church
and state (in our sense of the word). Art, philosophy, and religion,
though *in* the state, were not subordinate to it. He had a basic confidence
in the capacity of public opinion to support good laws. On grounds
similar to those of De Tocqueville he was sympathetic with the Americans and hopeful for their future. He sought to obtain the release from a
Prussian jail of the French liberal Victor Cousin. In a long and famous
footnote to *The Philosophy of Right*, Hegel attacks with remarkable vigor
and lucidity the "might makes right" views of K. L. von Haller and
stresses "how infinitely important and divine it is that the duties of the
state and the rights of the citizens, as well as the rights of the state and
the duties of the citizens, should be defined by law."[19]

Another misconception about Hegel is that his concern for history is
purely abstract and categorical. In fact his *Philosophy of History* is studded
with considerable historical detail, though less so in the often-repro-
duced Introduction than elsewhere. Man's thinking, says the author,
which includes "feeling, knowledge, and insight, desire and will," is what
distinguishes him from animals. History is past events, what has been.
The philosophy of history is merely thinking about history. Hegel finds,
as one might expect, a contradiction between the tasks of history and
philosophy that must be overcome. It is overcome in the "only thought
philosophy brings along" in approaching the materials of history,
"the very simple thought of reason, namely that reason rules the world.
. . . history is the rational and necessary way of the world spirit which
is the substance of history." Hegel sagely asserts that people do not study
history simply for information but for rational insight, yet many
historians for this reason necessarily do precisely what they criticize
the philosophers for, "namely the imparting of *a priori* inventions to
history."[20] Herbert Marcuse has pointed out how remarkable it is
that an idealistic philosophy should proceed empirically. The hypothesis
developed (and in one sense validated) in the *Logic* is here applied
to the data of history. But the structure of the dialectic transcends
both: "the 'negativity' that, in the *Logic*, determined the process of
thought appears in the *Philosophy of History* as the destructive power of
time."[21]

The task of the philosophy of history is, as we have seen, a deeply

19 *Philosophy of Right*, sec. 258.
20 *Philosophy of History*, Introduction, Friedrich trans., p. 6. Compare Sibree
trans., p. 9.
21 Herbert Marcuse, *Reason and Revolution; Hegel and the Rise of Social Theory*
(Toronto: Oxford Univ. Press, 1941), p. 224.

religious task for Hegel. He acknowledges the commandment of the Scriptures that it is a duty not only to love God but to know him. He seeks the penetrations of eternity within "the destructive power of time." Moreover, it is not enough to know God merely as a theological abstraction; indeed, "philosophy must guard religion against certain kinds of theology." Regarding nations and states as the individuals with which history deals, "we must make an earnest effort to understand the concrete as the means and ways of providence which are spread out openly before us as the phenomena of history." Hegel felt that his own time was "now at last . . . the right time to comprehend this rich production of creative reason which is world history."[22] The unfolding of creative reason—the world spirit—was inextricably bound up with enlarging conceptions of freedom—freedom that is simultaneously self-limitation and self-realization.

Hence, in *The Philosophy of History*, Hegel reviews the order of civilizations and tells his audience that the Orientals, who had only an external morality and were able to make of government only a coercive organ, did not know that "the spirit is free in itself, or that man is free in himself." For the Oriental, past and present, only one is free, and that one is the ruling despot, who, because he is only one and affected by "arbitrariness, ferocity, obtuseness of passion," is not really free and therefore not really a man. The Greeks and the Romans "knew only that a few are free, and not man as such" for they were tied to their slaves and could not rise above the accidental and contingent, which made their freedom a "passing and limited flower."

"Only the Germanic nations have in and through Christianity achieved the consciousness that man *qua* man is free and that freedom of the spirit constitutes his very nature."[23] The task of extending this principle to the secular realm is, however, not even yet completed. Hegel asserts his theological proposition despite and not in ignorance of the various qualifications that could be made:

. . . what constitutes the final end of the world we claim to be the spirit's consciousness of its freedom and thus the actualization of its freedom. That this [concept of] freedom is still indeterminate and ambiguous in definitions; that freedom, being the highest [good] implies infinitely many misunderstandings, confusions, and errors; that it involves all kinds of commotions—this one has never known better nor experienced more clearly than in our time. But right now we shall be content with the general notion, just the same. . . .[24]

22 *Philosophy of History*, Friedrich trans., pp. 9-10. See also *Hegel on Christianity: Early Theological Writings*, trans. by T. M. Knox (New York: Harper, 1961).
23 *Philosophy of History*, Friedrich trans., pp. 11-12.
24 *Ibid.*, pp. 12-13.

Spirit

SPIRIT has been referred to many times in the foregoing. As with many other Hegelian terms, to define spirit in a brief phrase such as "self-contained existence" helps hardly at all; nevertheless, if we are to do justice to the over-all unity of the Hegelian system, we must see how spirit at the personal level is related to spirit at the level of world history and hence world politics. For this we must look briefly to *The Phenomenology of Spirit*. The influence of Plato and Aristotle on Hegel is much in evidence in this work. From Plato comes a sense of the distinction between surface appearance and the reality lying beneath and beyond, the world of philosophical knowledge that is truth. The "we" Hegel uses, as Marcuse notes, is addressed to philosophers and not to ordinary readers. Plato's *Parmenides* is suggested by Hegel's concern for consciousness and otherness, that by which consciousness knows itself. But like Aristotle, Hegel sees a continuity rather than an unbridgeable gulf between the material and the nonmaterial worlds. Sense leads to thought. Going beyond both the Greeks and Kant, Hegel seeks to transcend the subject-object dichotomy. It is spirit (comparable to the Platonic soul, the self-moved mover) that accomplishes this transcendence through its own self-consciousness, which is the true reality. We begin with pure subjectivity, a self not conscious of itself. To become self-conscious, spirit must go outside of itself, so to speak, and make the objective world its own in order that it may know itself and its own power.

Since the process of becoming fully self-conscious involves this reciprocal relationship of self and the other, and of subjectivity and objectivity, there are no fixed limits to the sources of knowledge and "The process of knowledge becomes the process of history. . . . Hegel links the epistemological process of self-consciousness (from sense-certainty to reason) with the historical process of mankind from bondage to freedom."[25]

Hegel's treatment of the French Revolution in terms of history, freedom, and consciousness is instructive. It will be remembered that *The Phenomenology of Spirit* was written in the midst of the Thermidorian reaction to the French Revolution. Hegel called the Revolution the symbol of self-destructive freedom because the state created by it was merely external. Law freely willed by man, involving a unity of the subjective and the external, had not yet been achieved. Hence the promise of a more genuine internalized freedom of the German idealist-romantic school loomed all the more attractively on the horizon. Hegel's politics were

25 Marcuse, *Reason and Revolution*, p. 95.

inescapably related to his whole philosophical system. Some critics have charged Hegel with the confusion of mixing historical and philosophical concepts indiscriminately. Hegel does indeed mix them, but not indiscriminately. All post-Hegelian attacks on conventional epistemology for its failure to take into account the historical (and therefore continually shifting and relational) character of knowledge (e.g., those of Dilthey, Collingwood, Mannheim) owe a great deal to Hegel.

The gap between epistemology and history Hegel bridges brilliantly, but a parallel or at least related gap he does not bridge. In *The Phenomenology of Spirit* he is primarily looking at the absorption of historical knowledge by the spirit manifest in the human individual's psyche. In *The Philosophy of History* the individual is replaced by nations and states (in the special Hegelian sense of state, which we will discuss in a moment). To Hegel, no doubt, spirit cannot be confined to one or the other, but absorbs them both; a purely individualistic philosophy is, for Hegel, a contradiction in terms. So far so good. But there is a concreteness about the human individual that is not possessed by nations or states, and there is an arbitrariness about the selection of the latter as bearers of the world spirit that Hegel never seems to face up to. From the point of view of the almost Godlike stance Hegel is required to take, it is not at all clear why nations are more significant groupings of human beings than families, or towns, or religious groups, or occupational groups, or happy people, or right thinkers, each of which (even granting the reality of some kind of collective will) could be as "natural" a collectivity in the eyes of God as a nation or nation-state. If history is national history to Hegel, should he not be somewhat more modest in his belief that history is national history to God? Still, twentieth-century man, for whom nation has in many respects become God, is ill-prepared to judge Hegel on the point and has reason to feel some kinship with the old philosopher who felt that true freedom could only exist within the nation-state.

The State

THE concept of the State is the heart of Hegel's political philosophy, but it can scarcely be understood if pulled out of its elaborate context. If we turn back to the diagram of the Hegelian system, we note that the State is within the dialectical chain leading to Objective Spirit. The first term of the triad of which this concept is a part is Subjective Spirit, spirit in its inwardness and immediacy, the subcategories of which pertain to what we might call psychology in its broadest sense. Subjective Spirit "passes over" to Objective Spirit, spirit in its otherness, its mediateness.

The latter pertains to the whole area of sociology, politics, economics, law, and ethics—the subjects discussed in *The Philosophy of Right*. And so on into the synthesis of Absolute Spirit containing the highest expressions of art, religion, and philosophy.

But the State is two levels below the triad Subjective Spirit–Objective Spirit–Absolute Spirit. The triad of which it is a part feeds into Ethical Life, which is the third term of the triad Abstract Right (Law)–Morality –Ethical Life. Abstract Right is the sphere of rights and duties that attach to persons as persons (those who are conscious of their consciousness) considered singly, abstractly, and in isolation from their capacity as citizens. The law with which it is concerned is that of property, contract, and external right and wrong. Morality (*Moralität*), on the other hand, is higher than this (though why more mediate is not clear) and includes acts properly motivated along with the individual's inner awareness of conflict between law and the desire to break it. Instead of abstract right and wrong, it involves concrete goodness and wickedness. Finally there is a synthesis in Ethical Life (*Sittlichkeit*) in which the lower forms merge into a larger conception of the good of the whole, which is symbolized by the State. It may be significant that Hegel devotes about thirty pages to Morality and one hundred and twenty pages to Ethical Life.

The State is the apex of the triad that begins with the family as an immediate form, passes over into the mediate form of "civil society" (a crude translation of *burgerliche Gesellschaft*), and proceeds to the ethical community that is the State. Unless one understands that what we today generally understand by the word "state" largely corresponds to Hegel's conception of the civil society, great confusion results. The civil society includes all that we would place in the political system and more, including the economy, the administration of justice, and bureaucratic officialdom.

The relationship between property (which Hegel discusses under the heading of Abstract Right), the civil society, and the concept of freedom is difficult to grasp but important.[26] Man's will has simultaneously universal and particular aspects. Property is identified with the particular aspect of man's will because it is the result of the individual's appropriation of the "other." Even though directed toward particular ends, this assertion is nevertheless the "first phase of freedom."[27] The resulting situation is paradoxical. Private property is essential to the freedom of the subject; but the competitive claims of private property tend toward

26 It has been illumined for us in Herbert Marcuse's fine study, *Reason and Revolution*, Ch. 6.
27 *Philosophy of Right*, sec. 33A.

anarchy and work against the higher freedom of a truly unified social order. The first is negative freedom; the second is positive freedom. They work against each other, but the first must be experienced before the second can be understood. Man must have some freedom in order to want any freedom. This is what Hegel means by "the free will which wills the free will."[28] In the civil society the free play of private interests must be tolerated; their integration, if any, is a matter of chance and not rational choice.[29] To this extent Hegel is strictly middle-class in his economic orientation. But at the same time he sees the consequences for civil society as fortuitous necessity rather than true freedom. Hegel shares none of the liberals' easy optimism about a "natural" harmony between individual and general interests. Hence there is the need for the higher power of the State, which exists in a relationship of tension with the civil society. The State must dominate the civil society for the sake of the free individual (which, incidentally, is quite at odds with fascist theory). Guido de Ruggiero deals with the same issue in a different way:

Society is the intermediate factor between the individual and the State. That is Hegel's great discovery and the turning point of all German nineteenth-century political science. The social organism, inserting itself between the two extreme terms which revolutionary theory had brought too perilously face to face, makes it possible not only to place the idea of the State in a region secure against the assaults of the individual, but also to canalize into that idea in an organic and disciplined form, all the claims and aspirations that spring spontaneously out of the individual life. It parts the two protagonists in the struggle, and at the same time unites them by a firmer bond. It destroys the Revolutionary fancy that the State is a product of convention and caprice, but it equally rejects the reactionary fallacy that the State is identical with the prince and stands over against the consciousness of the people as an external object.[30]

Whether the civil society most usefully separates State and individual, or whether the State saves the individual from civil society, the distinction is not irrelevant, even today. Some such distinction as that between State and civil society permits present-day patriots to love America while hating the government and also permits constitutionalists to question the Supreme Court without questioning the rule of law.

Hegel's State as an ethical community has obvious parallels with the *polis* in Plato's ideal state. In a brilliant comparative study of the two,

28 *Ibid.*, sec. 27.   29 *Ibid.*, secs. 186, 229A.
30 *History of European Liberalism*, trans. by R. G. Collingwood, (Boston: Beacon Press, 1959), p. 231.

Michael Foster has shown the degree to which Hegel has improved upon yet confused the issue in Plato's formulation. As one capable of assimilating the liberating effect of the Enlightenment, Hegel both criticized and confused the relation of "subjective freedom" to Plato's *polis*. Plato's ruler has the subjective freedom to grasp universal forms. To this end, he is denied property and all that may conduce merely to sensual desire. Plato's subject does not have, in the ideal state, the subjective freedom to direct his soul toward any particulars, that is, toward the gratifications of sensuous desire. He has only the objective freedom derived from being tied to an all-wise ruler by external duty. In attacking Plato's exclusion of "subjective freedom" from the *polis*, Hegel, says Foster, confused this distinction. In claiming for his own state the capacity to assimiliate subjective freedom for everyone he seems to be asking for incompatibles—the freedom that comes from following universal law and freedom seen as independence from universal law.[31] In his powerful drive to transcend and unite categories of subjective and objective, freedom and determination, law and liberty, Hegel undoubtedly sought to be more systematic than is humanly possible and, as we shall see, was at points forced to come down on the side of preferred positions for rulers.

This general dilemma is illustrated especially in the problem of the relationship between the civil society and the State. Once again we can refer to the illuminating study by Foster.[32] In his concept of Absolute Right Hegel tried to subsume two quite disparate entities, both of which in earlier thought went under the name state of nature. (The juxtaposition of both meanings in the same writer and under the same label appeared most conspicuously in Hobbes.) On the one hand, it referred to a condition in which the laws of passion dominated—"natural" in the sense of universally operative; for example, economic laws. On the other hand, it referred to a condition in which the laws of reason dominated either actually or potentially. In this case, "natural" meant universally valid. The sphere in which both of these conditions obtained was for Hegel the civil society.

But how, then, does one get from the civil society to the State? Civil society is still a sphere of particularity. Law may be fulfilled, but not necessarily as a result of the conscious intention of the subjects to fulfill it. Civil society can, then, be seen as the level of operative economic laws, and the State as the ideal level at which ethical will dominates, the same ethical will that is only latent in civil society. Seen in this way, the mistake

31 Michael Foster, *The Political Philosophies of Plato and Hegel* (Oxford: Clarendon Press, 1935), Ch. 3.
32 *Ibid.*, Ch. 5.

of comparing the relationship between Hegel's civil society and State
to, say, the relationship between Locke's society and his state is obvious.
It would be more correct to think of civil society as an empiricist conception of society and State as a rationalist conception of society. Through
moral education, members of the empirical society can be lifted from
the level of economic necessity and sensual gratification to a higher level
of voluntary obedience to law as a system of reason. In this way they
achieve true freedom.

Hegel, however, does not explain the relationship of civil society to
State in quite this way and, indeed, is not a consistent rationalist. The
action of concrete will, quite apart from abstract reason, is important
in moral choice to Hegel, and there remains the ambiguity as to whether
both ruler and subject must participate in this exercise of moral will
before the State is achieved. In his discussion of the role of police powers
(broadly conceived) and guilds and corporations,[33] Hegel suggests that the
understanding of the moral order and the will to control affairs in its
service is the basic requirement of leadership. But, says Foster, "This
will which wills the universal and is therefore free, is the will which
regulates, not which submits to regulations; a ruler's and not a subject's
will."[34] This interpretation would suggest that the governing class alone
has a life in the State, and if so, Hegel has no grounds for trying to
lift anyone else out of the life of material passion in civil society.

Certainly in one sense the distinction between civil society and State is
metaphysical and not physical, and the division of classes is that of logical
rather than historical classes. Yet Hegel does go beyond Plato in that
he tries to relate his logical distinctions to existential historical classes and
divisions. He does try to identify the State with existing power. He does
discuss such concrete institutions as parliament, parties, public opinion,
and free speech.[35] He tries to relate them to the possibility of "subjective
freedom" for subjects. He takes public education very seriously and
favors extensive publicity for parliamentary debate. But here as elsewhere,
Hegel displays a fascination for the mixture of opposites that is the heart
of the dialectic, coated over with the affection for moral oneness associated
with Plato, Rousseau, and Kant:

316. The formal subjective freedom of individuals consists in their having
and expressing their own private judgements, opinions, and recommendations
on affairs of state. This freedom is collectively manifested in what is called
"public opinion" in which what is absolutely universal, the substantive and true,
is linked with its opposite, the purely particular and private opinions of the

33 *Philosophy of Right*, secs. 231 ff, 250 ff.
34 *Political Philosophies of Plato and Hegel*, p. 158.
35 *Philosophy of Right*, secs. 272 ff, 288 ff, 301, 308.

Many. Public opinion as it exists is thus a standing self-contradiction, knowledge as appearance, the essential just as directly present as the inessential.

317. Public opinion, therefore, is a repository not only of the genuine needs and correct tendencies of common life, but also, in the form of common sense (i.e., all-pervasive fundamental ethical principles disguised as prejudices), of the eternal, substantive principles of justice, the true content and result of legislation, the whole constitution, and the general position of the state. At the same time when this inner truth emerges into consciousness and, embodied in general maxim, enters representative thinking . . . it becomes infected by all the accidents of opinion, by its ignorance and perversity, by its mistakes and falsity of judgement. . . . because the bad is that which is wholly private and personal in its content.[36]

The fearfulness Hegel has about the political bargaining and compromise we would associate with "free" political institutions suggests that he is thinking in terms quite alien to our free-wheeling democratic tradition. On the other hand, his hope that the wide dissemination of public information could give the citizen understanding not only of the historical situation but of the philosophic conception of the State strikes us as excessively optimistic, perhaps even more liberal than the liberals. In both emphases the influence of Rousseau is evident. Here is a simple antithesis of pessimism and optimism concerning "the people" implicit in Hegel's political theory, which he did not successfully synthesize. But with it he drove to a central question which plagues us even more in an age of mass democracy: Are there philosophic prerequisites for self-rule? Actually, despite the amount of attention Hegel pays to his crowning idea of the State, its derivation within the framework of the dialectic is one of the least satisfying aspects of Hegel's work. The family represents unity and universality, which passes over into the particularity and diversity of the civil society, which culminates in the unity-in-diversity of the State. But, as W. T. Stace notes: "We see that *if* we advance from the idea of civil society to that of the state a reconciliation of the particular and the universal is found. But we cannot see any logical necessity why we *must* advance."[37]

We know that the State is "the actuality of the ethical Idea,"[38] and "mind objectified."[39] We know that it exists immediately in custom, mediately in individual self-consciousness, and essentially as "substantive freedom."[40] But we do not know exactly *how* power and ethical idea become one. This gap lays Hegel open to the criticism that his doctrine is one "that misses the tragedy of history and is the equivalent to

36 *Ibid.*, secs. 316-17.   37 *The Philosophy of Hegel*, p. 424.
38 *Philosophy of Right*, sec. 257.   39 *Ibid.*, sec. 258.   40 *Ibid.*, sec. 257.

Napoleon's dictum that God is on the side of the heaviest artillery."[41]
There is enough of a sense of tragedy elsewhere in Hegel to make us
wonder why he seemed to lose it in discussing the State. Even at the end
of *The Philosophy of Right*, after making the victorious nation-state the
bearer of the World Spirit, and making world history the final court of
judgment[42] Hegel nevertheless feels obliged to assure us that "world
history is not the verdict of mere might."[43]

Institutions of the State

IT REMAINS to look briefly at Hegel's constitutional views, examining
them as parts of an elaborate system, but also evaluating their empirical
realism. In taking up the constitution "on its internal side,"[44] Hegel picks
from "amongst current ideas" discussed with much "babble" and
"undigested chatter" the idea of separation of powers. It is, says Hegel,
"if taken in the true sense" the "guarantee of public freedom" but a
dangerously static equilibrium, a denial of "living unity" results if
"abstract Understanding handles it" and "reads into it the false doctrine
of the absolute self-substance of each of the powers against the other. . . ."

The three powers have, however, quite different purposes. The
Legislature is to "establish the universal." The Executive is to "subsume
single cases and the spheres of particularity under the universal." And
the Crown is to represent the "power of subjectivity" to bind into an
individual unity all powers and thus constitute at once the base and
the apex of the whole. Hegel's belief in constitutional monarchy was
demonstrated by his assertion of the necessity to symbolize, as only a
solitary individual can do, the moment of individuality, of subjectivity,
in the notion of the State. Yet it is by a quite unconvincing deduction
that this single figure is more "naturally" a hereditary monarch than one
chosen by other means. Constitutional monarchy nevertheless "is the
achievement of the modern world, a world in which the substantial
Idea has won the infinite form [of subjectivity] . . . the history of this
genuine formation of ethical life is the content of the whole course of
world-history."[45] The ancient distinctions between monarchy, aristocracy,
and democracy are merely quantitative and therefore superficial. Hegel
pays tribute to Montesquieu for his insight into the qualitative substance
of different forms, but disparages his feudal conception of monarchy in
which not duty but honor holds the state together.

41 Cohen, "Hegel," in *Encyclopaedia of the Social Sciences*, Vol. VII, p. 313.
42 *Philosophy of Right*, sec. 342.   43 *Ibid.*, sec. 343.
44 *Ibid.*, secs. 272 f.   45 *Ibid.*, sec. 273.

Hegel's view of representation as it comes out in his discussion of the Idea of the Corporation turns out to be feudal in character (even though he has, unlike some figures in the Reaction, accepted the irreversible transformation of feudal institutions by the rising middle class). The three estates receiving representation are the "substantial" or agricultural class, which lives within "concrete universals"; the "reflected," industrial and service groups, the business class directed to the particular; and the "thinking" estate, which is the determiner of the general interest. The last seems to endow with special prerogatives the professors, the bureaucrats, and the Junker class in general.[46]

The question of framing an original charter or constitution, the question that took on so much significance for the contractualists, is viewed almost with indifference by Hegel. His discussion, he says, presupposes an existent constitution. And, then, in a passage that reminds one of the myths of Plato and Rousseau's civil religion, "In any case, however, it is absolutely essential that the constitution should not be regarded as something made, even though it has come into being in time. It must be treated as something existent in and by itself, as divine therefore. . . ."[47] In fact, the constitution of any nation is a product of history and depends upon the development of that nation's self-consciousness. "Hence every nation has the constitution appropriate to it and suitable for it."[48]

Conclusion

THE flaws in the Hegelian system are many. We have examined some and can glance again at them here.

(1) Hegel asked too much of his new logic when he presented it not only as a new descriptive language but as a new view of the life that the language was supposed to describe. Nothing, not a scrap of reality, was left outside the system.[49]

(2) Without explicit defense, Hegel simply identified the more general with the more good; the more private and particular with the more bad. If general motivations are the prerequisite of greatness, it is questionable whether he will find any great men to lead the State.

(3) The recognition of the desirability of "subjective freedom" for subjects as distinguished from rulers was left ambiguous.

46 *Ibid.*, sec. 250ff., 201ff.   47 *Ibid.*, sec. 273.   48 *Ibid.*, sec. 274.
49 "[Hegel's] system must be pantheistic precisely on account of its finality. Existence must be revoked in the eternal before the system can round itself out; there must be no existing remainder, not even such a little minikin as the existing Herr Professor who writes the system." Søren Kierkegaard, *Concluding Unscientific Postscript*, trans. by David F. Swenson (Princeton: Princeton Univ. Press, 1941), p. 111.

(4) The conditions whereby a union of subjective freedom and objective freedom could be achieved never became concrete.

(5) The transition from civil society to the State remained ambiguous.

(6) The union of power and right in the State (as, indeed, the whole attempt to fuse is and ought), remained so unstable as to be hardly a union, and some of Hegel's references to the Crown were not reassuring to enemies of despotism.

(7) The selection of nation-states as the only true bearers of the World Spirit was at the least arbitrary and at the most blasphemous.

Many more criticisms and a good many rebuttals could no doubt be made. But we should not at this point care too much about Hegel's shortcomings, inasmuch as virtually all his disciples had more. His contribution to our processes of thought about political questions is what is important. He contributed great quantities of raw material for lesser minds to exploit as ideologies—the fascistic "myth of the state," the romantic glorification of war, the Marxian faith in the clash of opposites, the nationalistic fever that still rages around the globe—all have affected our recent history and our recent thinking, and all owe much to what Hegel did.

But beyond the level of ideological expropriation Hegel gave us new and profound insights without which it would be virtually impossible to speak as we do of ideologies. The impact of historicism and relativism has been felt especially in the social sciences and philosophy, more recently, perhaps, in theology, but not even yet with full force in science. In a sense, the completeness and linguistic abstractness of Hegel's system, when taken together with his epistemological historicism, puts him in a class by himself. He can be regarded as progressive or reactionary depending upon the society to which his system is applied.

Finally, the new logic of the dialectic, whatever its shortcomings, was a brilliant invention. The search for geometric laws of society stopped, and the search for processual or biological laws of society began in the nineteenth century. The gap between the Bentham of the preceeding chapter and the Marx of the following chapter is appropriately filled by our discussion of Hegel. But, as well, Social Darwinists, lawyers of the historical school, evangelizing Social Gospel men, and many others felt the tug of "creative evolution" set loose in the world by the hard, dry Herr Professor of Jena and Berlin.

CHAPTER

13 | *Marx*

T HAT the work of Karl Marx is relevant to twentieth-century politics scarcely requires labored demonstration to the present-day reader. Indeed, an overwhelming sense of this relevance may for many actually be a barrier to understanding what Marx did and did not say. There are a good many theoretical deviations along the path that runs between the *Communist Manifesto* and Communism today. Not all that is important as theory in Marx is today politically relevant; and not all that is today politically relevant in Marx is important as theory. Let us attempt a proper scholarly attitude, one which places the value of understanding a theory ahead of the value of outwitting an enemy (although the latter, needless to say, is not in all cases to be disparaged).

Early Life

KARL MARX was born in May, 1818, in Trier, in the German Rhineland, the eldest son and the second of eight children in his family. The area had been occupied by the French under Napoleon but was now, following the Congress of Vienna, part of Prussia. Marx's parents were Jews who had been segregated and discriminated against until the imposition of the Napoleonic Code introduced a new era of equalitarianism. During the period of new-found freedom Heinrich Marx, Karl's father, built up a successful law practice and lived the life of the respectable, liberal bourgeoisie. Then Napoleon withdrew some of the liberties granted to the Jews, and finally the Prussian princes cut off the rest with the anti-Jewish laws of 1816. The abrupt retreat to a position of inferior legal status was psychologically more damaging to the Jews than constant repression might have been. Karl was thus born in the midst of a period of intense frustration. Due to his close relationship with his father, he undoubtedly absorbed much of the latter's bitterness toward authority. Shortly after Karl's birth, possibly to achieve a kind of security, his father, and later his mother, became Christians. When Karl was sixteen, his father made a speech advocating certain mild governmental reforms. The Prussian police descended upon the home. The elder Marx recanted and begged forgiveness. Apparently this behavior was a source of great shame to Karl and further stimulated his attitude of resentment.

Young Marx was a precocious and brilliant student, especially in literature. Ahead of his years, he entered the Faculty of Law at the University of Bonn in 1835, at the age of seventeen. There he led the "gay and dissipated life of the ordinary German student"[1] and was once arrested for riotous behavior. Even at this time the powerful self-assurance that would later impress his followers was apparent. Reflecting a turn toward the serious, in the autumn of 1836, Marx transferred from Bonn to the University of Berlin to study jurisprudence. The attractions of Berlin were many: it was a big city, the center of the government, the hub of intellectual radicalism, and the fount of Hegelianism. Marx absorbed Hegel's system as deeply as anyone, but his interest in materialism, through which he came to refashion Hegel, was in early evidence. His doctoral dissertation, written after a move to Jena in 1840-41, was "The Difference Between the Natural Philosophy of Democritus and Epicurus."

Marx had planned to follow an academic career but instead in 1841 took a job as a reporter for the *Rheinische Zeitung*. The next year he became editor. The paper was bourgeois, but critical of the Prussian government, and Marx found himself writing radical but strictly capital-istic editorials, for which the journal was suppressed by the authorities in 1843. This turn of events embittered Marx, but had the effect of stimulating his interest in politics and economics. An article written in 1844 is one of the first to reveal the germ of Marx's idea of the economic interpretation of history:

. . . legal relations and political forms cannot be conceived as autonomous phenomena, nor as manifestations of the so-called general unfolding of the human spirit. They are, rather, rooted in the material conditions of life. . . . the anatomy of . . . civic society is to be sought in its economics.[1a]

    1 Isaiah Berlin, *Karl Marx* (New York: Oxford Univ. Press, 1959), p. 33.
    1a Quoted in *Encyclopaedia of the Social Sciences* (New York: Macmillan, 1933), Vol. X, p. 172.

Marx went to Paris to study economics and found there a job with the Paris magazine for German exiles, *Deutsche-Französische Jahrbücher*. While in Paris he met Friedrich Engels, a young German radical and son of a wealthy cotton manufacturer. Here began a close friendship and a great collaboration. So intertwined was the intellectual activity of Marx and Engels from this point on that when most people today speak of Marxism they are speaking of the joint output of Marx and Engels. Engels did not have as creative a mind as Marx, but he possessed a vast historical knowledge and a forceful, driving character. Moreover, Engels' periodic loans enabled Marx to write with greater concentration and at greater length than would otherwise have been possible, for Marx was to be frequently on the edge of poverty.

At the request of the Prussian government, France expelled Marx in 1845. He went to Brussels to study until the fateful year 1848. While in Brussels Marx and Engels reorganized the German Workers Educational Association (*Deutscher Arbeiterbildungsverein*), which allied itself with a secret federation called the Communist League (*Bund der Kommunisten*). Michael Bakunin, in Brussels at the time, could not understand why Marx and Engels were wasting their time with a group of ignorant workmen, filling their minds with obscure theories they could not understand. The reaction was symbolic of Bakunin's anarchist impotence and Marx's powerful sense of the necessity for joining theory and practice. As Marx said in his famous comment on Feuerbach, "[Until now] philosophers have only *interpreted* the world in various ways; the point however is to *change* it."[2] At the request of the Communist League, Marx and Engels wrote, in 1848, one of the most important documents of modern times, *The Communist Manifesto*.

The Communist Manifesto and Beyond

ALTHOUGH written in a passionate rhetorical style, the *Manifesto* contained in nascent form many of the theoretical principles that, taken together, were to comprise the Marxian system. "A spectre is haunting Europe," it began, "—the spectre of Communism." And after thus trying (perhaps with some success) to strike terror in the hearts of respectable readers, it went on to explain why and how "The history of all hitherto

2 *Theses on Feuerbach*, XI, in Émile Burns, ed., *A Handbook of Marxism* (New York: Random House, 1935), p. 231. This collection is still the handiest source for many Marxian materials, some of which are not even yet translated elsewhere. But see also Marx and Engels, *Basic Writings on Politics and Philosophy*, Lewis S. Feuer, ed. (New York: Doubleday [Anchor Books], 1959).

existing society is the history of class struggles," and how "The executive of the modern state is but a committee for managing the common affairs of the whole bourgeoisie."[3] The bourgeoisie has served its useful purpose in the history of class struggles, but its time is now past, and through exploitation of the very proletariat it has created it is blindly trying to hold onto its out-of-joint power, not realizing that "What the bourgeoisie therefore produces, above all, are its own grave-diggers. Its fall and the victory of the Proletariat are equally inevitable."[4]

On the grounds "that intellectual production changes its character in proportion as material production is changed. . . . The ruling ideas of each age have ever been the ideas of its ruling class,"[5] Marx and Engels laid out what the new ruling class, the proletariat, had in store for the world. Some planks of their platform—for example, the abolition of the family —would become an embarrassment to the cause. Others, such as the progressive income tax and free public education, seem less shocking to our day than to theirs. But abolition of private property in land, state ownership of basic instruments of production, and abolition of inheritance remain radical and remain communist planks today. When, as a result of these measures, class distinction shall have disappeared, politics as it has been known will disappear, and "we shall have an association in which the free development of each is the condition for the free development of all."[6] Following a critique of what they regard as spurious alternatives to their valid socialism—feudal socialism, "true" socialism of the German *literati*, Christian socialism, utopian socialism—Marx and Engels end with the ringing words: "The proletarians have nothing to lose but their chains. They have a world to win. Workingmen of all countries, unite!"[7] The assumptions underlying this great tract furnish us with more than enough problems to deal with in one chapter.

Even tolerant Belgium was obliged to expel Marx when the *Manifesto* came to light. But revolution was breaking out in Paris, so Marx felt safe in returning there. Revolts sprang up in Milan, Rome, Venice, Berlin, Vienna, and Budapest. To some this looked like the great proletarian revolution Marx had predicted. But Marx took no part in the formation of a legion of revolutionaries to fight in Germany and coolly said they would be mercilessly beaten by the Royal Prussian Army. They were. Later in the year Marx went back to Berlin and persuaded some liberal industrialists to back a new version of his old paper, to be known as the *Neue Rheinische Zeitung*. Again the journal was pro-bourgeoisie and

3 *The Communist Manifesto*, authorized English trans. (New York: International Publishers, 1932), pp. 8-9.

4 *Ibid.*, p. 21.   5 *Ibid.*, p. 29.   6 *Ibid.*, p. 31.

7 *Ibid.*, p. 44. The *Manifesto* was immediately translated into English, French, Italian, Flemish, and Danish, but not, please note, into Russian.

antigovernment, and again (May, 1849) it was suppressed by the author-ities. Marx (who had been participating in secret Communist League activities while editing this business-oriented paper) printed the last issue of the *Zeitung* in red ink. He was arrested for sedition, but made a long and powerful speech at his trial that led, to everyone's surprise, to his acquittal. Marx's position at this time is critical for the exegesis of later Marxians. The right-wingers pointed to this time to show that violent revolution was not necessarily the first consideration of Marx; he could and did work for reform with groups other than the proletariat. Such was the view expressed by the so-called revisionists, Eduard Bernstein and Karl Kautsky. Lenin and the left-wingers pointed out that Marx had not let his right hand know what his left hand was doing, and that the logic of the dialectic required a bourgeois revolution before a true prole-tarian revolution could take place. Hence he was conscientiously en-couraging a bourgeois revolution while also secretly keeping the prole-tarian revolution simmering. Marx's later writings would seem to confirm this interpretation. In *The Eighteenth Brumaire of Louis Napoleon* (1852) he spoke of the Paris situation in 1848: "Upon the *bourgeois monarchy* of Louis Philippe, only the *bourgeois republic* could follow. . . . The demands of the Parisian proletariat are utopian tom-fooleries that have to be done away with."[8]

Expelled from Prussia in July, 1849, Marx had only one place left to go: England. He expected to spend only a few weeks there, but instead spent the rest of his life. He lived with his large but devoted family in London, in what was frequently miserable squalor. Mainly he lived off loans from Engels, though in the fifties and sixties he was a corre-spondent for the New York *Tribune*. His typical day from 10 A.M. to 7 P.M. was spent in the reading room of the British Museum, where he ground out his heavy prose. In one two-year period he produced 1,472 pages organized into twenty-three books, only two chapters of which were published. Sometimes he lacked money for postage to send his manuscripts to the publishers. Afflicted with boils, eye trouble, and liver trouble, proud, contentious, uncompromising, he was not a prepossessing sight during his last years. Virtually unknown in England, he neverthe-less enjoyed a tremendous reputation on the Continent, participating in the formation of the First Workers International in 1864. In 1867 the first volume of Marx's greatest work, *Capital (Das Kapital)*, was pub-lished. The second, third, and incomplete fourth volumes did not come out until after Marx's death in 1883.

8 Trans. by Daniel DeLeon (1897), in Samuel Beer, ed., *The Communist Mani-festo with Selections from The Eighteenth Brumaire of Louis Napoleon* (New York: Appleton-Century-Crofts, 1955), p. 53.

Historical Materialism and the Dialectic

IRRITATED by the convolutions of his disciples, Marx once said in the later years of his life, "I am not a Marxist." Most founders of systems are to some extent betrayed by their progeny. But in another sense, the Marxian system was really built by those who followed, for Marx never worked out a complete, well-rounded theoretical "system." The theory of dialectial materialism upon which all of Marxism seems to rest was given very little direct attention by Marx. *Capital*, his great theoretical work, assumed dialectical materialism and worked instead on the theories of surplus value and capitalist accumulation. He left to Engels, in *Socialism, Utopian and Scientific* and *The Origin of the Family*, speculation on a theory of the state.

Marx's tendency to bypass philosophical questions makes Hegel's influence all the more relevant for us. From Hegel came the dialectic. It is not enough to say that Marx took the Hegelian dialectic (see Chapter 12) and by substituting the materialist concept of class for the idealist concept of spirit made it explain historical process materialistically rather than idealistically. This explanation is not wrong; it is merely too simple. For one thing, Hegel, we may remember, had not thought of himself as an idealist, if this term implies a simple dualism between matter and idea. Marx spoke of finding Hegel on his head and proceeding to "set him the right way up"; but no such either/or would have satisfied Hegel. The dialectic transcended and absorbed idea *and* nature *and* spirit.

Moreover, Marx differed from Hegel not only with reference to the object of philosophic discourse, but with reference to its function as well —although the two were bound together. For Hegel, philosophy "always comes too late." It can only understand the world, not change it. But the point of philosophy for Marx was precisely to change the world; for all philosophy was class philosophy and classes were the fulcrum of history. In the day when classes would be no more, Marx believed that social philosophy would literally cease and become descriptive social science.

In criticizing Hegel, Marx and Engels adopted many of the arguments of Ludwig Feuerbach (1804-72), a "Young Hegelian" who, with *Zur Kritik der Hegelschen Philosophie* (1839) and other books published in the following decade, became a prominent philosophical materialist. Feuerbach incisively demonstrated that in deducing the ideal from the real, Hegel ended with nothing but what he had been forced to assume at the outset, and charged that Hegel's disregard for the problem of sense perception had been cavalier. Feuerbach rejected traditional theism and traditional philosophy ("My philosophy is no philosophy," he said rather misleadingly), and sought to unite the scientific with the speculative, to theorize about the ordinary experience of ordinary men. Especially useful to Marx and Engels was Feuerbach's penetrating analysis of the psychology, sociology, and anthropology of religion. But Marx criticized Feuerbach for neglecting the concrete historical analysis his own assumptions seemed to require, and for his lack of appreciation of the dialectic itself.[9]

In breaking with idealism, Marx did not go back to a simple materialism that could evade the question of the nature of human thought. Idealists from Kant to Hegel had struggled with the problem of the extent to which thought is an activity of the mind depending upon pre-existing consciousness as well as mere external stimuli, and Marx could not dismiss it. He agreed with Feuerbach that Hegel's identification of this pre-existing consciousness with a timeless divine Subject was mythological nonsense. But having said that, Feuerbach, confined, as Marx thought, to academic speculations, was up a blind alley. Marx tried to get out of the blind alley by turning to history unencumbered by Hegel's metaphysical trappings, and there solved the problem of consciousness by finding that it was not pre-existing at all but was itself a part of the historical process. "In direct contrast to German philosophy, which descends from heaven to earth, here the ascent is made from earth to heaven. . . . men, developing their material production and their material intercourse, change, along with this their real existence, also their thinking and the products of their thought. It is not consciousness that determines life, but life that determines consciousness."[10]

The process of thought, in other words, is a part of the process of nature, a hypothesis that cannot be proved by speculation but can be proved by practice (*Praxis*). Feuerbach's "contemplative materialism" failed to see this. We do not discover the truth. History proves the truth for us, through "human, sensuous activity, practice." Hegel saw the role of activity in thought but not in sense. Feuerbach saw the role of sense in thought but not in activity. The insights of the two are combined in Marx's "dialectical materialism."

Compared to this fundamental tenet, the dialectical "laws" of Hegel —e.g., the transformation of quantity into quality, the unity of opposites, the negation of the negation—were important but subsidiary propositions.[11] They were invoked, sometimes metaphorically, more by Marx's followers than by Marx himself. In the history of the Communist Party

9 For a much fuller examination of these questions, see Sidney Hook's excellent *From Hegel to Marx* (London: Gollancz, 1936), especially Chs. 1-3, 7, 8.
10 Marx and Engels, *German Ideology* (1846), in Burns, *Handbook*, pp. 212-13.
11 See the discussion of Marx's use of these laws in R. N. Carew Hunt, *The Theory and Practice of Communism* (5th ed.; New York: Macmillan, 1957), Ch. 4.

their chief use has been to enable party officials to follow from one day
to the next, and sometimes on the same day, wholly contradictory policies
in the complete faith that "history" will resolve the discrepancy with a
new synthesis. Sometimes they have been right. This faith in "action"
may help explain why Marxists are so suspicious of the words of others.
Words, they believe, are not action. Engels in *Anti-Dühring* (1877) tried
to apply the dialectic to biology, using the life cycle of barley seed (as
Hegel had done) to demonstrate the "negation of the negation." Marx himself was not much interested in these biological excursions and preferred
to stay in the realm of social theory, where his heart was.

Historical Materialism and the Theory of
Objective Development

IT SHOULD be clear by now that, despite some caricatures of Marx's
system, Marx did not deny the capacity of men to think. He denied the
autonomy of thought and felt that he had discovered the hitherto unrecognized power of economics to shape it. In the famous words of the Preface
to *The Critique of Political Economy* (1859):

I was led by my studies to the conclusion that legal relations as well as forms
of state could neither be understood by themselves, nor explained by the
so-called general progress of the human mind, but that they are rooted in
the material conditions of life, which are summed up by Hegel . . . under the
name "civic society;" the anatomy of that society is to be sought in political
economy. . . . In the social production which men carry on they enter into
definite relations that are indispensable and independent of their will; these
relations of production correspond to a definite stage of development of
their material powers of production. The sum total of these relations of
production constitutes the economic structure of society—the real foundation,
on which rise legal and political superstructures and to which correspond
definite forms of social consciousness. The mode of production in material life
determines the general character of the social, political, and spiritual processes
of life. It is not the consciousness of men that determines their existence, but,
on the contrary, their social existence determines their consciousness.[12]

We may note in passing that the *general* and not the special character
of social, political, and spiritual processes of life is determined by the
mode of production. Marx is talking here about men in general in the
broad sweep of history. What is important in this passage is the distinction

12 *The Critique of Political Economy*, 2nd ed. trans. by N. I. Stone (Chicago:
C. H. Kerr, 1904), pp. 11-12.

between the "relations" or the "mode" of production—men working with men—and the "powers" or, in the sentence which follows, the "forces" of production—men working with coal, ships, machines, that is, technology in general. In the course of history there arises between these two complementary systems a lag and eventually conflict. But let Marx continue in his own behalf; for this is the heart of Marxism:

At a certain stage of their development, the material forces of production in society come in conflict with the existing relations of production, or—what is but a legal expression for the same thing—with the property relations within which they had been at work before. From forms of development of the forces of production these relations turn into their fetters. Then comes the period of social revolution. With the change of the economic foundation the entire immense superstructure is more or less rapidly transformed. In considering such transformations the distinction should always be made between the material transformation of the economic conditions of production which can be determined with the precision of natural science, and the legal, political, religious, aesthetic or philosophic—in short, ideological forms in which men become conscious of this conflict and fight it out. Just as our opinion of an individual is not based on what he thinks of himself, so can we not judge of such a period of transformation by its own consciousness; on the contrary, this consciousness must rather be explained from the contradictions of material life, from the existing conflict between the social forces of production and the relations of production. No social order ever disappears before all the productive forces, for which there is room in it, have been developed; and new higher relations of production never appear before the material conditions of their existence have matured in the womb of the old society. Therefore mankind always takes up only such problems as it can solve; since, looking at the matter more closely, we will always find that the problem itself arises only when the material conditions necessary for its solution already exist or are at least in the process of formation.[13]

The stages of history that this theory requires, each producing its own grave-diggers, each jerking itself through revolutions to the next "higher" stage, bear a striking resemblance to Hegel's stages, or Comte's, or even, for that matter, Condorcet's. In the Marxian view of history, the primitive agrarian economy was followed by the slave economy of the ancient world, then by the feudal economy, and finally by the socialist economy, now in the throes of being born. It is Enlightenment progressivism made "objective" by being attributed to inevitable and ultimately uncontrollable material forces, rather than human thought and initiative. As has often been pointed out, the classical laissez-faire economists, without the same sense of historical development, also had a faith in an economic system

13 *Ibid.*, pp. 12-13.

not controlled by conscious individual discretion. As is frequently the case, here a theorist and his enemies shared a basic presupposition. Another shared belief was that "better" meant more efficient. The periodic disjunctions between the technology and the social system that ran it were presumably intolerable because the social system ("relations of production") could no longer efficiently run the technology ("forces of production"). To be sure, there was in Marx's analysis, as we shall see, a half-hidden moral judgment against continuing in the lower stage when the higher stage was ripe for birth, but the praise Marx heaped upon the efficiency of early capitalism indicates that he shared some of the economic biases of the class he denounced—which, of course, only tends to confirm what he was saying about social existence determining consciousness.

The conception of "legal, political, religious, aesthetic or philosophic" enterprises as nothing more than superstructures built upon the economic substructure was as close to a wholly original contribution as one is likely to find in social theory. Its effect on our thinking is demonstrated every time an anti-Marxist historian decides to include a few statistics on diamond-mining in a chapter on the Boer War. Before Marx, the decisions of kings and generals tended to be the stuff of history. Today we all apologize for our economic biases, and even the unlettered know that oil has something to do with our foreign policy in the Middle East. Similarly, Marx can take no small amount of credit for our concern with the problem of ideology. The present age has been called "the age of ideology." Even Christianity, an "opium of the people" to Marx, has been examined as ideology. We now go back and look anew at settled figures of past scholarship. We ask how Locke's position as a Whig landlord affected his epistemology, a question no one had thought to ask before. Some fear, and with justification, that we have grown accustomed to regarding all classical theory as mere ideology, i.e., as mere rationalization, so that the most sophisticated of us are afraid to theorize in the grand manner of the past, and become instead narrow technicians of language. The sense that politics is but the visible part of a deeply submerged iceberg carried by little-known tides may also be partly responsible for the political apathy characteristic of citizens in some of our most culturally advanced democracies.

But why this concern with economics in the first place? Marx, the methodological enemy of apriorism, presumably did not set out to prove that economics was a more fundamental determinant of thought than age, nationality, blood chemistry, musical training, annual rainfall, or any other of an infinite number of "fundamentals." Hegel at least pretended to have surveyed and synthesized all human knowledge; not so

Marx. The empirical pragmatism of his methodology was both his strength and his weakness: his strength in that scholars could not and did not disregard his monumental research; his weakness in that the correlations he discovered between economic class and ideology could not properly be regarded as a primary historical cause until the same monumental research had been applied to all other possible causes in all periods of history. This, of course, was impossible, and though analogies were drawn from ancient and medieval times, major Marxian analysis was confined to the modern period.

It is often said that Marxism fails most conspicuously in being unable to explain the class position of its own advocates. Marx, like Engels, Lenin, Trotsky, and many others, was of middle-class, not proletarian, background. Actually, this is not a great difficulty for Marx. The theorist is always to some extent the exception to the social generalizations he produces. In seeing the system he stands outside of it. Marx was not at all concerned to prove the power of class consciousness with individual psychology. He was interested in the large-scale social forces that move history, forces powerful enough to tap as spokesmen persons who, by a legalistic definition, are outside the emerging class. In the course of discussing the French peasantry in *The Eighteenth Brumaire*, Marx reveals his sensitivity to this problem. The French peasantry, he says, both is and is not a class.

Insofar as millions of families live under economic conditions that separate their mode of life, their interests and their culture from those of the other classes, and that place them in an attitude hostile toward the latter, they constitute a class; insofar as there exists only a local connection among these peasants, a connection which the individuality and exclusiveness of their interests prevent from generating among them any unity of interest, national connections, and political organization, they do not constitute a class. Consequently they are unable to assert their class interests in their own name, be it by a parliament or by convention. They cannot represent one another, they must themselves be represented. Their representative must at the same time appear as their master, as an authority over them. . . .[14]

Although such empirical modifications of the theory of class and class ideology solve one problem, they create another. In showing how it is that external interpreters of class interest may see historical reality more clearly than members of the class itself, Marx comes close to saying that *only* such trained "scientific" interpreters as himself can know true class interest. Although Lenin was to develop it much further, there was an

14 *The Eighteenth Brumaire*, in Beer, *Manifesto and Eighteenth Brumaire*, pp. 63-64.

incipient elitism in Marx himself. His vicious personal attacks on theoretical deviates and former friends such as Bruno Bauer and Arnold Ruge suggest a closed circle of dogmatism, by which the true criterion of class and class interest was known only to the insiders. The claim to scientific validity for his interpretation was and is weakened so long as large numbers of reputable but independent scholars find the criteria of class either ambiguous or esoteric.

Marx's conception of class interest, said Joseph Schumpeter, was "nearly as valuable as was the economic interpretation of history itself." Yet, "Curiously enough, Marx has never, as far as we know, worked out systematically what it is plain was one of the pivots of his thought. It is possible that he deferred the task until it was too late, precisely because his thinking ran so much in terms of class concepts that he did not feel it necessary to bother about definitive statement at all. It is equally possible that some points about it remained unsettled in his own mind, and that his way toward a full-fledged theory of classes was barred by certain difficulties he created for himself by insisting upon a purely economic and over-simplified conception of the phenomenon."[15]

Without objective scientific criteria of class, it can hardly be established that class is a fundamental motive force in history (not that this is all that is required). Marx's theory of the objective development of history is marred by factors of subjective interpretation. Indeed, "class" in the Marxian scheme may turn out to be just as metaphorical as *Die Weltgeist*, *Der Volk*, or the American Way of Life.

If class is the key to the economic interpretation of history and the concept of class is ambiguous, we are brought back to the earlier question: Why is economics itself so important to Marx? We find, paradoxically, that economics was important to Marx because capitalism had made economics too important. Beneath his veneer of scientific detachment (a thick veneer, and useful) we find a deep, bitter, and possibly confused moral indignation that human beings were being used in the industrial process as mere economic commodities. The evidence for such dehumanizing mistreatment was presented in the form of the most technical and sometimes abstruse economic language. The argument was given the name of the theory of surplus value.

The Theory of Surplus Value

THE first thing to be said about the theory of surplus value is that while it depends upon the labor theory of value, it is not the same thing as the

15 Joseph A. Schumpeter, *Capitalism, Socialism, and Democracy* (3rd ed.; New York: Harper, 1950), pp. 14-15.

labor theory of value. Students are frequently confused on this point. The labor theory of value dates back to Locke and found full expression in David Ricardo and the so-called classical economists. It holds that the value of every commodity is proportional to the quantity of labor necessary to produce it, quantity being measured in man-hours, and the labor assumed to be "socially useful" (i.e., a tree chopped down in the middle of a dense forest, if it cannot be removed or used on the spot, has no economic value however many hours were devoted to the felling). The theory also assumes, of course—and this is its weakness—perfect competition in the labor market and in the commodity market.

As a tool for economic analysis the theory was never very good. Even assuming perfect competition, it would only work where labor was the only significant factor in production (for what happens if weather and soil conditions mean that one hour of labor produces five boxes of luscious strawberries in one place and two boxes of scrawny inedibles in another? Will their economic value be the same?); and where different types of laboring activity were similar enough to be comparable (for what happens if we try to compare a diagnosing doctor with a pig-iron-shoveling laborer?). Time spent in training could of course be made to explain wage differentials between skilled and unskilled workers ("skilled labor counts only as simple labor intensified"[16]), and even a labor-replacing machine could be viewed as the embodiment of labor, but these adjustments did not meet the basic difficulties.

Marx, then, began with a strictly orthodox and rather inadequate economic doctrine that was rapidly becoming irrelevant to the real conditions of imperfect competition. Evidently Marx wanted to show up the capitalists using their own favorite theory, to build a model they could not ignore because it was based on their own assumptions. Perhaps he also clung to the labor theory of value because it was a necessary foundation for his truly inventive theory of surplus value. According to the latter, labor is a commodity like any other commodity; therefore, following the labor theory of value, it must be valued by the man-hours devoted to its "production"—that is, to feeding, clothing, and sheltering the worker in order to maintain life at subsistence level (which was, as a matter of fact, the level at which many workers were living in Marx's day). It could be said that labor is bought just as any other commodity is bought, and valued in the same way. Marx meant it as almost more than a metaphor, therefore, when he spoke of "wage slavery." But, unlike other commodities, labor is not consumed in a clearly determinable period of time. A worker is "bought" (or more precisely his "labor force" or "labor potential"—*Arbeitskraft*—is bought) for the price of sustaining

16 *Capital*, Vol. I, Ch. 1, trans. by Samuel Moore and Edward Aveling (Chicago: C. H. Kerr, 1919), p. 51.

him physically, prorated in hours or days or weeks. But he may produce the equivalent of this price in economic value in six or eight hours of work, whereas the factories of Marx's day kept men going for ten, twelve, or fourteen hours a day. The difference between what the worker does (set by arbitrary standards of the work day) and what he is paid for (set by competition) is surplus value (*Mehrwert*), the source of all capitalist profits.[17] The labor power consumed has produced value in excess of its own replacement value.

Please note that surplus value is not just a matter of "cheating." The aim of Marx was to avoid such crass moralistic charges (at least in *Capital; The Communist Manifesto* may be another matter). Given perfect competition, the capitalist can pay workers at the *correct* value of their labor potential, charge the customer the *correct* price for producing the commodity, and still have a margin left over—a thin layer of cream he skims off the top of the economic system. The system is at fault and not the employer, who, given the ideological basis of all social thinking, can literally conceive of no other way of operating; for no other way of operating can succeed within the capitalistic system. Marx eats his cake and has it too. He has inferentially revealed the injustice heaped upon the workers; but he has shown it to be the result not of bad men, but of a particular system. Reform within the system, therefore, however well-intentioned, is doomed to failure. The state, being but the "executive committee of the ruling class," is powerless. Only revolutionary overthrow of the whole system can succeed. Only a new synthesis can overcome the contradiction between thesis and antithesis.

Accumulation, Immiserization, Revolution

CAPITALISTS accumulate surplus value not because they enjoy champagne and yachting on the Riviera, but because they need to accumulate in order to remain capitalists. Capitalist accumulation is both necessary and, by the rather unreal logic of perfect competition, in the long run disastrous. The continual pressure of competition means that firms must always be expanding production and producing technological innovations if they are to keep ahead of their competitors and maintain income. To do this they must accumulate capital. The best way to accumulate capital is through surplus value. Since what Marx called "constant capital" (machinery, plant, and so forth) produces no surplus value, the pressure is toward hiring more and more exploitable workers, whose labor is "variable

17 It must be noted that Marx did not deny to managerial talent its proper share of labor costs. Surplus value was over and above legitimate managerial reward.

capital." As the pace of competition in the consumer's market quickens, prices go down; as the pace of competition in the labor market quickens, wages go up (but only for the short run, as we will see).[18]

To meet the crisis of lower prices and higher wages, capitalists try to economize by introducing labor-saving machinery; but this, while it may produce a temporary gain in the market, only accelerates the drying up of the surplus value that is needed for subsequent expansion. It is as if a cruel and mocking Fate wheedles the capitalist into building his own trap without knowing what he is doing. The firm lags behind, struggling, and when it can no longer survive in the desperate life of the economic jungle, it is swallowed up by a larger firm that is capable of consolidating units of control and increasing the size of plants. This theory of "expropriation" is but a corollary of the theory of "concentration," as the many become the few in the capitalist elite. The uneven progress of consolidation and collapse means alternating periods of boom and bust, which come with increasing rapidity and cause greater and greater panic.

The denouement of all this is described in the theory of *Verelendung* (which Joseph Schumpeter, with admirable literalness, translates as "immiserization"). The introduction of labor-saving machinery means that men are laid off, unemployment results, and wages fall. Now when he needs a substitute for Malthus' population pressure Marx invents the term "industrial reserve army" to describe the unemployed. As workers become more miserable, as they are herded into larger and in a sense "socialized" work units, the breaking point approaches. There is a "contradiction between the socialized organization in the individual factory and the social anarchy in production as a whole."[19] Let Marx describe the process:

As soon as this process of transformation has sufficiently decomposed the old society from top to bottom, as soon as the labourers are turned into proletarians, their means of labour into capital, as soon as the capitalist mode of production stands on its own feet, then the further socialisation of labour and further transformation of the land and other means of production, as well as the further expropriation of private proprietors, takes a new form. That which is now to be expropriated is no longer the labourer working for himself, but the capitalist exploiting many labourers. The expropriation is accomplished by the action of the immanent laws of capitalistic production itself, by the centralisation of capital. One capitalist always kills many. Hand in hand with this centralisation, of this expropriation of many capitalists by

18 If Marx had not rejected Malthus' theories of population pressure, wages would not have gone up at this point.

19 Engels, *Socialism: Utopian and Scientific*, trans. by Edward Aveling (New York: International Publishers, 1935), p. 74.

few, develop, on an ever extending scale, the co-operative form of the labour-process, the conscious technical application of science, the methodical culti-vation of the soil, the transformation of the instruments of labour into instruments of labour only usable in common, the economising of all means of production by their use as the means of production of combined, socialised labour, the entanglement of all peoples in the net of the world-market and this, the international character of the capitalistic regime. Along with the constantly diminishing number of the magnates of capital, who usurp and monopolise all advantages of this process of transformation, grows the mass of misery, oppression, slavery, degradation, exploitation; but with this too grows the revolt of the working-class, a class always increasing in numbers, and disciplined, organised by the very mechanism of the process of capitalist production itself. The monopoly of capital becomes a fetter upon the mode of production, which has sprung up and flourished along with it, and under it. Centralisation of the means of production and socialisation of labour at last reach a point where they become incompatible with their capitalist integu-ment. This integument is burst asunder. The knell of capitalist private property sounds. The expropriators are expropriated. . . . It is the negation of negation.[20]

In this way the forces of production and the relations of production are brought back into harmony.

There is a difficulty if not an inconsistency in this process. Earlier Marx had said that factory owners were reluctant to introduce new machinery, since it produces no surplus value. Now he is saying that they *must* add new machinery in order to compete, even though they are dooming themselves in so doing. At several turns in the Marxian sys-tem we seem to find the equivalent of Adam Smith's "invisible hand" skillfully manipulating the vast congeries of forces to assure, not, this time, that things will get better and better, but that they will get worse and worse. Marx has a cataclysmic view of history. Things must get worse before they can get better. Eventually, they will get very good indeed.

Despite all his empirical evidence, despite his vast historical researches into the world-wide depredations of capitalistic enterprise, Marx's over-all economic system rested upon deduction rather than induction and in the course of time turned out not to fit the real world very well. Workers' wages did not go down and down;[21] more machines did not mean fewer workers; and, finally, the predicted revolution never came—anywhere.

20 *Capital*, Vol. I, Ch. 32, pp. 836-37.
21 In time, workers' wages went up and up. Even in his own lifetime Marx had to explain how this could be. He tried the tricky way out of saying that though concrete wages had risen, still, relative to the capitalist, the worker was worse off: ". . . although the comforts of the labourer have risen, the social satisfaction which they give has fallen in comparison with those augmented comforts of the capitalist.

What happened in Russia in 1917 or China in 1949 has very little similarity to the revolution Marx described. And the industrially advanced countries—England, the United States, Germany—where by Marx's logic the proletarian revolution would be most likely to occur, now seem to be the least likely environment for such an event.

On the other hand, Marx's prediction of the growth of big business at a time when most enterprise was quite small and widely expected to stay that way was remarkably prescient. Nor was his general assumption that recurring slumps, panics, and depressions would become a chronic problem for a free-market economy too far off the mark. The pressing need for continual growth and expansion to prevent such depressions is now accepted by almost all economists, and departure from the unregulated market in order to stimulate such growth by government expenditures is, in greater or lesser degree, today accepted by most. Though Marx's abstract, theoretical system was built on assumptions of perfect competition that never prevailed in actuality and even became irrelevant as business consolidations brought about the imperfect competition of oligopoly, we must remember that Marx was relying on the Hegelian dialectic in more than a technical way, and expected the capitalist system, both as a theoretical model and as a set of practices, to contradict itself; hence, the "negation of the negation." If he offered next to nothing by way of an adequate economic theory of monopoly, he did not feel obliged to. In a sense, his self-destructive economic theory had done its work. By the time he was talking about the final stages of capitalistic monopoly he had left economic theory behind and was once again immersed in the philosophy of history.

Belief in the inability of class-conscious capitalists[22] and their political representatives either to prevent the demise of unfettered competition or to abandon their ideological affection for such a system rests not upon economic theory but upon social and political theory, and in this, too, Marx was not completely in error. If capitalism did not perish by violent revolution as he predicted, neither did it survive in the form in which its nineteenth-century defenders knew it.

... Our wants and their satisfaction have their origin in society, and not in relation to the objects which satisfy them. Since their nature is social, it is therefore relative." Quoted in Abram L. Harris, "The Social Philosophy of Karl Marx," *Ethics*, Vol. 53 (1948), Part 2, p. 25. If our "social satisfactions" are this far divorced from material reward, what happens to economic determinism?

22 One of the major weaknesses of Marx's view was his failure to make a clear distinction between the "capitalist" who puts up the money to run the show and the "entrepreneur" who may also put up some money but actually manages the business. In time, of course, the investing and managerial functions would become much more distinct than they were in Marx's day.

Communism and the Classless Society

NEITHER Marx nor Engels had much to say about what happens after the revolution, but Engels said the most, in *Anti-Dühring* (1877) (and in *Socialism: Utopian and Scientific* [1892], which included one section relevant to this problem among the three lifted *in toto* from *Anti-Dühring*). Comes the revolution and:

The proletariat seizes the State power, and transforms the means of production in the first instance into State property. But in doing this, it puts an end to itself as the proletariat, it puts an end to all class differences and class antagonisms, it puts an end also to the State as the State. Former society, moving in class antagonisms, had need of the State. . . . [Now] The interference of State power in social relations becomes superfluous in one sphere after another, and then ceases of itself. The government of persons is replaced by the administration of things and the direction of the process of production. The State is not "abolished," *it withers away.*[23]

It is apparent that the word *state* has such evil connotations for Engels that a proletarian state is not even a rational possibility for him. Yet, evil though it may be, the meaning of the state is never made precise in either Marx or Engels, suggesting that political theory was not their primary interest. In *The Origin of the Family, Private Property and the State* (1884) Engels discusses the growth of institutions beginning with primitive communalism (relying heavily on Lewis Morgan's *Ancient Society*, published in 1877). Whether or not a state even existed in that stage of history remains ambiguous in Engels' treatment. In general terms, the rise of the state is identified with the rise of private property, and the whole network of law that constitutes the sinews of the modern state is regarded as an instrument of the ruling class.

Whether or not Hegel can be said to have stopped the dialectic with the Prussian state of his day, Marx and Engels certainly stopped the dialectic with the statelessness of proletarian triumph. The state, insofar as it suggested coercive class power, could logically have no existence in a condition of classlessness. Marx and Engels undoubtedly deserve to be placed with the utopians in their apparently sincere belief that coercive social power was tied to a particular culture and would disappear when that culture disappeared. To speak of the "administration of things" and the "direction" of production as if no human conflict, and hence no politics, were involved, can be regarded as nothing less than naïve. Of course coercive regulatory power could not be wished away all at once,

23 *Anti-Dühring*, in Burns, *Handbook*, pp. 295-96. Italics in original.

so Marx and Engels in a few places referred to the transitional stage as "the dictatorship of the proletariat." Marx apparently regarded the concept as one of his basic contributions: ". . . no credit is due to me for discovering the existence of classes in modern society, nor yet the struggle between them. . . . What I did that was new was to prove: (1) that the *existence of classes* is only bound up with *particular, historic phases in the development of production;* (2) that the class struggle necessarily leads to the *dictatorship of the proletariat;* (3) that this dictatorship itself only constitutes the transition to the *abolition of all classes* and to a *classless society.*"[24]

In Lenin, as we shall see, the phrase "dictatorship of the proletariat" became a basic concept for the strategy of practical politics. It did not have such a precise meaning for Marx and Engels. It did not mean the dictatorship of a small cadre of the party elite, but simply the coming into its own of the proletarian class as a whole, crushing out in all areas the remnants of bourgeois mentality. *The Communist Manifesto* implied that the proletariat did not need to be organized into one centralized party to gain victory. Later Marx and Engels supported the idea of a world-wide Communist party, but they did not conceive of it as the disciplined action group that Lenin made it. To Engels the dictatorship of the proletariat would be without "exploitation" and therefore without the oppression of the bourgeois state, but it would not be free of all coercion; therefore it would be "a half-state," "not a state in the proper sense of the word."[25] In *Anti-Dühring* Engels suggested that during this period the slum-ridden industrial cities as they were in his day would be taken apart, piece by piece, and industry decentralized all over the landscape.

Looking at much more concrete, short-run aims, Marx in his 1852 *Address to the Communist League* told his hearers how they must beware of the "bourgeois democrats" who after the revolution would try to give land to the peasants as private property. Marx would nationalize the land

---

24 *Letter to Georg Weydemeyer,* March 5, 1852, in *Selected Correspondence of Marx and Engels 1846-95,* trans. by Dona Torr (New York: International Publishers, 1942), p. 57. Italics in original.

25 Quoted in Henry B. Mayo, *Introduction to Marxist Theory* (New York: Oxford Univ. Press, 1960), p. 158. Engels was not utopian enough to identify classlessness with complete equality: "There will always exist a certain inequality in the conditions of life. . . . the notion of socialist society as the realm of equality is a superficial French idea resting upon the old 'liberty, equality, fraternity.' " *Letter to August Bebel,* March 28, 1875, in *Selected Correspondence of Marx and Engels,* p. 231. In his essay "On Authority" (1874), Engels ridiculed those who thought socialism meant the end of authority. The factory system itself, he said, creates an inescapable need for authority. Moreover, "A revolution is certainly the most authoritarian thing there is; it is the act whereby one part of the population imposes its will upon the other part. . . ." But after the revolution, *political* authority will be progressively "transformed into simple administrative functions." Feuer, *Basic Writings,* p. 485.

and organize it into "settlements for the associated groups of the landed proletariat."[26] He would in every way attack the "reactionaries" and go one step further on every reform proposal of the "democrats." Workers' clubs should be centralized under an Executive Committee with head-quarters in Germany. All workers should take immediate steps to insure that the "trickery" of local authorities does not deny them the vote. Apparently Marx accepted some usage of parliamentary machinery, for he talked of putting up working-class candidates in all constituencies. But he also spoke of arming the workers and of confiscating factories and railways. At any rate, there was enough flexibility in his words so that Lenin could make much expedient use of them. In fact, the basic problem of the status of state power in the dictatorship of the proletariat can be deferred to Chapter 16, for it was Lenin who from necessity took these fragments of political theory in Marx and made the most of them.

Suffice it to say that this transition period—as seen by Marx in *Critique of the Gotha Program*—would be a hard but glorious period for the faithful, eventuating in the establishment of an ideal Communism, when the rule of "from each according to his ability, to each according to his work" would be replaced by the traditional communist goal of "from each according to his ability, to each according to his needs."[27] Bakunin had accused Marx of wishing to impose a new form of repressive state on the workers, and perhaps Marx was at this point attempting to show that he, too, envisioned a free, libertarian order—in the long run. But he qualified this long-run utopianism (which had also flavored *The Communist Manifesto*) with some short-run realism suggesting that inequalities in both effort and reward would persist for some time under the new socialist rule. Lenin was most grateful, later, to be able to fall back on this concession to reality by the old master.

Conclusion: Ideology and Ideals in Social Change

AS ECONOMIST, Marx was brilliant but unsuccessful. The theory of surplus value was an ingenious but faulty construction, and with the passage of

26 In Burns, *Handbook*, p. 69.

27 *Critique of the Gotha Program*, in Feuer, *Basic Writings*, p. 119. In this work Marx vehemently attacked what he regarded as the sentimental vagaries of the unity program adopted by two German socialist parties at Gotha in 1875. The quoted phrase is enshrined in the present Soviet Constitution as the ultimate Marxist goal. The period of the dictatorship of the proletariat is not a period of "Communism" even though we popularly call the Soviet Union a Communist system. To the orthodox Marxist, Communism is the end condition; the means is "socialism." Like the Communists, right-wing spokesmen frequently employ this verbal distinction in trying to discredit non-Communist socialism.

time Marxian economics, as a technical science, has become not so much empty as irrelevant.

As theologian, Marx was naïve but notoriously successful (even to the point of suggesting a correlation between naïveté and success). The comfort of dogmatic belief in an absolutely inevitable process is not unrelated to the religious loyalty with which Marxists cling to their system. The eschatology of Marx accounts for no small part of his historic success, even though from the standpoint of the outsider his utopian theology must be regarded as a thin and emaciated myth by comparison with, say, the robust images of the Book of Revelation.

As social theorist, Marx was both provocative and influential. His fundamental conviction that class is the basic determinant of modes of human thought stimulated generations of scholars to look at social causation in a new light. Was Marx right? Few independently minded persons today would say yes. We can look at the bourgeois class that was the target of Marx's critique and find that many of its characteristic ideas— an atomistic conception of society, limited government, and so forth —far antedated the existence of the class as such. On the other hand, some of what are taken to be its characteristic ideas will undoubtedly persist long after the class itself has dissolved or been transformed by historical forces into something else. In fact, to speak of two and only two classes, bourgeois and proletariat, toward which everyone and everything is being pushed, is to make a statement with no empirical basis then or now. Like every philosophy of history, Marx's grand explanatory principle required an oversimplification of the infinitely complex pattern of action and response that is the substance of history. Communists to this day are victims of this oversimplification when they say, in effect, "if you're not for us, you're against us." Yet the dramatic way in which Marx pointed to class as a determinant of thought has made us realize that class is important. If not a determinant of thought, it is at least a conditioner.

That broad ideals familiar to many classes at many different times in history have affected the worldly success of Marxism seems indubitable. Apart from all the trappings of economic analysis, there was in Marx's treatment of the theory of surplus value an underlying passion that bubbled to the surface from time to time. It was the sense of injustice born of contemplating the treatment of men as mere commodities. Exploitation in Marx's sense was inefficient, yes; but worse, it was dehumanizing. Yet bourgeois liberals like William Cobbett and John Stuart Mill also spoke out against the dehumanizing evils of an irresponsible factory system. As against this negative ideal, Marx briefly flashed to his readers a positive ideal of a classless society where social harmony and individual fulfillment would characterize an entire epoch. Yet the much-ridiculed utopian socialists had a no less striking vision of what the future might be, and for a time struck a response in members of almost every class and station as widespread as that of Marxism.

Finally, Marx stood for one ideal more powerful, perhaps, than justice or social harmony, an ideal implicit in everything he wrote. It is what has sometimes been called the need to "get in step with history." To this day the great emotional appeal of Marxism is its own conviction of historical truth, the negation of finitude contained in its assurance that the "scientific" key to the historical process has at last been discovered. Hence it gives to its advocates the self-satisfying dogmatism of those who know they are right and know they will win. This is what has made Marxism one of the great "secular religions" of modern times. Without such nonmaterial and nondialectical aspirations, aspirations that cannot be understood simply by ideological analysis, dialectical materialism, paradoxically, would not have become the powerful ideology we know it to be.

CHAPTER

14 | *Nietzsche*

O F ALL the writers to whom we give special attention, Nietzsche is the most apolitical, the least
concerned with governmental policies for a whole public. Two justifications may be offered for his inclusion in a political study. First, we may
note that many lesser minds who were intensely interested in what we
commonly call politics were profoundly interested by Nietzsche. We
may rightfully look, therefore, to the source of their inspiration. Second,
we sometimes find even in relatively apolitical writers (St. Augustine
would be another) so fundamental a challenge to existing political norms
that our understanding of those norms is clarified by examining the
challenge. Such is singularly the case with Nietzsche.

Life

FRIEDRICH WILHELM NIETZSCHE was born in 1844 in the village of
Rocken, Saxony, which was then in Prussia. His father was a successful
and respected Lutheran pastor who died from a fall off a horse when
Friedrich was still an infant. The family background was Polish, but
Nietzsche was never able to substantiate his claim that his ancestors were
Polish noblemen.

Nietzsche was brought up in an atmosphere of great piety and overwhelming femininity provided by a grandmother, a mother, a sister, and
two aunts. They all meant well, but the poor boy never had a chance.
His classmates at school ridiculed him as the "Little Minister." In 1864

he went to the University of Bonn to study philosophy and, ostensibly, theology. Using up more of the family funds than was prudent, he made his last great effort to be one of the boys and threw himself into the gay social life of one of the *Burschenschaften*: going on excursions up the Rhine, drinking beer, singing lusty songs, even engaging in what turned out to be a mockery of a duel. According to one theory, during this time he picked up a case of syphilis that explains his later insanity. At any rate, it was largely a lost year as far as studies were concerned and not really a happy year, for student revelry was not natural to Nietzsche's temperament.

The next year he went to Leipzig where the great classicist Friedrich Ritschl had just been appointed to a chair. Ritschl was not only a great scholar but a great teacher who knew that his duty, as Nietzsche was later to express it, was to "find [the] chief talent in his pupil, and to assist the latter in organizing his whole life by means of it."[1] With only his love of music and solitary walks for diversion, Nietzsche buried himself in classical philology. With Ritschl's encouragement he wrote and published learned articles. Already his Lutheran orthodoxy had left him and he had set upon the lonely course suggested in a letter to his sister written at the end of his year at Bonn: "Certainly faith alone saves. . . . Every true faith is indeed infallible: it accomplishes that which the believer concerned hopes to find in it; it does not offer the least support for the establishment of an objective truth. It is here then that the ways of men divide: do you wish to strive after peace of mind and happiness, well then believe; do you wish to be a disciple of truth, then inquire."[2] The alternatives were too sharply posed; but the quest of honesty at all costs was to become a Nietzschean trademark.

More important than Ritschl's influence on Nietzsche, at least during his first year at Leipzig, was his discovery of Schopenhauer,[3] whose Eastern quietism resulting from his pessimistic philosophy of blind will that rules the world, seemed to the young Nietzsche the height of wisdom. Having accidentally come across *The World as Will and Idea* in a bookstore, Nietzsche took it home and devoured it, finding it a mirror of his own self.

Serving his year of required military service, Nietzsche, in the autumn of 1867, fell off a horse as his father had and was severely injured. He was given a medical discharge and was never again in good health. Affected

---

1 H. A. Reyburn, *Nietzsche* (London: Macmillan, 1948), p. 44.
2 June 11, 1865. Quoted in Reyburn, *Nietzsche*, p. 36.
3 Arthur Schopenhauer (1788-1860) of Danzig, Hamburg, and Frankfurt. Independently wealthy, Schopenhauer studied at several universities, and wrote his philosophy untroubled by the need of gainful employment. He was a brilliant linguist.

with migraine headaches and weak eyesight, he became more and more hypochondriac and more and more dependent upon drugs. He went back to Leipzig, indulged his musical tastes, and was blessed with a meeting with Richard Wagner, whose music he loved. The meeting led to a great but short friendship, a romance with Wagner's wife Cosima, and a long and bitter quarrel over Wagner's violent racism and nationalism.[4]

Thanks to the reputation of his articles and the support of Ritschl, Nietzsche was asked to become professor of Greek at the University of Basel in 1869. At not quite twenty-five, Nietzsche accepted a position that many older men coveted. He held the post until 1879, when ill health forced his resignation, and was reasonably successful as a teacher. When the Franco-Prussian war came in 1870, Nietzsche was eager to fight for his fatherland against the "cursed French tiger," but since he was now a Swiss national, the most he could do was serve as a volunteer ambulance attendant. His service was brief but bloody and ended when he picked up dysentery and diphtheria from his wounded patients. Despite his patriotism, he wept when he heard of the Germans burning the Louvre in Paris, and openly questioned whether Prussia might be a danger to culture.

Nietzsche returned to Basel, gave some widely heralded public lectures, and on the last day of 1871 held in his hands the first copy of the newly published *Birth of Tragedy*. This began a series of memorable publications. According to Charles Andler,[5] Nietzsche's work can be put into two cycles, each consisting of a period of mystical intuition followed by a period of rigorous analysis. The first period, which he calls "Wagnerian revaluation," lasted from 1869 to 1876. During this time Nietzsche felt that the great age of Greek tragedy and philosophy was being reborn in Germany. The music of Wagner and the philosophy of Schopenhauer were, to him, symptomatic of this rebirth. Nietzsche felt that neither science nor the state had done anything to promote the arts, and advocated the establishment of a new institute of culture. There followed a period of "intellectualistic evolutionism" from 1876 to 1881. During this period, says Andler, Nietzsche seemed to turn against the state as an institution of force and to seek instead a "society of free spirits" created as a work of art by some transcendent genius, a pan-European rather than a nationalistic society.

Next came the period of "lyrical affirmation," 1882 to 1885, during which was produced the best known of Nietzsche's works, *Thus Spake*

4 The "Wagner Circle" of racist intellectuals, later called the "Bayreuth Circle," lasted with scarcely a break in continuity into the 1920's, when Eckhart, Hitler, Goebbels, and Rosenberg were members.

5 In *Encyclopaedia of the Social Sciences* (New York: Macmillan, 1933), Vol. XI, pp. 373-75; see also his *Nietzsche: Sa vie et sa pensée* (Paris: Bossard, 1920-31).

Zarathustra, a poem with great poetic imagery and not a small amount of nonsense. The final period was "critical reflection on the values of decadence and renaissance," 1885 to 1888. This time critical reflection seemed to confirm rather than dissolve Nietzsche's mystical insights.

After 1879 Nietzsche wandered from Sils-Maria, in the Alpine valley of the Engadine, in the summer to Genoa or Nice in the winter, living a drab, impoverished life. In 1889 he cracked up. Embracing a horse being flogged in the street, he prayed for its beatification by God, then collapsed. A Basel friend, church historian Franz Overbeck, came to get Nietzsche and found him pounding a piano with his elbow, shrieking. Going by train to a clinic in Basel, Overbeck could not prevent the usually soft-spoken Nietzsche from shouting out his poetry. From the clinic he was taken to an asylum in Jena and finally to Weimar, where he died half paralyzed by a stroke and "sunk in a docile imbecility." It was only after his insanity that his fame grew, and then it was impossible to prevent exploitation of his name by his sister.

After Nietzsche's insanity came *Anti-Christ* (written 1885), and, published posthumously, *The Will to Power* (Vol. I 1901, Vol. II 1906) and *Ecce Homo* (written 1888, published 1908).[6] Nietzsche's sister had much to do with *The Will to Power,* to its detriment. A woman of great zeal but limited intelligence, she married a rabid anti-Semite named Förster who committed suicide after trying to organize a Teutonic colony in Paraguay. Changing her name to Elizabeth Förster-Nietzsche, the sister became a dedicated manager of her brother's reputation. She cornered and hoarded his manuscripts and in an arbitrary and biased way put together the fragments that were published as *The Will to Power.* She lived to know Hitler and was in large part responsible for Nietzsche's spurious reputation as an anti-Semite and for the attempts to link him to Nazism.

Nietzsche had a gentle laugh and a fragile politeness that attracted people yet kept them at a distance. He always seemed to feel alone and to convey that feeling. He wore a very long military mustache almost as a mask to hide his inner turmoil. The most introspective of philosophers —in this lay the essence of his contribution—and an advocate of painful candor, he nevertheless probably failed to see the degree to which his praise of noble bestiality concealed his own effeminate reserve, and his role of Anti-Christ mirrored a deep spiritual longing.

6 *Ecce Homo,* Nietzsche's autobiography, features as opening chapters "Why I Am So Wise," "Why I Am So Clever," "Why I Write Such Excellent Books." These titles are more cynical than vain, claims Walter Kaufmann, and take their inspiration from Socrates in Plato's *Apology. Ecce Homo* is Vol. XVII of *The Complete Works* of Friedrich Nietzsche, Oscar Levy, ed., Anthony Ludovici and others, trans. (London: Allen & Unwin, 1910-11). Hereafter cited as *Complete Works.*

Nietzsche as Philosopher

ONE scholar, as we have seen, finds that Nietzsche's work fits into a neat pattern of cycles. Another, however, finds only a pattern of irrational patternlessness:

Try the following experiment: take any one of his [Nietzsche's] works and open it at random. Start reading. Aphorism *n* has an electrifying effect. With enthusiasm we approve the correctness of what it says. Aphorism *n* plus 1 also calls forth our vivid assent. This goes on for a while until suddenly, while reading Aphorism *nn'*, we realize that somewhere something has got out of control, that the author has started raving, that something must have happened. . . . The solution of the puzzle is that we are dealing with a man who is seriously ill.[7]

Another scholar sees in Nietzsche a subtle, truly philosophic mind at work. Although granting Nietzsche's disdain for the pretense of "objectivity" and his dislike of scientific dogmatism, George Morgan sees his work as that of a "growing system" that could attain a completeness, if at all, only at the end. "In his last self-comments Nietzsche not only affirms but specifies the essential identity in his thinking. . . . the problem of good and evil occupied him continually from his fourteenth year. . . . Nietzsche of course does not claim an absolute identity in all his writings; rather, his ideal of philosophy as a fruit of life implies change, including the discard of things outgrown." Morgan, too, acknowledges different periods of Nietzsche's development, with dramatic turning points, but he claims they were not accidental, but "a dialectical pattern with cumulative effect." Morgan concludes that "there can be no doubt that he deserves to be read seriously as a philosopher."[8] Likewise, Walter Kaufmann says "he embodied the true philosophic spirit."[9]

Hannah Arendt, on the other hand, sees Nietzsche, along with Kierkegaard and Marx, as a symbol of the end of philosophy. Although it was, in Arendt's view, twentieth-century totalitarianism that shattered the Western philosophical tradition, Nietzsche's "leap from the non-sensuous transcendent realm of ideas and measurements into the sensuousness of

7 Robert Rie, "Nietzsche and After," *Journal of the History of Ideas*, Vol. 13 (1952), p. 353.
8 George Allen Morgan, Jr., *What Nietzsche Means* (Cambridge: Harvard Univ. Press, 1941), pp. 25, 26, 29.
9 Walter A. Kaufmann, *Nietzsche: Philosopher, Psychologist, Anti-Christ* (Princeton: Princeton Univ. Press, 1950), p. x.

life, his 'inverted Platonism' or 'trans-valuation of values' " was the means whereby he "tried desperately to think against the tradition using its own conceptual tools."[10] Karl Jaspers attributes to Nietzsche the same radical position, but sees it as a new beginning rather than an end to philosophy:

The contemporary philosophical situation is determined by the fact that two philosophers, Kierkegaard and Nietzsche, who did not count in their times and for a long time remained without influence in the history of philosophy, have continually grown in significance. . . . They stand today as the authentically great thinkers of their age. . . . Their thinking created a new atmosphere. They passed beyond all of the limits then regarded as obvious. It is as if they no longer shrank back from anything in thought.[11]

In the tradition of philosophy from Parmenides to Hegel, says Jaspers, Being is discovered in thought. With Kierkegaard Being is discovered in faith, and in Nietzsche it is discovered in the "will-to-power." But beyond this surface definitional distinction is the methodologically significant point that neither faith nor will-to-power are concepts in the traditional sense, but mere *signa*. They do not connote, but point to, and are hence "capable of endless explication."[12]

Obviously, estimates of the philosophical significance of Nietzsche turn on judgments not only of the nature of philosophy, but of what he was trying to do, and he himself was perhaps not too sure of this. To say that he was in "revolt against reason" is suggestive but too simple. What people mean when they say that Nietzsche was not a philosopher is that he was an impulsive artist with words who strung no beads of logical propositions. He communicated to his select followers by allusion and metaphor rather than by definition and demonstration. He tried, not to transcend sensation as did Plato, or to unite sensation and thought as did Hegel, but to burrow into sensation as far as he could go—beyond reflection and beyond thought. Through his discussion of guilt and dreams and instinct he was a contributor to Freudian psychology. Through his subjectivism he was a strong influence on contemporary existentialism. He was also a moralist, though a perverse one. He was perplexed by the problems of good and evil, and an inspired if incautious student of the cultural origin of social values. He believed in and practiced the use of etymology to teach us about ourselves—as individuals and as societies. In these respects surely he can be called a philosopher.

10 "Tradition and the Modern Age," *Partisan Review*, Vol. 21 (1954), pp. 63, 60.
11 Karl Jaspers, *Reason and Existence*, trans. by William Earle (New York: Noonday Press, 1955), pp. 23-24.
12 *Ibid.*, p. 27.

The Dionysian Myth

IN *The Birth of Tragedy from the Spirit of Music*, Nietzsche traces, by striking leaps of imagination, the interrelationships of the Apollonian and Dionysian myths in ancient Greece, relationships generally confirmed by later scholarship. Both Apollo and Dionysus were art-sponsoring deities, but, said Nietzsche, Dionysus was closer to the primal urges expressed in music and in the transport of intoxication. Apollo was the sponsor of the visual, plastic arts, whose spirit appeared in the more detached, personalized imagery of dreams. Apollo spoke for individuation and separateness and quiet balance. Dionysus symbolized a wild plunge into the flux of life, the unity and community of all things. The Apollonian, as in Doric art, tended to discipline the Dionysiac, somewhat at the latter's expense, according to Nietzsche. Already in this, his first book, Nietzsche is revealing his nihilistic bent, or perhaps more accurately his "immoralist" bent. The high point of Greek culture, he says, came in the great amoral art (all art for him was amoral by any conventional standard of morality) of Aeschylean tragedy, which was the union of Dionysian and Apollonian elements. Philistine interpreters saw tragedy as justifying a moral order. Aristotle saw tragedy as a purgative for pity and fear. Schopenhauer saw tragedy as a lesson in resignation. Nietzsche rejected all of these. He saw tragedy as a tonic for life, an affirmation of joy in existence, which included evil as well as good. In a sense therefore, tragedy justified evil: "We may express the Janus face, at once Dionysiac and Apollonian, of the Aeschylean Prometheus in the following formula: 'Whatever exists is both just and unjust, and equally justified in both.' What a world!"[13]

Tragedy began to perish with Euripides, who was infected with the optimistic, rationalistic spirit of Socrates, "the great exemplar of the theoretical man." This spirit tried to make reasonable everything that was beautiful, held that virtue is knowledge and that only the virtuous are happy, and tried to overcome death with this cheery faith. Hence real tragedy was gone. The grand illusion of Socrates "that thought, guided by the thread of causation, might plumb the farthest abysses of being and even correct it,"[14] persists to the present day, weakening the hold of nonrational myth, without which every culture loses its creativity. But

13 *The Birth of Tragedy*, Ch. 9, in Francis Golffing, trans., *The Birth of Tragedy and The Genealogy of Morals* (New York: Doubleday [Anchor Books], 1956), p. 65. This is a sprightly, useful, and convenient translation.

14 *Ibid.*, p. 93. In later years Nietzsche came to have greater respect for Socrates' position.

the dark powers of Dionysian feeling are still latent and spring forth in every truly artistic act, and the memory of great tragedy lingers in and gives "supreme significance" to dissonance in modern music.

Eternal Recurrence and Superman

CONVALESCING in the Alps in 1881 Nietzsche was struck with an idea of such emotional force that he wept in great gushes. It was the idea which came to be known as "eternal recurrence." In brief it is simply that since there is only so much energy in the universe, all possible combinations of it have occurred in the past and will recur in the future. Life, in short, is not a matter of infinite expansion, but an endless cycle. There is nothing very precise in this concept. It is a matter of mood rather than hypothesis, and the physical questions raised by such a theory, the nature of space and matter, are pushed aside or ignored. What was more important for Nietzsche was that it removed purpose from the world but also created a kind of timelessness that has been called Christian immortality in a new form.[15] Man makes his own purposes, but they are not trivial, for one's own "highest feeling" and the means necessary to achieve it are in a way part of nature's plan. The doctrine of eternal recurrence was for Nietzsche a substitute for the religion and the universalistic ethics he had thrown out.

The great expression of the idea of eternal recurrence was in Nietzsche's most popular book, the poem *Thus Spake Zarathustra*, written in 1883. Also introduced in *Zarathustra* was the idea of the Superman, the one who could take the empty freedom of the universe and by sheer exertion of courage make of it what he would, thereby surpassing the ordinary timid breed of man:

I teach you the Superman. Man is something that is to be surpassed. What have ye done to surpass man?

All beings hitherto have created something beyond themselves: and ye want to be the ebb of that great tide, and would rather go back to the beast than to surpass man? . . .

Lo, I teach you the Superman!

The Superman is the meaning of the earth. Let your will say: The Superman *shall be* the meaning of the earth!

I conjure you, my brethren, *remain true to the earth* and believe not those who speak unto you of superearthly hopes! Prisoners are they, whether they know it or not.[16]

15 See Jacob Taubes, "Community—After the Apocalypse," in Carl J. Friedrich, ed., *Community* (New York: Liberal Arts Press, 1959).

16 *Thus Spake Zarathustra*, Prologue, sec. 3, trans. by Thomas Common (London: Allen & Unwin, n.d.), pp. 6-7.

The comic strip character Superman, who, after changing clothes in a phone booth, smashes down walls, repels bullets, and rescues girl reporters, is a testament to the perverse effect of literary appropriation; but he may also have rendered more difficult an American's understanding of Nietzsche. *Übermensch* is literally "overman," but *über* has at least two meanings in this context. One is "ruling over" and the other is "higher than." We could with justification therefore translate *Übermensch* as "looked-up-to-man," a higher creation because it is a self-creation, one who has overcome man because "man is something that must be overcome." The implausibility of this "answer" to the despair Nietzsche found in life is matched only by the depth of that despair. For even the great men of the past were miserable creatures:

Ah, man returneth eternally! The small man returneth eternally!
Naked had I once seen both of them, the greatest man and the smallest man: all too like one another—all too human, even the greatest man!
Ah, Disgust! Disgust! Disgust![17]

It is not fair to say of Nietzsche or his Superman as Crane Brinton does, "A thousand Nietzsches have written a thousand appeals to create the Superman, and a thousand more will write again the same appeal, world without end and words without end. But no Nietzsche will ever have the slightest memory of another Nietzsche."[18] Nietzsche's memory was more acute and his Superman was less unoriginal than this implies. As a figure apart, the Superman can only appear excruciatingly paradoxical: Godlike, yet wholly of this earth; wholly new, yet eternally recurring; a man set apart, yet, because he is needed, somehow a cultural creation. That he is wholly different from ordinary men, even "great" men of the past, becomes more apparent when we note how, in his aphorisms, Nietzsche can penetrate human foibles with an almost cynical clarity: "One uses one's principles to tyrannize or justify or honor or affront or conceal one's habits." "Who has not at some time or other sacrificed himself in order to save his reputation?" "A great man, did you say? All I ever see is the actor creating his own ideal image."[19]

The Superman cannot be God, for "God is dead" as Nietzsche many times says."[20] Kant and Hegel, with their elaborate reconciliations of

17 *Ibid.*, Part 3, Disc. 57, sec. 2, p. 268.
18 Crane Brinton, *Nietzsche* (Cambridge: Harvard Univ. Press, 1941), pp. 140-41.
19 *Beyond Good and Evil*, Art. 4, Nos. 77, 92, 97, trans. by Marianne Cowan (Gateway ed., Chicago: Regnery, 1955), pp. 76, 78.
20 *Zarathustra*, Prologue, sec. 2, p. 5. See also Nietzsche, *Nachgelassene Werke, Gross-oktav Ausgabe* (Leipzig: Alfred Kröner, 1901-26), Vol. V, pp. 147, 271; Vol. VI, p. 12; Vol. XIII, p. 316; Morgan, *What Nietzsche Means*, pp. 36ff. Nietzsche is speaking of the Christian God. About other gods, he seems to agree with Epicurus: "If there are gods, they do not care for us."

NIETZSCHE

technical philosophy with Christian theology, were merely "procrastinators" of atheism. The death sentence imposed on God is more than a personal judgment. It is, for Nietzsche, the end of a civilization. Yet Nietzsche knows that life is not possible without illusion, that "the sincere person ends by realizing that he always lies."[21] And so he deliberately creates and gives us an illusion born of his own experience of reflection six thousand feet high in the Alps. He calls it *Übermensch*. The term points to a man apart who is also not apart. The *Übermensch* is not only some future race of giants; it is also the higher selves in each of us. Original as its form may be, Nietzsche does not claim newness for the idea itself. In essence it comes from classical literature and may be found in the earliest Dionysian joy in life as it is. Thus Superman and "eternal recurrence" are not as antagonistic as they might seem at first.[22]

Nietzsche's Superman is explicitly distinguished from the historical-political heroes of Carlyle, "that great counterfeiter," as Nietzsche called him. If Superman is apolitical and ahistorical, yet does not reside in some transcendental sphere, he must reside in us as individuals. That he is not a political leader is clear from *Zarathustra*:

> Somewhere there are still peoples and herds, but not with us, my brethren: here there are states. . . . the coldest of all cold monsters. Coldly lieth it also; and this lie creepeth from its mouth: "I, the state, am the people."
> It is a lie! . . .
> There, where the state ceaseth—there only commenceth the man who is not superfluous. . . . Do ye not see it, the rainbow and the bridges of the Superman?[23]

Nietzsche as Critic

DURING the writing of *Zarathustra*, Nietzsche broke away to write *The Gay Science* (1882),[24] which was aphoristic, worldly-wise, and auto-

21 *Nachgelassene Werke*, Vol. XII, p. 293. Cited in Morgan, *What Nietzsche Means*, p. 51. Hans Vaihinger puts great importance on Nietzsche's "doctrine of conscious illusion" in the development of his own "philosophy of 'as if.'" See *The Philosophy of "As If,"* trans. by C. K. Ogden (London: Routledge & Kegan Paul, 1935), pp. 341-42.

22 The evidence for this interpretation of *Übermensch* is well stated by Walter Kaufmann, *Nietzsche*, Ch. 11.

23 *Zarathustra*, Part 1, Disc. 11 ("The New Idol"), pp. 54, 57. Note that it is not a bridge *to* Superman, but a bridge *of* Superman. The metaphor suggests that we may use the illusion-myth-symbol of the Superman to move up out of our lesser selves.

24 *Die Fröhliche Wissenschaft* is sometimes translated *The Joyful Wisdom*, a less revealing title.

374

biographical, forming a sequence with the earlier *Human All Too Human* (1878), and *The Dawn of Day* (1881). In a more mordantly practical approach than that of *Zarathustra*, Nietzsche in *The Dawn of Day* suggests that one way the individual may lift the weight of customary morality with which society oppresses him is to achieve the great prestige of madness. In *The Gay Science* a calmer Nietzsche brings the doctrine of eternal recurrence once more to the fore, and at the end brings in the prophet Zarathustra, who now deigns to leave his solitary height and go down into the world of men to distribute his riches—not, however, as an exercise of charity, but as an exercise of power. The "gaiety" of the science Nietzsche approved of lay in its willingness to experiment fearlessly and to take lightly any settled opinion. Nietzsche was not hostile to science, only to dogmatic science.

After the great effort of finishing *Zarathustra*, Nietzsche was again full of dejection. But he bounced back and set aside his next six years to write *Zarathustra*'s prose counterpart his great work of philosophy, which was to be called *The Will to Power: Attempt at the Transvaluation of All Values*. As we have seen, it was not completed in his lifetime. Again he kept breaking off to include portions of the greater work in smaller versions, some of which overlapped, and some of which were written at high speed. The best known is *Beyond Good and Evil* (1886), which was followed by *The Genealogy of Morals* (1887), *The Case of Wagner* (1888), *The Twilight of Idols* (1889) and *The Anti-Christ*.

By the time of *Beyond Good and Evil* Nietzsche seemed somewhat less the scholarly philologist and more the colorful essayist, although he had never been colorless. Here he plays with the reader, purposely leaving crucial thoughts in mid-air, toying with words, making tongue-in-cheek exaggerations. Almost surreptitiously he notes that most of the time when he is saying terrible things about "women as such" he is talking about himself. Even the form is playful. The 296 paragraphs are divided into nine scholastic-like articles with faintly ironic titles, "We Intellectuals," "Our Virtues," "Peoples and Fatherlands," "What Does 'Distinguished' Mean?" Article Four is "Aphorisms and Entr'actes," pithy and powerful assertions ranging all over the landscape; and elsewhere as well, the sudden, barely relevant insight flashes before the eye: "It was a masterpiece of *British* instinct to sanctify and dullify the Sunday to such a degree that the Briton quite unnoticeably begins to yearn for his workaday week."[25]

If the work is impossible to summarize, the themes are clear enough. They have appeared before and will appear again: what is often taken to be morality is merely timidity, an inability to face up to the fact

25 *Beyond Good and Evil*, Art. 5, No. 189, p. 95.

that one's guidelines to life are based upon illusion; comprehension is but the tool of desire, reason a pawn of instinct; the self-deception of philosophers is one of the most amusing phenomena of intellectual life. Kant's categorical imperative mainly tells us that Kant wanted to be a dutiful person. Schopenhauer could not be a consistent pessimist because he enjoyed playing the flute too much. Descartes was "superficial" in claiming that reason was his only authority. Spinoza "naively recommended destruction of the passions through analyzing and vivisecting them." Aristotle with his golden mean would tone down the passions "till they reach a harmless mediocrity." Much of this was *ad hominem* forensics, but Nietzsche's wild slashes at the stupid arrogance of those who claim a "science of morality" come close to the jugular, and when he much too briefly draws upon linguistics to demonstrate how much of our supposedly hard knowledge depends upon uncontrollable intuitive leaps, we have the feeling that he could, if he would, take everyone apart analytically as he has done rhetorically.

As he criticized everything else, Nietzsche criticized German culture. No nationalist, he. And the opposite of an anti-Semite, saying that "the Jews are beyond doubt the strongest, toughest, purest race now living in Europe." It is a sign of the weakness and insecurity of German nationhood that Germans are "afflicted now by the anti-French stupidity, now by the anti-Semitic, now the anti-Polish. . . . I hope that I shall be forgiven if I, too, during a brief reckless sojourn in this infected country, did not remain entirely free of the disease; if I too, like everybody else, began to have thoughts about things which are none of my business—the first symptom of political infection."[26] "It would be useful to banish from the country the anti-Semitic cry-babies."[27] Nietzsche thought of national political problems as petty problems, beneath his gaze, and after discussing this one, he quickly jumps back to "my *serious* problem: the European problem as I understand it: the breeding of a new caste which is to rule Europe."[28]

The thrust of disillusionment once more having dissolved politics, we are confronted again with the necessity of a Superman, the "natural master" who knows what he wants, takes it, and holds it. ". . . when such a man feels compassion, then such compassion is worth something! But of what use is the compasion of those who suffer? Or even worse of those who *preach* compassion?"[29] But as disillusionment dissolved politics so

26 *Ibid.*, Art. 5, No. 251, pp. 187, 186.
27 *Ibid.*, p. 188.
28 *Ibid.*, p. 189. Although there are passages which suggest the literal eugenic breeding of a new caste, Nietzsche here must be taken to mean breeding in a metaphorical sense.
29 *Ibid.*, Art. 9, No. 293, p. 234.

also in the end it dissolves philosophy, and even the counterpart of Zarathustra's Superman here adumbrated does not evoke great conviction. Candor seems to be the only virtue left, says Nietzsche, and laughter the only action. Though Hobbes tried to ruin the reputation of laughter, "I should permit myself an ordering of the ranks of philosophers according to the quality of their laughter—all the way up to those who are capable of *golden* laughter. And if the gods, too, philosophize . . . I do not doubt that they also know how to laugh in superhuman and original fashion—and at the expense of all serious things!"[30] There is more consistency in Nietzsche than one might think. The tragicomic symphony never stops.

Good and Evil, Good and Bad

THE prose work of Nietzsche most compelling to contemporary readers is probably *The Genealogy of Morals: An Attack* (1887). The thesis of the work still has the power to shock. Nietzsche raises the question of the value of values, and how man has come to invent judgments of good and evil. He boldly asserts that in the dim dawn of history the strong simply created those conceptions of "good" which would be of most use to them and imposed them on the weak. But from time to time the weak outsmart the strong and sell their ideas to civilization, a maneuver most notably illustrated by the history of Christianity. The crisis of the present age, which is really the crisis behind everything Nietzsche wrote, is the decay of judgmental language, the irrelevance of moral standards, and the lack of strong men to impose a new standard. Nietzsche is a nihilist not in the sense that he is one who says men do not need moral standards, but rather in the sense that he is one who says moral standards have no intrinsic morality. The many, the vulgar, will never be able to understand this.

After a swipe at the English utilitarians' lack of historical sense, Nietzsche concedes the relevance of their criterion of practicality to morals, even though they do not understand what this relevance is. Nietzsche does turn to history in general and etymology in particular to demonstrate that the word "good" almost invariably originated from a word meaning "noble" in the class sense. Or, to put it another way, "Political supremacy always gives rise to notions of spiritual supremacy."[31] Two qualifications need to be thrown into this equation. While the

30 *Ibid.*, No. 294, p. 235.
31 *The Genealogy of Morals*, Essay 1, sec. 6, in Golffing, trans., *The Birth of Tragedy and The Genealogy of Morals*, p. 165.

noble were basically the strong, Nietzsche did not make sheer physical force alone the determinant of right. Class power, even the power of military conquerors, existed in a context that imposed conditions. Secondly, the sometimes subtle modes of resistance of the weak, especially the admonitions of priests and seers, are what have most contributed to make man an "interesting" creature. Had there been nothing but the depredations of the powerful to contend with in history, man could not have become profound as well as evil. "The greatest haters in history—but also the most intelligent haters—have been priests. Beside the brilliance of priestly vengeance all other brilliance fades. Human history would be a dull and stupid thing without the intelligence furnished by its impotents."[32]

The most brilliant case of the weak outsmarting the strong was what the Jews did with Jesus. They first dared to invert all the basic values: the good became not the powerful, the noble, the privileged, the healthy, but the weak, the ignoble, the poor, the suffering. Then they took the most conspicuous prophet of this doctrine, Jesus of Nazareth, and nailed him to a cross "like a mortal enemy, so that 'the whole world' (meaning all the enemies of Israel) might naively swallow the bait. . . ."[33] As a result, the slaves, the mob, the herd, democrats, Christians, Jews—they are all very much the same for Nietzsche—have more and more taken over from aristocrats and imposed their cringing, negative ethics. They are not necessarily stupid. Their kind of life breeds a kind of sharp-wittedness. But such a person's "soul squints."

The noble classes or races live by a distinction between good and bad, by which the good—what they want—is uppermost and its opposite, the bad, is almost an afterthought. The slave morality pervading the modern world is that of good and evil, in which a deified evil born of rancor, bitterness, vengeance, *ressentiment*, dominates the whole mentality, and good is only the passive, sugar-coated restraint of these feelings. The true noble spirits bear no grudges. They are positive thinkers. They can return "from an orgy of murder, arson, rape, and torture, jubilant and at peace with themselves as though they had committed a fraternity prank."[34]

The phrase "beyond good and evil" has at least three meanings in Nietzsche. It means first, as appears here, that true noble spirits are unconfined by conventional morality. But it also suggests that the role of the critic, i.e., Nietzsche, is to conduct inquiries without regard to

32 *Ibid.*, p. 167.   33 *Ibid.*, sec. 8, p. 169.
34 *Ibid.*, sec. 11, p. 174. Such admirably uninhibited fellows could be found almost anywhere. Nietzsche mentions the Roman, Arabian, German, Japanese, and Scandinavian nobles, as well as the Homeric heroes, who, one suspects, were his models.

current moralisms, to penetrate behind and beyond them. Finally, there is, standing by itself as a reminder of the tender side of Nietzsche, Aphorism 153 of *Beyond Good and Evil:* "What is done out of love always happens beyond good and evil." Here we find a special morality not apart from but deeper than ordinary morality.

The noble spirit of *The Genealogy of Morals* is called the "autonomous" man, one who is "more than moral." Here more clearly than elsewhere in Nietzsche's writings he is recognized as the end product of a long and pain-racked history, pain-racked because it is only through the infliction of great pain that ordinary men could be made to remember their race's history and do what society demanded of them. In modern times the rack, boiling in oil, and flaying alive have been abandoned; but punitive and festival cruelties have now simply been replaced by psychological ones. As a community becomes full of pride and power its penal code becomes more lenient, but when the community is threatened, the code becomes harsh again. Justice itself may be canceled out under the name of mercy, but mercy as well as justice is still defined by the man outside the law, the strong, the autonomous, the "active man" rather than the "reactive man."

Nietzsche ridicules the historians of law for their easy acceptance of the original purpose of laws as exhaustive of their present meaning. They tend to ignore the constant transmutations of function as legal institutions are used differently by each ascending generation. He loosely links this distortion with "The democratic bias against anything that dominates or wishes to dominate. . . ." Herbert Spencer's faith in progressive adaptation of the species "misjudges the very essence of life; it overlooks the intrinsic superiority of the spontaneous, aggressive, overreaching, reinterpreting and re-establishiing forces, on whose action adaptation gradually supervenes."[35] The spontaneous expression of instinct is creative; its repression as encouraged by religion produces a sense of indebtedness to higher powers, the "bad conscience" which is "the wellspring of all altruistic values." Therefore "Atheism and a kind of 'second innocence' go together."[36]

The third part of *The Genealogy of Morals* is an examination of the "ascetic ideal," which concludes that man's capacity to suffer, to be cruel to himself, has been a part of all the great cultural achievements upon which lesser men today complacently feed. ". . . learning today is a hiding place for all manner of maladjustment, lukewarmness, self-depreciation, guilty conscience. Its restless activity thinly veils a lack of ideals, the want of a great love. . . ."[37] Yet beneath the falsity and hypocrisy of society

35 *Ibid.*, Essay 2, sec. 12, p. 211.   36 *Ibid.*, sec. 20, p. 224,
37 *Ibid.*, Essay 3, sec. 23, p. 285.

persists a driving human will not so much troubled by suffering as by its meaning. *The Genealogy of Morals* concludes:

. . . the ascetic ideal arose to give it [suffering] meaning—its only meaning, so far. But any meaning is better than none and in fact, the ascetic ideal has been the best stopgap that ever existed. . . . It signifies, let us have the courage to face it, a will to nothingness, a revulsion from life, a rebellion against the principal conditions of living. And yet, despite everything, it is and remains a *will*. Let me repeat, now that I have reached the end, what I said at the beginning: man would sooner have the void for his purpose than be void of purpose. . . .[38]

In spite of himself, Nietzsche was a social theorist, concerned with the values which can give meaning not to one man but to all men.

Will-to-Power

"WILL-TO-POWER" is on a par with eternal recurrence and Superman as a basic concept (or, remembering Jaspers, *signa*) for Nietzsche. It served in Nietzsche's later writings as a unifying agent, bringing together earlier dualisms such as Dionysus and Apollo, nature and value, empirical self and true self. As Walter Kaufmann explains,[39] this duality persists in Nietzsche's first explorations with the will-to-power. On the one hand, he seems to see will-to-power as a craving after worldly success, which Nietzsche deplored; on the other, it was a basic psychological drive, by which even pity and humility could be explained as the assertion of self and the desire to hurt others. In neither sense, then, is will-to-power at this point a virtue to Nietzsche.

The term itself first breaks onto the scene, as did "eternal recurrence" in *Zarathustra*. Beginning with assertions of the relativism of all values, the Prophet says that nevertheless "A table of excellencies hangeth over every people. Lo! it is the table of their triumphs; lo! it is the voice of their Will to Power."[40] But the crucial transition comes in *Dawn of Day*, where Nietzsche acknowledges that power itself ennobles even though the will-to-power may lead to degraded behavior. At this point there is still a trace of dualism, which *Zarathustra* seems to resolve in favor of making quantity of power a measure of value.

Actual power, it would seem, is, for Nietzsche, neither physical nor material; nor is it metaphysical. It is, rather, a capacity for self-discipline, a capacity of "giving style to one's character," probably what Nietzsche

38 *Ibid.*, Essay 3, sec. 28, p. 298.   39 *Nietzsche*, Ch. 6.
40 *Zarathustra*, Part 1, Disc. 15, p. 66.

meant in *The Genealogy of Morals* by an "instinct of freedom." ". . . one thing is needed: that a human being attain his satisfaction with himself . . . only then is a human being at all tolerable to look at. Whoever is dissatisfied with himself is always prepared to revenge himself therefore: we others will be his victims."[41] The effect of the will-to-power is thus not to pit person against person and nation against nation, but every person against himself and every nation against itself. "In Nietzsche's vision the globe became a Greek gymnasium where all nations vie with each other, each trying to overcome itself and thus to excel all others."[42]

The boldness of Nietzsche's concept of will-to-power poses an ironic threat to his consistency, inasmuch as he had often castigated philosophers for their grand explanatory concepts and advocated piecemeal experimentation. Moreover there seemed to be a classic paradox built into the inference that the will-to-power lies behind all motivations, for then Nietzsche's own assertion of the concept would be nothing but an act of the will-to-power and it would invalidate itself. But at least one can say that Nietzsche never pretends that the concept is more than a hypothesis drawn from his own experience. He offers no deductive proofs, no claim of transcendental revelation. Perhaps the ultimate faith of Nietzsche is not so much will-to-power as "will-to-truth." " 'I will not deceive, not even myself': and herewith we are on the ground of morality."[43]

Conclusion

IN THE brief half-century since his death a fantastic collection of distortions and myths has grown up around Friedrich Nietzsche. By concentrating on what Nietzsche really said, this chapter, it is hoped, has discredited what is merely attributed to him. He was not anti-Semitic. He was not a German nationalist. He was not a statist. His Superman was not a political leader. His will-to-power had nothing to do with military might or material success. His sister helped the myths along by mistakenly attributing the birth of the will-to-power idea to Nietzsche's observation of loyal German troops in the Franco-Prussian war. But consider one who could write this:

And there comes perhaps a day when a people, distinguished by wars and victories and by the highest development of a military order and intelligence,

41 *The Gay Science*. Quoted in Kaufmann, *Nietzsche*, p. 367.
42 Kaufmann, *Nietzsche*, p. 173.
43 *Anti-Christ*. Quoted in Kaufmann, *Nietzsche*, p. 314.

and accustomed to make the heaviest sacrifices for all these things, will exclaim of its own free will: *"we break the sword"*—and will smash its entire military establishment down to its last foundations. *Rendering itself unarmed while one was the best armed,* out of the *height* of a feeling—that is the means to real peace which must always rest on a peace of mind: while the so-called armed peace, as it exists now in all countries, is the lack of peace of mind which does not trust itself nor its neighbor and, half from fear, does not lay down arms. Rather perish than hate and fear, and *twice rather perish than make oneself be hated and feared*—this must also some day become the highest maxim of every single commonwealth![44]

Nietzsche's direct influence on psychoanalysis and existentialism is infinitely greater than his direct influence on fascism. His political significance stems not from what he was for, but from what he was against. Existing European parties, parliaments, laws, all come under his scathing ridicule. He heaps contempt on monarchy as well as democracy.[45] They are partners in an empty, smug, false, and mediocre culture. The *Bildungsphilister,* the culture philistines, were his prime target. He offered no political "solutions." According to his "hammer philosophy" destruction was better than mediocrity. His attempt at a transvaluation of all values was a radical and rather heroic attempt to overcome what he regarded as a deep crisis in civilization.[46] And this was not so much the construction of a new system of ethics as it was the creation of a wholly new personality.

We cannot say that Nietzsche succeeded in being much more than provocative in these constructive efforts. But in his attacks and prophecies he created a mood which somehow seems strangely akin to that of the twentieth century. In an apocalyptic vision[47] he prophesied that great and horrible wars would follow the rapid deterioration of basic values. Whatever one may say about the deterioration of our values, we have had great and horrible wars. Nietzsche's radical anti-politicism spoke for a moral emptiness at the root of the political order that, in Germany, at least, in time led to a radical pro-politicism. Neither moral nor political anarchy is a viable condition. If nothing else, Nietzsche's historical generalization that "political supremacy always gives rise to notions of spiritual supremacy" can lead us to conclude that perhaps the reverse order can and ought to obtain. To say as Nietzsche does that God is dead at least implies that once he was alive.

44 *Der Wanderer und sein Schatten.* Quoted in Kaufmann, *Nietzsche,* p. 160.
45 See *The Will to Power,* Bk. 3, Part 3, in *Complete Works,* Vol. XV, pp. 183-238.
46 See Eric Voegelin, "Nietzsche, The Crisis and the War," *Journal of Politics,* Vol. 6 (1944), pp. 177-212.
47 *Ecce Homo,* in *Complete Works,* Vol. XVII, Ch. 4.

As the liberal faith in the equal reason of independent individuals was beginning to wane and the socialist faith in the justice of the social group was beginning to burgeon, Nietzsche undercut both with a devastating critique of both individual rationality and wisdom in the mass. If he has not given us solutions, he has recognized and defined some of our problems, in particular the problem we have yet to do much with in the twentieth century: How can truths of man without which a political order destroys its own subjects, be embodied in that order without being transformed into falsehoods by the process of political embodiment? Plato had an answer, but we, like Nietzsche, seem to have none.

15 | *The Twentieth Century*

Who Is Important?

PHILOSOPHY has never been popular and political theory has never been free of ideology, but the curious thing about these two subjects in the twentieth century to date is that in forms of expression they draw further apart, philosophy becoming more narrowly technical and political theory becoming more ideological. If we look at the philosophical movements we see pragmatism, logical positivism, and existentialism, all difficult and subtle movements, holding the stage. In political theory, the textbook headings tend to read "fascism," "communism," "the new liberalism," "democratic socialism," "nationalism,"—all "isms," patterns of thought better designed to sway crowds than to reach truth. Hobbes, Rousseau, and Hegel were simultaneously philosophers and political theorists, but Martin Heidegger and Ludwig Wittgenstein are not very political, and Leon Trotsky and Harold J. Laski were not very philosophical.

Political philosophy in the grand manner is not altogether lacking on the contemporary scene. There is Eric Voegelin's *Order and History*, Hannah Arendt's *The Human Condition*, and possibly in this category, the scholarship of Bertrand de Jouvenel and Leo Strauss. But except for Strauss, these writers do not seem to evoke a following. No doubt it is too soon to look for "followings" as it is too soon for any solid judgment on the "greats" of an age that is our own. Without pretending to establish their greatness thereby, we shall examine in subsequent chapters three figures who represent some of the dominant trends in twentieth-century political theorizing.

Though not, perhaps, qualified as a philosopher, V. I. Lenin (Chapter 16) is an intellectual force that must be reckoned with. His election to special chapter status should find few objectors.

John Dewey (Chapter 17) is an exception to the just-noted tendency of philosophers and political theorists to part company in the twentieth century. This characteristic in itself is a mark of his distinction. Dewey in retrospect appears more conditioned by nineteenth-century ideas than he did when pragmatism flourished in the schools, but still he is a twentieth-century figure and a major theorist on anyone's list. No matter that his philosophy was antiphilosophical; he nevertheless fits the tradition of the philosopher–political theorist.

Reinhold Niebuhr (Chapter 18) is a symbol of the most serious reunion of political and orthodox Christian categories since the sixteenth century. This reunion may be a flash in the pan or it may be what the twentieth century will be known for. It is too early to tell. There are more original contemporary theologians than Niebuhr (Barth or Tillich, say); there may be more perceptive social critics (Max Weber, David Riesman) or more archetypal political theorists (Eric Voegelin, Hannah Arendt). But Niebuhr, like Lenin and Dewey, can stand for what is important in twentieth-century thought so far. In addition to the new-found strength of theological thinking, he reflects the eclipse of liberalism, the rise of existentialism, and the transcending of the outworn categories of capitalism and socialism.

The contents of this chapter will necessarily be as arbitrarily chosen as the subjects of the three that follow. We shall first look at the theory of totalitarianism, for the fact of totalitarianism is as deep in our twentieth-century consciousness as any social fact can be. Next we shall examine some aspects of twentieth-century liberalism. Third, we shall look at the political impact of existentialism. And finally, we shall have a word to say about the new interest of the West in Eastern political thought.

Totalitarianism

SOME theorists explain; other theorists justify; some do both. In few cases is the line between these types of theorists sharper than in the case of totalitarianism, at least from the standpoint of the western democratic biases most of us hold. Adolf Hitler, in *Mein Kampf*, was no doubt "explaining" Nazism when he said of the masses: ". . . in view of the primitive simplicity of their minds, they more easily fall a victim to a big lie than to a little one, since they themselves lie in little things, but would be ashamed of lies that were too big." He was "justifying" it in saying, "All who are not of good race in this world are chaff."[1] While both were statements of some power, neither was of a high order of theoretical insight. The antirational tendencies of fascist brands of totalitarianism worked against first-rate theory in its behalf. And among nontotalitarian interpreters of totalitarianism there has been the widest divergence of views as to its essence. Early interpreters tended to stress the state and its role as a total entity. Alfred Cobban in 1939 linked totalitarianism to very old theories of the organic state: ". . . the liberal state proclaims itself as organic. Until recently the organic idea of the state was no more than a theory, but the progress of what we have called the internal aspect of nationalism has produced a vigourous attempt to transfer this theory into practice, and of this attempt totalitarianism is the result."[2] In the same year Emil Lederer pointed to the destruction by the state of classes and other forms of social stratification as the essence of totalitarianism, and even saw, apart from war, internal tensions ahead for totalitarianism. The bureaucratic agents of this "destruction of society" would in time themselves become entrenched and hence antipathetic to the principle of the "amorphous mass"—the "people," who, under totalitarianism, are denied a tradition and a social structure and hence become dependent upon raw emotion.[3]

Recent theorists of totalitarianism have moved in the direction of stressing its character as *movement*, as a dynamic emotional force, which, as Lederer suggested, is antithetical to the orderliness inherent in well-established governmental forms. This view would seem to represent a consensus drawn from the many stimulating hypotheses developed and tested at a three-day conference held in Boston in 1953.[4] If the conferees agreed on totalitarianism as movement, they did not agree on much else. Some thought terror was a calculated policy for the maintenance of a position of leadership; others thought it had a more irrational basis. Some regarded totalitarian ideologies as hypocritical tools of leadership; others felt that the leaders, too, were generally infected with ideological belief. Some thought of totalitarianism as an enemy of all religion; others thought of it as a secular religion itself. Some thought fascist and communist forms of totalitarianism were quite similar, others stressed their differences (though none as much as was customary among scholars when the

1 *Mein Kampf*, trans. by Ralph Manheim (Boston: Houghton Mifflin, 1943), pp. 231, 296.

2 *Dictatorship, Its History and Theory* (New York: Scribner, 1939), p. 177.

3 *State of the Masses, the Threat of the Classless Society* (New York: Norton, 1940).

4 Carl J. Friedrich, ed., *Totalitarianism*. Proceedings of a conference held at the American Academy of Arts and Sciences, March, 1953 (Cambridge: Harvard Univ. Press, 1954).

U.S.S.R. and Nazi Germany were fighting each other in World War II).

On the basis of empirical evidence from those societies of recent experience that have been labeled totalitarian (Fascist Italy, 1922–43; Nazi Germany, 1933–45; the Soviet Union, 1917– ; Communist China, 1949– ; and the various Soviet satellites), Carl J. Friedrich and Zbigniew Brzezinski list six features that, taken together, must be regarded as the typological signs of a totalitarian regime: (1) an official ideology broad enough to cover the "vital aspects of man's existence," which is usually focused on some future ideal state of mankind; (2) a single mass party, usually led by one man, the "dictator," composed of a select and small percentage of the population, organized hierarchically, and superior to or intertwined with the government organization; (3) "a system of terroristic police control"; (4) a monopoly control of the media of mass communication (press, radio, cinema) by the party; (5) a similar monopoly of all means of effective armed combat; (6) "central control and direction of the entire economy" with bureaucratic coordination of formerly independent associations and groups.[5]

While these authors give us a carefully worked-out description of totalitarianism, they do not try long-range speculation or an inquiry into ideological genesis. The shattering newness of totalitarianism has inhibited studies along these lines. Friedrich points out that not a single one of the great scholars of social institutions at the beginning of this century was able to foresee the rise of totalitarianism in anything approximating its actual form.

THE GENESIS OF TOTALITARIANISM: ARENDT

Undoubtedly the major work so far produced that does attempt to move back into the historical, philosophical, and ideological roots of the subject is Hannah Arendt's *The Origins of Totalitarianism*.[6] At the descriptive level Arendt would agree with much of the foregoing, but stresses especially the transvaluation of values inherent in the totalitarian way of life. For example, totalitarian regimes deliberately seek out the innocent for abuse, punishment, and even death, while the guilty go free or are treated more respectfully. This tactic shatters the sense of order and the reliability of law, creating a helpless insecurity and dependence even in those who are not punished, and giving the latter, in addition, a collective guilt that binds them together into an amorphous mass. She

5 In *Totalitarian Dictatorship and Autocracy* (Cambridge: Harvard Univ. Press, 1956), pp. 9-10.

6 *The Origins of Totalitarianism* (New York: Harcourt, Brace, 1951). The second edition (New York: Noonday Press [Meridian Books], 1958) has additional chapters on "Ideology and Terror" and the Hungarian Revolution of 1956. Subsequent quotations are from this edition.

notes that as against political and racial prisoners, the common criminal was in almost every Nazi and Soviet concentration camp part of the elite group, because the common criminal had at least the status of a conviction under law. He had not been deprived of his "juridical person." The whole paraphernalia of Nazi repression—the uniforms, the shaving of heads, the shipment of masses of persons by boxcar, and finally the factory-like process of execution in gas chambers—were well suited to the destruction of any sense of uniqueness in individual persons, again not only in the victims but in the population as a whole who were aware of the boxcars moving through the night.

More than being indifferent to moral values, totalitarianism tends to establish a new, inverted morality. "Thou shalt not kill" gives away to "Thou shalt kill." Whereas older forms of tyranny imposed an order resistant to change, totalitarianism has been dependent upon disorder and continual change. It is expansiveness of power for no rational end, elevated to a principle. Whereas followers of pragmatism and even of Leninism believed that reality could be known only by action rather than by thought, Arendt's model of totalitarianism goes further: the search for reality ceases. The belief that literally "everything is possible" leads totalitarian rulers to invent a policy and force social conditions to conform to it, rather than the reverse. Legislation tends to mean nothing and offers no guide to the populace or administrators. Survival in a totalitarian regime depends upon the development of a sixth sense as to which order or official to follow and which to disregard. In this way every individual tends to be isolated from every other individual by a veil of suspicion. It is "a permanent state of lawlessness."[7]

Arendt is more successful in capturing the acrid flavor of totalitarianism[8] than in explaining its historical genesis, but her ambitious attempt to do the latter is filled with brilliant insights and juxtapositions. Her strength is at the point of interpenetration between historical events, articulate theories, and subconscious popular moods. The historical tendencies that "crystallized" into totalitarianism came, she finds, out of the racism and imperialism of the late nineteenth century and from the growing irrelevance of abstract conceptions of human rights. As long as economies were largely confined within the nation-state system the bourgeoisie tended to leave politics to others. As economics in the age of imperialism (1885–1914) moved abroad, the bourgeoisie found it necessary to involve themselves with politics in order to influence domes-

7 *Ibid.*, p. 394
8 See also Ceslaw Milocz, *The Captive Mind* (New York: Knopf [Vintage Books], 1953); Eugen Kogon, *The Theory and Practice of Hell*, trans. by Heinz Norden (New York: Farrar, Straus, 1950); David Rousset, *The Other Kingdom*, trans. by Ramon Guthrie (New York: Reynal, 1947); Raul Hilberg, *The Destruction of the European Jews* (New York: Quadrangle Books, 1961).

tically minded statesmen like Richter, Gladstone, and Clemenceau. The supposedly "international" Jews, who had been identified as money-lenders to the absolute monarchs of the past, became convenient targets of resentment.[9] But anti-Semitism was not the only racism to contend with.

When the Europeans discovered what a "lovely virtue" a white skin could be in Africa, when the English conqueror in India became an administrator who no longer believed in the universal validity of law, but was convinced of his own innate capacity to rule and dominate . . . when the British Intelligence services began to attract England's best sons, who preferred serving mysterious forces all over the world to serving the common good of their country, the stage seemed to be set for all possible horrors. Lying under anybody's nose were many of the elements which gathered together could create a totalitarian government on the basis of racism."[10]

Imperialism incorporated a mood of continual expansionism justified by mysterious forces of history, which became the heart of both Nazi and Communist totalitarianism.

The growing nationalistic feeling attending this imperialist thrust was a sign not of the strength of the nation-state system, but rather of its weakness, for "the nation-state cannot exist once its principle of equality before the law has broken down,"[11] and the attempt to rule "inferior nations" was destroying this principle. Without the advantages of a Roman *imperium* of law, the imperialist states were equipped only with very troublesome doctrines of consent of the governed, which they did not care to apply to native populations. From this loss of community, and the context of free speech that community provides, followed a loss of humanity. The supposedly inalienable Rights of Man that had been intended to replace the security of feudal station proved unenforceable outside of a national context. Paradoxically, human rights are lost at that moment when one becomes a human being in general, without citizenship, a profession, or group support. When nothing but equality as a human being is left, one's humanity is destroyed. Hence the terrible plight of contemporary "stateless" persons ("displaced persons," thinks Arendt, is a euphemism), who are the peculiar products of totalitarianism.

Denationalization became a powerful weapon of totalitarian politics, and the constitutional inability of European nation-states to guarantee human rights

9 Arendt milks for all they are worth the many-sided implications of the Dreyfus Affair, in which a Jewish officer in the French Army was falsely convicted of espionage for Germany in 1894, creating a *cause célèbre* for a decade thereafter.

10 Arendt, *Origins*, p. 221.   11 *Ibid.*, p. 290.

to those who had lost nationally guaranteed rights, made it possible for the persecuting governments to impose their standard of values even upon their opponents. Those whom the persecutor had singled out as the scum of the earth—Jews, Trotskyites, etc.—actually were received as scum of the earth. . . . a practical demonstration of the totalitarian movement's cynical claims that no such thing as inalienable human rights existed.[12]

Hence, thinks Arendt, Burke was right in his attacks upon the abstract rights of the French Revolution. We are not born equal; we are *made* equal by political organization, by the protections of law. The private realm of uniqueness and difference is always something of a threat to the public realm, the political. But the private realm needs the protection and encouragement of the public if human uniqueness is to be maintained. In totalitarianism, the public realm not only absorbs the private, it seeks to destroy it and thereby transform human nature itself, to prove "everything is possible." It seeks to produce a system in which "all men [are] equally superfluous"—even the leaders of the system. The most terrifying of Arendt's many pessimistic conclusions is that totalitarianism cannot finally prove itself until it has global control and all men are equally dehumanized.[13]

ITALIAN FASCISM

Although going beyond the limits of empirical data,[14] Arendt is rich and compelling by contrast with most of the theorists who have tried to justify totalitarianism, since the movement rides so heavily on non-rational assumptions. For intellectual nourishment the Italian Fascists leaned heavily on Giovanni Gentile (1875–1944), Professor of Philosophy at Pisa and Rome, and Mussolini's Director of the Institute of Fascist Culture. An almost mystical disciple of Hegel, Gentile made the "State" the embodiment of all things good, its force a mode of discipline not only consistent with individual well-being but necessary to achieve the citizen's "true" personality and freedom. Another theorist, Alfredo Rocco (1875–1935), stressed "society" more than the "State," but, using a biological analogy, he meant by this term national society, which had unity, purpose, and direction transcending the lives of its individual members. The appeal of the Fascists was to a public interest painted

12 *Ibid.*, p. 269.

13 Arendt observes that totalitarianism only works in very large countries where there are large undifferentiated masses of people. Totalitarian regimes in smaller countries like Yugoslavia or Albania tend to revert to old-fashioned tyranny and dictatorship.

14 Empirical studies of phenomena peculiar to mass societies are becoming more available. See William Kornhauser, *The Politics of Mass Society* (Glencoe, Ill.: Free Press, 1959), and the bibliography therein.

in bright hues, contrasted with petty, competing private interests, and to an expansive, heroic national pride that glorified war and the will to dominate. What the Fascists were against may have been more important than what they were for. They opposed flabby and decadent liberalism that pandered to individual comfort and license. They opposed parliamentarianism, with its indecent welter of conflicting groups. Mussolini tried to bring these groups under control with what he called the "corporate state" after his march on Rome in 1922. Before this time he had fooled around with Marxist socialism and the French syndicalist ideas of Georges Sorel. His economic positions were inconsistent; yet inconsistency itself was supposed to be consistent with the spontaneity and antirationalism upon which Fascist men of power (and even philosophers like Gentile) prided themselves. Nothing could have been further from the truth than Mussolini's assertion that "Fascism has a doctrine, or, if you will, a particular philosophy with regard to all the questions which beset the human mind today."[15]

NAZISM

In any narrow sense of "political," the Nazis scarcely had a political theory at all, since what they glorified was not the state but the nation, *der Volk*. Perhaps the most sophisticated of Nazi theorists was Carl Schmitt (1888–   ), a professor of law and from 1933 to 1945 a Prussian State Councilor. In the essay "The Concept of the 'Political'" (1927) he makes the distinction between friend and enemy the core distinction of politics, comparable to that between good and evil in morals or beautiful and ugly in aesthetics. We find in Schmitt the previously mentioned totalitarian tendency to make everything of importance public in that he defines "enemy" not as those we may individually hate, but as that collectivity of men who as a real possibility will fight one's nation. "Enemy is only the public enemy, because everything that relates to such a collectivity, especially a whole nation, becomes *public*." And he later continues, "The genuine concept of the enemy thus implies the eventual reality of a struggle." The antagonistic relationship is essential to any political order, for "Political unity presupposes the real possibility of an enemy."[16] Compared to Schmitt, the wild Nordicism of the Nazis'

15 Quoted in Rocco, *The Political Doctrine of Fascism*, trans. by Bigongiari (Washington: Carnegie Endowment for International Peace, International Conciliation Bulletin No. 223, 1926), p. 7. For Gentile's ideas see "The Philosophical Basis of Fascism," *Foreign Affairs*, Vol. 6 (1928), pp. 290-304; Benito Mussolini, *The Political and Social Doctrine of Fascism*, English trans. (London: Hogarth Press, 1933). See also Herbert W. Schneider, *Making the Fascist State* (New York: Oxford Univ. Press, 1928).

16 The quotations are from William Ebenstein's translation, reprinted in his *Modern Political Thought* (New York: Rinehart, 1954), pp. 327-28. To overcome

"official" philosopher, Alfred Rosenberg (1893–1946), is extremely super-ficial. His *Myth of the Twentieth Century* is a mish-mash of Treitschke, Nietzsche, Chamberlain, and Gobineau. And even Rosenberg never really understood the purposefulness of Hitler's policy of extermination.

Though theory must come to grips with totalitarianism, and con-temporary scholarship has only begun to probe its depths, it is action and not theory that gives totalitarianism its character. Hitler's policy of *Lebensraum* (living space) needed only a mystique of German expansion-ism and not fancy geopolitical rationalizations to keep the Wehrmacht pushing on. His *Fuehrerprinzip* (leadership principle) described but did not ennoble the self-selection of power-wielders and their disregard for the traditional forms of election and majority vote. The interesting theoretical justifications for totalitarian rule are found in Communist theories. But these we shall leave until we look at what Lenin did to Marx (see Chapter 16). For the moment it is enough to reflect that anti-intellectual ideologies of action often have special appeal to intellectuals and others caught in a social bankruptcy of traditional ideals. Above all, we must not think that totalitarianism as a phenomenon is relevant only to other places and other times. Insofar as its legacy is the evisceration of human rights and the derangement of orderly relationships between public and private categories, totalitarianism as a problem is likely to be distressingly close to us for some time to come.

Liberalism in the Twentieth Century

AS the twentieth century began, political liberalism was riding high. Now, in the mid-twentieth century, it is in retreat. Liberalism as a be-lief in the ultimacy of individual conscience and as a movement directed to freeing the individual from archaic social restraints and his own ir-rationalities had and still has many forms. To William Graham Sumner, the free individual was the economically unrestricted individual, at liberty to compete in a dog-eat-dog world. At the other extreme, in the writings of idealists like Bernard Bosanquet or William Hocking, he was one whose potentialities could only be developed within the framework of a state or social order that evoked his higher loyalties. In between we find a Leonard Hobhouse, defending greater state activity but in the name of

---

what he regards as the unresolved dualisms of anarchic liberalism (state/individual; state/society; law/politics; legislative/executive), Schmitt substitutes what Ernest Barker has called a "trialism": ". . . the party stands at the centre of the common life, reaching out on the one hand into the state . . . and reaching out on the other into the People or Volk." Ernest Barker, *Reflections on Government* (Galaxy ed., New York: Oxford Univ. Press, 1958), p. 289. See entire Part 4 on totalitarianism.

essentially utilitarian values; or a Justice Holmes, for whom duty to nation could take on almost mystical overtones, but who was nonetheless a champion of the maximum of individual liberty and tolerance of diversity, for reasons that were based on the too-literal economic analogy of the "free marketplace of ideas." There were in the first decades of the twentieth century few new philosophical inquiries dedicated to the under-girding of the liberal faith. Intellectually, liberalism was riding on the momentum of Locke, the Enlightenment, and Adam Smith. But the faith was still there.

The twentieth century has seeen a continual battering of this liberal faith.[17] The hard, inescapable fact of totalitarianism is no doubt the greatest of all challenges to the hopefulness that liberalism blended into the politics of Western democracies. Not all pre-World War I liberals were bland optimists, by any means, but the mood of that time was indubitably progressive: science, industry, popular education, government by the people were moving us toward a better, freer life for all. Totalitarianism shattered that mood.

The shock of totalitarianism turned theologians from liberal preachments of the Social Gospel to reinterpretations of original sin. The political significance of the irrational in man was freshly demonstrable, and Freudian psychology became a tool of political analysis.

Meanwhile the disastrous economic conditions of the twenties, which helped make totalitarianism in Germany possible, were making the tenets of laissez-faire liberalism increasingly irrelevant. Socialism (meaning the nationalization of productive units) did not fare well in all places, but the welfare state (meaning redistribution of income and a managed economy) moved ahead without let across the western world. Politically, the welfare state has deen defended mainly with mellow clichés about liberty and equality drawn from the old liberal arsenal. But attackers of the welfare state[18] were forced to draw their clichés from the same warehouse and with them did poorly in elections. The deep thinkers, meanwhile, seemed to be working on other issues.

Granting the wisdom of selecting John Dewey as the most philosophically eminent representative of twentieth-century liberalism, we may look briefly here at four men chosen not because they are great political

17 See Judith Shklar's study of the decline of Enlightenment faith as revealed in the philosophy, poetry, and theology of the late nineteenth century, *After Utopia; The Decline of Political Faith* (Princeton: Princeton Univ. Press, 1958).

18 E.g., Friedrich von Hayek, *The Road to Serfdom* (Chicago: Univ. of Chicago Press, 1944) and *The Constitution of Liberty* (Chicago: Univ. of Chicago Press, 1960); John T. Flynn, *The Road Ahead* (New York: Devin-Adair, 1949); Ludwig von Mises, *The Anti-Capitalist Mentality* (Princeton: Van Nostrand, 1956); Henry C. Simons, *Economic Policy for a Free Society* (Chicago: Univ. of Chicago Press, 1948).

theorists and not even because they span the range of contemporary liberalism, but simply because they suggest its diversity and uncertainty. The four are Laski, Keynes, Galbraith, and Lippmann.

LASKI

Harold J. Laski (1893–1950) may at first glance appear far more a critic of liberalism than a liberal. A lifelong activist in the Labor Party and an inveterate crusader against the injustices of capitalism, he became in the 1930's an avowed though unorthodox Marxist. But in 1920, the year he returned to England from a dazzling teaching stint at Harvard, he criticized Fabian Socialist Sidney Webb for an excessive faith in governmental regulation and attacked Fabian and Marxist Socialists alike for assuming that the nationalization of industry was a cure-all.

Laski at this time[19] occupied a position reflecting both the syndicalists and the guild socialists on one side and the pluralists of the historical school of jurisprudence on the other side. That is, he held with the former that workers ought to have a greater direct say in the determination of industrial policy, and held with the latter that the state should be viewed as but one association among many associations. Consequently sovereignty became for Laski merely the ability of the state to induce the obedience of members to its rules, a relationship present in other associations as well. One difficulty of the former position was frequently the vagueness of the proposals to increase popular participation in industrial control. A difficulty of the latter position was the easy assumption that in case of a conflict arising from differing loyalties to state, church, union or other group, a harmonious ordering could be worked out without the superior imposition of one group's will on the others. Laski's thought shared these difficulties.

The pluralist position emerges from the precocious Laski's four earliest and most intellectually rigorous books: *Studies in the Problem of Sovereignty* (1917), *Authority in the Modern State* (1919), *Foundations of Sovereignty and Other Essays* (1921), and *A Grammar of Politics* (1925), which is probably his most significant book. Accepting the Benthamite formula of the greatest good for the greatest number, Laski rejected the egoism of its earlier applications: "If man is to live in community with his fellows it is a necessary condition of his life that what he attains should, at least in the long run, involve benefit also to others."[20]

19 At Harvard "Laski was a liberal in the American sense. He was for the underdog, for trade unions, and collective bargaining, mildly socialist in a fashion that lay between a liberal pluralism, tinged with Fabian ideas, and the Guild Socialism then fashionable among progressive intellectuals in Britain." Kingsley Martin, *Harold Laski (1893–1950), A Biographical Memoir* (London: Gollancz, 1953), p. 33.
20 *A Grammar of Politics* (1st ed.; London: Allen & Unwin, 1925), p. 25.

Yet by 1930, when the second edition of the *Grammar of Politics* and Laski's *Liberty in the Modern State* appeared, he had moved away from the pluralist conception of the state and also (though there seems to be no logical connection between the two) toward an older, more individualistic view of liberty: "Let me remind you of the essence of my argument. I have taken the view that liberty means that there is no restraint upon those conditions which, in modern civilization, are the necessary guarantees of individual happiness."[21]

From the first edition of the *Grammar of Politics* on, Laski became more and more busy with popularizing ventures, and more and more eclectic, and his intellectual powers declined.[22] The conscious adoption of a watered-down Marxism in the 1930's was more a sign of flagging originality than a conversion. Laski's consistency was in his passionate concern for social justice, the freedom to express ideas, and the opportunity for ordinary people to have a decent existence. That he did not harness these concerns to a systematic theoretical position is a failure of the man, but also a failure of contemporary liberalism. For, as Herbert Deane says, "Marxism and classical liberalism are philosophies poorly equipped to deal with the central political issues of our times. Both are fundamentally concerned with the society and the economy rather than the polity."[23]

KEYNES

John Maynard Keynes (1883–1946) was one of the most versatile men of his age—British public official, scholar, essayist, patron of the arts, businessman, speculator, theater director. As prophet he gave the world a grim insight into disaster in *The Economic Consequences of the Peace* (1919), "bursting into international fame when men of equal insight but less courage and men of equal courage but less insight kept silent."[24] As economist, in *The General Theory of Employment, Interest and Money* (1935), he gave capitalism a theoretical and highly technical rationale for accepting the governmental intervention it needed to survive after the disaster of depression struck.

But he was not a political philosopher, even though a liberal (in ideas and in party registration). Beyond his monumental role as economic innovator, a role which ranks him with Adam Smith and Karl Marx, his political ideas were perhaps most substantial in their negative aspect,

21 *Liberty in the Modern State* (rev. ed.; New York: Viking, 1948), p. 129
22 Herbert Deane has documented this decline in his excellent *The Political Ideas of Harold J. Laski* (New York: Columbia Univ. Press, 1955).
23 *Ibid*, p. 342.
24 Joseph A. Schumpeter, *History of Economic Analysis* (New York: Oxford Univ. Press, 1954), p. 1170.

that is, in their corrosive impact on outworn doctrines still appended to western industrial activity:

Let us clear from the ground the metaphysical or general principles upon which, from time to time, laissez-faire has been founded. It is *not* true that individuals possess a prescriptive "national liberty" in their economic activities. There is *no* "compact" conferring perpetual rights on those who Have or on those who Acquire. The world is *not* so governed from above that private and social interest always coincide. It is *not* so managed here below that in practice they coincide. It is *not* a correct deduction from the Principles of Economics that enlightened self-interest always operates in the public interest. Nor is it true that self-interest generally *is* enlightened; more often individuals acting separately to promote their own ends are too ignorant or too weak to attain even these. Experience does *not* show that individuals, when they make up a social unit, are always less clear-sighted than when they act separately. We cannot therefore settle on abstract grounds, but must handle on its merits in detail what Burke termed "one of the finest problems in legislation, namely, to determine what the State ought to take upon itself to direct by the public wisdom, and what it ought to leave, with as little interference as possible, to individual exertion." We have to distinguish between what Bentham, in his forgotten but useful nomenclature, used to term *Agenda* and *Non-Agenda,* and to do this without Bentham's prior assumption that interference is, at the same time, "generally needless" and "generally pernicious." Perhaps the chief task of Economists at this hour is to distinguish afresh the *Agenda* of Government from the *Non-Agenda;* and the companion task of Politics is to devise forms of Government within a Democracy which shall be capable of accomplishing the *Agenda.*[25]

In his affirmative declaration "Am I a Liberal?" (1925), he moved away from economic issues with some reluctance and aligned his liberal faith with such broad goals as "stability" and "justice." At bottom, it was experimentalism to which he was committed: "Our programme must deal not with the historic issues of Liberalism, but with those matters—whether or not they have already become party questions—which are of living importance and urgency today."[26]

But Keynes did express some hope that altruistic impulses natural to man would increasingly find expression at a level between that of the strictly individual and that of the state as a whole, namely, in the modern corporation (which had in fact long ago become nonindividualist, nonprivate enterprise), a possible bearer of a new public spirit. Government, he felt, should not try to replace corporations, or to do what

25 *The End of Laissez-Faire* (1926), in Alan Bullock and Maurice Shock, eds., *The Liberal Tradition from Fox to Keynes* (Edinburgh: A. & C. Black, 1956), pp. 254-55.
26 *Ibid.,* p. 284.

individuals were already doing, but it should do what no one in the 1920's was doing—manage the whole economy through fiscal and monetary controls.

A generation later this new but no less "true" liberalism—antisocialist but pro-governmental regulation—found expression in another economist, less brilliant in the technicalities of the discipline but somewhat more willing to theorize about the political whole.

GALBRAITH

The writings of John Kenneth Galbraith (1908–   ) have an edge of irony reminiscent of Thorstein Veblen or Thurman Arnold.[27] Especially in his *American Capitalism* (1952) and *The Affluent Society* (1958), he challenged Americans to look again at the stereotypes of capitalism and socialism. In the first, he substituted a concept of "countervailing power" for traditional price competition in the market. In the present-day welfare state, economic and political policy alike is, he feels, a resultant of the bargaining between the big power blocs of government, labor, business, and sometimes agriculture. As between the unrestricted price competition presumed to be normal under classical economic theories and the oligopolistic conditions of modern industry, the latter is much to be preferred, says Galbraith. In *American Capitalism*, Galbraith chides economic thinkers for not taking the problem of power seriously. In *The Affluent Society* he chides the makers of public policy for not taking seriously the productivity of the economic system. In effect, he is saying to Americans that we have not learned how to live with, and use, wealth. Our past thinking has been so oriented toward first production, then consumer products marketable on an individual basis, that important expenditures on such public works as schools, hospitals, and urban renewal have been neglected. We have been blinded by the conception of how an individualistic society works long after an individualistic society is impossible. The net effect of all this is that the union of business and government turns out to be more than a temporary antidepression expedient. It is here to stay even in a United States that is regarded as the last bastion of private-enterprise capitalism.

Without making more of Galbraith's somewhat optimistic conception of countervailing power than it deserves, we can at least say that it tends to bring economic considerations into a position subordinate to political considerations—but not all the way, for Galbraith is still a liberal in the manner in which he values economic well-being and political pluralism. The full-scale subordination of economic to political values appears in those who are neither liberal nor socialist. They cannot simply be called

27 See Arnold's *Folklore of Capitalism* (New Haven: Yale Univ. Press, 1937).

conservatives, for the varieties of conservatives are too numerous. Perhaps "anti-liberals" or "half-liberals" will do.

LIPPMANN

One such "half-liberal" is Walter Lippmann (1889–   ). A socialist as an undergraduate at Harvard, he soon moved into more conventional channels of protest. His first book, *A Preface to Politics* (1913), showed the influence of both Graham Wallas and Freud as Lippmann protested against the empty formalism and legalism of earlier political studies. The Walter Lippmann of *The Good Society* (1935) was a champion of an open and unplanned society in the best liberal tradition. But one writer has found that *Public Opinion* (1922) was "the liberal Lippmann's farewell to liberalism."[28] It might best be said that while Lippmann's concerns were and are shaped by a liberal outlook, some of his remedies have illiberal, elitist characteristics. In *Public Opinion*, probably the best of his twenty-three books, the problem was the extreme difficulty of keeping a democratic people informed through news media, and the eradication of the misshapen stereotypes that form in people's heads in the absence of insistent signals from the real world. His remedies included a government news bureau dedicated to "objectivity" and the filling in of gaps left by commercially minded interpreters of the news.

Lippmann's recent book, *The Public Philosophy* (1955), begins with an analysis of a problem that had long bothered him, the ponderous emotionalism by which democratic publics tie the hands of executive leaders trying to cope with crises in foreign affairs. But with much less precision than he displayed in some of his earlier philosophical writings, Lippmann attributes this and the widest variety of other social evils to what he calls the philosophy of "Jacobinism" (Rousseau, Andrew Jackson, Marx, and progressive education are all included in this category), and proposes as an antidote an eclectic brand of natural law with definite elitist implications. His "public philosophy" and Rousseau's "civil religion" are first cousins.

That liberalism in the twentieth century has had so few spokesmen of profundity must be taken as a sign of its decline as a political philosophy.

FREUDIAN LIBERALISM

To speak of Freud and liberalism in the same breath may seem to many a contradiction. But Freud himself was more of a liberal than

---

28 Heinz Eulau, "From Public Opinion to Public Philosophy: Walter Lippmann's Classic Reexamined," *American Journal of Economics*, Vol. 15 (1956), p. 450. But see Lippmann's "Conservative, Liberal, Progressive," *The New Republic*, Vol. 146 (Jan. 22, 1962), pp. 10-11.

many who link his name with dark and irrational passions will concede. He was liberal in that a liberated individual was the *raison d'être* of his work. He was liberal in that he believed in the power of reason—not, to be sure, reason disembodied as rational idealists had tended to conceive of it, but reason as an aspect of man's emotional life, an ego controlling an id.[29] As a scientist, he was obliged to operate on deterministic assumptions, but he was not far from Kant in the seriousness with which he took the problem of personal moral obligation. In the Freudian view character was formed early in life. Men were not remade as adults. Yet he never doubted that knowledge could contribute to any man's therapy. His one unshakable faith was in science, and a progressive science at that, This, surely, was liberal.

His liberalism did not, however, lead Freud to become an optimist or a sentimentalist. He stopped short of cynicism, but he had few illusions, and courted none. As he somewhere put it, his aim was to "transform neurotic despair into the general unhappiness which is the usual lot of mankind." Concerned as he was with individual patients, he had little sympathy with grand, overarching nationalistic or class explanations of human behavior as given by a Hegel or a Marx. As many commentators have observed, his pessimism shared something with that of Hobbes: in the views of both, it was the misery of men that required, and possibly was sufficient to sustain, a social order. In Hobbes it was a more or less rational fear of death that showed men the inexorable need for authority. In Freud it was an irrational death wish, the basis of aggression, that created the need for authority. In one the myth of the social contract rationalized political power; in the other the myth of the slaying by Oedipus of his father rationalized the guilt that binds men to their brothers.

On this basis Freud was more of an elitist and less of an equalitarian than Hobbes. But Freud's natural elite, the strong and self-knowledgeable, were cut down to human size by the drive of sex that stamped all men with a biological commonality; and even the most pathetic, self-deceiving neurotic was granted some capacity for rational control. If man was not blessed with innate goodness, neither was he cursed with innate depravity. The neurotic might not be free; but even the normal man did not have *much* freedom.

29 It is barely possible that the reader is unfamiliar with Freudian terms like id, ego, and superego; Eros and Thanatos; Oedipus and Electra complexes. It is even imaginable that the reader might not know that Sigmund Freud (1856–1939), Viennese psychiatrist, was the founder of psychoanalysis. If so, it is suggested he consult the family magazine section of a Sunday newspaper, any issue. Then again, *The Basic Writings of Sigmund Freud*, trans. by A. A. Brill (New York: Modern Library, 1938), might be more helpful.

Freud, of course, was not a political theorist at all, and not much of a social thinker. His early explorations into primitive anthropology[30] have been much criticized. His study of religion[31] misunderstands elemental doctrines of the Judeo-Christian tradition. Yet all this testified to the power on Freud of nineteenth-century historicism and its search for genetic roots. Although concerned with the problems of individuals, Freud wanted to explain essences by primitive origins. Faced with an individual who knew no father, he could fall back on "racial memory" to provide Oedipal feelings.[32] On the occasions when he does speak of whole cultures, he leaps if anything too easily from the individual to the mass. After discussing the struggle between Eros and Thanatos, the life urge versus the death instinct, Freud observes, "When . . . we compare the cultural process in humanity with the process of development or upbringing in an individual human being, we shall conclude without much hesitation that the two are very similar in nature, if not in fact the same process applied to a different kind of object."[33]

In *Civilization and Its Discontents* Freud discusses guilt and conscience, that part of guilt stimulated by the superego. The superego is the internalization of the moral demands of society, what Riesman has called "the walking delegate from ideology." Contrary to some vulgarizations of Freud, the liberation of the life force in the dark places of the id from the restraint of guilt was not the primary object of Freud. Indeed, "the price of progress in civilization is paid in forfeiting happiness through the heightening of the sense of guilt."[34] But this is not an easy progress. Though disclaiming a prophet's role, Freud raises the question of whether a whole people can become neurotic—"possibly even the whole of humanity"—under the pressure of these civilizing trends. And so at the very end he returns to the struggle between the life force and the death force and, in a statement even more appropriate to the post-atomic age, says:

Men have brought their powers of subduing the forces of nature to such a pitch that by using them they could now very easily exterminate one another to the last man. They know this—hence arises a great part of their current unrest, their dejection, their mood of apprehension. And now it may be expected that the other of the two "heavenly forces," eternal Eros, will put

30 See *Totem and Tabu* (1913) in *Basic Writings*.

31 See *The Future of an Illusion*, trans. by W. D. Robson-Scott (London: Hogarth Press, 1928). See also the essays by Will Herberg and Reinhold Niebuhr in Benjamin Nelson, ed., *Freud and the Twentieth Century* (New York: Noonday Press [Meridian Books], 1957).

32 See David Riesman, "Authority and Liberty in the Structure of Freud's Thought," in his *Individualism Reconsidered* (Glencoe, Ill.: Free Press, 1954).

33 *Civilization and Its Discontents*, trans. by Joan Rivière (London: Hogarth Press, 1939), p. 133.

34 *Ibid.*, p. 122.

forth his strength so as to maintain himself alongside his equally immortal adversary.[35]

The important contributions of Freud to twentieth-century political thinking were not made directly through his own semi-political writings but indirectly through the changed conception of man-the-political-animal resulting from the increased use of psychoanalytic categories.[36] A certain tolerance and flexibility in penal procedures accompanied the recognition that the ego (the rational self) is not unlimited in its capacity to control the id (the subconscious). This affected standards of responsibility in law and expectations of self-direction in education, and in some respects led to a reduction in the perfectionist moral demands made by the superego (the culture) on the individual. Our dependence upon parents as authority figures and our capacity to transfer this dependence to surrogates who may be political leaders have been observed,[37] and the observation has affected not only our understanding but our leadership. (At least among sophisticates, however, the biologically equalizing tendencies of the Freudian approach referred to above probably has inhibited the possibility of regarding leaders as truly noble figures in any classical sense of the word "noble.") Finally, the Freudian insight into the rationalizing propensities of the human being, transferred to politics, makes ideology as compared to "pure" ideals all the more pervasive and, as well, suggests the possibility of "subliminal" manipulations, which has been lost on neither advertisers nor political manipulators. The capacity of individuals for the repression, suppression, and displacement of aggressive feelings, whatever it has suggested by way of mass manipulation, also has revealed to us the depth of the problem of rational social control.

NEO-FREUDIANISM: FROMM

Freud, of course, is not the only contemporary psychological influence,[38] and the so-called Freudian revisionists have departed from the

35 *Ibid.,* p. 144.

36 This is not to suggest that Freudian concepts have not been directly applied to political subjects, and usefully so. See especially the work of Harold Lasswell: *Psychopathology and Politics* (Chicago: Univ. of Chicago Press, 1930), *World Politics and Personal Insecurity* (New York: McGraw-Hill, 1935), *Power and Personality* (New York: Norton, 1948), *The Analysis of Political Behavior: An Empirical Approach* (New York: New York Univ. Press, 1948).

37 See Sebastian de Grazia, *The Political Community, A Study of Anomie* (Chicago: Univ. of Chicago Press, 1948); Robert E. Lane, "Fathers and Sons: Foundations of Political Belief," *American Sociological Review,* Vol. 24 (1959), pp. 502-11.

38 See, for example, C. G. Jung, *Modern Man in Search of a Soul* (London: Kegan Paul, Trench, Trübner, 1933), and Ira Progoff, *Jung's Psychology and Its Social Meaning* (New York: Grove Press [Evergreen Books], 1957).

master in many repects. Perhaps the most politically minded of these neo-Freudians is *Erich Fromm* (1900–   ), whose reputation was made by *Escape from Freedom*.[39] In that work, well timed to confront readers when the Nazis' power was at its height, he reminded liberals of the negative possibilities of freedom. Tracing the alienation of the individual from his primary social groups since the Renaissance and the Reformation, Fromm analyzed the sadistic and masochistic feelings generated by the loneliness of a competitive industrial society. Modern man finds that he has negative freedom, freedom *from*, but he does not know what to do with it. He yearns to be a unique and different self, and to be accepted as a whole person. But a fragmented and mechanical culture treats him as a cog in a machine. He is like everyone else. "The despair of the human automaton is fertile soil for the political purposes of Fascism." He needs somehow to achieve positive freedom, freedom *to*, which is synonymous with "the spontaneous activity of the total integrated personality."[40]

In pursuit of this laudable goal Fromm explicitly criticized Freud for his narrow biologism and like his psychiatric colleague Harry Stack Sullivan stressed the importance of interpersonal relations in shaping character well beyond childhood. He also emphasized the affirmative and unifying rather than the cathartic side of love.

If Freud can be criticized for neglecting social institutions, Fromm can be criticized for making the community responsible for almost everything. Like the nineteenth-century utopian socialists, Fromm takes an extremely optimistic view of natural man, and the way in which he offers his "humanitarian communitarianism" as a solution to "robotism" and the most complex socio-psychological problems is engagingly naïve. On man: ". . . the striving for mental health, for happiness, harmony, love, productiveness, is inherent in every human being who is not born a mental or moral idiot. Given a chance, these strivings assert themselves forcefully, as can be seen in countless situations."[41] On solutions: "Changes in ownership must be made to the extent to which they are necessary to create a community of work. . . . Man must be reinstituted to his supreme place in society, never being a means, never a thing to be used by others or by himself. Man's use by man must end, and economy must become the servant for the development of man. Capital must serve labor, things must serve life."[42]

39 *Escape from Freedom* (New York: Rinehart, 1941). See also Karen Horney, *The Neurotic Personality of Our Time* (New York: Norton, 1937). A new study of Fromm's political thought is John Schaar, *Escape from Authority* (New York: Basic Books, 1961).

40 *Escape from Freedom*, pp. 256, 258.
41 *The Sane Society* (New York: Rinehart, 1958), p. 275.
42 *Ibid.*, p. 361. With more thoroughness than any other recent writer Christian

Existentialism

EXISTENTIALISM is a much misunderstood but highly important twentieth-century phenomenon, perhaps the most significant philosophic movement yet to rise up in this century.[43] Its forms are various and subtle, and insofar as it has common tenets they are apolitical, if not antipolitical. Yet its political consequences are tremendous.

KIERKEGAARD

The starting point of contemporary existentialism is in the Platonic distinction between existence and essence, more particularly in the reaction of the Danish theologian Soren Kierkegaard (1813–1855) against Hegel's attempt to make rational essence embrace all that is. The search for essence is both a rational and a definitional exercise. Existence does not need to be—indeed, cannot be—defined, analyzed, plotted out, or reduced to abstractions: it is simply *there*. We know it not by intellectual inquiry but by a transrational "encounter." It is concrete rather than abstract, spontaneous rather than predictable, free rather than determined, subjectively rather than objectively known.

According to Kierkegaard, the separation of existence from essence

---

Bay has taken the liberal tenet of the free individual and has tried to work out a set of propositions appropriate to a social policy based on this ideal, postulating a "humanitarian loyalty" that is "compatible with a maximal level of *psychological freedom*." In *The Structure of Freedom* (Stanford: Stanford Univ. Press, 1958), he employs the latest findings of psychology, social psychology, and sociology, and tries, with some difficulty, to follow a "value-free" methodology in so doing. See Walter Berns, "The Behavioral Sciences and the Study of Political Things: The Case of Christian Bay's *The Structure of Freedom*," *Am. Pol. Sci. Rev.*, Vol. 55 (1961), pp. 550-59. The concern for the political *as* the political in Berns' criticism of Bay represents a new and essentially nonliberal, or transliberal, tendency in contemporary political thinking. Liberals have generally thought of politics as the resultant of conflicting "interests," either individual or group, a kind of superstructure built on nonpolitical forces. This assumption is challenged in such writings as Norman Jacobson, "The Unity of Political Theory: Science, Morals, and Politics," in Roland Young, ed., *Approaches to the Study of Politics* (Evanston, Ill.: Northwestern Univ. Press, 1958), pp. 115-24; Joseph Cropsey, "On the Relation of Political Science and Economics," *Am. Pol. Sci. Rev.*, Vol. 54 (1960), pp. 3-14; and works by Sheldon Wolin and Hannah Arendt cited above.

43 The bibliography of existentialism is already immense. See Kenneth Douglas, *A Critical Bibliography of Existentialism (The Paris School)*, Yale French Studies Special Monograph No. 1 (New Haven: Yale Univ. Press, 1950); Victor Vanitelli, S.J., "A Bibliographical Introduction to Existentialism," *The Modern Schoolman*, Vol. 26, No. 4 (May 1949). Some important studies since these dates are: William Barrett, *Irrational Man* (New York: Doubleday, 1958); Frederick Heinemann, *Existentialism and the Modern Predicament* (2nd ed.; Edinburgh: A. & C. Black, 1954), H. J. Blackham, *Six Existentialist Thinkers* (London: Routledge & Kegan Paul, 1953).

is most apparent to a man in moments of personal crisis. At such a time definitions, abstract concepts, "principles," seem especially unreal. They do not satisfy. Yet man's intellect is trapped within the sphere of essences, for that is all intellect can know. We depend upon our intellectual constructions even in times of crisis, but they are found wanting and great tension and frustration result. This is the anguish *(Angst)* Kierkegaard described as "metaphysical sickness," which was for him the precursor of religious faith. For when one is at the end of his intellectual rope he is forced either to dangle helplessly or to take the "leap of faith" and grasp "the absurd," which is beyond reason, but restores wholeness of spirit. The paradox (among the many that delighted Kierkegaard) is that until one knows he is sick, he cannot be well.

Since the leap can be in any direction, since it is, from the pre-leap outlook, a leap into darkness and nothingness, the freedom that liberals once prized so highly now becomes terrifying. It is a "dizziness." The optimistic view of freedom that had become part of modern man's inheritance was in Kierkegaard (and Dostoevsky and Nietzsche) shattered. The incidence of personal crises that makes freedom so terrifying may be more characteristic of twentieth-century life than of nineteenth-century life, which may help to explain why Kierkegaard's writings lay in limbo for the second half of the nineteenth century only to be rediscovered and spread over the globe in the twentieth.

JASPERS

One of many influenced by Kierkegaard is Karl Jaspers (1883–   ), psychiatrist and professor of philosophy at Heidelberg and, since 1948, Basel. More directly concerned than many other existentialists with the political environment as a matter of theory, Jaspers outlines the present historical condition of man in *Man in the Modern Age (Die geistige Situation der Zeit)*.[44] Jaspers finds a threat to the selfhood of every man in the giant impersonal machine of modern mass society. The Nietzschean influence is obviously cast over the following passages, yet their content seems fully as relevant to the 1960's as to the Weimar Republic days when Jaspers first wrote them:

Essential humanity is reduced to the general; to vitality as a functional corporeality, to the triviality of enjoyment. The divorce of labour from pleasure deprives life of its possible gravity: public affairs become mere entertainment; private affairs, the alternation of stimulation and fatigue, and a craving for novelty whose inexhaustible current flows swiftly into the waters of oblivion.

44 *Man in the Modern Age*, trans. by Eden and Cedar Paul (New York: Doubleday [Anchor Books], 1957). See also his *The Future of Mankind*, trans. by E. B. Ashton (Chicago: Univ. of Chicago Press, 1961).

. . . Youth as the period of highest vital efficiency and of erotic exaltation becomes the desired type of life in general. Where the human being is regarded only as a function, he must be young; and if youth is over he will try to show its semblance. . . . Great men pass into the background as contrasted with the efficient. . . . Without the support of the mass will he is of no account. What he can be is not measured by an ideal, is not related to a genuinely present Transcendence, but is based upon his conception of the fundamental qualities of mankind as manifested in the majority. . . . Now the result of "leadership" of this kind is inextricable confusion. . . .

With the unification of our planet there has begun a process of levelling-down which people contemplate with horror. That which has today become general to our species is always the most superficial, the most trivial, and the most indifferent of human possibilities. Yet men strive to effect this levelling-down as if, in that way, the unification of mankind could be brought about. . . . People dress alike. . . . the same dances, the same types of thought, and the same catchwords. . . .45

Politics is always, says Jaspers, a concrete activity taking place within a vast and incomprehensible whole, full of obscure motives. But political claims are couched in terms of abstract generality and drilled into citizens "with the fixity of religious dogmas." The concept "nation" is one of the best, that is, worst, examples of this, and the bolsheviks and fascists are the most adept at the drilling.

How does Jaspers help us overcome these suffocating forces? His means obviously cannot be the construction of a new system. In his gigantic three-volume *Philosophy* (1932) he noncommittally examined the possibilities of transcending material knowledge and the realm of objects. Being more "representational" than other existentialists would approve, Jaspers surveyed a variety of philosophical world views. He was trying to help man become aware of himself and to help him face his free decision. After his enforced "inside exile" under the Nazis, he came up with a massive (1,103 large-sized pages!) volume that was supposed to be the first of three in a new *Philosophical Logic*. Its title was *Of Truth (Von der Wahrheit)*. Despite its name, it was not a logic, but ironically, in spite of himself, Jaspers had now produced a system of sorts; and, also in spite of himself, he had come close to a religious faith. Seeing him move from Nietzschean defiant doubt to Kierkegaardian faith, some critics marked this as a sign of strength, others as a sign of weakness.46 If one contribution of Jaspers stands out it is his treatment of the problem

45 *Ibid.*, pp. 48, 55, 85. See also Jose Ortega y Gasset, *The Revolt of the Masses* (New York: Norton, 1932).

46 Compare Heinemann, *Existentialism*, p. 76, with Walter Kaufmann, ed., in the Introduction to *Existentialism from Dostoevsky to Sartre* (New York: Noonday Press [Meridian Books], 1956), p. 33.

of communication between persons beyond the limits of rational knowledge, that is, beyond the realm of the essential. He speaks of a "rise into transcendence" where by "evocation" one recreates in another a crisis similar to one's own. Transrational "signs" are in this way "decoded" and a meeting of the minds is achieved. This is the level of being Jaspers calls "The Encompassing" *(das Umgreifende)* and it is with this level that authentic philosophy deals.

Like other existentialists, Jaspers would bring philosophy back from the technicism of logical positivism to the central moral concerns of concrete living. Still basically without the guidance of metaphysical principles, "It remains," says Heinemann, "a venture of radical openness."[47]

SARTRE

Possibly the most difficult of twentieth-century philosophers of existence is Martin Heidegger (1889–   ). Utterly neglectful of the problem of community, he has been absorbed by the ontology of man's "encounter with nothingness." Heidegger's thought need not detain us here, but the name serves to introduce his more politically minded student, Jean-Paul Sartre (1905–   ), one of few contemporary philosophers who willingly accepts the name "existentialist" (Jaspers is an advocate of *Existenzphilosophie*). Sartre tries to bring Heidegger's detached ontologizing down to the problems of the subjective self.

Heidegger, Jaspers, and Sartre all agree that the philosophy of existence must be lived to have meaning. All agree that man makes himself by his choices. It is doubly interesting to note, thus, the divergent courses they followed when faced with the crisis of Nazism. Heidegger joined the Nazi party to keep his university post. Jaspers, who had a Jewish wife, lost his professorship, but kept silent and continued working in seclusion. Sartre fought in the French resistance and after the war on impulse joined the Communist Party as a protest against the status quo—while defiantly claiming that should the Communists ever come to power in France he would be among the first to be liquidated.

The absolute self-dependence of each man would seem to have nihilistic and hence anarchistic political implications. But Sartre does not see it this way. Simply because there is no transpersonal standard of values to which all men can repair, a man's choice of values, observes Sartre, is an expression of the values he feels all men should choose. "My commitments commit all men." Since we are totally responsible for ourselves, we are responsible for all men. Thus one goes on, "condemned to be free," acting without hope, a self that is a bubble, empty in the middle, expanding itself. Sartre's wartime Resistance experience clearly

47 *Existentialism*, p. 67.

has dominated his very conception of life. This was a life of hopeless struggle in which the struggle gave meaning to everything. The ultimate freedom was the cry of "No" to the Gestapo torturer. Every act was heightened in intensity by the imminent threat of death. Every man was on his own but bound to other men by being on his own. Sartre tells the story of a boy torn between staying in France to fight the Germans or fleeing for the sake of his ailing mother to England. Sartre was moved, but unable to make the decision for him. We are moved, but the story offers no substantiation of an existentialist view of life, only case materials for a classroom exercise in ethics.

There is little basis for a theory of natural community in Sartre's thought. The exercise of personal freedom is characteristically described as isolated, defiant revolutionary activity. Even his emphasis on "making oneself" through conscious choices seems to exaggerate the possibility of individual autonomy and assumes too easily an intellect detachable from the unconscious.[48] That community is artificial rather than natural in Sartre is made clear in his recent book *Critique de la raison dialectique*.[49] The parallel with Hobbes is striking as Sartre explains that leaders and the groups they lead are established out of the fear men have of each other in the "serial" condition of natural equality. The establishment is maintained and sanctioned by "terror" and "oath."

Sartre's psychology is a narrow ego psychology. The egocentricity of his outlook is apparent in his rationale for the distrust of party platforms, abstract principles, masses of people, or any group. The distrust may be well founded, but not his explanation: "I cannot count on men whom I do not know. . . . I must confine myself to what I can see."[50] It can surely be argued that the fabric of trust we have in people we cannot see, if torn asunder, would make life not only grim, as Sartre claims, but impossible. Imagine our utter dependence upon unknown bank clerks, mailmen, printers, government officials, newspaper writers, pharmacists, food processors. Were this trust thoroughly broken not even the most rigid totalitarian regime could survive, and it is the relative lack of such

48 Freedom understood as a yielding to the nature that "flows through us at the borders of consciousness and the unconscious" is, says William Barrett, unknown to Sartre. *Irrational Man*, Ch. 10. Herbert Read attacks the same problem in a different way and shows that, etymologically, "free" and "friend" come from the same root. A communitarian "liberty" is what is really concrete and existential, he says; the "freedom" existentialists brood over is really abstract and essential. *Existentialism, Marxism, and Anarchism* (London: Freedom Press, 1950), pp. 21-24.

49 *Critique de la raison dialectique* (Paris: Gallimard, 1960). See the long review by Édouard Morot-Sir in *Journal of the History of Ideas*, Vol. 22 (1961), pp. 573-81.

50 *Existentialism and Humanism* (1948), trans. by Philip Mairet, in Morton White, ed., *The Age of Analysis* (New York: New American Library [Mentor Books], 1955), p. 133.

trust which makes totalitarian regimes weaker than they seem on the surface. With this question of communion at the level of the existential we
have arrived at a link with the so-called existentialist theologians, Berdyaev,
Buber, Marcel, Tillich and others. But mention of their contribution can
wait until Chapter 18.

CAMUS

Finally, a word on Camus. Albert Camus (1913–1959), Nobel prize-
winning novelist and essayist, was closely associated with Sartre, but
broke with him when the latter joined the Communist Party. Sharing
the existentialist vision of the absurd and, in particular, Sartre's atheism,
Camus nevertheless strikes a different and more affirmative note than most
of his peers. In his famous essay "The Myth of Sisyphus," the condemned
Sisyphus, who must roll a great rock to the top of the mountain only
to have it fall back of its own weight, is referred to as "the absurd hero."
Yet he is a tragic hero because, unlike many modern workmen whose task
is no less futile, Sisyphus is *conscious* of his absurdity. He learns that
"There is no fate that cannot be surmounted by scorn." His discovery
of the absurd is enough by itself to bring happiness. "Happiness and the
absurd are two sons of the same earth." For at least Sisyphus' "fate
belongs to him. His rock is his thing."[51]

In *The Rebel*, the most consciously political of contemporary existentialist writings and one of the most brilliantly anti-ideological books of
our time, Camus makes a case for the view that by rebelling we assert
the worth of the society against which we rebel. It is the very act of
rebelling that creates the value society has for us. Camus explicitly distinguishes his position from nihilism through the idea of "limits." For
rebellion without a sense of limit is a form of slavery and is self-
defeating. Inherent in Camus' rebellion is the idea of restraint and the
rejection of absolutes. For absolute justice is always unfree and absolute
freedom is alway unjust. Only through restraint can rebellion be kept
alive and constant and pertinent, which it must be to be meaningful.

Along the way Camus throws off dazzling critiques of, among others,
Rousseau, Saint-Just, Sade, Hegel, Marx, Nietzsche, and the entire
socialist movement. He gives us many vignettes of what in contemporary
society can be rebelled against: authoritarianism, systematic violence, the
centralized state, colonization, human misery, the persecution of innocents.
But any such check-list is superficial in relation to the deeper thrust
of Camus' attack: the utopian valuing of the future over the present,
the use of ideology to delay human decency:

51 "The Myth of Sisyphus," in Kaufmann, ed. *Existentialism from Dostoevsky
to Sartre*, pp. 314-15.

The men of Europe, abandoned to the shadows, have turned their backs on the fixed and radiant point of the present. They forget the present for the future, the fate of humanity for the delusion of power, the misery of the slums for the mirage of the Eternal City, ordinary justice for an empty promised land. They despair of personal freedom and dream of a strange freedom of the species; reject solitary death and give the name of immortality to a vast collective agony. They no longer believe in the things that exist in the world and in living man; the secret of Europe is that it no longer loves life. Its blind men entertain the puerile belief that to love one single day of life amounts to justifying whole centuries of oppression. That is why they wanted to efface joy from the world and to postpone it until a much later date. Impatience with limits, the rejection of their double life, despair at being a man have finally driven them to inhuman excesses. Denying the real grandeur of life, they have had to stake all on their own excellence. For want of something better to do, they deified themselves and their misfortunes began; these gods have had their eyes put out. . . . we offer as an example, the only original rule of life to-day: to learn to live and to die, and in order to be a man, to refuse to be a god.[52]

Thus, finally, the struggle to keep rebellion alive yet within limits is a struggle within man and not outside him. In the face of the hard fact that in twenty centuries the sum total of evil has not diminished and probably will not diminish one understands why "rebellion cannot exist without a strange form of love." But the love Camus asks for is not a form of resignation. Indeed, his final words are an exultant clarion call of hope: ". . . it is time to forsake our age and its adolescent rages." For the "love of the earth" we must fit a new arrow to the bow, "the bow bends; the wood complains. At the moment of supreme tension, there will leap into flight an unswerving arrow, a shaft that is inflexible and free."[53]

A Note on Eastern and Western Political Thought

THIS is a book on the history of *Western* political theory not because the West alone is important but because the book is written by a Westerner for Westerners in the conviction that we must first know what we are before we can know what we may be. So far, at least, "the West can interpret the West; it can only describe the East."[54]

52 *The Rebel*, trans. by Anthony Bower (London: Hamish Hamilton, 1953), pp. 272-73.
53 *Ibid.*, p. 273.
54 John Lukacs. Quoted in Norman D. Palmer, "Indian and Western Political Thought: Coalescence or Clash?" *Am. Pol. Sci. Rev.*, Vol. 49 (1955), p. 745.

While Western man has been aware of Eastern thought for centuries, it has taken the world-shrinking conflicts and technological revolutions of the twentieth century to give it common relevance. Culturally, and especially technologically, Eastern nations ("nation" is itself a Western concept) are becoming Westernized at an accelerating rate. The newer constitutions of Asia reflect Western political ideas far more than Eastern. And insofar as the great political struggle of the present in Asia may be described as that between liberal democracy and Communism, it must be noted that both are Western importations.

The reverse—East to West—influence seems hardly equivalent. But no commerce can be wholly unilateral, and a new interest, especially among Americans, in Eastern religion, art, and culture may be detected. Professor K. P. Mukerji has argued that ancient Hindu philosophy integrated socio-political theory more successfully with "a morally valid . . . view of life" than Western thinkers have ever done, a fact Westerners are only beginning to recognize.[55] Without question we can and shall learn much from Eastern concepts of "community without collectivism" and "personality without individualism."

The outcome of this commerce is, however, by no means clear. The consequences for political theory are clouded by the fact that typical Eastern philosophy is generally apolitical and often antipolitical. Eastern philosophy still has a dominant purpose: escape from the miseries of worldly existence and a loss of self in mystical detachment. As worldly miseries become less miserable, if they do, no one can be quite sure what will happen. Meanwhile it is not to be wondered at that the worldly and politically expansive West has contributed more to a consistent body of political doctrine. Ironically, part of the current American interest in Zen Buddhism undoubtedly stems from a general disenchantment with the political, a disenchantment of which existentialism may be another expression.

Another factor worth noting is that Eastern thought at its root is so different from Western modes of thought that significant communication in political or other theory remains difficult and frustrating. Western thought, even that employed against the dominance of logic, is geared to logical progression. It "zeroes in" on its object. As Lili Abegg observes in her rewarding *The Mind of East Asia*,[56] Eastern thinking is "envelopmental thinking," taking the form of a series of encircling thrusts around its object, trying to open up as many avenues to comprehension as possible, trying to intimate a wholeness that can never be encapsuled in propositional and logical form. To the Westerner, Eastern thought,

55 *Ibid.*, p. 757.
56 A. J. Crick and E. E. Thomas, trans. (London: Thames & Hudson, 1952).

even at its most erudite, often seems meandering, undisciplined, inconclusive. To the Easterner, Western thought, even when most diligently in search of some kind of *Gestalt*, often seems incomplete and pedantically rigorous.

We can agree with India's great scholar and Vice-President, Sarvepalli Radhakrishnan, when he says: "Mankind stems from one origin from which it has figured out in many forms. It is now striving toward the reconciliation of that which has been split up. The separation of East and West is over. This history of the new world, the one world, has begun."[57] But we are not yet capable of the intellectual and spiritual leap necessary to ratify the end of this separation by a serious history of the political thought of the world. Not yet; but undoubtedly soon in this century of phenomenal cultural assimilation.

57 *East and West, Some Reflections* (London: Allen and Unwin, 1955), p. 131. Other works on the same theme are: *The East and West Must Meet*, A symposium (Lansing: Michigan State Univ. Press, 1959); S. Hofsra, ed., *Eastern and Western World* (The Hague: Van Hoeve, 1953); F. S. C. Northrop, *The Meeting of East and West* (New York: Macmillan, 1946); Arnold Toynbee, *The World and the West* (New York: Oxford Univ. Press, 1953).

CHAPTER

16 | *Lenin*

W E NEED NOT TRY to prove that Vladimir Ilich Ulianov, more commonly called V. I. Lenin, was one of the most skillful revolutionists in history. Many detailed histories of the Bolshevik Revolution do that. It is enough to assert that Lenin was a rare combination of theorist and activist without whose efforts the Bolshevik Revolution would probably have failed. Most theorists are uncomfortable organizing people. Most organizers are impatient with theory. Lenin was neither. By no stretch of the imagination could he be called a major philosopher. He was invariably too close to action decisions to be thoroughly reflective. His one work devoted to philosophic subjects, *Materialism and Empirio-Criticism* (1908), was written for political purposes and contained a number of deviations from ideas expressed in private writings. But there is no question that Lenin took seriously the theoretical problems of Marxism, especially the nature of the dialectic of history. Again and again he went back to the works of Marx and pored over them, setting a pattern for subsequent generations of Marxists.

Life

His father and his brother contributed a good bit to Lenin's seriousness of purpose, revolutionary zeal, and theoretical inventiveness. His father had been a director of schools in Simbirsk and a Councilor of State, a practicing Christian who had worked against considerable odds to build schools and spread education. Though frequently away from home, the father imposed on the household his reformist liberalism and solid middle-class virtues. He died after seeing his life work go down the drain with the surge of feeling against popular education that followed the assassination of Czar Alexander II in 1881. The brother, Alexander, whom Lenin had emulated as a child, went away to the university in St. Petersburg, was involved in a plot to assassinate the new Czar, Alexander III, and was hanged for his involvement. The older brother was twenty-one at the time; Vladimir was seventeen. The event, according to his sister, noticeably "hardened" Vladimir. A short while later, largely because he was the brother of "the other Ulianov," he was expelled from the University of Kazan.

Lenin now began to read Marx. Thanks to his mother's efforts, he was permitted to take the law examination at the University of St. Petersburg, and though his only training was a limited amount of self-education, he passed ahead of all the other examinees. His legal career was short and unsuccessful, for he soon found himself a political prisoner and was later exiled to Siberia. There he married Nadezhda Konstantinova (in later years simply "Krupskaya"), a fellow Marxist he had met in St. Petersburg, and spent a happy honeymoon copying the text of *The Development of Capitalism in Russia*, his first major work. In 1899 he went abroad and began to publish, in Munich, *Iskra* ("The Spark"), at which time he began to use the name N. Lenin.

For seventeen years Lenin was in exile, writing, talking, thinking. Through the vehicle of *Iskra*, printed on onionskin paper and smuggled into Russia, Lenin waged relentless war on the various other groups seeking the leadership of revolutionary sentiment in Russia, groups such as the People's Will (*Narodnaya Volya*), whose chief policy was assassination, or the Economists, who ignored Marxism to concentrate on attaining free speech and the right to strike. Lenin, of course, was not alone in editing *Iskra*. Among the exiled Social Democrats, as they were called, Lenin, Julius Martov, and A. H. Potresov regarded themselves as a *troika*, a three-man editorial team. Helping with *Iskra* from Switzerland, Georgi Plekhanov, with his followers Pavel Axelrod and Vera Zasulich, served as an inspiration to Lenin's group by virtue of Plekhanov's rigorous application of Marxist principles to Russia. By 1903 dissension had risen between the Lenin group, which was by that time in London, and the Plekhanov group in Switzerland. This was neither the first nor the last of the almost infinite number of schisms and divisions within the Marxist movement.

While in London, Lenin had met and was impressed by Lev Davidovich Bronstein, who would be known to the world as Leon Trotsky. Plekhanov did not like Trotsky very much, but when the division over the editing of *Iskra* became so deep that Lenin resigned, Trotsky stayed with Plekhanov, as did almost everyone else. Lenin was cut off and alone. But he had a remarkable capacity for believing himself right even in these circumstances, which was a basic factor in his subsequent strength. Lenin wrote feverishly, attacking his old friends publicly and privately. This period produced *One Step Forward, Two Steps Back* (1904), which stands with *What Is To Be Done?* (1902) as two of Lenin's greatest organizational monographs. Although his fortunes were at a low ebb, Lenin was tremendously heartened when the Marxist writer Bogdanov came over to his side. Together they published in Switzerland *Proletarii*, a counterpart of *Iskra*.

Because of early majorities in the tempestuous voting at the 1903 Social Democratic Party Congress in Brussels, Lenin's faction had been called the "Bolsheviks," from *bolshinstvo* ("majority"), and the group that grew up around Martov (which Plekhanov later joined) was called the "Mensheviks" from *menshinstvo* ("minority"). The Bolsheviks held their own Third Party Congress in London in 1905 while the Mensheviks were holding their session in Geneva. Two months later Lenin tore into the Mensheviks in *Two Tactics of Social Democracy in the Democratic Revolution*.

Meanwhile a general strike in Russia had led to the Revolution of 1905. Determined to be a part of it, Lenin slipped back into the country with a forged passport. A first Russian Duma, or parliament, was called. Lenin would have nothing to do with it, and when in 1907 the Duma was finally dissolved and its Social Democratic members were arrested and incarcerated, the Bolshevik faction was in a position to dominate the party. But Lenin was forced to flee to Finland, then to Switzerland, and finally, in 1909, to Paris. The intrigues of this ten-year exile are intricate and fascinating. The plots and the counterplots, the arrests and the escapes provide a treasury of melodramatic material. All the while Lenin was writing. In Zurich in 1916 he wrote *Imperialism. State and Revolution* was written during the summer of 1917 while its author was in hiding in Helsingfors. Shortly thereafter, through the assistance of the German authorities, who knew that a Lenin in Russia was infinitely more troublesome to their enemy the Czar than a Lenin out of Russia, he was returned to his homeland aboard a special train. Preaching "Peace, Bread, and Land" to the Petrograd proletariat and surrounding peasantry, Lenin was in a position to make the Petrograd Soviet of Workers' and Soldiers' Deputies the seat of authority when Kerensky's Provisional Government collapsed.

The rest of Lenin's story is too familiar to need detailed repeating here: the vigorous pursuit of "war communism" until the White Russian armies were defeated; the retreat into the "New Economic Policy" (NEP) of modified capitalism that Lenin had to defend against the purists of Marxist theory; the would-be assassin's bullet that accelerated the breakdown of Lenin's already failing health; the ultimate doubts about Party Secretary Stalin who was now dug in in preparation for his forthcoming battle with Trotsky. Lenin died of a massive sclerosis of the brain on January 21, 1924. Even in death his image continued to inspire the faithful, for his embalmed body is still on display at the Kremlin.

Lenin is a herald not only of Communism but of the age of ideology itself. For, facile as was his mind, ideas were for him weapons and only weapons. He took Marxism with utter seriousness—as a set of axioms to be applied rather than as a set of propositions to be examined. Bright, ruthless, single-minded, his task was to lead and to train in the manner of the stern headmaster to whom Edmund Wilson compared him.[1] Few have demonstrated more convincingly how philosophy can become an instrument in the struggle for political power.

Lenin as Philosopher

LENIN'S major contributions to Marxist theory are three in number: (1) his theory of the organization and functioning of the party as an integral part of the revolutionary occurrence; (2) his concept of capitalistic imperialism; (3) his concept of the dictatorship of the proletariat. With his typically hollow air of profundity, Stalin wrote in *The Foundations of Leninism* (1924), "What, then, in the last analysis, is Leninism? Leninism is Marxism of the era of imperialism and of the proletarian revolution."[1a]

A fourth contribution, though not a major one, was represented by Lenin's writings on the philosophy of materialism *per se*, especially his attack on the Russian philosopher Bogdanov in *Materialism and Empirio-Criticism* (1908). Like virtually all of Lenin's works, the book was politically inspired. Bogdanov's philosophy had been expounded in *Empiriomonism*, which appeared in three volumes from 1904 to 1906. Lenin read the books as they came out but waited to attack them until 1908, when for factional reasons he broke with Bogdanov. (Plekhanov, by contrast, had attacked Bogdanov's works at the time of their publication.) Lenin had made common cause with Bogdanov and his poet and philosopher friends in the face of the turmoil surrounding the 1905 revolution.

1 Edmund Wilson, *To the Finland Station* (New York: Harcourt, Brace, 1940), Part 3. See also David Shub, *Lenin* (Garden City: Doubleday, 1948); Leon Trotsky, *Lenin*, authorized trans. (New York: Minton, Balch, 1925); Bertram D. Wolfe, *Three Who Made a Revolution* (New York: Dial, 1948).

1a Josef Stalin, *The Foundations of Leninism* (new trans.; New York: International Publishers, 1939), p. 10.

But now, in 1908–09, Lenin was impatient with this group for its ostensible deviation from hard Marxist materialism. He accused them of "fideism" or the substitution of faith for knowledge, on the grounds that some of them (least of all, ironically, Bogdanov) were flirting with religion and religious metaphor. Bogdanov was the principal target because Lenin was trying to oust him from the editorial board of *Proletarii*. In April, 1909, when the book was in process of publication, Lenin wrote: "It is hellishly important for me that the book should come out at the earliest possible date, not only for literary but also for political reasons."[2]

Lenin's principal thrust was against the "Machians," supposed followers of the Viennese physicist and positivist Ernst Mach. In a rather strange juxtaposition, the Machian and the "god-builders" were regarded as "one essential whole." As against Engels, who argued that the reality of the external world was provable by the continual application of science and industry, the Machians postulated a realm of the unknowable, a factor of indeterminacy, which precluded categorical knowledge of the reality of the material world. This presumably enabled them to be classed with the agnostics who became religious in Lenin's eyes simply because they had rejected pure materialistic atheism.

The polemical character of Lenin's work is apparent throughout. He constantly refers to various arguments as "tricks" or "betrayals" and impugns the motives of those he criticizes. He helps the reader to "see with what sophistry 'recent' empirio-critical philosophy operates. We shall compare the argument of the idealist Berkeley with the *materialist* argument of Bogdanov, as a kind of punishment for the latter's betrayal of materialism!"[3] The arguments of his opponents he variously labels as "trash," full of "indecency," "extremely naive," "a cunning and refined form of fideism," and "destined to find their way into the museum of reactionary exhibits manufactured by the German professordom." To the inference drawn from "the humanitarian Philistines in Europe with their freethinking sympathies and their ideological slavery . . ." that philosophy is properly above partisan strife, Lenin answers: "Non-partisanship in philosophy is only a contemptible cloak of servility to idealism and fideism." The statement is not only polemical; it is parochial.

The book is also authoritarian in the sense that the final appeal in almost every case is to a quotation from Friedrich Engels. Marx is frequently mentioned, but Engels provides the text. Engels, it is true, offers a more

2 Quoted in Wolfe, *Three Who Made a Revolution*, p. 509. Later in 1909 Bogdanov and his followers were just outside the "faction" but explicitly not outside the "party." In 1912 Lenin's faction would declare itself the party!

3 All quotations in this paragraph are from *Materialism and Empirio-Criticism*, trans. by David Kvitko (New York: International Publishers, 1927), pp. 30, 132, 183, 179, 311, 179, and 308, respectively. Italics in original.

substantial case for dialectical materialism than Lenin was apparently capable of, a case designed to prove that those who questioned the externality of "objective" matter were in a solipsistic trap; but Lenin seems unable to cope with the necessity of a fundamental reexamination of Marxist tenets. When he rather self-consciously raises the question of his appeals to authority, he almost pathetically tries to down it with one more appeal to authority:

And do not cry out, you Machians, that I resort to 'authorities'; your clamour against the argument from authority is only a screen to conceal the fact that you substitute for the socialist authorities Marx, Engels, Lafargue, Mehring, Kautsky, the bourgeois authorities (Mach, Petzoldt, Avenarius, and the immanentists). It would have been much better if you had not raised the question of "authorities" and "authoritarianism."[4]

Perhaps the most substantial and fair-minded chapter in the book is Chapter 5, in which Lenin summarizes current developments in physics and shows how the conclusions of some physicists that "matter has disappeared" when conceived as the particles heretofore postulated, does no damage to the Marxist assumption of a "world existing and developing independently of the mind" which appears to be the heart of Marxist materialism.

All in all, *Materialism and Empirio-Criticism* is significant not so much for the technical philosophy tossed violently around, as for the evidence it gives of Lenin's intense dedication to the goal of organizational and ideological unity. Lenin spent considerable time and mental energy in studying philosophical and scientific writings. But he did so not so much out of the love of learning and speculation (though this motive was no doubt present), but in order to use philosophy for nonphilosophical ends.

Party and Revolution

LENIN's theory of the party was developed in the continuous outpouring of tracts, pamphlets, and articles that occupied so many of his prerevolutionary days. A synthesis of most of his early ideas on the subject appeared in the monograph *What Is To Be Done?* (1902). It still stands as a monument to the tenets that came in time to be called Leninism. The need for a hard, dedicated, disciplined party, flexible in action but inflexible in lines of authority: this was and is the essence of Leninism. The first chapter is an attack on the idea of "freedom of criticism" within a revolutionary party, and is directed against the "English Fabians, the French

4 *Ibid.,* p. 210.

Ministerialists, the German Bernsteinists" as well as the Russian "Critics." Lenin expresses gratitude for the new international flavor of the basic conflict between his position and that of all other socialists, a gratitude eventually turned to bitterness by the latent nationalism that World War I brought out in European socialists.

Already the problem of the supposed spontaneity of the dialectical process was creating psychological and philosophical problems that Lenin felt obliged to meet. He attacked *khvostism*—following in the tail—the view that regarded the party as a mere passive force following in the wake of the predetermined events of history. The party must be, he said, not in the tail of history but in the vanguard, and the party as the "vanguard of the proletariat" henceforth became a symbol of great force in the Communist movement. The intelligentsia who, Lenin frankly conceded, did not come out of the proletariat, were vitally necessary to keep the Communist movement related to Marxist theory, the railroad into the future. "Without revolutionary theory there can be no revolutionary movement. This cannot be insisted upon too strongly at a time when the fashionable preaching of opportunism is combined with absorption in the narrowest forms of practical activity."[5] By themselves, peasants and workers at the present stage, he wrote, could at best achieve a consciousness of the need for low-level trade-union reformism. Only those trained to see further into history could grasp the full sweep of the required revolution, "the task of emancipating the whole people from the yoke of autocracy," and develop the organizational means to carry this through; for "the role of vanguard can be fulfilled only by a party that is guided by an advanced theory."[6]

What may be the most fundamental Marxist characteristic, the tendency to dichotomize everything, is apparent throughout *What Is To Be Done?*: "... *the only choice is:* Either bourgeois, or Socialist ideology. There is no middle course (for humanity has not created a 'third' ideology, and, moreover, in a society torn by class antagonisms there can never be a non-class or above-class ideology). Hence, to belittle Socialist ideology *in any way*, to *deviate from it in the slightest degree* means strengthening bourgeois ideology."[7] The target of this outburst was the group called the Economists, those who, favoring the line of least resistance, believed that while the proletariat could be successful with forays into politics in the West, this was a fruitless course in Russia. Their faith in the spontaneous working out of the Marxian dialectic led them to urge, instead, the gradual building up of worker strength through trade-union organiza-

5 *What Is To Be Done?* Ch. 1, sec. D in *Collected Works*, authorized trans. (New York: International Publishers, 1929), Vol. IV, p. 110.
6 *Ibid.*   7 *Ibid.*, Ch. 2, sec. B, p. 123. Italics in original.

tion. Lenin was infuriated by expressions of this position and led what he himself called "a desperate struggle against spontaneity." At this date Lenin was still able to welcome as an ally the scholarly Karl Kautsky (1854-1938), German Marxist and editor of *Neue Zeit*. Both had attacked the conciliatory "revisionism" of the German Social Democrat Eduard Bernstein (1850-1932), and now Bernstein was linked to the Economists.[8]

Nowhere is Lenin's prose stronger than in the passage where, gibing at "infantile playing at 'democracy,'" he calls for a greater sense of "professional" party work (the first time he uses the word in this connection), i.e., finding able agitators, seeing that they are put in the kinds of jobs where they can do the most good—or damage—and paying for their subsistence from party funds if necessary. The organizational discipline and self-sacrificial zeal that later generations would associate with Communist Party activity were already apparent in *What Is To Be Done?* But it is fair to say that the quotation on the title page, an excerpt from a letter of Lassalle to Marx, which says, "A party becomes stronger by purging itself," did not in 1902 have the ominous overtones that in time would come to be identified with the word "purge."

The battle continued with the publication two years later of *One Step Forward, Two Steps Back*. But this time the object of attack—always there was an object of attack—is not the Economists but the Mensheviks who came out of the Second Party Congress (1903), "the opportunist wing of our party," as Lenin unabashedly called them. Through a close examination of the minutes of the Second Congress, Lenin brings to light a tangle of factional conflict that can only fill the present-day reader with bewilderment. Forty-three delegates, representing twenty-six different organizations, cast fifty-one votes. There were Bundists and *Rabocheye Dyelo*-ites and the *Yuzhny Rabochy* group and many others. Thirty-three delegates supported *Iskra* to begin with. But, as Stalin's official *History of the Communist Party of the Soviet Union (Bolshevik)* quaintly puts it, "not all those who considered themselves *Iskra*-ists were real Leninist *Iskra*-ists."[9] To maintain the ideological offensive against

8 Bernstein held that evolution rather than revolution would lead to communism, and over a much greater time span than Marx had assumed. He repudiated the predestinarian implications of the early materialist conception of history. He criticized the theory of surplus value not only on the grounds that it too simply explained an entire economy in terms of one phase of industrial production; but also on empirical grounds: industries with a high rate of surplus value in fact often had the highest-paid workers. In general, Bernstein faced the uncomfortable un-Marxist fact of a growing differentiation of industrial function that did not confirm the prophecy of the poor getting poorer while the rich got richer.

9 *History of the Communist Party of the Soviet Union (Bolshevik)* (New York: International Publishers, 1939), p. 40. The Second Party Congress began in Brussels but moved *en masse* to London when the Brussels police became troublesome.

the articulate Mensheviks, Lenin lashed out at their broad conception of party membership, which would allow every striker to consider himself a member. Such looseness would only lower the party's vitality and ultimately destroy its effectiveness, argued Lenin. The party must not lose its connections with the whole working class, it must not become an ivory-tower elite, Lenin agreed, but it appears that the constant connection with the proletariat he called for was not to be so much for the sake of nourishing the party on new ideas and challenges as to provide an avenue whereby the right answer already possessed by the party could be transmitted to the masses.

Lenin's excursions into the theory of the dialectic are but shallow dips that season the essentially practical argument:

... the great Hegelian dialectics which Marxism made its own, having first turned it right side up again, must never be confused with the vulgar trick of justifying the zigzags of politicians who swing over from the revolutionary wing to the opportunist wing of the Party. ... Genuine dialectics does not justify individual errors, but studies the inevitable turns, proving that they were inevitable by a detailed study of the process in all its concreteness. The basic principle of dialectics is that there is no such thing as abstract truth, truth is always concrete. ... [10]

The principle of the "negation of the negation" was used to explain how, in the Second Party Congress, majorities become minorities and vice versa, and the offensive position became the defensive position.[11] But the underlying circularity of Lenin's reasoning is never overcome, for the right side in the struggles that make up this inevitable process is ultimately defined as the side represented by the Party, and the Party is that faction of the Social Democrats led by Lenin. Despite his praise of concreteness, Lenin could not even accept revolutionary success as a test of rightness:

... there are revolutions which are more like reaction. ... We must know whether it was a revolutionary wing or the opportunist wing of the Party which was the actual force that made the revolution, we must know whether it was revolutionary or opportunist principles that inspired the fighters, before we can determine whether the "world" (our Party) was moved forward or backward by any concrete revolution.[12]

10 *One Step Forward, Two Steps Back*, sec. R, in *The Essentials of Lenin* (London: Lawrence & Wishart, 1927). Vol. I, pp. 344-45.

11 Lenin was no doubt recalling the crucial 28-to-22 defeat he suffered in the Second Party Congress concerning what seemed to many a minor difference with Menshevik Martov over the broad versus the narrow definition of party membership. To the detached observer, Lenin's reversal of this trend seems much more a matter of his own tenacity and cleverness and not a few "zigzags," than an inevitable process.

12 *One Step Forward, Two Steps Back*, p. 345.

How truly revolutionary principles may be distinguished from merely opportunist principles never becomes clear. Indeed, given a dedication to "concreteness," it is not clear how principles enter into the matter at all.

The last monograph worth mentioning that belongs to this period and this genre is *Two Tactics of Social Democracy in the Democratic Revolution* (1905). This work was addressed to the difficult problem of the relationship between the bourgeois revolution and the proletarian revolution as applied to backward Russia. There were two basic positions, as we have seen above, on the nature of the party. There were three basic positions on the nature of the forthcoming revolution.[13] The Mensheviks were closest to Marxian orthodoxy, believing that a proletarian revolution would have to wait until an authentic bourgeois revolution had occurred. They recognized that the proletariat in Russia was nowhere near a majority and in no position to take over the government. The Social Democratic Party, they felt, should stay out of any provisional government. Trotsky and his followers felt, on the other hand, that the bourgeois and proletarian revolutions could be telescoped into one. The weak Russian middle class could manage no revolution on its own. Socialist-proletarian leadership would have to make a "bourgeois" revolution that almost simultaneously would become the proletarian revolution. This was Trotsky's "permanent revolution" predicted on the basis of his own inventive modification on Marx, the "law of combined development," as he called it.

Lenin's was a shifting, intermediate position. "In formulae, Lenin sounded much like the Mensheviks; in spirit he was forever attracted to the Trotskyist pole."[14] Ironically, as Trotsky had warned Lenin of the dangers of factional dictatorship and the need for democracy within the party in 1904, Lenin was warning Trotsky of the dangers of party dictatorship (though not put in these words) and the need for democracy within the state in 1905. Lenin's uncertainty is revealed in the *Two Tactics*. The question, he says, is not whether there will be a revolution, but whether the party can "put a proletarian imprint" on it in order to overcome the "half-heartedness and treachery" of the democratic bourgeoisie. Should the work of the party in the present moment emphasize organizing trade unions and educating the masses, or should it move im-

13 See Wolfe, *Three Who Made a Revolution*, pp. 289ff.
14 *Ibid.*, p. 291. The theory of "permanent revolution" was a joint product of Trotsky and his friend and mentor, Parvus (Alexander L. Gelfand), though the concept was used by Marx in his *Address to the Communist League* (1850). Implying as it did the necessity of sustaining an ever-expanding network of revolutions around the world, it became anathema to Stalin, whose idea of "socialism in one country" was a useful shibboleth in the expedient persecution of Trotsky.

mediately to the building up of a revolutionary army? Both are necessary, says Lenin, and seems to hedge. But the weight of his remarks is clearly on the side of moving rapidly ahead with militant organization and action so that the bourgeoisie will not be able to stop the revolution short of socialist goals. To this end, Lenin focuses the whole monograph on the proper formulation of "correct tactical slogans" in order to keep the revolution on the right track and keep the initiative in the hands of the Bolsheviks.

The essence of the tactics proposed was a deft management of a simultaneous attraction-repulsion effort. The peasantry was to be attracted, for the Bolsheviks needed an ally if they were to be successful in this not-yet-industrialized country. The repulsion was directed to the liberal bourgeois democrats who were not to be trusted with the leadership of the revolution, even though, in one sense, it was their revolution:

Marxism has irrevocably broken with the ravings of the Narodniks and the anarchists to the effect that Russia, for instance, can avoid capitalist development, jump out of capitalism, or skip over it, along some path other than the path of the class struggle on the basis and within the framework of this same capitalism. . . . the idea of seeking salvation for the working class in anything save the further development of capitalism is *reactionary*. In countries like Russia, the working class suffers not so much from capitalism as from the insufficient development of capitalism. . . . The bourgeois revolution is precisely a revolution which sweeps away the survivals of the past, the remnants of serfdom (which include not only autocracy but monarchy as well) and which most fully guarantees the broadest, freest and most rapid development of capitalism.

That is why a bourgeois revolution is *in the highest degree advantageous to the proletariat*. A bourgeois revolution is *absolutely* necessary in the interests of the proletariat. The more complete, determined and consistent the bourgeois revolution, the more assured will be the proletarian struggle against the bourgeoisie for Socialism. Such a conclusion will appear new, or strange or paradoxical only to those who are ignorant of the rudiments of scientific Socialism.[15]

Since Marxism prescribed that the bourgeois revolution precede the socialist revolution, Lenin was stuck with the sequence. But he was determined not to let the bourgeois manage such a bourgeois revolution. Some would call this brilliant theorizing. Others would call it ideological rationalizing. Still others would say Lenin wanted to eat his cake and have it, too. The amazing thing is that he did.

15 *Two Tactics of Social Democracy*, sec. 6, in *The Essentials of Lenin*, Vol. I, p. 376. Italics in original.

Imperialism

FOLLOWING his formulation of a new and more crucial role for the party as the "vanguard of the proletariat," Lenin made a second major contribution to Marxist theory in *Imperialism, The Highest Stage of Capitalism,* written in Zurich in the spring of 1916. In a preface to the Russian edition of 1917, Lenin complained about the need to write in 1916 "in that cursed Aesopian language" of indirection and allusion necessary to get by the Czarist censors. "It is very painful, in these days of liberty, to read these cramped passages . . . , crushed, as they seem, in an iron vise, distorted on account of the censor."[16] In the text he gives Japan as an example of how "social-chauvinist deserters . . . lie on the question on annexations," but in the preface he says he was really talking about Russia.

Like Lenin's other writings, *Imperialism* was a *pièce d'occasion,* but such was his skill that he could write a work of compelling directness that also spoke to several different problems simultaneously. Lenin was explaining World War I in the light of Marxist doctrine ("I proved that the war of 1914-18 was imperialistic."). He was explaining how it was possible during the war for workers in belligerent countries to abandon the cause of the proletariat in a mood of patriotic nationalism. He was attacking the "revisionist" theories of former ally Karl Kautsky (and, in passing, scoring thrusts against leaders of labor in various countries: Otto Bauer in Austria, Ramsay MacDonald in England, Samuel Gompers in the United States).

Lenin's primary task was to account for the refusal of workers to put class above country. Although Lenin was capable of becoming technical at times, the heart of his argument was quite simple: a handful of states, less than one tenth of the world's population, "very rich and very powerful," were plundering the whole world "simply by clipping coupons." Out of "such enormous super-profits" drawn off colonial lands over and above what is made by the exploitation of workers in their home country, "it is quite *possible to bribe* the labour leaders and the upper stratum of the labour aristocracy." Capitalists "bribe them in a thousand different ways, direct and indirect, overt and covert."[17]

Imperialism is loaded with statistics demonstrating the growing concentration of productive facilities in the hands of a few, the sharp increase in the export of capital abroad, and the economic division of the world

16 *Imperialism, The Highest Stage of Capitalism* (new rev. trans.; New York: International Publishers, 1939), p. 7.

17 *Ibid.,* pp. 13-14.

into cartels by the political division of the world into areas ruled by a few great powers. Above all, Lenin emphasized that old-fashioned bank capital had more and more been merged with industrial capital to create what he called "finance capital," the control of which, as symbolized by the J. P. Morgan interests, led to new and hitherto undreamed-of power.

Much of this had already been described by non-Marxist scholars, foremost of whom was the English economist J. A. Hobson (a "bourgeois social reformer" from Lenin's view), whose *Imperialism* had been published in 1902. Lenin at least gave him a reasonable share of the credit. The real issue as far as Lenin was concerned was how this development was to be interpreted within the framework of the Marxist world view. Hence, Lenin was far more vituperative in discussing Kautsky, with whom he shared basic theoretical positions, than he was in discussing Hobson, who was, presumably, beyond saving. Lenin accused Kautsky not of failing to see the facts, but of failing to see what they meant. Kautsky, according to Lenin, saw the expansion of finance capital around the world as a matter of national policy by which more advanced nations annexed less advanced countries. Lenin saw this process not simply as a matter of governmental policy but as a necessary stage of capitalist development, an inexorable phase of the Marxist dialectic.

In a 1919 article Kautsky had defined imperialism as "the striving of every industrial capitalist nation to bring under its control and to annex increasingly big *agrarian* regions. . . ."[18] Lenin, in a 1920 preface, is enraged by this seemingly innocuous definition. "Kautsky's definition is not only wrong and un-Marxian. It serves as a basis for a whole system of views which run counter to Marxian theory and Marxian practice all along the line." It is "a mockery of historical concreteness."[19] It seems that to emphasize the acquisition of agrarian areas by industrial states is to minimize unduly the inevitable conflict between industrial states and to overlook the forces driving them to absorb one another. Kautsky, claims Lenin, does not see that industrial states are inexorably led to devour one another and hence that World War I had to come. Kautsky is also charged with the failure to attach sufficient significance to the new dominance of the financier over the producer and merchant (although in fact Kautsky did recognize the role of finance capital).

Because, from his viewpoint, imperialism is only one and not the

18 Quoted in *Imperialism*, p. 91.
19 *Imperialism*, p. 92. To the end, Kautsky adhered to the basic tenets of Marxism: historical materialism, the concentration of capital, class struggle, and the rest; but he argued cogently against the necessity or desirability of violent revolution. The revolution could and should come through democratic processes, he maintained. After the Bolshevik Revolution, Kautsky became an outspoken critic of Soviet autocracy.

essential policy of modern capitalism, Kautsky thought the world might see an era of "ultra-imperialism" in which the big powers unite peacefully for the sake of joint exploitation. Lenin cannot abide "Kautsky's silly little fable about 'peaceful' ultra-imperialism. This is not the reactionary attempt of a frightened philistine to hide from stern reality?"[20] In short, there *must* be wars and capitalism *must* be the cause.

International war was in this way made to be a kind of substitute for inevitable internal revolution in those countries where the internal revolution that Marx predicted seemed less and less likely to occur. In England, contrary to every prophecy based upon Marxist tenets, the standard of living was rising. But Lenin was able to note that both immigration into and emigration out of England were declining, in effect contributing even among English working people themselves to a sense of being a privileged class because they were members of a privileged nation. The bribery earlier referred to now becomes understandable. It was the seduction of the workers into a kind of proletarian bourgeoisie by virtue of their participation in the exploitation of less fortunate brethren overseas. The explanation is ingenious and not without a certain amount of truth. The sense of national superiority in workers and especially civil servants was an essential part of nineteenth- and early twentieth-century imperialism. Lenin managed to find three letters of Engels that commented upon the special bourgeois attitudes of English workers, so it was possible to invoke the blessing of the highest—or next to the highest—authority to bolster Lenin's orthodoxy.

Lenin's fighting spirit carries through on every page. He concludes *Imperialism* like a football coach speaking to his team or a general admonishing his troops. Those people are "dangerous," he says, who do not understand that the "fight against imperialism is a sham and humbug unless it is inseparably bound up with the fight against opportunism."[21] To Lenin, neglect of the war against capitalism on either the home front or the foreign front, or the attempt to make it less warlike, was opportunism.

The State and the Dictatorship of the Proletariat

THE third theoretical contribution of Lenin was his handling of the transition period between capitalism and communism and the role of the state in this transition period. We have already seen to what extent the party was the center of all decision-making power during this transition, but not until *State and Revolution* (1917), was it clear to what ex-

20 *Ibid.,* p. 96.   21 *Ibid.,* p. 126.

tent the state was identified by Lenin with coercive power and regarded as a transitional institution that would disappear once the revolution was fully consummated. Indeed, *State and Revolution* stands in some degree of isolation from Lenin's thought both before and after its writing.

In this work the party as a causal force is scarcely mentioned. Lenin speaks, rather, of the necessity of smashing the bourgeois state in order that power may be not so much transferred as eliminated. Following Engels, Lenin portrays the elimination of the state as the elimination of coercion of man over man. Government gives way to the administration of "things," and the working people are set free. *State and Revolution* represents a sharp swing to the left by Lenin, partly at least due to the influence of N. I. Bukharin during the winter of 1916-17.[22] A swing to the left meant a swing to utopian categories. A strong factor affecting the tone of this book was the imminence of the Revolution itself, which forced Lenin to turn from thoughts of undercover revolutionary activity to questions of what happens after revolutions. His answers were fairly unoriginal as well as being utopian. He apparently consulted in some haste Engels' *Origin of the Family* and Marx's *Critique of the Gotha Program*, for he repeated many of their vague postrevolutionary formulations.

The ostensible purpose of *State and Revolution* was to "*resuscitate* the real teachings of Marx on the state." Mainly on the basis of Engels' *Origin of the Family*, Lenin concludes that "the state is a product and the manifestation of the *irreconcilability* of class antagonisms. The state arises when, where and to the extent that the class antagonisms *are* irreconcilable.[23] There are, to Lenin's way of thinking, two distortions of this truth about the state, one gross and one subtle. The gross distortion is that of "petty-bourgeois politicians" who see that the state brings about order but cannot see that it does so only by suppressing class antagonisms. The subtle distortion is that of Kautsky and the "Kautskyists" who are said to gloss over the implications of the doctrine that the state is an instrument for the suppression of class antagonisms, namely, that the apparatus of state power is necessarily so contaminated by its function of suppression that after the revolution the apparatus itself must be destroyed. Even the institution of universal suffrage shares in this contamination and must be destroyed. Lenin simply postulates that it is a "wrong idea that universal suffrage 'in the *modern* state' is really capable of expressing the will of the majority of the toilers and of assuring its realization."[24]

22 See Robert V. Daniels, "*State and Revolution:* A Case Study in the Genesis and Transformation of Communist Ideology," *American Slavic and Eastern European Review*, Vol. 12 (1953), pp. 22-43.

23 *State and Revolution* (New York: International Publishers, 1932), p. 8.

24 *Ibid.*, p. 14.

Lenin must reconcile this position with the famous statement of Engels in *Anti-Dühring* that "The state is not 'abolished,' it *withers away*." The popular conception of this is "the crudest distortion," says Lenin. What Engels really means is that the proletarian semi-state, the "special repressive force" that takes over in the transition period, withers away. The bourgeois state, the real state, is "done away with" by the revolution.

In place of the bourgeois state, the "dictatorship of the bourgeois," we shall find the well-known "dictatorship of the proletariat." But by contrast with its earlier identifications with the party, Lenin here curiously omits mention of the party and speaks of the political rule of the proletariat as "power shared with none and relying directly upon the armed forces of the masses."[25] But shortly thereafter there is a passage that sounds like the Lenin of old, in which the party as the vanguard is seen as "leading the whole people to Socialism" and acting as "teacher, guide, and leader of all the toiling and exploited."[26]

Considering the fierce realism of his conspiratorial activities, it comes as a surprise to find Lenin as utopian and as anarchistic as he appears to be in *State and Revolution*. He states that the growth of literacy and the training and discipline required in an industrialized society have already created the conditions whereby the whole mass of the people can govern themselves, since most of the functions of an industrialized society are mechanical and routine:

It is perfectly possible, immediately, within twenty-four hours after the overthrow of the capitalists and the bureaucrats, to replace them, in the control of production and distribution, in the business of *control* of labour and products, by the armed workers, by the whole people in arms. (The question of control and accounting must not be confused with the question of the scientifically educated staff of engineers, agronomists, and so on. These gentlemen work today, obeying the capitalists; they will work even better tomorrow, obeying the armed workers.) . . . *All* citizens become employees and workers on *one* national state "syndicate." All that is required is that they should work equally, should regularly do their share of work, and should receive equal pay. The accounting and control necessary for this have been *simplified* by capitalism to the utmost, till they have become the extraordinarily simple operations of watching, recording and issuing receipts, within the reach of anybody who can read and write and knows the first four rules of arithmetic. . . . The whole society will have become one office and one factory, with equal work and equal pay.[27]

This vision of technocratic paradise seems to us absurdly simple and romantic, somewhat like the quaint Victorian narratives of Edward

25 *Ibid.,* p. 23.   26 *Ibid.,* p. 24.   27 *Ibid.,* pp. 83-84.

Bellamy. Surely Lenin could not have believed all this; surely he must have been writing consciously hypocritical pap for the consumption of emotionally volatile revolutionaries; surely he could not place so much trust in the people as to think that an armed and unfettered mass of them would be models of decorum.

We underestimate the power of the nineteenth-century faith in industrial progress if we do not concede that Lenin could very well have believed some of this nonsense. If we think back on Owen, Fourier, Comte, and many others, we recall a similar faith that the right organization of society would liberate an essentially good human nature and that scientific management would virtually eliminate the need for the hard moral choices among competing alternatives that we call politics. The difference between Lenin and the other utopians was that, partly because of his own propensities and partly because of historic circumstances, he found himself with a government to run and could not in the long run remain content with simple formulas.

Conclusion

LENIN demonstrates at once the forces of ideas and their weaknesses. Less paradoxically, we can say that Lenin demonstrates the instrumental but not the substantial force of ideas. Because he was skillful with words, because he could sniff out the crux of a factional dispute and neatly fit the Marxist categories to his own position, we can call him a theorist of influence. But inasmuch as he failed to push beyond the urgent to the enduring issue, failed to construct a standard of governmental reality and purpose of truly general applicability, he was no theorist at all.

The development of Marxism since Lenin has not been much more auspicious. Once Marxists gained massive blocs of political power they made of Marxism an orthodoxy hardly stimulating to creative thought. Even in countries far removed from the Kremlin the weight of this orthodoxy could be felt, in large part because its institutionalization transformed Marxism into a creedal religion. At the same time the hostility of traditional institutions to Marxism made it a religion embroiled in a political fight, and from our own experience it is easy to conclude that political fights over religion are not conducive to philosophical creativity.

One thing Lenin accomplished was to create a tradition of "theorist leaders," which dictated that Stalin should be known as a theorist even though in many regards he was the antithesis of the man of thought. So from his pen, or those of his ghostwriters, came Stalin's *Marxism and the*

National and Colonial Questions, written before the Revolution; *Dialetical Materialism,* written as part of the official history of the Communist Party published in the mid-thirties; and *The Foundations of Leninism* (1924). These works, primerlike in tone, now stand as useful guides to some of the inarticulate preconceptions of the Marxist, but as theory are anemic. In China in the 1920's and after, Mao Tse-tung, with a more facile mind than Stalin's, took up the old Marxist problems and tried to fit them to a feudal agrarian society even less developed than Russia.[28]

In underdeveloped countries the appeal of Lenin, especially in those of his writings that justify the simultaneous existence of capitalist and socialist institutions, is not so much due to his intrinsic merits as a theorist as to the usefulness of his thought in meeting the psychological demand for rebellion against colonial institutions. Paradoxically, the most backward nations economically have become the most "advanced" agencies of "proletarian class consciousness."

Marxism is a product of the industrial age, and all its ideas about society arise from an acceptance of the machine as the most basic fact of modern life. At the same time, it is radically critical of the social institutions and relationships of the industrial age. Transformed into the theory of imperialism, this ambivalence toward industrial capitalism turns into an ambivalence toward the West, and this mixture of hostility and admiration develops naturally among politically conscious men in underdeveloped areas. In espousing Leninism, such men can advocate a program of westernization without abandoning their hatred and fear of the West.[29]

Perhaps no better demonstration of the distinction between ideology and theory could be advanced than this use of a theory of advanced industrialism as a rationale for nationalist revolt.

28 See Mao Tse-tung, *Let a Hundred Flowers Bloom* (1957), reprinted as a special supplement to the *New Leader,* Vol. 40 (Sept. 9, 1957), sec. 2; Benjamin I. Schwartz, *Chinese Communism and the Rise of Mao* (Cambridge: Harvard Univ. Press, 1951).

29 Alfred G. Meyer, *Leninism* (Cambridge: Harvard Univ. Press, 1956), p. 267. See also David G. Smith, "Lenin's Imperialism: a Study in the Unity of Theory and Practice," *Journal of Politics,* Vol. 17 (1955), pp. 546-69.

CHAPTER

17 | *Dewey*

JOHN DEWEY has often been called a typical American with a typically American philosophy. How typical he or his philosophy were may be questioned, but he was one of the first scholars to get a Doctor of Philosophy degree in the United States and one of the last native philosophers to have a widespread public reputation.

Life

HE WAS born and educated in Vermont, and got out as soon as he could, as he later told a friend, displaying a certain earthiness that Americans like to think is typical. The year of his birth was 1859, the year of Marx's *Critique of Political Economy,* Mill's "On Liberty," Darwin's *Origin of Species,* and the birth of Henri Bergson and Havelock Ellis. Nothing close to home foreshadowed the distinction that was later to come to John Dewey. His father ran a general store in Burlington. As a boy, John delivered newspapers, worked in a lumber yard, and made an unexceptional record in the local grammar and high schools. Even after entering the University of Vermont at the age of fifteen, Dewey did not give promise of great academic prowess until his senior year, when Thomas Huxley's physiology textbook aroused his interest in science and jarred his complacency by creating concern for the supposed conflict between revealed religion and scientific method. Dewey received his Bachelor's degree at the University, then taught high school in Pennsylvania and in a country school in Vermont. Meanwhile he was reading philosophy, ever more voraciously. His first published journal article came out the year he entered The John Hopkins University to begin work on the doctorate. It was entitled "The Metaphysical Assumptions of Materialism." Two years later, in 1884, he had his degree and was off to the University of Michigan as a young instructor.

After a year at the University of Minnesota in 1888, Dewey returned to Michigan as head of the department of philosophy. In 1895 President Harper asked him to come to the newly established University of Chicago to head the departments of philosophy, psychology, and education. With the help of Mrs. Dewey he there established what later would be famous as the Experimental or Laboratory School, starting progressive education on its long and controversial career. The University was not as happy as the Deweys over their experiment, and in 1904 Dewey resigned to go to Columbia as professor of philosophy, a post he held until his retirement in 1930.

Before his death in 1952 at the venerable age of ninety-two, Dewey had written more than thirty books, and had worked on behalf of many liberal political causes. His name had become widely known for his advocacy of child-centered, democratic, nonformal education. He spoke out against the conviction of Sacco and Vanzetti. He worked in the League for Industrial Democracy and supported the American Civil Liberties Union. He helped found the Liberal Party of New York and the New School for Social Research. In 1937, at the age of seventy-eight, he went to Mexico to investigate the guilt of Leon Trotsky, who had been exiled there by a Soviet tribunal. As a result of his investigations, he roundly denounced the Soviet government, upon whose experiments he had at one time looked with considerable interest. In 1941, along with several others, he produced an angry defense of Bertrand Russell against the bigots who kept him out of The College of the City of New York.

At Johns Hopkins, studying under G. S. Morris, Dewey was introduced to Hegel. The latter's opposition to dualism, his emphasis on process and the historical approach to knowledge, had immediate appeal for Dewey, and Hegel's influence remained with him all his life, despite his specific rejection of the Hegelian dialectic early in his career. At the same time, the down-to-earth, problem-solving orientation of what came to be called instrumentalism led Santayana to regard Dewey as typifying the spirit of modern industrial enterprise. Dewey never cared much for this description. And, indeed, Dewey's challenge to tradition included a departure from traditional American thought, even though the spirit of his antiphilosophical philosophy indubitably was American to the core.

Antiformalism

DEWEY was a leader in what Morton White has called the "revolt against formalism," expressed not only in philosophy by Dewey but in law by Holmes, in history by Beard and Robinson, in economics by Veblen. On the theoretical level the revolt was hostile both to the scientific rigidities of British empiricism and to the dogmatic abstractions of traditional metaphysics. On the political level the revolt was directed against the excessively legalistic interpretations of American political society characteristic of the late nineteenth century.

The central theme of the revolt, and especially Dewey's part in it, was growth. Dewey is said to have said that the statement in *Reconstruction in Philosophy*, "Growth itself is the only moral end," was central to his whole intellectual life.[1] There was in this emphasis a good bit of Hegelian process and Darwinist natural selection. It is not irrelevant that Dewey was a youthful admirer of Hegel and that one of his early books was entitled *The Influence of Darwin on Philosophy* (1910). By lifting Social Darwinism out of the realms of atomistic competition and adapting it to the idea of problem-solving communities, Dewey was able to transform it from an ideology of laissez faire to an ideology of the welfare state.

At the level of epistemology, this processual emphasis led to the substitution of the concept of "inquiry" for that of "truth." "Inquiry," wrote Dewey in his best known epistemological work, *Logic: The Theory of Inquiry*, "is the controlled or directed transformation of an indeterminate situation into one that is so determinate in its constituent distinctions and relations as to convert the elements of the original situation into a unified whole."[2] Bertrand Russell, whose epistemological realism always put him at odds with Dewey in these matters, commented snidely that this definition would fit a bricklayer converting a pile of bricks into a wall. Russell, representing a correspondence theory of truth, was interested at getting at the reality of the facts "out there," which were assumed to exist independently of the observer. Dewey, representing a coherence theory of truth, was interested in the mutual adjustment between an organism and its environment; this relationship, rather than something wholly outside the observer, or, for that matter, wholly within him, was the basic factor to be considered. The test of any proposition was the consequence of following it. This is what gave it "warranted assertability," not something more ultimate or unchange-

[1] Cited by James T. Farrell in Corliss Lamont, ed., *Dialogue on Dewey* (New York: Horizon Press, 1959), p. 53.
[2] *Logic: The Theory of Inquiry* (New York: Holt, 1939), pp. 104-05.

ably real. "An idea is true so long as it is profitable to our lives," said William James (1842–1910), who had an unfortunate habit of using monetary metaphors. Dewey preferred not to use the word truth at all, but rather "inquiry." The quest for certainty, he often said, was incompatible with the self-corrective process of scientific method. When the indeterminate situation has been transformed into a determinate situation, inquiry is simply terminated. This is as close to knowledge (or "warranted assertability") as we can get.

The revolt against formalism, the new emphasis upon process, adjustment, problem-solving, indeterminacy—or, better, always provisional determinacy—that we associate with Dewey had its most conspicuous impact in the rejection of a good many traditional philosophic dichotomies, among them theory-practice, percept-concept, learning-doing. We shall look especially at four: subject-object; value-fact; past-present; individual-society.

Subject and Object

MUCH of Dewey's position on subjective-objective relationship and indeed much of his whole technical philosophy came from Charles Sanders Peirce (1839–1914; pronounced "purse"), now generally credited with being the founder of pragmatism, although during his lifetime he was little known. Peirce held a university chair only briefly and published no books in his lifetime; his thought is contained in a vast and exceedingly diverse array of journal articles, most of which were published in six volumes by Harvard University in 1931. His 1877 paper "How To Make Our Ideas Clear" attracted little attention until William James made much of it in a lecture at the University of California in 1898. After some of his ideas were picked up and distorted, Peirce publicly denounced "pragmatism" and coined "pragmaticism," a term, he said, "ugly enough to be safe from kidnappers."

In the essay "How To Make Our Ideas Clear" Peirce attacks Leibnitz's method of abstract definition and Descartes' a priori appeal to self-evidence. One does not learn anything new, he argues, simply by refining and analyzing definitions. In the past, philosophers have mainly disputed meanings, and have been led into nothing but disagreement. Scientists conduct investigations rather than disputations, and their method has led to wider and wider areas of agreement. This, then, is the course that philosophers ought to follow. The rationalist conception of "true ideas" as some kind of "mind stuff" is useless. With such a method there is an inevitable confusion between that which seems clear subjectively and that which *is* clear objectively. By focusing on the consequences of an idea or concept this dilemma is overcome. Hence the "pragmatic maxim" formulated by Peirce: "Consider what effects, which might conceivably have practical bearings, we conceive the object of our conception to have. Then, our conception of these effects is the whole of our conception of the object."[3]

It is important to note that this emphasis upon effects as the test of validity had little in common with the merely "practical" in the sense of the expedient, that which is conducive to success. Some of Peirce's friends wanted him to call his methodology "practicalism" but he vigorously repudiated the implication. The Kantian terms *praktisch* and *pragmatisch*, observed Peirce, "were as far apart as the two poles," the latter referring to controlled, purposeful experimental observation.[4] William James was largely responsible for the materialist overtones given some of the tenets of pragmatism, and this more by inadvertence than by intent.

Pragmatism tended to lead away from concern for the problem of subjectivity and objectivity. The concepts in themselves were of course abstract and could be placed in the catalogue of empty symbols of the past such as mind and matter and substance. But in fact, the pragmatists, Dewey as well as Peirce, could be said to have evaded the old problem simply by assuming that out of observation, experiment, and an operational orientation the agreement of observers would emerge.

Facts and Values

PRAGMATISM was also an assault upon the dichotomy between facts and values. It is important to note that this union of the is and the ought was quite different from the comparable union in the natural-law tradition. There, reason liberated from the drag of appetite and passion was assumed to be capable of glimpsing the nature of ultimate reality, which included a simultaneous vision of the good and the true. Dewey and the pragmatists, as we have seen, made no such assumption about universal goodness or universal truth. Dewey, like Hume, believed thought was stimulated by the nonintellectual side of man. Moreover, there is no "Good" or "True," only goods and truths that are invariably relative to a particular historical situation. Dewey was a thoroughgoing "con-

---

3 *Values in a Universe of Chance, Selected Writings of Charles S. Peirce*, Philip Wiener, ed., (New York: Doubleday [Anchor Books], 1958), p. 124.
4 "What Pragmatism Is" (1905), in *Values in a Universe of Chance*, p. 183.

textualist." Neglect of the historic situation, the concrete problem at hand, in pursuit of a standard supposedly set by pure, abstract reason is, he thought, illusory and dangerous. He sought always to serve "ends in view" rather than ends so exalted as to be out of view.

In a practical way, there is much to recommend this attitude. It is the pragmatist's contention that intellectual and social conflicts are unarbitrable if the arguer on each side—or for that matter on only one side—of a dispute asserts that his position stems from a true perception of reality, or if he asserts, in a manner consistent with the emotive-imperative school of ethics, that his position stems from a wholly subjective emotion that can have no rational defense. The logic of either position, the pragmatist argues, is that social disputes can be settled only by violence or superior power, since genuine conciliation requires a modification of the values of both sides. The pragmatic alternative is to apply the test of a critical examination of the probable consequences of proposed policies, and let the needs of each ongoing situation, as determined by scientific methodology, decide the best policy.

. . . the idea of actively adopting experimental method in social affairs, in the matters deemed of most enduring and ultimate worth, strikes most persons as a surrender of all standards and regulative authority. But in principle, experimental method does not dignify random and aimless action; it implies direction by ideas and knowledge. . . .

Where will regulation come from if we surrender familiar and traditionally prized values as our directive standards? Very largely from the findings of the natural sciences. . . . a moral that frames its judgments on value on the basis of consequences must depend in a most intimate manner upon the conclusions of science. For the knowledge of the relations between changes which enable us to connect things as antecedents and consequences *is* science. . . .

Another great difference to be made by carrying the experimental habit into all matter of practice is that it cuts the roots of what is often called subjectivism, but which is better termed egoism.[5]

The critic may well ask: Can social conflicts really be expected to wait until all the evidence is in? In the face of ambiguity will not decisions have to be made upon the basis of the subjective—or objective—standards of the participants, and are these not in every case assertions of what they feel to be ultimately important? To this Dewey would undoubtedly say that since the truly ultimate cannot in any case be reached with certainty, it is not necessary to pursue problems that far. Consensus on the desirability of certain consequences over other consequences can hold for the

5 *The Quest for Certainty* (New York: Minton, Balch, 1929), pp. 273-74.

sake of solving a particular concrete problem about which all are agreed, after which we all move on to the next problem requiring solution. This may, in fact, be the way society tends to deal with its problems, whether or not it is scientific about the determination of consequences. But this method must be regarded as an evasion of the question above, which turns on the validity of one's grounds for moral choice in the face of ambiguity —perhaps the inevitable condition of moral choice.

Dewey was conscious of the problem and recognized the need for some kind of ethical theory to bridge the gap between what is desired (which might include "the free play of impulse") and what ought to be desired. "The fact that something is desired only raises the *question* of its desirability," wrote Dewey, "it does not settle it."[6] He proposed the application of scientific tests to help people determine if what they seemed to desire was what they really desired. In the last analysis, however, he was still forced to equate the desirable with the desired, the flaw in all naturalistic theories of ethics. Dewey did not wish to be simply a naturalist in ethics. He did not wish to recognize raw emotion as a self-validating source of value. Neither could he honestly hope to eliminate emotion from values. What he hoped to do was purify values by subjecting them to a rigorous test of consequential relevance. He put his faith, then, more in a process of handling values than he did in any particular acknowledged value. He never did, indeed never tried to, work out a hierarchy of scientifically approved values. The pragmatic orientation to values is as opposed to hierarchies of values as it is to the dichotomy between facts and values.

Most conflicts of importance are conflicts between things which are or have been satisfying, not between good and evil. And to suppose that we can make a hierarchical table of values at large for once and for all, a kind of catalogue in which they are arranged in an order of ascending or descending worth, is to indulge in a gloss on our inability to frame intelligent judgments in the concrete. Or else it is to dignify customary choice and prejudice by a title of honor.[7]

Dewey is never willing to say what values we should follow, because he does not believe that valid values can be meaningfully expressed in the abstract. He gives us, rather, a method for the refinement and improvement and validation of whatever values presently exist, or will exist in the concrete situation to which the method will be applied. The method is, of course, the method of Deweyan "inquiry" already referred to. Perhaps the only abstract value Dewey explicitly assumes is "intellectual honesty." Beyond that, he says, "inquiry should follow the lead of subject

6 *Ibid.*, p. 260.   7 *Ibid.*, p. 266.

matter." But, in general, it can be said that this is the experimental, scientific method. ". . . an idea [we could as well substitute "value"] in experiment is tentative, conditional, not fixed and rigorously determinative. It controls any action to be performed, but the consequences of the operation determine the worth of the directive idea; the latter does not fix the nature of the object."[8]

In the phraseology of his critic Morton White,[9] Dewey recognizes that "X is desired" is not a synonym for "X is desirable." But in the long run he comes out with a position by which "X is desirable" *is* the equivalent of "X is desired under normal conditions" where normal conditions suggest full and rational reflection on the causes and consequences of the particular act in question. In this way, says White, the factual statement slips confusingly over into the normative statement, somewhat in the manner of traditional natural-law theories: *de facto* becomes *de jure.*

Sidney Hook, a defender of Dewey, contends that this is not a careless slip, but a significant move. White, he says, tries to put Dewey's dynamic, concrete analysis into static and abstract terms. The *de facto* becomes *de jure,* the desired becomes the desirable, not by abstract rationalization of its consequences, but by being rationally examined in a context of actual choice, a context which can never be fully anticipated. "The normative element in the conclusion is in a sense provided by that which distinguishes the situation as a practical one from one that is purely logical or theoretical. The underlying premise is: that should be done which appropriately meets the needs and requirements of the situation, broadly conceived to include the demands and expectations of the community or traditions in which we find ourselves."[10]

From this excellent statement of the pragmatic position in ethics we may draw several not altogether reassuring conclusions. (1) In repeatedly deferring to the "needs" of a not-yet-arrived "situation" the issue of the ground of moral choice is evaded rather than met. Perhaps this is only to say that one cannot make a satisfactory abstract ethical statement demonstrating that ethical statements can never be abstract. (2) When asked what the needs of some future situation might be, pragmatists usually defer to the "demands and expectations of the community or traditions in which we find ourselves." While they rarely draw this implication, such an approach can result in not merely a conservative bias but a frightfully

8 *Ibid.*, pp. 68, 288.

9 See Morton G. White, "Value and Obligation in Dewey and Lewis," *Philosophical Review*, Vol. 53 (1949), pp. 321-29; *Social Thought in America: The Revolt Against Formalism* (New York: Viking, 1949), Ch. 13.

10 Sidney Hook, "The Desirable and Emotive in Dewey's Ethics," in Sidney Hook, ed., *John Dewey, Philosopher of Science and Freedom, A Symposium* (New York: Dial Press, 1950), pp. 204-05.

reactionary position. Reason and scientific method become prisoners of the situation rather than masters of it.

An excursion into technical ethical theory may seem out of place in an examination of political theories; but Dewey's ethic is fundamental to his orientation toward public policy and, indeed, to the whole character of his influence. His was a profound rationale for avoiding profound moral discourse. It seemed to fit an optimistic nation more interested in doing than in thinking. Although their appearance is perhaps inconsistent with his noncommittalism, his desire to close no doors, his hope of bringing immediate, concrete empirical data into the very vortex of moral choice and keeping them there, certain constant values, abstractions if you will, do nevertheless emerge from Dewey's language. They include science, community, growth, education, liberalism, democracy, openness, freedom, "thinking which is operative." Some of these we shall examine later in this chapter.

Past and Present

ANOTHER dichotomy battered by the pragmatists was that between the past and the present. It is not surprising that, given a dynamic and wholly interrelational union of subject and object, value and fact, we find the past seen in the light of the present and the present seen in the light of the past. Like Charles A. Beard, Dewey believed that history is necessarily written from the standpoint of the present. At the same time, the validity of historical propositions could, he thought, be subjected to the same kind of evidential tests as any other kind of proposition. Indeed, history was regarded as but another medium of problem-solving, and "the writing of history is an instance of judgment as a resolution through inquiry of a problematical situation." Again, "That which is now past was once a living present, just as the now living present is already in course of becoming the past of another present. There is no history except in terms of movement toward some outcome, something taken as an issue, . . ." And finally, "history cannot escape its own process. It will therefore, always be rewritten. As the new present arises, the past is the past of a different present."[11]

The sense of fluidity and wholeness that characterizes other aspects of Dewey's thought is markedly apparent in his treatment of history. His view is best called contextualist, because he continually emphasizes the unity of history with other forms of inquiry, and recognizes that the his-

11 *Logic*, pp. 231, 238-39. See this same passage from the *Logic* reprinted in Hans Meyerhoff, ed., *The Philosophy of History in Our Time* (New York: Doubleday [Anchor Books], 1959), pp. 163-72, and the comment of Arthur O. Lovejoy upon it, pp. 173-87.

torian invariably plucks out of a mass of detail those facts that serve a present interest.

Individual and Society

THE Dewey-dissolved dichotomy most closely related to the subject matter of traditional political theory is that between the individual and society. No human mind, thought Dewey, could be completely known when separated from society.

The interaction of human beings, namely, association, is not different in origin from other modes of interaction. There is a peculiar absurdity in the question of how individuals become social, if the question is taken literally. Human beings illustrate the same traits of both immediate uniqueness and connection, relationship, as do other things. No more in their case than in that of atoms and physical masses is immediacy the whole of existence and therefore an obstacle to being acted upon by and effecting other things. Everything that exists in as far as it is known and knowable is in interaction with other things. It is associated, as well as solitary, single. The catching up of human individuals into association is thus no new and unprecedented fact; it is a manifestation of a commonplace of existence.[12]

Habits, upon which we depend for existence, are acquired functions that are picked up only through the medium of the surrounding social environment. "There are specific good reasons for the usual attribution of acts to the person from whom they immediately proceed. But to convert this special reference into a belief of exclusive ownership is as misleading as to suppose that breathing and digesting are complete within the human body. To get a rational basis for moral discussion we must begin with recognizing that functions and habits are ways of using and incorporating the environment in which the latter has its say as surely as the former."[13]

Although prior in time, instincts, or to use a term that Dewey preferred, impulses, were not prior in action, but secondary. For the social medium is what gives them meaning and direction. Take anger, for example. "Human displays of anger are not pure impulses; they are habits formed under the influence of association with others who have habits already and who show their habits in the treatment which converts blind physical discharge into a significant anger."[14] Hence, in a sense, virtually all psychology becomes for Dewey social psychology.

12 *Experience and Nature* (Chicago: Open Court Publishing Co., 1925), pp. 174-75.
13 *Human Nature and Conduct* (New York; Modern Library, 1930), p. 15.
14 *Ibid.*, p. 90.

At times there seems to be something almost Rousseauistic in Dewey's
conception of impulse shaped by a social medium. For while he placed a
higher value on society than did Rousseau, still he talked as if there were
a natural man encapsuled in a crust of social convention: ". . . there are
always intrinsic forces of a common human nature at work; forces which
are sometimes stifled by the encompassing social medium but which also
in the long course of history are always striving to liberate themselves
and to make over social institutions so that the latter may form a freer,
more transparent and more congenial medium for their operation."[15]
Dewey rejects with some vehemence theories of intuitional moral knowledge which set moral judgments against man's natural tendencies. There
is no "separate agent of moral knowledge" Dewey insists. Even the utilitarians were guilty of this error in trying to trace morality from sensations. Morality is not a set of fixed principles, or a faculty of mind, or a
dictate of innate and constant conscience. It is a matter of the adjustment
of the organism to the environment in such a way that what was formerly
a problem is no longer a problem. When Dewey comes at the question
from a different angle it would appear that intelligence likewise is the
process of satisfactory adjustment of an organism to its environment:

Deliberation needs every possible help it can get against the twisting, exag-
gerating and slighting tendency of passion and habit. To form the habit of
asking how we should be treated in a similar case—which is what Kant's
maxim amounts to—is to gain an ally for impartial and sincere deliberation
and judgment. It is a safeguard against our tendency to regard our own
case as exceptional in comparison with the cases of others. . . . Demand for
consistency, for "universality," far from implying a rejection of all consequences, is a demand to survey consequences broadly, to link effect to effect
in a chain of continuity. Whatever force works to this end *is* reason. For
reason, let it be repeated, is an outcome, a function, not a primitive force.[16]

Morality and intelligence, in other words, are, for all practical purposes,
synonyms.

Such a theory of morality and human nature necessarily puts a heavy
burden on the environment, for what is right for an individual would seem
to be determined by what is right in terms of a particular social environment. As we shall see, this conclusion has tremendous significance for
Dewey's views on education and politics and the relations between the
two. It also leads him to place a very high value on community as a
norm. He would not like this phraseology; but what else can one say in
contemplating, say, the final words of *Human Nature and Conduct*:
"Within the flickering inconsequential acts of separate selves dwells a

15 *Ibid.*, pp. viii-ix.   16 *Ibid.*, p. 247.

sense of the whole which claims and dignifies them. In its presence we put off mortality and live in the universal. The life of the community in which we live and have our being is the fit symbol of this relationship."[17] The phrasing is religious if not mystical, and the universal that Dewey has been so concerned to avoid comes lumbering up to attach itself to the social order, one is tempted to say *any* social order, though this would hardly be fair to Dewey's intent. Religionists, however, are either amused or irritated by seeing Dewey make the secular community a "fit symbol" of the universal. He gives no reason why it should be; indeed, he cannot, without throwing away the core of pragmatism.

Community

SINCE Dewey is unwilling (passages such as the above apart) to come down on either horn of the individual-society dilemma, it follows that communication, the means whereby individuals become a society and society shapes its individuals, is an especially important subject for him. The political aspects of this concern are displayed most tellingly in *The Public and Its Problems* (1927). Dewey begins by showing what fallacious quests most searches for a theory of the state have been. They have drawn us away from the facts and into a labyrinth of mythological constructions. Despite their variety, they all "spring from a root of shared error: the taking of causal agency instead of consequences as the heart of the problem." The fiction of the state has tended to be a mask for private ambition, and "society itself has been pulverized into an aggregate of unrelated wants and wills."[18] What the public is, or what the state (conceived as a public organized by officials) is, is a matter for empirical investigation, not abstract speculation.

Dewey proceeds to sketch the outlines of what constitutes the state on the basis of what he takes to be empirical evidence, but actually in a manner not much different from that of many "abstract" political theorists of the past. He then turns to the problem of the democratic state, which consists of finding a way for the public itself to make its weight felt in the determination of public policy. In practice this means overcoming the tendency for political power to be acquired by "accidental and irrelevant factors" and for officials to employ such power for private rather than public ends (any transactions "which affect others beyond those immediately concerned" are earlier referred to as public). Dewey establishes the fact of a greatly broadened range of public transactions in recent times by reference to the interdependence of modern industrial society, and

17 *Ibid.*, pp. 331-32.
18 *The Public and Its Problems* (Chicago: Gateway, 1946), pp. 20-21.

discusses "the enormous ineptitude of the individualistic philosophy [of Locke, Adam Smith, and the utilitarians] to meet the needs and direct the factors of the new age."[19] The primary need is to regain a sense of community: ". . . the machine age in developing the Great Society has invaded and partially disintegrated the small communities of former times without generating a Great Community." "Till the Great Society is converted into a Great Community, the Public will remain in eclipse. Communication can alone create a great community."[20]

Dewey is generally regarded as a theorist of democracy, or, which may not be quite the same, a democratic theorist. The appellation is not inappropriate. His repeated emphasis upon a fluid, adaptable, problem-solving community built out of the sinews of constant communication between individuals as citizens and officials as agents of the public, is little more than a description of a functioning democracy. But perhaps he gives the term more than it can carry. "Regarded as an idea, democracy is not an alternative to other principles of associated life. It is the idea of community life itself. . . . The clear consciousness of a communal life, in all its implications, constitutes the idea of democracy."[21] This sounds both ideal and idealistic, in the popular sense; but Dewey, as always, insists upon staying close to "the facts":

Only when we start from a community of fact, grasp the fact in thought so as to clarify and enhance its constituent elements, can we reach an idea of democracy which is not utopian. The conceptions and shibboleths which are traditionally associated with the idea of democracy take on a veridical and directive meaning only when they are construed as marks and traits of an association which realizes the defining characteristics of a community. Fraternity, liberty and equality isolated from communal life are hopeless abstractions.[22]

An adequate set of community symbols is necessary, Dewey feels, to transmute the "order of energies" that is a human association into the "order of meanings" that is a human community. Intelligence, in Dewey's sense of inquiry, and education were key factors in this transformation. One is tempted to see parallels between the community of symbols Dewey calls for and many of the mythical structures used to bolster previous ideal communities: Plato's golden lie, or Rousseau's civil religion, or Comte's religion of humanity. But, though Dewey regards communication as an art, he would certainly not see it as a manipulative art: "Opinion casually formed and formed under the direction of those who have something at stake in having a lie believed can be *public* opinion only in name."[23]

19 *Ibid.,* p. 96.   20 *Ibid.,* pp. 126-27, 142.   21 *Ibid.,* pp. 148-49.
22 *Ibid.,* p. 149.   23 *Ibid.,* p. 177.

A basic assumption of Dewey, acknowledged but scarcely explored in *The Public and Its Problems*, is that the common perceptions brought about by communication will create common interest. His unwillingness to postulate any long-run ends in so many words makes it imperative for him to adopt this faith in what certain instrumental means will do. Logically it must be a rather blind faith, trusting serenely in the wisdom of a future generation liberated from past dogma and with nothing else to guide its members but the canons of science. Actually, of course, certain long-run and rather abstract values, the kind in which Dewey is not supposed to indulge himself, can be found in many of Dewey's pages. The old French ideal of fraternity seems to have special importance for Dewey. He speaks of utilizing government as "the genuine instrumentality of an inclusive and fraternally associated public." He speaks warmly of sustaining "fraternally shared experience." He talks of the need for the kind of face-to-face community that can grow only in small towns or in neighborly relationships.[24]

This emphasis upon community-mindedness is consistent with Dewey's theories of education in both their narrow and their broad applications. His view of education is democratic, first, in respect to what is supposed to go on in the classroom. The experimental elementary school at the University of Chicago illustrated this. Traditional education was oriented around passive listening to authoritative exposition. Dewey wanted to make each child an active contributor. He wanted the fixed curriculum to be supplanted by projects that arose out of the "felt personal and group needs" of the children themselves, with regimentation and discipline minimized for the sake of spontaneous expression by the pupils. Second, Dewey's view of education is democratic with respect to the relationship between the classroom and the larger society beyond. As the growth of the individual child should be uppermost in the classroom, so should the growth and reconstruction of the social order be uppermost in society. One learns by doing, and the citizen learns how to be a citizen by continually examining and questioning the political institutions of his society. The aim of the educational system should not therefore be—as it usually is—to habituate the young to the status quo. Even if the status quo is admirable, change is inevitable, and "the problem is not whether the schools *should* participate in the production of a future society (since they do so anyway), but whether they should do it blindly and irresponsibly or with the maximum possible of courageous intelligence and responsibility."[25]

24 *Ibid.*, pp. 109, 218.
25 "Education and Social Change," *The Social Frontier*, Vol. 3, (1937), pp. 235-38. Quoted in Joseph Ratner, ed., *Intelligence in the Modern World* (New York: Modern Library, 1939), p. 692.

Social Planning

AS ONE who spoke of the indeterminacy of the situations to be dealt with in the future and the need for discussion, communication, and openness, it might seem that Dewey was in a poor position to be an advocate of planning. But a notable advocate of planning he was. Some would say that Dewey did not reconcile successfully the discrepancy implied in belief in indeterminacy, on the one hand, and advocacy of social planning, on the other. But at least we can say that the ubiquitous concept of consequences was the link Dewey tried to forge:

. . . in practice, if not in so many words, it has been denied that man has any responsibility for the consequences that result from what he invents and employs. The denial is implicit in our widespread refusal to engage in large-scale collective planning. Not a day passes, even in the present crisis, when the whole idea of such planning is not ridiculed as an emanation from the brain of starry eyed professors or of others equally inept in practical affairs. And all of this in the face of the fact that there is not a successful industrial organization that does not owe its success to persistent planning within a limited field—with an eye to profit—to say nothing of the terribly high price we have paid in the way of insecurity and war for putting our trust in drift.

Refusal to accept responsibility for looking ahead and for planning in matters national and international is based upon refusal to employ in social affairs, in the field of human relations, the methods of observation, interpretation, and test that are matters of course in dealing with physical things, and to which we owe the conquest of physical nature. The net result is a state of imbalance, of profoundly disturbed moral knowledge.[26]

Dewey was concerned basically with methodology. But underlying this concern was a hearty belief that his methodology would produce a certain kind of society of which he approved. It would be a democratic society, with widespread and active discussion of political and economic matters by all the people, where capitalistic enterprise would be restrained by intelligent centralized planning to make sure that the great community that had emerged out of all this discussion was moving the great society in the direction it ought to go. Dewey was not, supposedly, prejudging this direction; but it would seem that the old revolutionary goals of liberty, equality, and fraternity, so long as they were not treated as "hopeless abstractions," had much to recommend them. In the semipopular essays and articles collected in *The Problems of Men*, we can, if we wish, point out certain highly concrete evils that Dewey sniped at, and which may

26 *Problems of Men* (New York: Philosophical Library, 1946), pp. 26-27.

tell us as much as or more than the abstractions of his antiabstractionist philosophy: these include the Hearst press, Tammany Hall, the "spurious liberalism . . . represented by the Liberty League and ex-President Hoover," dictatorships, the educational philosophy of Robert Maynard Hutchins, the use of press and radio for "propaganda," loyalty oaths for teachers, racial discrimination.

Dewey was in a somewhat anomalous position, although perhaps he never fully realized it. He had certain values that in practice he advanced with vigor, both through his institutional associations and through his more popular writing. But philosophically, he defended none of them; indeed, he could not consistently defend them, since his *sine qua non* was a methodology that deferred to the values of each emerging situation rather than some fixed catalogue of ends. Dewey's great contribution, it must be said, was negative rather than positive, though this is not to say it was a small one.

Conclusion

IN looking over the bulk of Dewey's writing on political subjects it seems clear that he stands hip-deep in the mainstream of the Western liberal tradition and that many of the values attached to it, which he espouses, not only have never been subjected to an experimental scientific test, but probably could not be. In a chapter on "Democracy and America" in *Freedom and Culture*, he speaks with great praise of Jefferson and the ideals of the Declaration of Independence. Because, he says, we are wary today of "self-evident truths," it is necessary to translate eighteenth-century ideals into twentieth-century symbols, for which purpose he suggests the substitution of "moral rights" for "natural rights."

Nature and the plans of a benevolent and wise Creator were never far apart in his [Jefferson's] reflections. But his fundamental beliefs remain unchanged in substance if we forget all special associations with the word *Nature* and speak instead of ideal aims and values to be recognized—aims which, although ideal, are not located in the clouds but are backed by something deep and indestructible in the needs and demands of humankind.[27]

This identification of the traditional ideals of liberal thought with certain attributes of human nature that seem to be virtually permanent would not appear to be consistent with basic pragmatic assumptions; but it can-

27 *Freedom and Culture* (New York: Putnam, 1939), p. 156. See also Milton R. Konvitz, "Dewey's Revision of Jefferson," in Hook, ed., *John Dewey, A Symposium,* pp. 169-76.

not be dismissed as a mere lapse. Again and again Dewey makes this point. In the conclusion of *Liberalism and Social Action*: ". . . the cause of the liberty of the human spirit, the cause of opportunity of human beings for full development of their powers, the cause for which liberalism enduringly stands, is too precious and too ingrained in the human constitution to be forever obscured. Intelligence after millions of years of errancy has found itself as a method and it will not be lost forever in the blackness of night."[28]

Dewey assumed that experimentalism as a method would in time validate the traditional values he already held. It would be unfair to say that Dewey did not make concrete application of these abstract ideals in his own life, for he did. The indictment runs the other way, namely, that the theory of experimentalism, useful as a critical tool, was not helpful in supporting many of the values Dewey most wished to support. It permitted, and perhaps made imperative, begging off from the task of working out a program for practical reform that could stand on a platform of philosophically solid principles. Dewey was not unwilling to tackle the program, but he could not consistently build the platform. As Morton White has suggested, there were two Deweys, one who was opposed to any fixed ends for society, the other who wanted to engineer the construction of a liberal society.

Writing in 1935, Dewey could sketch with accuracy the threat to liberal ideals posed by Communism and Fascism and issue a rallying cry to liberalism's banner:

The eclipse of liberalism is due to the fact it has not faced the alternatives and adopted the means upon which the realization of its professed aims depends. Liberalism can be true to its ideals only as it takes the course that leads to their attainment. The notion that organized social control of economic forces lies outside the historic path of liberalism shows that liberalism is still impeded by remnants of its earlier *laissez faire* phase, with its opposition of society and the individual. The thing which now dampens liberal ardor and paralyzes its efforts is the conception that liberty and development of individuality as ends exclude the use of organized social effort as means . . . socialized economy is the means of free individual development as the end.[29]

We may note the reification involved in the continual reference to liberalism as an "it" that can be true, and therefore presumably false, to its ideals, which are presumably justified by applying the theory of inquiry. But a few sentences later in *Liberalism and Social Action* Dewey seems

28 Reprinted by permission of G. P. Putnam's Sons from *Liberalism and Social Action* by John Dewey. Copyright 1935 by John Dewey.
29 *Ibid.*, p. 90. See also *A Common Faith* (New Haven: Yale Univ. Press, 1934).

not so much to be justifying liberalism as taking it as a "given," either for the sake of using it as an example of the method of inquiry or, possibly, using it as a means to the higher end of "unity": "by concentrating upon the task of securing a socialized economy as the ground and medium for release of the impulses and capacities *all men agree to call ideal,* the now scattered and often conflicting activities of liberals can be brought to effective unity."[30] The italicized phrase is typical of Dewey's ambiguity at the crucial points where one might determine what values he finally chooses to defend. Does he mean that all men, literally all men, agree to make liberalism their social ideal? Surely he cannot seriously mean this as a factual statement. Does he mean, then, that all men *ought* to agree to make liberalism their ideal? If so, *why* ought they? Dewey nowhere explicitly prescribes a social ought for all men, because to do so would be to violate his instrumentalist premise, namely that theories, including ideals, are products of emerging concrete historical situations good only for their own time and place just as mechanical inventions are good only for their own time and place.

Indeed, he seems suddenly to shy away from the very activity he has entered into. In the next sentence he says, "It is no part of my task to outline in detail a program for renascent liberalism."[31] But he begins almost immediately to berate liberals once again, this time, however, for their weakness in organization, rather than for their failure to agree on socialization of the economy. This, in a sense, is a revival of a methodological issue; but it is a quite different issue, appropriate for the practical level that assumes we all agree on our objective (though he has earlier suggested that all are not agreed on the middle-level objective of socialization) and wants to find the best way to achieve it. But all of a sudden it turns out that the cause to be served by this better organization, this hypothetical "concrete program of action," is not the socialization of the economy at all, not even liberalism in general, but "democratic ideals." ". . . without this organization there is danger that democratic ideals may go by default. Democracy has been a fighting faith. When its ideals are reënforced [not, please note, established] by those of scientific method and experimental intelligence, it cannot be that it is incapable of evoking discipline, ardor and organization."[32] Why can it not be? All the tenets of instrumentalism would seem to indicate that it could very well not be.

Perhaps we are to dismiss all this confusion as a mere example of the hyperbole even philosophers indulge in when speaking to popular audiences (this was a lecture given at the University of Virginia). One would be inclined to take this way out upon reading on the same page: "I for one do not believe that Americans living in the tradition of Jefferson and

30 *Ibid.,* p. 91. Italics added.   31 *Ibid.*   32 *Ibid.,* pp. 91-92.

Lincoln will weaken and give up without a whole-hearted effort to make democracy a living reality. This, I repeat, involves organization." But unless one can assume a duplicity wholly alien to Dewey's known character, one must take all his writings seriously, and grant as well that what one says in a mood of exhortation is often more revealing of one's underlying position than arid pedagogical utterance. And, moreover, Dewey in the passage under review is not wholly forgetful of the philosophic position he is bound to uphold. We push on to the next sentence: "The question [presumably of whether democracy can be a "living reality"] cannot be answered by argument. Experimental method means experiment, and the question can be answered only by trying, by organized effort."[33] We are carried back to Peirce's contention that philosophers have only disputed and found disagreement, while scientists have investigated and found agreement.

It would seem that Dewey's basic faith is in the capacity of scientific method to bring men together into a common life of progressively revealed and shared insight. Around this faith he gathered in somewhat haphazard fashion, as befits one who does not believe in hierarchies of value, all sorts of more or less well-defined value concepts, including those of democracy and liberalism.

Dewey turns out to be an important symbol of American political existence after all. He was impatient of delay, he was willing to run some risks out of confidence in the future, and he took his thoroughly American liberalism largely for granted.

33 *Ibid.*, p. 92.

18 | *Niebuhr*

To say that there has been a great "return to religion" in the post-World War II period of Western civilization would, by itself, be misleading. The religious picture is rather more cloudy than such a statement implies. After the war, European and American theologians who had been writing for a number of years —Barth, Brunner, Buber, Maritain, Niebuhr, Tillich—began to be listened to with greater interest than before. Billy Graham revivals seemed to flourish as they could not have in the nineteen-thirties. Church membership in America rose sharply and piety at times threatened to become a political necessity. On the other hand, the continuing spread of Communist influence around the world put churches, especially Christian churches, on the defensive. Although quarrels between fundamentalist churchmen and natural scientists over evolution seemed a thing of the past, and more scientists than before were able to be practicing churchmen, the widespread scientific revolution of automation, space flights, and electronic social analysis elevated the scientific, "objective" mind to which religion seemed frequently irrelevant.

Nevertheless, it does not seem inappropriate to conclude a volume on modern political thought with consideration of the work of a theologian, especially one who has been concerned with the effect of scientific assumptions on political thinking and who has been in touch with such contemporary currents of thought as existentialism and depth psychology. These currents may or may not lead to clear-cut alternatives to the by now traditional liberal categories. We have not yet entered a new age of faith. But most observers concede that we have begun to leave the great age of reason dominated by Enlightenment optimism.

Life

REINHOLD NIEBUHR was born in Wright City, Missouri, in 1892. His father, Gustave Niebuhr, was a scholarly German preacher who died when Reinhold and his younger brother, Helmut Richard (now a professor in the Yale Divinity School) were still young. A frugal and industrious childhood preceded their enrollment in Elmhurst College in Illinois. Reinhold left that school without a degree in 1910 to enroll in Eden Theological Seminary, St. Louis, and transferred from there to the Yale Divinity School, from which he received Bachelor of Divinity and Master of Arts degrees. He has since received honorary degrees from Yale, Harvard, Princeton, Oxford, Glasgow, and other institutions.

In 1915 he was ordained in the Evangelical Synod of North America and accepted his first pastorate at the Bethel Evangelical Church of Detroit, a church with a small working-class congregation, mainly auto workers. Here he came to identify with the fight against the depersonalizing influences of modern industrial society and became involved with working-class interests. During this period he once commented that "the lowliest peasant of the Dark Ages had more opportunity for self-expression than the highest paid employee in the Ford factory." Niebuhr's championing of labor's cause led to overt conflicts with employers and the conservative churches of the area.

In 1928 he left Detroit to become associate professor of the philosophy of religion at Union Theological Seminary, New York City, and remained at Union for the rest of his active career, retiring as dean of the faculty in 1960. In his early days in New York he was an active member of the Socialist Party and editor of a Socialist publication, *The World Tomorrow*. In June of 1940 he resigned in protest against the party's pacifist position.[1]

Niebuhr has been a prolific writer, the author of seventeen books and countless articles. He was a contributing editor of *The Christian Century* and *The Nation*, and editor or co-editor of *Christianity and Society* and *Christianity and Crisis*. The first of his books to attract wide attention was *Moral Man and Immoral Society* (1932), a searing blast at the sentimental assumptions of the social gospel. In 1939 he was named the fifth American to deliver the famous Gifford Lectures at the University of Edinburgh. In published form, the lectures became his *magnum opus, The Nature and Destiny of Man* (1941, 1943).

Always active in practical politics, Niebuhr was one of the organizers

---

[1] See his *Christianity and Power Politics* (New York: Scribner, 1940), Ch. 1, for a statement of his antipacifist position at that time.

of Americans for Democratic Action, and worked for the Liberal Party in New York. For years he maintained an intensive preaching schedule, frequently appearing at eastern centers of higher education. His tone was prophetic and his pungent, slightly rasping style unforgettable. A severe stroke in 1956 ended his preaching but not his writing.

Neo-orthodox Theology

NEO-ORTHODOX Christian theologians of the twentieth century are set apart by the effort to take seriously the fundamental theological concepts that had tended to be neglected by the liberal religionists of the late nineteenth and early twentieth centuries: original sin, grace, atonement, resurrection, last judgment. Their attempts to make the theological tradition represented by such terms relevant to the present day range from the Biblicism of Karl Barth, whose God is "wholly other" rather than immanent, and who must be taken in the language of the Bible or not taken at all, to Paul Tillich, whose attempt at a rational explication of theological categories in a manner that absorbs a vast array of modern knowledge has led some to call him a pantheist. Niebuhr is less architectonic than Tillich, more worldly than Barth, and probably less original than either. His method is built upon a fundamental dualism that tends toward contradiction, paradox, and irony. The dialectical tendencies of St. Paul, Pascal, Hegel, Kierkegaard, and Heidegger appear in his work.

Niebuhr sees "contradictions" in both the psyche of the individual and in the human historical communities of which he is a part. In the individual he finds both love and self-love. In historical existence he finds both fate and freedom. Being by inclination an incisive critic, Niebuhr examines a variety of supposed attempts to find coherence and purpose in human history, such as Enlightenment rationalism, Communism, Freudianism, and logical positivism, and argues that these attempts all fail to see, or misinterpret, the "contradictions" recognized by traditional Christian interpretations.

Christian faith, as Niebuhr conceives of it, does not eliminate these contradictions, for they are woven into the fabric of existence, but it transmutes them into meaningful paradox. Man's ability to "accept by faith" the Christian interpretation of human existence represents "self-transcendence," perhaps the most difficult term in Niebuhr's lexicon. Within history, within logic, within reason, there is no resolution of these basic conflicts. Niebuhr, of course, grants that there can be no formal conflict between logic and truth. "The laws of logic are reason's guard against chaos in the realm of truth." Yet he asserts that while rationally understanding and accepting the limits of rationality, man may find in faith "that a rationally irresolvable contradiction may point to truth which logic cannot contain."[2]

A primary example of such a "dialectical" truth is the contradiction between fate and freedom, which finds its personal expression in original sin. Sin is rebellion against God and therefore rebellion against one's true self, either in the form of affirming one's animality at the expense of one's humanity (sins of the flesh); or denying one's animality at the expense of imitating God (sins of pride). Man is free not to sin. But he is fated to sin. In the origin of his being there is a "bias in the will," "something more than ignorance and something less than malice," which pulls him apparently inevitably, yet through a process of responsible choice (what psychology calls "rationalizing"), to a defiance of God's sovereignty over the world. This is a contradiction, says Niebuhr, overcome not by reason but by grace.

That man has a considerable affinity with lower animals has been apparent to almost all philosophers. It has been the magnitude and character of man's dissimilarity from other animals that has caused contention. In his typical dichotomizing manner, Niebuhr classifies the efforts to understand man as basically two: those that see man primarily in terms of his animal nature, and those that find in the excellencies of his rational faculties his primary character. In the former category fall those who seek in impulses, drives, instincts, and so on, the key to man's fundamental nature—or, which may be more relevant today, those who by their devotion to the study of man from a psycho-biological point of view imply that these are the keys to man's nature. Niebuhr welcomes the findings of modern psychology, but contends that its failure to explain how subliminal factors are transmuted into "highly complex spiritual phenomena" marks the limitations of psychology as a science. "Man is never a simple two-layered affair who can be understood from the standpoint of the bottom layer should efforts to understand him from the standpoint of the top layer fail."[3]

Niebuhr's criticism falls no less heavily upon the rationalists, those who, presumably, concentrate only upon the "top layer." They not only assume a greater emancipation from the limitations of physical nature than actually exists, but fail to see that there is more to man than the rational capacity of surveying the world and forming general concepts about it. Man, says Niebuhr, possesses the capacity of "self-transcendence," that is, the capacity to stand outside his own rational processes to ask questions about the relation of rational to natural processes and the limits of his

2 *The Nature and Destiny of Man* (New York: Scribner, 1949), Vol. I, pp. 263, 262.
3 *Ibid.*, p. 40.

own reason. The distinction between man and animal, therefore, is not fully explained by the distinction between reason and no reason, for "animal consciousness is merely the expression of a central organic unity of an organism in relation to its immediate environment. Human consciousness invokes a sharp distinction between the self and the totality of the world."[4] It is this distinction between the self and the totality of the world, man's realization of his finitude, that is, paradoxically, the greatest clue to man's potentialities of infinitude, says Niebuhr. Man tries, however imperfectly, to stand off and look at himself self-consciously, and not only at himself but at his place in history. The rational mind can contemplate "nature" as a collection of objective phenomena, but the whole self "with all its hopes, fears, and ambitions" becomes involved in any reflection on human history. This cosmic relationship, Niebuhr insists, is not encompassed by the classic Greek conception of reason. "Dialogue" is a word Niebuhr favors. The uniqueness of the human self is found in its constant dialogue with itself, with its fellows, and with God.[5]

In constructing his theory of self-transcendence Niebuhr acknowledges the work of Martin Heidegger, who used the idea of transcendence to denote man's attempt to reach beyond rationality, and Max Scheler, who used the word "spirit" (Geist) to denote both the Greek nous (man's particular rational qualities, his technical intelligence) and a higher type of comprehension, requiring certain volitional capacities, that can make the whole world, including the self, an object of knowledge. The relationship would seem to be hierarchical: "What is ordinarily meant by 'reason' does not imply 'spirit,' but 'spirit' does imply 'reason.' "[6]

Reason is inadequate to satisfy man's innate quest for the "unconditioned ground of existence," since the only unconditioned statement man can rationally make is that all human truth is relative to changing historical and cultural situations. We can say absolutely only that nothing in our rational consciousness is absolute. Reason exposes but does not overcome the ambiguities of man's nature and his historic position. Two centuries ago Western society felt otherwise, but the faith in progressive revelation through reason found in the Enlightenment has been shattered by the fruits of nineteenth-century biology and psychology and by "sci-

4 Ibid., p. 55.
5 The Self and the Dramas of History (New York: Scribner, 1955), Ch. 1. Niebuhr defers to modern empiricists in granting that the third dialogue cannot be subject to empirical verification in precisely the same way as the first two. But at the least, he says, it can be taken as an empirical datum that the human self persistently imagines itself in dialogue with God. "The anatomy of human selfhood distinguishes itself by a yearning for the ultimate." (p. 5.)
6 Nature and Destiny of Man, Vol. I, p. 162n. It should be noted that St. Augustine and Kierkegaard were more significant influences on Niebuhr's over-all thought than either Heidegger or Scheler.

entific" but demonically irrational forces in the twentieth century. Today we are quicker to acknowledge that reason is used more than it uses.

Reason by itself, then, can dissolve hope but can no longer sustain it. Yet man, led by rational analysis to the "abyss of meaninglessness" (here the existentialist influence shows through), must nevertheless, Niebuhr believes, construct a world of meaning:

Implicit in the human situation of freedom and in man's capacity to transcend himself and his world is his inability to construct a world of meaning without finding a source and key to the structure of meaning which transcends the world beyond his own capacity to transcend it. The problem of meaning, which is the basic problem of religion, transcends the ordinary rational problem of tracing the relation of things to each other as the freedom of man's spirit transcends his rational faculties.[7]

Niebuhr calls himself a "Christian realist," by which he means to suggest emancipation from the naïve hope of "even the most consistent naturalists" that scientific development within history will provide "an ultimate triumph of the rational over the irrational."[8] The varieties of naturalism, Niebuhr asserts, start with an avowed concern for nothing beyond causal explanation, but end by elevating finite elements of existence—reason, sex, the survival impulse, economic relationships, biological growth, nation, race—into ultimate explanations, and hence bestow upon them the eminence of the divine.[9] The "hidden dogmas" of social science, as, for example, the view that the realm of history is for purposes of study virtually identical with the realm of nature, are all the more potent, he thinks, for being hidden.

The innate tendency of human beings to seek unity with greater and greater wholes would, if carried to the nth degree, destroy individuality. The natural desire to establish and protect one's individual identity thus stands in a contradictory relationship with the impulse toward the divine, according to Niebuhr. The result is a tension infecting all human endeavors, a tension that constitutes a "bias toward sin" and is manifest in man's perennially uneasy conscience. (This is not, Niebuhr insists, a Rousseauistic or Hegelian dichotomy between a particular self and a universal self.) Out of this tension come not only man's rebelliousness, which mani-

7 *Ibid.*, p. 164.

8 *Faith and History* (New York: Scribner, 1949), p. 67. The attack is here directed against John Dewey. See also Paul Tillich, *Systematic Theology* (Chicago: Univ. of Chicago Press, 1951-   ), Vol. I, pp. 71-105.

9 Whether all men or only some men share this yearning for ultimate meaning is, of course, the question that most clearly divides religionists and nonreligionists. And, in the nature of the case, neither can answer the question in terms satisfactory to the other.

fests itself in the various forms of sin, but man's creativity. Both the sin and the creativity have collective as well as individual manifestations.[10]

Group Morality

THAT groups can become extensions of the personal egos of their members is hardly a new insight. What Niebuhr has done with this phenomenon is to discuss it in terms of traditional Christian symbolism. The effect has been to make both Christians and non-Christians look anew at some old behavior patterns. The Philistine seismograph registered the highest shock waves in 1932, when Niebuhr published *Moral Man and Immoral Society*. Americans were in this year facing the bottom of the Great Depression. Those putting inordinate hope in new forms of collective action were laced by Niebuhr's icy blast. Without in the least suggesting that we could do without collective action, indeed, suggesting the exact reverse, Niebuhr nevertheless threw cold water on any hope for an easy collective morality:

Individual men may be moral in the sense that they are able to consider interests other than their own in determining problems of conduct, and are capable, on occasion, of preferring the advantages of others to their own. They are endowed by nature with a measure of sympathy and consideration for their kind. . . . Their rational faculty prompts them to a sense of justice which educational discipline may refine and purge of egoistic elements. . . .

But all these achievements are more difficult, if not impossible, for human societies and social groups. In every human group there is less reason to guide and check impulse, less capacity for self-transcendence, less ability to comprehend the needs of others, and therefore more unrestrained egoism than the individuals who compose the group reveal in their personal relationships.[11]

The larger the group the more selfish, by and large. The larger the group the more difficult the achievement of a genuine moral relationship with another group. The unifying principle in large organizations is more likely to be basic but unreflective impulses. The impulse to national survival that operates in war most clearly unifies a national community and most inhibits altruistic behavior toward rival nations. "It is a rather pathetic aspect of human social life that conflict is a seemingly unavoidable prerequisite of group solidarity."[12] Even small groups, even intimate groups like the

10 For an extended discussion of man as sinner, see *Nature and Destiny of Man*, Vol. I, Chs. 7-9.
11 *Moral Man and Immoral Society* (New York: Scribner, 1932), pp. xi-xii.
12 *Ibid.*, p. 48.

family, characteristically display a marked selfishness in protecting their interests vis-à-vis the interests of other groups, and the leadership of even small groups (e.g., the father in a patriarchal society) is rarely as benevolent as individual persons defending purely individual interests can be. An individual may literally sacrifice himself on an heroic impulse. A group almost never does or can, figuratively or literally.

The tendency to couch group aims in the language of noble and altruistic ideals only makes matters worse. Niebuhr does not believe in a group mind existing apart from the individuals who make up the group, but the existence of the group enables persons to lose themselves, even to sacrifice themselves, in the name of a nominally laudable end, while participating in an emotional enterprise whose genuine purposes are anything but laudable.[13] The sins of the flesh may be less dangerous simply because they tend to be individual in manifestation, while the sin of pride is, above all, a collective phenomenon. American Protestant churches have often evaded the danger of the sins of collective pride, thinks Niebuhr, by overconcentrating attention on sins of the flesh. But liberal political theories generally have tended to underestimate the difficulties created by group pride:

> Our contemporary culture fails to realize the power, extent and persistence of group egoism in human relations. It may be possible, though it is never easy, to establish just relations between individuals within a group purely by moral and rational suasion and accommodation. In intergroup relations this is practically an impossibility. The relations between groups must therefore always be predominantly political rather than ethical; that is, they will be determined by the proportion of power which each group possesses at least as much as by any rational and moral appraisal of the comparative needs and claims of each group.[14]

Niebuhr is not saying that all politics is unethical or that ethics is unrelated to politics. He is saying that the spokesmen of the liberal heritage, those who have been "children of light" less wise in their generation than the "children of darkness," have tended to overestimate the degree to which personal ethics can be fulfilled or at least not damaged by group action. They have underestimated the degree to which group loyalties tend to degenerate into irrational faith in "false absolutes"—the contingent norms of race, class, nation, even religious sect, which become spuriously absolutized.

Critics of Niebuhr suggest that the gap between his impossible transcendent ideal and the realities of earthly political existence is so great that Christian ethics becomes virtually irrelevant to politics in the Niebuhrian

---

13 See Eric Hoffer, *The True Believer* (New York: Harper, 1951).
14 *Moral Man and Immoral Society*, pp. xxii-xxiii.

system. He is so realistic, they say, that he slides into a Burkean conservatism in which prudence is all.[15] Niebuhr sometimes seems to invite this criticism by his stubborn penchant for rhetorical paradoxes, and by his emphasis on divine perfection and human depravity. Of course his own political activism and reformism would seem to belie the quietistic or conservative implications some would draw from his thought. But the logical implication of his theory rather than his own personal behavior is the crucial factor at this point. (See, however, the concluding section of this chapter.) The question of whether Niebuhr's tension ethics results in a hopeless compartmentalization dividing Christian ethics from practical politics may, perhaps, be clarified by looking at Niebuhr's treatment of the relationship between the Christian norm of love, and political justice as dealt with by courts of law.

The Christian ethic is summed up in the *agape* of Christ, a sacrificial, outward-moving, selfless, ecstatic love that regards other individuals as objects of God rather than as objects of the self. It is intensely personal. Justice in its everyday connotation is thought of as the "rightness" of the rewards and punishments a community formulates and administers to preserve its order and cohesiveness. Such justice is rational and calculating; it cannot be wholly personal, nor is it easily subject to the ecstatic illuminations of the spirit. Were legal justice dispensed by agapic individuals, unreasonable disorder would result. Even—or especially—a town full of saints would require a dispassionately administered set of traffic laws. Spontaneous love and public order are, therefore, separable if not at odds.

Seen as a norm of justice (Christian "brotherhood" can be regarded as a collective approximation of *agape*), *agape* is a standard by which all earthly systems of justice are found wanting. Some such spirit of love must, however, accompany and animate rational calculation in the establishment and maintenance of earthly systems if they are not to become purely mechanical and inhuman: ". . . justice which is only justice soon degenerates into something less than justice."[16] Yet the rational calculation of rights and interests, which are so intrinsic a part of the judicial process, remains antithetical to the spirit of Christian ethics—at least to the ethics of the New Testament, which is not all that Christians claim, but is the most that they can agree upon as authoritative. This standard is quite heedless of rights and interests and is wholly beyond the rational appeal for equal treatment:

15 See Holtan P. Odegard, *Sin and Science, Reinhold Niebuhr as Political Theologian* (Antioch, Ohio: Antioch Press, 1956), especially p. 197; Morton G. White, *Social Thought in America: The Revolt Against Formalism* (rev. ed.; Boston: Beacon Press, 1958), Epilogue; Robert E. Fitch, "Reinhold Niebuhr as Prophet and as Philosopher of History," *Journal of Religion*, Vol. 32 (1952), pp. 31-36.

16 *Moral Man and Immoral Society*, p. 258.

You have heard that it was said "An eye for an eye and a tooth for a tooth." But I say to you, Do not resist one who is evil. But if any one strikes you on the right cheek, turn to him the other also; and if any one would sue you and take your coat, let him have your cloak as well; and if any one forces you to go one mile, go with him two miles. . . . Love your enemies. . . . do not be anxious, saying, "What shall we eat?" or "What shall we drink?" or "What shall we wear?" . . . Judge not that you be not judged. . . ."[17]

Human survival and strict obedience to these commandments are not consistent, thinks Niebuhr; but the spirit of the commandments, a spirit not derivable from the rational faculty, is necessary to prevent the deterioration of human society to a subhuman level.

But it is not enough simply to say, "We shall adopt the spirit of the New Testament while recognizing the irrelevance of its concrete standards." This would be the opposite of the more common ethical dilemma of trying to follow a set of rules without participating in the spiritual force that gives them sanction—legalism, or goodness by the numbers. Niebuhr insists that these commandments must be understood by the Christian as ultimately realizable even though provisionally unrealizable. Hence the Christian concern for eschatology, the doctrine of last things, has important ethical consequences. Goodness is sustained by a hope strong enough to overcome a despairing present. The Christian ethic and the perfection of the moral life are what Niebuhr calls the "impossible possibility," a possibility without which the Christian is unable to reject the normativeness of the merely normal.[18]

Critics coming out of the natural-law tradition would be inclined to say, of course, that reason is much more than prudential calculation, and that while in the last analysis revelation may sustain the norms of the New Testament, they are not the contradictions to reason that Niebuhr assumes. From a quite different direction the scientific humanist is apt to agree with Niebuhr that the norms of the New Testament are, in their literal extremity, beyond rational demonstration, and on these grounds deny their validity in favor of moral norms validated by scientific inquiry, experiment, or some other means. More technically minded students of ethics might argue that Niebuhr's tension ethics keeps in suspension and needlessly confuses two different types of ethical system: the ethics of proper motive, which is essentially personal, and the ethics of proper consequences, which is essentially social. To this

17 Matthew 5:38-41, 44; 6:31; 7:1 (Revised Standard Version).
18 See *Nature and Destiny of Man*, Vol. II, Ch. 3; *Faith and History*, Ch. 13; *Christianity and Power Politics*, pp. 214ff. The American Protestant church, thinks Niebuhr, is not eschatological enough. It has participated too fully in America's naïve confidence in a "redemptive history."

Niebuhr would no doubt reply that the logical separation of the two, which in different language he fully concedes, is not a separation in life. There, each exists in a sort of hostile dependence on the other. Indeed, this is the problem; this is the continuous ethical tension of man in society as Niebuhr sees it.

The tension is reflected in Niebuhr himself in a more acute form than is likely to occur in those able to be more consistently optimistic or pessimistic. He explicitly acknowledges that the "highest satisfactions of the inner life" from an aloof, ascetic viewpoint may be enjoyed at the expense of tragic social injustice, while attempts to maintain order through proximate norms of justice may undermine personal moral idealism. The human situation is one in which it is necessary to see "love exploited to the full yet discounted."[19] There is even a note of despair in the earlier Niebuhr of *Moral Man and Immoral Society*: ". . . justice cannot be approximated if the hope of its perfect realization does not generate a sublime madness in the soul. The illusion is dangerous because it encourages terrible fanaticisms. It must therefore be brought under the control of reason. One can only hope that reason will not destroy it before its work is done."[20]

Nation, Community, History

GROUP ethics, as we have seen, is a fundamental concern for Niebuhr. When the group is the modern nation-state, special factors come into play. The size, the longevity, the coercive power, the traditional symbolism of the nation-state is apt to make it an object of worship or an object of fear, or both. Since awe and fear are basic emotions evoked by divinity, the state has frequently been one of the "false gods" worshipped by men. German idealism and German political practice are alike frequently mentioned by Niebuhr as examples of state worship in which the particular is absolutized. The United States, with its early heritage of "that government is best which governs least," is, on the other hand, cited as an example of fear of the state which sometimes approaches the edge of anarchy and often downgrades the valid and necessary element of majesty in government.[21] Niebuhr's German-American background is perhaps reflected in these two examples.

19 *Christianity and Power Politics*, p. 39. See also *Beyond Tragedy* (New York: Scribner, 1937), Ch. 8.
20 *Moral Man and Immoral Society*, p. 277.
21 *The Irony of American History* (New York: Scribner, 1952). The religious factor in the majesty of state and its neglect by Western democratic theory is discussed in *The Structure of Nations and Empires* (New York: Scribner, 1959), Chs. 4, 11.

The exaggerations of the positive and the negative aspects, respectively, of state control in these two traditions both reveal excessively rigid conceptions of the relationship of the individual to his larger political community, thinks Niebuhr. In *The Children of Light and the Children of Darkness* (1944), he sets forth his understanding of this relationship in three propositions. In the first place the individual is so related to his community that "the highest reaches of his individuality are dependent upon the social substance out of which they arise."[22] A great artist like Shakespeare may achieve a perspective approaching universal dimensions, but he remains a product of his community, and his community limits every choice he makes, not least through the language it provides. There is freedom in history, but no absolute freedom. There is self-transcendence, but no removal from social limitations. The juridical norms behind positive law may be conditioned by profound religious insights, but any statement of them is conditioned to a greater extent than natural-law advocates are willing to acknowledge by the shifting historical milieu.

In the second place, "Both individual and collective centers of human vitality may be endlessly elaborated," and any premature attempt to define the limits of these vitalities suppresses the "indeterminate creativity" of man and society as well as their destructive possibilities.[23] Such premature definitions are found, thinks Niebuhr, in the natural harmony of the economic order presupposed by classical economics and the inevitable class conflict (and harmony "on the other side of the revolution") presupposed by Marxian theory. At the level of individual vitality, Niebuhr finds similar attempts in Freudian and behaviorist psychologies in their attempt to explain man in terms of the sex impulse or various reflexes. Man's freedom allows "indeterminate elaboration" of any natural impulse, perhaps aesthetically, perhaps perversely.

Finally, "individual vitality rises in indeterminate degree over all social and communal concretions of life,"[24] and is not ultimately fulfilled within the historical process. This third contention, which brings us back to the difficult problem of "self-transcendence" is probably most subject to dispute; for at this point Niebuhr himself seems to be standing outside history to speak of an ultimate that cannot be fulfilled within history. This is the position of anyone who asserts a philosophy of

22 *The Children of Light and the Children of Darkness* (New York: Scribner, 1944), p. 48.
23 *Ibid.*
24 *Ibid.*, p. 49. In *The Self and the Dramas of History* Niebuhr employs a different terminology, speaking of the "vertical" and the "horizontal" dimensions of the individual's relationship to the community. In the former, the individual looks down on the community from a position of moral transcendence. In the latter, he is made aware of conflict with other communities.

history, whether secular or religious—if, indeed, a secular philosophy of history is not a contradiction in terms. Such a position can never be compelling to the skeptic. None of us has experienced or can experience more than an indeterminate part of history. "History as a whole," therefore, is a category beyond empirical knowledge, and its use implies some sort of revelation.

Niebuhr uses what he regards as the Christian view of history as a fulcrum by which to pry up at their roots modern secular democratic theories. The failure to understand "the full height of . . . human self-transcendence," says Niebuhr, has led such theories to oscillate between excessively individualistic and excessively collectivistic emphases. The individualism of a democratic Bentham can eventuate in a disorder, especially in the neglected economic realm, which actually constricts individual freedoms. The communitarianism of a democratic Dewey, thinks Niebuhr, places such faith in political communities, whose life is "even more contingent than that of the individuals who are able to survey their relations to them,"[25] as to make possible the cutting off of the "pinnacle of individuality" by the community.

Both of these theories, indeed all those that Niebuhr would put in the category of "modern" thought, as distinguished from the classical view and the Biblical view, are guilty of treating history as "redemptive." That is, they can operate only on the assumption that man and society are capable of being redeemed by the triumph of processes already at work within history. ". . . modern culture, despite its diversities, has a common confidence in the temporal process as that which gives meaning to our existence."[26] In the time that man controls, therefore, rather than in the eternity that he does not control, man's error can in some way or other be made self-liquidating.

In *Faith and History* (1949) Niebuhr contrasts the modern view with the classical view, in which reality is a fixity above and apart from the realm of historical flux and change. Niebuhr contends that the modern view is truer than the classical in seeing "that both nature and historic institutions are subject to development in time," but that from this truth two illusions developed. "Modern culture . . . consistently exaggerated the degree of growth in human freedom and power" and made the "second mistake of identifying freedom with virtue."[27] Both classical and modern views are, of course, contrasted with what Niebuhr identifies as the Biblical view, which recognizes historical process but does not deify it, because it acknowledges a diety outside of historical process.

The United States is the national representative *par excellence* of the essentially optimistic view of history as redemptive. The success of

[25] *Faith and History*, p. 156.   [26] *Ibid.*, p. 45.   [27] *Ibid.*, p. 69.

our national experiment surely helps explain this. In *The Irony of American History* (1952), Niebuhr fits the United States into the Niebuhrian system, with illuminating results for those complacent about the clichés by which America lives. Niebuhr argues that America's constantly expanding economy, "a gift of providence" thanks to a small population on a large, rich continent, is primarily responsible for the fluidity of our class structure. This has enabled capitalism to take credit for economic productivity without having to take the blame for hardened class lines. The theory remains relatively unspotted and hence unexamined, while the practice of American capitalism goes its own unorthodox way. Marxism criticizes the error of a false individualism used as a rationalization for collective oppression and "substitutes a more grievous error for the error which it challenges," namely, the view that class interest as interpreted by an elite party is synonymous with the interest of the whole and is the very purpose of historical movement.

Liberals in general, of whom Americans are such good examples, Niebuhr calls "soft utopians." Communists he calls "hard utopians." One group mistakenly regards property as the primary instrument of justice, the other mistakenly regards property as the primary instrument of injustice. The utopianism is also reflected in the impatient desire to solve political problems "once and for all." "In this debate between errors, or between half-truth and half-truth, America is usually completely on the side of the bourgeois credo in theory; but in practice it has achieved balances of power in the organization of social forces and a consequent justice which has robbed the Marxist challenge of its sting."[28]

Although granting a providential basis to America's material position, Niebuhr by no means equates this, as an older Calvinism might have done, with divine sanction for America's ideological position. It is precisely this erroneous equation that Niebuhr attacks in *The Irony of American History*. It is this error that liberalism and Communism alike, using the secular language of "progress" (i.e., redemptive history) have committed. Niebuhr's view of history is not progressive, but tragic and ironic in almost equal proportions. This view suggests not a quickness to identify historical causes as God's causes, but a great reluctance to do so. In the American political past, Niebuhr finds Lincoln a rather solitary example of this kind of restraint. His Second Inaugural with its "malice toward none, charity for all" and its reference to the God to whom South as well as North pray, Niebuhr compares with the scriptural injunction to "judge not that you be not judged." "Lincoln's model . . . rules out our effort to establish the righteousness of our cause by a monotonous reiteration of the virtues of freedom compared with the evils of tyranny. . . .

28 *Irony of American History*, p. 91.

it is very dangerous to define the struggle as one between a God-fearing and a godless civilization."[29] Russia is worshipping a god, albeit a different one from ours, and we are not so God-fearing as we pretend. In the Marxist liturgy, Engels' "withering away of the state" is the

. . . anarchistic pinnacle on top of the collectivist structure of utopia which makes the Leninist dream at once so implausible and so attractive to the victims of injustice. It provides the ideological basis for the power system which has developed in the communist world. If we remember that power is never merely force but always a combination of force and prestige it must become apparent that the ideological framework for the communist power structure has some striking similarities with—as well as differences from— the traditional power structures which are maintained through the millennia of human history. In these the gradations of authority and the centralization of power in government were presented as consonant with the cosmic order as enjoined by the divine will."[30]

Conclusion: Theology and Politics

IN rather rapid order we have now moved from the sinful nature of man to United States–Russian relations, a movement typical of Niebuhr himself. The most perplexing question emerging from this chapter concerns the tensile strength of the links connecting these two poles.

The essence of Niebuhr's argument may be summed up as follows: The "soft utopianism" of liberal politics and religion and the "hard utopianism" of Communist politics and religion alike underestimate the depth of self-love and overestimate the possibility that scientific knowledge will defeat the sinful propensities of man at some point in history. The former tends toward a sentimental view of the force of individual good will in coping with perverse institutional structures; the latter places too much confidence in institutional structures (and, after the withering away of the state, in naturally virtuous individuals). By contrast with these diverse "children of light," the cynical "children of darkness" give up all pretense of moral aspiration and yield to Machiavellian pessimism in politics.

The "Christian realist," while acknowledging the ambiguity of his own standards and actions, avoids the liberal temptation to put his faith in a redemptive history as well as the cynical temptation to disengage himself from the moral conflicts of his community. He is willing to balance power against power in the interests of a tolerable order and a

29 *Ibid.*, p. 173.
30 *Structure of Nations and Empires*, p. 227.

provisional justice, without expecting personal or social redemption from them. The Christian realist does not look to pure democracy to overcome the ingrained shortcomings of the *demos*; but finds it desirable as "a method of finding proximate solutions for insoluble problems," for "Man's capacity for justice makes democracy possible; but man's inclination to injustice makes democracy necessary."[31]

As Niebuhr readily acknowledges, there is much of St. Augustine in all this:

Modern realists know the power of collective self-interest as Augustine did; but they do not understand its blindness. Modern pragmatists understand the irrelevance of fixed and detailed norms; but they do not understand that love as the final norm must take the place of these inadequate norms. Modern liberal Christians know that love is the final norm for man; but they fall into sentimentality because they fail to measure the power and persistence of self-love. A generation which finds its communities imperiled and in decay from the smallest and most primordial community, the family, to the largest and most recent, the potential world community, might well take counsel of Augustine in solving its perplexities.[32]

Granted his definitions and assumptions, especially that liberals err on the side of sentimentality and "modern" realists err on the side of cynicism, it is not hard to agree with Niebuhr. It is, in fact, difficult to argue that we should be more sentimental, that we should hope for nothing less than perfection in politics, that we should be either more utopian or less moral. But who other than nitwits would so argue? With some justification, critics of Niebuhr accuse him of putting too many people in too few categories. His victims are too often strapped to a Procrustean bed. Rousseau gets thrown in with the liberals because he used social-contract terminology. Locke is pictured as naïve about the ease of determining consent. Bentham is portrayed as unable to see the need for social controls. Hegel believed in a redemptive history and so, apparently, does Bertrand Russell. Niebuhr sometimes seems more interested in massive differences than in fine distinctions. As a matter of fact, liberals, however much they have deified nature, have frequently been much less sentimental about human nature than Niebuhr indicates.

Is it possible that Niebuhr merely provides us with a gigantic tautological system built upon the cornerstone of man's sinfulness and then gives it the semblance of empirical validity by picking and choosing among the facts of intellectual history and current events? If so, Niebuhr would not be the first philosopher to do so. Nor would his company

31 *The Children of Light and the Children of Darkness*, pp. 118, xi.
32 *Christian Realism and Political Problems* (New York: Scribner, 1953), p. 146.

necessarily be undistinguished. Tautological, pseudo-empirical systems can be both profound and helpful. Indeed, it may be that all philosophic thought is tautological insofar as it is truly systematic and no more than pseudo-empirical insofar as it strains for universality. A system, even one that acknowledges religious mystery, can hardly incorporate religious mystery. Niebuhr has oversold and overextended his system—but it is a good system, as systems go.

But Niebuhr is not only a system-builder. He practices what he preaches about involvement in the crucial political issues of the day, and this involvement includes for him analysis, commentary, and prescription. Though they might not meet all the tenets of contemporary scientific empiricism, his analyses in a periodical like *Christianity and Crisis* of, say, the Teamsters Union, Charles de Gaulle, or the Berlin crisis (any Berlin crisis) are certainly empirical in one legitimate sense of the term. Our question, then, should perhaps be rephrased: Is the system, whether or not invariably *supported by* the empirical analysis, invariably *related to* the empirical analysis? Or are there two Niebuhrs, Niebuhr the theologian and Niebuhr the political analyst?

Examination of Niebuhr's more political writings reveals a remarkable consistency of style and approach. There have been, of course, changes in point of view. But after the big changes in the 1930's, first away from pacifism, then away from socialism, they have been marginal. Some articles are devoid of theological language, some are not. What makes even the former peculiarly Niebuhrian in flavor is: (1) Their pungency, frequently attained through the use of irony, paradox, and the close juxtaposition of logical antinomies. (2) Their unblinking attention to power factors in the situation under scrutiny. (3) Their uniform level of generality. Instead of concentrating on factual details and local color, Niebuhr is almost always chiefly concerned with the ends decision-makers were trying to achieve and the reasons people reacted as they did to the situation. (4) Their uniform level of normativeness. Niebuhr is not only unafraid to use "value-laden" words ("freedom," "justice," "tyranny"), but he does so easily and consistently, at a level somewhere between manifestly judgmental and manifestly descriptive usages.

Let us look, for example, at two statements on race relations, the first more or less theoretical, the second more or less empirical:

Christianity's resources for approaching the problem of race relations do not stop short with a mere statement of the ideal of equality. Christian insights into the human situation afford, for instance, a much more profound illumination of the sources of racial prejudice than does the analysis of secular liberalism. Generally, American liberals have regarded racial prejudices as vestiges of barbarism, which an enlightened education was in the process of overcoming. . . . Our anthropologists rightly insisted that there were no biological roots of inequality among races; and they wrongly drew the conclusion from this fact that racial prejudice is a form of ignorance which could be progressively dispelled by enlightenment.[33]

. . . counties which comply [with the Supreme Court decision requiring school integration] are usually those in which Negroes are a minority of 25 per cent or less. On the other hand, counties which approach the 50 per cent ratio almost invariably seek some form of evasion. . . . It is easier for a majority to be tolerant of a small minority than of a large minority. . . . This is a phenomenon of all group relations and does not apply solely to Negro-white relations. It may lead to pessimistic conclusions in regard to certain counties in the South. But it prompts to optimism when we consider the nation as a whole, where Negroes are in an obvious minority. The relation of morals to percentage points is a reminder to all of us of the frailty of our conscience and the limits of our tolerance.[34]

The first statement, while not wholly devoid of factual references, is essentially an assertion that race prejudice is more than ignorance (how much more is dealt with elsewhere at length), and that "Christian insights" recognize this but "secular liberalism" does not. This statement is prophetic and apologetic, in the Christian sense, and may be summed up more bluntly in Niebuhr's own words: "Race bigotry is, in short, one form of original sin."[35] This is not the conclusion of a sociologist. The statement on the correlation of the size of minorities with the intensity of racial tensions is, on the other hand, the kind of observation a sociologist might make. But again, in prophetic fashion Niebuhr cannot help but remind us of what this suggests concerning our own frail consciences.

Whatever other purposes they serve, these two quotations do illustrate a point. Whether he is being theoretical or empirical, Niebuhr is perennially and indubitably a Christian prophet, calling men and nations to think upon the condition of their souls. What, then, do Niebuhr's critics mean when they question the relation of his theology to his politics? Perhaps all that they mean is that his prophetic conclusions do not necessarily follow from the data. Indeed, they do not *of necessity* follow, or else no nontheistic sociologist would be in a position to say anything significant about race relations, a proposition which even theologians would find

33 *The Children of Light and the Children of Darkness*, pp. 138-39.
34 "Morals and Percentages," *Christianity and Society*, Vol. 20 (1955), pp. 3-4. In Harry R. Davis and Robert C. Good, eds., *Reinhold Niebuhr on Politics* (New York: Scribner, 1960), p. 230.
35 "Christian Faith and the Race Problem," *Christianity and Society*, Vol. 10 (1945), p. 23. In Davis and Good, p. 232.

hard to accept. The function of prophets may be to point a spotlight of urgency at deeply shadowed truths, while that of theologians is to switch on a floodlight of significance.

Some critics attack not so much the overconclusiveness of Niebuhr as the underconclusiveness. He uses theological language, yes, but mainly to show how murky and involved problems are rather than how to resolve those problems. Since Niebuhr does not offer "Christian answers" at the practical political level, so this criticism runs, he is party to a divorce between politics and theology. This argument suffers from the widespread misconception that Christianity is mainly concerned to prescribe "answers" to men's practical problems, rather than to illumine the true character of these problems in their broadest dimensions. Some Christians by their evangelical excesses certainly encourage this error, but since Niebuhr's view of history is a tragic-ironic view, he can hardly be expected to apply Christian doctrine as some kind of magic formula that provides simple solutions to complex problems. The burden of his whole argument is that Christians ought to be better able to live with the ambiguities of political life without loss of hope, and to endure provisional solutions, arrived at by men of many viewpoints, to intractable problems. Critics who indict Niebuhr for not providing certified Christian solutions to everyday problems, therefore, only indicate that they have not understood him.

But we must get back to the main issue. There remains a valid question about the relationship of theology to politics. It involves neither the extent to which Niebuhr employs theological language, nor the extent to which he prescribes Christian answers, but the degree to which his theological position enhances the value of his admittedly useful political commentaries. In a sense, all of Niebuhr's political commentaries are but illustrations of the most general kind of theological propositions—about man's sin, man's fate, God's way of working in the world. The value of the illustration is not wholly dependent upon the theological context, but the full value of the illustration cannot be appreciated without sharing to some extent the presuppositions on which it is based. The non-Christians are no doubt right in suggesting that Niebuhr's political writings can stand alone; but they are not right in concluding from this that they can "just as well" stand alone—that the theology is superfluous. It is superfluous to them, of course, and this is a difficulty.

Like every theologian, Niebuhr is speaking from a base of prerational commitment and can communicate fully only to those who to some extent, perhaps even half-consciously, share such a commitment. To say this will seem to some a hopeless confusion of private subjective feelings with the criteria of objective demonstration that political theory should supposedly display. There is in this criticism, however, a bias (a liberal bias?)

toward viewing religion as private because subjective and therefore presumably less significant than objective, hence public, knowledge. In Niebuhr's view, religious commitment precedes and transcends categories of public and private, objective and subjective, interests and obligations, art and science, without necessarily annulling them. Every statement, "factual" or otherwise, presupposes an ultimate concern that makes it worth stating. Indeed, significant thought itself proceeds from religious commitment in this sense.

The editors of Niebuhr's collected political philosophy agree that the understandings that we label Niebuhr's political science and his political ethics are in neither case verifiable apart from highly personal involvement: "To freeze these understandings into a rigid, completely coherent system, would do violence to their spirit. At the center is no system, but the concerned, searching, believing, understanding and acting person."[36] Thus even Niebuhr's action in the field of politics, his work for this cause or that candidate, is inseparable from his theorizing about man and God in history, simply because actor and thinker are one person. To point to Druid-worshippers who support the same political causes as Niebuhr, or to men of other political beliefs who use similar language to describe God in history, with the implication that religious faith and politics are separable, is to miss the point. They are always logically separable and never, short of schizophrenia, personally separable.

Niebuhr is not primarily proving a set of precepts, though he may sometimes appear to be. He is describing the world, including the political world, as seen from a particular vantage point. In this he is, to use Christian terminology, witnessing to a faith; and part of the faith is that what he sees of the world of politics from his particular vantage point is not illusory. All who write of politics, whatever their viewpoint may be, all who have been discussed in this book, act from a similar ground of faith in their "given" viewpoint. And so do all who read what they have written.

36 Davis and Good, p. xi. See also Charles W. Kegley and Robert W. Bretall, eds., *Reinhold Niebuhr, His Religious, Social, and Political Thought* (New York: Macmillan, 1956), especially essays by Emil Brunner, Kenneth Thompson, and Alan Richardson.

19 | *Political Theory and the Science of Politics*

ONTRARY to the impression left by some partisans of scientific method in matters political, interest in a science of society or a science of politics is not new. It was a major concern of Aristotle and Machiavelli. It agitated the seventeenth, eighteenth, and nineteenth centuries. Moreover, its practitioners in those periods were not altogether unsuccessful. Their propositions can be dismissed because they were not quantifiable, testable, and repeatable; but the "scientific" political hypotheses of, say, Hume, may possibly stand up to any yet produced in the twentieth century.

What is new in the twentieth century is the split between what is claimed to be *the* scientific approach to politics and the great tradition of political theory. Many political science faculties in our larger universities know this split, and though graduate students, perhaps to alleviate an otherwise humdrum existence, like to magnify the disagreement among their mentors, it is surely there. The behavioralists, as they are sometimes called, may think that their historically oriented theorist colleagues are wasting their time with grand but empty metaphors, while the theorists may think the behavioralists are wasting their time with precise but trivial data and formulas.

The issue needs to be seen in the context of the whole ethos of twentieth-century thought, including the fact of totalitarianism and the decline of liberalism. The development has, very likely, the most far-reaching consequences for political theory—or at least for the way political theorizing is received by Western society. "Science" is a term of considerable popular authority and what is done in its name gains some standing thereby. But the issue of a science of politics involves judgments on the significance of trends not yet revealed in anything like their fullness. Therefore a chapter separated from the themes of our discussion of twentieth-century political thought in Chapter 15 seems warranted.[1]

The definition of the problem we have raised in this chapter, as well as our general understanding of social processes, owe much to the great European sociologists of this century. Of these we will look at four, in the order of their deaths; Durkheim, Weber, Pareto, and Mannheim.

European Sociology

DURKHEIM

Émile Durkheim (1858–1917) led French sociology away from the cosmological dogmatism of Comte toward a more solid grounding in empirical fact. He studied, for one example (but not a random example), the statistics of suicide, and found that an increase in suicides occurred not only in times of depression, as one might expect, but also in times of sudden prosperity. He concluded from this that a rapid change in social norms and a discrepancy between aspirations and the ability to gratify them were more important than external privation or plenty.[2] In this way he brought social theory back to the problem of community. For he found that the suicide-prone individual was, in essence, a community-less individual, one whose identification with a tangible group was defective and who displayed the drifting and helpless characteristics of a man

1 Literature devoted to the issue of political science in relation to political theory is voluminous. See the bibliography prepared by Charles Hyneman and Ruth Driscoll, "Methodology for Political Scientists," *Am. Pol. Sci. Rev.*, Vol. 49 (1955), pp. 192-217, and Hyneman's *The Study of Politics* (Urbana: Univ. of Illinois Press, 1959). See also Vernon Van Dyke, *Political Science: A Philosophical Analysis* (Stanford: Stanford Univ. Press, 1960); Roland Young, ed., *Approaches to the Study of Politics* (Evanston: Northwestern Univ. Press, 1958), Part 1; Harry Eckstein, *rapporteur*, "Political Theory and the Study of Politics," *Am. Pol. Sci. Rev.*, Vol. 50 (1956), pp. 475-87; J. Roland Pennock, "Political Science and Political Philosophy," *Am. Pol. Sci. Rev.*, Vol. 45 (1951), pp. 1081-85.

2 *Suicide: A Study in Sociology* (1897), trans. by J. A. Spaulding and George Simpson (Glencoe, Ill.: The Free Press, 1951). See also *The Division of Labor in Society* (2nd ed., 1902), trans. by George Simpson (Free Press, 1949). In the latter Durkheim argues that in primitive, kinship-based societies, where the individual's role is not differentiated, there is a strong common conscience and all law tends to be punitive; whereas in the advanced society with a division of labor, the common conscience is weakened and law becomes more cooperative and regulative. Durkheim's use of the terms "mechanical solidarity" to explain the former society and "organic solidarity" to explain the latter may be misleading. See also Sebastian De Grazia, *The Political Community, A Study of Anomie* (Chicago: Univ. of Chicago Press, 1948).

with ambiguous and shifting norms. This was the "anomic" individual. His condition was "anomie."

The power of the community-group without which the individual became anomic fascinated Durkheim. He found that nonanomic individuals bear within them a "collective consciousness" (in French, *conscience*) through which the group transmits "collective representations" to its members. These include, as one might expect, standards of behavior, but so inclusive did the influence of some groups seem to Durkheim that society itself was held to have created concepts of space and time, and all religious beliefs, in each case with the underlying aim of social solidarity. Whether this belief implies a disembodied "group mind" is a moot point in interpreting Durkheim, because he was sometimes given to generous metaphor. Society has within it both ugliness and grandeur, but "It is society that has freed us from nature. Is it not then to be expected that we think of it as a mental being higher than ourselves from which our mental powers emanate? This explains why it is that when it demands of us those sacrifices, great or small, that make up our moral life, we bow before its demands with deference."[3]

At any rate, what Durkheim saw most clearly was that under the division of labor and specialization characteristic of modern industry, workers come to lack a sense of performing meaningful work and a sense of belonging to the corporate enterprise. A common purpose is needed to show the relationship between the otherwise disjointed parts. Hence what is taken for granted today, namely, that individuals must learn to "adjust" to their groups if they are to avoid anxiety, and leaders must pay attention to subordinates' feelings of belonging if the enterprise is to function smoothly, was implicit in the sociology of Durkheim. We have so far accepted these conclusions, indeed, that today their unthinking application is being looked at by fresh and critical eyes.[4] Not only social science is today community-minded.

WEBER

Max Weber (1864–1920) is often called the greatest of the twentieth-century sociologists, for no one else tried so hard to combine the rigor of method so much admired today with the rich historical insight and sensitivity to human feelings that have given scholars of the past their standing. Weber's insistence on a hard distinction between "value judgments"

3 *Sociology and Philosophy* (1924), trans. by D. F. Pocock (London: Cohen & West, 1953), p. 73.

4 Widely read books such as William H. Whyte's *The Organization Man* (New York: Doubleday, 1957) not long ago reminded us that "togetherness" had become a way of life. Indeed, we became so aware of this that groupness is now a standard source of popular humor.

and empirical fact is the premise of "value-free science" accepted as axiomatic in most social research today; but mistaken conclusions are often drawn from this by supporters as well as critics. Metaphysically minded critics[5] find nihilism in the implication that because the choice of values is outside rational method and hence presumably arbitrary, the ordering of life by some kind of hierarchical principles is impossible. Some pragmatists, though hostile to metaphysics, hope to verify values scientifically, at least as "ends in view," and so reject the value-fact dichotomy.

Arnold Brecht has recently examined this whole question in his ambitious *Political Theory: The Foundations of Twentieth Century Political Thought* (1959). He vigorously asserts that the value-fact dichotomy does not mean and did not mean to Weber the suspension of critical judgment in inquiry pertaining to values, nor, on the other hand, does it make impossible an operative hierarchy of values. In his 1904 article "Die 'Objectivität' in sozialwissenschaftlicher und sozialpolitischer Erkenntnis" Weber explicitly said that his position "is certainly not that value judgments are to be withdrawn from scientific discussion in general. . . . Practical action . . . would always reject such a proposition." Again, "criticism is not to be suspended in the presence of value judgments. The problem is rather what is the meaning and purpose of the scientific criticism of ideals and value judgments."[6] What "value-free" science could do for values was to examine the rationality of *means* to any given posited *end*, and to examine the probable consequences of any policy. To this extent Weber's position has something in common with pragmatism. But it is in every case the personal conscience of the acting individual that decides what to do with this knowledge. "An empirical science cannot tell anyone what he *ought* to do, but rather what he *can* do and, under certain circumstances, what he wishes to do."[7]

But what is forgotten by those who would make Weber into a scientific pragmatist is that the value-fact dichotomy as a logical proposition was meant not only to protect science from the intrusions of warping values, but as well to protect the realm of personal affirmation from spurious scientific direction. The methodological problem becomes acute only when we take account of the personal affirmations of the individual scholar, for to say that he will stoically do the best he can to keep his

5 See Leo Strauss, *Natural Right and History* (Chicago: Univ. of Chicago Press, 1953), Ch. 2; Eric Voegelin, *The New Science of Politics* (Univ. of Chicago Press, 1952), pp. 13-22.

6 Quoted in Brecht, *Political Theory: The Foundations of Twentieth Century Political Thought* (Princeton: Princeton Univ. Press, 1959), p. 223. See also *Max Weber on the Methodology of the Social Sciences* (1922), trans. by Edward A. Shils and Henry A. Finch (Glencoe, Ill.: Free Press, 1949). Originally trained in law, Weber was a professor at Berlin, Freiburg, and Heidelberg.

7 Quoted in Brecht, p. 225.

own feelings out of the investigation does not answer all the questions in the field of social studies. As revealed in Weber's studies of Chinese culture or his famous *Protestant Ethic and the Spirit of Capitalism*, it is necessary to immerse oneself in the ethos of the culture, actually to feel the culture. The result is a profound methodological tension.

This methodological tension was reflected in (possibly created by) the extreme psychological tensions Weber felt in himself, and, more importantly for our concerns, reflected also in the substance of his descriptive conclusions. Whereas Marx could see ideas as mere reflections of social interests and Nietzsche could see ideas as reflection of psychic interests, Weber could see the interdependence, the correspondence, and the tensions between ideas in history and interests in history.[8] The satisfactions and simplifications of single-factor analyses were not to be his.

One of the best known of Weber's projects was the development of an "ideal-type" bureaucratic structure, that is, the distillation of the essence of bureaucracy from the murky vapors of contemporary historical reality (actually, the term "descriptive model" might be closer to our understanding than "ideal type"). He worked out various principles (centralization, integration, hierarchy, qualification for office, standardization of forms, and so forth) by which casual organization became bureaucratized organization. The one term that would describe the whole process was rationalization. This in turn was seen as itself the tendency of the whole of modern industrial society.[9] Weber distinguished three types of leaders: the traditional, such as a hereditary monarch; the "charismatic," the leader touched by a divine spark who galvanizes his followers; and the bureaucratic, who controls by superior organization. The last type, he felt, was coming to dominate more and more in a modern world of big organizations.

Here again Weber's tensions, which may today have their counterpart in popular feeling, are apparent. He admired the efficiency of bureaucratic leadership, but felt that this efficiency and orderliness was achieved at the expense of "the disenchantment of the world," a loss of heroic grandeur. "The fate of the classical hero was that he could never overcome contingency or *fortuna;* the special irony of the modern hero is that he strug-

8 H. H. Gerth and C. Wright Mills, in the Introduction to their edition of *From Max Weber: Essays in Sociology* (London: Routledge & Kegan Paul, 1948), p. 62. The statement is well illustrated in Weber's *Protestant Ethic and the Spirit of Capitalism*, trans. by Talcott Parsons (London: Allen & Unwin, 1930), in which Weber shows how the Calvinists' passion for otherworldly blessedness and their ascetic discipline made possible this-worldly capitalist accumulation and a remarkable degree of materialistic success.

9 See *The Theory of Social and Economic Organization*, trans. by A. M. Henderson and Talcott Parsons (New York: Oxford Univ. Press, 1947).

gles in a world where contingency has been routed by bureaucratized procedures and nothing remains for the hero to contend against."[10] In the famous essay "Politics as a Vocation" this conflict manifests itself between the new bureaucratic party official and the politician-leader who is part hero—or would-be hero. And there is internal conflict within the politician who acts on the "ethic of responsibility" while acknowledging an "ethic of ultimate ends." Somewhat like Weber himself, the politician —the real politician, not the nine out of ten who are "windbags"—must be one who can accomplish the almost impossible combination of passionate involvement in the issues of his day (for only this attracts followers), and the cool detachment to see where the real power is (for only this produces success). Such a man will see and appreciate the "ethic of ultimate ends," the call to perfection, even if he cannot live by it:

. . . it is immensely moving when a *mature* man—no matter whether old or young in years—is aware of a responsibility for the consequences of his conduct and really feels such responsibility with heart and soul. He then acts by following an ethic of responsibility and somewhere he reaches the point when he says: "Here I stand; I can do no other." That is something genuinely human and moving. And every one of us who is not spiritually dead must realize the possibility of finding himself at some time in that position. In so far as this is true, an ethic of ultimate ends and an ethic of responsibility are not absolute contrasts but rather supplements, which only in unison can constitute a genuine man—a man who *can* have the "calling for politics."[11]

Like Durkheim, Weber saw the moral element in society as that most worthy of study; but even more than Durkheim did he appreciate the quality of ambiguity and mystery in social morality, a quality, he was aware, that might be destroyed by the very methodology he espoused.

PARETO

No such qualms inhibited Vilfredo Pareto (1848–1923), professor of political economy at the University of Lausanne and one-time teacher of Mussolini. Pareto was so bent upon becoming scientific and detached in his study of society that he fell into the trap of cynicism, holding little sacred but his own views. This post-Machiavelli Machiavellianism had a certain vogue among hard-boiled social scientists of the complacent twenties and frantic thirties. The urge to "see through" our fellows, what Riesman would later call the "inside-dopester" mentality, is no doubt always a factor in social science, and Pareto, quite apart from whatever influence he may have had on fascism, exemplified this mentality. He was scornful

10 Sheldon Wolin, *Politics and Vision* (Boston: Houghton Mifflin, 1960), p. 423.
11 *From Max Weber*, p. 127.

of natural law, metaphysics, and a priori reasoning in general.[12] But Pareto's own social views got in the way of the pure detachment he no doubt genuinely sought.[13] He was attracted to logical fallacy in the collective thought of the world as a moth is attracted to flame, and he pointed out fallacies with such thoroughness that some readers wondered if logical thought was humanly possible. He opposed democracy, humanitarianism, and socialism as naïve and futile. But clearly, social stability was his implicit good, and capitalism was his favorite economic system.

All this is not to say that Pareto's theoretical work was negligible. Although the Pareto vogue has passed, his distinction between "residues," "derivatives," and "derivations" still holds interest. George Homans and Charles P. Curtis, Jr.[14] illustrate the relationship by means of a triangle. Angle *A* is what inclines men to action—"sentiments," "instincts," "drives." The words are immaterial, but Pareto generally preferred "sentiments." Angle *B* is the action itself. Angle *C* is what men say about what they do. Since what men say influences what sentiments they feel and possibly act upon, the triangle is closed from *C* to *A* as elsewhere; all angles interact on each other. This is social reality as Pareto sees it, a network of interactions against which a search for unilateral causation is futile. The most that the social scientist can hope to do is describe certain relationships in human behavior, what might be called variables and functions.

The uniformities that can be observed, whether of action or speech, Pareto called "residues," that is, the things that have *remained* constant in variable phenomena. (He also lapses at times into a looser usage in which "residues" is almost a synonym for "sentiments"—the *A* of the triangle.) The things men say about what they do—the *C* of the triangle—are "derivatives." Reluctantly, Pareto was forced to recognize that some of the derivatives should also be called residues, for there are uniformities of speech and behavior that can be observed. The rest of the derivatives, which he called "derivations," are what we would call rationalizations, nice words that do not really affect our behavior. This designation applied to almost all historical political theories.

The object of all this was not simply to express in other language the belief that most of what men said and wrote was irrelevant nonsense

12 His scorn may have been a displacement of some of the hostility Pareto showed against his idealistic father. The senior Pareto had been exiled from Italy for his support of Mazzini's liberal *Risorgimento* movement.

13 To help assure this detachment, most of the historical illustrations in Pareto's monumental *Trattato di sociologia* (1916) were drawn from ancient and medieval times, even though their import was often contemporary. The English translation of this work is *The Mind and Society*, Arthur Livingston, ed. (New York: Harcourt, Brace, 1935).

14 In *An Introduction to Pareto* (New York: Knopf, 1934), Ch. 4.

(though this motive may have been present). It was to display a kind of epistemological self-denial, a recognition that the scientific observer must work within the limits of his observation and the student of society cannot go much beyond words and overt actions. The method of residues was one way of canceling out the fortuitous cause at the same time one disregarded the irrelevant utterance. It was a way of getting at what really could be known. Pareto was willing to dismiss much of reality in order to get one part of it in an iron grip. And it must be admitted he did thus manage to conceive of society as a system without the organic or mechanistic metaphors characteristic of most such attempts.

We need not discuss the elaborate extrapolations of Pareto's system, the six classes of residues, the four classes of derivations, the attempts at graphic representation of society as an equilibrium situation. We may note in passing the "circulation of elites." With a certain fatalism Pareto adds to the many theories of inevitable elite rule the view that elites are never permanent but are continually being displaced from below by rising classes. None, however, can disrupt for long the basic social equilibrium, and survival is the only utilitarian value they or the system can know.[15]

MANNHEIM

A far more optimistic, yet in one way more profound political sociologist of twentieth-century Europe was Karl Mannheim (1893–1947). Mannheim posed the problem of historical relativism more acutely than any other contemporary social scientist, yet, ironically, none struggled with greater determination to escape from its implications. Mannheim's most important work was *Ideology and Utopia*,[16] the first major statement of his "sociology of knowledge."

After the breakdown of feudalism, Mannheim argued, philosophers,

15 *Mind and Society*, Vol. IV, pp. 1787ff. Two noted scholars of the inevitable elite-rule persuasion who were contemporaries of Pareto were Gaetano Mosca (1858–1941) and Roberto Michels (1876–1936). See Mosca's *Elementi di scienza politica* (1896), trans. by Hannah D. Kahn as *The Ruling Class*, Arthur Livingston, ed. (New York: McGraw-Hill, 1939). Livingston, the editor of both Pareto and Mosca, claims their ideas were arrived at independently. *Ibid.*, pp. xxxvi-xxxix. See also James H. Meisel, *The Myth of the Ruling Class* (Ann Arbor: Univ. of Michigan Press, 1957). Michels' famous "iron law of oligarchy," expounded despite his democratic leanings, is found in *Political Parties: A Sociological Study of the Oligarchical Tendencies of Modern Democracy* (1915), trans. by Eden and Cedar Paul (Glencoe, Ill.: Free Press, 1949). See also his *First Lectures in Political Sociology* (1927), trans. by Alfred De Grazia (Minneapolis: Univ. of Minnesota Press, 1949).

16 *Ideology and Utopia*, trans. by Louis Wirth and Edward Shils (New York: Harcourt, Brace, 1949). The book consists of a translation of *Ideologie und Utopie* (1929), a 1931 article, and a specially written introduction. Mannheim was a professor at Heidelberg, Frankfurt, and, after the Nazis came to power, the London School of Economics.

as always, reflected the social situation in which they found themselves. Modern epistemology and psychology approached the individual mind as if it could be separated from group influences. Infected by an individualistic and a rationalistic bias, a Descartes or a Locke thought he could approach the truth of the mind free of the superstitions and authoritarian restraints of the past. But, says Mannheim, knowledge is partly a group product that presupposes a community and a "collective unconscious."

Even mathematical knowledge, perhaps the least obviously influenced by group norms, is a function of such norms. But the "irrational foundation of rational knowledge" is most conspicuously demonstrated by political thought:

Politics is conflict and tends increasingly to become a life-and-death struggle. . . .

Political discussion possesses a character fundamentally different from academic discussion. It seeks not only to be in the right but also to demolish the basis of its opponent's social and intellectual existence. Political discussion therefore penetrates more profoundly into the existential foundation of thinking. . . .

In political discussion in modern democracies where ideas were more clearly representative of certain groups, the social and existential determination of thought became easily visible. In principle it was politics which first discovered the sociological method in the study of intellectual phenomena. Basically it was in political struggles that for the first time men became aware of the unconscious collective motivations which had always guided the direction of thought.[17]

If, then, all thought is socially conditioned, there is no fixed point in historical existence by reference to which all thought may be judged. We are all prisoners of the age in which we live. Relativism was, of course, not an invention of Mannheim. But he pushed its implications a bit further. The older relativism recognized that the content of human thought was relative to the social position of the thinker, but took for granted that the structure of thought was constant and could be understood categorically by a permanently true epistemology. Yet, "Actually, epistemology is as intimately enmeshed in the social process as is the totality of our thinking."[18] To differentiate it from the older relativism, Mannheim calls his view "relationism." "Relationism signifies merely that all of the elements of meaning in a given situation have reference to one another and derive their significance from this reciprocal interrelationship in a given frame of thought. Such a system of meanings

17 *Ibid.*, pp. 34-35.   18 *Ibid.*, p. 70.

is possible and valid only in a given type of historical existence, to which, for a time, it furnishes appropriate expression. When the social situation changes, the system of norms to which it had previously given birth ceases to be in harmony with it."[19]

The transience of human thought revealed by this position would seem to pose insuperable barriers to significant social reform, not only with reference to obtaining rational guidance of the direction of reform, but also with reference to the elemental problem of maintaining community morale in the face of cosmic ambiguity. It was precisely to this problem that Mannheim gave the bulk of his energies. The morale problem had been faced many times before. In every age, Mannheim could easily demonstrate, certain beliefs, suppositions, and myths had been absolutized and used as instruments for leadership, as tools whereby contingent policies were given the sanction of eternal truths. Where these were used to maintain the status quo, Mannheim called them "ideologies." Where they were used to change the social system, he called them "utopias" (we need to remember that the vernacular use of "ideology" would include both "ideology" and "utopia" in Mannheim's sense).

The thorny problem was how to achieve some kind of rational guidance for the social scientist or the would-be leader. How could he avoid being the victim of his own group's ideology, his own false absolutes? Mannheim's first answer to this was to recognize them. The more one is able in retrospect to probe one's own motives and interests "the more it is apparent that this empirical procedure (in the social sciences at least) can be carried on only on the basis of certain meta-empirical, ontological, and metaphysical judgments. . . . He who makes no decisions has no questions to raise."[20]

It is not possible to prove the validity of these basic ontological assumptions; but it may be possible to recognize some of them and thereby cast light on differing systems of thought so that they may be seen more clearly for what they are. In this way group, class, and national biases may be slowly stripped away so that the social scientist can determine "which of all the ideas current are really valid in a given situation"— although in a footnote Mannheim admits that "exposure of ideological and utopian elements in thought is effective in destroying only those ideas with which we ourselves are not too intimately identified."[21]

It can be argued that this rather pragmatic "validity" is nothing but old-fashioned rational truth by a different name, now limited more severely than ever to the rare social scientist (could Aristotle have been such?) who is most fortunate in purging himself of bias. The description of

19 *Ibid.*, p. 76. The influence of Marx on Mannheim is clear in this passage.
20 *Ibid.*, p. 79.   21 *Ibid.*, pp. 84, 79*n*.

such a person, a member of the so-called socially unattached intelligentsia, comes remarkably close to a description of Mannheim himself.

Yet however detached and however intellectual the scholar on whom Mannheim depends, he cannot really lead us out of the dilemma of relationism Mannheim has described. If you are asked whether a painting of a person you have never seen is a good likeness, you have no way of answering. And it matters not how many paintings of him you see. You still cannot answer until you see the person himself. Mannheim's "valid" ideas would seem to be very much like the unseen portrait subject. The "socially unattached intellectual" is only offering one more portrait, a composite of all the rest.[22]

Without trying to summarize Mannheim's provocative discussion of the requirements for a science of politics (*Ideology and Utopia*, Chapter 3), it can be said that despite what might seem to be the tragic implications of his relationism, he is optimistic rather than pessimistic over the possibilities of such a science. Further, he contends that to the degree that a science of politics is possible, politics in the sense of group conflict will disappear and ideological warfare will be replaced by rational "administration," a "purely technical" operation.

The means to this end of endless means were treated by Mannheim in a number of writings, most notably *Man and Society in an Age of Reconstruction* (1940) and *Freedom, Power, and Democratic Planning* (1950). He argued that democracy and planning were compatible and even necessary, that an open society as far as ultimate ends were concerned was consistent with the rational direction of means. Such rational "non-political" direction would, however, require both increased centralization and a deflection of the "artificial" consumer wants stimulated by the "psychological anarchy of liberal capitalism."[23] "Everything connected with the reorganization of industry and the encouragement and discouragement of investment will take precedence, for the effect on the whole cycle is more important than the satisfaction of individual desires. . . . People will learn that consumer choice is not sacred and the entrepreneur will find that he has more control over his business, if he can be guided in his investments by a central plan." Mannheim hoped the transition could be accomplished "without much fuss or propaganda."[24]

Whether taking the form of the cynical conservatism of Pareto or the optimistic reformism of Mannheim, the common tendency of

22 I am indebted for the portrait analogy to Gustav Bergmann, *The Metaphysics of Logical Positivism* (New York: Longmans, Green, 1954), p. 316.

23 *Man and Society in an Age of Reconstruction*, trans. by Edward Shils (New York: Harcourt, Brace, 1940), p. 352.

24 *Ibid.*, p. 347.

European and much of American sociology has been antiliberal. The concept of the group has gained the ascendancy over the concept of the autonomous individual.

While European sociology was giving political science a new appreciation of group influences in the formation of individual values, an important European philosophical movement was doing its utmost to free the methodology of science, including social science, from the taint of subjective values.

Logical Positivism

THE historical roots of positivism go back through Comte and Mill and Hume, but the springboard of action in the twentieth century was clearly the so-called Vienna Circle, which grew up under the leadership of Moritz Schlick at the University of Vienna in the early 1920's. The influence of the group was dispersed westward by the migrations of Otto Neurath to England, Rudolph Carnap to the University of Chicago, Felix Kaufmann to the New School for Social Research in New York, and, via Berlin, Hans Reichenbach to the University of California at Los Angeles. Other centers developed around Ludwig Wittgenstein at Cambridge University and A. J. Ayer at Oxford. The terminology changed, to "logical empiricism," or "neo-positivism," or simply "analytic philosophy," but few doubt that the labels designate a major intellectual movement.

Logical positivism represents one of the most consistent attempts to transfer the rigorous methodology of the physical sciences to philosophic inquiry, if not, indeed, to make the two disciplines one (Schlick, like his predecessor at Vienna, Ernst Mach—jet pilots will know the name if not the man—was trained in physics). To begin with the negative, logical positivists rejected as hopelessly imprecise the formulations of "speculative" philosophy, the metaphysical questions that have been the chief occupation of philosophers since the classical period: the one and the many, the nature of reality, the problem of evil, the nature of the true, the beautiful, and the good. These are put aside as pseudo-questions, beyond the realm of meaning. Logical positivists deny not only that "eternal questions" are eternal; they deny that they are questions! In a striking reversal of Plato's distinction between knowledge and opinion, logical positivists hold that answers to these alleged questions can never be more than opinion, for "meaningful propositions," the only basis of knowledge, are those that can be verified by the methods of the natural sciences, that is, experimentation with data derived from direct sensory perception and/or logical inference from those data. Early members of the Circle held that conclusive scientific verification was the only condition of significance. Ludwig Wittgenstein, whose *Tractatus Logico-Philosophicus* (1922) was a bible for the group, there held (he later recanted) that the complete body of natural science would exhaust the totality of true propositions. Later disciples have softened to the extent of accepting as sufficient a high degree of probability, and admitting a few non-scientific statements into their lexicon.

All acknowledged positivists agree with the basic tenet of the *Tractatus* that philosophy is not a subject matter but an activity. Its purpose is not to construct propositions (the scientist does this) or to ascribe value to them (everyone does this), but to clarify them. The analysis of the logical syntax of language, thus, has been one of their central occupations. For the positivist there are two fundamental types of "meaningful statements." One is the empirical, "I see the satellite," and the other is the logical, "two plus two is four." Statements of value, "I like the satellite. The satellite is good," fall into neither of these categories. Statements of value have no empirical content or logical structure. They are expressions of emotional preference. However much they must live as *men* by valuing, as *philosophers*, the logical positivists feel they are bound to regard value statements as meaningless—one is tempted to say as valueless. The stringency with which they identify this Weberian distinction between the "positive" fact and values with the distinction between knowledge and nonknowledge is what most distinguishes them from their next of kin, the pragmatists. Finally, logical positivism is marked by the tendency to avoid the question of causation and substitute the concept of function, to speak of "correlations" and "probabilities" rather than "causes."

The continual reduction of traditional philosophic questions to questions of scientific methodology would seem to have the effect of particularizing inquiry to such an extent that broad-gauge generalizations become impossible. Some critics of positivism have felt that this was the case. Yet, despite this tendency, the drive toward the unity of all scientific thought has been powerful within the logical positivist movement, as shown by the *International Encyclopedia of Unified Science* begun in 1938 under the editorship of Neurath, Carnap, and Charles W. Morris.

To speak of logical positivist political theory is to speak of a movement that makes political theory and political science synonymous and makes the political theorist simply an articulate, generalizing political scientist. Three examples may be found in the work of Herbert S. Simon, Harold D. Lasswell, and Robert A. Dahl. All three are Americans, which may be more than accidental. Judged by their willingness to bother with traditional political theories, they could possibly be thought of, respectively, as left-wing, middle-of-the-road, and right-wing representatives of the logical positivist influence.

SIMON

Herbert Simon, professor of administration at the Carnegie Institute of Technology, is a social scientist often better understood by mathematicians than by colleagues in his own discipline. His introduction to what we might call scientific theorizing was by way of the problems of administrative decision-making,[25] but he can hardly be restricted to a designation more narrow than social theorist. Of his essays in *Models of Man* he says, ". . . economists are aware of them chiefly as they impinge upon the theory of the firm, social psychologists and sociologists as they relate to the small group theory, learning theorists as they relate to problem solving, political scientists as they relate to the phenomena of power, and statisticians as they relate to the identification problem."[26] The two basic concerns that unite these apparently diverse threads are, he says, the "mechanism of influence" and the "mechanism of choice." In both cases, he has arrived at a middle ground between the assumptions that man has a high degree of rationality (economics) and that man's behavior is basically a product of emotions (psychology). But the median assumption is itself only an assumption and Simon, to his credit, does not claim that his models are more than models. This epistemological self-denial is no doubt a reflection of his acknowledged debt to logical positivism, especially on the matter of causation.

Accepting the Humean critique of causation as necessary connection and wishing to avoid the ontological overtones of traditional views on the subject, Simon nevertheless finds that "working scientists" cannot seem to get along without using the word "cause." His aim is to make the word "operational" by keeping its usage strictly within the logical model, thus implying, as we have seen, nothing of necessity about the empirical world. In other words, he is willing to say, "Sentence A stands in a causal relation to sentence B," but he is not willing to say, "That which is denoted by sentence A *causes* that which is denoted by sentence B." So conceived, "Causality is an asymmetrical relation among certain variables, or subset of variables, in a self-contained structure. There is no necessary connection between the asymmetry of this relation and the asymmetry in time. . . ."[27] Although, he goes on to say, it may be useful to asume that "lagged" relations are causal relations.

What does this have to do with politics? Of course, any contribution

25 See his *Administrative Behavior* (1947) (2nd ed.; New York: Macmillan, 1956).
26 *Models of Man* (New York: Holt, 1957), p. vii.
27 *Ibid.*, pp. 34-35.

to the methodology of the social sciences is a contribution to political theory. But the connection is much closer than that. In the first part of *Models of Man*, Simon attempts to relate three questions that, on the face of it, seem wholly unrelated:

(1) How should we define influence, power, and authority, and measure the strength of influence relations? This is a question central to political science.

(2) ". . . in determining the relationship between two variables by the method of least squares, which variable should be taken as independent and which as dependent?" This is a problem in statistics.

(3) If a prediction in the social sciences is published so that the people whose behavior is predicted know about it, is the prediction thereby falsified? This is a long-standing problem of general social science methodology.

It was about 1950, Simon says, that he began to put these questions together:

. . . influence, power, and authority are all intended as *asymmetrical* relations. When we say that A has power over B, we do not mean to imply that B has power over A. The mathematical counterpart to this asymmetrical relation appeared to be the distinction between independent and dependent variable —the independent variable determines the dependent, and not the converse. But in algebra, the distinction between independent and dependent variable is purely conventional—we can always rewrite our equations without altering their content in such a way as to reverse their roles. Thus, if $y = ax$, it is equally true that $x = by$, where $b = 1/a$. Neither way of writing the equation is preferred to the other.

When I had stated the question in this form—as a problem in giving operational meaning to the asymmetry of the relation between independent and dependent variable—it became clear that it was identical with the general problem of defining a *causal relation* between two variables. That is to say, for the assertion, "A has power over B," we can substitute the assertion, "A's behavior causes B's behavior." If we can define the causal relation, we can define influence, power, or authority, and *vice versa*.[28]

In other words, Simon is seeking and thinks he has found, a method for handling data on power relations at a very high degree of generality, so high, in fact, that the same operation that isolates the independent variable among a collection of abstract integers can isolate the power-holder and, given the right data, measure his power. We can scarcely follow through on the implications of this juxtaposition of the political with the statistical, and, indeed, it cannot be said that Simon does; but

28 *Ibid.*, p. 5.

obviously handling descriptions of power relations at this level not only of generality but of precision would have far-reaching implications for the development of a unified body of scientific social knowledge.

There is still, however, question (3) and its correlates. Power relations cannot be dealt with like inert algebraic relations, because, while abstract symbols A and B may be perfectly asymmetrical, Mr. Able and Mr. Baker are never in a wholly asymmetrical or unilateral relationship. There is almost always the softening effect of compassion or the hardening effect of fear. There are what Carl J. Friedrich calls "anticipated reactions" or what others call "feedback," which make the hypothecated asymmetry (or symmetry) of human relations in fact ambiguous. Human beings may, for example, turn honest prophecies into self-fulfilling prophecies by conforming to what is predicted of them. With the help of an elaborate statistical exercise, Simon has claimed to have minimized the descriptive errors resulting from this tendency.[29] He also has some useful suggestions on how political scientists can beat the rule of anticipated reactions by taking advantage of the errors of public officials.[30]

Obviously, what Simon gives us is not the confirmation of substantive hypotheses about politics but the confirmation of statistical methods of analysis that may give us more precise knowledge about politics. That more can be done with the mathematical approach to social phenomena goes without saying. That it can do as much as positivistic admirers of natural science think it can may be another question. "Mathematics," says Simon, "has become the dominant language of the natural sciences not because it is quantitative—a common delusion—but primarily because it permits clear and vigorous reasoning about phenomena too complex to be handled in words. This advantage of mathematics over cruder languages should prove of even greater significance in the social sciences, which deal with phenomena of the greatest complexity, than it has in the natural sciences."[31] Whether the subtleties of English or any other verbal language are as crude as Simon suggests is open to question. And whether his optimism concerning what the social sciences will become is free of the distorting influence of his own infectious enthusiasm for mathematical manipulations seems quite dubious. But then, without enthusiastic confrontation, would we even take seriously the prospects of a mathematical political theory, as now we must?

LASSWELL

Harold D. Lasswell, professor of law and political science at Yale, stepped into the positivists' circle with *Power and Society: A Framework*

29 *Ibid.*, Ch. 5.   30 *Ibid.*, Ch. 4.   31 *Ibid.*, p. 89.

for Political Inquiry,[32] a kind of *Tractatus Logico-Philosophicus* for political scientists. The book was written with Abraham Kaplan, a University of California philosopher and colleague of Reichenbach. Lasswell had earlier made his mark as an empirically oriented theorist with a 1936 book, *Politics: Who Gets What, When, How*, an elite model analysis emphasizing as motive forces of politics the drives of income, safety, and deference to a degree perhaps more cynical than skeptical. Lasswell is also known for his studies of political language and the application of Freudian concepts to politics, especially the judicial decision-making process. Like others influenced by positivism, Lasswell has been attracted to the world of science and the behavioral sciences. It may be more than merely accidental that his presidential address to the American Political Science Association in 1956 was entitled "The Political Science of Science" and called attention to the discipline's neglect of policy problems and opportunities created by scientific change.

Power and Society is a series of definitions and propositions dovetailed together in such a way that an almost self-contained language results. For example: to know what it means to say that authority is "formal power" we must know that *power* is "participation in the making of decisions," a *decision* is "a policy involving severe sanctions," and a *policy* is "a projected program of goal values and practices." We must also know that *formal* is "pertaining to the political formula," the political *formula* is "the part of the political myth describing and prescribing in detail the social structure," the political *myth* is "the pattern of basic political symbols current in a society," and so on. For their purposes it might have been better if Lasswell and Kaplan had used much more esoteric symbols than English words for the subjects of their definitions. When students genuinely try to use this set of definitions as a "framework for political inquiry" they almost always lapse into ordinary English from time to time, so that "decision" or "formula" on one page has a Lasswellian meaning and on another page a more common meaning. The result is often hopeless confusion. Lasswell and Kaplan cannot really be blamed if others misuse their terminology; but on the other hand, even in natural science the most important words are defined by usage and not by pronouncement. Impatience with ambiguity seems to be a characteristic of modern positivism, and indeed the very purpose of a precisely defined (and authoritative) lexicon and a logically interrelated set of operational propositions reflects the positivistic tenor of the enterprise.

The positivistic orientation is also evident in the authors' conception

32 *Power and Society: A Framework for Political Inquiry* (New Haven: Yale Univ. Press, 1950).

of values. Their commitment to "objective" analysis requires a prefatory confession of their own subjective values ("those of the citizen of a society that aspires toward freedom") along with the disclaimer that these values will not affect the book's findings. As between empirical propositions and value judgments, "Only statements of the first kind are explicitly formulated in the present work."[33] Despite the fact that this book is in large part concerned with the operation of certain "welfare values" and "deference values" in the political arena, these are viewed from the outside, so to speak; they are viewed as "goal events" whose fulfillment can be checked off by a detached observer. "Value" itself is one of the undefined terms of the lexicon.

Again, as in the case of Simon, what this positivistic endeavor offers is not so much significant knowledge, not so much the fruits of research, but stimulation to research. In natural science, system-building has come after the amassing of a pressing quantity of nonself-evident or even contradictory "facts." In political science, as many critics of this book have pointed out, system-building has seemed to come before the facts. There is no doubt more attraction in being a political Einstein than in being a political Michelson and Morley. Yet it would be unfair to suggest that this criticism lies with particular force against Lasswell. Despite *Power and Society*, he cannot be written off as a nonempirical empiricist. More than many other theorists he has immersed himself in concrete studies within what he calls the "policy sciences," thereby qualifying himself as an empiricist as well as a theorist of empiricism. He has deigned to deal with quite ordinary historical and even impressionistic data.[34] He has encouraged more than one approach to political reality. Positivism can easily become a cult. If Lasswell has been one of the leading cult figures, he has at least kept himself from becoming a cultist.

DAHL

Robert A. Dahl is a young political scientist at Yale who would no doubt shy away from the designation positivist, and we should not quibble about it. Whereas Simon is not much concerned with thinkers who thought before the days of the chi-square test, whereas Lasswell nods to Plato, Locke, and Rousseau and puts them under the heading of "political doctrine," Dahl pays political theorists of the past the honor of analyzing them into a shambles. He is positivistic perhaps only in the sense that the logical analysis of language is his critical weapon and the reconstruction of propositions to make them "operational" and "testable"

33 *Ibid.*, p. xiii.
34 See his *National Security and Individual Freedom* (New York: McGraw-Hill, 1950).

is his constructive task. Although *Politics, Economics, and Welfare* (1953), written with his economics colleague Charles E. Lindblom, would mark him as a system-builder, *A Preface to Democratic Theory*[35] is a more modest venture, yet of considerable significance. In that work Dahl subjects the allegedly democratic theories of Madison, Rousseau and others to meticulous linguistic analysis. The logical implications of words, phrases, and sentences are drawn out, in some cases reduced to nonverbal symbols, and compared with the implications of other words, phrases, and sentences. The result is that the Madisonian or natural-rights view of democracy and the Rousseauistic-majoritarian view of democracy (Dahl calls it "populistic") look a bit tattered. Dahl does not belittle their historical significance, emotive import, or richness of language, but he pitilessly exposes their defective logic and operational limitations.

After the demolition operation, Dahl turns to the constructive task of devising a concept of democracy precise enough to permit its meaningful application to a series of discrete, empirical events. The task is not easy and it cannot be said that Dahl altogether succeeds—but he certainly tries. His concept of "polyarchal democracy" is defined by a set of eight criteria with at least hypothetically quantifiable indices. He even provides a suggested classification of polyarchies. "Egalitarian polyarchies" are those in which the eight conditions are scaled at values equal to or greater than 0.75, "nonegalitarian polyarchies" fall between 0.50 and 0.75; "oligarchies" between 0.25 and 0.50; and "dictatorships" below 0.25. If all this sounds a bit premature, or even futile, it must be said that Dahl is well aware of the hypothetical nature of what he is doing and tempers every proposition with a commendable awareness of the "real world." In fact, his great virtue is the degree to which he has sought to bridge the gap between traditional historical political theories and the solid empirical data of hard-headed political researchers like V. O. Key of Harvard, Paul Lazarsfeld of Columbia, and Angus Campbell of Michigan and Berkeley. The softening of the partisan positivist temper without loss of logical vigor and operationalism is a welcome contribution of Professor Dahl's writings.

Toward a Science of Law

JURISPRUDENCE is a complicated and heavily chronicled subject that has not figured prominently in these pages. Seventy-five years ago it would have been otherwise. Then, the prevailing conception of the nature of political theory made it almost synonymous with legal theory. Today

35 *A Preface to Democratic Theory* (Chicago: Univ. of Chicago Press, 1956).

not only political theory but legal theory itself is heavily weighted with sociological and psychological terminology. The positivistic emphasis has been felt in law, too. But even as we say this, we must note that the trend is by no means unilateral. A reaction against legal positivism and the relativism it implies began almost as soon as it had reached full tide. The reaction took the form of a return to natural-law thinking, but not always natural law in traditional dress. The lawlessness of totalitarianism accelerated the reaction. "In the secure days of constitutional order during the last century, there was a general inclination to transfer such [higher law] standards, even when recognized, from jurisprudence into ethics or religion. The lawless rule of totalitarian power has made it evident that jurisprudence once again must consider the development of such standards as one of its most essential tasks.[36]

A leader of the relativists was Gustav Radbruch (1878–1949)[37] of Heidelberg. His basic premise was that of the positivists, namely that a system built on value preferences must give up any claim to scientific validity. A science of law required, he felt, the development of a "system of systems" with no attempt to express preferences among them. Radbruch thereupon tried to describe and organize all previous types of legal theories around three presumably impartially chosen categories of value: the individual; human collectivities; and human works or culture. Significantly, the rise of Nazism, under which Radbruch personally suffered, led him to unfortunately uncompleted postwar attempts to overcome some of the limitations of relativism.

Another and better known legal positivist who has tried to purge his theory of all value judgments is Hans Kelsen (1881–   ),[38] father of the "pure theory of law." The "purity" is found in the system's complete formalism. Kelsen is as uninterested in the content of law as one can be. He is uninterested in speculations about the will behind law. Rather, he takes for granted in any given society a basic norm *(Grundnorm)* with coercive sanctions behind it, from which flows everything that can be called law. He proceeds to develop a system of logical correlates

36 Carl J. Friedrich, *The Philosophy of Law in Historical Perspective* (Chicago: Univ. of Chicago Press, 1958), p. 182.

37 See his *Rechtsphilosophie* (3rd ed., 1932), trans. by Kurt Wilk, Twentieth Century Legal Philosophy Series, Vol. II (Cambridge: Harvard Univ. Press, 1950). See also Anton-Hermann Chroust, "The Philosophy of Law of Gustav Radbruch," *Philosophical Review*, Vol. 53 (1944), pp. 23-45; *The Legal Philosophies of Lask, Radbruch and Dabin*, trans. by Kurt Wilk, intro. by Edwin W. Patterson. Twentieth Century Legal Philosophy Series, Vol. IV (Cambridge: Harvard Univ. Press, 1950); Brecht, *Political Theory*, pp. 233-36, 357-61.

38 See his *General Theory of Law and the State*, trans. by Anders Wedberg (Cambridge: Harvard Univ. Press, 1945). A former professor at Vienna, Kelsen has been in the United States since 1940. An important precursor of Kelsen was Rudolph Stammler (1856-1938) of Halle and Berlin, a leading neo-Kantian.

built upon such a norm—whatever its specific content may be. In a sense, the whole operation is a tautology. It pretends to do no more than provide a structure that may help one think about law. There is no law but positive law, and any state can be a *Rechtsstaat*. But since other organizations exercise coercive power over its members and law is wholly relative to such power, the boundaries of statehood are not altogether clear in Kelsen's system.

Kelsen has been a defender of philosophical relativism in its more extreme form and remains a forthright critic of natural-law doctrines. He argues that if natural law were in any meaningful sense "self-evident," positive law would be superflouous; and if natural law is open to interpretation, the only interpretation that counts is that approved by the authorities established by positive law. He grants that natural-law doctrines may serve a function in giving people a sense of deep-seated moral justification as they obey laws. In this respect, natural law is a kind of Platonic myth: "That the natural-law doctrine, as it pretends, is able to determine in an objective way what is just, is a lie; but those who consider it useful may make use of it as a useful lie."[39]

Less philosophically minded, but also defenders of a form of legal positivism, are the so-called legal realists of American jurisprudence. Their origins go back at least to Professor John Chipman Gray's *Nature and Sources of the Law* (1909) and the earthy naturalism of Justice Oliver Wendell Holmes' miscellaneous essays. Later candidates for the school would be Thurman Arnold and Karl Llewellyn. One member deeply influenced by the findings of social science was Jerome Frank (1889–1957),[40] who found in Freudian psychology an explanation of the almost universal tendency to deify the law and dignify judges beyond their normal human stature. Frank's aim was to use the resources of social science to demythologize the popular image of the legal system in order that mature—that is to say, modern—men will accept responsibility for the fact that law is really made and not discovered: ". . . this Blackstonian lie (or myth) serves to shield the courts from popular understanding and criticism by making their work a mystery; and, in a democracy, no part of government should be mysterious."[41]

39 "The Natural-Law Doctrine Before the Tribunal of Science," *Western Political Quarterly*, Vol. 2 (1949), p. 513. See also Kelsen's *What Is Justice?* (Berkeley: Univ. of California Press, 1957).

40 See *Law and the Modern Mind* (New York: Brentano, 1930), *If Men Were Angels* (New York: Harper, 1942), *Fate and Freedom* (New York: Simon & Schuster, 1945).

41 "A Sketch of an Influence," in Paul Sayre, ed., *Interpretations of Modern Legal Philosophy, Essays in Honor of Roscoe Pound* (New York: Oxford Univ. Press, 1947), p. 233. Against these attacks on natural law, Catholic neo-Thomism of course maintained a solid front. Some writers in this school are: Victor Cathrein, Giorgio

Pound.   A more moderate position is exemplified in the United States by Roscoe Pound (1870–   ), great Harvard law dean and founder of the "sociological" theory of law.[42] The essence of his position is that law is not, as it was for the nineteenth century, a set of deductions; it is, as Pound said, "social engineering." Law should be conceived always in light of the social conditions within which it is expected to operate. Pound criticized the way private litigation operating under an unrealistic but protective cloak of abstract individual rights was used to settle social issues of major importance to the community. Pound was the enemy of pharisaical artificiality, Germanic hair-splitting, and nostalgic devotion to natural-law doctrines. Above all, he took the social sciences seriously.

In one chapter of *Social Control Through Law* Pound sketches the changes in the conceptions of law characteristic of the twentieth century; the list reads like a statement of Pound's own tenets. This is not prejudicial reporting; it is a testament to his own influence. He mentions, for example, a pragmatic concern for function, legal action aiming at the satisfaction of concrete human wants rather than serving an abstract freedom of will. He speaks of a recognition of the problem of value as both integral to the judicial process (in contrast to the "pure theory of law") and wider than the judicial process (in contrast to the judicial "realists"). It is, he said, "a problem of all the social sciences."

. . . we have to note the movement for teamwork with the other social sciences; the study of law as part of a whole process of social control. This is an essential point in the twentieth-century sociological jurisprudence. Compare it with the characteristic noncooperation of the social sciences in the nineteenth century. This ignoring by each of the social sciences of each of the others was by no means wholly due to the exigencies of university organization and academic courtesy, requiring each scholar to keep off his neighbor's premises. It was in the very spirit of the last century—every man for himself, every subject for itself. It was in the spirit of the atomistic conception of humanity as an aggregate of individuals engaged, with a minimum of organization, in a competitive acquisitive struggle for existence.[43]

---

del Vecchio, François Geny, Jacques Maritain, Heinrich Romman, and Jacques Leclerq. Other anti-positivist writers sought an ethical basis for law without relying on traditional natural-law concepts. The Dutchman Hugo Krabbe (1857-1936) found it in an instinctive sense of right in the community; the Frenchman Léon Duguit (1859-1928) found it in *solidarité*.

42 Sociological jurisprudence is obviously not without many antecedents, especially in the theories of Rudolf von Ihering and Ludwig Gumplowicz. Of Pound's many works see *An Introduction to the Philosophy of Law* (1924) (rev. ed.; New Haven: Yale Univ. Press, 1954); *Social Control Through Law* (New Haven: Yale Univ. Press, 1942); *Contemporary Juristic Theory* (Claremont, Calif.: Claremont Colleges, 1940); *Justice According to Law* (New Haven: Yale Univ. Press, 1951). Perhaps the classic example of Pound's attempt to relate legal abstraction to hard social realities was his article "Liberty of Contract," *Yale Law Journal*, Vol. 18 (1909), pp. 454-87.

43 *Social Control Through Law*, pp. 124-25.

Pound once proposed that courts should be fully staffed with social scientists to compile the background data necessary for sound judicial decisions (a technique followed on his own initiative by Justice Brandeis).

In his later years Pound has criticized some of those who have carried the sociological principle of law too far.[44] The Freudian analysis of judicial motives identified with Jerome Frank is not, in Pound's view, a fruitful course. A proper concern for the law involves finding standards that can restrain and nullify personal idiosyncrasy rather than magnify it. The purpose of law is distorted if it is treated only as subjective preference. While judges have access to no absolute standards, they have an obligation to serve standards outside themselves. But Pound, as a pragmatist, is perhaps most weak on this very question of values, deferring at various times to "harmony," "consensus," and "social needs" without offering any higher criterion by which the harmony and consensus and fulfilled social need of a group of opium smokers is distinguished from that of Plato's Academy. One of Pound's concluding admonitions to the courts represents a typical pragmatic statement of value, or evasion of value: ". . . the courts must . . . go on finding out by experience and developing by reason the modes of adjusting relations and ordering conduct which will give the most effect to the whole scheme of interests with the least friction and the least waste."[45]

The positivists, both legal and logical, continue their attack on metaphysical standards of right. But in the mid-twentieth century social scientists seem more concerned than ever before to find some rapprochement between those who would make science the only metaphysics and those who would make metaphysics the only science.[46]

Toward System, and Beyond

THE political science fraternity numbers among its members the devoted fact-gatherers, those practicing empiricists who provide the grist for the theoretical mills of others. Theirs is a necessary and sometimes unrewarding job, and who can blame them if a few feel that they are the only

44 See *Justice According to Law*, 1951.

45 *Social Control*, p. 134. See also *Introduction to the Philosophy of Law*, pp. 45-47.

46 The counterattack on positivism has come not only from Thomists, but from non-Catholic Christian theists like Eric Voegelin and John Hallowell and from Jewish classical natural-law scholars like Leo Strauss and Harry Jaffa. For two scholarly debates in which, as usual, each side is brilliant, but the issue is not quite squarely joined, see Felix Oppenheim, "The Natural Law Thesis: Affirmation or Denial?" Harry Jaffa, "Comment on Oppenheim"; Oppenheim, "Non-Cognitivist Rebuttal," *Am. Pol. Sci. Rev.*, Vol. 51 (1957), pp. 41-66; and Hans Kelsen, "The Natural Law Doctrine Before the Tribunal of Science," and Edgar Bodenheimer, "The Natural Law Doctrine Before the Tribunal of Science: A Reply to Hans Kelsen," *Western Political Quarterly*, Vols. 2, 3 (1949, 1950), pp. 481-513, and 335-63, respectively.

political scientists, that others gather wool while they gather facts. Without "facts," as we all know, no body of truly scientific knowledge can be built. There are also among us the theorists who have nothing but disdain for this "raw empiricism," who believe that much current research is a process of gathering facts on the basis of fuzzy and inarticulate criteria of selection, and that this is a futile operation, leading to full files but empty heads. These two extreme positions, fortunately, are not typical. Most political scientists, like most working men, do the jobs they can do best and welcome whatever help their colleagues can provide.

But delicately balanced between the polar extremes of antitheoretical empiricists and antiempirical theorists stand a few theoretical empiricists who are trying to construct value-free theoretical systems—with facts and for facts. It is not our place to outline such systems here. But we may note a few by way of indicating to the interested reader what is going on.

Lasswell and Kaplan's *Power and Society* was discussed earlier in this chapter, and Dahl and Lindblom's *Politics, Economics, and Welfare* was mentioned. Anthony Downs, in *An Economic Theory of Democracy*,[47] takes the competitive economic model, substitutes vote-getting for money-getting, and on this basis constructs a competitive model for the political system. The author grants that the system is but a logical construct that cannot be applied directly to every facet of current political life, but suggests that it may be useful for the stimulation and ordering of future research. Critics contend that it cannot serve this function since the model assumes a type and consistency of motivation alien to the actual behavior of voters and vote-getters.

Basing his work on a general theory of action, Talcott Parsons has for some time been the leading system-builder in the sociological fraternity.[48] According to those who have mastered the system, Parsons' statement of it has moved from a focus on action conceived through a rather narrow behavioralist orientation to an emphasis on "macro-functionalism" in which the equilibrium pattern of stable groups is the center of attention. The latter has provided a used and therefore useful framework for what has sometimes been criticized as a rather static analysis of stabilizing cultural norms. The system has been less useful in dealing with the generation of groups and group conflict. Those outside the sociological guild have most often accused Parsons of laboring the ob-

---

47 *An Economic Theory of Democracy* (New York: Harper, 1957).
48 See his *Structure of Social Action* (New York: McGraw-Hill, 1937), and *The Social System* (Glencoe, Ill.: Free Press, 1951). See also *The Alpha Kappa Deltan*, Vol. 29, No. 1 (Winter, 1959) pp. 2-80, a whole issue devoted to Parsons' work. With Edward Shils, Parsons edited *Toward a General Theory of Action* (Cambridge: Harvard Univ. Press, 1951).

vious with fancy words, to which Parsons, in effect, replies that the obvious has been neglected too long already. For our purposes it is important to note that from the beginning Parsons, due no doubt to the Weberian influence upon him, has subsumed political phenomena within his analytical system. And he has given special attention to a model of the two-party system in the United States.[49] To the extent that he and other generalists are successful, political sociology and political science will become indistinguishable, which perhaps they have been in essence all along.

One of the best known systematizers in current political science is Chicago's David Easton. In *The Political System*[50] Easton assaulted not only raw empiricism—"hyperfactualism" he called it—but the "historicism" of such widely respected works as George Sabine's *History of Political Theory*, which becomes, in Easton's view, little more than the history of ideology, presented non-committally. While Easton accepts the fundamental difference between factual and value propositions, he rejects the idea of a wholly value-free social science. He calls instead for an explicit and thorough exposition of value premises as a prerequisite for any systematic study. This should not inhibit the possibility of the truly general theory political science needs. He speaks of the possibility rather than the actuality, for most of what has passed for theory in the recent past he regards as moralizing and low-level descriptive propositions. Easton does not himself provide a theoretical system—he and his students are continuing to work on this—but makes a case for its possibility. But he intimates that the concept of general equilibrium, with some analogies drawn from economics, might be the key concept in such a system.[51]

All theoretical systems in the social sciences have been influenced by the models of the natural sciences. Hobbes built such a system in the seventeenth century based upon the crude physics of his day. Later, biology was the template. Now, once again, the new physics has an exemplary appeal. Economics, blessed with massive flows of quantitative and impersonal units, can, in its econometrics branch, become what amounts to a nonsocial social science. Some political scientists look on with envy. One has the feeling that however modest the tone of their

49 See his "'Voting' and the Equilibrium of the American Political System," in Eugene Burdick and Arthur Brodbeck, eds., *Studies of Voting Behavior*, Vol. III in *Continuities of Social Research* (Glencoe, Ill.: Free Press, 1958).

50 *The Political System* (New York: Knopf, 1953).

51 Robert Dahl has chided Easton for the labored attempt of *The Political System* to provide an adequate definition of political science. "It is," he says, "an almost medieval search for essences." Do physicists, he asks, spend much time and energy arguing over "What is physics?" "The Science of Politics: New and Old," *World Politics*, Vol 7 (1955), pp. 479-89.

utterances, proponents of large and logical systems believe that once the slots are filled in, mankind will be closer to Truth, or truth, or reality, than was Hobbes in his day. They feel that their system will serve much more than the ideological-mythological function that, in retrospect, it can be shown, Hobbes' creation served. Every theoretical political system communicates a sense of being on a threshold as was Einstein with $E = mc^2$.

It has become typical for critics of the systematizers to point out that the social and the physical worlds are different because a stubborn, irascible humanity populates the former and not the latter. They note that a method designed for one world may not fit another. It is also worth noting that systems of physical science are not changeless. Our builders of social systems are more sophisticated and have a greater body of data to draw on than did Hobbes. Our physicists are more sophisticated and have a greater body of data to draw on than did Newton. But a creative genius like Hobbes or Newton is as rare today as in the seventeenth century. Our system-builders can regard themselves as fortunate if they have a fraction of Hobbes' historical significance, and genius rather than effort will probably determine the fraction.

Rather than regard systems as threats to historical theory, however, we who dabble in history ought to accept them for what they can do, and by putting them in historical context show how thoroughly historical is even the most ardent ahistoricism.

CHAPTER 20 | *Conclusion: Theory and Ideology*

THE problem of concluding a history of political theory is similar to that of introducing it. Before one has entered into the dialogue that makes up that history little can be said, and afterward little need be said. Why conclude at all, then? One concludes out of a decent respect for all that has not been said and all that might have been said. One concludes, in other words, in order not to leave a false impression of conclusiveness.

If an elaborate defense of the best political theory would, at this point, be gratuitous, a defense of political theory itself as a worthy enterprise might be in order. In Chapter 1 we suggested that theory aims at the truth and ideology aims at victory over human opponents. Such victory is fairly determinate; one either wins or loses. But the truth of a political theory is elusive, personal, and infinitely complex. It may be destroyed by an overrigid formulation. It may be missed by not "getting inside" the theorist to understand what, exactly, he was driving at. Even after considerable effort, we are never quite sure we understand a theorist who looked upon a world that is not ours. How much less are we able to summarize his kernel of truth in an easily digestible, preservative-coated capsule. Second-rate political thinkers engage in a somewhat too self-conscious debate on how men are and ought to be governed. The first-rate thinkers, those we have included in this book, are engaged in a dialogue[1] in which opposing ideas are absorbed and transformed instead of being beaten down or evaded. Debates can be summarized

---

1 From the Greek *dia logos*, "through words"; hence, not merely battling *with* words but clarifying one's point *through* words.

fairly easily by simple score-keeping, but dialogues are not easy to summarize. Too much of their character resides in the flavor, the subtle shading, the play of idea upon idea.

There is much talk in the 1960's about ideological counteroffensives against the Communist threat, doing a better job of selling America abroad, and the like. Sometimes this sort of enterprise, which no doubt has its own quite legitimate justification, is confused with political theorizing. It is important that it not be. Whether ideologies as such can account for the rise and fall of nations is doubtful. Ideologies as justifications for mass behavior are obviously tremendously important to the morale of individuals in large groups (more important to the less emotionally stable, no doubt). But the content of a particular ideology is probably less important than its availability. The ideologically zealous opponents of increased federal intervention in local public education do not seem bothered by the intervention of Congressional investigating committees in local public education. The ideologically zealous advocates of proletarian democracy do not seem bothered by one-party rule within their own labor unions. The ideology is available for use against opponents but it is not, merely for the sake of consistency, used against allies. What is democracy to one group is tyranny to another group. An imaginative leader will find adequate verbal symbols almost anywhere to give his followers the verbal equipment necessary to rationalize their support of him. Given the choice of a better ideology or a better leader, a nation is well advised to choose the latter, for good leadership implies the proper use and non-use of ideology, whereas a good ideology (whatever that may mean) does not necessarily imply good leadership.

But even granting for the moment that a better ideology might be necessary for national survival, this would in no way invalidate the distinction between ideology and theory. For if, by our definition (and the definition seems relevant to practice) a political ideology aims first and foremost at political victory, and if a nation is victorious in some contest thanks to an ideology, once victory has been achieved the ideology is dead. By doing its appointed job it has killed itself. First-rate political theory has value precisely because it outlives the crises that may have generated it. Victories may be and often are won in pursuit of an illusion. But in the long run neither personal nor collective life can go on unless there exists some hold on reality strong enough to survive the shock of disillusion. Political ideologies dominate the stage; but political theories are with the actors and theater-goers as they walk out into the chill night air.

Some say that the condition of free inquiry and free expression, which enables political theorists to practice their trade openly, is itself a product of ideology, in this case the ideology of the Western liberal tradition. Therefore, it is biting the hand that feeds him for a theorist to attack this ideology. The Western liberal tradition has indeed permitted and even encouraged the open pursuit of political theory. But we should not forget that political theory in the disguise of history, fables, children's stories, and advice to the monarch has been produced under all sorts of repressive conditions. As theory, it is no less valid because of its disguise; there is, in fact, a certain esoteric quality to all original theorizing that the Western liberal tradition has sometimes failed to appreciate. But in any case a clear distinction must be drawn between liberalism as a tradition and liberalism as an ideology. A tradition includes all sorts of customary behavior patterns not reducible to the structured intellectual formulas of an ideology. We can rise above ideologies in a way that we cannot rise above traditions. If an ideology is a deliberately prefabricated set of answers whose effect is to close off inquiry, it is difficult to call the tradition of free inquiry an ideology. There are certainly ideologies that include free inquiry as one of their positive symbols, but the authentic practice of free inquiry tends to be corrosive of ideological cohesion since it generates embarrassing questions asked in unlikely places at unlikely times.

A lack of ideological cohesion is not necessarily the equivalent of anarchy. People who have developed the ability to live with a variety of conflicting ideologies are able, as it is often put, to agree to disagree. This ability, which would seem to be essential to both the representative and the libertarian aspects of Western democracy, implies a degree of consensus about social goals and a certain trust in the reasonableness of others. But it would be a mistake to call such consensus and such trust ideological. The trust is prerequisite to, and more important than, the consensus. It is the cement of the social fabric. Trust grows out of an experience of honest relationships. What meaning could there be to "common social goals" if we could not trust as honest those things told us by parents, friends, teachers, authors of books, newspapers, political leaders? Part of the horror of a totalitarian regime is that no one can trust anyone else. The network of honest reports is broken down. More or less spontaneous personal confidence is dissolved and has to be replaced by an implacable, impersonal ideology—the "logic" of an idea bent and twisted into an all-purpose guide to everything from personal relations to the purpose of history.

Citizens are less likely to succumb to frantic appeals for political uniformity, however, if they understand the degree of unity involved in their merely being citizens of a common *res publica* with a tradition of its own. This is why totalitarian movements try to undermine a sense of tradition and historical continuity and to encourge an irrational dependence upon the achievement of a glorious plan for the future. A regime impelled to claim omniscience in seeing the good and forseeing the future may win support, but it courts eventual disorder. Ordinary people with ordinary skepticism are dubious of the moral and intellectual pretenses of such regimes. Ordinary people tend to seek a more enduring source of meaning and morality than a transient political order can provide. They turn to tradition or religious faith or both. Political ideologies sometimes try to make use of tradition and often seek the status of religious faiths. But neither the past nor the stirrings of divinity are, one hopes, controllable by the men who manufacture ideologies. We must wish them failure in their attempt to transform the human community into the political community and the political community into their private cult.

The role of the political theorist is not to concoct an ideology that can substitute for lost trust after other ideologies have helped destroy it. His role is not even to create trust through philosophy. Trust is a relationship of personal confidence between persons seen or unseen. It is a willingness to concede unproven qualities. It is a capacity to act beyond the point at which intellectual assurance guarantees the results of action. It is, if you will, the capacity to act on faith. Theories and philosophies and theologies rarely instill this capacity in large numbers of people, since theories and philosophies and theologies (and, yes, ideologies) are the very intellectual assurances beyond which trustful action occurs. But theories can clarify the meaning of what men have done, and this enriched knowledge of past action can influence future action. The political theorist has, in a way, the same responsibility as that of newspapers, to inform the public honestly. His immediate public is smaller, however, and he informs it not of the transient facts but of the more enduring meanings behind them. He is obliged to penetrate the illusions he can recognize and to disclose the reality he can understand. If power has no reality to him but the public good does—or vice versa—that is what he must honestly report. Good theories, it is our thesis, are honest reports. Bad theories (ideologies) are dishonest reports.

Granted these distinctions, the more widespread the habit of honest reporting the more likely is theory to be encouraged and ideology to be discouraged. To call for collective honesty is to call for something at once complex and simple. How many individuals can live without self-deception and the deception of others? To tell nothing but the truth is difficult enough, but to tell the whole truth is probably impossible. The desire to tell people what they want to hear often springs from a laudable compassion but it leads to false impressions. For each role that we play—son, father, husband, executive, churchman, socializer, leader, follower—a different standard of honesty tends to apply. And many are the occasions when a fragment of the truth, honest in itself, betrays the larger truth of which it is a part.

If honesty is this great a challenge to the well-integrated individual, how much greater a challenge is it to a whole society. In our present society, half-truths and untruths scream at us and plead with us unendingly in commercial advertising, political advertising, religious advertising, eductional advertising, and various other forms of distortion. Most people accept all this quite blandly, the naïve because they think it part of the natural environment, the sophisticated because they know each age has its own form of untruth.

And yet simple honesty is not an illusion. There are moments of truth when it breaks through even in totalitarian societies steeped in ideological pretense. A worker accosts a lavishly dressed member of the Supreme Soviet in Red Square and taunts him for his nonproletarian clothes. A young girl being feted in Moscow for winning a prize is handed a prepared statement to read over the state radio and refuses because the statement is not true. In our country, an agency head says what everyone knows is true even when it offends his "clients" and their Congressional allies. A Congressman overcomes the temptation to win votes with a flamboyant speech on a delicate international situation on which he does not yet have adequate information. A newsman admits his bias. A voter admits he is voting for the party rather than the man.

There is no assured salvation in countless such acts of individual honesty (honesty can be cruel and agitational, too); but it is by virtue of them that reality is known and the world of illusion is dissipated. Sometimes we wonder if political theory does as much. We look back on the manifest illusions about quantifiable units of pleasure and pain in Bentham and think his functon must have been other than to dispel illusion. But in so doing we forget the seriousness and pungency of his critique of obscurity and flabbiness in eighteenth-century legal thinking. We look at the obscurities in Hegel and say wistfully that a lot of nonsense would have been spared the world had Hegel not inspired so many disciples. But in so doing we forget that he saw process where none had been seen before. Even the good is less than perfect. All theories unintentionally build up illusions that must be torn apart by the next generation. Like thought itself, political theory is a never-ending process.

There will be political theory as long as people live outside of caves and as long as there are men with the ability and courage to think for themselves. The degree to which the fruits of their best thought will permeate the body politic depends upon a variety of factors. Many forces in our present world will continue to inhibit this permeation. The increasing complexity of the subject matter of politics places a great strain on the institutions of popular consultation. Defective theories of democracy, often transformed into ideologies, do not help. The democratic politician frequently exaggerates the degree to which he must be a crowd-pleaser. But politicians may be more honest about their role—at least when talking among themselves—than are many average citizens, who, confused by the view that they-the-people are supposed to know all about running a government, try to reassure themselves and impress others by mouthing second-hand political slogans as if they were scientific dogma. The more unsure one is of his own beliefs, or of whether they are really his own, the more likely he is to insist that everyone else agree with him. Excessive confidence in mass wisdom can actually induce a falling away from that degree of political excellence attainable under more realistic assumptions.

Rousseau's poignant goal that "every citizen should speak his opinion entirely from himself" is still a valid democratic goal. But an opinion is more genuine if it expresses an honest but limited competence than if it pretends to omnicompetence. This statement is as applicable to the opinions of experts who manage the routine of public affairs as it is to those of the citizens who set the general direction of political life. It is especially hard to speak one's opinions entirely from oneself in an age of insistent electronic communication, when news is fast-moving, information is overcondensed, and standardized opinions, neatly packaged, emanate from highly centralized agencies of transmission. The continuing internationalization of politics will no doubt complicate the task of achieving collective honesty. Nationalist pride will garble facts with emotion, and the high stakes of nuclear war or peace may be used as an end to justify deceptive means. Some Americans, unable to carry the weight of starving and rebellious foreigners on their well-padded shoulders, will eagerly accept dishonestly simple answers to excruciating problems. They will also accept the scapegoats who invariably accompany the too-simple answer.

Meanwhile, the painful search for political reality will go on, and some solitary searchers will continue to ask why rather than how. Some future Socrates will care more for truth than safety. Some future Plato will have a vision of political perfection. Some future Hegel will put it all in a system. These will be the political theorists, and to them, as to their predecessors, we shall owe such knowledge as we have of the latent body politic to which we all are bound.

Selected Readings

Chapter 1, Introduction

Bowle, John. *Western Political Thought; An Historical Introduction from the Origins to Rousseau*. London: Cape, 1947; New York: Barnes and Noble (University Paperbacks), 1961. Both scholarly and lucid.

Ebenstein, William, ed. *Great Political Thinkers*. 3rd ed. New York: Rinehart, 1960. Selections from leading political theorists with prefatory statements. Good bibliography, pp. 869-974.

————, ed. *Political Thought in Perspective*. New York: McGraw-Hill, 1957. Writings *on* great political thinkers *by* great political thinkers.

Parkinson, C. Northcote. *The Evolution of Political Thought*. Boston: Houghton Mifflin, 1958; New York: Viking (Compass Books), 1960. Iconoclastic, amusing, quaint, unreliable.

Russell, Bertrand. *A History of Western Philosophy*. New York: Simon and Schuster, 1945. Somewhat opinionated and partial, but good reading.

Sabine, George H. *A History of Political Theory*. 3rd ed. New York: Holt, Rinehart and Winston, 1961 (orig. ed., 1937). Probably the best of the standard textbooks.

Watkins, Frederick M. *The Political Tradition of the West*. Cambridge, Mass.: Harvard U. Press, 1948. An enlightening essay on our liberal heritage.

Wolin, Sheldon S. *Politics and Vision; Continuity and Innovation in Western Political Thought*. Boston: Little, Brown, 1960. Brilliant reinterpretations of certain political thinkers and movements.

CHAPTER 2, The Seventeenth Century

GENERAL

BOULENGER, JACQUES. *The Seventeenth Century*. The National History of France. New York: Putnam, 1920.

CARRÉ, MAYRICK. *Phases of Thought in England*. Oxford: Clarendon, 1949.

CLARK, G. N. *The Seventeenth Century*. Oxford: Clarendon, 1929. An intellectual survey of Europe.

GOOCH, G. P. *Political Thought in England from Bacon to Halifax*. London: Butterworth, 1914.

GUÉRARD, ALBERT. *The Life and Death of an Ideal; France in the Classical Age*. London: Benn, 1929.

STANKIEWICZ, W. J. *Politics and Religion in Seventeenth-Century France*. Berkeley: U. of California Press, 1960.

WILLEY, BASIL. *The Seventeenth Century Background; Studies in the Thought of the Age in Relation to Poetry and Religion*. New York: Columbia U. Press, 1934; New York: Doubleday (Anchor Books), n.d.

THE POLITICAL OBLIGATION OF SUBJECTS

ALLEN, J. W. *English Political Thought, 1603-1644*. London: Methuen, 1938.

BACON, FRANCIS. *Essays or Counsels Civil and Moral*. London: Dent (Everyman), 1906. This is a reprint of the fifth and last edition written by Bacon and published in 1625. The first edition was published in 1597.

FIGGIS, J. N. *The Theory of the Divine Right of Kings*. 2nd ed. Cambridge, Eng.: Cambridge U. Press, 1914.

FILMER, ROBERT. *Patriarcha and Other Political Works*. Peter Laslett, ed. Oxford: Blackwell, 1949.

GROTIUS, HUGO. *De juri belli et pacis*. 3 vols. Cambridge, Eng.: Cambridge U. Press, 1853. Latin text of 1625 with translation by William Whewell.

JAMES I, *The Political Works of James I*. Charles H. McIlwain, ed. Cambridge, Mass.: Harvard U. Press, 1918.

KNIGHT, W. S. M. *The Life and Work of Hugo Grotius*. London: Sweet, 1925.

PUFENDORF, SAMUEL. *De officio hominis et civis* (1673). Carnegie Classics in International Law. 2 vols. New York: Oxford U. Press, 1921. Vol. 2, F. G. Moore, trans.

———. *De jure naturae et gentium* (1688). Carnegie Classics in International Law. 2 vols. Oxford: Clarendon, 1934. Vol. 2, C. H. and W. A. Oldfather, trans.

SPINOZA, BENEDICT DE. *Writings on Political Philosophy*. A. G. A. Balz, ed. New York: Appleton-Century, 1937. Contains the *Tractatus politicus* of 1677 in full in the R. H. M. Elwes translation of 1883.

———. *The Political Works*. A. G. Wernham, ed. and trans. Oxford: Clarendon, 1958. Contains the *Tractatus politicus* in full and the *Tractatus theologico politicus* (1670) in part.

SYKES, NORMAN. "Bossuet," Ch. 2 in F. J. C. Hearnshaw, ed., *The Social and Political Ideas of Some Great French Thinkers of the Age of Reason*. London: Harrap, 1930.

VREELAND, HAMILTON. *Hugo Grotius*. New York: Oxford U. Press, 1917.

RESTRAINTS UPON RULERS: CONSTITUTIONALISM

ALTHUSIUS, JOHANNES. *Politica methodica digesta*. Carl J. Friedrich, ed. Cambridge, Mass.: Harvard U. Press, 1932.

BARKER, ARTHUR. *Milton and the Puritan Dilemma, 1641-1660*. Toronto: U. of Toronto Press, 1942.

BOWEN, CATHERINE DRINKER. *The Lion and the Throne; The Life and Time of Sir Edward Coke*. Boston: Little, Brown, 1956.

CLARK, G. N. *The Later Stuarts, 1660-1714*. 2nd ed. Oxford: Clarendon, 1955.

COKE, EDWARD. *The First Part of the Institutes of the Laws of England*. Francis Hargrove and Charles Butler, eds. London: Clarke, 1832.

CROMWELL, OLIVER. *The Writings and Speeches of Oliver Cromwell*. Wilbur C. Abbott, ed. 4 vols. Cambridge, Mass.: Harvard U. Press, 1937-47.

DAVIES, GODFREY. *The Early Stuarts, 1603-1660*. Oxford: Clarendon, 1937.

GARDINER, SAMUEL RAWSON, ed. *The Constitutional Documents of the Puritan Revolution*. Oxford: Clarendon, 1889.

GERBRANDY, P. S. *National and International Stability; Althusius, Grotius, Van Vollenhoven*. London: Oxford U. Press, 1944.

GOOCH, G. P. *English Democratic Ideas in the Seventeenth Century*. 2nd ed. Cambridge, Eng.: Cambridge U. Press, 1927.

MILLER, PERRY. *Orthodoxy in Massachusetts; A Genetic Study*. Cambridge, Mass.: Harvard U. Press, 1933.

———. *The New England Mind; The Seventeenth Century*. New York: Macmillan, 1939.

MILTON, JOHN. *Areopagitica*. New York: Dutton (Everyman), 1927.

PERRY, RALPH BARTON. *Puritanism and Democracy*. New York: Vanguard, 1944.

WILLIAMS, ROGER. *Works.* 6 vols. Providence, R. I.: Narragansett Club, 1866. The standard edition.

———. *Roger Williams; His Contribution to the American Tradition.* Indianapolis: Bobbs-Merrill, 1953.

WOODHOUSE, A. S. P., ED. *Puritanism and Liberty; Being the Army Debates (1647-1649) from the Clarke Manuscripts.* 2nd ed. Chicago: U. of Chicago Press, 1951.

ZAGORIN, PEREZ. *A History of Political Thought in the English Revolution.* London: Routledge and Kegan Paul, 1954.

THE GROUND OF POLITICAL AUTHORITY: POPULISM

FRANK, JOSEPH. *The Levellers; A History of the Writings of Three Seventeenth-Century Social Democrats: John Lilburne, Richard Overton, William Walwyn.* Cambridge, Mass.: Harvard U. Press, 1955.

GIBB, M. A. *John Lilburne the Leveller; A Christian Democrat.* London: Drummond, 1947.

HALLER, WILLIAM. *Liberty and Reformation in the Puritan Revolution.* New York: Columbia U. Press, 1955.

———. *The Rise of Puritanism.* New York: Columbia U. Press, 1938.

———, ED. *Tracts on Liberty in the Puritan Revolution, 1638-1647.* 3 vols. New York: Columbia U. Press, 1934.

——— AND GODFREY DAVIES, EDS. *The Leveller Tracts, 1647-1653.* New York: Columbia U. Press, 1944.

HARRINGTON, JAMES. *Political Writings; Representative Selections.* Charles Blitzer, ed. New York: Liberal Arts, 1955.

HOLORENSHAW, HENRY. *The Levellers and the English Revolution.* London: Gollancz, 1939.

JONES, RUFUS M. *Mysticism and Democracy in the English Commenwealth.* Cambridge, Mass.: Harvard U. Press, 1932.

ROBERTSON, D. B. *The Religious Foundations of Leveller Democracy.* New York: King's Crown, 1951.

SMITH, H. F. RUSSELL. *Harrington and His Oceana.* Cambridge, Eng.: Cambridge U. Press, 1914.

WINSTANLEY, GERRARD. *Works,* George H. Sabine, ed. Ithaca: Cornell U. Press, 1941.

WOLFE, DON M. *The Leveller Manifestoes of the Puritan Revolution.* New York: Nelson, 1944.

NATURAL LAW, REASON OF STATE, AND COMPARATIVE POLITICS

D'ENTRÈVES, ALEXANDER PASSERIN. *Natural Law.* London: Hutchinson's U. Library, 1952.

GIERKE, OTTO. *Natural Law and the Theory of Society, 1500-1800.* 2 vols. Cambridge, Eng.: Cambridge U. Press, 1934; 1 vol. ed., 1950, Boston: Beacon, 1957.

HALIFAX, LORD. *The Complete Works of George Savile, First Marquess of Halifax.* Walter Raleigh, ed. Oxford: Clarendon, 1912.

MEINECKE, FRIEDRICH. *Machiavellism; The Doctrine of Raison d'État and Its Place in Modern History.* Douglas Scott, trans. New Haven: Yale U. Press, 1957 (orig. German ed., 1924).

CHAPTER 3, Hobbes

WORKS BY HOBBES

The English Works of Thomas Hobbes. William Molesworth, ed. 11 vols. London: Bohn, 1839-45.

Behemoth, or The Long Parliament. F. Tonnies, ed. London: Simpkin, Marshall, 1889.

De cive, or The Citizen. Sterling P. Lamprecht, ed. New York: Appleton-Century-Crofts, 1949.

The Elements of Law, Natural and Politic. F. Tonnies, ed. London: Simpkin, Marshall, 1889.

Leviathan. Michael Oakeshott, ed. Oxford: Blackwell, 1946. See J. M. Brown, "A Note on Professor Oakeshott's Hobbes"; Dorothea Krook, "Mr. Brown's Note Annotated"; J. M. Brown, "Mr. Brown Answers Miss Krook"; *Political Studies,* Vol. 1, 1953, pp. 53-64, 216-27; Vol. 2, 1954, pp. 168-72.

Leviathan. A. D. Lindsay, ed. New York: Dutton (Everyman), 1950.

Selections. Frederick J. E. Woodbridge, ed. New York: Scribner, 1930.

SECONDARY WORKS

BRANDT, F. *Thomas Hobbes' Mechanical Conception of Nature.* V. Maxwell and A. I. Frausbøll, trans. Hachette, 1928; Copenhagen: Leven & Munksgaard, 1928.

BOWLE, JOHN. *Hobbes and His Critics; A Study in Seventeenth Century Constitutionalism.* London: Cape, 1951.

CATLIN, G. E. C. *Thomas Hobbes; An Introduction.* Oxford: Blackwell, 1922.

LAIRD, JOHN. *Hobbes.* London: Oxford U. Press, 1934.

LYON, GEORG. *La Philosophie de Hobbes.* Paris: Alcan, 1893.

PETERS, RICHARD. *Hobbes.* London: Penguin, 1956.

ROBERTSON, C. CROOM. *Hobbes.* Edinburgh: Blackwood, 1886.

STEPHEN, LESLIE. *Hobbes.* New York: Macmillan, 1904.

STRAUSS, LEO. *The Political Philosophy of Hobbes.* Elsa M. Sinclair, trans. Oxford: Clarendon, 1936.

TONNIES, FERDINAND. *Thomas Hobbes—Leben und Lehre.* 3rd ed. Stuttgart: Fromman, 1925 (1st ed., 1896).

WARRENDER, J. HOWARD. *The Political Philosophy of Hobbes; His Theory of Obligation.* Oxford: Clarendon, 1957. See John Plamenatz, "Mr. Warrender's Hobbes," *Political Studies,* Vol. 5 (1957), 295-308.

CHAPTER 4, Locke

WORKS BY LOCKE

The Works of John Locke. 10 vols. London: Tegg, 1823.

An Essay Concerning Human Understanding (1690). Alexander Campbell Fraser, ed. 2 vols. Oxford: Clarendon, 1894. A convenient abridged edition is Russell Kirk, ed. Chicago: Regnery (Gateway Books), 1956.

Essays on the Law of Nature. Wolfgang von Leyden, ed. Oxford: Clarendon, 1954. Latin with English translation. These are Locke's early essays, c. 1670's. See Leo Strauss's criticism of this edition, "Locke's Doctrine of Natural Law," *American Political Science Review,* Vol. 52 (1958), pp. 490-501.

A Letter Concerning Toleration (1685). J. W. Gough, ed. Oxford: Blackwell, 1947. See also entry below under *Two Treatises.*

The Reasonableness of Christianity (1695). I. T. Ramsey, ed. Library of Modern Religious Thought. Stanford, Cal., Stanford U. Press, 1958.

Some Thoughts Concerning Education. Intro. and notes by R. H. Quick. Cambridge, Eng.: Cambridge U. Press, 1895.

Two Treatises of Government. Intro. and Apparatus Criticus by Peter Laslett. Cambridge, Eng.: Cambridge U. Press, 1960. This is the definitive edition, incorporating for the first time Locke's final revisions. See also Thomas I. Cook, ed. New York: Hafner, 1947. See also *A Treatise of Civil Government and A Letter Concerning Toleration.* Charles L. Sherman, ed. New York: Appleton-Century-Crofts, 1937; and *Of Civil Government.* Chicago: Regnery (Gateway Books), 1955.

The Correspondence of John Locke and Edward Clarke, Benjamin Rand, ed. London: Oxford U. Press, 1927.

SECONDARY WORKS

AARON, R. I. *John Locke.* 2nd ed. New York: Oxford U. Press, 1955 (orig. ed., 1937).

COX, RICHARD H. *Locke on War and Peace.* New York: Oxford U. Press, 1960.

CRANSTON, MAURICE. *John Locke; A Biography*. New York and London: Macmillan, 1957.

CZAJKOWSKI, C. J. *The Theory of Private Property in Locke's Political Philosophy*. South Bend, Ind. U. of Notre Dame Press, 1941.

FOX-BOURNE, H. R. *The Life of John Locke*. 2 vols. London: King, 1876.

GOUGH, JOHN W. *John Locke's Political Philosophy; Eight Studies*. Oxford: Clarendon, 1950.

HOFSTADTER, ALBERT. *Locke and Scepticism*. New York: Albee, 1935.

LAMPRECHT, STERLING P. *The Moral and Political Philosophy of John Locke*. Archives of Philosophy, No. 11. New York: Columbia U. Press, 1918.

LASLETT, PETER. Intro. to his ed. of Robert Filmer's *Patriarcha*. Oxford: Blackwell, 1949.

McLACHLAN, H. *The Religious Opinions of Milton, Locke, and Newton*. Manchester: Manchester U. Press, 1941.

VAUGHN, C. E. *Studies in the History of Political Philosophy Before and After Rousseau*. 2 vols. Manchester: U. of Manchester Press, 1925. Vol. 1, pp. 130-204.

YOLTON, JOHN Y. *John Locke and the Way of Ideas*. London: Oxford U. Press, 1956. Excellent bibliography.

CHAPTER 5, The Eighteenth Century

THE ENLIGHTENMENT

BECKER, CARL L. *The Heavenly City of the Eighteenth-Century Philosophers*. New Haven: Yale U. Press, 1932.

CASSIRER, ERNST. *The Philosophy of the Enlightenment*, F. C. A. Koelln and J. P. Pettegrove, trans. Princeton, N. J.: Princeton U. Press, 1951; Boston: Beacon, 1955 (orig. German ed., 1932).

DE TOCQUEVILLE, ALEXIS. *The Old Regime and the French Revolution* (1856). Stuart Gilbert, trans. New York: Doubleday (Anchor Books), 1955.

FLEISHER, DAVID. *William Godwin: A Study in Liberalism*. London: Allen and Unwin, 1951.

FRANKEL, CHARLES. *The Faith of Reason; The Idea of Progress in the French Enlightenment*. New York: King's Crown, 1948.

GAY, PETER. *Voltaire's Politics; The Poet as Realist*. Princeton, N. J.: Princeton U. Press, 1959.

GODWIN, WILLIAM. *An Enquiry Concerning Political Justice*, 2 vols. 3rd ed. F. E. L. Priestly, ed. Toronto: U. of Toronto, 1946.

GROSSMAN, MORDECAI. *The Philosophy of Helvetius*. New York: Teacher's College, Columbia U., 1926. Stresses theory of education.

HAZARD, PAUL. *European Thought in the Eighteenth Century; From Montesquieu to Lessing.* J. Lewis May, trans. New Haven: Yale U. Press, 1954.

HEARNSHAW, F. J. C., ED. *Social and Political Ideas of Representative Thinkers of the Revolutionary Age.* New York: Barnes and Noble, 1950.

———, ED. *Social and Political Ideas of Some Great French Thinkers of the Age of Reason.* New York: Barnes and Noble, 1950.

KEGAN PAUL, C. *William Godwin.* 2 vols. London: King, 1876.

LASKI, HAROLD J. *The Rise of European Liberalism.* London: Allen and Unwin, 1936.

———. *Political Thought in England; Locke to Bentham.* London: Oxford U. Press (Home University Library), 1920.

MARTIN, KINGSLEY. *French Liberal Thought in the Eighteenth Century.* Boston: Little, Brown, 1929. 2nd ed. titled *The Rise of French Liberal Thought; A Study of Political Ideas from Bayle to Condorcet.* J. P. Mayer, ed. New York: New York U. Press, 1954.

MORLEY, JOHN. *Diderot and the Encyclopedists.* 2 vols. London: Chapman and Hall, 1878.

ROBBINS, CAROLINE. *The Eighteenth Century Commonwealthenan; Studies in the Transmission, Development, and Circumstance of English Liberal Thought from the Restoration of Charles II until the War with the Thirteen Colonies.* Cambridge, Mass.: Harvard U. Press, 1959.

ROCKWOOD, RAYMOND O., ED. *Carl Becker's Heavenly City Revisited.* Ithaca: Cornell U. Press, 1958.

ROWE, CONSTANCE. *Voltaire and the State.* New York: Columbia U. Press, 1955.

STEPHEN, LESLIE. *History of English Thought in the Eighteenth Century.* 2 vols. 3rd ed. London: Smith, Elder, 1902.

VOLTAIRE, *Oeuvres complètes.* Louis Moland, ed. 52 vols. Paris: Garnier, 1883-85.

———. *Philosophical Dictionary.* H. I. Woolf, sel. and ed. New York: Knopf, 1938.

———. *Selections,* George R. Havens, ed. New York: Century, 1925.

VYVERBERG, HENRY. *Historical Pessimism in the French Enlightenment.* Cambridge, Mass.: Harvard U. Press, 1958.

WICKWAR, W. H. *Baron d'Holbach.* London: George Allen, 1935.

WILLEY, BASIL. *The Eighteenth Century Background; Studies on the Idea of Nature in the Thought of the Period.* London: Chatto and Windus, 1940.

ECONOMICS AND POLITICS:
THE PHYSIOCRATS AND ADAM SMITH

BEER, MAX. *An Inquiry into Physiocracy*. New York: Macmillan, 1940.

CROPSEY, JOSEPH. *Polity and Economy; An Interpretation of the Principles of Adam Smith*. The Hague: Nijhoff, 1957.

GINZBERG, ELI. *The House of Adam Smith*. New York: Columbia U. Press, 1934.

HEILBRONER, ROBERT L. *The Worldly Philosophers*. New York: Simon and Schuster, 1953. Chs. 1-4.

HIGGS, HENRY. *The Physiocrats*. New York: Macmillan, 1897.

McCULLOCH, JOHN R. *Treatises and Essays on Money, Exchange, Interest*. . . . 2nd ed. Edinburgh: Black, 1859. On Quesnay, Smith, and Ricardo.

POLANYI, KARL. *The Great Transformation*. Boston: Beacon, 1957.

SCHNEIDER, HERBERT W., ED. *Adam Smith's Moral and Political Philosophy*. New York: Hafner, 1948.

SCHUMPETER, JOSEPH A. *A History of Economic Analysis*. New York: Oxford U. Press, 1954. Part 2.

SMITH, ADAM. *An Inquiry into the Nature and Causes of the Wealth of Nations*. E. B. Bax, ed. 2 vols. London: Bell, 1896.

HISTORY AND POLITICS:
CONDORCET, BOLINGBROKE, VICO

ADAMS, H. P. *The Life and Writings of Giambattista Vico*. London: Allen and Unwin, 1935.

BOLINGBROKE, LORD (HENRY ST. JOHN). *A Dissertation on Parties*. 10th ed. London: Davies and Cadell, 1775 (orig. ed., 1734).

———. *Letters on the Spirit of Patriotism; On the Idea of a Patriot King*. 2nd ed. London: Davies, 1775 (orig. ed., 1738).

———. *Letters on the Study and Use of History*. 2nd ed. London: Cadell, 1770 (orig. ed., 1735).

CAPONIGRI, A. R. *Time and Idea; The Theory of History in Giambattista Vico*. Chicago: Regnery, 1953.

CONDORCET (MARIE JEAN ANTOINE NICHOLAS DE CARITAT). *Outlines of an Historical View of the Progress of the Human Mind*. Philadelphia: Carey, Rice, Orwood, Bache, and Fellows, 1796.

CROCE, BENEDETTO. *The Philosophy of Giambattista Vico*. R. G. Collingwood, trans. New York: Macmillan, 1913.

JAMES, D. G. *The Life of Reason; Hobbes, Locke, Bolingbroke*. London: Longmans, Green, 1949, Ch. 4.

PETRIE, CHARLES. *Bolingbroke*. London: Collins, 1937. A critical biography.

SCHAPIRO, J. SALWYN. *Condorcet and the Rise of Liberalism.* New York: Harcourt, Brace, 1934.

VICO, GIAMBATTISTA. *The New Science.* Thomas G. Bergin and Max H. Fisch, trans. Ithaca: Cornell U. Press, 1948 (from 3rd ed. of 1744).

LAW AND CONSTITUTIONALISM

ADAMS, JOHN. "A Defense of the Constitution" in *Works,* Charles Francis Adams, ed. Boston: Little and Brown, 1851. Vol. 6.

BLACKSTONE, WILLIAM. *Commentaries on the Laws of England.* William G. Hammond, ed. 8th ed. San Francisco: Whitney, 1890. Also 4 vols., Oxford, Clarendon, 1765-69.

BOORSTIN, DANIEL J. *The Mysterious Science of the Law; An Essay on Blackstone's Commentaries.* Cambridge, Mass.: Harvard U. Press, 1941; Boston: Beacon, 1958.

FARRAND, MAX, ED. *The Records of the Federal Convention of 1787,* 2 vols. New Haven: Yale U. Press, 1911.

The Federalist. New York: Random House (Modern Library), 1937.

FRIEDRICH, CARL J. *The Philosophy of Law in Historical Perspective.* Chicago: U. of Chicago Press, 1958.

GOOCH, G. P. *Frederick the Great.* New York: Knopf, 1947.

GOUGH, JOHN. *Fundamental Law in English Constitutional History.* Oxford: Clarendon, 1955.

HARTZ, LOUIS. *The Liberal Tradition in America.* New York: Harcourt, Brace, 1955.

LOCKMILLER, DAVID A. *Sir William Blackstone.* Chapel Hill: U. of North Carolina Press, 1938.

MAESTRO, M. T. *Voltaire and Beccaria as Reformers of Criminal Law.* New York: Columbia U. Press, 1942.

OTIS, JAMES. *Rights of British Colonies Asserted and Proved.* London: Williams, 1766.

WHITE, ANDREW DICKSON. *Seven Great Statesmen in the Warfare of Humanity with Unreason.* New York: Century, 1912. Ch. 3 is on Thomasius.

WILSON, JAMES. *Works.* 2 vols. J. D. Andrews, ed. Chicago: Callaghan, 1896.

THEORY OF REVOLUTION

ACTON, LORD (JOHN E. E. D. ACTON). *Lectures on the French Revolution.* London: Macmillan, 1910.

BEST, M. A. *Thomas Paine; Prophet and Martyr of Democracy.* New York: Harcourt, Brace, 1927.

BRINTON, CRANE. *The Anatomy of Revolution.* New York: Norton, 1938.

Conway, M. C. *The Life of Thomas Paine*. 2 vols. New York: Putnam, 1892.

Jefferson, Thomas. *Life and Selected Writings*. Adrienne Koch and William Peden, eds. New York: Random House (Modern Library), 1944.

———. *Political Writings*. Edward Dumbauld, ed. New York: Liberal Arts, 1955.

Paine, Thomas. *The Complete Writings*, Philip Foner, ed. 2 vols. New York: Citadel, 1945.

Palmer, Robert R. *The Age of the Democratic Revolution; A Political History of Europe and America, 1760-1800*. Princeton: Princeton U. Press, 1959.

Vallentin, Antonina. *Mirabeau*. E. W. Dickes, trans. New York: Viking, 1948.

Chapter 6, Montesquieu

WORKS BY MONTESQUIEU

Oeuvres complètes. Édouard Laboulaye, ed. 7 vols. Paris: Garnier, 1875-79.

Cahiers, 1716-1755. Bernard Grasset, ed. Paris: Grasset, 1941.

Considerations on the Causes of the Grandeur and the Decadence of the Romans, Jehu Baker, trans. New York: Appleton, 1894.

Persian and Chinese Letters. John Davidson, trans. New York: Dunne, 1901.

The Spirit of the Laws. Franz Neumann, ed. Thomas Nugent, trans. New York: Hafner, 1949. Many other editions.

SECONDARY WORKS

For an extended and excellent annotated bibliography, see David C. Cabeen, *Montesquieu Bibliography*. New York: New York Public Library, 1947.

Collins, J. Churton. *Voltaire, Montesquieu, and Rousseau in England*. London: Nash, 1908.

Dedieu, Joseph. *Montesquieu; L'Homme et l'oeuvre*. Paris: Boivin, 1943. (orig. ed., 1913).

Durkheim, Émile. *Montesquieu et Rousseau; Precurseurs de la sociologie*. Intro. by Georges Davy. Paris: Rivière, 1953 (written, 1892 and 1918).

Faguet, Émile. *La Politique comparée de Montesquieu, Rousseau, et Voltaire*. Paris: Société d'imprimerie et de librairie, 1902.

Fletcher, F. T. H. *Montesquieu and English Politics, 1750-1800*, London: Arnold, 1939.

FLINT, ROBERT. *Montesquieu.* New York: Scribner, Welford, and Armstrong, 1875. Highly critical of Montesquieu.

GRANT, A. J. "Montesquieu" in F. J. C. Hearnshaw, ed., *The Social and Political Ideas of Some Great French Thinkers in the Age of Reason.* London: Harrap, 1930. Pp. 114-35.

HOLMES, OLIVER WENDELL. "Montesquieu" in *Collected Legal Papers.* New York: Appleton, 1921. Pp. 250-65.

LEVIN, LAWRENCE MEYER. *The Political Doctrine of Montesquieu's Esprit des Lois; Its Classical Background.* New York: The Institute of French Studies, 1936.

MARTIN, KINGSLEY. *French Liberal Thought in the Eighteenth Century,* Boston: Little, Brown, 1929. Ch. 6.

SOREL, ALBERT. *Montesquieu,* M. B. Anderson and E. P. Anderson, trans. Chicago: McClurg, 1888 (orig. French ed., 1887). An exemplary study.

TEBERT, COURTENAY. *Montesquieu.* Oxford: Clarendon, 1904.

VAUGHN, C. E. *Studies in the History of Political Philosophy Before and After Rousseau.* 2 vols. Manchester: U. of Manchester Press, 1939. Vol. 1, pp. 253-302.

CHAPTER 7, Rousseau

WORKS BY ROUSSEAU

Oeuvres complètes. 13 vols. Paris: Hachette, 1886-1911.

The Confessions. Edmund Wilson, trans. 2 vols. New York: Knopf, 1923. Many other editions.

Émile. Barbara Foxley, trans. New York: Dutton (Everyman), 1948.

The Political Writings of Jean-Jacques Rousseau. C. E. Vaughn, ed. 2 vols. Cambridge, Eng.: Cambridge U. Press, 1915. Note Vaughn's introduction.

Rousseau; Political Writings. Frederick W. Watkins, trans. London: Nelson, 1953.

The Social Contract and Discourses. G. D. H. Cole, trans. New York: Dutton (Everyman), 1950. Note Cole's introduction.

The Social Contract. Charles Frankel, ed. New York: Hafner, 1947. An eighteenth-century translation revised by Frankel.

SECONDARY WORKS

BABBITT, IRVING. *Rousseau and Romanticism.* Boston: Houghton Mifflin, 1919; New York: Meridian, 1955.

CASSIRER, ERNST. *The Question of Jean-Jacques Rousseau,* trans., ed., and with an intro. by Peter Gay. New York: Columbia U. Press, 1954.

CHAPMAN, JOHN W. *Rousseau—Totalitarian or Liberal?* New York: Columbia U. Press, 1956.

COBBAN, ALFRED. *Rousseau and the Modern State.* London: Allen and Unwin, 1934.

DERATHÉ, ROBERT. *Jean-Jacques Rousseau et la science politique de son temps.* Paris: Presses Universitaires, 1950.

———. *Le Rationalism de Jean-Jacques Rousseau.* Paris: Presses Universitaires, 1948.

GREEN, F. C. *Jean-Jacques Rousseau; A Critical Study of His Life and Writings.* Cambridge, Eng.: Cambridge U. Press, 1955.

GROETHUYSEN, BERNARD. *Jean-Jacques Rousseau.* Paris: Gallimard, 1949.

HENDEL, CHARLES W. *Jean-Jacques Rousseau, Moralist.* 2 vols. London: Oxford U. Press, 1934.

HØFFDING, HARALD. *Jean-Jacques Rousseau and His Philosophy*, trans. from the Danish by William Richards and Leo Saidla. New Haven: Yale U. Press, 1930.

HUDSON, WILLIAM HENRY. *Rousseau and Naturalism in Life and Thought.* Edinburgh: Clark and Clark, 1903.

JOSEPHSON, MATTHEW. *Jean-Jacques Rousseau.* London: Gollancz, 1932.

MORLEY, JOHN. *Rousseau.* 2 vols. London: Macmillan, 1905.

OSBORNE, ANNIE M. *Rousseau and Burke.* London: Oxford U. Press, 1940.

SCHINZ, ALBERT. *La Pensée de Jean-Jacques Rousseau.* Northampton, Mass.: Smith College, 1929.

WRIGHT, ERNEST HUNTER. *The Meaning of Rousseau.* London: Oxford U. Press, 1929.

CHAPTER 8, Hume

WORKS BY HUME

Dialogues Concerning Natural Religion. Norman Kemp Smith, ed. 2nd ed. London: Nelson, 1947.

An Enquiry Concerning Human Understanding. L. A. Selby-Bigge, ed. Oxford: Clarendon, 1894. From the 1777 edition.

Essays and Treatises on Several Subjects. 2 vols. Edinburgh: Bell and Bradfate, 1800. Vol. 1 is *Essays, Moral, Political, and Literary.* Vol. 2 contains, among other works, *An Enquiry Concerning the Principles of Morals* and *The Natural History of Religion.*

The History of England from the Invasion of Julius Caesar to the Revolution of 1688. 8 vols. London: Cadell and Davies, 1802 (orig. ed., 1754-62).

The History of England from the Revolution to the Death of George II. T. G. Smollett, ed. 5 vols. London: Cadell and Baldwin, 1804.

Treatise of Human Nature. L. A. Selby-Bigge, ed. Oxford: Clarendon, 1896.

David Hume's Political Essays. Charles W. Hendel, ed. New York: Liberal Arts, 1953. From the 1777 edition of *Essays, Moral and Political.*

Hume; Theory of Politics. Frederick Watkins, ed. Austin, Tex.: U. of Texas, 1953. Note Watkins' introduction.

Moral and Political Philosophy. Henry Aiken, ed. New York: Hafner, 1948.

SECONDARY WORKS

BRYSON, GLADYS. *Man and Society; The Scottish Inquiry of the Eighteenth Century.* Princeton: Princeton U. Press, 1945.

HUXLEY, THOMAS. *Hume.* London: Macmillan, 1881.

KNIGHT, WILLIAM A. *Hume.* Edinburgh: Blackwood, 1886.

KYDD, RACHEL M. *Reason and Conduct in Hume's Treatise.* London: Oxford U. Press, 1946.

LAING, B. M. *David Hume.* London: Benn, 1932.

LAIRD, JOHN. *Hume's Philosophy of Human Nature.* London: Methuen, 1932.

MOSSNER, ERNEST C. *The Life of David Hume.* Austin, Tex.: U. of Texas, 1954.

ROSS, WILLIAM G. *Human Nature and Utility in Hume's Social Philosophy.* Garden City, N. Y.: published by the author, 1942.

SMITH, NORMAN KEMP. *The Philosophy of David Hume.* London: Macmillan, 1941.

CHAPTER 9, Burke

WORKS BY BURKE

The Writings and Speeches of Edmund Burke. 12 vols. Boston: Little, Brown, 1901.

Reflections on the Revolution in France. Russell Kirk, ed. Chicago: Regnery, 1955.

Burke's Politics. Ross Hoffman and S. J. Levack, eds. New York: Knopf, 1949.

The Philosophy of Edmund Burke; A Selection from His Speeches and Writings. L. I. Bredvold and R. G. Ross, eds. Ann Arbor: U. of Michigan Press, 1961.

Selected Writings of Edmund Burke. Walter J. Bate, ed. New York: Random House (Modern Library), 1960. "Appeal from the New to the Old Whigs" is a conspicuous omission from this collection.

SECONDARY WORKS

BARKER, ERNEST. *Essays on Government*. London: Oxford U. Press, 1945. Chs. 6, 7.

CANAVAN, FRANCIS, S. J. *The Political Reason of Edmund Burke*. Durham; N. C.: Duke U. Press, 1960.

COBBAN, ALFRED. *Edmund Burke and the Revolt Against the Eighteenth Century*. New York: Macmillan, 1929. Esp. Chs. 2-4.

COPELAND, THOMAS W. *Edmund Burke; Six Essays*. London: Cape, 1950.

GRANBARD, STEPHEN A. *Burke, Disraeli, and Churchill; The Politics of Perseverance*. Cambridge: Harvard U. Press, 1961.

KIRK, RUSSELL. *The Conservative Mind; From Burke to Santayana*. Chicago: Regnery, 1953.

LASKI, HAROLD J. *Political Thought in England; Locke to Bentham*. London: Hutchinson's U. Library, 1937. Ch. 6.

MACCUNN, JOHN. *The Political Philosophy of Burke*. New York: Longmans, Green, 1913.

MAGNUS, PHILIP. *Edmund Burke; A Life*. London: Murray, 1939.

MORLEY, JOHN. *Burke*. New York: Knopf, 1924 (orig. ed., 1867).

MURRAY, ROBERT H. *Edmund Burke; A Biography*. Oxford, Clarendon, 1931.

PARKIN, CHARLES. *The Moral Basis of Burke's Political Thought; An Essay*. Cambridge, Eng.: Cambridge U. Press, 1956.

STANLIS, PETER J. *Edmund Burke and the Natural Law*. Ann Arbor: U. of Michigan Press, 1958.

CHAPTER 10, The Nineteenth Century

GENERAL

BARKER, ERNEST. *Political Thought in England, 1848-1914*. 2nd ed. London: Oxford U. Press (Home University Library), 1928.

BOWLE, JOHN. *Politics and Opinion in the Nineteenth Century*. New York: Oxford U. Press, 1954. See bibliography, pp. 500-02.

BRINTON, CRANE. *English Political Thought in the Nineteenth Century*. Cambridge, Mass.: Harvard U. Press, 1933.

FAGUET, ÉMILE. *Politiques et moralistes du dix-neuvième siecle*. 3 vols. Paris: Boivin, 1899.

HEARNSHAW, F. J. C. ED. *Essays in the Social and Political Ideas of the Age of Reaction and Reconstruction*. London: Harrap, 1932.

————, ED. *Social and Political Ideas of the Victorian Age*. London: Harrap, 1933.

KRIEGER, LEONARD. *The German Idea of Freedom*. Boston: Beacon, 1957. See bibliography, pp. 529-33.

MAYER, J. P. *Political Thought in France from Sieyès to Sorel.* London: Faber and Faber, 1948.

MURRAY, R. H., ED. *Studies in English Social and Political Thinkers of the Nineteenth Century.* 2 vols. London: Heffer, 1929. Vol. 1 contains selections from Malthus, Bentham, James Mill, John Stuart Mill, Owen, Coleridge, Disraeli, Carlyle, Cobden, and Kingsley. Vol. 2 contains selections from Spencer, Maine, Ruskin, Arnold, Seeley, Bagehot, Green, Bryce, Maitland, and assorted socialists.

REISS, H. S., ED. *The Political Thought of the German Romantics, 1793-1815.* Oxford: Blackwell, 1955. Selections from Fichte, Novalis, Müller, Schliermacher, Savigny.

RUGGIERO, GUIDO DE. *A History of European Liberalism.* R. G. Collingwood, trans. London: Oxford U. Press, 1927. Boston: Beacon, 1959. See bibliography, pp. 445-63.

SCHAPIRO, J. SALWYN. *Liberalism and the Challenge of Fascism; Social Forces in England and France, 1815-1870.* New York: McGraw-Hill, 1949. See bibliography, pp. 405-13.

SOLTAU, ROGER. *French Political Thought in the Nineteenth Century.* New Haven: Yale U. Press, 1931.

SOMERVELL, D. C. *English Thought in the Nineteenth Century.* New York: Longmans, Green, 1938.

WILLEY, BASIL. *Nineteenth Century Studies; Coleridge to Matthew Arnold.* London: Chatto and Windus, 1949.

ENGLISH UTILITARIANISM

[See also the bibliography for Chapter 11, "Bentham."]

AUSCHUTZ, R. P. *The Philosophy of John Stuart Mill.* Oxford: Clarendon, 1953.

AUSTIN, JOHN. *Austinian Theory of Law.* W. Jethro Brown, ed. London: Murray, 1906.

———. *The Providence of Jurisprudence Determined* and *The Uses of the Study of Jurisprudence,* H. L. A. Hart, ed. London: Weidenfeld and Nicolson, 1954.

BAIN, ALEXANDER. *John Stuart Mill; A Criticism.* London: Longmans, Green, 1882.

BRITTON, KARL. *John Stuart Mill.* London: Penguin, 1953.

MILL, JAMES. *Essays on Government, Jurisprudence, Liberty of the Press, and Law of Nations.* Philip Wheelwright, ed. Garden City, N. Y.: Doubleday, Doran, 1935. Bound with works by Bentham and John Stuart Mill.

MILL, JOHN STUART. *Disquisitions and Discussions.* 4 vols. London: Longmans, Green, Reader, and Dyer, 1859-75.

———. *A System of Logic.* 8th ed. London: Longmans, Green, 1925. Book 6.

———. *Utilitarianism, Liberty, and Representative Government.* New York, Dutton (Everyman), 1951. Many other editions.

MORLAN, GEORGE K. *America's Heritage from John Stuart Mill.* New York: Columbia U. Press, 1936.

CONTINENTAL LIBERALISM

CONSTANT, BENJAMIN. *Principes de politique* in *Oeuvres,* Alfred Roulin, ed. Paris: Gallimard, 1957. Pp. 1099-1249.

DE TOCQUEVILLE, ALEXIS. *Democracy in America.* H. S. Commager, ed. Henry Reeve, trans. London: Oxford U. Press, 1946. Many other editions.

———. *The Old Regime and the French Revolution.* Gilbert Stuart trans. from 4th French ed. (1858). New York: Doubleday (Anchor Books), 1955.

GUIZOT, FRANÇOIS. *Democracy in France.* Trans. anon. New York: Appleton, 1849.

MAZZINI, JOSEPH. *The Duties of Man and Other Essays.* New York: Dutton (Everyman), 1929.

ROYER-COLLARD, PIERRE PAUL. *Les Fragments philosophiques.* Intro. by André Schimberg. Paris: Alcan, 1913.

SCHERMERHORN, ELIZABETH W. *Benjamin Constant.* London: Heinemann, 1924.

VON TREITSCHKE, HENRICH. *Politics.* Blanche Dugdale and T. de Bille, trans. 2 vols. New York: Macmillan, 1916.

SOCIAL DARWINISM

BAGEHOT, WALTER. *Physics and Politics.* New York: Appleton, 1873.

DEWEY, JOHN. *The Influence of Darwin on Philosophy.* New York: Holt, 1910.

HOBHOUSE, LEONARD. *Social Evolution and Political Theory.* New York: Columbia U. Press, 1911.

HOFSTADTER, RICHARD. *Social Darwinism in American Thought.* Philadelphia: U. of Pennsylvania, 1944. Boston: Beacon, 1955. See bibliography, pp. 205-16.

RITCHIE, DAVID G. *Darwinism and Politics.* London: Sonnenschein, 1889.

RUMNEY, JUDAH. *Herbert Spencer's Sociology.* London: Williams and Norgate, 1934.

SPENCER, HERBERT. *First Principles.* New York: Appleton, 1864.

———. *The Man Versus the State.* Caldwell, Idaho: Caxton, 1940.

———. *Social Statics.* New York: Appleton, 1864.

STARR, HARRIS. *William Graham Summer.* New York: Holt, 1925.

SUMNER, WILLIAM GRAHAM. *The Challenge of Facts and Other Essays.* New Haven: Yale U. Press, 1914.

————, *Essays.* A. G. Keller and M. R. Davie, eds. 2 vols. New Haven: Yale U. Press, 1934.

CONSERVATISM

[See also the bibliography for Chapter 12, "Hegel"]

BERLIN, ISAIAH. *The Hedgehog and the Fox; An Essay on Tolstoy's View of History.* New York: Simon and Schuster, 1953. Relates De Maistre to Stendahl and Tolstoy.

CAIRD, EDWARD. *The Social Philosophy and Religion of Comte,* London: Macmillan, 1885.

COMTE, AUGUSTE. *A General View of Positivism* (1848). J. H. Bridges, trans. Stanford: Academic Reprints, n. d.

DE BONALD, LOUIS. *Legislation primitive.* 5th ed. Paris: Le Clere, 1857.

DE MAISTRE, JOSEPH. *Du Pape.* Paris: Garnier, n. d.

————, *Soirées de St. Petersberg.* 2 vols. Lyon: Vitte, 1924.

BUTLER, ROHAN D'O. *The Roots of National Socialism.* London: Faber and Faber, 1941.

FICHTE, JOHANN G. *Addresses to the German Nation.* R. F. Jones and G. F. Turnbull, trans. Chicago: Open Court, 1922.

GIANTURCO, ELIO. *Joseph de Maistre and Giambattista Vico.* Washington, D. C.: published by the author, 1937.

LASKI, HAROLD J. *Authority in the Modern State.* New Haven: Yale U. Press, 1919. Ch. 1.

MILL, JOHN STUART. *Auguste Comte and Positivism.* 3rd ed. London: Turner, 1882.

BRITISH IDEALISM

BOSANQUET, BERNARD. *Philosophical Theory of the State.* 4th ed. London: Macmillan, 1923 (orig. ed., 1899).

BRADLEY, F. H. *Ethical Studies; Selected Studies.* Ralph Ross, intro. New York: Liberal Arts, 1951 (orig. ed., 1876).

GREEN, THOMAS HILL. *Lectures on the Principles of Political Obligation* (1879). Intro. by A. D. Lindsay. London: Longmans, Green, 1941.

————, *Works.* R. L. Nettleship, ed. 3 vols. London: Longmans, Green, 1889-90.

HOBHOUSE, LEONARD. *The Metaphysical Theory of the State.* London: Allen and Unwin, 1918.

RITCHIE, DAVID G. *Natural Rights.* London: Allen, 1894.

ELITISM

CARLYLE, THOMAS. *Critical and Miscellaneous Essays,* 2nd ed. New York: Appleton, 1871.

———, *Heroes, Hero-Worship, and the Heroic in History.* New York: Burt, n. d. (orig. ed., 1841).

CASSIRER, ERNST. *The Myth of the State.* New Haven: Yale U. Press, 1946, 1960. Ch. 15 is on Carlyle.

CHAMBERLAIN, HOUSTON STEWART. *The Foundations of the Nineteenth Century.* John Lees, trans. 2 vols. London: Lane, 1911.

DE GOBINEAU, ARTHUR. *The Inequality of Human Races.* Adrian Collins, trans. New York: Putnam, 1915.

LIPPINCOTT, BENJAMIN E. *Victorian Critics of Democracy.* Minneapolis: U. of Minnesota Press, 1938. On Carlyle, Ruskin, Arnold, Stephen, Maine, and Lecky.

ROE, FREDERICK WILLIAM. *The Social Philosophy of Carlyle and Ruskin.* New York: Harcourt, Brace, 1921.

RUSKIN, JOHN. *The Seven Lamps of Architecture, Sesame and Lilies, Unto This Last.* Sterling edition. Boston: Estes, n. d.

SOCIALISM

[See also the bibliographies for Chapter 13, "Marx," and Chapter 16, "Lenin."]

BAKUNIN, MICHAEL. *Marxism, Freedom, and the State.* K. J. Kenafick, trans. and ed. London: Freedom, 1950.

BELLAMY, EDWARD. *Looking Backward* (1887). Memorial edition. Boston: Houghton Mifflin, 1898. Many other editions.

BERNERI, MARIE LOUISE. *Journey Through Utopia.* London: Routledge and Kegan Paul, 1950. See bibliography, pp. 320-29.

BRISBANE, ALBERT. *The Social Destiny of Man.* Philadelphia: Stollmeyer, 1840. By Fourier's chief American disciple.

BROGAN, DENIS W. *Proud'hon.* London: Hamilton, 1934.

BUBER, MARTIN. *Paths in Utopia,* R. F. C. Hull, trans. London: Routledge and Kegan Paul, 1949.

CARR, E. H. *Michael Bakunin.* London: Macmillan, 1937.

———, *Studies in Revolution.* London: Macmillan, 1950.

COLE, G. D. H. *A History of Socialist Thought.* 6 vols. London; Macmillan, 1953-58. A monumental work covering the period from 1789 to 1931. See the bibliographies in each volume.

———. *Robert Owen.* London: Benn, 1925.

FOOTMAN, DAVID. *Ferdinand Lassalle, Romantic Revolutionary.* New Haven: Yale U. Press, 1947.

FOURIER, CHARLES. *Selections from the Works of Fourier.* Julia Franklin, trans. London: Swan, Sonnenschein, 1901.

GEORGE, HENRY. *Progress and Poverty* (1881). New York: Vanguard, 1929.

GRAY, ALEXANDER. *The Socialist Tradition from Moses to Lenin.* London: Longmans, Green, 1946.

HALÉVY, ELIE. *Histoire du socialisme europeen.* Paris: Gallimard, 1948.

JAURÈS, JEAN, ED. *Histoire socialiste, 1789-1900.* 4 vols. Paris: Rouff, 1901-08.

KROPOTKIN, PETER. *Mutual Aid.* Rev. ed. London: Heinemann, 1904.

LAIDLER, HARRY. *A History of Socialist Thought.* New York: Crowell, 1927. New edition titled *Social Economic Movements,* 1944.

LLOYD, HENRY DEMAREST. *Wealth Against Commonwealth.* New York: Harper, 1894.

MANUEL, FRANK E. *The New World of Henri Saint-Simon.* Cambridge, Mass.: Harvard U. Press, 1956.

OWEN, ROBERT. *Book of the New Moral World.* London: Wilson, 1836.

———. *A New View of Society and Other Writings* (1813). New York: Dutton (Everyman), 1927.

PLAMENATZ, JOHN. *The Revolutionary Movement in France, 1815-1871.* London: Longmans, Green, 1952.

PROUD'HON, PIERRE JOSEPH. *What Is Property?* Benjamin R. Tucker, trans. New York: Humboldt, 1876.

SAINT-SIMON, COMTE DE (CLAUDE DE ROUVROY). *Selected Writings.* F. M. H. Markham, trans. Oxford: Blackwell, 1952. See introduction.

WILSON, EDMUND. *To the Finland Station; A Study on the Writing and Acting of History.* New York: Harcourt, Brace, 1940; New York: Doubleday (Anchor Books), 1959. Part 2, Chs. 1-4.

WOODCOCK, GEORGE. *Pierre-Joseph Proud'hon.* London: Routledge and Kegan Paul, 1956.

CHAPTER 11, Bentham

An excellent bibliography on Bentham is contained in Halévy, *The Growth of Philosophic Radicalism* (see below), pp. 522-46.

WORKS BY BENTHAM

The Works of Jeremy Bentham. John Bowring, ed. 22 vols. Edinburgh: Tait, 1838-42.

A Fragment on Government. F. C. Montague, ed. Oxford: Clarendon, 1891.

A Fragment on Government and Introduction to the Principles of Morals

and Legislation. Wilfred Harrison, ed. Oxford: Blackwell, 1948.
Handbook of Political Fallacies. Harold A. Larrabee, ed. Baltimore: Johns Hopkins U. Press, 1952.
Introduction to the Principles of Morals and Legislation. Oxford: Clarendon, 1879. New ed., 1907.
Introduction to the Principles of Morals and Legislation. Lawrence J. Lafleur, ed. New York: Hafner, 1948.
Theory of Legislation. C. K. Ogden, ed. London: Routledge and Kegan Paul, 1950.

SECONDARY WORKS

ALBEE, ERNEST. *A History of English Utilitarianism*. London: Swann, Sonnenschein, 1900.
BAUMGART, DAVID. *Bentham and the Ethics of Today*. Princeton, N.J.: Princeton U. Press, 1952.
DAVIDSON, WILLIAM L. *Political Thought in England; The Utilitarians from Bentham to J. S. Mill*. New York: Oxford U. Press, 1950.
EVERETT, CHARLES W. *The Education of Jeremy Bentham*. New York: Columbia U. Press, 1931.
HALÉVY, ELIE. *The Growth of Philosophic Radicalism*. Mary Morris, trans. Boston: Beacon, 1955 (orig. ed., New York: Macmillan, 1928).
KEETON, G. W., AND GEORGE SCHWARZENBERGER, EDS. *Jeremy Bentham and the Law*. London: Stevens, 1948.
LEAVIS, F. R., ED. *Mill on Bentham and Coleridge*. London: Chatto and Windus, 1950.
MacCUNN, JOHN. *Six Radical Thinkers*. London: Arnold, 1907.
OGDEN, C. K. *Bentham's Theory of Fictions*. New York: Harcourt, Brace, 1932.
PLAMENATZ, JOHN. *The English Utilitarians*. London: Oxford U. Press, 1949.
STEPHEN, LESLIE. *The English Utilitarians*. 3 vols. London: Duckworth, 1900. Vol. 1 is on Bentham.

CHAPTER 12, Hegel

WORKS BY HEGEL

Samtliche Werke. J. Hoffmeister, ed. 35 vols. projected. Hamburg: Meiner, 1952–. A new critical edition, the best of several collected works.
Early Theological Writings. T. M. Knox, trans. Chicago: U. of Chicago

Press, 1948. Reprinted as *On Christianity*. New York: Harper (Torchbooks), 1961. In the latter see Richard Kroner's introduction, pp. 1-66.

Phenomenology of Mind. J. B. Baillie, trans. 2nd ed. London: Macmillan, 1931.

Philosophy of History. J. Sibree, trans. London: Bell, 1905; New York: Dover, 1955.

Philosophy of Right. T. M. Knox, trans. Oxford: Clarendon, 1942. Corrected eds., 1945, 1949, 1953.

Science of Logic. W. H. Johnston and L. G. Struthers, trans. London: Allen and Unwin, 1929.

The Philosophy of Hegel. Carl J. Friedrich, ed. New York: Random House (Modern Library), 1954.

Selections. J. Loewenberg, ed. Rev. ed. New York: Wiley, 1944.

Reason in History. R. S. Hartman, trans. New York: Liberal Arts, 1953. Contains introduction to *Philosophy of History*.

SECONDARY WORKS

CAIRD, EDWARD. *Hegel*. Edinburgh: Blackwood, 1883.

CROCE, BENEDETTO. *What Is Living and What Is Dead in Hegel's Philosophy?* D. Ainslie, trans. London: Macmillan, 1915. (orig. Italian ed., 1906.)

FINDLAY, JOHN N. *Hegel: A Re-examination*. New York: Macmillan, 1958.

FOSTER, MICHAEL B. *The Political Philosophy of Plato and Hegel*. Oxford: Clarendon, 1935.

HYPPOLITE, JEAN. *Introduction à la philosophie de l'histoire de Hegel*. Paris: Rivière, 1948.

MACINTOSH, ROBERT. *Hegel and Hegelianism*. New York: Scribner, 1903.

MCTAGGART, JOHN M. E. *Studies in the Hegelian Dialectic*. Cambridge, Eng.: Cambridge U. Press, 1896.

MARCUSE, HERBERT. *Reason and Revelation; Hegel and the Rise of Social Theory*. London: Oxford U. Press, 1941; 2nd ed., New York: Humanities Press, 1954.

MURE, G. R. G. *An Introduction to Hegel*. Oxford: Clarendon, 1940.

REYBURN, HUGH A. *The Ethical Theory of Hegel; A Study of the Philosophy of Right*. Oxford: Clarendon, 1921.

ROSENZWEIG, FRANZ. *Hegel und der Staat*. 2 vols. Munich: Oldenbourg, 1920.

STACE, W. T. *The Philosophy of Hegel*. London: Macmillan, 1924; New York: Dover, 1955.

WEIL, ERIC. *Hegel et l'état*. Paris: Vrin, 1950.

CHAPTER 13, Marx

PRIMARY WORKS

Selected Works of Marx and Engels, C. P. Dutt, ed., 2 vols. New York: International Publishers, 1936.

Selected Correspondence of Marx and Engels, 1846-1895. Dona Torr, trans. New York: International Publishers, 1942.

Handbook of Marxism, Emile Burns, ed. New York: Random House, 1935.

Marx and Engels; Basic Writings on Politics and Philosophy, Lewis S. Feuer, ed. New York: Doubleday (Anchor Books), 1959.

Marx on Economics, Robert Freedman, ed. New York: Harcourt, Brace & World (Harvest Books), 1961.

MARX, KARL, AND FRIEDRICH ENGELS. *The Communist Manifesto.* Eden and Cedar Paul, trans. New York: International Publishers, 1930.

——————. *The Communist Manifesto, with Selections from the Eighteenth Brumaire of Louis Napoleon.* Samuel Beer, ed. New York: Appleton-Century-Crofts, 1955. There are countless editions of the *Manifesto.*

——————. *The German Ideology* (1845-46). W. Looch and C. P. Magill, trans. London: Lawrence and Wishart, 1938.

——————. *The Civil War in the United States* (1861-66). Richard Emmale, ed. New York: International Publishers, 1937.

MARX, KARL. *Critique of Political Economy* (1859) translated from the second German edition by N. I. Stone. Chicago: Kerr, 1904.

——. *Capital* (1867-94). Samuel Moore and Edward Aveling, trans. 3 vols. Chicago: Kerr, 1906-09.

——. *Value, Price, and Profit* (1865). Eleanor Marx Aveling, ed. New York: International Publishers, 1935.

——. *Wage-Labour and Capital* (1849). Intro. by Friedrich Engels. New York: International Publishers, 1933.

——. *The Poverty of Philosophy* (1847). H. Quelch, trans. Chicago: Kerr, 1920.

——. *A Critique of the Gotha Program* (1891). C. P. Dutt, ed. New York: International Publishers, 1938.

——. *The Civil War in France* (1871). Intro. by Friedrich Engels. New York: International Publishers, 1933.

ENGELS, FRIEDRICH. *Herr Eugen Dühring's Revolution in Science* [*Anti-Dühring*] (1877-78). London: Lawrence, 1894. Three chapters of *Anti-Dühring* were published separately as *Socialism, Utopian and Scientific* in 1880 and subsequently.

———. *Socialism, Utopian and Scientific.* Edward Aveling, trans. Chicago: Kerr, 1912.

———. *The Origin of the Family, Private Property, and the State* (1884), Ernest Untermann, trans. Chicago: Kerr, 1902.

SECONDARY WORKS

BERLIN, ISAIAH. *Karl Marx; His Life and Environment,* 2nd ed. New York: Oxford U. Press, 1948 (Galaxy Books, 1959). See bibliography, pp. 269-73.

BÖHM VON BAWERK, E. *Karl Marx and the Close of His System.* Paul M. Sweezy, ed. New York: Kelley, 1949.

BOBER, M. M. *Karl Marx's Interpretation of History.* Rev. ed. Cambridge, Mass.: Harvard U. Press, 1948.

CARR, E. H. *Karl Marx; A Study in Fanaticism.* London: Dent, 1935.

COLE, G. D. H. *A History of Socialist Thought.* London: Macmillan, 1954. Vol. 2, Ch. 11.

———. *The Meaning of Marxism.* London: Gollancz, 1950.

CROCE, BENEDETTO. *Historical Materialism and the Economics of Karl Marx,* C. M. Meredith, trans. London: Allen and Unwin, 1922.

HOOK, SIDNEY. *From Hegel to Marx.* London: Gollancz, 1936.

———. *Towards the Understanding of Karl Marx.* New York: Day, 1933.

HUNT, R. N. CAREW. *The Theory and Practice of Communism,* 5th ed. New York: Macmillan, 1957.

KAUTSKY, KARL. *The Economic Doctrines of Karl Marx.* London: Black, 1925.

LICHTHEIM, GEORGE. *Marxism; An Historical and Critical Study.* New York: Praeger, 1961.

LINDSAY, A. D. *Karl Marx's Capital: An Introductory Essay.* 2nd ed. London: Oxford U. Press, 1947 (orig. ed., 1925).

MAYO, HENRY B. *Introduction to Marxist Theory.* New York: Oxford U. Press, 1960. Note Mayo's excellent bibliography, pp. 310-25.

MEYER, ALFRED G. *Marxism.* Cambridge, Mass.: Harvard U. Press, 1954.

ROBINSON, JOAN. *An Essay on Marxian Economics.* London: Macmillan, 1947.

SCHLESINGER, RUDOLPH. *Marx; His Time and Ours.* London: Routledge and Kegan Paul, 1950.

SCHUMPETER, JOSEPH A. *Capitalism, Socialism, Democracy.* 3rd ed. New York: Harper 1950. Part 2.

WILSON, EDMUND. *To the Finland Station; A Study in the Writing and Acting of History.* New York: Harcourt, Brace, 1940; New York: Doubleday (Anchor Books), 1959.

Chapter 14, Nietzsche

See Herbert Reichert and Karl Schlechta, eds., *International Nietzsche Bibliography*. Chapel Hill: U. of North Carolina Press, 1960.

WORKS BY NIETZSCHE

Werke. 15 vols. Leipzig: Naumann, 1899-1904.

Complete Works. Oscar Levy, trans. 18 vols. New York: Macmillan, 1924.

Beyond Good and Evil. Helen Zimmern, trans. New York: Boni and Liveright, 1917. Marianne Cowan, trans. Chicago: Regnery, 1955.

The Birth of Tragedy and *The Genealogy of Morals.* Francis Goeffing, trans. Garden City: Doubleday (Anchor Books), 1956.

The Genealogy of Morals; A Polemic. Horace B. Samuel, trans. New York: Macmillan, 1924.

The Joyful Wisdom. Thomas Common, trans. 2nd ed. London: Foulis, 1918.

Thus Spake Zarathustra. Thomas Common, trans. New York: Macmillan, 1911; New York: Random House (Modern Library), n. d.

The Use and Abuse of History. Adrian Collins, trans. New York: Liberal Arts, 1949.

The Will to Power. Anthony M. Ludovici, trans. Edinburgh: Foulis, 1910.

The Philosophy of Nietzsche. New York: Random House (Modern Library), 1937.

The Portable Nietzsche. W. Kaufmann, ed. New York: Viking, 1954.

SECONDARY WORKS

BRINTON, CRANE. *Nietzsche.* Cambridge: Harvard U. Press, 1941.

JASPERS, KARL. *Reason and Existenz*, William Earle, trans. New York: Noonday, 1955. Nietzsche and Kierkegaard.

KAUFMANN, WALTER A. *Nietzsche; Philosopher, Psychologist, Anti-Christ.* Princeton: Princeton U. Press, 1950. See bibliography, pp. 383-95.

LEA, FRANK A. *The Tragic Philosopher; A Study of Friedrich Nietzsche.* New York: Philosophic Library, 1957.

LÖWITH, KARL. *Nietzsche's Philosophie der ewigen Wiederkehr des Gleichen.* Stuttgart: Kohlhammer, 1956.

MENCKEN, H. L. *The Philosophy of Friedrich Nietzsche.* 3rd ed. Boston: Luce, 1913.

MORE, PAUL ELMER. *Nietzsche.* Boston: Houghton Mifflin, 1912.

MORGAN, GEORGE ALLEN, JR. *What Nietzsche Means.* Cambridge, Mass.: Harvard U. Press, 1941.

REYBURN, HUGH A. *Nietzsche; The Story of a Human Philosopher.* London: Macmillan, 1948.

CHAPTER 15, The Twentieth Century

The multiplicity of books and the uncertainty of criteria of importance makes this selection even more arbitrary than those for other chapters. For more extended bibliographies, see Albert R. Chandler, ed., *The Clash of Political Ideals*, 3rd ed. (New York: Appleton-Century-Crofts, 1957), pp. 334-74; J. Roland Pennock, *Liberal Democracy* (New York: Rinehart, 1950), pp. 373-94; Christian Bay, *The Structure of Freedom* (Stanford: Stanford U. Press, 1958), pp. 391-408; William Kornhauser, *The Politics of Mass Society* (Glencoe, Ill.: Free Press, 1959), pp. 239-47.

TOTALITARIANISM

ARENDT, HANNAH. *The Origins of Totalitarianism.* New York: Harcourt, Brace, 1951; 2nd ed., New York: World Pub. (Meridian Books), 1958.

COBBAN, ALFRED. *Dictatorship; Its History and Theory.* New York: Scribner, 1939.

FRIEDRICH, CARL J., ED. *Totalitarianism.* Cambridge, Mass.: Harvard U. Press, 1954.

———, AND ZBIGNIEW BRZEZINSKI. *Totalitarian Dictatorship and Autocracy.* Cambridge, Mass.: Harvard U. Press, 1956.

GENTILE, GIOVANNI. "The Philosophical Basis of Fascism," *Foreign Affairs*, Vol. 6 (1928), pp. 290-304.

HITLER, ADOLF. *Mein Kampf.* Ralph Manheim, trans. Boston: Houghton Mifflin, 1943.

HOFFER, ERIC. *The True Believer.* New York: Harper, 1951.

KORNHAUSER, WILLIAM. *The Politics of Mass Society.* Glencoe, Ill.: Free Press, 1959.

LEDERER, EMIL. *The State of the Masses.* New York: Norton, 1940.

MILOCZ, CESLAW. *The Captive Mind.* Jane Zielonko, trans. New York: Knopf (Vintage), 1953.

MUSSOLINI, BENITO. *The Political and Social Doctrine of Fascism.* Jane Soames, trans. London: Hogarth, 1933.

ROCCO, ALFREDO. "The Political Doctrine of Fascism," D. Bigongiari, trans. Carnegie Endowment for International Peace, *International Conciliation Bulletin,* No. 223, 1926.

SCHNEIDER, HERBERT W. *Making the Fascist State.* New York: Oxford U. Press, 1928.

LIBERALISM-CONSERVATISM

[For Socialism, see the bibliography for Chapter 16, "Lenin."]

ARNOLD, THURMAN. *The Folklore of Capitalism.* New Haven: Yale U. Press, 1937.

BAY, CHRISTIAN. *The Structure of Freedom.* Stanford: Stanford U. Press, 1958.

CRANSTON, MAURICE. *Freedom; A New Analysis.* 2nd ed. London: Longmans, Green, 1954.

DEUTSCHER, ISAAC. *Two Concepts of Liberty.* Oxford: Clarendon, 1958.

GALBRAITH, JOHN KENNETH. *The Affluent Society.* Boston: Houghton Mifflin, 1958.

———. *American Capitalism.* Boston: Houghton Mifflin, 1952; rev. ed., 1956.

DE GRAZIA, SEBASTIAN. *The Political Community; A Study in Anomie.* Chicago: U. of Chicago Press, 1948.

VON HAYEK, FRIEDRICH A. *The Constitution of Liberty.* Chicago: U. of Chicago Press, 1960.

HEIMANN, ÉDUARD. *Reason and Faith in Modern Society; Liberalism, Marxism, and Democracy.* Middletown, Conn: Wesleyan U. Press, 1961.

HOOVER, HERBERT. *The Challenge to Liberty.* New York: Scribner, 1934.

KALLEN, HORACE M. *The Liberal Spirit.* Ithaca: Cornell U. Press, 1948.

———. *A Study of Liberty.* Yellow Springs, Ohio: Antioch Press, 1959.

KEYNES, JOHN MAYNARD. *The Economic Consequences of the Peace.* New York: Harcourt, Brace, 1920.

———. *The General Theory of Employment, Interest, and Money.* London: Macmillan, 1936; New York: Harcourt, Brace, 1936.

LASKI, HAROLD J. *A Grammar of Politics.* London: Allen and Unwin, 1925.

———. *Liberty in the Modern State.* New York: Harper, 1930.

———. *The State in Theory and Practice.* New York: Viking, 1935.

LIPPMANN, WALTER. *Essays in the Public Philosophy.* Boston: Little, Brown, 1955; New York: New American Library (Mentor Books), 1957.

———. *An Inquiry into the Principles of the Good Society.* Boston: Little, Brown, 1937.

———. *Public Opinion.* New York: Harcourt, Brace, 1922; New York: Penguin, 1946.

McGOVERN, WILLIAM M., AND DAVID S. COLLIER. *Radicals and Conservatives.* Chicago: Regnery, 1957.

MARITAIN, JACQUES. *Man and the State.* Chicago: U. of Chicago Press, 1951.

NISBET, ROBERT. *The Quest for Community.* New York: Oxford U. Press, 1953.

ORTEGA Y GASSET, JOSÉ. *The Revolt of the Masses.* New York: Nelson, 1932.

RUSSELL, BERTRAND. *Authority and the Individual.* New York: Simon and Schuster, 1945.

Simons, Henry C. *Economic Policy for a Free Society*. Chicago: U. of Chicago Press, 1948.

FREUDIANISM

Birnbach, Martin. *Neo-Freudian Social Philosophy*. Stanford: Stanford U. Press, 1961.

Brown, Norman. *Life Against Death; The Psychoanalytic Meaning of History*. Middletown, Conn.: Wesleyan U. Press, 1959.

Freud, Sigmund. *Civilization and Its Discontents* (1930). Joan Rivière, trans. London: Hogarth, 1939, 1951.

———. *Civilization, War, and Death*. John Rickman, ed. London: Hogarth, 1939. Consists of three essays written in 1915, 1929, 1933.

———. *The Future of an Illusion*. W. D. Robson-Scott, trans. London: Hogarth, 1928; New York: Doubleday (Anchor Books), 1957.

Fromm, Erich. *Escape from Freedom*. New York: Rinehart, 1941.

———. *The Sane Society*. New York: Rinehart, 1955.

Horney, Karen. *The Neurotic Personality of Our Time*. New York: Norton, 1937.

Jung, Carl G. *Modern Man in Search of a Soul*. London: Kegan Paul, Trench, Trübner, 1933.

Lasswell, Harold D. *Psychopathology and Politics*. Chicago: U. of Chicago Press, 1930.

———. *Power and Personality*. New York: Norton, 1948.

———. *World Politics and Personal Insecurity*. New York: McGraw-Hill, 1935.

Progoff, Ira. *Jung's Psychology and Its Social Meaning*. New York: Grove, 1957.

Schaar, John H. *Escape from Authority; The Perspectives of Erich Fromm*. New York: Basic Books, 1961.

EXISTENTIALISM

See Kenneth Douglas, *A Critical Bibliography of Existentialism (The Paris School)*. Yale French Studies, Special Monograph No. 1, 1950.

Arendt, Hannah. *Between Past and Future; Six Exercises in Political Thought*. New York: Viking, 1961.

———. *The Human Condition*. Chicago: U. of Chicago Press, 1958.

Barrett, William. *Irrational Man*. New York: Doubleday, 1958.

Blackham, H. J. *Six Existentialist Thinkers*. London: Routledge and Kegan Paul, 1953.

Camus, Albert. *The Myth of Sisyphus and Other Essays*. Justin O'Brien, trans. New York: Knopf, 1955.

————. *The Rebel*. Anthony Bower, trans. London: Hamilton, 1953. New York: Vintage, 1959.

HEINEMANN, FREDERICK. *Existentialism and the Modern Predicament*. 2nd ed. London: Black, 1954. New York: Harper (Torchbook), 1958.

JASPERS, KARL. *The Future of Mankind*. E. B. Ashton, trans. Chicago: U. of Chicago Press, 1961.

————. *Man in the Modern Age*. Eden and Cedar Paul, trans. London: Routledge and Kegan Paul, 1951. New York: Doubleday (Anchor Books), 1957 (orig. German ed., 1931).

KAUFMANN, WALTER A., ED. *Existentialism from Dostoevsky to Sartre*. New York: Meridian, 1956.

READ, HERBERT. *Existentialism, Marxism, and Anarchism*. London: Freedom, 1950.

SARTRE, JEAN-PAUL. *Critique de la raison dialectique*. Paris: Gallimard, 1960.

————. *Existentialism and Humanism*. Philip Mairet, trans. London: Methuen, 1948.

CHAPTER 16, Lenin

Useful bibliographies may be found in Henry B. Mayo, *Introduction to Marxist Theory* (New York: Oxford U. Press, 1960), pp. 310-25; and Harry and Bonaro Overstreet, *What We Must Know about Communism* (New York: Norton, 1958), pp. 314-24. See also works listed below by Daniels, Haimson, Hammond, and Meyer.

WORKS BY LENIN

Sochineniya (Works), 30 vols., 3rd ed. (Moscow: Marx-Engels-Lenin Institute, 1928-37. For readers of Russian, this edition is regarded as more complete and reliable than later ones. A forthcoming edition of fifty-five volumes has been announced in Moscow. Many of the various Lenin tracts have been published separately in English by International Publishers, New York.

Collected Works. New York: International Publishers, 1927-42. Vols. 4, 13, 18–20, 21 only are translated (badly) into English.

Essentials of Lenin. 2 vols. London: Lawrence and Wishart, 1947.

Marx-Engels-Marxism. 3rd English ed. Moscow: Foreign Languages Publishing House 1947. Includes excerpts from "State and Revolution," "What Is to Be Done?" and most of the major tracts.

Selected Works. 12 vols. New York: International Publishers, 1935-43.

Selected Works. 2 vols. Moscow: Foreign Language Publishing House, 1946.

The Suppressed Testament of Lenin; The Complete Original Text with Two Explanatory Articles by L. Trotsky. New York: Pioneer, 1935. Lenin's famous criticism of Stalin, not published in the Soviet Union until 1956.

SECONDARY WORKS

BUKHARIN, NIKOLAI I. *Historical Materialism.* Auth. trans. from 3rd. Russian ed. New York: International Publishers, 1925.

CARR, EDWARD H. *The Bolshevik Revolution, 1917-1923.* 3 vols. New York: Macmillan, 1954.

DANIELS, ROBERT V. *The Conscience of the Revolution; Communist Opposition in Soviet Russia.* Cambridge, Mass.: Harvard U. Press, 1960. Bibliography, pp. 439-48. Note Daniels' imaginative diagrams of Communist factionalism, pp. 435-38.

DEUTSCHER, ISAAC. *The Prophet Armed; Trotsky, 1879-1921.* London: Oxford U. Press, 1954.

————. *Stalin; A Political Biography.* New York: Oxford U. Press, 1949.

EASTMAN, MAX. *Marx, Lenin, and the Science of Revolution.* London: Allen and Unwin, 1926.

HAIMSON, LEOPOLD H. *The Russian Marxists and the Origins of Bolshevism.* Cambridge: Harvard U. Press, 1955. Bibliography, pp. 235-40.

HAMMOND, THOMAS TAYLOR. *Lenin on Trade Unions and Revolution, 1893-1917.* New York: Columbia U. Press, 1957. Bibliography, pp. 130-50.

HILLQUIT, MORRIS. *From Marx to Lenin.* New York: Hanford, 1921.

History of the Communist Party of the Soviet Union (Bolsheviks): Short Course. New York: International Publishers, 1939. The so-called Stalin history.

KAUTSKY, KARL. *The Economic Doctrines of Karl Marx.* H. J. Stenning, trans. London: Black, 1925.

————. *Terrorism and Communism; A Contribution to the Natural History of Revolution.* W. H. Kerridge, trans. London: Allen and Unwin, 1920.

MEYER, ALFRED G. *Leninism.* Cambridge, Mass.: Harvard U. Press, 1957. See bibliography, pp. 295-98.

PLAMENATZ, JOHN. *German Marxism and Russian Communism.* London: Longmans, Green, 1954.

PLEKHANOV, GEORGI. *The Development of the Monist View of History* (1895). Andrew Rothstein, trans. Moscow: Foreign Language Publishing House, 1956.

SCHWARTZ, BENJAMIN. *Chinese Communism and the Rise of Mao*. Cambridge, Mass.: Harvard U. Press, 1951.

SHUB, DAVID. *Lenin; A Biography*. Garden City, N. Y.: Doubleday, 1948.

STALIN, JOSEPH. *Problems of Leninism*. 11th ed. Moscow: Foreign Language Publishing House, 1941. Moscow-published works by Stalin tend to be unreliable.

TREADGOLD, D. W. *Lenin and His Rivals*. New York: Praeger, 1955.

TROTSKY, LEON. *Lenin*. Auth. trans. New York: Minton, Balch, 1925.

———. *My Life; An Attempt at an Autobiography*. New York: Scribner, 1931.

———. *The Permanent Revolution*. Max Schachtman, trans. New York: Pioneer, 1931.

WILSON, EDMUND. *To the Finland Station; A Study in the Writing and Acting of History*. New York: Harcourt, Brace, 1940. New York: Doubleday (Anchor Books), 1959.

WOLFE, BERTRAM D. *Three Who Made a Revolution*. New York: Dial, 1948; Boston: Beacon, 1956.

CHAPTER 17, Dewey

WORKS BY DEWEY

School and Society. Chicago: U. of Chicago Press, 1900; rev. ed., 1915.

Ethics, with James H. Tufts. New York: Holt, 1908; rev. ed., 1932.

The Influence of Darwin on Philosophy. New York: Holt, 1910.

German Philosophy and Politics. New York: Holt, 1915; Boston: Beacon, 1945.

Democracy and Education. New York: Macmillan, 1916.

Reconstruction in Philosophy. New York: Holt, 1920; enl. ed., Boston: Beacon, 1949.

Human Nature and Conduct. New York: Holt, 1922; New York: Random House (Modern Library), 1930.

Experience and Nature. Chicago: Open Court, 1925.

The Public and Its Problems. New York: Holt, 1927. Chicago: Gateway, 1946; Denver: Swallow, 1957.

The Quest for Certainty. New York: Minton, Balch, 1930.

Liberalism and Social Action. New York: Putnam, 1935.

Freedom and Culture. New York: Putnam, 1939.

Logic: The Theory of Inquiry. New York: Holt, 1938.

Intelligence in the Modern World. Joseph Ratner, ed. New York: Random House (Modern Library), 1939.

SECONDARY WORKS

See the Symposium on Dewey, *Journal of the History of Ideas*, Vol. 20 (1959), pp. 515 ff.

EDMAN, IRWIN. *John Dewey; His Contribution to the American Tradition*. New York: Bobbs-Merrill, 1955.

Essays in Honor of John Dewey on the Occasion of His Seventieth Birthday, New York: Holt, 1929.

FELDMAN, W. T. *The Philosophy of John Dewey*. Baltimore: Johns Hopkins U. Press, 1934.

GEIGER, GEORGE R. *John Dewey in Perspective*. London: Oxford U. Press, 1958.

HOOK, SIDNEY. *John Dewey; An Intellectual Portrait*. New York: Day, 1939.

——, ED. *John Dewey; Philosopher of Science and Freedom*. New York: Dial, 1950.

JOHNSON, A. H., ED. *The Wit and Wisdom of John Dewey*. Boston: Beacon, 1949.

LAMONT, CORLISS, ED. *Dialogue on Dewey*. New York: Horizon, 1959.

LEANDER, FOLKE. *The Philosophy of John Dewey*. Göteborg, Sweden: Elanders, 1939.

MOORE, EDWARD C. *American Pragmatism; Peirce, James, and Dewey*. New York: Columbia U. Press, 1961.

RATNER, SIDNEY, ED. *The Philosopher of the Common Man*. New York: Putnam, 1940.

SCHILPP, PAUL, ED. *The Philosophy of John Dewey*. Evanston, Ill.: Northwestern U. Press, 1939.

WHITE, MORTON G. *The Origin of Dewey's Instrumentalism*. New York: Columbia U. Press, 1943.

CHAPTER 18, Niebuhr

For a complete bibliography of the writings of Reinhold Niebuhr to 1956, see Kegley and Bretall, *Reinhold Niebuhr* (listed below), pp. 455-78. Issues of *Christianity and Crisis* from the early 1940's on provide a record of Niebuhr's political commentary.

WORKS BY NIEBUHR

Moral Man and Immoral Society. New York: Scribner, 1932.
Reflections on the End of an Era. New York: Scribner, 1934.
An Interpretation of Christian Ethics. New York: Harper, 1935.
Christianity and Power Politics. New York: Scribner, 1940.

The Nature and Destiny of Man. 2 vols. New York: Scribner, 1941.
The Children of Light and the Children of Darkness. New York: Scribner, 1944.
Faith and History. New York: Scribner, 1949.
The Irony of American History. New York: Scribner, 1952.
Christian Realism and Political Problems. New York: Scribner, 1953.
The Self and the Dramas of History. New York: Scribner, 1955.
Pious and Secular America. New York: Scribner, 1958.
The Structure of Nations and Empires. New York: Scribner, 1959.
Reinhold Niebuhr on Politics, Harry R. Davis and Robert C. Good, eds. New York: Scribner, 1960. On page 359 Davis and Good give a complete list of Niebuhr's books.

SECONDARY WORKS

BENNETT, JOHN C. *Christians and the State.* New York: Scribner, 1958.
———. *Social Salvation.* New York: Scribner, 1935.
BINGHAM, JUNE. *The Courage to Change; An Introduction to the Life and Thought of Reinhold Niebuhr.* New York: Scribner, 1961.
BRUNNER, EMIL. *The Divine Imperative.* Olive Wyon, trans. Philadelphia: Westminster, 1947.
BUBER, MARTIN. *Between Man and Man.* R. G. Smith, trans. Boston: Beacon, 1955.
CARTER, PAUL A. *The Decline and Revival of the Social Gospel; Social and Political Liberalism in American Protestant Churches, 1920-1940.* Ithaca: Cornell U. Press, 1954. See bibliography, pp. 251-60.
HOFMAN, HANS. *The Theology of Reinhold Niebuhr.* New York: Scribner, 1956.
HUTCHISON, JOHN A., ED. *Christian Faith and Social Action.* New York: Scribner, 1953.
KEGLEY, CHARLES W., AND ROBERT W. BRETALL, EDS. *Reinhold Neibuhr; His Religious, Social, and Political Thought.* New York: Macmillan, 1956.
MARITAIN, JACQUES. *Man and the State.* Chicago: U. of Chicago Press, 1951.
MEYER, DONALD. *The Protestant Search for Political Realism, 1919-1941.* Berkeley: U. of California Press, 1960.
ODEGARD, HOLTAN P. *Sin and Science; Reinhold Niebuhr as Political Theologian.* Yellow Springs, Ohio: Antioch Press, 1956. See bibliography, pp. 221-34.
SCHNEIDER, HERBERT W. *Religion in Twentieth Century America.* Cambridge, Mass.: Harvard U. Press, 1952.

THELEN, M. F. *Man as Sinner in Contemporary American Realistic Theology*. New York: King's Crown, 1946.

TILLICH, PAUL. *Love, Power, and Justice*. New York: Oxford U. Press, 1954.

WHITE, MORTON G. *Social Thought in America; The Revolt Against Formalism*. Rev. ed. Boston: Beacon, 1958. Epilogue contains a critique of Niebuhr.

CHAPTER 19, Political Theory and the Science of Politics

In addition to the works cited in the text consult the following:

BENDIX, REINHARD. *Social Science and the Distrust of Reason*. Berkeley: U. of California Press, 1951.

COHEN, MORRIS. *Reason and Nature*. 2nd ed. New York: Harcourt, Brace, 1953.

FESTINGER, B. L., AND DANIEL KATZ, EDS. *Research Methods in the Behavioral Sciences*. New York: Dryden, 1953.

HAYEK, FRIEDRICH A. *The Counterrevolution of Science; Studies in the Abuse of Reason*. Glencoe, Ill.: Free Press, 1952.

HYDE, LAWRENCE. *The Learned Knife*. New York: Scribner, 1928.

KEY, V. O., *A Primer of Statistics for Political Scientists*. New York: Crowell, 1954.

MACIVER, ROBERT. *Social Causation*. Boston: Ginn, 1942.

MERTON, ROBERT. *Social Theory and Social Structure*. Rev. ed. Glencoe, Ill.: Free Press, 1957.

MOORE, BARRINGTON, JR. *Political Power and Social Theory; Six Studies*. Cambridge, Mass.: Harvard U. Press, 1958.

NORTHRUP, F. S. C. *The Logic of the Sciences and the Humanities*. New York: Macmillan, 1947.

STRAUSS, LEO. *What Is Political Philosophy?* Glencoe, Ill.: Free Press, 1960.

VOEGELIN, ERIC. *The New Science of Politics*. Chicago: U. of Chicago Press, 1953.

Index

THIS is primarily an index of proper names. Major book titles are indexed under authors and are grouped together alphabetically at the end of the entry for a given author. Pages in which the chief discussion of a topic appears are printed in **boldface**.